Cultural Studies

Cultural Studies

Theory and Practice

3rd edition
Chris Barker

with a foreword by Paul Willis

SAGE Publications
Los Angeles · London · New Delhi · Singapore

© Chris Barker 2008

First published 2000
Second edition published 2003
This edition published 2008

 SAGE Publications Ltd
1 Oliver's Yard
55 City Road
London EC1Y 1SP

SAGE Publications Inc.
2455 Teller Road
Thousand Oaks, California 91320

SAGE Publications India Pvt Ltd
B 1/I 1 Mohan Cooperative Industrial Area
Mathura Road, New Delhi 110 044

SAGE Publications Asia-Pacific Pte Ltd
33 Pekin Street #02-01
Far East Square
Singapore 048763

Library of Congress Control Number: 2007927246

British Library Cataloguing in Publication data

A catalogue record for this book is available from the British Library

ISBN 978-1-4129-2415-3
ISBN 978-1-4129-2416-0 (pbk)

Typeset by C&M Digitals (P) Ltd, Chennai, India
Printed in Great Britain by TJ International Ltd, Padstow, Cornwall
Printed on paper from sustainable resources

Contents

Foreword

Paul Willis

'Culture' is a strange and capacious category. It's one of those concepts, perhaps the best example, that we simply cannot do without – it is used everywhere – but which is also very unsatisfactory and cries out for betterment. No one can define it exactly, say what it 'really' means. That's partly why it's so useful of course, because we can always say later we meant something slightly different whilst getting on for now saying something nearly right of great importance. So many things are contained in the word.

At an everyday and human level, cultural interests, pursuits and identities have never been more important. This has to be broadly considered, of course, as individuals and groups bearing a felt responsibility for and wanting a hand in the making of the self as something more than a passive or unconscious acceptance of a historically/socially pre-scribed identity (simply *being* working class, black or white, young or old, etc.). Everyone wants to have, or make, or be considered as possessing cultural *significance*. No one knows what the social maps are any more, so it is more important not be left out, overlooked or misrepresented. Everyone wants a stake in the action, though no one is quite sure where the party is.

At the same time and in a connected way, 'culture' has become an important and much used theoretical and substantive category of connection and relation. Both in academic and popular writing and commentary we see countless references to 'cultures of … schools, organizations, pubs, regions, sexual orientations, ethnicities, etc.' You name it and you can add, 'culture of …'. All those evoked domains of 'culture' are seen as containing a multiplicity of human forms and relations: from micro-interpersonal interactions to group norms processes and values to communicative forms, provided texts and images; wider out to institutional forms and constraints, to social representations and social imagery; wider out still to economic, political, ideological determinations. All can be traced back for their cultural effects and meanings, all traced for their mutual interactions from the point of view of how the meanings of a particular 'culture' are formed and held to operate.

Small wonder, then, that the mode of academic enquiry that seeks to comprehend some of this, 'cultural studies', should be a field of at times intractable complexity and perhaps the first great academic experiment in the attempted formation of a 'non-disciplinary' discipline. No single approach can hope to comprehend the above in one sweep; no one sweep producing some partial understanding can fail to notice what other sweeps might produce. We are condemned to a kind of eclecticism because of the very eclecticism and indissoluble combinations of the dissimilar in the increasingly complex 'real' world around us.

Whatever its complexity and disputed origins, cultural studies is now coming, perhaps, to a kind of maturity, a special kind of maturity, of course, in light of the above: the coming to majority of the first of the 'non-disciplinary' disciplines! Clearly we need new measures of maturity. The fullest test of maturity will be whether cultural studies is to be without discipline (bad), or capable of avoiding the pitfalls and really exploiting the advantages of 'postdisciplinarity' (good) to produce genuinely new and 'connected-up' knowledge. Previous cultural studies textbooks have made worthy and illuminating attempts to give a history of the subject, to plot its growth through successive waves of new thought and critique. But that kind of narration cannot give the essence of the nature of cultural studies' ambition to found a new disciplinarity of the disciplines. For in this endeavour even a notion of 'multidisciplinarity', of the tracing of multiple linear paths, will not really do. What is needed is openness to and choice from strands (both past and present) within and between inherited fields of method, enquiry and theory. Their ability to illuminate complex empirical subjects of study, rather than their conformity to the particular tests and procedures of founding academic traditions, should govern these choices. Though welcome, it is hardly surprising that the early 'textbook' attempts to chart 'a cultural studies discipline' through a historical route should have engendered their own towers of Babel, combusting with fierce debate and bad-tempered rivalries over true ownership and alternative myths of origin.

Chris Barker has pioneered a new and promising course. Clearly and coherently expressed, it is likely to be an exceptionally useful one for those confronting the undoubted difficulties of teaching cultural studies and cultural studies approaches. Rather than attempting to show another version of the provenance of cultural studies, he has plumped for breadth and the collecting together of relevant theoretical and empirical strands, from wherever they might come. He presents a whole cluster of modern perspectives judged for their usefulness to the understanding of contemporary cultural forms. In doing this, Chris Barker certainly draws from theorists and writers who would not necessarily situate themselves in cultural studies, thereby providing a whole range of theoretical resources, methodological options and empirical connections which are useful for the understanding of any particular focus and which far outstrip those available in any one traditional discipline. This leads him to grapple with deeper and more serious concerns than would a conventional 'introduction to …'. In reverse direction, it might be noted that the variable and contested importation of cultural studies' perspectives into other disciplines and domains shows their own struggle, from their own positions and histories, to achieve greater adequacy and purchase in comprehending multifaceted and ruptural cultural change. There is, of course, no guarantee that cultural studies will indeed be the privileged site for the emergence of a discipline of the disciplines, or even that, though necessary, the latter is even possible. There are and certainly will be other contenders.

However, Chris Barker has made a bold thrust to grab the prize. I was particularly impressed by the sections on contemporary issues and problematics – 'World Disorder', 'Sex and Subjectivity', 'Space', 'Cultural Policy', as well as the more well-trodden ones of 'Identity', 'Youth Culture', 'Television', 'Ethnicity and Race' – which reveal some concrete grounds of a complex and rapidly changing 'real' world within which all approaches must now situate themselves if they hope to contend with the contradictory currents of contemporary change. At the same time, though, these connected 'sites' are presented in selected theoretical contexts of what has gone before and in the light of a constellation of theoretical insights, 'cultural studies' or not, which help to illuminate, connect and place them.

One of the crucial issues in trying to produce a textbook for a (first-stage) mature cultural studies is to find and argue for a supra-disciplinary base, a loose coherence of connecting tissue or metaphor, which is capable of anchoring a principled eclecticism (rather than a theoretical anarchism) whilst still retaining a wide empirical grasp. Here I have an uncertainty or perhaps lack of competence in judging Chris Barker's path. Although a colleague and a friend, certainly honoured in the asking, I was in some ways a strange choice to be invited to provide this Foreword. I have been (rightly) generally associated with an ethnographic/qualitative approach and (misleadingly) associated with a 'culturalist' formation within cultural studies, both of which are granted important but only finally subordinate status within this book. Like Chris Barker, I am not fussed about disciplinary boundaries, less fussed than he is actually about the privileged status of cultural studies, but I would seek to ground the complex, unwieldy and weighty category of 'culture' ultimately upon notions of 'experience' and 'practice', sensuously understood and (ethnographically) studied.* Contrastingly, Chris Barker proposes a 'language-game' account of the 'discursive formation' of cultural studies, seeing all cultural forms as structured like language, and ends, tellingly, with a Rortian emphasis on pragmatism within cultural studies as that which can influence 'reality', 'learning how best to cope with the world', but in no way 'reflecting' it. I have doubts about a model derived from language

---

* See issues of the Sage journal *Ethnography*, edited by myself and Mats Trondman, and *The Ethnographic Imagination* (Willis, P. [ed.] (2000), Cambridge Polity Press).

for understanding sensuous aspects of experience and lived practice, and cannot wean myself from a notion that in order to change reality, something of its actual music must first somehow be recorded and appreciated (ethnographically) in its own terms, even as, learning from Chris Barker, 'fractured subjects' and 'anti-essentialism' must hold some sway in how this is understood and presented.

Chris Barker wants his book to engender debate. It's worked already! I have learned a great deal from this book and respect its breadth and fairness, as well as finding points of difference and new departure for my own thinking. There is much here to help me develop more adequacy and elegance in my own work, continuous with and by no means contradicting that of Chris Barker. There is an excellent basis and framework here to help teachers lead students to an understanding of the necessary ambition of the cultural studies project and to make their own *informed and knowledgeable* decisions about how to approach and understand the importance, fullness, variety and pace of contemporary cultural change.

PART ONE

CULTURE AND
CULTURAL STUDIES

1 An Introduction to Cultural Studies

Given the title of this book – *Cultural Studies: Theory and Practice* – it would be reasonable to expect a comprehensive account of cultural studies, including summaries and discussions of its main arguments and substantive sites of intellectual enquiry. Indeed, this is what has been attempted. However, I want to open this account of cultural studies with a kind of 'health warning' regarding the scope of the book.

CONCERNING THIS BOOK

Selectivity

Any book about cultural studies is necessarily selective and likely to engender debate, argument and even conflict. To offer a truly comprehensive account of cultural studies would be to reproduce, or at least to summarize, every single text ever written within the parameters of cultural studies. Not only would this be too mammoth a task for any writer, but also the problem would remain of deciding which texts warranted the nomination. Consequently this book, like all others, is implicated in constructing a *particular version* of cultural studies.

I do offer, under the rubric of 'culture and cultural studies', some (selective) history of the field. However, most of the later chapters, the *sites* of cultural studies, draw on more contemporary theory. Indeed, in order to make the book as useful as possible in as many different geographical places as possible, there is a stress on theory over context-specific empirical work (though theory is also context-specific and the text does try to link theory with empirical work). In doing so, I deploy a good number of theorists who would not describe themselves as working within cultural studies but who have something to say which has informed it. Thus, writers like Tony Bennett, Paul Gilroy, Lawrence Grossberg, Stuart Hall, Meaghan Morris and Paul Willis would probably accept a description of their work as 'cultural studies'. However, though extremely influential, neither Foucault, Derrida nor Barthes would have described himself in this way, just as Giddens would not adopt this self-nomination today.

This book is a selective account because it stresses a certain type of cultural studies. In particular, I explore that version of cultural studies which places language at its heart. The kind of cultural studies influenced by poststructuralist theories of language, representation and subjectivity is given greater attention than a cultural studies more concerned with the ethnography of lived experience or with cultural policy. Nevertheless, both do receive attention and I am personally supportive of both.

✓ *Cultural studies does not speak with one voice, it cannot be spoken with one voice, and I do not have one voice with which to represent it.*

The title of this book is somewhat over-ambitious in its claims. Not only is this a selective account of cultural studies, it is one that draws very largely from work developed in Britain, the United States, Continental Europe (most notably France) and Australia. I draw very little from a growing body of work in Africa, Asia and Latin America. As such, it would be more accurate to call this text western cultural studies. I simply do not feel qualified to say how much cultural studies, as I understand it, is pertinent to the social and cultural conditions of Africa.

The language-game of cultural studies

Further, this book tends to gloss over differences within western cultural studies, despite doubts about whether theory developed in one context (e.g. Britain) can be workable in another (e.g. Australia) (Ang and Stratton, 1996; Turner, 1992). Nevertheless, I want to justify this degree of generalization about cultural studies. I maintain that the term 'cultural studies' has no referent to which we can point. Rather, cultural studies is constituted by the language-game of cultural studies. The theoretical terms developed and deployed by persons calling their work cultural studies is what cultural studies 'is'. I stress the language of cultural studies as constitutive of cultural studies and draw attention at the start of each chapter to what I take to be important terms. Subsequently, each of these concepts, and others, can be referred to in the Glossary at the end of the book.

These are concepts that have been deployed in the various geographical sites of cultural studies. For, as Grossberg et al. have argued, though cultural studies has stressed conjunctural analysis, 'which is embedded, descriptive, and historically and contextually specific', there are some concepts in cultural studies across the globe which form 'a history of real achievements that is now part of the cultural studies tradition', and to do without which would be 'to willingly accept real incapacitation' (Grossberg et al., 1992: 8). Concepts are tools for thinking and acting in the world.

Cultural studies as politics

It remains difficult to pin down the boundaries of cultural studies as a coherent, unified, academic discipline with clear-cut substantive topics, concepts and methods that differentiate it from other disciplines. Cultural studies has always been a multi- or post-disciplinary field of enquiry which blurs the boundaries between itself and other 'subjects'. Yet cultural studies cannot be said to be anything. It is not physics, it is not sociology and it is not linguistics, though it draws upon these subject areas. Indeed, there must be, as Hall (1992a) argues, something at stake in cultural studies that differentiates itself from other subject areas.

For Hall, what is at stake is the connection that cultural studies seeks to make to matters of power and cultural politics. That is, to an exploration of representations of and 'for' marginalized social groups and the need for cultural change. Hence, cultural studies is a body of theory generated by thinkers who regard the production of theoretical knowledge as a political practice. Here, knowledge is never a neutral or objective phenomenon but a matter of positionality, that is, of the place from which one speaks, to whom, and for what purposes.

THE PARAMETERS OF CULTURAL STUDIES

There is a difference between the study of culture and institutionally located cultural studies. The study of culture has taken place in a variety of academic disciplines – sociology, anthropology, English literature, etc. – and in a range of geographical and institutional spaces. However, this is not to be understood as cultural studies. The study of culture has no origins, and to locate one is to exclude other possible starting points. Nevertheless this does not mean that cultural studies cannot be named and its key concepts identified.

Cultural studies is a discursive formation, that is, 'a cluster (or formation) of ideas, images and practices, which provide ways of talking about, forms of knowledge and conduct associated with, a particular topic, social activity or institutional site in society' (Hall, 1997a: 6). Cultural studies is constituted by a *regulated* way of speaking about objects (which it brings into view) and coheres around key concepts, ideas and concerns. Further, cultural studies had a moment at which it named itself, even though that naming marks only a cut or snapshot of an ever-evolving intellectual project.

KEY THINKERS

Stuart Hall (1932–)

A West Indian born British thinker initially associated with the 'New Left' of the late-1960s, Hall was the Director of the Birmingham Centre for Contemporary Cultural Studies from 1968 to 1979. It was during this time that an identifiable and particular field called cultural studies began to emerge. Stuart Hall is perhaps the most significant figure in the development of British cultural studies. Hall's work makes considerable use of Gramsci and the concepts of ideology and hegemony, though he also played a significant part in deploying poststructuralism in cultural studies.

Reading: Morley, D. and Chen, D.-K. (eds) (1996) *Stuart Hall.* London: Routledge.

The Centre for Contemporary Cultural Studies

Cultural studies has been reluctant to accept institutional legitimation. Nevertheless, the formation of the Centre for Contemporary Cultural Studies at Birmingham University (UK) in the 1960s was a decisive organizational instance. Since that time, cultural studies has extended its intellectual base and geographic scope. There are self-defined cultural studies practitioners in the USA, Australia, Africa, Asia, Latin America and Europe, with each 'formation' of cultural studies working in different ways. While I am not privileging British cultural studies *per se*, I am pointing to the formation of cultural studies at Birmingham as an institutionally significant moment.

Since its emergence, cultural studies has acquired a multitude of institutional bases, courses, textbooks and students as it has become something to be taught. As McGuigan (1997a) comments, it is difficult to see how it could be otherwise, despite the concern that professionalized and institutionalized cultural studies may 'formalize out of existence the critical questions of power, history and politics' (Hall, 1992a: 286). Cultural studies' main location has always been institutions of higher education and the bookshop. Consequently, one way of 'defining' cultural studies is to look at what university courses offer to students. This necessarily involves 'disciplining' cultural studies.

Disciplining cultural studies

Many cultural studies practitioners oppose forging disciplinary boundaries for the field. However, it is hard to see how this can be resisted if cultural studies wants to survive by attracting degree students and funding (as opposed to being only a postgraduate research activity). In that context, Bennett (1998) offers his 'element of a definition' of cultural studies:

- **Cultural studies is an interdisciplinary field in which perspectives from different disciplines can be selectively drawn on to examine the relations of culture and power.**

- **'Cultural studies is concerned with all those practices, institutions and systems of classification through which there are inculcated in a population particular values, beliefs, competencies, routines of life and habitual forms of conduct' (Bennett, 1998: 28).**

- **The forms of power that cultural studies explores are diverse and include gender, race, class, colonialism, etc. Cultural studies seeks to explore the connections between these forms of power and to develop ways of thinking about culture and power that can be utilized by agents in the pursuit of change.**

- The prime institutional sites for cultural studies are those of higher education, and as such, cultural studies is like other academic disciplines. Nevertheless, it tries to forge connections outside of the academy with social and political movements, workers in cultural institutions, and cultural management.

With this in mind, we may consider the kinds of concepts and concerns that regulate cultural studies as a discursive formation or language-game. Each of the concepts introduced here is developed at greater length throughout the book and can also be referred to in the Glossary.

KEY CONCEPTS IN CULTURAL STUDIES

Culture and signifying practices

Cultural studies would not warrant its name without a focus on culture (Chapter 2). As Hall puts it, 'By culture, here I mean the actual grounded terrain of practices, representations, languages and customs of any specific society. I also mean the contradictory forms of common sense which have taken root in and helped to shape popular life' (Hall, 1996c: 439). Culture is concerned with questions of shared social meanings, that is, the various ways we make sense of the world. However, meanings are not simply floating 'out there'; rather, they are generated through signs, most notably those of language.

Cultural studies has argued that language is not a neutral medium for the formation of meanings and knowledge about an independent object world 'existing' outside of language. Rather, it is constitutive of those very meanings and knowledge. That is, language gives meaning to material objects and social practices that are brought into view by language and made intelligible to us in terms that language delimits. These processes of meaning production are signifying practices. In order to understand culture, we need to explore how meaning is produced symbolically in language as a 'signifying system' (Chapter 3).

Representation

A good deal of cultural studies is centred on questions of representation. That is, on how the world is socially constructed and represented to and by us in meaningful ways. Indeed, the central strand of cultural studies can be understood as the study of culture as the signifying practices of representation. This requires us to explore the textual generation of meaning. It also demands investigation of the modes by which meaning is produced in a variety of contexts. Further, cultural representations and meanings have a certain materiality. That is, they are embedded in sounds, inscriptions, objects, images, books, magazines and television programmes. They are produced, enacted, used and understood in specific social contexts.

THE PLANET

© Photographer: Svetlana Prevzentseva | Agency: Dreamstime.com

- *Is this image a reflection of the natural world or a cultural representation?*

- *This picture was only possible with the advent of space travel. How might its appearance in our culture have changed the way we think about ourselves?*

- *Can you imagine cultural life without this picture in our minds?*

Materialism and non-reductionism

Cultural studies has, for the most part, been concerned with modern industrialized economies and media cultures organized along capitalist lines. Here representations are produced by corporations who are driven by the profit motive. In this context, cultural studies has developed a form of cultural materialism that is concerned to explore how and why meanings are inscribed at the moment of production. That is, as well as being centred on signifying practices, cultural studies tries to connect them with political economy. This is a discipline concerned with power and the distribution of economic and social resources. Consequently, cultural studies has been concerned with:

- **who owns and controls cultural production;**
- **the distribution mechanisms for cultural products;**
- **the consequences of patterns of ownership and control for contours of the cultural landscape.**

Having said that, one of the central tenets of cultural studies is its non-reductionism. Culture is seen as having its own specific meanings, rules and practices which are not reducible to, or explainable solely in terms of, another category or level of a social formation. In particular, cultural studies has waged a battle against economic reductionism. That is, the attempt to explain what a cultural text means by reference to its place in the production process. For cultural studies, the processes of political economy do not determine the meanings of texts or their appropriation by audiences. Rather, political economy, social relationships and culture must be understood in terms of their own specific logics and modes of development. Each of these domains is 'articulated' or related together in context-specific ways. The non-reductionism of cultural studies insists that questions of class, gender, sexuality, race, ethnicity, nation and age have their own particularities which cannot be reduced either to political economy or to each other.

Articulation

Cultural studies has deployed the concept of articulation in order to theorize the relationships between components of a social formation. This idea refers to the formation of a temporary unity between elements that do not have to go together. Articulation suggests both expressing/representing and a 'putting-together'. Thus, representations of gender may be 'put-together' with representations of race or nation so that, for example, nations are spoken of as female. This occurs in context-specific and contingent ways that cannot be predicted before the fact. The concept of articulation is also deployed to discuss the relationship between culture and political economy. Thus culture is said to be 'articulated' with moments of production but not determined in any 'necessary' way by that moment, and vice versa. Consequently, we might explore how the moment of production is inscribed in texts but also how the 'economic' is cultural, that is, a meaningful set of practices.

Power

Cultural studies writers generally agree on the centrality of the concept of power to the discipline. For most cultural studies writers, power is regarded as pervading every level of social relationships. Power is not simply the glue that holds the social together, or the coercive force which subordinates one set of people to another, though it certainly is this. It is also understood in terms of the processes that generate and enable any form of social action, relationship or order. In this sense, power, while certainly constraining, is also enabling. Having said that, cultural studies has shown a specific concern with subordinated groups, at first with class, and later with races, genders, nations, age groups, etc.

Popular culture

Subordination is a matter not just of coercion but also of consent. Cultural studies has commonly understood popular culture to be the ground on which this consent is won or lost. As a way of grasping the interplay of power and consent, two related concepts were repeatedly deployed in cultural studies' earlier texts, though they are less prevalent these days, namely ideology and hegemony.

By ideology is commonly meant maps of meaning that, while they purport to be universal truths, are historically specific understandings that obscure and maintain power. For example, television news produces understandings of the world that continually explain it in terms of nations, perceived as 'naturally' occurring objects. This may have the consequence of obscuring both the class divisions of social formations and the constructed character of nationality.

Representations of gender in advertising, which depict women as housewives or sexy bodies alone, reduce them to those categories. As such, they deny women their place as full human beings and citizens. The process of making, maintaining and reproducing ascendant meanings and practices has been called hegemony. Hegemony implies a situation where a 'historical bloc' of powerful groups exercises social authority and leadership over subordinate groups through the winning of consent.

Texts and readers

The production of consent implies popular identification with the cultural meanings generated by the signifying practices of hegemonic texts. The concept of text suggests not simply the written word, though this is one of its senses, but all practices that signify. This includes the generation of meaning through images, sounds, objects (such as clothes) and activities (like dance and sport). Since images, sounds, objects and practices are sign systems, which signify with the same mechanism as a language, we may refer to them as cultural texts.

However, the meanings that critics read into cultural texts are not necessarily the same as those produced by active audiences or readers. Indeed, readers will not necessarily share all the same meanings with each other. Critics, in other words, are simply a particular breed of reader. Further, texts, as forms of representation, are polysemic. That is, they contain the possibility of a number of different meanings that have to be realized by actual readers who give life to words and images. We can examine the ways in which texts work, but we cannot simply 'read-off' audiences' meaning production from textual analysis. At the very least, meaning is produced in the interplay between text and reader. Consequently, the moment of consumption is also a moment of meaningful production.

Subjectivity and identity

The moment of consumption marks one of the processes by which we are formed as persons. What it is to be a person, viz. subjectivity, and how we describe ourselves to each other, viz. identity, became central areas of concern in cultural studies during the 1990s. In other words, cultural studies explores:

- **how we come to be the kinds of people we are;**
- **how we are produced as subjects;**
- **how we identify with (or emotionally invest in) descriptions of ourselves as male or female, black or white, young or old.**

The argument, known as *anti-essentialism*, is that identities are not things that exist; they have no essential or universal qualities. Rather, they are discursive constructions, the product of discourses or regulated ways of speaking about the world. In other words, identities are constituted, made rather than found, by representations, notably language.

Overall, some of the key concepts that constitute the discursive formation of cultural studies are:

KEY CONCEPTS

Active audiences	*Politics*
Anti-essentialism	*Polysemy*
Articulation	*Popular culture*
Cultural materialism	*Positionality*
Culture	*Power*
Discourse	*Representation*
Discursive formation	*Signifying practices*
Hegemony	*(the) Social*
Identity	*Social formation*
Ideology	*Subjectivity*
Language-game	*Texts*
Political economy	

✓ *Cultural studies writers differ about how to deploy these concepts and about which are the most significant.*

THE INTELLECTUAL STRANDS OF CULTURAL STUDIES

The concepts we have explored are drawn from a range of theoretical and methodological paradigms. The most influential theories within cultural studies have been: Marxism, culturalism, structuralism, poststructuralism, psychoanalysis and the politics of difference (under which heading, for the sake of convenience, I include feminism, theories of race, ethnicity and postcolonialism). The purpose of sketching the basic tenets of these theoretical domains is to provide a signpost to thinking in the field. However, each is developed in more detail throughout the text and there is no one place in the book to look for theory. Theory permeates all levels of cultural studies and needs to be connected to specific issues and debates rather than be explored solely in the abstract.

Marxism and the centrality of class

Marxism is, above all, a form of historical materialism. It stresses the historical specificity of human affairs and the changeable character of social formations whose core features are located in the material conditions of existence. Marx (1961) argued that the first priority of human beings is the production of their means of subsistence through labour. As humans produce food, clothes and all manner of tools with which to shape their environment, so they also create themselves. Thus labour, and the forms of social organization that material production takes, a mode of production, are central categories of Marxism.

The organization of a mode of production is not simply a matter of co-ordinating objects; rather, it is inherently tied up with relations between people. These relationships, while social, that is, co-operative and co-ordinated, are also matters of power and conflict. Indeed, Marxists regard social antagonisms as being the motor of historical change. Further, given the priority accorded to production, other aspects of human relations – consciousness, culture and politics – are said to be structured by economic relations (see Chapter 2).

For Marxism, history is not a smooth evolutionary process. Rather, it is marked by significant breaks and discontinuities of modes of production. Thus, Marx discusses the transformations from an ancient mode of production to a feudal mode of production and thence to the capitalist mode of production. Different forms of material organization and different social relations characterize each mode of production. Further, each mode of production is superseded by another as internal contradictions, particularly those of class conflict, lead to its transformation and replacement.

Capitalism

The centrepiece of Marx's work was an analysis of the dynamics of capitalism. This is a mode of production premised on the private ownership of the means of production (in his day, factories, mills, workshops; and in a more contemporary vein, multinational corporations). The fundamental class division of capitalism is between those who own the means of production, the bourgeoisie, and those who, being a propertyless proletariat, must sell their labour to survive.

The legal framework and common-sense thinking of capitalist societies declare that the worker is a free agent and the sale of labour a free and fair contract. However, Marx argues that this appearance covers over a fundamental exploitation at work. Capitalism aims to make a profit and does so by extracting surplus value from workers. That is, the value of the labour taken to produce a product, which becomes the property of the bourgeoisie, is less than the worker receives for it.

The realization of surplus value in monetary form is achieved by the selling of goods (which have both 'use value' and 'exchange value') as commodities. A commodity is something available to be sold in the marketplace. Thus, commodification is the process associated with capitalism by which objects, qualities and signs are turned into commodities. The surface appearance of goods sold in the marketplace obscures the origins of those commodities in an exploitative relationship, a process Marx calls commodity fetishism. Further, the fact that workers are faced with the products of their own labour now separated from them constitutes alienation. Since the proletariat are alienated from the core of human activity, namely the labour process, so they are alienated from themselves.

Capitalism is a dynamic system whose profit-driven mechanisms lead to the continual revolutionizing of the means of production and the forging of new markets. For Marx, this was its great merit in relation to feudalism. This is because it heralded a massive expansion in the productive capacities of European societies. It dragged them into the modern world of railways, mass production, cities and a formally equitable and free set of human relations in which people were not, in a legal sense, the property of others (as were serfs in feudal societies).

However, the mechanisms of capitalism also give rise to perennial crises and will ultimately lead, or so Marx argued, to its being superseded by socialism. Problems for capitalism include:

- **a falling rate of profit;**

- **cycles of boom and bust;**

- **increasing monopoly;**

- **the creation of a proletariat which is set to become the system's grave-digger.**

Marx hoped that capitalism would be rent asunder by class conflict. He envisaged the proletariat's organizations of defence, trade unions and political parties, overthrowing and replacing it with a mode of production based on communal ownership, equitable distribution and ultimately the end of class division.

Marxism and cultural studies

Cultural studies writers have had a long, ambiguous, but productive relationship with Marxism. Cultural studies is not a Marxist domain, but has drawn succour from it while subjecting it to vigorous critique. There is little doubt that we live in social formations organized along capitalist lines that manifest deep class divisions in work, wages, housing, education and health. Further, cultural practices are commodified by large corporate culture industries. In that context cultural studies has been partisan in taking up the cause of change.

However, Marxism has been critiqued for its apparent teleology. That is, the positing of an inevitable point to which history is moving, namely the demise of capitalism and the arrival of a classless society. This is a problem on both theoretical and empirical grounds. Theoretically, a determinist reading of Marxism robs human beings of agency or the capacity to act. This is so because the outcomes of human action appear to be predetermined by metaphysical laws (ironically posing as objective science) that drive history from outside of human action. It is a problem on empirical grounds because of the failure of significant numbers of proletarian revolutions to materialize and the oppressive totalitarian outcomes of those that made claims to be such revolutions.

In its engagement with Marxism, cultural studies has been particularly concerned with issues of structure and action. On the one hand, Marxism suggests that there are regularities or structures to human existence that lie outside of any given individual. On the other hand, it has a commitment to change through human agency.

Cultural studies has resisted the economic determinism inherent in some readings of Marxism and has asserted the specificity of culture. Cultural studies has also been concerned with the apparent success of capitalism. That is, not merely its survival but its transformation and expansion. This has been attributed in part to the winning of consent for capitalism on the level of culture. Hence the interest in questions of culture, ideology and hegemony (see Chapter 2) which were commonly pursued through perspectives dubbed culturalism and structuralism (see Hall, 1992a).

Culturalism and structuralism

In the collective mythology of cultural studies, Richard Hoggart (1957), Raymond Williams (1965, 1979, 1981, 1983) and Edward Thompson (1963) are held to be early figureheads representing the moment of 'culturalism'. This perspective is later contrasted with 'structuralism'. Indeed, culturalism is a *post hoc* term that owes its sense precisely to a contrast with structuralism.

Culture is ordinary

Culturalism stresses the 'ordinariness' of culture and the active, creative capacity of people to construct shared meaningful practices. Empirical work, which is emphasized within the culturalist tradition, explores the way that active human beings create cultural meanings. There is a focus on lived experience and the adoption of a broadly anthropological definition of culture which describes it as an everyday lived process not confined to 'high' art.

Culturalism, particularly for Williams and Thompson, is a form of historical cultural materialism that traces the unfolding of meaning over time. Here culture is to be explored within the context of its material conditions of production and reception. There is an explicit partisanship in exploring the class basis of culture that aims to give 'voice' to the subordinated and to examine the place of culture in class power. However, this form of 'left culturalism' is also somewhat nationalistic, or at least nation-centred, in its approach. There is little sense of either the globalizing character of contemporary culture or the place of race within national and class cultures.

Structuralism

Culturalism takes meaning to be its central category and casts it as the product of active human agents. By contrast, structuralism speaks of signifying practices that generate meaning as an outcome of structures or predictable regularities that lie outside of any given person. Structuralism searches for the constraining patterns of culture and social life which lie outside of any given person. Individual acts are explained as the product of social structures. As such, structuralism is anti-humanist in its decentring of human agents from the heart of enquiry. Instead it favours a form of analysis in which phenomena have meaning only in relation to other phenomena within a systematic structure of which no particular person is the source. A structuralist understanding of culture is concerned with the 'systems of relations' of an underlying structure (usually language) and the grammar that makes meaning possible.

Deep structures of language

Structuralism in cultural studies takes signification or meaning production to be the effect of deep structures of language that are manifested in specific cultural phenomena or human speakers. However, meaning is the outcome not of the intentions of actors *per se* but of the language itself. Thus, structuralism is concerned with how cultural meaning is generated, understanding culture to be analogous to (or structured like) a language (Chapter 3).

The work of Ferdinand de Saussure (1960) was critical in the development of structuralism. He argued that meaning is generated through a system of structured differences in language. That is, significance is the outcome of the rules and conventions that organize language (*langue*) rather than the specific uses and utterances which individuals deploy in everyday life (*parole*).

According to Saussure, meaning is produced through a process of selection and combination of signs along two axes, namely:

1 the syntagmatic (linear – e.g. a sentence);

2 the paradigmatic (a field of signs – e.g. synonyms).

The organization of signs along these axes forms a signifying system. Signs, constituted by signifiers (medium) and signifieds (meaning), do not make sense by virtue of reference to entities in an independent object world; rather, they generate meaning by reference to each other. Meaning is a social convention organized through the relations between signs.

In short, Saussure, and structuralism in general, are concerned more with the structures of language which allow linguistic performance to be possible than with actual performance in its infinite variations. Structuralism proceeds through the analysis of binaries: for example the contrast between *langue* and *parole* or between pairs of signs so that 'black' only has meaning in relation to 'white' and vice versa.

KEY THINKERS

Ferdinand de Saussure (1857–1913)

Saussure was a Swiss linguist whose posthumously published work laid the basis for structural linguistics or semiotics, the 'science' of signs. Saussure's influence on cultural studies comes indirectly through the work of other thinkers, like Roland Barthes, who were influenced by him. The central tenet of Saussure's argument is that language is to be understood as a sign system constituted by interrelated terms without positive values (that is, meaning is relational). *Langue*, or the formal structure of signs, is said to be the proper subject of linguistics. Cultural studies commonly explores culture as a grammar of signs.

Reading: Saussure, F. de (1960) *Course in General Linguistics*. London: Peter Owen.

Culture as 'like a language'

Structuralism extends its reach from 'words' to the language of cultural signs in general. Thus human relations, material objects and images are all analysed through the structures of signs. In Lévi-Strauss (see Leach, 1974), we find structuralist principles at work when he describes kinship systems as 'like a language'. That is, family relations are held to be structured by the internal organization of binaries. For example, kinship patterns are structured around the incest taboo that divides people into the marriageable and the prohibited.

Typical of Lévi-Strauss's structuralism is his approach to food, which, he declares, is not so much good to eat, as good to think with. That is, food is a signifier of symbolic meanings. Cultural conventions tell us what constitutes food and what does not, the circumstances of their eating and the meanings attached to them. Lévi-Strauss tends towards the structuralist trope of binaries: the raw and the cooked, the edible and the inedible, nature and culture, each of which has meaning only in relation to its opposite. Cooking transforms nature into culture and the raw into the cooked.

The edible and the inedible are marked not by questions of nutrition but by cultural meanings. An example of this would be the Jewish prohibition against pork and the necessity to prepare food in culturally specific ways (kosher food). Here, binary oppositions of the edible–inedible mark another binary, insiders and outsiders, and hence the boundaries of the culture or social order. Later, Barthes (see Chapter 3) was to extend the structuralist account of culture to the practices of popular culture and their naturalized meanings or myths. Barthes was to argue that the meanings of texts are to be grasped not in terms of the intentions of specific human beings but as a set of signifying practices.

In sum:

- **Culturalism focuses on meaning production by human actors in a historical context.**

- **Structuralism points to culture as an expression of deep structures of language that lie outside of the intentions of actors and constrain them.**

- **Culturalism stresses history.**

- **Structuralism is synchronic in approach, analysing the structures of relations in a snapshot of a particular moment. As such, it asserts the specificity of culture and its irreducibility to any other phenomena.**

- **Culturalism focuses on interpretation as a way of understanding meaning.**

- **Structuralism has asserted the possibility of a science of signs and thus of objective knowledge.**

Structuralism is best approached as a method of analysis rather than an all-embracing philosophy. However, the notion of stability of meaning, upon which the binaries of structuralism and its pretensions to surety of knowledge are based, is the subject of attack by poststructuralism. That is, poststructuralism deconstructs the very notion of the stable structures of language.

Poststructuralism (and postmodernism)

The term poststructuralism implies 'after structuralism', embodying notions of both critique and absorption. That is, poststructuralism absorbs aspects of structural linguistics while subjecting it to a critique that, it is claimed, surpasses structuralism. In short, poststructuralism rejects the idea of an underlying stable structure that founds meaning through fixed binary pairs (black–white; good–bad). Rather, meaning is unstable, being always deferred and in process. Meaning cannot be confined to single words, sentences or particular texts but is the outcome of relationships between texts, that is, intertextuality. Like its predecessor, poststructuralism is anti-humanist in its decentring of the unified, coherent human subject as the origin of stable meanings.

Derrida: the instability of language

The primary philosophical sources of poststructuralism are Derrida (1976) and Foucault (1984d) (see Chapter 3). Since they give rise to different emphases, poststructuralism cannot be regarded as a unified body of work. Derrida's focus is on language and the deconstruction of an immediacy, or identity, between words and meanings.

Derrida accepts Saussure's argument that meaning is generated by relations of difference between signifiers rather than by reference to an independent object world. However, for Derrida, the consequence of this play of signifiers is that meaning can never be fixed. Words carry many meanings, including the echoes or traces of other meanings from other related words in other contexts. For example, if we look up the meaning of a word in a dictionary, we are referred to other words in an infinite process of deferral. Meaning slides down a chain of signifiers abolishing a stable signified. Thus, Derrida introduces the notion of *différance*, 'difference and deferral'. Here the production of meaning in the process of signification is continually deferred and supplemented.

Derrida proceeds to deconstruct the 'stable' binaries upon which structuralism, and indeed western philosophy in general, relies. He argues for the 'undecidability' of binary oppositions. In particular, deconstruction involves the dismantling of hierarchical conceptual oppositions such as speech/writing, reality/appearance, nature/culture, reason/madness, etc., which exclude and devalue the 'inferior' part of the binary.

For Derrida, 'we think only in signs' and there is no original meaning circulating outside of 'representation'. It is in this sense that there is nothing outside of texts or nothing but texts (by which it is *not* meant that there is no independent material world). That is, the meanings of texts are constitutive of practices.

BUDDHIST SHRINE

© **Photographer: Freya Hadley**

- *What cultural practices take place around this Japanese Buddhist shrine?*

- *What is the meaning of the sign on the 'flags'? This sign was rotated and used in a different context. What meaning did it have in that context?*

- *What conclusion can you draw from this about the meanings of signs?*

Foucault and discursive practices

Like Derrida, Foucault (1972) argues against structuralist theories of language which conceive of it as an autonomous, rule-governed system. He also opposes interpretative or hermeneutic methods that seek to disclose the hidden meanings of language. Foucault is concerned with the description and analysis of the surfaces of discourse and their effects under determinate material and historical conditions. For Foucault, discourse concerns both language and practice. The concept refers to the regulated production of knowledge through language which gives meaning to both material objects and social practices.

Discourse constructs, defines and produces the objects of knowledge in an intelligible way while at the same time excluding other ways of reasoning as unintelligible. Foucault attempts to identify the historical conditions and determining rules of formation of regulated ways of speaking about objects, that is, discursive practices and discursive formations. He explores the circumstances under which statements are combined and regulated to form and define a distinct field of knowledge/objects requiring a particular set of concepts and delimiting a specific 'regime of truth' (i.e. what counts as truth).

For Foucault, discourse regulates not only what can be said under determinate social and cultural conditions but also who can speak, when and where. Consequently, much of his work is concerned with the historical investigation of power and the production of subjects through that power. Foucault does not formulate power as a centralized constraining force; rather, power is dispersed through all levels of a social formation and is productive of social relations and identities (i.e. generative).

Foucault conceives of the subject as radically historized, that is, persons are wholly and only the product of history. He explores the genealogy of the body as a site of disciplinary practices that bring subjects into being. Such practices are the consequences of specific historical discourses of crime, punishment, medicine, science and sexuality. Thus, Foucault (1973) analyses statements about madness which give us knowledge about it, the rules that prescribe what is 'sayable' or 'thinkable' about madness, subjects who personify madness, and the practices within institutions that deal with madness (see Chapter 3).

Anti-essentialism

Perhaps the most significant influence of poststructuralism within cultural studies is its anti-essentialism. Essentialism assumes that words have stable referents and that social categories reflect an essential underlying identity. By this token there would be stable truths to be found and an essence of, for example, femininity or black identity. However, for poststructuralism there can be no truths, subjects or identities outside of language. Further, this is a language that does not have stable referents and is therefore unable to represent fixed truths or identities. In this sense, femininity or black identity are not fixed universal things but descriptions in language which through social convention come to be 'what counts as truth' (i.e. the temporary stabilization of meaning).

Anti-essentialism does not mean that we cannot speak of truth or identity. Rather, it points to them as being not universals of nature but productions of culture in specific times and places. The speaking subject is dependent on the prior existence of discursive positions. Truth is not so much found as made and identities are discursive constructions. That is, truth and identity are not fixed objects but are regulated ways that we speak about the world or ourselves. Instead of the scientific certainty of structuralism, poststructuralism offers us irony: that is, an awareness of the contingent, constructed character of our beliefs and understandings that lack firm universal foundations.

Postmodernism

There is no straightforward equation of poststructuralism with postmodernism, and the sharing of the prefix 'post' can lead to unwarranted conflation of the two. However, they do share a common approach to epistemology, namely the rejection of truth as a fixed eternal object. Derrida's assertion of the instability of meaning and Foucault's awareness of the historically contingent character of truth are echoed in Jean-François Lyotard's postmodern 'incredulity towards metanarratives'. Lyotard (1984) rejects the idea of grand narratives or stories that can give us certain knowledge of the direction, meaning and moral path of human 'development'. Lyotard has in mind the teleology of Marxism, the certainty of science and the morality of Christianity.

Postmodern writers like Lyotard (1984) or Rorty (1989) share with Foucault the idea that knowledge is not metaphysical, transcendental or universal but specific to particular times and spaces. For postmodernism, knowledge is perspectival in character. That is, there can be no one totalizing knowledge that is able to grasp the 'objective' character of the world. Rather, we have and require multiple viewpoints or truths by which to interpret a complex, heterogeneous human existence. Thus, postmodernism argues that knowledge is:

- **specific to language-games;**
- **local, plural and diverse.**

One strand of postmodernism is concerned with these questions of epistemology, that is, questions of truth and knowledge. However, an equally significant body of work is centred on important cultural changes in contemporary life. Postmodern culture is said to be marked by a sense of the fragmentary, ambiguous and uncertain quality of the world along with high levels of personal and social reflexivity. This goes hand in hand with a stress on contingency, irony and the blurring of cultural boundaries. Cultural texts are said to be typified by self-consciousness, bricolage and intertextuality. For some thinkers, postmodern culture heralds the collapse of the modern distinction between the real and simulations (see Chapter 6).

✓ *Poststructuralism and postmodernism are anti-essentialist approaches that stress the constitutive role of an unstable language in the formation of cultural meaning.*

Poststructuralism and postmodernism argue that subjectivity is an effect of language or discourse and also that subjects are fractured – i.e. we can take up multiple subject positions offered to us in discourse. However, rather than rely on an account that stresses 'subjection' by external discourses, some writers have looked to psychoanalysis, and particularly Lacan's poststructuralist reading of Freud, for ways to think about the 'internal' constitution of subjects.

Psychoanalysis and subjectivity

Psychoanalysis is a controversial body of thought. For its supporters (Chodorow, 1978, 1989; Mitchell, 1974), its great strength lies in its rejection of the fixed nature of subjects and sexuality. That is, psychoanalysis concentrates on the construction and formation of subjectivity.

The Freudian self

According to Freud (1977), the self is constituted in terms of:

- *an ego*, **or conscious rational mind;**
- *a superego*, **or social conscience;**
- *the unconscious* **(also known as the id), the source and repository of the symbolic workings of the mind which functions with a different logic from reason.**

This structuring of the human subject is not something we are born with; rather, it is something we acquire through our relationships with our immediate 'carers'. Here the self is by definition fractured; consequently we must understand the unified narrative of the self as something we attain over time. This is said to be achieved through entry into the symbolic order of language and culture. Through processes of identification with others and with social discourses, we create an identity that embodies an illusion of wholeness.

Within Freudian theory, the libido or sexual drive does not have any pregiven fixed aim or object. Rather, through fantasy, any object, which includes persons or parts of bodies, can be the target of desire. Consequently, an almost infinite number of sexual objects and practices are within the domain of human sexuality. However, Freud's work is concerned to document and explain the regulation and repression of this 'polymorphous perversity' through the resolution (or not) of the Oedipus complex into 'normal' heterosexual gendered relationships.

The Oedipus complex

In classical Freudian thought, the Oedipus complex marks the formation of the ego and of gendered subjectivity. Prior to the Oedipal moment, we are unable to distinguish clearly between ourselves and other objects, nor do we have a sense of ourselves as male or female. An infant's first love-object is its mother, whom it both identifies with and desires. That is, the child wants both to 'be' the mother and to 'possess' the mother. The resolution of the Oedipus complex involves the repudiation of the mother as a love-object and the separation of the subject from the mother.

For boys, the incest taboo, symbolized by the power of the father as Phallus, means that desire for the mother is untenable and threatened by punishment in the form of castration. As a consequence, boys shift their identification from the mother to the father and take on masculinity and heterosexuality as the desirable subject form. For girls, the separation from the mother is more complex and arguably never completed. Girls do not entirely repudiate mother identification nor do they take on father identification. However, they do recognize the power of the Phallus as something which they do not have (penis envy) but which the father does. Since they do not have a penis (or symbolic Phallus), and thus cannot ever 'be' it, they cannot identify with it. However, they can set out to possess it. This they do by seeking to have a child by the father or, more accurately, other men who stand in for the father as Phallus.

Psychoanalysis can be understood to be an ahistorical universal account of subjectivity marking the psychic processes of humankind across history. Furthermore, for many critics it is inherently patriarchal and phallocentric. As such it has proved to be unacceptable within cultural studies. However, sympathetic critics have suggested that psychoanalysis can be reworked as a historically contingent account of subject formation. That is, one that describes it only under specific historical circumstances. Changes in the cultural and symbolic order are said to lead to changes in subject formation, and vice versa. The subversiveness of psychoanalysis would then lie in its disruption of the social order, including gendered relations, by trying to bring new kinds of thinking and subjectivities into being. Thus, psychoanalysis could, it is argued, be stripped of its phallocentrism and be made appropriate to the political project of feminism (Chapter 9).

The politics of difference: feminism, race and postcolonial theory

A theme of structuralism and poststructuralism is the idea that meaning is generated through the play of difference down a chain of signifiers. Subjects are formed through difference, so that what we are is constituted in part by what we are not.

✓ *There has been a growing emphasis on difference in the cultural field, and in particular on questions of gender, race and nationality.*

Feminism

Feminism (Chapter 9) is a field of theory and politics that contains competing perspectives and prescriptions for action. However, in general terms, we may locate feminism as asserting that sex is a fundamental and irreducible axis of social organization which, to date, has subordinated women to men. Thus, feminism is centrally concerned with sex as an organizing principle of social life where gender relations are thoroughly saturated with power. The subordination of women is argued to be evident across a range of social institutions and practices, that is, male power and female subordination are structural. This has led some feminists to adopt the concept of patriarchy, with its derivative meanings of the male-headed family, 'mastery' and superiority.

Liberal feminism stresses equality of opportunity for women. This is held to be achievable within the broad structures of the existing legal and economic frameworks. In contrast, socialist feminists point to the interconnections between class and gender, including the fundamental place of gender inequalities in the reproduction of capitalism. Instead of liberal and socialist feminism's stress on equality and sameness, difference or radical feminism asserts essential differences between men and women. These are celebrated as representing the creative difference of women and the superiority of 'feminine' values.

Problems with patriarchy A criticism of the concept of patriarchy is its treatment of the category of 'woman' as undifferentiated. That is, all women are taken to share something fundamental in common in contrast to all men. This is an assumption continually challenged by black feminists, amongst others, who have argued that the movement has defined women as white and overlooked the differences between black and white women's experiences. This stress on difference is shared by poststructuralist and postmodern feminists who argue that sex and gender are social and cultural constructions, which cannot be adequately explained in terms of biology or reduced to functions of capitalism. This is an anti-essentialist stance that argues that femininity and masculinity are not essential universal categories but discursive constructions. That is, gender is constituted by the way we talk about and perform it. As such, poststructuralist feminism is concerned with the cultural construction of subjectivity *per se* and with a range of possible masculinities and femininities.

Race, ethnicity and hybridity

Another 'politics of difference' which has received increasing attention within cultural studies is that of race and ethnicity in postcolonial times (see Chapters 8 and 14). Ethnicity is a cultural concept centred on norms, values, beliefs, cultural symbols and practices that mark a process of cultural boundary formation. The idea of 'racialization' has been deployed to illustrate the argument that race is a social construction and not a universal or essential category of either biology or culture. Races do not exist outside of representation but are formed in and by it in a process of social and political power struggle.

There are two key concerns that have emerged in and through postcolonial theory (Williams and Chrisman, 1993), namely those of domination–subordination and hybridity–creolization. Questions of domination and subordination surface most directly through colonial military control and the structured subordination of racialized groups. In more cultural terms, questions arise about the denigration and subordination of 'native' culture by colonial and imperial powers along with the relationship between place and diaspora identities.

The question of hybridity or creolization points to the fact that neither the colonial nor colonized cultures and languages can be presented in 'pure' form. Inseparable from each other, they give rise to forms of hybridity. In metropolitan cultures like America and Britain, this concept is reworked to include the hybrid cultures produced by, for example, Latino-Americans and British Asians.

CENTRAL PROBLEMS IN CULTURAL STUDIES

Over the past 30 years or so, cultural studies has developed to a stage where similar problems, issues and debates have emerged from within the literature. A 'problem' in cultural studies is constituted by a field of recurrent doubts and puzzles in the literature. Although such problems are discussed throughout this book it is worth crystallizing some of the key points at this stage.

Language and the material

A long-running debate within cultural studies concerns the relationship between culture as signification and culture as material. This debate is located in the triangular confrontation between:

1 **the legacy of Marxism within cultural studies;**

2 **the development of an anti-reductionist strain within cultural studies;**

3 **the recent ascendancy of poststructuralism.**

For Marxism, culture is a corporeal force locked into the socially organized production of the material conditions of existence. Marxism has argued that the material mode of production is 'the real foundation' of cultural superstructures. That is, the material – understood here as the economic – determines the cultural. However, this orthodox reading of Marx proved to be too mechanical and deterministic in exploring the *specific* features of culture. Consequently, the narrative of cultural studies involves a distancing of itself from Marxist reductionism. Instead, the analysis of the autonomous logic of language, culture, representation and consumption was placed in the foreground. Structuralism provided the means by which to explore language and popular culture as autonomous practices by emphasizing the irreducible character of the cultural (as a set of distinct practices with their own internal organization).

Some critics have felt that cultural studies has gone too far in its assertion of the autonomy of culture and has abandoned political economy. Although this argument has some merit, it is not the case in the multiperspectival approach offered by Hall et al.'s 'circuit of culture' (see Figure 2.2 on p. 60). Here a full analysis of any cultural practice requires discussion of both 'economy' and 'culture' and articulation of the relations between them. Accordingly, the material as political economy vs. cultural autonomy debate represents an unnecessary binary division.

The textual character of culture

The machinery and operations of language are central concerns for cultural studies. Indeed, the investigation of culture has often been regarded as virtually interchangeable with the exploration of meaning produced symbolically through signifying systems that work 'like a language'. This turn to studying language within cultural studies represents a major intellectual gain and research achievement. It has also involved some partial sightedness.

Most students of cultural studies are aware that culture can be read as a text, using concepts like signification, code or discourse. However, an emphasis on structuralist and poststructuralist accounts of signification has sometimes led cultural studies to reify language as a 'thing' or 'system' rather than grasp it as a social practice. The danger here is a kind of textual determinism. That is, textual subject positions are held to be indistinguishable from, and constitutive of, speaking subjects. The living, embodied speaking and acting subject may be lost from view.

The metaphor of culture as 'like a language' has a great deal to recommend it. However, there is also much to be gained by describing culture in terms of practices, routines and spatial arrangements. Not only is language always embedded in practice, but also all practices signify. Further, the identification of textual codes and subject positions does not guarantee that the proscribed meanings are 'taken up' by concrete persons in daily life (see Ang, 1985; Morley, 1992). In sum, the study of language is absolutely critical to cultural studies as an ongoing project. At the same time, there remain some significant blind-spots in the field, including:

- the positing of language as a free-floating system rather than a human social activity;
- the elevation of semiotic theory over the linguistic competencies of living persons.

Name three different types of cultural text.

— What are the common elements that make up a cultural text?
— What different features of each of the three texts can you identify?
— Can you distinguish any differences between a text and a practice?

The location of culture

For Raymond Williams (1981, 1983) culture is located, for all intents and purposes, within flexible but identifiable boundaries. That is, culture is understood to be a facet of place. Indeed it is constitutive of place. In so far as culture is a common whole way of life, its boundaries are largely locked into those of nationality and ethnicity, that is, the culture of, for example, the English or perhaps the British. However, globalization has made the idea of culture as a whole way of life located within definite boundaries increasingly problematic.

In particular, that which is considered to be local is produced within and by globalizing discourses. These include global corporate marketing strategies that orient themselves to differentiated 'local' markets. Much that is considered to be local, and counterpoised to the global, is the outcome of translocal processes (Robertson, 1992). Place is now forged globally by virtue of the movement of cultural elements from one location to another. For example, population movement and electronic communications have enabled increased cultural juxtapostioning, meeting and mixing. These developments suggest the need to escape from a model of culture as a locally bounded, 'whole way of life'.

The processes of globalization suggest that we need to rethink our conception of culture. Culture is not best understood in terms of locations and roots but more as hybrid and creolized cultural routes in global space. Indeed, the prominence given to difference in cultural theory has led many writers to think of culture, identities and identifications as always a place of borders and hybridity rather than fixed stable entities (Bhabha, 1994).

✓ *Cultures are not pure, authentic and locally bounded. They are the syncretic and hybridized products of interactions across space.*

KEY THINKERS

Homi K. Bhabha (1949–)

Homi Bhabha was born in India and educated at Bombay University and Christ Church College, Oxford University. He is currently Professor in the Humanities at the University of Chicago, where he teaches in the Departments of English and Art. Strongly influenced by poststructuralism, Bhabha argues against the tendency to essentialize 'Third World' countries into a homogeneous identity, claiming instead that all sense of nationhood is narrativized. For Bhabha, the instability of meaning in language leads us to think of culture, identities and identifications as always a place of borders and hybridity rather than of fixed stable entities, a view encapsulated in his use of concepts such as mimicry, interstice, hybridity and liminality.

Reading: Bhabha, H. (1994) *The Location of Culture.* London and New York: Routledge.

Yet there remains a value in locating culture in-place in order to be able to say things like 'this is a valued and meaningful practice in Australian culture' or that the cultural flows of the 'Black Atlantic' involve musical forms of 'West African origin'. The *duality of culture* lies in its being both 'in-place' and of 'no-place'. Global culture can be understood as a series of fluid and overlapping fields (or language-games) marked out with the temporary knots or nodal points of place. Phrases like 'a whole way of life' or a 'local culture' no longer signify cultural entities but are expressions that mark out analytic boundaries drawn for particular purposes.

Consider what kind of a place you call 'home'.

— What feelings do you associate with 'home'?
— What symbols, practices and emotions give 'home' meaning and significance for you?

Consider the phrase 'homeland'.

— What are the elements that give this term meaning for you?
— How many of the symbols and practices associated with your homeland originated from outside of its borders?

How is cultural change possible?

Cultural studies writers have consistently identified the examination of culture, power and politics as central to the domain. Indeed, cultural studies can be understood as a body of theory generated by thinkers who regard the production of theoretical knowledge as a political practice. Many cultural studies writers have wanted to link their work with political movements. This followed the model of the 'organic' intellectuals, who were said to be the thinking and organizing elements of the counter-hegemonic class and its allies.

However, there is little evidence to suggest that cultural studies writers have ever been 'organically' connected with political movements in any significant way. Rather, as Hall (1992a) has commented, cultural studies intellectuals acted 'as if' they were organic intellectuals, or in the hope that one day they could be. Originally cultural studies writers imagined themselves organically linked to revolutionary class factions. Later, as class declined as a political vehicle and socialism receded as an immediate goal, New Social Movements (NSMs) took on the mantle of political agents. However, cultural studies has not been especially successful in forging links with such movements either.

Indeed, there is little evidence of popular support for radical political change in the west at all, let alone 'cultural revolution'. Reform seems to be the only possible way to move forward within western liberal democracies. This does not mean that we have to accept liberal democracy as it stands. On the contrary, one of our aims must be to push for the extension of democratic practices within the liberal democratic framework. This has led some in the field to argue for cultural policy that is specifically and carefully targeted with a clear sense of the intended outcomes and mechanisms of transformation. Overall cultural studies has not developed a general political strategy but engages where it can on a contingent basis.

Rationality and its limits

Western cultures mostly assume that human life is explicable in terms of the rational choices of individual actors. Rational action is that which can be justified within a specific cultural context. Cultural studies would not want to adopt the notion of the rational actor who calculates the means to maximize his or her interests. Nevertheless, there has been an implicit assumption that rationality could provide logical explanations for cultural phenomena. For example, a common assumption has been that racism and sexism would dwindle in the face of rational argument.

Often absent from cultural studies are the non-linear, non-rational and emotionally driven aspects of human behaviour. The exception to this observation is the import of psychoanalysis into the field. For example, Hall (1990, 1992b, 1996a) and Butler (1993) have profitably explored Lacanian psychoanalysis and the processes by which our psychic identifications, or emotional investments, are attached to disciplinary discourses. Yet psychoanalysis has its own problems, not least its phallocentrism and spurious claims to objective science (see Chapters 2 and 9). But still, there are very good reasons why cultural studies as a discipline needs to further develop issues of affect and emotion. Many of the horrors of our world are driven by emotional responses and social change is never going to be a simple matter of argument and analysis.

The exploration of emotion is one route by which to dethrone the ascendancy and authority of the rational mind. Another is pursued by a postmodern philosophy that has turned reason against itself. For over 200 years reason and rationality have been championed as the source of progress in knowledge and society. However, a range of postmodern thinkers have criticized the impulses of modern rationality. They argue that it brings us not so much progress as domination and oppression. The very impulse to control nature through science and rationality is, it is argued, an impulse to control and dominate human beings. This is an instrumental rationality whose logic leads not only to industrialization but also to concentration camps.

Foucault, for example, argues that:

- **Knowledge is not metaphysical, transcendental or universal.**
- **Knowledge is a matter of perspective.**
- **Knowledge is not pure or neutral but is always from a point of view.**
- **Knowledge is itself implicated in regimes of power.**

However, Foucault also questions the idea of a clear and final break between enlightenment and post-enlightenment thought, or between the modern and postmodern. It is not a question of accepting or rejecting enlightenment rationality but of asking: 'What is this reason that we use? What are its historical effects? What are its limits, and what are its dangers?' (Foucault, 1984c: 249).

The character of truth

How can we ground or justify cultural theory and cultural politics? This is one of the central problems of cultural studies. For modernists, the adoption of a realist epistemology has allowed writers and researchers to make universal truth claims. It follows that once we know the truth about the workings of the social world, then we can intervene strategically in human affairs with confidence. All the social sciences, from sociology to economics and psychology, were founded on the premise that conceptual and empirical truth can be discovered.

However, realist epistemologies have largely been displaced within cultural studies. This is a consequence of the influence of poststructuralism, postmodernism and other anti-representationalist paradigms. These widely accepted (within cultural studies) strands of thinking have undermined the notion of objective and universal truth.

For the philosopher Nietzsche (1968) truth is expressed in language so that sentences are the only things that can be true or false. Truth is a 'mobile army of metaphors and metonyms'. An acculturated authority arbitrates between these sentences. Thus 'truth' is a question of whose interpretations count as truth. Truth is embroiled in power. Foucault

(1972, 1973), whose work was greatly informed by Nietzsche, argues that different epistemes, or configurations of knowledge, shape the practices and social order of specific historical periods. In place of Truth, Foucault speaks instead about particular 'regimes of truth'. Similarly, Rorty (1980, 1989) argues that all truth is culture-bound and specific to times and places. Knowledge and values are located in time, space and social power.

✓ *Truth is understood to be a social commendation rather than an accurate picture of an independent object world.*

For its critics, this anti-representationalism is a form of *relativism* that posits the existence of a series of epistemologically equal truth claims. This situation has led, or so it is said, to a fatal inability to make judgements between forms of knowledge. Relativism *per se* is a self-contradictory and self-undermining position for its own claims are also subject to relativity; consequently, it must be rejected. However, to argue that all knowledge is positional or culture-bound is not to embrace relativism. Relativism would imply the ability to see across different forms of knowledge and to conclude that they are of equal value. Instead, as Rorty argues, we are always positioned *within* acculturated knowledge. There is no final vocabulary of language that is 'true' in the sense of accurately picturing an independent object world called reality. Our vocabularies are only final in the sense of currently being without tenable challenge. Thus our best bet is to go on telling stories about ourselves that aim to achieve the most valued description and arrangement of human actions and institutions.

QUESTIONS OF METHODOLOGY

Cultural studies has not paid much attention to the classical questions of research methods and methodology. Thus, methodological texts by Alasuutari (1995), McGuigan (1997b) and Gray (2003) are exceptions to the rule. Further, most of the debates in cultural studies have not been concerned with the technicalities of method but with the philosophical approaches that underpin them, that is, methodology. The most significant methodological debates within cultural studies have centred on the status of knowledge and truth, as discussed above. These are issues of epistemology, or the philosophy of knowledge. As we have seen, the realist argument is that a degree of certain knowledge about an independent object world (a real world) is possible even though methodological vigilance and reflexivity need to be maintained. Within cultural studies this point of view has more often than not appeared in a quasi-Marxist guise. In contrast, for post-structuralists knowledge is not a question of discovering objective and accurate truth but of constructing interpretations about the world which are 'taken to be true'.

Key methodologies in cultural studies

Despite disputes about the status of knowledge, it is reasonably clear which methods are most widely deployed within cultural studies, though researchers disagree about their relative merits. We may start with the standard methodological distinction between quantitative and qualitative research methods. That is, between, respectively, methods that centre on numbers and the counting of things (e.g. statistics and surveys) and those that concentrate on the meanings generated by actors gathered through participant observation, interviews, focus groups and textual analysis. On the whole, cultural studies has favoured qualitative methods with their focus on cultural meaning.

Work in cultural studies has centred on three kinds of approach:

1 *ethnography*, which has often been linked with culturalist approaches and a stress on 'lived experience';

2 a range of *textual* approaches, which have tended to draw from semiotics, post-structuralism and Derridean deconstruction;

3 a series of *reception* studies, which are eclectic in their theoretical roots.

Ethnography

Ethnography is an empirical and theoretical approach inherited from anthropology which seeks detailed holistic description and analysis of cultures based on intensive fieldwork. In classical conceptions, 'the Ethnographer participates in people's lives for an extended period of time, watching what happens, listening to what is said, asking questions' (Hammersley and Atkinson, 1983: 2). The objective is to produce what Geertz (1973) famously described as 'thick descriptions' of 'the multiplicity of complex conceptual structures'. This would include the unspoken and taken-for-granted assumptions that operate within cultural life. Ethnography concentrates on the details of local life while connecting them to wider social processes.

Ethnographic cultural studies has been centred on the qualitative exploration of values and meanings in the context of a 'whole way of life'. That is, ethnography has been deployed in order to explore questions about cultures, life-worlds and identities. As Morley remarks, 'qualitative research strategies such as ethnography are principally designed to gain access to "naturalized domains" and their characteristic activities' (Morley, 1992: 186). However, in the context of media-oriented cultural studies, ethnography has become a code-word for a range of qualitative methods, including participant observation, in-depth interviews and focus groups. Here, it is the 'spirit' of ethnography (i.e. qualitative understanding of cultural activity in context) which is invoked polemically against the tradition of quantitative communications research.

The problem of representation   Ethnography has tried to 'represent the subjective mean-ings, feelings and cultures of others' (Willis, 1980: 91). In this way, ethnography has relied on an implicitly realist epistemology. This assumption that it is possible to represent in a naturalistic way the 'real' experience of people has been the subject of considerable critique.

- **First, it is argued that the data presented by ethnographers are always already an interpretation made through that person's eyes. That is, interpretation is not objec-tive but rather is positional. However, this is an argument that can be directed at all forms of research. Here it simply gives rise to 'interpretative ethnography'.**

- **Second, there has been a brand of more telling postmodern critique. Here, in addition to pointing to the problems of realist epistemology, it is argued that ethnography is a genre of writing that deploys rhetorical devices, often obscured, to maintain its realist claims (Clifford and Marcus, 1986). In other words, the products of ethnography are always texts.**

Clifford poses the second issue thus:

> If ethnography produces interpretations through intense research experiences, how is unruly experience transformed into an authoritative written account? How, precisely, is garrulous, overdetermined cross-cultural encounter shot through with power relations and personal cross-purposes circumscribed as an adequate version of a more or less dis-crete 'other world' composed by an individual author? (Clifford, 1988: 25)

This argument leads to the examination of ethnographic texts for their rhetorical devices. It also suggests the need for a more reflexive and dialogical approach to ethnography which demands that writers elaborate on their own assumptions, views and positions. Further, consultation with the 'subjects' of ethnography is required so that ethnography becomes less an expedition in search of 'the facts' and more a conversation between par-ticipants in a research process.

The critique of the epistemological claims of ethnography does not mean that it is of no value or that it should be abandoned. There is no fundamental epistemological dis-tinction between ethnography and a multi-layered novel. For both, the purposes do not lie in the production of a 'true' picture of the world but in the production of empathy and the widening of the circle of human solidarity (Rorty, 1989). Thus, ethnography has personal, poetic and political, rather than epistemological, justifications.

In this view, ethnographic data can be seen as giving poetic expression to voices from other cultures or from the 'margins' of our own cultures. However, representing such voices is no longer to be regarded as a 'scientific' report. Rather, it is to be understood as a poetic exposition and narration that bring new voices into what Rorty calls the 'cosmopolitan conversation of humankind'. Thus, ethnographic data can be the route by which our own culture is made strange to us, allowing new descriptions of the world to be generated.

The continued redescription of our world, which ethnographic research can achieve, is a desirable thing to do because it offers the possibility of an improvement of the human condition. The route for such an improvement would be through comparison between different representations of social practices. Different practices and descriptions of the world can be played off against each other, compared and juxtaposed. This process would itself generate yet more new descriptions within the ongoing conversation of humanity as we search for improvements to the human condition. For example, ethnographic research may help us to learn from other cultures, to supply those 'toeholds for new initiatives' and 'tensions which make people listen to unfamiliar ideas' which combat ethnocentrism and help enrich our own culture with new ideas (Rorty, 1989).

None of this means that we can abandon all methodological rigour for the following reasons:

1 Evidence and poetic style are pragmatically useful warrants for truth and action epistemologically equivalent to the procedural agreements of the physical sciences. That is, scientific 'objectivity' is to be read as social solidarity and truth signals maximum social agreement (Rorty, 1991a).

2 The language of observation and evidence are among the conventions that divide the genre of ethnography from the novel.

3 The rejection of a universal objective truth is based on the impossibility of word–world correspondence and therefore of accurate or adequate representation. This does not mean that we have to abandon word–word translation. That is, we can achieve 'good enough' reporting of the speech or action of others without making claims to universal truth. Thus, it is better to use a tape recorder to document the utterances of research subjects rather than make it up because:

   (a) we will be better able to translate and understand the words of others for practical purposes;

   (b) we will be better able to predict the actions of others.

The problems of ethnography are problems of translation and justification rather than of universal or objective truth. We can consider languages (and thus culture and knowledge) to be constituted not by untranslatable and incompatible rules but as learnable *skills*. According to Davidson (1984), there can be no such thing as an unlearnable language for this would mean we were unable to recognize the 'other' as a language user at all. Ethnography now becomes about dialogue and the attempt to reach pragmatic agreements about meaning between participants in a research process. There is no *a priori* reason why this should succeed, agreement may never be reached, but there is no *a priori* reason why it should fail either (Rorty, 1991a).

I have discussed ethnography at greater length than I am about to devote to textual and reception studies, for two reasons. First, ethnography raises crucial epistemological issues that are relevant and, to a degree, generalizable to other methods. That is, questions about realism, interpretation and representation are also applicable to textual and reception methodology. Second, the vast majority of 'evidence' provided in this book comes from textual, reception or theoretical work. It thus seemed reasonable to devote more space here to the somewhat neglected strand of ethnographic cultural studies.

Textual approaches

Although textual work comes in many guises, including 'literary criticism', the three outstanding modes of analysis in cultural studies draw from:

- **semiotics;**

- **narrative theory;**

- **deconstructionism.**

Texts as signs   Semiotics explores how the meanings generated by texts have been achieved through a particular arrangement of signs and cultural codes (Chapter 3). Such analysis draws attention to the ideologies or myths of texts. For example, semiotic analysis illustrates the case that television news is a constructed representation and not a mirror of reality (Chapter 10). The media's selective and value-laden representations are not 'accurate' pictures of the world. Rather, they are best understood as the site of struggles over what counts as meaning and truth. Television may appear to be 'realistic' because of its use of seamless editing and the 'invisible' cut. However, such realism is constituted by a set of aesthetic conventions rather than being a reflection of the 'real world'.

Texts as narratives   Texts tell stories, whether that is Einstein's theory of relativity, Hall's theory of identity, or the latest episode of *The Simpsons*. Consequently, narrative theory plays a part in cultural studies. A narrative is an ordered sequential account that makes claims to be a record of events. Narratives are the structured form in which stories advance explanations for the ways of the world. Narratives offer us frameworks of understanding and rules of reference about the way the social order is constructed. In doing so they supply answers to the question: How shall we live?

Stories take different forms and utilize a variety of characters, subject matters and narrative structures (or ways of telling a story). However, structuralist theory has concerned itself with the common features of story formation.

According to Todorov (1977), narrative minimally concerns the disruption of an equilibrium and the tracing of the consequences of said disruption until a new equilibrium is achieved. For example, an established soap opera couple are shown in loving embrace as a prelude to the later revelation that one of them is having an affair. The question is posed: will this spell the end of the relationship? A good deal of talk, emotion and explanation takes place before the characters are either reconciled or go their separate ways. Soap opera is the name of a genre. Genres structure the narrative process and contain it; they regulate it in particular ways using specific elements and combinations of elements to produce coherence and credibility. Genre thus represents systemizations and repetitions of problems and solutions in narratives (Neale, 1980).

Deconstruction   Deconstructionism is associated with Derrida's 'undoing' of the binaries of western philosophy and the extension of this procedure into the fields of literature (e.g. De Man) and postcolonial theory (e.g. Spivak). To deconstruct is to take apart, to undo, in order to seek out and display the assumptions of a text. In particular, deconstruction involves the dismantling of hierarchical conceptual oppositions such as man/woman, black/white, reality/appearance, nature/culture, reason/madness, etc. Such binaries are said to 'guarantee' truth by excluding and devaluing the 'inferior' part of the binary. Thus, speech is privileged over writing, reality over appearance, men over women.

The purpose of deconstruction is not simply to reverse the order of binaries but to show that they are implicated in each other. Deconstruction seeks to expose the blindspots of texts, the unacknowledged assumptions upon which they operate. This includes the places where a text's rhetorical strategies work against the logic of a text's arguments. That is, the deconstruction seeks to expose the tension between what a text means to say and what it is constrained to mean.

One of the central problems faced by the process of deconstruction is that it must use the very conceptual language it seeks to undo. For example, to deconstruct western philosophy is to use the very language of western philosophy. To mark this tension, Derrida places his concepts under erasure. To place a word under erasure is first to write the word and then to cross it out, leaving both the word and its crossed-out version. As Spivak explains: 'Since the word is inaccurate, it is crossed out. Since it is necessary, it remains legible' (Spivak, 1976: xiv). The use 'under erasure' of accustomed and known concepts is intended to destabilize the familiar. As such it marks it as useful, necessary, inaccurate and mistaken. Thus does Derrida seek to illuminate the undecidability of meaning.

Reception studies

Exponents of reception or consumption studies argue that whatever analysis of textual meanings a critic may undertake, it is far from certain which of the identified meanings, if any, will be activated by actual readers/audiences/consumers. By this is meant that audiences are active creators of meaning in relation to texts. They bring previously acquired cultural competencies to bear on texts so that differently constituted audiences will work with different meanings.

On the theoretical front, two fields of study have proved to be particularly influential: first, Hall's (1981) 'Encoding–Decoding' model; and, second, hermeneutic and literary reception studies. Hall argues that the production of meaning does not ensure consumption of that meaning as the encoders might have intended. This is so because (television) messages, constructed as a sign system with multi-accentuated components, are polysemic. That is, they have more than one potential set of meanings. To the degree that audiences participate in cultural frameworks with producers, then audience decodings and textual encodings will be similar. However, where audience members are situated in different social positions (e.g. of class and gender) from encoders, and thus have divergent cultural resources available to them, they will be able to decode programmes in alternative ways.

Work within the tradition of hermeneutics and literary reception studies (Gadamer, 1976; Iser, 1978) argues that understanding is always from the position and point of view of the person who understands. This involves not merely reproduction of textual meaning but the *production* of meaning by the readers. The text may structure aspects of meaning by guiding the reader, but it cannot fix the meaning. Rather, significance is the outcome of the oscillations between the text and the imagination of the reader (Chapter 10).

The place of theory

A significant strand of work in cultural studies is not empirical but theoretical.

✓ *Theory can be understood as narratives that seek to distinguish and account for general features which describe, define and explain persistently perceived occurrences.*

Theory does not picture the world more or less accurately; rather, it is a tool, instrument or logic for *intervening* in the world. This is achieved through the mechanisms of description, definition, prediction and control. Theory construction is a self-reflexive discursive endeavour that seeks to interpret and intercede in the world.

Theory construction involves the thinking through of concepts and arguments, often redefining and critiquing prior work, with the objective of offering new ways to think about our world. Thus, theoretical concepts are tools for thinking. This process has maintained a high-profile position within cultural studies. Theoretical work can be thought of as a crafting of the cultural signposts and maps by which we are guided. Cultural studies has rejected the empiricist claim that knowledge is simply a matter of collecting facts from which theory can be deduced or tested against. Rather, theory is always already implicit in empirical research through the very choice of topic, the focus the research takes, and the concepts through which it is discussed and interpreted. That is, 'facts' are not neutral and no amount of stacking up of 'facts' produces a story about our lives without theory. Indeed, theory is precisely a story about humanity with implications for action and judgements about consequences.

Cultural studies seeks to play a de-mystifying role, that is, to point to the constructed character of cultural texts and to the myths and ideologies that are embedded in them. It has done this in the hope of producing subject positions, and real subjects, who are enabled to oppose subordination. As a political theory, cultural studies has hoped to organize disparate opposition groups into an alliance of cultural politics. However, Bennett (1992, 1998) has argued that the textual politics which much cultural studies produces is (a) not connected to many living persons and (b) ignores the institutional dimensions of cultural power. Consequently, he urges cultural studies to adopt a more pragmatic approach and to work with cultural producers in the construction and implementation of cultural policy (Chapter 14).

SUMMARY

Cultural studies:

- is a plural field of contesting perspectives which through the production of theory has sought to intervene in cultural politics;
- explores culture as the signifying practices of representation within the context of social power;
- draws on a variety of theories, including Marxism, structuralism, poststructuralism and feminism;
- is eclectic in its methods;
- asserts the positionality of all knowledge, including its own;
- coheres conceptually around the key ideas of culture, signifying practices, representation, discourse, power, articulation, texts, readers and consumption;
- is an interdisciplinary or post-disciplinary field of enquiry which explores the production and inculcation of maps of meaning;
- can be described as a language-game or discursive formation concerned with issues of power in the signifying practices of human life.

Above all, cultural studies is an exciting and fluid project that tells us stories about our changing world in the hope that we can improve it.

2 Questions of Culture and Ideology

KEY CONCEPTS

Articulation	*Mass culture*
Culturalism	*Popular culture*
Hegemony	*Poststructuralism*
Ideology	*Social formation*
Marxism	*Structuralism*

The concept of culture is by definition central to cultural studies. Yet there is no 'correct' or definitive meaning attached to it. In describing it as 'one of the two or three most complicated words in the English language', Williams (1983) indicates the contested character of culture and cultural studies. Culture is not 'out there' waiting to be correctly described by theorists who keep getting it wrong. Rather, the concept of culture is a tool that is of more or less usefulness to us. Consequently, its usage and meanings continue to change as thinkers have hoped to 'do' different things with it.

✓ *We should not ask what culture 'is'. Rather, we need to enquire about how the language of culture is used and for what purposes.*

The study of culture within sociology, anthropology, literature, etc., predates cultural studies as a stream of thought with particular themes and theoretical leanings. Indeed, the study of culture has no origins. However, cultural studies as an institutionalized discursive formation does have a particular history, albeit one that takes on the status of myth. British cultural studies, as exemplified by Hoggart, Williams and Hall, can be regarded as a crucial moment in the trajectory of cultural studies. In tracing the ways in which the concept of culture has been defined and deployed by them, we are in effect exploring the changing concerns of cultural studies.

KEY THINKERS

Raymond Williams (1921–88)

Raymond Williams was born and raised in working-class rural Wales before attending Cambridge University as both student and professor. The experience of working-class culture and a commitment to democracy and socialism are themes of his writing. William's work was extremely influential in the development of cultural studies through his understanding of culture as constituted by 'a whole way of life'. His anthropologically inspired grasp of culture as ordinary and lived legitimized the study of popular culture. His work engages with Marxism but is critical of its economic reductionism.

Reading: Williams, R. (1981) *Culture*. London: Fontana

CULTURE WITH A CAPITAL C: THE GREAT AND THE GOOD IN THE LITERARY TRADITION

According to Williams (1981, 1983), the word 'culture' began as a noun of process connected to growing crops, that is, cultivation. Subsequently, the idea of cultivation was broadened to encompass the human mind or 'spirit'. This gave rise to the idea of the cultivated or cultured person. However, during the nineteenth century a more anthropological definition of culture emerged. Here culture was understood to be 'a whole and distinctive way of life'. This understanding of culture emphasized 'lived experience'. It is within these definitional tensions that British cultural studies has its discursive and mythological origins.

The nineteenth-century English writer Matthew Arnold has taken on iconic status within the narrative of cultural studies. He famously described culture as 'the best that has been thought and said in the world' (Arnold, 1960: 6). Here 'reading, observing and thinking' were said to be the means toward moral perfection and social good. Culture as the form of human 'civilization' is to be counterposed to the 'anarchy' of the 'raw and uncultivated masses'. As such, Arnold's aesthetic and political arguments are a justification for what we commonly call 'high culture'.

Leavisism

The work of Arnold was influential upon the other icons of culture with a capital C, F.R. and Q.D. Leavis. Their work opens in the 1930s and spans four decades. Leavisism shares with Arnold the notion that culture is the high point of civilization and the concern of an educated minority. F.R. Leavis argued that, prior to the industrial revolution, England had an authentic common culture of the people and a minority culture of the educated elite. For Leavis, this was a golden age of an 'organic community' with a 'lived culture' of 'Folk-songs and Folk-dance' (Leavis and Thompson, 1933: 1). This authentic culture has, it is argued, now been lost to the 'standardization and levelling down' (ibid.: 3) of industrialized mass culture. The purpose of high or minority culture, now reduced to a literary tradition, is to keep alive, nurture and disseminate the ability to discriminate between the best and the worst of culture. For Leavisism, the important tasks are:

- **to define and defend the best of culture represented by the canon of good works;**
- **to criticize the worst of mass culture represented by advertising, films and popular fiction.**

It was *against* such definitions of culture that cultural studies struggled and through which it defined itself. In Britain, Arnold and F.R. Leavis were the critical figures. However, similar arguments were embodied by other writers in other countries and continue to be repeated today. With hindsight it is not difficult to criticize the arbitrary and elitist character of Arnold and Leavis's work. However, they can also be said to have opened up the terrain of popular culture for study by bringing the tools and concepts of 'art and literature' to bear on it.

CULTURE IS ORDINARY

Raymond Williams developed an understanding of culture that is in stark contrast to Arnold's aesthetic and elitist conception. He stresses the everyday lived character of culture as 'a whole way of life'. Williams was particularly concerned with working class experience and their active everyday construction of culture. As such, his view of culture is no less political than Arnold's. However, it is, crucially, a different kind of politics which stresses democracy, education and 'the long revolution' (Williams, 1965), that is, the march of the working class through institutions of contemporary life leading to the democratization of culture and politics. For Williams:

A culture has two aspects: the known meanings and directions, which its members are trained to; the new observations and meanings, which are offered and tested. These are the ordinary processes of human societies and human minds, and we see through them the nature of culture: that it is always both traditional and creative; that it is both the most ordinary common meanings and the finest individual meanings. We use the word culture in these two senses: to mean a whole way of life – the common meanings; to mean the arts and learning – the special processes of discovery and creative effort. Some writers reserve the word for one or other of these senses; I insist on both, and on the significance of their conjunction. The questions I ask about our culture are questions about our general and common purposes, yet also questions about deep and personal meanings. Culture is ordinary, in every society and in every mind. (Williams, 1989: 4)

Culture is both the 'arts' and the values, norms and symbolic goods of everyday life. While culture is concerned with tradition and social reproduction, it is also a matter of creativity and change.

Consider the following questions. Discuss them with another person.

— Why is meaning central to the concept of culture?
— In what way can culture be considered 'ordinary'?
— What are the connections between culture and communication?
— By what methods do we construct meaning?

The anthropological approach to culture

Williams's concept of culture is 'anthropological' since it centres on everyday meanings: values (abstract ideals), norms (definite principles or rules) and material/symbolic goods.

✓ *Meanings are generated not by individuals alone but by collectives. Thus, the idea of culture refers to shared meanings.*

To say that two people belong to the same culture is to say that they interpret the world in roughly the same ways and can express themselves, their thoughts and feelings about the world, in ways which will be understood by each other. Thus culture depends on its participants interpreting meaningfully what is happening around them, and 'making sense' of the world, in broadly similar ways. (Hall, 1997a: 2)

The adoption of an anthropological version of culture would be something of a banality were it not being applied to the lives and social organization of modern western industrialized cultures rather than to the cultures of colonized peoples (McGuigan, 1992). Further, within the context of English literary criticism, an anthropological definition of culture offered a critical and democratic edge. Comprehending culture as a 'whole way of life' had the pragmatic consequence of splitting off the concept from the 'arts'. It helped to legitimize popular culture and opened up television, newspapers, dancing, football and other everyday artefacts and practices to critical but sympathetic analysis.

FAST FOOD

© Photographer: Wael Hamdan | Agency: Dreamstime.com

- *The anthropologist Claude Lévi-Strauss once said that 'food is good to think by'. What do you think he meant by that?*

- *What culture(s) do we associate with this type of food? What does it tell us about the lifestyles and values of this culture?*

- *Many health experts are critical of fast food. How powerful is this message in our culture compared to the advertising that promotes burgers?*

Culturalism: Hoggart, Thompson, Williams

The retrospective narrative of cultural studies credits Richard Hoggart, Edward Thompson and Raymond Williams with having forged an anthropological and histori-cally informed understanding of culture. This perspective has been dubbed 'culturalism' (Hall, 1992a). There are significant differences between Hoggart, Thompson and Williams. However, what they have in common is a stress on the 'ordinariness' of culture. This includes the active, creative, capacity of common people to construct shared meaningful practices. Further, all three are particularly interested in questions of class culture, democracy and socialism.

In this case the context is that of the history of the English working class. For Williams and Thompson, there is an engagement with Marxism. In particular they are concerned with the notion that 'men [*sic*] make their own history, but they do not make it just as they please; they do not make it under circumstances chosen by themselves, but under circumstances directly encountered, given and transmitted from the past' (Marx, 1961: 53).

Richard Hoggart: *The Uses of Literacy*

Hoggart's (1957) *The Uses of Literacy* explores the character of English working-class culture as it developed and changed from the 1930s through to the 1950s. The book is divided into two parts: (a) 'An "Older" Order' and (b) 'Yielding Place to the New'. This partition indicates the historical and comparative approach that Hoggart brings to bear. In the first part, based on memories of his own upbringing, Hoggart gives a sympathetic, humanist and detailed account of the lived culture of the working class. This includes a day at the seaside and the creative appropriation and uses of popular song. To those of us brought up with commercial culture and pop music, Hoggart's view of working-class culture sounds tinged with nostalgia. He appears to mourn a lost authenticity of a culture created from below.

In Part Two, Hoggart gives a rather acid account of the development of 'commercial culture'. This is figured by the 'jukebox boy', the 'American slouch' and loud music. Despite its romanticism, however, *The Uses of Literacy* is an important book.

✓   *Hoggart's legacy is the legitimacy accorded to the detailed study of working-class culture, that is, to the meanings and practices of ordinary people as they seek to live their lives and make their own history.*

Edward Thompson: *The Making of the English Working Class*

'History from below' is the central theme of Thompson's (1963) *The Making of the English Working Class*. This book concerns the lives, experiences, beliefs, attitudes and practices of working people. Thompson, along with Williams, conceives of culture as lived and ordinary. However, he is also concerned with what he sees not so much as cultural but as socio-economic. For Thompson, class is a historical phenomenon forged and created by people. It is not a 'thing' but a set of social relations and experiences.

> Class happens when some men [*sic*], as a result of common experiences (inherited or shared), feel and articulate the identity of their interests as between themselves, and as against other men whose interests are different from (and usually opposed to) theirs. (Thompson, 1963: 8–9)

Thompson stresses the active and creative role of the English working class in bringing themselves into being (though not under conditions of their own making). He seeks to secure working-class experience in historical understanding so that, as he famously remarked, 'I am seeking to rescue the poor stockinger, the Luddite cropper, the "obsolete" hand-loom weaver, the "utopian" artisan, and even the deluded follower of Joanna Southcott, from the enormous condescension of posterity' (Thompson, 1963: 12).

Raymond Williams and cultural materialism

Hoggart and Thompson have been influential figures in the development of cultural studies. However, the legacy of Raymond Williams has been the more enduring. For Williams, culture as everyday meanings and values is part of an expressive totality of social relations. Thus, 'the theory of culture' is defined as 'the study of relationships between elements in a whole way of life' (Williams, 1965: 63).

> We need to distinguish three levels of culture, even in its most general definition. There is the lived culture of a particular time and place, only fully accessible to those living in that time and place. There is the recorded culture, of every kind, from art to the most everyday facts: the culture of the period. There is also, as the factor connecting lived culture and period cultures, the culture of the selective tradition. (Williams, 1965: 66)

For Williams, the purpose of cultural analysis is to explore and analyse the recorded culture of a given time and place. In doing so he seeks to reconstitute the 'structure of feeling', or shared values and outlooks, of a culture. At the same time, we need always to be aware that cultural records are part of a selectively preserved and interpreted 'tradition'.

Williams insists that culture be understood through the representations and practices of daily life in the context of the material conditions of their production. This Williams calls cultural materialism, and involves 'the analysis of all forms of signification ... within the actual means and conditions of their production' (Williams, 1981: 64–5). Thus, Williams (1981) suggests that we explore culture in terms of:

- *institutions* of artistic and cultural production, e.g. artisanal or market forms;

- *formations* or schools, movements and factions of cultural production;

- *modes of production*, including the relations between the material means of cultural production and the cultural forms which are made manifest;

- *identifications* and *forms of culture*, including the specificity of cultural products, their aesthetic purpose and the particular forms that generate and express meaning;

- *the reproduction*, in time and space, of a selective tradition of meanings and practices involving both social order and social change;

- the *organization* of the 'selective tradition' in terms of a 'realized signifying system'.

Such a strategy might be applied to contemporary music and its associated images and practices. For example Rap, Hip-Hop or Rave can be understood as formations of popular music produced within the institutions of record companies and advertising agencies. The mode of production of popular music would include the technical means of studio recording and the capitalist social relations within which such practices are embedded. Clearly, Hip-Hop or Rave are musical forms that involve the specific organization of sounds, words and images with which particular social groups form identifications. Hence one could analyse the specific organization of sounds and signs as a signifying system. This could be connected with the way in which Hip-Hop, for example, reproduces and changes aspects of African-American musical forms and the values of its historically developed lived culture, that is, what Hip-Hop means to young African-Americans.

Culture as lived experience   In sum, culture for Williams is constituted by:

- **the meanings generated by ordinary men and women;**

- **the lived experiences of its participants;**

- **the texts and practices engaged in by all people as they conduct their lives.**

Meanings and practices are enacted on terrain not of our making even as we struggle to creatively shape our lives. Culture does not float free of the material conditions of life. On the contrary, for Williams,

✓ *The meanings of lived culture are to be explored within the context of their conditions of production. In this sense culture is understood as 'a whole way of life'.*

HIGH CULTURE/LOW CULTURE: AESTHETICS AND THE COLLAPSE OF BOUNDARIES

Leavis and Arnold distinguish between the good and the bad, the high and low. Their distinctions centre on questions of aesthetic quality; that is, on judgements about beauty, goodness and value. Historically, the policing of the boundaries of a canon of 'good works' led to the exclusion of popular culture. This is because judgements of quality have derived from an institutionalized and class-based hierarchy of cultural taste.

Such a hierarchy, formed within particular social and historical contexts, is employed by its apologists as representative of a universal set of aesthetic criteria. However, judgements about aesthetic quality are always open to contestation. With the passing of time and the increased interest in popular culture, a new set of theorists argued that there were no legitimate grounds for drawing these lines between the worthy and the unworthy. Evaluation was not a sustainable task for the critic. Rather, the obligation was to describe and analyse the cultural production of meaning. This stance had the great merit of opening up a whole new array of texts for legitimate discussion, for example the soap opera (Brunsdon, 1990).

A question of quality

'Until recently', argues Allen, 'the aesthetic discourse on soap operas has been marked by near unanimous disdain of the form' (Allen, 1985: 11). For mainstream criticism, the romantic idea of the 'artistic object', produced by the 'artistic soul', is allied to a sense of the complexity and authenticity of the work of art. This in turn requires necessary skills and work by readers in order to access a genuine aesthetic experience. From within this paradigm the soap opera, as an expression of mass culture, was seen as superficial and unsatisfying.

However, neither the form of art nor its context can secure universal meaning. The concepts of beauty, harmony, form and quality can be applied as much to a steam train as to a novel or a painting. Thus, concepts of beauty, form and quality are culturally relative. Beauty in western thought may not be the same as that found in other cultures. Art can be understood as a socially created category that has been attached to certain external and internal signals. These are the signs by which art is recognized; hence the 'art gallery' and the theatre. Art as aesthetic quality is that which has been so labelled by western cultural and class elites. To see art as 'a uniquely different kind of work, with a unique, indeed transcendent, product is a mistaken notion, wrongly generalized and taken to be essential to the value of art' (Wolff, 1980: 17).

Popular cultural forms such as the television soap opera have been bypassed for social as much as 'creative' reasons. Further, we may note similarities between high art and popular forms. Neither the *Mona Lisa* nor *The OC* is the outcome of the mystical practices of geniuses. Rather, each is the product of work, a human transformation of the material environment through labour. Art is an industry with its owners, managers and workers operating according to the law of profit. In this it does not differ radically from commodity culture and popular commercial television.

✓ *There is little justification for excluding the soap opera from the artistic domain on the grounds that art, i.e. aesthetic quality, is a different kind of activity.*

Form and content

Some critics offer formal criteria for distinguishing work of quality from that which is inferior. They have argued that the quality work is more subtle, complex and adequate in its formal expression of content. However, the form–content division upon which this argument relies is hard to sustain. They are indistinguishable aspects of the same object.

One might argue that the quality work is that which is most adequate and expressive in relation to its referent. That is, good art is superior to bad art in its illumination of the real world. However, many writers would have difficulty in supporting the epistemology of realism that underpins the argument. Art is not a copy of the world but a specific socially constructed representation.

Ideological analysis

The attempt to produce universal criteria for aesthetic judgements inevitably falls foul of relativism, that is, the argument that alternative criteria apply in different times and places. Instead cultural studies has developed arguments that revolve around the social and political *consequences* of constructing and disseminating specific representations of the world.

Cultural studies has developed evaluative criteria based on political values and ideological analysis rather than on aesthetics. Here the role of criticism becomes the development of a more profound understanding of the way our cultural and symbolic processes are connected to social, political and economic power (Eagleton, 1984). From this perspective, it makes little sense to discuss whether culture is formally and aesthetically 'good' or 'bad'. Rather, we need to consider, from an inevitably value-laden position, its 'ideological' construction and potential consequences.

For example, Cantor (1991) argues that domestic drama on American television is primarily a morality play about how we should live. In particular it seeks to inform us about how to bring up children and about what constitutes appropriate love relationships. Airtime, according to Cantor, is devoted to representations of mainstream norms. There have been changes in the representation of families and an increase in the range of types of families. Nevertheless, the TV ideal remains the married couple/nuclear family. Even with the development of 'off-beat' families in the American sitcom, problems are always resolved in terms of the values of caring, togetherness, love and peace.

The consequences of television's discourse of the family may be to:

- **demonize the majority of us who do not live in nuclear families;**
- **support the main institution of the patriarchal oppression of women;**
- **suggest that we seek solutions to social problems within the family (by making it responsible for 'crime' or 'social care').**

The problem of judgement

The relativity of 'value' within cultural studies leads discussion into a dilemma. On the one hand, there is a desire to legitimize popular and non-western culture as valuable in the face of a traditional western high cultural aesthetic discourse. On the other hand, there is a reluctance to sanction a position in which we are disbarred from making judgements.

If we cannot judge cultural products, then we have to accept that whatever is produced by corporations of the culture industries is acceptable because popular. Hence the argument that discourses of power rather than aesthetic evaluations are the legitimate target of criticism. Here we are still making value judgements. However, these conclusions are political rather than aesthetic. We cannot escape moral and political judgements nor should we seek to do so. Human life is centrally concerned with decision-making based on our values.

A universal distinction between high culture and low culture is unsustainable. This argument, combined with the rise in visibility and status of popular culture, has led critics to suggest that 'High culture becomes just one more sub-culture, one more opinion, in our midst' (Chambers, 1986: 194).

However, though cultural analysts may question the universal validity of high–low cultural boundaries, this does not mean that such distinctions are not actively utilized to maintain social power. As Pierre Bourdieu (1984) has argued:

✓ *Taste and cultural judgement mark out class boundaries, cultural competencies and cultural capital.*

Mass culture: popular culture

A variant of the high–low cultural boundary is that which decries commodity-based culture as inauthentic, manipulative and unsatisfying. This perspective reproduces again the 'inferiority' of popular culture. The argument is that commodified capitalist 'mass culture' is:

- **inauthentic because not produced by 'the people';**
- **manipulative because its primary purpose is to be purchased;**
- **unsatisfying because it requires little work to consume and thus fails to enrich its consumers.**

These views are held both by conservative critics like Leavis and by the Marxist-inspired Frankfurt School. Thus, Adorno and Horkheimer coined the phrase 'the culture industry' to suggest that culture is now totally interlocked with political economy. That is, culture is held to be a production of capitalist corporations. In this context, the authors seek to explore the meanings of mass-produced culture and the kinds of people and social order in which, they claim, such a culture is implicated.

Culture as mass deception

Adorno and Horkheimer's attitude towards mass culture is stated clearly and boldly in the title of their essay 'The Culture Industry – Enlightenment as Mass Deception' (Adorno and Horkheimer, 1979). They argue that cultural products are commodities produced by the culture industry. These commodities, while purporting to be democratic, individualistic and diversified, are in actuality authoritarian, conformist and highly standardized. Thus, 'Culture impresses the same stamp on everything. Films, radio and magazines make up a system which is uniform as a whole in every part' (ibid.: 120). The apparent diversity of the products of the culture industries is an illusion for 'something is provided for all so none may escape' (ibid.: 123).

Adorno (1941) regarded popular music, and jazz in particular, as stylized, lacking in originality and requiring little effort by its audience. For Adorno, the aim of standardized music is standardized reactions that affirm life as it is. This involves not just overt meanings but the structuring of the human psyche into conformist ways. Adorno displaces notions of ideology (as ideas) with those of Freudian psychology. He argues that the culture industries, in tandem with the family, produce 'ego weakness' and the 'authoritarian personality'.

In contrast, critical art for Adorno is that which is not oriented to the market but challenges the standards of intelligibility of a reified society. An example would be the atonal music of Schoenberg which, Adorno argues, forces us to consider new ways of looking at the world. We may note that critique here is largely a question of form rather than content. Specifically, Adorno praises non-realism and the 'alien' nature of art which, it is argued, inspires us through its 'utopian negativity'.

Criticisms of the Frankfurt School

The Frankfurt School analysis is pessimistic. It holds to an overly monolithic view of the culture industries and denies the effectivity of popular cultural politics. Popular culture is regarded as inferior and contaminated both aesthetically and politically. The Frankfurt School shares with Leavis, from whom it is otherwise quite different, a reliance on textual analysis. This it calls 'immanent criticism', that is, the critique of the 'internal' meanings of cultural products. In doing so, the Frankfurt School makes the assumption that the meanings so identified are taken up by audiences in an unproblematic fashion.

The School is thus subject to the criticism that it over-emphasizes aesthetics and the internal construction of cultural products. It assumes audience reaction from immanent criticism. This is a position challenged by later cultural studies research within the active audience paradigm. Indeed, the arguments that surround the Frankfurt School analysis are indicative of a wider discussion. This involves the debate between those who locate the generation of meaning at the level of production/text and those who perceive it at the moment of consumption.

Creative consumption

The production of popular music, film, television and fashion is in the hands of transnational capitalist corporations. However, consumption-oriented cultural studies argues that meanings are produced, altered and managed at the level of use by people who are active producers of meaning. This is particularly significant in an environment of 'semiotic excess', that is, one in which the widespread circulation of polysemic signs makes it harder for any dominant meaning to stick.

Writers like Chambers (1987, 1990), Fiske (1989a, 1989b) and Hebdidge (1988) have discussed the creative meaning-producing activities of consumers. Here buyers become bricoleurs, selecting and arranging elements of material commodities and meaningful signs. Likewise, Willis (1990) argues that, rather than being inherent in the commodity, meaning and value are constructed through actual usage. In general, it is argued that people range across a series of terrains and sites of meaning, which, though not of their own making, are ones within which they can actively produce sense.

> To a rationalized, expansionist and at the same time centralized, clamorous and spectacular production corresponds another production, called 'consumption'. The latter is devious, it is dispersed, but it insinuates itself everywhere, silently and almost invisibly, because it does not manifest itself through its own products, but rather through its ways of using the products imposed by a dominant economic order. (De Certeau, 1984: xii–xiii)

Following de Certeau, Fiske argues that popular culture is constituted by the meanings that people make with it rather than those identifiable within texts. He is clear that popular culture is very largely produced by capitalist corporations. However, he 'focuses rather upon the popular tactics by which these forces are coped with, are evaded or are resisted' (Fiske, 1989a: 8). Fiske finds 'popular vitality and creativity' leading to 'the possibility of social change and the motivation to drive it' (ibid.: 8). Further, he argues that 'between 80 and 90 per cent of new products fail despite extensive advertising'. His point is that the culture industries have to work hard to get us to consume mass culture. Consumers are not passive dopes but discriminating active producers of meaning.

It is worth noting that while critics who stress production talk of 'mass culture', writers who stress consumption prefer to call it 'popular culture'. The very terms 'mass culture' and 'popular culture' are evaluative with regard to the worth of commodities and the capacities of consumers.

Popular culture

There are a number of ways in which the term 'popular culture' has been used (see Storey, 1993). For example:

- **It may refer to that which is 'left over' after the canon of high culture has been decided upon.**
- **It may pertain to the mass-produced culture of the culture industries.**

These perspectives chime with the work of Leavis and Adorno. In both cases popular culture is regarded as inferior to its partner in the binary division. In taking popular culture seriously, cultural studies works against the grain of these elitist definitions. Some critics dislike commodity culture but don't want to decry the popular completely. Their strategy is to contrast mass culture with an authentic folk culture produced by the people. This view haunts the search for a golden age exhibited by both conservative cultural theorists and left-leaning critics of the commodification of culture. However, as Fiske argues, 'in capitalist societies there is no so-called authentic folk culture against which to measure the "inauthenticity" of mass culture, so bemoaning the loss of the authentic is a fruitless exercise in romantic nostalgia' (Fiske, 1989a: 27).

Contemporary popular culture is, primarily, a commercially produced one and there is no reason to think that this is likely to change in the foreseeable future. However, it is argued that popular audiences make their own meanings with the texts of popular culture. They bring to bear their own cultural competencies and discursive resources to the consumption of commodities. Popular culture can be regarded as the meanings and practices produced by popular audiences at the moment of consumption. Thus the study of popular culture becomes centred on the uses to which commodities are put.

✓ *These arguments represent a reversal of the traditional question: how do the culture industries turn people into commodities that serve their interests? Instead there is exploration of how people turn the products of industry into their popular culture serving their interests.*

SYMPHONY ORCHESTRA

© Photographer: Pavel Losevsky|Agency: Dreamstime.com

THE CAVERN CLUB

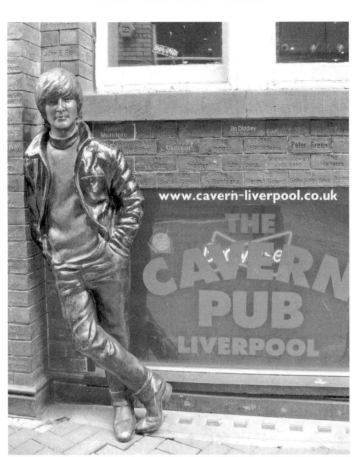

© Photographer: Freya Hadley

- *What elements in the photograph on p. 52 tell us that this is a high cultural event? Who would value this occasion?*

- *The Beatles first played at the Cavern Club. How were they first greeted in British culture? Who like them and who rejected them?*

- *How are the Beatles now regarded in western culture? What does this tell us about popular culture today?*

- *What cultural features do both photographs have in common?*

The popular is political

Cultural studies works with a positive conception of popular culture by which it is both valued and critically analysed. Cultural studies rejects elitist notions of high–low culture or the critiques of mass culture. As McGuigan has argued, cultural studies has a populist bent: 'cultural populism is the intellectual assumption, made by some students of popular culture, that the symbolic experiences and practices of ordinary people are more important analytically and politically than culture with a capital C' (McGuigan, 1992: 4).

Popular culture is constituted through the production of popular meaning located at the moment of consumption. Such meanings are the site of contestation over cultural and political values. As Hall (1977, 1981, 1996c) has argued, popular culture is an arena of consent and resistance in the struggle over cultural meanings. It is the site where cultural hegemony is secured or challenged.

Hall returns us to a *political* conception of popular culture as a site for the struggle over meaning. Judgements about popular culture are not concerned with questions of cultural or aesthetic value (good or bad culture). They are interested in power and the place of popular culture within the wider social formation. The concept of the popular challenges not only the distinctions between high and low culture but also the very act of cultural classification by and through power (Hall, 1996e).

Try writing a dictionary-style definition of the word 'culture'.

— First, as an individual.
— Then, with another person.
— Finally, in a group of four people.

CULTURE AND THE SOCIAL FORMATION

The political conception of culture that cultural studies employs has its roots in debates about the place of culture in a social formation and its relationship to other practices, notably economics and politics. This debate developed historically in the context of cultural studies' Marxist legacy.

Marxism and the metaphor of base and superstructure

Marxism, or historical materialism, is a philosophy that attempts to relate the production and reproduction of culture to the organization of the material conditions of life (Chapter 1). Culture is a corporeal force tied into the socially organized production of the material conditions of existence. The concept of culture refers to the forms assumed by social existence under determinate historical conditions. The idea that culture is determined by the production and the organization of material existence has been articulated in Marxism through the metaphor of the base and the superstructure, which is drawn from the following passage.

> In the social production which men [*sic*] carry on they enter into definite relations that are indispensable and independent of their will; these relations of production correspond to a definite stage of development of their material powers of production. The totality of these relations of production constitute the economic structure of society – the real foundation, on which legal and political superstructures arise and to which definite forms of social consciousness correspond. The mode of production of material life determines the general character of the social, political and spiritual processes of life. It is not the consciousness of men that determines their being, but, on the contrary, their social being determines their consciousness. (Marx, 1961: 67)

The foundations of culture

A mode of production is constituted by the organization of the means of production (factories, machinery, etc.) together with the specific social relations of reproduction (e.g. class) which arise from the organization of those productive forces. It is noteworthy that this mode of production is held to be 'the real foundation' of legal and political superstructures and that it '*determines*' the social, political and spiritual. Thus, the economic mode of production shapes the cultural superstructure (see Figure 2.1).

Here culture, the consequence of a historically specific mode of production, is not understood to be a neutral terrain. This is because 'the existing relations of production between

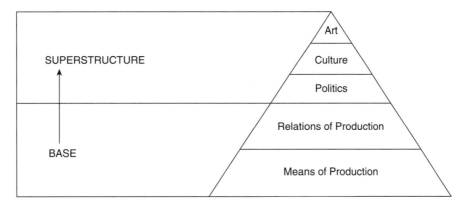

Figure 2.1   Base and superstructure in Marxist theory

Note: Arrow indicates relations of determination

individuals must necessarily express themselves also as political and legal relations' (Marx, 1961: 92). Culture is political because it is expressive of relations of power. Thus 'the ideas of the ruling class are, in every age, the ruling ideas, i.e., the class which is the dominant material force in society is at the same time its dominant intellectual force' (Marx, 1961: 93).

In addition, the taken-for-granted nature of capitalist social relations in the sphere of the market obscures its exploitative base in the realm of production, i.e., the use of 'free' labour covers over economic exploitation. Further, an apparent market sovereignty and equality (we are all consumers) obscures the 'real' foundations of inequality on the level of production. What is a historically specific set of social relations between people appears as a natural, universal set of relations between things. That is, contingent social relations are reified (naturalized as fixed things).

Culture as class power

In short, for Marxism, culture is political because:

1 **It is expressive of social relations of class power.**

2 **It naturalizes the social order as an inevitable 'fact'.**

3 **It obscures the underlying relations of exploitation.**

As such, culture is ideological. In this case, the concept of ideology refers to maps of meaning which, while they purport to be universal truths, are historically specific understandings that obscure and maintain power. Or, to put it more crudely, the ruling ideas are the ideas of the ruling class.

Expressed in this way, the relationship between the economic base and the cultural superstructure is a mechanical and economically deterministic one. By economic determinism is meant the idea that the profit motive and class relations *directly* determine the form and meaning of cultural products. Economic determinism would mean that because a television company is driven by the need to make a profit, all the programmes made within that company will be pro-capitalist. The influence of such a mechanistic and deterministic model has long waned in cultural studies. Rather, the narrative of cultural studies involves a moving away from economic reductionism towards an analysis of the autonomous logics of language, culture, representation and consumption. This has been the subject of much debate within cultural studies.

The specificity of culture

Most thinkers in cultural studies have rejected economic reductionism as simplistic in failing to grant cultural practices any specificity of their own. The analysis of economic determinants may be necessary to any understanding of culture. It is not, and cannot be, self-sufficient. We need to examine cultural phenomena in terms of their own rules, logics, development and effectivity. This argument points to the desirability of a multidimensional and multiperspectival approach to the understanding of culture. This approach would seek to grasp the connections between economic, political, social and cultural dimensions without reducing social phenomena to any one level. Again the work of Raymond Williams (1965, 1979, 1981, 1989) proved to be influential in developing a non-reductionist understanding of the relationship between the material/economic and the cultural.

Williams: totality and the variable distances of practices

For Williams (1981), culture is both constitutive and expressive of a social totality of human relations and practices. He discusses the relations between the economic and the cultural in terms of 'setting limits'. By this he means that the economic sets limits to what can be done or expressed in culture. However, it does not determine the meaning of cultural practices in a direct one-to-one relationship. Rather, Williams speaks of 'the variable distance of practices'. By this he means that the social relationships embedded in the wage labour process are the critical and dominant set of social relations. Other relations and practices are set at 'variable distances' from this central set of practices allowing for degrees of determination, autonomy and specificity. In short, the closer a cultural practice is to the central economic relations, the more they will directly determine it. The further cultural practices are away from the core capitalist production process, the more they can operate autonomously. By this reasoning, individually produced art is more autonomous than mass-produced television.

Williams's arguments are suggestive and represent a move away from crude economic reductionism. However, while the production of television may be more embedded in capitalist production than painting, it is by no means certain that painting is any the less ideological or political. Nor does 'setting limits' tell us much about the form that television takes and why it is different from painting. Williams understood this and devoted much time to analysing the specificity of cultural forms. However, he did not adequately resolve or conceptualize the relationship between culture and economics. Within Williams's schema, a crude base–superstructure model has been displaced in favour of a conception of society as an 'expressive totality'. Here all practices – political, economic, ideological – interact, mediate and affect each other. As Hall (1992a) has remarked, the phase of theoretical development within cultural studies that followed that of Williams interrupted this search for underlying totalities. This is the moment of structuralism (Chapters 1 and 3) in cultural studies and, in particular, of Althusser's structuralist Marxism.

Relative autonomy and the specificity of cultural practices

✓ *Structuralism describes social formations as constituted by complex structures or regularities. It is concerned with how cultural meaning is produced. Structuralism regards culture as analogous to (or structured like) a language.*

Structuralism does not dissolve culture back into the economic (as in a base–superstructure model). Instead the emphasis is on the irreducible character of the cultural as a set of distinct practices with its own internal organization or structuration. Social formations are analysed in terms of how the various elements that make up structures are articulated or linked together.

Althusser and the social formation

Althusser (1969, 1971) did not conceive of a social formation as a totality of which culture is an expression. Rather, he understood it to be a complex structure of different instances (levels or practices) that are 'structured in dominance'. That is, the different instances of politics, economics and ideology are articulated together to form a unity. This totality is not the result of a single, one-way, base–superstructure determination. Rather, it is the product of determinations emanating from different levels. Thus a social formation is the outcome of 'over-determination'. By this is meant the idea that any given practice or instant is the outcome of many different determinations. These distinct determinations are levels or types of practice with their own logic and specificity. This specificity cannot be reduced to, or explained by, other levels or practices. This formulation was hailed by Hall (1972) as a 'seminal advance'. This is so because it allows us to examine a cultural phenomenon as a separate signifying system with its own effects and determinations. Culture is irreducible. Indeed, the cultural and ideological can be seen as constitutive of our understandings of what the economic is.

KEY THINKERS

Althusser, Louis (1918–90)

Althusser was a Marxist philosopher and theorist of the French Communist Party who attempted to produce a structuralist Marxism. His argument that a social formation was constituted by a set of complex overdetermined relationships between different autonomous levels of practice was influential within cultural studies. In particular, he was a significant figure in cultural studies' break with economic determinism and the granting of theoretical autonomy to the levels of culture and ideology. A thinker of considerable influence during the late 1960s and 1970s his star has now waned somewhat.

Reading: Althusser, L. (1971) *Lenin and Philosophy and Other Essays*. London: New Left Books.

Relative autonomy

Despite the specificity granted to different levels or practices, Althusser does not grant each instance total autonomy. Instead he describes the economic level as having determination in the 'last instance'. Culture is then 'relatively autonomous' from the economic (a rather vague and problematic formulation which was once the subject of considerable debate). Althusser gives an example of what is meant. He explains that in the context of feudal societies it was politics, and not economics, which was the dominant and determining instance. However, this is said to be itself a result of economic determination 'in the last instance'. That is, it was the very mode of economic organization of feudal society, its mode of production, which determined that politics became the dominant practice.

The intricacies of the Althusserian debate no longer command much attention within cultural studies. Nevertheless, the attempt to get away from economic reductionism by conceiving of social formations in terms of relatively autonomous practices articulated together in complex and unevenly determining ways has been of lasting significance. For example, it is the basis of Hall's formulation that: 'We must "think" a society or social formation as ever and always constituted by a set of complex practices; each with its own specificity, its own modes of articulation; standing in an "uneven development" to other related practices' (Hall, 1977: 237). By articulation is meant:

- **a temporary unity of discursive elements that do not have to 'go together';**
- **the form of connection that *can* make a unity of two different elements, under certain conditions;**
- **expressing/representing;**
- **a joining together.**

Here, that unity thought of as 'society' is considered to be the unique, historically specific, temporary stabilization of the relations and meanings of different levels of a social formation (Chapters 3 and 14).

Articulation and the circuit of culture

Hall and his colleagues (Du Gay et al., 1997) discuss the 'circuit of culture' and the articulation of production and consumption. In this model, cultural meaning is produced and embedded at each level of the circuit. The meaningful work of each level is necessary, but not sufficient for or determining of, the next instance in the circuit. Each moment – production, representation, identity, consumption and regulation – involves the production of meaning which is articulated, linked with, the next moment. However, it does not determine what meanings will be taken up or produced at that level (see Figure 2.2).

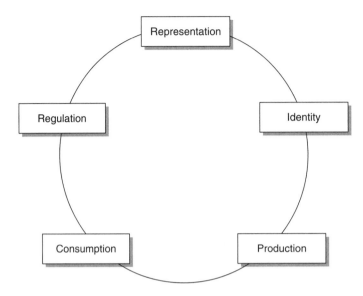

Figure 2.2   The circuit of culture

For example, the Sony Walkman is initially analysed in terms of the meanings embedded at the level of design and production. These are then modified by the creation of new meanings as the Walkman is represented in advertising. In turn, the meanings produced through representation connect with, and help constitute, the identities of Walkman users. Meanings embedded at the moments of production and representation may or may not be taken up at the level of consumption, where new meanings are again produced. Thus, meanings produced at the level of production are available to be worked on at the level of consumption. However, they do not determine them. Further, representation and consumption shape the level of production through, for example, design and marketing.

Two economies

Hall maintains the need to understand the articulation of the different moments of the cultural circuit. Other writers wishing to maintain a non-reductionist stance have separated the realms of the economic and cultural/ideological altogether. For example, Fiske (1987, 1989a, 1989b) describes two separate economies: a financial economy of production and a cultural economy of consumption. The former is primarily concerned with money and the exchange value of commodities. The latter is the site of cultural meanings, pleasures and social identities.

According to Fiske, the financial economy 'needs to be taken into account' in any investigation of the cultural. However, it does not determine it nor invalidate the power audiences have as producers of meaning at the level of consumption. Indeed, popular culture is seen as a site of semiotic warfare involving popular tactics deployed to evade or resist the meanings produced and inscribed in commodities by producers.

Throughout this debate the concept of ideology played a crucial mediating role between the economic and the cultural. As Turner (1990) has commented, ideology was perhaps the most important concept in the foundation of British cultural studies.

KEY THINKERS

John Fiske (1939–)

Fiske was a significant voice in the dissemination of cultural studies throughout the 1980s and 1990s. His work concerns the character of popular culture, and television in particular, laying stress on the uses that people make of texts as active readers or producers of meaning. While he is clear that popular cultural texts are very largely produced by capitalist corporations, he has been more concerned with the popular tactics by which these forces are coped with, evaded or resisted so that popular culture is understood to be a site of 'semiotic warfare'.

Reading: Fiske, J. (1989) *Understanding Popular Culture*. London: Unwin Hyman.

— What do you understand by the concept 'reductionist'?
— In what way can culture be said to have its own specificity?

Devise an explanation of a mobile phone that is:

- economically reductionist;
- culturally specific;
- multiperspectival.

THE QUESTION OF IDEOLOGY

The Marxist concern with the concept of ideology was rooted in the failure of proletarian revolutions to materialize and the inadequacy of historical materialism in relation to questions of subjectivity, meaning and cultural politics. Put simply, the concern with ideology began as an exploration into why capitalism, which was held to be an exploitative system of economic and social relations, was not being overthrown by working-class revolution.

- **Was the failure of proletarian revolution therefore a failure of the proletariat to correctly understand the world they lived in?**

- **Did the working class suffer from 'false consciousness': a mistaken world view that served the interest of the capitalist class?**

Marxism and false consciousness

There are two aspects of Marx's writing which might be grounds for pursuing a line of thought that stresses 'false consciousness'. First, Marx (1961; Marx and Engels, 1970) argues that the dominant ideas in any society are the ideas of the ruling class. Second, he suggests that what we perceive to be the true character of social relations within capitalism are in actuality the mystifications of the market. That is, we accept the idea that we are free to sell our labour, and that we get a fair price for it, since this is the way the social world appears to us.

However, Marx argues that capitalism involves exploitation at the level of production. This involves the extraction of surplus value from the proletariat. Consequently, the appearance of market relations of equality obscures the deep structures of exploitation. We have two versions of ideology here both functioning to legitimate the sectional interests of powerful classes, namely:

- **ideas as coherent statements about the world and the dominance of bourgeois or capitalist ideas;**

- **world views which are the systematic outcome of the structures of capitalism which lead us to inadequate understandings of the social world.**

For Marxism, ideas are not independent of the material and historical circumstances of their production. On the contrary, people's attitudes and beliefs are held to be systematically and structurally related to the material conditions of existence. However, this broad conception of ideas and material circumstances leaves crucial questions unanswered:

- **Just how are ideas related to the material conditions of existence?**

- **If a base–superstructure model is inadequate, as most thinkers within cultural studies would say, then what kind of relationship do ideas have to material conditions?**

- **To what extent is it the case that ideology is 'false'?**

- Can we all be said to be living false lives? How would we know?

- Who has the ability to perceive the 'truth' and separate it from ideology? How would that be possible?

- If the problem of ideology is not so much truth *per se*, but adequacy, that is to say, ideology is not so much false but partial, from what vantage point would an adequate explanation be forthcoming?

These are the kinds of questions that the concept of ideology poses for us as it was developed by Althusser and Gramsci.

Althusser and ideology

For Althusser, ideology is one of the three primary instances or levels of a social formation. As such, it is relatively autonomous from other levels (e.g. the economic), though it is determined by it 'in the last instance'. Here ideology, 'a system (with its own logic and rigour) of representations (images, myths, ideas or concepts)' (Althusser, 1969: 231), is conceived as a practice that is lived and transforms the material world. There are four aspects of Althusser's work which are core to his view of ideology:

1 Ideology has the general function of constituting subjects.

2 Ideology as lived experience is not false.

3 Ideology as misrecognition of the real conditions of existence is false.

4 Ideology is involved in the reproduction of social formations and their relations of power.

Ideological state apparatuses

For Althusser, our entry into the symbolic order (of languages), and thus our constitution as subjects (persons), is the work of ideology. In his essay 'Ideology and the Ideological State Apparatuses' (1971), he argues that 'ideology hails or interpellates concrete individuals as concrete subjects'. Ideology 'has the function of constituting concrete individuals as subjects'. This argument is an aspect of Althusser's anti-humanism whereby the subject is seen not as a self-constituting agent but rather as the 'effect' of structures. In this case, it is the work of ideology to bring a subject into being because 'there is no practice except by and in ideology'.

✓ *In short, for Althusser, ideological discourse constructs subject positions or places for the subject from which the world makes sense.*

Subjects are the effects of discourse because subjectivity is constituted by the positions which discourse obliges us to take up. Discourse refers to production of knowledge through language that gives meaning to both material objects and social practices (Chapter 3). Discourse constructs, defines and produces objects of knowledge in an intelligible way. At the same time it excludes other ways of reasoning as unintelligible. In this way, discourse is ideological because it is a partial view. Further, these incomplete ways of understanding the world, by which subjects are constituted, serve to reproduce the social order and the interests of powerful classes.

Fragmented subjects

Within the Althusserian paradigm, subjects formed in ideology are not unitary wholes but fragmented subjects who take up plural subject positions. For example, class is not an objective economic fact but a discursively formed collective subject position. Consequently, class consciousness is neither an inevitability nor a unified phenomenon. Classes, while sharing certain common conditions of existence, do not automatically form a core unified class consciousness. Instead they are cross-cut by conflicting interests as they are formed and unformed in the course of actual historical development. Class consciousness is likely to be cross-cut by questions of gender, race and age, at the very least.

The double character of ideology

Ideology is double-edged for Althusser.

- **On the one hand, it constitutes the real conditions of people's lives and is not false.**

- **On the other hand, ideology is conceived of as a more elaborate set of meanings which make sense of the world (an ideological discourse) in ways that misrecognize and misrepresent power and class relations. In this sense ideology is false.**

In the first sense ideology constitutes the world views by which people live and experience their lives. Here, ideology is not false for it forms the very categories and systems of representation by which social groups render the world intelligible. Ideology is lived experience. However, in its second usage, ideology is said to represent the *imaginary* relationship of individuals to their real conditions of existence. Thus, if I mistake the class relations of exploitation within capitalism for the free and equal relations of humans to each other, then I am subject to and subjected by the illusions and delusions of ideology.

For Althusser, ideology exists in an apparatus and its associated practices. Thus he designates a series of institutions, as 'ideological state apparatuses' (ISAs), namely:

- **the family;**
- **the education system;**

- the church;

- the mass media.

Althusser regards the church as the dominant pre-capitalist ISA. However, he argues that within the context of capitalism, it has been replaced by the educational system. Thus schools and universities are implicated in the ideological (and physical) reproduction of labour power along with the social relations of production. Ideology, he argues, is a far more effective means for the maintenance of class power than physical force.

For Althusser, education transmits a general ruling-class ideology that justifies and legitimates capitalism. It also reproduces the attitudes and behaviour required by major class groups within the division of labour. Ideology teaches workers to accept and submit to their own exploitation while teaching managers and administrators to practise the craft of ruling on behalf of the dominant class. According to Althusser, each class is practically provided with the ideology required to fulfil its role in a class society.

Further, ideology performs the function of what Poulantzas (1976) called 'separation and uniting'. That is, ideology masks the 'real' exploitative foundations of production by displacing the emphasis of thought from production to exchange. It stresses the character of people as individuals, thereby fragmenting a vision of class. It then welds individuals back together again in an imaginary coherence as a passive community of consumers or behind the concept of nation.

Althusser and cultural studies

Althusser's work was significant in elevating the debate about ideology to the forefront of thinking within cultural studies. Further, the legacy of Althusserian thinking about social formations as a complex structure of related but relatively autonomous instances can be seen in the work of Stuart Hall, Ernesto Laclau and Chantal Mouffe, amongst others (below and Chapter 14). However, much of Althusser's thinking about ideology is now regarded as problematic for the following reasons:

- **Althusser's view of the operation of ISAs is too functionalist in orientation. Ideology appears to function behind people's backs in terms of the 'needs' of an agentless system. The Althusserian formulation of the question of ideology is also too coherent (despite the fragmented character of the subject). The educational system, for example, is the site of contradictory ideologies and of ideological conflict rather than a place for the unproblematic and homogeneous reproduction of capitalist ideology.**

- **Althusser's formulation of the place of ideology within a social formation, that is, as relatively autonomous but determined in the last instance, is imprecise and threatens to return analysis to the very economic reductionism that it hoped to escape.**

- Althusser's work is dogged by an important epistemological problem, that is, a problem of truth and knowledge. If we are all formed in ideology, how can a non-ideological view be generated which would allow us to deconstruct ideology or even recognize it as such? Althusser's answer, that the rigours of science (and of his science in particular) can expose ideology, is both elitist and untenable (see Chapter 3).

Though the work of Gramsci was written prior to Althusser's, its influence within cultural studies postdates the former's enterprise (itself indebted to Gramsci). Indeed, the popularity of Gramsci within cultural studies was in partial response to the problems of Althusserian theory. In particular, Gramsci appeared to offer a more flexible, sophisticated and practical account of the character and workings of ideology.

Gramsci, ideology and hegemony

Culture is constructed in terms of a multiplicity of streams of meaning and encompasses a range of ideologies and cultural forms. However, it is argued (Williams, 1973, 1979, 1981; Hall, 1977, 1981) that there is a strand of meaning that can be called ascendant. The process of making, maintaining and reproducing these authoritative sets of meanings and practices has been called hegemony.

Cultural and ideological hegemony

For Gramsci, hegemony implies a situation where a 'historical bloc' of ruling-class factions exercises social authority and leadership over the subordinate classes. This is achieved through a combination of force and, more importantly, consent (see also Chapter 14). Thus,

> the normal exercise of hegemony on the classical terrain of the parliamentary regime is characterized by the combination of force and consent, which balance each other reciprocally without force predominating excessively over consent. Indeed, the attempt is always to ensure that force would appear to be based on the consent of the majority expressed by the so-called organs of public opinion – newspapers and associations. (Gramsci, 1971: 80)

Within Gramscian analysis, ideology is understood in terms of ideas, meanings and practices which, while they purport to be universal truths, are maps of meaning that sustain powerful social groups. Above all, ideology is not separate from the practical activities of life. Rather, it is understood to be a material phenomenon rooted in day-to-day conditions.

Ideologies provide people with rules of practical conduct and moral behaviour equivalent 'to a religion understood in the secular sense of a unity of faith between a conception of the world and a corresponding norm of conduct' (ibid.: 349). For example, the representation of the formal education system as a meritocracy which offers all an equal chance in a fair society can be described as ideological. Likewise the representation of people of colour as by 'nature' inferior and less capable than white people.

A hegemonic bloc never consists of a single socio-economic category. Rather, it is formed through a series of alliances in which one group takes on a position of leadership. Ideology plays a crucial part in allowing this alliance of groups (originally conceived in class terms) to overcome narrow economic-corporate interest in favour of 'national-popular' dominance. Thus, 'a cultural-social unity' is achieved 'through which a multiplicity of dispersed wills, with heterogeneous aims, are welded together with a single aim, as the basis of an equal and common conception of the world' (ibid.: 349). The building, maintenance or subversion of a common conception of the world is an aspect of ideological struggle involving a transformation of understanding through criticism of the existing popular ideologies.

Ideology and popular culture

Ideology is lived experience. It is also a body of systematic ideas whose role is to organize and bind together a bloc of diverse social elements. Ideology acts as social cement in the formation of hegemonic and counter-hegemonic blocs. Though ideology can take the form of a coherent set of ideas, it more often appears as the fragmented meanings of common sense inherent in a variety of representations.

For Gramsci, all people reflect upon the world and, through the 'common sense' of popular culture, organize their lives and experience. Thus, common sense becomes a crucial site of ideological conflict and, in particular, the struggle to forge 'good sense'. This involves, for Gramsci, the recognition of the class character of capitalism. Common sense is the most significant site of ideological struggle because it is the terrain of the 'taken-for-granted', that is, a practical consciousness which guides the actions of the everyday world. More coherent sets of philosophical ideas are contested and transformed in the domain of common sense. Thus, Gramsci is concerned with the character of popular thought and popular culture.

> Every philosophical current leaves behind it a sediment of 'common sense'; this is the document of its historical effectiveness. Common sense is not rigid and immobile but is continually transforming itself, enriching itself with scientific ideas and with philosophical opinions which have entered ordinary life. Common sense creates the folklore of the future, that is as a relatively rigid phase of popular knowledge at a given place and time. (Gramsci, 1971: 362)

Complete this activity in groups of three or four.

— How does crime drama act as ideology in relation to the law?
— How do soap operas present ideology about the family?

The instability of hegemony

✓ *Hegemony can be understood in terms of the strategies by which the world views and power of ascendant social groups are maintained.*

However, hegemony has to be seen in relational terms and as inherently unstable. Hegemony is a *temporary* settlement and series of alliances between social groups that is won and not given. Further, it needs to be constantly re-won and re-negotiated. Thus culture becomes a terrain of conflict and struggle over meanings. Consequently hegemony is not a static entity; it is marked by a series of changing discourses and practices intrinsically bound up with social power. Gramsci characterizes hegemony as

> a continuous process of formation and superseding of unstable equilibria ... between the interests of the fundamental group and those of the subordinate groups ... equilibria in which the interests of the dominant group prevail, but only up to a certain point. (Gramsci, 1968: 182)

Since hegemony has to be constantly re-made and re-won, it opens up the possibility of a challenge to it, that is, the making of a counter-hegemonic bloc of subordinate groups and classes. For Gramsci, such a counter-hegemonic struggle must seek to gain ascendancy within civil society before any attempt is made on state power. Civil society is constituted by affiliations outside of formal state boundaries, including the family, social clubs, the press, leisure activities, etc.

Gramsci makes a distinction between:

- the '*war of position*': the winning of hegemony within the sphere of civil society; and

- the '*war of manoeuvre*': the assault on state power.

For Gramsci, success in 'the war of manoeuvre' is dependent on attaining hegemony through the 'war of position'.

Gramscian cultural studies

The introduction and deployment of Gramscian concepts within cultural studies proved to be of long-lasting significance. This was so (see Chapter 14), because of the central importance given to popular culture as a site of ideological struggle. In effect, Gramsci makes ideological struggle and conflict within civil society the central arena of cultural politics, with hegemonic analysis the mode of gauging the relevant balance of forces. Gramsci argued that 'it would be interesting to study concretely the forms of cultural organization which keep the ideological world in movement within a given country and to examine how they function in practice' (Gramsci, cited in Bennett et al., 1981: 195–6). This could be read as a virtual campaign slogan for cultural studies, at least until the debates about poststructuralism and postmodernism gained ascendancy (Chapters 6 and 14).

For example, early work on advertising was cast within the problematic of ideology and hegemony. Textual and ideological analysis of advertising stressed the selling not just of commodities but also of ways of looking at the world. The job of advertising was to create an 'identity' for a product amid the bombardment of competing images by associating the brand with desirable human values. Buying a brand was not only about buying a product. It was also about buying into lifestyles and values. As Winship argues, 'A woman is nothing more than the commodities she wears: the lipstick, the tights, the clothes and so on are "woman"' (Winship, 1981: 218).

For Williamson (1978), objects in advertisements are signifiers of meaning that we decode in the context of known cultural systems. In doing so, we associate products in adverts with other cultural 'goods'. An image of a particular product may denote only beans or a car. However, it is made to connote 'nature' or 'family'. Thus advertising creates a world of differences between products and lifestyles which we 'buy into'. In purchasing products we also buy the image and so contribute to the construction of our identities through consumption. For Williamson, advertising is ideological in its obscuring of economic inequality at the level of production by images of free and equal consumption.

The problems of hegemony and ideology

Hegemony and fragmentation

Although neo-Gramscian hegemony theory has been a strong mode of analysis within cultural studies since the late 1970s, it has not gone unchallenged. Collins (1989) rejects the notion of hegemony on the grounds that culture is heterogeneous. This is said to be so both in terms of the variety of texts produced and the different meanings that compete within texts. For Collins, contemporary (postmodern) culture no longer has a centre in terms either of industrial production or of the generation of meaning. Right across the western world, it is argued, we have been witnessing the end of anything remotely resembling a 'common culture'.

The notion of a hegemonic culture is also made problematic in terms of the lived cultures of social groups. In particular, the last 30 years have seen the fragmentation of lifestyle cultures. This has been a consequence of:

- **the impact of migration;**
- **the 're-emergence' of ethnicity;**
- **the rise and segmentation of youth cultures;**
- **the impact of gender politics;**
- **the creation of an array of lifestyles centred on consumption.**

The consumption-centredness of the working class becomes the medium and instrument of its fragmentation. The choice between values and lifestyles becomes a matter of taste and style rather than being forged by an authentic, cultural authority that could be called hegemonic.

Hegemony and power

The concept of hegemony 'contains' or connotes issues of power. If the play of power is removed from the notion of hegemony, it ceases to have any validity at all. However, the notion of power that it infers through its usage in cultural studies remains that of the exercise of constraint by the powerful over the subordinate. That is, the concept of hegemony connotes an undesirable 'imposition' disguised as widespread consent. If the argument is that consent represents misrecognition of the real relations of power and interest in play, then we are faced with the problem of ideology understood as false consciousness (see below).

Some usages of the concept of hegemony are more effective than others. For example, reference to the 'hegemony' of free enterprise and free trade philosophies amongst the powerful economic nations seems to have merit. However, allusion to the 'hegemony' of particular notions of masculinity and femininity are of more doudtful value given the increasing complexity and fragmentation of gender identities.

Laclau and Mouffe (1985) have put forward a revised concept of hegemony. They put aside the final determination of class and the economic. That is, ideology has no 'class-belonging'. Instead, hegemonic and counter-hegemonic blocs are formed through temporary and strategic alliances of a range of discursively constructed subjects and groups of interest. Here, the 'social' is understood to be not an object but rather a field of contestation in which multiple descriptions of the self and others compete for ascendancy. For Laclau and Mouffe, it is the role of hegemonic practices to try to fix difference, to put closure around the unstable meanings of signifiers in the discursive field.

However, it is unclear that the term hegemony is required at all when it continues to carry connotations of dominance. It might be better to deploy concepts like 'explanatory authority', and power/knowledge in the context of descriptions of cultural alliances.

Ideology as power

The whole concept of ideology has come under scrutiny for it involves at least two central problems:

1 the problem of *scope.*

2 the problem of *truth.*

Early Marxist and sociological versions of the concept of ideology restricted its usage to ideas associated with, and maintaining the power of, the dominant class. Later, more extended versions of the concept added questions of gender, ethnicity, age, etc., to that of class. Giddens argues that ideology should be understood in terms of 'How structures of signification are mobilized to legitimate the sectional interests of hegemonic groups' (Giddens, 1979: 6). This is a contemporary definition of ideology that attenuates the concept. In other words, while ideology refers to the way meaning is used to justify the power of ascendant groups, this definition encompasses social groups based on race, gender, age, etc., as well as those of class.

While Giddens's definition of ideology refers only to the ideas of the powerful, other versions, including Althusser's, see ideology as justifying the actions of *all* groups of people. In other words, marginal and subordinate groups also have ideologies. Here ideology means the organizing and justifying ideas that groups of people hold about themselves and the world. Of course, this wider version of the concept of ideology can also embrace the narrower one in that we are all, as Foucault (1980) argued, implicated in power relations. The difference between the dominant and subordinate groups is one of degrees of power and differing substantive world views. It is not a question of ideological versus non-ideological ideas.

— How does one class justify domination over another?
— How does one sex justify dominating another?
— How does one 'race' justify domination over another?

In each case give examples from popular culture.

Discuss your work with other people.

Ideology and misrecognition

The second fundamental problem with the concept of ideology refers to its epistemological status, that is, the relation of ideology to truth and knowledge. These questions will be discussed at greater length in Chapters 3 and 6. However, we may note that ideology has commonly been counterpoised to the truth. For example, Althusser compares ideology with science, casting the former as 'misrecognition'. However, science is a mode of thinking and a set of procedures that produce certain kinds of knowledge. It is not an elevated, God-like form of knowledge that produces objective truth beyond dispute.

Most versions of the concept of ideology cast it as falsity. To do so, one must employ a representationalist epistemology. That is, one must be able to represent the true (understood to be an accurate picture of the world) in order to be able to compare it with the 'false' ideology. However, representationalist epistemology has largely been displaced within cultural studies by the influence of poststructuralism, postmodernism and other anti-representationalist paradigms.

These widely accepted (with cultural studies) strands of thinking have undermined the notion of objective and universal truth. Instead, it is now commonplace to talk of 'regimes of truth', being 'in the true', 'multiple truth claims', 'the social construction of truth', etc. In this view no universally accurate picture of the world is possible, only degrees of agreement about what counts as truth. For this reason, thinkers like Foucault (1980) and Rorty (1989, 1991a, 199lb) have rejected the concept of ideology altogether. Foucault certainly regards knowledge as implicated with power, hence his concept of power/knowledge. By power/knowledge is meant a mutually constituting relationship between power and knowledge, so that knowledge is indissociable from regimes of power. Knowledge is formed within the context of the relationships and practices of power and subsequently contributes to the development, refinement and proliferation of new techniques of power. However, no simple uncontaminated 'truth' can be counterposed to power/knowledge for there is no truth outside of it.

Rorty (1989) understands knowledge to be a series of descriptions of the world that have practical consequences. They can be judged in terms of values but not in terms of absolute truths. For Rorty, 'truth' is a social commendation. Truth is a cultural 'good', rather than a form of universal knowledge. One can compare world views (ideologies) in terms of their values, consequences and social/historical conditions of production. However, we cannot contrast them in terms of ultimate truth versus untruth.

Nevertheless, the concept of ideology remains strongly entrenched within cultural studies. Many writers persist in discovering ideology lurking beneath the surface of texts. Further, these ideologies continue to be regarded as the self-serving and false claims of the powerful. Cultural studies is faced with a dilemma. If one holds to an anti-representationalist position in relation to language, it is inconsistent to deploy a concept of ideology as falsehood. In order to continue to use the concept of ideology, we need to redefine the concept of ideology.

What is ideology?

Assuming that ideology is not confined to questions of class, and few would argue that it should be, then ideology can be seen in the following ways:

- **world views of dominant groups that justify and maintain their power and that are counterposed to truth;**

- **world views of any social groups that justify their actions and that are counterposed to truth;**

- **world views of dominant groups that justify and maintain their power but which cannot be counterposed to truth; however, they can be subject to redescription and thus do not have to be accepted;**

- world views of any social groups that justify their actions but that cannot be counterpoised to truth; however, they can be subject to redescription and thus do not have to be accepted.

It would be unwise to suggest that any particular version of ideology is the 'correct' one. Nevertheless, if writers use the concept, it is beholden on them to clarify what they mean by the term.

My own view is that it is untenable to counterpoise the concept of ideology to truth (see Chapter 3) and that all social groups have ideologies. In this sense, the only acceptable concept of ideology is one that is interchangeable with the Foucauldian notion of power/knowledge. As such, ideology cannot be seen as a simple tool of domination but should be regarded as discourses that have specific *consequences* for relations of power at all levels of social relationships (including the justification and maintenance of ascendant groups).

✓ *The concept of ideology need only be understood as the 'binding and justifying ideas' of any social group. This definition of ideology requires no concept of the truth.*

DECONSTRUCT THIS: FORM VS. CONTENT

- *How does form shape content?*
- *How does content shape form?*
- *Is there a borderline between form and content?*

SUMMARY

The first story of cultural studies concerns the move from perceiving culture as the 'arts' to seeing culture as being 'ordinary' and encapsulating 'a whole way of life'. This represents the move from a broadly literary to an anthropological definition of culture.

The second story of cultural studies concerns the place of culture in a social formation, that is, the relationship of culture to other social practices such as the economic and the political. Cultural studies has rejected the idea of culture as *determined* by economic forces. Instead culture is understood as an *autonomous* set of meanings and practices with its own logic. This logic is paralleled by the transformation of culture as a concept from the margins of the humanities and social sciences to one at its very heart.

(Cont'd)

Definitions of culture are all contestable. However, a widely accepted way of understanding the concept within cultural studies is in terms of 'maps of meaning'. Cultural studies asks questions about which meanings are put into circulation, by whom, for what purposes and in whose interests. As Fiske (1992) has argued, the concept of culture within cultural studies is above all a political one concerned with questions of *power*. Consequently, much of cultural studies work has been centred on questions of power, knowledge, ideology and hegemony.

Considerations of meaning have led cultural studies to be concerned with how our maps are produced and hence to culture as a set of signifying practices. That is, attention has been given to the organization of signs that generate meaning. The primary sign system in operation is language. This has led theorists to explore the idea of discourses or regulated ways of speaking. In short, cultural studies, along with the whole of the humanities and social sciences, has taken a 'linguistic turn', the subject of Chapter 3.

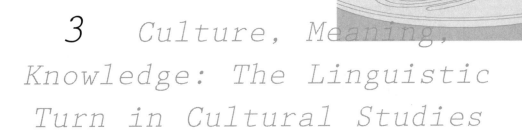

3 Culture, Meaning, Knowledge: The Linguistic Turn in Cultural Studies

The significance of the relationship between language and culture has risen to the top of the agenda within cultural studies. This is for two central and related reasons:

1 **Language is the privileged medium in which cultural meanings are formed and communicated.**

2 **Language is the means and medium through which we form knowledge about ourselves and the social world.**

Language is not a neutral medium for the formation and transfer of values, meanings and forms of knowledge that exist independently beyond its boundaries. Rather, language is constitutive of those very values, meanings and knowledges. That is, language gives meaning to material objects and social practices that are brought into view and made intelligible to us in terms which language delimits. Language is not best understood as an innocent reflection of non-linguistic meaning.

Nor is it to be grasped simply in terms of the intentions of language users. Rather,

✓ *Language constructs meaning. It structures which meanings can or cannot be deployed under determinate circumstances by speaking subjects.*

There is the 'suchness' of the world and there are linguistic descriptions of objects in the world. There is a rock and there is the word 'rock'. We are aware that there is a difference between the word and the object and yet we cannot easily distinguish between them. Once we talk about what a rock 'is', we are doing so from 'within' language. We are not in unmediated contact with the rock. Even if we can 'experience' the suchness of rocks, as Zen Buddhists urge us to do, we are stuck with a dualistic language.

SAUSSURE AND SEMIOTICS

To understand culture is to explore how meaning is produced symbolically through the signifying practices of language. This has been the domain of semiotics, broadly understood as the study of signs, and developed from the pioneering work of Saussure.

Ferdinand de Saussure (1857–1913) is a founding figure of structuralism. This is so because he explains the generation of meaning by reference to a system of structured differences in language. He explores the rules and conventions that organize language (*langue*) rather than the specific uses and utterances which individuals deploy in everyday life (*parole*). Saussure, and structuralism in general, is more concerned with the structures of language than actual performance. Structuralism is concerned with how cultural meaning is produced, holding it to be structured 'like a language'. A structuralist understanding of culture is concerned with 'systems of relations' of an underlying structure that forms the grammar which makes meaning possible.

Signifying systems

Saussure (1960) argued that language does not reflect a pre-existent and external reality of independent objects. Instead, a sign system like language constructs meaning from within itself through a series of conceptual and phonic differences. In language, he argued, there are only differences without positive terms. That is, meaning is not generated because an object or referent has an essential and instrinsic meaning. It is produced because signs are different from one another.

For Saussure, a signifying system is constituted by a series of signs that are analysed in terms of their constituent parts. These components of a sign are called the signifier and the signified. A signifier is taken to be the form or medium of signs, for example a sound, an image, the marks that form a word on the page. The signified is to be understood in terms of concepts and meanings.

The relationship between the sounds and marks of language, the signifiers, and what it is taken to mean, the signified, is not held in any fixed eternal relationship. Rather, their arrangement is *arbitrary* in the sense that the animal we call a 'cat' as it sits on the 'mat' could equally be signified by 'tac' and 'tam' or by 'el gato' and 'la estera'.

According to Saussure, meaning is produced through the selection and combination of signs along the syntagmatic and paradigmatic axis. The syntagmatic axis is constituted by the linear combination of signs that form sentences. Paradigmatic refers to the field of signs (i.e. synonyms) from which any given sign is selected. Meaning is accumulated along the syntagmatic axis, while selection from the paradigmatic field alters meaning at any given point in the sentence. Hartley (1982: 20) offers the following example:

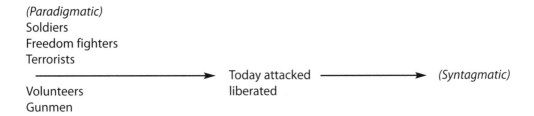

On the paradigmatic axis, the selection of freedom fighter or terrorist is of meaningful significance. It alters what we understand the character of the participants to be. Further, it will influence the combination along the syntagmatic axis since it is by convention unlikely, though grammatically acceptable, to combine terrorist with liberated. The arbitrary character of the signifier–signified relationship suggests that meaning is fluid because it is culturally and historically specific. It is not fixed in time and space, i.e it is not universal. However, the fact that terrorist and liberated is a rare combination does suggest that meaning is *regulated* under specific historical social conditions. As Culler puts it, 'Because it is arbitrary, the sign is totally subject to history and the combination at the particular moment of a given signifier and signified is a contingent result of the historical process' (Culler, 1976: 36).

Cultural codes

Signs are commonly organized into a sequence that generates meaning through the cultural *conventions* of their usage within a particular context. Such arrangements are called cultural codes. An illustration concerns the organization and regulation of colours into the cultural code of traffic lights.

Colours are breaks in the light spectrum that we classify with signs such as red, green, amber, and so forth. There is, of course, no universal reason why the sign 'red' should refer to a specific colour; rather, the relationship is arbitrary. The 'same' colour can be designated by the sign 'rojo'. It is central to Saussure's argument that red is meaningful *in relation* to the difference between red, green, amber, etc. These signs are then organized into a sequence – a code – that generates meaning through cultural *convention*. Thus, traffic lights deploy 'red' to signify 'stop' and 'green' to signify 'go'. This is the cultural code of traffic systems that temporally fixes the relationship between colours and meanings.

✓ *Signs become naturalized codes. Their apparent transparency of meaning is an outcome of cultural habituation. The effect of this is to conceal the practices of cultural coding.*

Saussure's contribution was to the study of a narrowly defined field of linguistics. Nevertheless, he predicted the possibility of a wider 'science that studies the life of signs within society'. This is possible because cultural objects convey meaning. Indeed, all cultural practices depend on meanings generated by signs. Consequently, culture is said to work 'like a language'. This makes all cultural practices open to semiotic analysis. Thus, Barthes (1967, 1972) takes Saussure's approach, amends it, and applies it to the practices of popular culture with an eye to showing how such events generate meaning.

DRESS CODES

What are the connotations of the following items?

- *tee-shirt;*
- *suspenders;*
- *bowler hat;*
- *briefcase;*
- *Doc Martens boots;*
- *wedding dress;*
- *bikini;*
- *black lace underwear;*
- *a red rose;*
- *pin-stripe suit.*

Write down combinations of items to produce:

- *socially acceptable and socially unacceptable dress for a man in (a) an office (b) a church (c) the beach (d) a bedroom;*
- *Socially acceptable and socially unacceptable dress for a woman in (a) an office (b) a church (c) the beach (d) a bedroom.*

Which items are socially acceptable in more than one context?
How do objects change their meanings in different contexts?

BARTHES AND MYTHOLOGY

Roland Barthes argues that we can talk of two systems of signification: denotation and connotation.

- *Denotation* is the descriptive and literal level of meaning shared by virtually all members of a culture. Thus, 'pig' denotes the concept of a useful pink farm animal with a snout and curly tail, etc.

- *Connotation* involves meanings that are generated by connecting signifiers to wider cultural concerns. Here, meaning involves the association of signs with other cultural codes of meaning. Thus, 'pig' may connote nasty police officer or male chauvinist according to the sub-codes or lexicons at work.

Connotation concerns meanings that multiply up from a given sign. Thus a single sign becomes loaded with many meanings. The expressive value of connotation can arise from the cumulative force of a sequence of signs (i.e. syntagmatically). However, it more usually arises by comparison with absent alternatives (i.e. paradigmatically). Where connotations have become naturalized, that is, as accepted as 'normal' and 'natural', they act as conceptual maps of meaning by which to make sense of the world. These are myths.

Though myths are cultural constructions, they may appear to be pre-given universal truths embedded in common sense. Myths are thus akin to the concept of ideology, which, it is argued, works at the level of connotation. Indeed, Vološinov (1973) was to argue that the domain of ideology corresponds to the field of signs. Where there are signs, so there is ideology.

For Barthes, myth is a second-order semiological system or metalanguage. It is a second language that speaks about a first-level language. The sign of the first system (signifier and signified) that generates denotative meaning becomes a signifier for a second order of connotative mythological meaning. Barthes (1972) represents this as a spatialized metaphor (Figure 3.1).

'Myth today'

In his essay 'Myth Today', Barthes gives an often quoted example of the work of signification, myth and ideology. The example refers to the cover of the French magazine *Paris Match*, featuring a young black soldier in French military uniform saluting the tricolour. His eyes are cast upward towards the French flag. On a denotative level this can be read as 'a black soldier salutes the French flag'. However, the repertoire of cultural codes available to Barthes and his contemporaries (which included French colonial history and their military involvement in Algiers) allowed them to interpret the image in a more ideological way. For Barthes, the connotations of the image suggest the loyalty of black French subjects to the French flag. In this way, the picture undermines criticism of French imperial activity. As Barthes explains:

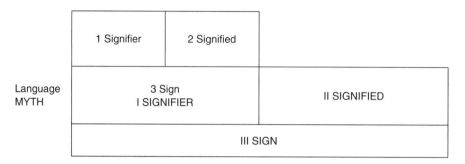

Figure 3.1   Barthes: the significations of myth

> I am at the barber's, and a copy of *Paris Match* is offered to me. On the cover, a young Negro in a French uniform is saluting, with his eyes uplifted, probably fixed on the fold of the tricolour. All this is the meaning of the picture. But, whether naïvely or not, I see very well what it signifies to me: that France is a great Empire, that all her sons, without colour discrimination, faithfully serve under the flag, and that there is no better answer to the detractors of an alleged colonialism than the zeal shown by this Negro in serving his so-called oppressors. (Barthes, 1972: 125–6)

According to Barthes, myth and ideology work by *naturalizing* the contingent interpretations of historically specific persons. That is, myth makes particular world views appear to be unchallengeable because natural or God-given. 'Myth has the task of giving an historical intention a natural justification, and making contingency appear eternal' (ibid.: 155). In another analysis, Barthes describes a French language advert thus:

> Here we have a Panzani advertisement: some packets of pasta, a tin, a sachet, some tomatoes, onions, peppers, a mushroom, all emerging from a half-open string bag, in yellows and greens on a red background. (Barthes, 1977: 33)

In his subsequent analysis, Barthes differentiates between

- a *linguistic code*: the French language, the Panzani label;
- a *visual code*: 'a half-open bag which lets the provisions spill out over the table'.

He reads the visual code as 'a return from market', with the overflowing supplies acting as a signifier that implies 'freshness' and 'domestic preparation'. A second sign brings together 'the tomato, the pepper and the tricoloured hues (yellow, green, red) of the poster' (ibid.: 34). This signifies Italy or rather '*Italianicity*'. (The composition of the image suggests a still-life painting, thereby adding to the 'Italianness' of the image.)

The work of Saussure and the early Barthes are amongst the founding texts of contemporary cultural studies. They represent the move away from culturalism towards structuralism. Both were influential within cultural studies in helping critics break with notions of the text as a transparent bearer of meaning. They illuminated the argument that all cultural texts are constructed with signs. However, the structuralist view of language has itself been the subject of critique. In particular, the idea that signs can have stable meanings, which is implied by the idea of binary pairs and denotation, was to be undermined in the work of the later Barthes, Vološinov/Bakhtin and Derrida.

KEY THINKERS

Roland Barthes (1915–80)

The French writer, critic, teacher and theorist Roland Barthes exerted a significant influence on bringing structuralism into cultural studies. In particular, he brought the methods of semiotics to bear on a wide range of cultural phenomena to illuminate the argument that all texts are constructed with signs in social contexts. Central to Barthes's work is the role of signs in generating meaning and framing the way texts are read. He explored the naturalization of connotative meanings into myths. He famously declared the 'death of the Author' in order to illustrate the intertextual character of meaning.

Reading: Barthes, R. (1972) *Mythologies*. London: Cape.

Polysemic signs

Instead of having one stable denotative meaning, signs are said by the later Barthes to be polysemic. That is, signs carry many potential meanings. Consequently, texts can be interpreted in a number of different ways. Meaning requires the active involvement of readers and the cultural competencies they bring to bear on the text-image. It is the readers of texts who temporally 'fix' meaning for particular purposes. Thus, interpretation of texts depends on readers' cultural repertoire and knowledge of social codes. These are differentially distributed along the lines of class, gender, nationality, etc.

This idea was carried forward within cultural studies through the work of Vološinov (1973). Of particular importance is his concept of the 'multi-accentuality' of the sign. For Vološinov, signs do not have one meaning but possess an 'inner dialectical quality' and an 'evaluative accent' which makes them capable of signifying a range of meanings. Signification changes as social conventions and social struggles seek to fix meaning. That is, the meanings of signs are not fixed but negotiable. They are fought over so that 'sign becomes the arena of class struggle' (Vološinov, 1973: 23). The ideological struggle is the contest over the significance of signs. Here power attempts to regulate and 'fix' the otherwise shifting meanings of signs.

As Hall (1996e) argues, the thrust of Vološinov's writing echoes Mikhail Bakhtin's (1984) argument that all understanding is dialogic in character. Bakhtin suggested that signs do not have fixed meanings; rather, sense is generated within a two-sided relationship between speaker and listener, addresser and addressee. Many critics hold that Bakhtin wrote under the name of Vološinov. In any case, both suggest that

 Meaning cannot be guaranteed; it is not pure but always ambivalent and ambiguous. Meaning is the inherently unstable domain of contestation not the product of a finished secure language.

Vološinov's work enabled cultural studies to take on board the idea of the multi-accentuality of the sign. It highlighted a sense that meaning was the outcome of politics and the play of power. The inherent undecidability of meaning and the place of regulative power are also themes within poststructuralism. Indeed, this theoretical perspective has had an even more enduring influence within cultural studies.

US FLAG

© **Photographer: Jenny Horne | Agency: Dreamstime.com**

Describe the following elements of this sign:

- *the signifiers;*
- *the signified at a denotive level;*
- *the signified at a connotative level.*

- *How easy was it to decide which meanings operate at which level?*
- *What does this tell us about the meanings of signs?*
- *In what contexts does this sign have different meanings for different people?*

Poststructuralism and intertextuality

The term poststructuralism implies 'after structuralism'. It embodies a notion of critique and absorption. That is, poststructuralism accepts and absorbs aspects of structural linguistics while subjecting it to a critique. This is a critical investigation which, it is claimed, surpasses structuralism. In short, poststructuralism rejects the idea of an underlying structure which founds meaning. For poststructuralism there can be no denotative meaning that is clear, descriptive and stable; rather, meaning is always deferred and in process. This is the position of the 'later' Barthes when he writes that

> a text is not a line of words releasing a single 'theological' meaning (the 'message' of the Author-God) but a multi-dimensional space in which a variety of writings, none of them original, blend and clash. The text is a tissue of quotations drawn from the innumerable centres of culture. (Barthes, 1977: 146)

In other words, textual meaning is unstable and cannot be confined to single words, sentences or particular texts. Meaning has no single originatory source. Rather, it is the outcome of relationships between texts, that is, intertextuality. It is argued that there can be no clear and stable denotative meanings (as in early Barthes), for all meaning contains traces of other meanings from other places.

These ideas make more sense if we explore the work of Jacques Derrida (1976), one of the most influential philosophers in cultural studies today. This poses a particular problem, for Derrida's work deliberately sets out to resist the stabilization of its meanings. Nevertheless, at the risk of simplification, I shall try to summarize key ideas in Derrida's writings as they have been taken up within cultural studies.

DERRIDA: TEXTUALITY AND *DIFFÉRANCE*

Nothing but signs

Derrida takes as axiomatic Saussure's claim (which, he argues, Saussure himself contradicts) that language generates meaning through difference rather than by correspondence with fixed transcendental meanings or referents to the 'real'. Consequently, 'From the moment that there is meaning there are nothing but signs. We think only in signs' (Derrida, 1976: 50).

In this argument there is no original meaning outside of signs. Since signs are a form of graphic 'representation', so writing is in at the origins of meaning. We cannot think about knowledge, truth and culture without signs, that is, writing. For Derrida, writing is a permanent trace that exists *always already* before perception is aware or conscious of itself. Thus, Derrida deconstructs the idea that speech provides an identity between signs and meaning. That is, signs do not possess clear and fixed meanings.

Derrida rehearses this argument in a number of places, for example in his discussion of the opposition between nature and culture. Derrida points out that nature is already a concept in language (i.e. culture) and not a pure state of being beyond signs. Likewise, Christianity claims to be based on the transcendental truth of the word of God. Yet the word of God is available only through the unstable signs of writing, that is, through the Bible. Ultimately, Derrida argues, the very idea of literal meaning is based on the idea of the 'letter', that is, writing. Literal meaning is always underpinned by metaphor – its apparent opposite. As Derrida puts it, 'All that functions as metaphor in these discourses confirms the privilege of the logos and founds the "literal" meaning then given to writing: a sign signifying itself signifying an eternal logos' (Derrida, 1976: 15).

Derrida critiques what he calls the 'logocentrism' and 'phonocentrism' of western philosophy.

- **By '*logocentrism*', Derrida means the reliance on fixed *a priori* transcendental meanings, that is, universal meanings, concepts and forms of logic that exist within human reason before any other kinds of thinking occur. This would include a universal conception of reason or beauty.**

- **By '*phonocentrism*', Derrida means the priority given to sounds and speech over writing in explaining the generation of meaning.**

According to Derrida, Socrates held speech to come directly from the heart of truth and the self. By contrast, writing was regarded as a form of sophistry and rhetoric. For Derrida, this signals Socrates's attempt to find wisdom and truth through reason unmediated by signification. This privileging of speech, argues Derrida, allows philosophers to regard the formation of subjectivity as unmediated agency. This would involve 'the unique experience of the signified producing itself spontaneously from within itself' (ibid.: 20).

The priority given to speech as a form of unmediated meaning is the search for a universal transcendental truth. This would be a truth that grounds itself as a source of the self. It would be pure spontaneity. Derrida argues that the privileging of speech relies on the untenable idea that there is direct access to truth and stable meaning. This idea is fallacious because, in representing a truth that 'exists' outside of representation, one must be re-representing it. That is, there can be no truth or meaning outside of representation. There is nothing but signs.

- Look up the word 'text' in a dictionary or in the thesaurus on your PC.
- Look up one of the words that you are referred to.
- Look up one of the words that you are next referred to.
- Continue this process until you have 20 words that are connected to the word 'text'.

— Can you write a stable definition of the word 'text'? Does the process ever stop?
— What does it tell us about the relationship between meanings and words?
— Explore what is meant by the phrase 'the text creates the context as much as the context creates the text'.

Différance

For Derrida, since meaning is generated through the play of signifiers not by reference to an independent object world, it can never be fixed. Words carry multiple meanings, including the echoes or traces of other meanings from other related words in other contexts. Language is non-representational and meaning is inherently unstable so that it constantly slides away. Thus, by *différance*, the key Derridean concept, is meant 'difference and deferral'.

✓ *The production of meaning in the process of signification is continually deferred and supplemented.*

Meaning is no longer fixed outside any textual location or spoken utterance and is always in relation to other textual locations in which the signifier has appeared on other occasions. Every articulation of a signifier bears a trace of its previous articulations. There is no fixed transcendental signified, since the meaning of concepts is constantly referred, via the network of traces, to their articulations in other discourses: fixed meaning is constantly deferred. (Weedon et al., 1980: 199)

Central to Derrida's project is the logic of the 'supplement' as a challenge to the logic of identity between signs and meanings. Our common-sense usage of language tells us that meaning is identical with a fixed entity to which a word refers. The sign 'dog' signifies the animal dog because a dog is a dog. It could be signified in no other way.

By contrast, Derrida argues that a supplement adds to and substitutes meanings. For example, writing supplements speech by adding to it and substituting for it. The meaning of a word is supplemented by the traces of other words. A dog is a dog because it is not a cat or a wolf (difference). However, the meaning of dog is unstable. Are we talking about guard dogs or guide dogs? Alsatians or Dalmatians?

If we look up the word 'dog' in a dictionary, we can follow the chain of signifiers thus:

— Dog–canine–hound–hybrid–crossbreed–composite
— If a dog is now a composite, is it still a dog? (Deferral)

Nevertheless, this use of 'the supplement' is problematic. This is so because the argument assumes that the supplement adds to an already existent, self-present, original meaning. That is, the signifier 'dog' has a stable meaning to which 'crossbreed' is added. Instead, the supplement is always already part of the thing supplemented. Meaning is always displaced and deferred. The signifier 'dog' and the signifier 'crossbreed' are always already a part of each other – they define each other. This continual supplementarity of meaning, the continual substitution and adding of meanings through the play of signifiers, challenges the identity of noises and marks with fixed meaning. There cannot be a final fixed meaning attached to the word dog.

Derrida's postcards

In *La Carte Postale* (1980), Derrida plays with the idea of postcards and postal systems which act as metaphors for the generation and circulation of meaning. The postcard motif allows him to challenge the idea that meaning operates within a closed circuit where intentions and messages are unambiguously sent and received. Rather, postcards may go astray, they may reach persons and generate meanings other than those that were intended. In this way the idea of 'true' meaning or communication is displaced. Meanings circulate without any absolutely authorized source or destination. Reason is unable to permanently fix and define the meaning of concepts. The particular character of postcard writing as destined for a specific person who understands Derrida's cryptic messages suggests the irreducible specificity of writing.

Strategies of writing

By writing, Derrida means not simply text on a page but what he calls *archewriting*. This concept reminds us that there is no 'outside' of the text. Writing is always already part of the outside of texts. Texts form the outside of texts. Texts are constitutive of their outsides. It is in this sense that there is nothing outside of texts or nothing but texts. This does not mean that there is no independent material world. However, it does suggest that texts are constitutive of meaningful practices.

The idea of writing plays an important part in Derrida's work:

- **Writing is seen not as secondary to speech (as self-present meaning) but as a necessary part of speech and meaning.**

- **Meaning and truth claims are always dependent on writing. They are subject to the rhetorical claims, metaphors and strategies of writing.**

First, writing is always already inside speech. Since writing is 'a sign of a sign', then the meaning of words cannot be stable and identical with a fixed concept. Rather, they must be deferred by dint of the traces of other words. Second, truths are not outside of a writing that tries to express them. Rather, the strategies of writing are constitutive of any truth claims and can be deconstructed in terms of those strategies.

Deconstruction

Derrida is widely associated with the practice of deconstruction.

✔ *To deconstruct is to take apart, to undo, in order to seek out and display the assumptions of a text.*

In particular, deconstruction involves the dismantling of hierarchical binary oppositions such as:

- **speech–writing;**
- **reality–appearance;**
- **nature–culture;**
- **reason–madness.**

Such binary divisions serve to 'guarantee' truth through excluding and devaluing the 'inferior' part of the binary. Thus within the conventions of western culture, speech is privileged over writing, reality over appearance, men over women.

Deconstruction seeks to expose the blind-spots of texts. These are the unacknowledged assumptions through which they operate. This includes those places where a text's rhetorical strategies work against the logic of its own arguments, that is, the tension between what a text means to say and what it is constrained to mean.

For example, Saussure claims that the relationship between the signifier and signified is arbitrary. However, in deconstructing Saussure's writing, Derrida attempts to show that his text operates with a different logic. According to Derrida, Saussure implicitly privileges speech over writing and thereby abandons the arbitrary character of the sign. This is so because speech is held to contain clear and fixed meanings.

However, Derrida faces a conceptual problem. He deconstructs the binaries of western philosophy and attacks the 'metaphysic of presence' (i.e. the idea of a fixed self-present meaning). Yet Derrida must use the very conceptual language of the western philosophy that he seeks to undo. In Derrida's view there is no escape from Reason, that is, from the very concepts of philosophy. This problem can be exposed by a strategy of reversal, that is, by putting writing before speech, appearance before reality, etc. However, it cannot be overcome or replaced. To mark this tension, Derrida places his concepts 'under erasure'.

> To place a word under erasure is to first write the word and then cross it out, leaving both the word and its crossed-out version. For example, R̶e̶a̶s̶o̶n̶ .

As Spivak explains. 'Since the word is inaccurate, it is crossed out. Since it is necessary, it remains legible' (Spivak, 1976: xiv). The use of accustomed and known concepts 'under erasure' is intended to destabilize the familiar as at one and the same time useful, necessary, inaccurate and mistaken. Derrida seeks to expose the *undecidability* of metaphysical oppositions, and of meaning as such. He does this by arguing within and against philosophy and its attempts to maintain its authority in matters of truth by dictating in advance what shall count as topics, arguments and strategies.

KEY THINKERS

Jacques Derrida (1930–2007)

Derrida was an Algerian-born French speaking philosopher whose work proved highly influential within cultural studies. He is associated with the themes of deconstruction and poststructuralism. Derrida's main influence on cultural studies is his anti-essentialism. Derrida undoes the structuralist trope of the stable binary structures of language, arguing that meaning slides down a chain of signifiers and is thus continually deferred and supplemented. Derrida seeks to deconstruct the epistemological base of western philosophy, including the idea that there can be any self-present transparent meaning outside of 'representation'.

Reading: Derrida, J. (1976) *Of Grammatology*. Baltimore: Johns Hopkins University Press.

Derrida and cultural studies

Derrida's work is complex, subtle, difficult and open to contested interpretations. For some (e.g. Norris, 1987), Derrida is taken to be an 'argumentative' philosopher who operates with a transcendental logic, that is, one which seeks to find the conditions for the existence of logic, the presuppositions on which reason is based. For others (notably Rorty, 1991b), Derrida is a poetic writer who displaces one intellectual world with another. Thus he gives us new ideas and new visions by making us dissatisfied with the old ways of thinking. For Rorty, Derrida makes the whole concept of representation unusable since there is never a stable referent to be represented nor any truth that is not re-presentation. Others, for example Hall (1997a), continue to use the term 'representation', while highlighting its constructed character. In this way, the concept of representation is put under erasure.

There is much that is valuable within cultural studies that is derived from poststructuralism. Cultural studies has taken from Derrida the key notions of writing, intertextuality, undecidability, deconstruction, *différance,* trace and supplement. These concepts all stress the instability of meaning, its deferral through the interplay of texts, writing and traces. Consequently, categories do not have essential universal meanings but are social constructions of language. This is the core of the anti-essentialism prevalent in cultural studies. That is, words have no universal meanings and do not refer to objects that possess essential qualities. For example, since words do not refer to essences, identity is not a fixed universal 'thing' but a description in language (Chapter 7).

However, the legacy of Derrida's work within cultural studies is not without its problems. For example, the relationship between signifiers and signifieds may be arbitrary in the sense of 'could have been otherwise'. That is, meaning is conventional rather than universal and essential. However, it is not arbitrary in the sense that, given the history of language and culture, words do have more or less fixed meanings and uses in practice. This 'fixing' is the consequence of the routine indissolubility of language and practice. To neglect this facet of language is to:

- posit language as an autonomous free-floating system rather than as a human tool;

- de-couple signification from other practices, habits and routines;

- undertake textual analysis that is divorced from any significant social implications;

- elevate the study of texts over the linguistic competencies of living persons;

- join sceptics in wondering about the disjunction between words and the world.

FOUCAULT: DISCOURSE, PRACTICE AND POWER

Alongside Derrida, Michel Foucault is the most influential anti-essentialist, poststructuralist thinker in cultural studies at present. His work is cited in many chapters of this text. Here we will focus on his conception of language and practice. This coheres around the concepts of discourse, discursive practice and discursive formation.

Foucault (1972) argues against formalist theories of language that conceive of it as an autonomous system with its own rules and functions (i.e. structuralist semiotics). He also opposes interpretative or hermeneutic methods that seek to disclose the 'hidden' meanings of language. Instead, he is concerned with the description and analysis of the surfaces of discourse and their effects.

Foucault is determinedly historical in his insistence that language develops and generates meaning under specific material and historical conditions. He explores the particular and determinate historical conditions under which statements are combined and *regulated*. Regulation forms and defines a distinct field of knowledge/objects constituted by a particular set of concepts. This ordered domain of language delimits a specific 'regime of truth' (i.e. what counts as truth). Foucault attempts to identify the historical conditions and determining rules of the formation of discourses or regulated ways of speaking about objects.

Discursive practices

For Derrida, meaning has the potential to proliferate into infinity. By contrast, Foucault explores how meanings are temporarily stabilized or regulated into a discourse. This ordering of meaning is achieved through the operation of power in social practice. For Foucault, discourse 'unites' both language and practice.

✓ *Discourse constructs, defines and produces the objects of knowledge in an intelligible way while excluding other forms of reasoning as unintelligible.*

The concept of discourse in the hands of Foucault involves the production of knowledge through language. That is, discourse gives meaning to material objects and social practices. Needless to say, material objects and social practices 'exist' outside of language. However, they are given meaning or 'brought into view' by language and are thus discursively formed.

Discourses provide ways of talking about a particular topic with repeated motifs or clusters of ideas, practices and forms of knowledge across a range of sites of activity. This phenomenon we may call a discursive formation. A discursive formation is a pattern of discursive events that brings into being a common object across a number of sites. They are regulated maps of meaning or ways of speaking through which objects and practices acquire meaning. For example, Foucault's (1973) study of discourses of madness included:

- statements about madness which give us knowledge concerning madness;
- the rules that prescribe what is 'sayable' or 'thinkable' about madness;
- subjects who personify the discourses of madness, i.e. the 'madman';
- the processes by which discourses of madness acquire authority and truth at a given historical moment;
- the practices within institutions that deal with madness;
- the idea that different discourses about madness will appear at later historical moments, producing new knowledge and a new discursive formation.

Discourse and discipline

Foucault argued that discourse regulates not only what can be said under determinate social and cultural conditions but also who can speak, when and where. Consequently, much of his work is concerned with the historical investigation of power. Foucault (1977) has been a prominent theorist of the 'disciplinary' character of modern institutions, practices and discourses. In particular, the 'regimes of truth' (what counts as truth) of modernity involve relations of power/knowledge. Foucault concentrates on three disciplinary discourses;

1 *the 'sciences'*, which constitute the subject as an object of enquiry;

2 *'dividing practices'*, which separate the mad from the sane, the criminal from the law-abiding citizen, and friends from enemies;

3 *technologies of the self*, whereby individuals turn themselves into subjects.

Disciplinary technologies arose in a variety of sites, including schools, prisons, hospitals and asylums. They produced what Foucault called 'docile bodies' that could be 'subjected, used, transformed and improved' (Foucault, 1977: 198). Discipline involves the organization of the subject in space through dividing practices, training and standardization. It produces subjects by categorizing and naming them in a hierarchical order through a rationality of efficiency, productivity and 'normalization'. By 'normalization' is meant a system of graded and measurable categories and intervals in which individual subjects can be distributed around a norm. For example, western medicine and judiciary systems have increasingly appealed to statistical measures and distributions to judge what is normal. This leads, for example, not only to classifications of what is sane and mad but also to degrees of 'mental illness'. Classificatory systems are essential to the process of normalization and thus to the production of a range of subjects.

The metaphor of disciplinary power commonly associated with Foucault is the 'Panopticon'. This is a prison design consisting of a courtyard with a tower in the centre capable of overlooking the surrounding buildings and cells, which have a window facing the tower. The inmates of the cells are visible to the observer in the tower but the onlooker is not seen by the prisoners. The cells became 'small theatres, in which each actor is alone, perfectly individualized and constantly visible' (Foucault, 1977: 200). The idea of the Panopticon is a metaphor (it is doubtful that the design was materialized) for a continuous, anonymous and all-pervading power and surveillance operating at all levels of social organization.

The productivity of power

For Foucault, power is distributed throughout social relations. It is not to be reduced to centralized economic forms and determinations nor to its legal or juridical character. Rather, power forms a dispersed capillary woven into the fabric of the entire social order. Further, power is not simply repressive but is *productive*. That is, power brings subjects into being. It is implicated in 'generating forces, making them grow, and ordering them, rather than one dedicated to impeding them, making them submit, or destroying them' (Foucault, 1980: 136).

For example, Foucault argues against the 'repressive hypothesis' whereby discourses of sexuality are said to be repressed. Instead, he suggests that there has been an 'incitement to discourse' about sex, that is, a proliferation of discourses about sex through for example, medicine, Christianity and population studies. These discourses about sex analyse, classify and regulate sexuality in ways that produce sexed subjects and make sexuality a cornerstone of subjectivity.

Foucault establishes a mutually constituting relationship between power and knowledge so that knowledge is indissociable from regimes of power. Knowledge is formed within the practices of power and is constitutive of the development, refinement and proliferation of new techniques of power. Hence the analytic term 'power/knowledge' (Foucault, 1980). For example, psychiatry emerges through the practices of trying to understand and control 'madness'. In doing so it classifies forms of madness, thereby bringing new forms of discipline and new kinds of subject into being. That is, psychiatry decides what madness and sanity are to be undertsood as, while enforcing that classification as 'natural' rather than cultural.

The subjects of discourse

For Foucault, bodies are 'subject to' the regulatory power of discourse by which they become 'subjects for' themselves and others. Here, he is concerned with subjectivity as formed within the subject positions of discourse. The speaking subject is not held to be the author or originator of a statement. Rather, subjectivity depends on the prior existence of discursive positions. These

> can be filled by virtually any individual when he formulates the statement; and in so far as one and the same individual may occupy in turn, in the same series of statements, different positions, and assume the role of different subjects. (Foucault, 1972: 94)

Foucault provides us with useful tools for understanding the way the social order is constituted by discourses of power. In particular, he describes the processes by which cultural regulation produces subjects who fit into, constitute and reproduce that order. Nevertheless, for some critics, Foucault's notions of subject positions and docile bodies deprives the self of any form of agency. However, in his later work, he does turn to questions of how subjects are 'led to focus attention on themselves, to decipher, recognize and acknowledge themselves as subjects of desire' (Foucault, 1987: 5); that is, how one recognizes oneself as a subject for oneself involved in practices of self-constitution, recognition and reflection.

This concern with self-production as a discursive practice is centred on the question of ethics as a mode of 'care of the self'. For Foucault, ethics is concerned with practical advice as to how one should concern oneself with oneself in everyday life. It centres on the 'government of others and the government of oneself' and forms part of our strategies for 'conduct about conduct' and the 'calculated management of affairs' (Foucault, 1979, 1984a, 1984b). (See Chapters 7 and 9.)

DISCOURSES OF GENDER

Consider each of the following categories (for each one try to give a contemporary example):

- *statements about men and women which give us knowledge concerning men and women;*
- *the rules that prescribe what is 'sayable' or 'thinkable' about men and women;*
- *subjects who personify the discourses of masculinity and femininity;*

(Cont'd)

- *the processes by which discourses of men and women acquire authority and truth at a given historical moment;*
- *the practices within institutions that deal with men and women.*

Discuss your thoughts with other people.

Write a paragraph summary of contemporary discourse on men and women. Try to link statements about men and women to particular persons and institutions.

How is power involved in discourses of men and women?

How do you think discourses about men and women have changed over the last 100 years?

Look at any magazine that is available to you. Discuss examples of how discourses of gender are manifested in the images that it contains.

POST-MARXISM AND THE DISCURSIVE CONSTRUCTION OF THE 'SOCIAL'

The considerable influence of Foucault within cultural studies might be taken to mark the abandonment of its Marxist legacy. Foucault was opposed to what he saw as the economic reductionism and historical *telos* (or inevitable unfolding of a purposeful history) of Marxism. However, Laclau and Mouffe (1985), amongst others, have been involved in the critique and reconstitution of Marxism through the application of post-structuralist theory to Marxism (Hall, 1997b). This perspective is sometimes called post-Marxism.

Deconstructing Marxism

Laclau and Mouffe are particularly critical of the essentialism, foundationalism and reductionism of Marxism (see Chapter 14). They reject the idea that there are any essential universal concepts (such as class, history, mode of production) that refer to unchanging entities in the world. Further, discursive concepts are not to be reduced to or explained solely in terms of the economic base as in reductionist forms of Marxism. Instead, Laclau and Mouffe argue that discourse constitutes the objects of its knowledge. Consequently, they analyse the 'social' (a concept they reject as being not a proper object of analysis) in terms of the discursive construction of reality. For them, 'society' is an unstable system of discursive differences in which socio-political identities represent the open and contingent articulation of cultural and political categories.

Class, in Marxist theory, is conceived of as an essential unified identity between a signifier and a specific group of people who share socio-economic conditions. By contrast, class is understood by Laclau and Mouffe to be the effect of discourse. Class is not simply an objective economic fact but a discursively formed, collective subject position. Class consciousness is neither an inevitability nor a unified phenomenon. Classes, while sharing certain common conditions of existence, do not automatically form a core, unified class consciousness. Rather, class and class consciousness are historically specific. Further, classes are cross-cut by conflicting interests, including those of gender, race and age. Thus, subjects are not unitary wholes; they are fragmented subjects who take up plural subject positions.

For Laclau and Mouffe, the 'social' involves multiple points of power and antagonism. It does not cohere around class conflict as it does in Marxism. The complex field of multiple forms of power, subordination and antagonisms are not reducible to any single site or contradiction. Consequently, any radical politics cannot be premised on the domination of any particular political project (e.g. the proletariat of Marxism). Instead it must be constructed in terms of the recognition of difference and the identification and development of points of common interest.

Laclau and Mouffe are critical of universal Reason and argue that all progressive values must be defended within the pragmatic context of particular moral traditions. There can be no appeal to absolute standards of legitimation. The formulation of what is equitable involves, for them, the recovery of modern political ideas of democracy, justice, tolerance, solidarity and freedom. Laclau and Mouffe could be said to be both modern and postmodern (Chapter 6) in their pursuit of radical democracy (Chapter 14).

The articulated social

Laclau and Mouffe argue that the 'social' is to be thought of not as a totality but rather as a set of contingently related aggregates of difference articulated or 'sutured' together. Laclau (1977) argues that there are no necessary links between discursive concepts. Those links that are forged are temporary and connotative. They are said to be articulated together and bound by the power of custom and opinion. Indeed, it is hegemonic practice that seeks to fix meaning 'for all time'. What we take to be the common-sense meanings of conceptual links are understood to be the outcome of a 'politics of articulation' (see Chapter 14).

As Hall suggests:

the term [articulation] has a nice double meaning because 'articulate' means to utter, to speak forth, to be articulate. It carries that sense of language-ing, of expressing, etc. But we also speak of an 'articulated' lorry (truck); a lorry where the front (cab) and the back (trailer) can, but need not necessarily, be connected to one another. The two parts are connected to each other, but through a specific linkage that can be broken. An articulation is thus the form of the connection that can make a unity of two different elements, under certain conditions. It is the linkage which is not necessary, determined, absolute and essential for all time. You have to ask, under what circumstances can a connection be forged or made? The so-called 'unity' of a discourse is really the articulation of different, distinct elements which can be rearticulated in different ways because they have no necessary 'belongingness'. The 'unity' which matters is a linkage between the articulated discourse and the social forces with which it can, under certain historical conditions, but need not necessarily, be connected. (Hall, 1996b: 141)

✓ *Those aspects of social life (identities or nation or society) which we think of as a unity (and sometimes as universals) can be thought of as a temporary stabilization or arbitrary closure of meaning.*

Put this way, it is possible to regard both individual identity and social formations as the unique, historically specific articulations of discursive elements. For example, there is no necessary or automatic connection between the various discourses of identity (e.g. of class, gender and race). Thus, working-class black women do not necessarily share the same identity and identifications any more than all middle-class white men do. Accordingly, the task of cultural studies is to analyse the articulations that have taken place. This involves illustrating how various contingent practices are 'put together' with each other through the operation of power.

The idea that subjectivity is a discursive construction has become widely accepted within cultural studies. However, for some writers (Hall, 1996a), the stress on the discursive 'outside' does not fully explain the affective 'inside'. That is, discourse analysis does not explain why particular subject positions are 'taken up' as the target of emotional investment by some subjects and not by others. Consequently, a number of cultural critics have turned to psychoanalysis to assist them in constructing an adequate account of language, subjectivity and identity. In particular, the work of Lacan, which seeks to unite poststucturalist understandings of language with Freudian psychoanalysis, has been influential, if contentious.

LANGUAGE AND PSYCHOANALYSIS: LACAN

According to Freud (1977), the self is constituted in terms of:

- *an ego*, or conscious rational mind;
- *a superego*, or social conscience;
- *the unconscious* (or id), the source and repository of the symbolic workings of the mind which functions with a different logic from reason.

In this model the self is by definition fractured into the ego, superego and unconscious. The unified narrative of the self is something we acquire over time through entry into the symbolic order of language and culture. Through processes of identification with others and with the subject positions of social discourses, we create an identity that embodies an illusion of wholeness.

According to Freud, the libido or sexual drive does not have any pre-given fixed aim or object. Rather, through fantasy, any object, which includes persons or parts of bodies, can be the target of desire. Consequently, an almost infinite number of sexual objects and practices are within the domain of human sexuality. Freud's work is concerned to document and explain the *regulation* and repression of this 'polymorphous perversity' through the resolution (or not) of the Oedipus complex. The outcome of regulation is said to be 'normal' heterosexual gendered relationships. It is in this sense that 'anatomy is destiny', for it is hard to escape the regulatory discourses that constitute bodily difference and the signification of sex and gender.

The mirror phase

In Lacan's (1977) reading of Freud, the resolution of the Oedipus complex marks the formation of the unconscious as the realm of the repressed. It establishes the very possibility of gendered subjects through entry into the symbolic order. Prior to the resolution of the Oedipus complex, infants are said to be unable to differentiate themselves from the surrounding world of objects, including other persons. Pre-Oedipal infants experience the world in terms of sensory exploration and auto-eroticism. The primary focus at this stage is the mother's breast as a source of warmth, comfort and food. This is a relationship that the child cannot control. Infants begin to regard themselves as individuated persons during what Lacan calls the 'mirror phase'. This involves identification with another person, primarily the mother, as being 'one' and/or recognition of themselves in a mirror as 'one'. However, since for Freud and Lacan we are fragmented subjects, such recognition of wholeness is 'misrecognition' and part of the infant's 'imaginary relations'.

The Oedipus complex involves a boy's desire for his mother as the primary love object. This is a desire that is prohibited by the symbolic order in the form of the incest taboo. Specifically, the father represents to boys the threat of castration that such prohibited desire brings forth. Consequently, boys shift their identification from the mother to father, who is identified with the symbolic position of power and control (the Phallus). For girls, this involves the acceptance that they have already been castrated. This leads to fury and partial identification with the mother as a gendered role together with the association of fathers with authority, domination and, indeed, mastery. For Lacan, as with poststructuralism, meaning is generated along a system of differences. Here the Phallus is the primary universal or transcendental signifier from which difference is generated. That is, the chain of difference begins with the stability of the Phallus as a sign. This arguably makes 'woman' a secondary signifier. That is, 'woman' becomes an adjunct to the symbolic man, acquiring meaning only by way of difference from masculinity.

The symbolic order

Language plays a critical role in Lacanian theory. Its formation is motivated by the pleasure that comes through feelings of control. Language acquisition represents the wish to regulate desire through occupying the place of symbolic power. In fact, language is the manifestation of the *lack* that Lacan sees at the core of subjects. Specifically, this is the lack of the mother as a result of separation at the mirror phase. More generally, it is the lack that human subjects experience by virtue of the prior existence of a symbolic order which they cannot control. Language is the symbolization of desire in a never-ending search for control.

It is through entry into the symbolic order that subjects are formed. Outside of the symbolic order lies only psychosis. For Lacan, the symbolic order is the overarching structure of language and received social meanings. It is the domain of human law and culture whose composition is materialized in the very structure of language. In particular, language enables subjectivity by virtue of the subject positions it provides from which one may speak. Crucially, these are gendered subject positions. This is a consequence of the fact that it is the Phallus that serves to break up the mother–child dyad and stands for entry into the symbolic order. Indeed, it is the Phallus as 'transcendental signifier' which enables entry to language (for both sexes). Further, by functioning as a 'unity', it stands in for the fragmented subject and allows the construction of a narrative of wholeness. The symbolic Phallus is the privileged and universal signifier because it is the law of the Name-of-the-Father. This is of course resonant of God as the place of creation and power in Judaic–Christian culture. As such, the Phallus organizes the symbolic order and the infant's entry into it.

The unconscious as 'like a language'

The unconscious is the site for the generation of meaningful representations. In Lacanian terms, the unconscious is structured 'like a language'. Not only is language the only route to the unconscious, but the unconscious is a site of signification. That is, the unconscious is a place of meaningful activity that works 'like a language'. In particular, the mechanisms of condensation and displacement, which Freud saw as the most important of the 'primary processes', are held by Lacan to be analogous to the linguistic functions of metaphor and metonymy.

- *Condensation* **is the mechanism by which one idea comes to stand for a series of associated meanings along a chain of signifiers.**

- *Displacement* **involves the redirection of energy due to one object or idea onto another.**

As an example of condensation, we might consider the sign – *rose* – as perfumed and petalled, as vagina, as female. Rose signifies female. Likewise, metaphor involves the replacement of one signifier by another – rose for female. While meaning is never fixed (or denotative) because generated through difference/*différance*, nevertheless, under the force of repression, a signifier comes to acquire the status of a signified. A conscious idea represents, as metaphor, a whole chain of unconscious meanings.

Metonymy is a process whereby a part stands for the whole. It is the displacement of energy and therefore meaning along a chain of signifiers. For example, burning cars can be seen as a metonym for urban riots and subsequently the 'state of the nation'. While meaning is differed, because generated by difference, displacement/metonymy is motivated by the desire for satisfaction that fixing meaning could bring. It involves the attempt to control the symbolic and overcome lack. The continual sliding of meaning is prevented, or temporarily stabilized, by its metonymic organization around key cultural *nodal points* which structure (and gender) the unconscious.

Problems with Lacan

Although influential in cultural studies, the Lacanian reading of Freud poses a number of unanswered questions:

- **Is the unconscious 'like a language' or is it a language?**

- **Is structuring of the symbolic order by the Phallus and the regulation of our entry into it by the law of the father a universal human condition, or is it culturally and historically specific? Is Lacanian theory phallocentric?**

- **How can gendered subjects be the outcome of subjection to the symbolic order and yet, at the same time, be a condition of the resolution of the Oedipus complex, which relies on male–female difference?**

- **Is it possible to struggle against, and change, the language and ideology of patriarchy, or are we forever formed in this way?**

These questions are of particular significance for feminism. Indeed, much of the debate which surrounds issues of language and subjectivity from a psychoanalytic perspective has been taken forward by feminist theorists. Feminism has been both attracted and repelled by psychoanalysis (and Lacan specifically). Feminists have been drawn to Lacanian theory because its seems to offer an account of the constitution of gendered subjects (Mitchell, 1974). However, it appears to locate the formation of subjectivity in a set of universal, ahistorical and patriarchal (i.e. male-dominated) processes (see Chapter 9).

Other writers have attacked psychoanalysis *per se* as being at best unnecessary and at worst a misguided and disciplinary mythology. For example, Rose follows Foucault in arguing that psychoanalysis is a particular, historically located way of understanding persons. It was carved out at the end of the nineteenth century and cannot be used 'as the basis for an investigation of the historicity of being human' (Rose, 1996: 142).

Indeed, whatever its strengths and weaknesses, psychoanalysis must be taken as a historically specific account of human sexuality and subjectivity. This is important if it is to maintain its connections with the idea of 'polymorphous perversity' and social regulation.

✓ *The particular kinds of psychic resolutions which psychoanalysis describes are not universals of the human condition but particular to specific times and places.*

LANGUAGE AS USE: WITTGENSTEIN AND RORTY

The work of Derrida, Foucault and Lacan represents the influence of poststructuralist theories of language and representation within cultural studies. However, there is another tradition which, though different in some respects, shares and indeed prefigures the anti-representationalist, anti-essentialist stance of poststructuralism. This tradition is personified by the philosopher Wittgenstein and the American tradition of pragmatism developed by Dewey and James. Richard Rorty has been the foremost contemporary exponent of this philosophical tradition. Though less influential in cultural studies than poststructuralism, this body of work is of growing significance, especially in relation to debates about postmodernism (Chapter 6).

Wittgenstein's investigations

Language as a tool

In his *Philosophical Investigations*, Wittgenstein suggests that looking for universal theoretical explanations for language is not the most profitable way to proceed. For Wittgenstein, language is not a metaphysical presence but a tool used by human animals to co-ordinate their actions in the context of social relationships. 'The meaning of a word is its use in the language' (Wittgenstein, 1953: §43: 20e). What is important is that we ask 'in what special circumstances this sentence is actually used. There does it make sense' (ibid.: §117: 48e). To see language as a tool is to suggest that we do things with language. Language is action and a guide to action. Language, in the context of social usage, can be temporarily stabilized for practical purposes. There are similarities between the writings of Derrida and Wittgenstein. For example, both stress:

- **the non-representational character of language;**
- **the arbitrary relationship between signs and referents;**
- **the contextual nature of 'truth'.**

However, Wittgenstein more than Derrida underlines the pragmatic and social character of language. This includes the significance of social relationships to language use, a point that sometimes slips away from the latter. For Wittgenstein, the meanings of language do derive from relations of difference. However, meanings are given a degree of stability by social convention and practice. The endless play of signification that Derrida explores is regulated and partially stabilized through the location of signs within pragmatic narratives.

For Wittgenstein, a meaningful expression is one that can be given a use by living human beings. That is, language is directly implicated in human 'forms of life'. Thus, in so far as the meaning of the word 'table' is generated through the relationship of signifiers – table, desk, counter, console, etc. – it is unstable. Nevertheless, it is stabilized by social knowledge of the word 'table', of what it is used for, when, under what circumstances and so forth; in other words, by the pragmatic narratives or language-games that the word 'table' appears in.

Language-games

Let us consider Wittgenstein's discussion of the word 'game', where he suggests that, in looking at games

> you will not see something that is common to all, but similarities, relationships, and a whole series of them at that. … Look for example at board-games, with their multifarious relationships. Now pass to card-games; here you find many correspondences with the first group but many common features drop out, and others appear. When we pass next to ball-games, much that is common is retained, but much is lost. … And the result of this examination is: we see a complicated network of similarities overlapping and criss-crossing: sometimes overall similarities, sometimes similarities of detail. (Wittgenstein, 1953: 31e–32e)

The meaning of the word 'game' does not derive from some special or essential characteristic of a game. It arises through a complex network of relationships and characteristics, only some of which are ever present in a specific game. Thus, games are constituted by a set of 'family resemblances'. Members of a family may share characteristics with one another without necessarily sharing any specific feature in common. In this sense the word 'game' is relational: the meaning of card-game depends on its relations to board-game and ball-game. Further, the word 'game' itself gains its meaning from its place in a specific language-game of games. It also depends upon the relation of the word 'game' to things that are not games.

Nevertheless, as Wittgenstein argues, when it comes to explaining the word 'game' to others, we are likely to show them different games and to say: 'this is what games are'. In doing so, we draw boundaries for specific purposes. We give examples not as 'meanings' generated by an abstract and reified 'language', but as practical explanation for specific purposes. In a sense, to know what games are is to be able to play games. While language-games are rulebound activities, those rules are not abstract components of language (as in structuralism). Rather, they are *constitutive rules*, that is, rules that are such by dint of their enactment in social practice. The rules of language constitute our pragmatic understandings of 'how to go on' in society.

In sum, Wittgenstein puts a greater emphasis on the indissolubility of language and practice than does Derrida. 'Language', as Wittgenstein remarks, 'did not emerge from reasoning. … Children do not learn that there are books, that there are armchairs etc. etc., but they learn to fetch books, sit in armchairs etc.' (Wittgenstein, 1969: 475–6). Similarly, instantaneous expressions of pain are not the outcome of thought; rather, they are spontaneous (biochemically motivated) actions. As a child develops language, so words replace actions like crying; to learn the language of pain is to learn 'new pain behaviour' (Wittgenstein, 1953: §244: 89). Understood in this way, language is not best described as a coherent system or set of structural relations but rather as an array of marks and noises used to co-ordinate action and to adapt to the environment. That does not mean that sometimes, for analytic purposes, it is not useful to treat language 'as if' it were a structured system.

> [Wittgenstein] believed that the correct method was to fix the limit of language by oscillation between two points. In this case the outer point was the kind of objectivism which tries to offer an independent support for our linguistic practices, and the inner point is a description of the linguistic practices themselves, a description which would be completely flat if it were not given against the background of that kind of objectivism. His idea is that the outer point is an illusion, and that the inner point is the whole truth, which must, however, be apprehended through its contrast with the outer point. (Pears, 1971: 170)

Lyotard and incommensurability

One of the better-known 'uses' of Wittgenstein (within cultural studies) is that of the postmodern philosopher Jean-François Lyotard. He argues that Wittgenstein has shown that 'there is no unity of language, but rather islets of language, each governed by a system of rules untranslatable into those of others' (Lyotard, 1984: 61). That is, truth and meaning are constituted by their place in specific local language-games and cannot be universal in character. Knowledge is specific to language-games. Consequently, postmodern philosophy embraces local, plural and heterogeneous knowledges. It rejects grand narratives or big totalizing explanatory stories (notably Marxism). In Lyotard's interpretation this implies the 'incommensurability' or untranslatability of languages and cultures. From this follows the celebration of difference and 'local' knowledge regimes. However, Rorty (1991a), a writer who has also been influenced by Wittgenstein, disagrees. He argues that we should see language as a practice that utilizes skills. Exact symbolic translation of languages or cultures as meaning may not be feasible. However, we can learn the skills of language to make cross-cultural communication possible.

TOKYO FISH MARKET

© **Photographer: Freya Hadley**

- *This image shows whale meat for sale at Tokyo fish market. How can we describe this as 'ordinary'?*

- *What is your reaction to the photograph? Do you find it strange?*

- *How might the concepts of 'cultural values', 'language-games' and 'incommensurability' be applied to the photograph?*

Rorty and the contingency of language

For Rorty (1980, 1989, 1991a, 1991b), human beings use noises and marks, which we call language, to co-ordinate action and to adapt to the environment. Here Rorty is making the Wittgensteinian point that language is a tool used by a human organism. In particular, language is 'a useful tactic in predicting and controlling its future behaviour' (Rorty, 1989: 52). In this view, the relationship between language and the rest of the material universe is one of causality. It is not one of adequacy of representation or expression. That is, we can usefully try to explain how human organisms come to act or speak in particular ways that have casual relationships. However, we cannot usefully see language as representing the world in ways that more or less correspond to the material world.

Anti-representationalism

For Rorty, '*no* linguistic items represent *any* nonlinguistic items' (Rorty, 1991a: 2). That is, no chunks of language line up with or correspond to chunks of reality. There is no Archimedean place from where one could independently verify the truth of a particular description of the world (if truth is taken to be the correspondence between the world and language). There is no God-like vantage point from which to survey the world and language separately in order to establish the relationship between them. This is so because we cannot escape using language itself if we try to establish such a relationship. We can describe this or that discourse, chunk of language, as being more or less useful and as having more or less desirable consequences. However, we cannot do so by reference to its correspondence with an independent reality but only in relation to our *values*. That is, we cannot lay claim to an objective truth but only to a justification.

Rorty argues that there is no 'skyhook – something which might lift us out of our beliefs to a standpoint from which we glimpse the relations of those beliefs to reality' (Rorty, 1991a: 9). However, that is not to say that no material reality exists or that by dint of being 'trapped' in language we are somehow out of sync with material reality (as sceptics might claim). On the contrary, since language is a tool for adapting to and controlling the environment, we are in touch with reality in all areas of culture. This argument holds as long as one takes the phrase 'in touch with' to mean 'caused by and causing' rather than 'representing reality'. Here the function of language is being understood in terms of representation. Consequently, it makes no sense, and is not useful, to think of language as being out of phase with the environment. As Rorty argues:

> We need to make a distinction between the claim that the world is out there and the claim that truth is out there. To say that the world is out there, that it is not our creation, is to say, with common sense, that most things in space and time are the effects of causes which do not include human mental states. To say that truth is not out there is simply to say that where there are no sentences there is not truth, that sentences are elements of human languages, and that human languages are human creations. Truth cannot be out there – cannot exist independently of the human mind – because sentences cannot so exist, or be

out there. The world is out there, but descriptions of the world are not. Only descriptions of the world can be true or false. The world on its own – unaided by the describing activities of human beings – cannot. (Rorty, 1989: 69)

> Consider the argument put by Rorty in the above quotation.
>
> — Explain it in your own words to another person.
> — Do you agree with Rorty's point of view?

Truth as social commendation

Rorty holds that most of the beliefs that we claim to be 'true' are indeed 'true'. However, the word true does not refer to a correspondence between language and reality. Rather, to say that most of our beliefs are true is to say that we agree with others regarding the character of an event. That is, 'true' is not an epistemological term referring to the relationship between language and reality but a consensual term referring to degrees of agreement and co-ordination of habits of action.

Truth is commendation. It is what we take to be good. To say that something is not true is to suggest that there is a better way of describing things. Here 'better' refers to a value judgement about the consequences of describing the world in this way (including its predictive power).

Truth, knowledge and understanding are located within particular language-games. Truth is the literalization (or temporary fixing through social convention) of metaphors within a language-game into what Rorty calls a 'final vocabulary'. What we take to be true and good is the consequence of our particular form of acculturation. As Rorty puts it,

> one consequence of antirepresentationalism is the recognition that no description of how things are from a God's-eye-view, no skyhook provided by some contemporary or yet-to-be developed science, is going to free us from the contingency of having been acculturated as we were. Our acculturation is what makes certain options live, or momentous, or forced, while leaving others dead, or trivial, or optional. We can only hope to transcend our acculturation if our culture contains (or, thanks to disruptions from outside or internal revolt, comes to contain) splits which supply toeholds for new initiatives. (Rorty, 1991a: 13–14)

Describing and evaluating

For Rorty, the contingency of language and the irony that follows from it lead us to ask about what kind of human being we want to be. Irony here means holding to beliefs and attitudes that one knows are contingent and could be otherwise, i.e. they have no universal foundations.

The necessity of asking ourselves questions about who we want to be follows from the fact that no transcendental truth and no transcendental God can answer this question for us. We ask questions about ourselves as individuals – who do I want to be? – and questions about our relations to other human beings – how shall I relate to others? These are pragmatic questions that bring forth political-value responses. They are not metaphysical or epistemological questions bringing forth truth-correspondence answers.

The consequences of an anti-representational view of language is to put aside appeals to truth as correspondence. Instead we must appeal to the pragmatic consequences of discourse and action. Truth, in William James's phrase, is 'what it is good for *us* to believe'. The evaluation and justification of claims about the self and courses of action are not to be done from the viewpoint of absolute metaphysical truth. Rather, they are to be conducted on the basis of the desirability of their pragmatic consequences judged in relation to our values. What constitutes the 'good' emerges through comparison between different *actual practices* or through comparing the actual good with the possible better. There is room for new ways of looking at things that may have consequences judged to be better when compared with other ways of doing things.

There remains the danger that truth acquired through acculturation becomes a narrow loyalty to a particular culture or way of being. In order to avoid this, Rorty argues that it is desirable to open ourselves up to as many possible descriptions and redescriptions of the world as possible. Hence, Rorty defends political-cultural pluralism and the enlargement of the self through the weaving in of new attitudes and beliefs.

There are pragmatic consequences to the adoption of multiple descriptions of the world, namely:

- **the greater likelihood of finding useful ways of adapting to and shaping our environment;**
- **the increased probability of being able to listen to the voices of others who may be suffering;**
- **the idea that individuals grow through the acquisition of new vocabularies.**

Both individual identity projects and the cultural politics of collectivities require us to forge new languages or final vocabularies, that is, new ways of describing ourselves which recast our place in the world with desirable consequences. We do not need universal foundations to validate political values or political action. Rather, political projects can be justified in terms of pragmatism related to our values (Chapter 14).

Culture as conversation

Rorty adopts the notion of a 'conversation' to grasp the dynamic and language-oriented character of culture. For Rorty (1980), we must set out to build the 'cosmopolitan conversation of human kind'. The metaphor of the conversation:

- allows us to consider the formation of meaning and culture as formed in the 'joint action' of social relationships;

- directs us to the constitutive and action-orientation of language in the context of social dialogue;

- underscores the importance of the social practice of reason-giving in the justification of action;

- allows us to think through cross-cultural communication in terms of the learning of language skills;

- highlights the variability of accounts to which any state of affairs can be put;

- points to culture as involving both agreement, contestation and conflict over meanings and actions.

Nevertheless, there are limitations to the analogy between culture and conversations. The commonly understood connotations of 'conversation' may lead us to prioritize declarative voice over conduct, the verbal above the visual, and the utterance before the body. Indeed, objects and spaces, which are very much part of cultural analysis, are in danger of disappearing from view. Further, what we say is only occasionally the product of self-conscious reflection. It is more often than not the outcome of pragmatic, ritualized or unconscious processes. That is, the undertone of the metaphor of conversation is one of intentionality when much of what we want to say about human culture includes routines, habits, compulsion and brain chemistry.

Culture as performance

Thus, according to the precise circumstances that confront us, we might also make use of the concept of performance. This aspect of culture directs our attention to the simultaneous production of the discursive, the body and a set of practices. That is, the metaphor of the performance engages with:

- the verbal and the visual;

- words and bodies;

- stasis and movement;

- objects and space;

- scripts and improvisation;

- intention and compulsion.

✓ *Nevertheless, we must get away from the idea that a performance is necessarily a consequence of intention. Rather, our stories are performative in that they enact and constitute that which they purport to describe.*

Like all metaphors, performance is better suited to some kinds of purpose or object than others. For example, the idea of culture as a performance works well for public and interactional situations. However, it may be less well suited to more contemplative zones of culture. Reading a book may fit the metaphor of performance less comfortably than does producing a film or popular music.

—   What are the advantages and disadvantages of using the metaphor of a conversation to understand the concept of culture?

—   What are the advantages and disadvantages of using the metaphor of a performance to understand the concept of culture?

—   What other useful metaphors can you think of to help us understand the concept of culture?

DISCOURSE AND THE MATERIAL

This chapter has stressed the significance of language and discourse in the constitution of culture and subjectivity. Some critics have feared that such a perspective is a form of idealism. Idealism is a view that regards the world as formed by language and mind outside of any material considerations. In its extreme form, 'everything is discourse'.

However, this is not what has been argued here. The materiality of the world is one of those things that is, in the Wittgensteinian sense, beyond doubt. That is, we cannot function without that assumption. As Wittgenstein argues, we may in principle imagine that every time we open a door there will be a bottomless chasm beneath us. However, it makes no sense to do so; it is unintelligible to us.

Indissolubility

Material objects and social practices are given meaning and brought into view by language. In this sense they are discursively formed. Discourse constructs, defines and produces the objects of knowledge in an intelligible way while excluding other ways of reasoning as unintelligible. This, for Foucault, is a historical and material process for language generates meaning under determinate conditions. As Butler (1993) argues, discourse and materiality are indissoluble. Discourse is the means by which we understand what material bodies are. It brings material bodies into view in particular ways. For example,

> sexed bodies are discursive constructions, but indispensable ones, which form subjects and govern the materialization of bodies. As such 'bodies will be indissociable from the regulatory norms that govern their materialization and the signification of those material effects'. (Butler, 1993: 2)

Languages for purposes

The opposition set up between the material and discourse is an unnecessary binary division. That we may think that there is a distinction to be made between them echoes the way that we talk about the world. It is not a reflection of a clear conceptual or material distinction as such.

The metaphor of the 'tool' captures the idea that we do things with language. That said, the concept of 'using a tool' should not be read as implying the intentionality of a pre-existent subject. Rather, 'use' is acquired through our acculturation and habituation into social practices and their associated justifications. The metaphor of the 'tool' does, however, direct us to the diverse functions words play in human life. 'We might think of words as the tools in a tool-box: there is a hammer, pliers, a screw-driver, a rule, a glue-pot, glue, nails and screws. The functions of words are as diverse as the functions of the objects' (Wittgenstein, 1953: 6).

This is an understanding of communication that places an emphasis on the variety of uses to which human beings put the marks and noises we call language. Humans produce various descriptions of the world and use those that seem best suited to our purposes. We have, as Rorty (1991a) argues, a variety of languages because we have a variety of purposes.

✔ *Knowledge is not a matter of getting an accurate picture of reality. Rather, it is a question of learning how to contend with the world in pursuit of those purposes.*

DECONSTRUCT THIS: THE OBJECT VS. THE WORD

- *Describe a rock. Describe the word 'rock'.*
- *Is it possible to distinguish between a rock and the word 'rock'?*

SUMMARY

Language is a central concern of cultural studies. It is the means and medium for the generation of significance or meaning. The concept of meaning is core to the explication of culture. To investigate culture is to explore how meaning is produced symbolically in language as a signifying system. Here, meaning is generated through difference, the relation of one signifier to another, rather than by reference to fixed entities in an independent object world.

If meaning resides in a chain of signifiers, that is to say, 'bad' has meaning only in relation to evil–naughty–disagreeable, etc., then meaning has the potential to proliferate into infinity. Meaning is never fixed but always in motion and continually supplemented. Hence, the key Derridean concept of *différance* – 'difference and deferral'. This notion centres on the instability and undecidability of meaning.

However, while this has proved to be a productive poetic of language, it was also argued that, in social practice, meanings are temporarily stabilized. For Wittgenstein, this occurs through language use, social convention and the embedding of words in pragmatic narratives. For Rorty, it involves the production of contingent 'final vocabularies'. For Foucault, it is the regulation of meaning by power into discourse and discursive formation. In any case, culture is a matter of practices as well as of meanings. Or, rather, meanings are forged in and through practices.

Culture can be regarded as regulated maps of meaning. These maps are constituted by criss-crossing discourses through which objects and practices acquire significance. Culture is a snapshot of the play of discursive practices within a given time and space. It can be understood as a map that temporarily freezes 'meaning-in-motion'. In addition, maps of meaning, and language in general, are infused with an affective dimension. In other words, culture is also a matter of emotion.

Cultures and cultural identities are temporarily stabilized at key 'nodal points'. In modern western societies these have historically formed around class, gender, ethnicity and age. The processes by which meaning becomes temporarily fixed are questions of power and cultural politics (Chapter 14).

4   Biology and Culture: Questions of Reductionism and Complexity

KEY CONCEPTS

Body (the)	*Genome*
Emotion	*Holism*
Epistemology	*Meme*
Evolution	*Phenotype*
Evolutionary psychology	*Reductionism*

One of the longest-running debates in the humanities and social sciences concerns the relationship between human biology and human culture or, as it is commonly posed, nature vs. nurture. This discussion has been particularly acute in relation to questions of sex and gender. That is, we ask the question as to whether men and women behave as they do as a consequence of their biology or as an outcome of their social and cultural construction (see Chapter 9).

Many practitioners within cultural studies dismiss physiological explanations of human behaviour as a form of biological reductionism, preferring instead those accounts that stress cultural constructionism. By contrast, I will be offering an explication that is sympathetic to evolutionary biology as an explanatory tool and suggests that we can work with both cultural studies and evolutionary biology in a productive alliance. Such a partnership collapses a number of dualistic distinctions such as the mind and the body, culture and biology, cognition and emotion.

In exploring these substantive issues, we necessarily encounter significant debates about explanatory mechanisms such as reductionism, constructionism and complex systems theory. In other words, an exploration of the relations between biology and culture is also an exercise in understanding how to understand. This chapter is as much about epistemology and reductionism as it is about culture and the body.

THE PROBLEM OF REDUCTIONISM

Reductionism is a dirty word in cultural studies. In particular, writers in the field have sought to resist the reduction of culture to economic factors. This has been on the grounds that understanding culture cannot take the form of an economic explanation alone, because culture has its own specific forms and its own particular mechanisms of operation. These specific features of culture cannot be reduced to (i.e. explained in terms of) the activities of wealth production and distribution (though these are important facets of any culture). Here, to reduce means to lessen, contract, diminish and degrade, since one component of human endeavour (culture) is deemed to be the product of another (e.g. economic activity or human anatomy).

In order that we can engage with human biology but also avoid accusations of biological reductionism, we need to 'deconstruct' the opposition of nature and culture from both directions. On the one hand, culture is an outgrowth of human beings learning and adapting within their natural ancestral environment. But, on the other hand, not only is nature already a concept in language (and not a pure state of being beyond signs), but also the natural world has come under the sway of human knowledge and institutions. Indeed, not only may we speak of the 'socialization of nature', but through the investigations of genetic science we are learning to intrude even further into the 'natural' human body.

Forms of reduction

Biological reductionism can be understood to mean that there are invariant features of human genetic endowment that are resistant to change. Thus, on this view, genetics could provide explanations for features of human culture, such as aggression, no matter what other factors are present. For example, a biological reductionist claim of this kind would involve saying that all men are more aggressive by nature, whatever the environment, than are women.

✓ *There are no real biological determinists who ignore environment completely.*

No one imagines that a seed will grow in the same way no matter what kind of environment it is planted in. Consequently, questions arise regarding the relationships between genes and the environment. It is useful to adopt a distinction put forward by Dennett (1995) between:

- *greedy reductionism*, which seeks to reduce all human behaviour to genes without recourse to intermediate causal steps; and

- *good reductionism*, which seeks to explain phenomena through causal chains without resort to mysteries or miracles.

Clearly, 'greedy reductionism' is unacceptable. The adoption of 'good reductionism' is merely to suggest that we can discover *causal chains* and explanations for human behaviour that include the place of genetic material.

Biologists agree that the body and behaviour of an organism are products of the interaction between genetic and environmental factors. A human genome is required if 'environment' is to produce a human being, while no organism can develop without suitable conditions. A stronger version of this argument would hold that not only are genetics and environment necessary, but also that a change in either one produces changes in the 'final' outcome. Thus, gene differences can contribute to widely varying phenotypes (the manifested morphology, physiology and behaviour of an organism) through environmental variation. Further, we cannot bracket off environment as a constant background, for a novel environment may produce a novel phenotype. That is, genes and other developmental factors interact with the environment in multi-factorial, non-additive ways to produce variable outcomes (Sterelny and Griffiths, 1999).

Culture forms an environment for the human body and feeds into evolutionary change. Hence environmental change, which includes the social and cultural aspects of human life, can change biological developmental outcomes. Of course, the time scales involved in human cultural change and evolutionary adaptations are radically different. The latter takes place over aeons of time, while the former is more obviously measured in decades. Thus, we currently operate with a human genome and brain structure that evolved a long time ago in quite different environmental (including cultural) circumstances from those that we live in today.

As Sterelny and Griffiths argue, philosophy (and here I would include cultural studies) is important to biology because the latter's conclusions do not follow from the 'facts' alone but require interpretation. Equally, biology is important to philosophy because these conclusions do depend on the scientific evidence.

In any case, that which makes human beings responsive to their immediate environment owes its existence to evolutionary processes. Consequently, as Buss (1999a, 1999b) argues, a whole series of binaries need to be jettisoned. These would include:

- **nature vs. nurture;**

- **culture vs. biology;**

- **genes vs. the environment.**

✓ *Human culture and human biology have co-evolved and are indivisible.*

Complexity and holism

Traditional science disciplines are reductionist in the sense that they break down objects of analysis into smaller and smaller parts. These are subsequently related to each other in an explanatory causal chain. However, human beings are both biological animals *and* cultural creatures. Any plausible attempt to understand them must embrace the idea of holism and complex system analysis. Here, objects of analysis are considered not only in isolation but also within their systemic context. Indeed, the human and physical worlds are so interconnected both within themselves and between each other that everything can be said to affect everything else.

✓ *We are interrelated beings in an interdependent world.*

A methodological individualist maintains that to study society is to investigate the behaviour of individuals. A methodological holist argues that this will have limited value in illuminating the workings of the social and cultural whole.

Methodological holism argues that the best way to study a complex system is to treat it as a whole. We cannot be content with analysis of the structure and 'behaviour' of its component parts. Indeed, the non-separability inherent to holism suggests that the properties of the whole are not fully determined by the properties of its parts. In this view, a human society always adds up to more than is stated by a description of the relationships of the parts or levels.

That is, in the context of methodological holism, one cannot meaningfully ascribe properties to an absolute 'level'. The designation of levels or parts is a device for understanding. It can be only used in the context of a well-defined analytic arrangement or metaphor designed to achieve particular purposes. For example, the linguistic holism of Wittgenstein, Rorty and Davidson, amongst others, suggests that an understanding of language requires utterances to be put in the context of the entire network of language. Meaning is always relational and context-specific. Indeed, the philosophy of language espoused by those writers who have been influential in cultural studies – Derrida, Bakhtin, Foucault – shares this emphasis on the relational character of language and the contextual nature of truth.

It was once argued that if you knew the 'laws' that held for the given parts of a whole, then you could predict its behaviour with certainty. Determination led to predictability. Thus, if you understood Newton's laws of physics, you could safely predict the outcomes of events at the level of the atom and above. The fundamentals of classical Newtonian science still hold for particular purposes. However, from the viewpoint of sub-atomic quantum mechanics and complex system science, unpredictability or chaos can be the outcome of otherwise predictable events. Chaos, as persistent instability, often arises when an 'object' feels the effect of more than one force, that is, it is over-determined (as we have noted biology–culture relations must be).

✓ *It is not possible to give absolute answers to enquiries concerning relations between biology and culture.*

These are undecidable questions because the conditions they ask about are complex and chaotic. However, saying this is of limited usefulness to us in terms of coping with the world. For example, we need to make decisions about how to treat depression or carry out sex changes. Thus we need to grasp what science can and cannot be asked to do.

— List three ways in which human beings are socially interrelated.
— List three ways in which human beings are culturally interrelated.
— List three ways in which human beings are biologically interrelated.
— Construct a list of these nine ways of being interrelated ranked 1–9 in terms of their importance to human life and development. What conclusions can you draw?

THE CAPABILITIES OF SCIENCE

The physical sciences are *cultural classification* systems with their own specialized languages. They consist of sets of *conceptual tools* that are of more or less usefulness to us. Thus, physics, chemistry, biology and genetics are constituted by particular vocabularies deployed for the achievement of specific purposes.

The arguments of the physical sciences should not be understood as the revelation of objective truth. Nor can they be grasped as the correspondence of language to an independent object world. Rather, the sciences represent the achievements of agreed procedures. These procedures have enabled us to produce levels of predictability that have underpinned a degree of consensus or solidarity amongst the scientific community, leading them to call particular statements true.

Here, science is not thought to have a privileged access to a deeper truth. That is,

✓ *Science cannot be founded on representationalism.*

However, as Gutting (1999) argues, the predictive success of science does make it a privileged form of knowledge. This is so not because science works with methods unknown to others. Rather, it is because science extends and makes effective those empirical trial-and-error methods that we all use. Further, it does so in ways that have yielded more workable knowledge of the material world.

The final test for science is not whether it can demonstrate adequacy of representation in relation to an independent object world but whether it works for specific purposes. That is, the sciences are subject to pragmatic testing. As eminent physicist Richard Feynman once argued,

> In general we look for a new law by the following process. First we guess it. Then we compute the consequences of the guess to see what would be implied if this law that we guessed is right. Then we compare the result of the computation to nature, with experiment or experience, compare it directly with observation, to see if it works. If it disagrees with the experiment it is wrong. (Feynman cited in Gribbin, 1998: 4)

Gribbin argues that even if the proposed model does agree with experiment, this does not mean that it represents a form of universal truth. For example, molecules can be described as 'little hard balls'. This does not mean they are such entities. Rather, it means that they behave, under specific circumstances, 'as if' they were little hard balls. For other purposes, or under different circumstances, atoms are described in terms of electromagnetic forces and the movement of electrons. As he goes on to suggest,

> even the best model is only a good one in its own context ... chisels should never be used to do the job of mallets. Whenever we describe something as being 'real', what we mean is that it is the best model to use in the relevant circumstances. (Gribbin, 1998: 7)

According to this line of argument, there is no fundamental *epistemological* distinction between cultural studies, physical science and a multi-layered novel; they all involve socially agreed procedures that produce texts of more or less use to us in guiding our conduct. The differences are not degrees of correspondence to reality but matters of purpose and genre. Science has proved itself to be good at prediction and control of the natural environment, while cultural studies and novels have amongst their achievements the production of empathy and the widening of the circle of human solidarity.

The logic of this argument is thus:

- **The relationship between biology and culture is not subject to greedy reductionism because it is a part of a complex system.**

Nevertheless ...

- **The relationship between biology and culture can be described in specific ways for particular purposes.**

Languages for purposes

Language does not accurately represent the world. Rather, it is a tool for achieving our purposes. Thus, knowledge is not a matter of getting an accurate picture of reality. Instead it is about learning how best to contend with the world. Since we have a variety of purposes, we develop a variety of languages. Hence, we cannot know what something 'is' when 'is' suggests an accurate representation of an independent object world, that is, a metaphysical universal truth. Thus we cannot say what the relationship between biology and culture 'really is'.

This argument is not the preserve of the philosophy of language but is one shared by the 'hard' sciences. For example, at the core of quantum physics is a wave–particle duality by which quantum entities can be treated as both waves *and* particles. Under some circumstances it is useful to regard photons (quantities of light) as a stream of particles. At other times they are best thought of in terms of wavelengths. Both descriptions 'work' according to the purposes one has in mind. Physical phenomena are put 'under the description' (Davidson, 1984) of different models to achieve divergent ends. Thus, we can recast questions about biology and culture. We do not ask the metaphysical and representationalist question 'What is?' We ask the more mundane and pragmatic question 'How do we talk about *X*?'

As Wittgenstein puts it 'Grammar tells what kind of object anything is. (Theology as grammar.)' (Wittgenstein, 1953: 373). What something 'is' becomes constituted by the use of language within specific language-games. The truth of a matter is culturally and historically specific and changeable. Hence the term a 'regime of truth' or a condition of being 'in the true' (Foucault, 1972). In this context, problems are 'solved' by being 'dissolved', that is, by redescribing them in a different language.

KEY THINKERS

Ludwig Wittgenstein (1889–1951)

The Austrian-born philosopher Ludwig Wittgenstein did much of his work at the University of Cambridge, England. His linguistic anti-essentialism and holism have been a significant 'behind-the-scenes' influence on constructionism, and thus on cultural studies. For Wittgenstein, 'language' is a tool used by human beings where the meaning of words is forged in use in the context of a language-game. While language-games are rule-bound activities, those rules are not abstract components of language (as in structuralism) but rather they are constitutive rules. That is, rules which are such by dint of their enactment in social practice.

Reading: Wittgenstein, L. (1953) *Philosophical Investigations*. Oxford: Basil Blackwell.

These arguments turn our attention away from the search for universal truth and towards justification as the giving of reasons. Reason-giving is a social practice, so that to justify a belief is to give reasons in the context of a tradition and a community. Here, reasons are objective in the sense that they have an intersubjective base. That is, the community operates with norms for reason-giving and tends towards agreement on claims that have been merited by practice. However, norms may be contradictory and understood in varying ways by the community. Further, it is possible to investigate an issue with varying degrees of conscientiousness. Thus, justification is a part of an ongoing 'conversation' of humanity.

✓ *However we characterize 'truth', we have no reliable source for it other than our ongoing conversation with each other.*

Having said that, some practices of knowledge formation have yielded more capacity for predictability and control of the material world than others. Thus, physical science has been more able to generate consensus about its forms of understanding than have the humanities, precisely because of its predictive reliability. Further, the languages of genetics, along with those of evolutionary biology and psychology, have proved more useful to us in dealing with these questions of biology, culture and language than has 'undecidability' or the Bible.

— Write two different 100-word, dictionary-style definitions of the word 'truth'.
— Form a group of four people and try to arrive at an agreed definition of the word 'truth'.

THE CULTURED BODY

The biological body is a clear sign that human beings are physical creatures. Traditionally this body has been the domain of science. However, in recent times the body has emerged as an important site of investigation in cultural studies not least because it represents the frontier point of cultural constructionism. For example, Bryan Turner claims that we live in a *somatic society*, that is, one in which 'major political and personal problems are both problematized within the body and expressed through it' (Turner, 1996: 1).

Here the body is not simply a biological given of nature but is worked over by culture. Indeed, radical formulations about the body argue that it is constructed by the forces of culture. In particular, the body is said to be so saturated with the floating cultural signs of consumption that a sense of the self traditionally based on the solidity of body has given way to fragmented, plural and shifting identities. Either way, the body is held to be plastic and malleable; it is something to be stylized and performed rather than being a fixed and eternal entity of physiology.

✓ *The idea of the body as a pre-social, pre-cultural object has become impossible to sustain.*

In the context of contemporary western culture, we need not look too far for empirical manifestations of a cultural concern with the body (see Hancock et al., 2000; Shilling 1993, 1997). Thus:

- Organ transplants raise questions about the ownership of bodies.

- Implants, from heart pacemakers to 'artificial' limbs, lead us to question the boundaries of the body.

- Regimes of diet, exercise and cosmetic surgery are testament to the disciplinary powers of discourse to successfully exhort us to shape and aestheticize the body to fit cultural norms.

- The medicalization of lifestyle is achieved through health promotion strategies that are invariably narratives of self-transformation through self-regulation.

- The requirement to have an acceptably shaped and healthy body now belongs not to the domains of health and aesthetics but to that of moral rectitude. Having the right kind of body is now a matter not only of tasteful and pleasing appearance, or even of longevity, but also of moral virtue.

- The transformation of the body through fashion and body decoration has become a significant aspect of contemporary identity projects.

- Sex is no longer the clear-cut issue of bodily organs and biochemistry that it was once thought to be. Not only is sex said to be a performance (see Butler, 1993, discussed in Chapter 9), but surgery and drug therapy have allowed the radical transformation of sex to occur.

- Categories such as the 'elderly' and the 'disabled', once thought to be straightforward descriptions of a biological process and deficiency, respectively, are increasingly argued, at least by activists and theorists, to be social and cultural productions.

TATTOOED MAN

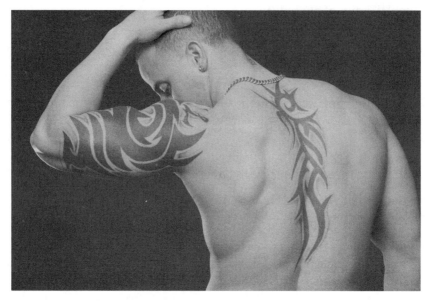

© Photographer: Les3photo8 | Agency: Dreamstime.com

- *Write a brief description of this photograph. What are its significant details?*
- *In what ways does the image represent the cultural transformation of the body?*
- *Are there specifically gendered dimensions to the body in this picture?*

A body of theory

In contemporary culture, we are constantly called upon to perform 'body work' that is dedicated to maintaining a particular and desirable state of embodiment. This process can be understood as being on the one hand, the passive consequence of disciplinary power, and, on the other hand, an active project of identity construction.

Foucault's body of work, which has been very influential in bringing the fleshly torso (or at least its representations) into the domain of cultural studies, encapsulates both these theoretical directions. The force of Foucault's thinking can be seen in Turner's (1996) influential work on the body, where he seeks to examine the tasks that societies set themselves in relation to the 'government of the body'.

A good deal of Foucault's writing (e.g. 1977) has been concerned with the 'disciplinary' character of modern institutions, practices and discourses. Discipline involves the organization of the subject in space through dividing practices, training and standardization (see Chapter 3). Disciplinary technologies appeared in schools, prisons, hospitals and asylums. They produced what Foucault called 'docile bodies' that could be 'subjected, used, transformed and improved' (Foucault, 1977: 198).

Discipline is part of a wider process of governmentality, that is, the mechanisms of 'policing' societies by which a population becomes subject to bureaucratic regimes and modes of discipline. Here a population can be categorized and ordered into manageable groups. Amongst the modes of regulation that concern Foucault are the ones that operate through:

- **medicine;**
- **education;**
- **social reform;**
- **demography;**
- **criminology.**

A common criticism of Foucault is that he turns men and women into acquiescent creatures that have no capacity to act; that is, they lack agency (Chapter 7). In response, some writers on the body (e.g. Frank, 1991) have turned to symbolic interactionism in general, and the work of Goffman in particular, to explore the active and interventionist body.

For Goffman (1969, 1974, 1979), the body enables people to intercede in the comings and goings of daily life. This includes the ways in which humans negotiate how they present themselves to others. For example, Goffman discusses the way that we communicate with our bodies through facial expression, dress and stance. These symbolic actions construct and deploy a shared cultural vocabulary or idiom of bodily communication. Thus,

✔ *The body is both a material entity and a set of cultural signs that categorize, train and cultivate people.*

Much of the criticism of Foucault's work on the body stems from reading his early works in isolation. This work apparently concentrated its attention on questions of passivity and docility. However, power in the work of Foucault is held to be productive or generative as well as being constraining. That is, the processes of social regulation do not simply stand over and against the individual but are constitutive of self-reflective modes of conduct, ethical competencies and social movements. In this sense, discipline is not simply constraining but also enabling. Further, in his later work (Foucault, 1986) he concentrates on 'techniques of the self' that reintroduce agency and 'self-fashioning'. In particular, in his studies of ancient Greek and Roman practices, he points to an ethics of 'self-stylization' as an aspect of the valued process of 'self-mastery'. In this sense, Foucault and Goffman share a concern with the mutual constitution of the individual body and the wider body of cultural practices.

The medical body

The manner in which the body has been understood by medical science illustrates the paradox of agency and discipline that is apparent in the work of both Foucault and Goffman. For example, there is little doubt that medicine has been heavily implicated in the disciplining and surveillance of modern populations.

For biologically based medicine (biomedicine), the body is understood to be a more or less fixed entity. It is constituted by unchanging necessities that exist prior to culture. Here disease is located in the pathology of human tissue. All human dysfunction can eventually be traced to the consequence of specific causal mechanisms within the physical organism. The prime concern of medicine, then, is the classification, documentation and elimination of disease. The job of a physician is to describe and evaluate the signs and symptoms of malfunction. There are three prime implications of this way of viewing the body:

1 **The causes of disease are internal to the body.**

2 **Disease is an outcome of the objective facts of biology.**

3 **The doctor knows best since s/he has gained the appropriate scientific knowledge.**

Amongst the consequences of this model are forms of social and cultural discipline. Thus,

✓ *Medicine began to describe and compare bodies in ways that produced normality and pathology.*

The central limitation of biomedicine is biological reductionism, for it has become apparent that ill health is distributed differentially by age, class, gender, place, etc. Sickness is not simply a consequence of the hermetically sealed workings of individual bodies. Ill health is a consequence of what we eat, where we work (e.g. stress or chemical poisoning), levels and types of exercise, the patterns of our thinking (generated in our childhood experiences) and so forth.

Thus, in the context of contemporary western culture, a more holistic understanding of health practice has begun to emerge. This has been called the bio-psychosocial model of medicine. The shift from biomedicine to bio-psychosocial medicine is marked by a change of language from talk of 'treatment' to that of 'health promotion'. Here we are all called upon to be *active* in relation to our own health. Public health campaigns advance the idea that we should take responsibility for our well-being. The movement from biomedicine to bio-psychosocial medicine is marked by *relative* shifts in focus from:

- **the isolated body to bodies in environmental contexts;**
- **the curative to the preventative;**
- **the dominance of medical authority to co-operation with active knowledgeable lay persons.**

In terms of the discipline/agency dichotomy discussed above, the body in medicine has become less disciplined and more active. Or has it? Paradoxically, health promotion can quite easily be understood as a new form of medical discipline. Health promotion extends the processes of medicalization into cultural organization and lifestyle management. Thus, we are exhorted, urged and disciplined into adopting the 'right' healthy attitude towards our bodies. We are expected to give up smoking, abstain from illegal drug use, keep fit, eat the 'right' food, etc. In some quarters, illness is a sign of moral and personality weakness indicative of a lack of self-control and moral fortitude. Health promotion strategies are clearly based on the division of actions into the 'good' and the 'bad', whose management is our ethical responsibility.

Hence, the circle turns and the active agent is once more in the domain of discipline. And yet, this apparent paradox is more a matter of styles of thinking imposed on the objects of knowledge than of objective description. Bodies are never simply the subjects of constraining disciple; nor do they *possess* agency. Rather, discipline generates agency and agency produces discipline. Discipline and agency can be understood as two sides of the same coin. Indeed, they are better understood not as qualities of objects but as ways of talking about and simultaneously constituting objects for particular purposes (see above).

— What is meant by the concept of a somatic society?
— Can you think of five ways in which 'major political and personal problems are both problematized within the body and expressed through it' (Turner, 1996: 1)?

THE EVOLVED BODY OF BIOLOGY

Evolutionary biology explores and explains the diversity of life on our planet, the processes of adaptation made by organisms in order to survive, and the long-term development of species. According to Dennett:

> The fundamental core of contemporary Darwinism, the theory of DNA-based reproduction and evolution, is now beyond dispute among scientists. It demonstrates its power every day, contributing crucially to the explanation of planet-sized facts of geology and meteorology, through middle-sized facts of ecology and agronomy, down to the latest microscopic facts of genetic engineering. It unifies all of biology and the history of our planet into a single grand story. (Dennett, 1995: 20)

As understood by Mayr (1982), the fundamentals of evolutionary theory can be grasped as a network of five components:

1 The living world is not constant; evolutionary change has occurred.

2 Evolutionary change has a branching pattern, indicating that contemporary species descended from remote ancestors.

3 New species form when a population splits and the fragments diverge. That is, new species are accounted for by the isolation of sub-populations.

4 Evolutionary change is gradual.

5 The mechanism of adaptive change is natural selection.

Natural selection and the place of genes

Natural selection is the process by which characteristics that enable organisms to thrive and reproduce are carried forward in a species. Richard Dawkins (1976, 1995) is the prime architect of the 'gene's-eye' view of evolution. Here evolution is understood as being constituted by a river of DNA that flows through time.

In Dawkins's terminology, genes are *replicators* that form a lineage or chain, with each link being a copy of its predecessor. This is something that organisms (and their traits) cannot do. That is, organisms are not copied, genes are. Of course, the successful reproduction of genes depends on their capacities for building robustly thriving bodies (vehicles or *interactors*) that survive their environment and reproduce. Thus, organisms mediate the relationship of genes to the environment and further replication. In this context, evolutionary change is a consequence of cumulative selection over a very long period of time.

DNA is responsible for the chemically unique structure of individual brains as they develop within singular environments. We may understand genes as long strings of digitally encoded information constructed from four symbols: A, T, G and C (Dawkins, 1995). This information can be encoded, recorded and decoded without degradation.

It is important to remember that genes occur in bodies and that physical forms inhabit environmental niches. In the long run, the genes that are good at surviving and reproducing are those that build bodies and traits that gather cumulative advantage in the environment. However, the specific phenotypic effects of genes are often variable depending on the environment (both the other genes in the body and the 'external' environment). Genes can then be seen as 'context-sensitive difference makers' (Sterelny and Griffiths, 1999: 99) that operate within a whole 'developmental matrix'. This matrix includes:

- **the inheritance of non-genetic factors;**

- **the modification of genetic consequences by developmental contexts.**

— The philosopher Daniel Dennett (1995) describes the process of evolution as mindless and purposeless. What do you think he means by this?

EVOLUTIONARY CULTURE

An evolutionary view of culture suggests that it is formed as the legacy of prior adaptations to our ancestral physical circumstances. Today culture represents the human creation of a new 'synthetic' environment. It is often said that the complex character of human language and culture is what distinguishes us most obviously from other animals. However, we cannot presuppose human language, co-operation and culture. Rather, they are built up from scratch over time within an evolutionary context. Human life is, after all, animal life.

The development of language, the foundation stone of culture, probably depends on the evolutionary development of a 'language acquisition device'. Additionally, the style and parameters of our thinking are shaped in part by the cognitive structures of the brain. Subsequently, we learn language as an integral part of learning how to do things within our environment. Thus, we develop language skills not so much through reasoning as through practice.

Evolutionary psychology

One of the more promising outcomes of the marriage of evolutionary theory and the study of human cultural behaviour is evolutionary psychology. Here, there has been a turn away from the idea that different behaviours can be accounted for directly and only by genetically inspired adaptive selection. Instead, an interest has developed in the evolution of *cognitive mechanisms* that oversee our behaviour. Subsequently, 'evolutionary psychology advocates integration and consistency of different levels of analysis, not psychological or biological reductionism' (Buss, 1999b: 20).

✓ *'By themselves, psychological theories do not, and cannot, constitute theories of culture. They only provide the foundations for theories of culture.' (Tooby and Cosmides, 1992: 88)*

The foundations of culture are the evolved psychological mechanisms that utilize and work over social and cultural inputs. It is the differential activation of these psychological mechanisms by divergent inputs in varied contexts that account for cultural diversity.

The concern of evolutionary psychology is to locate the cognitive mechanisms (and their functions) that underpin cultural behaviour. The aim is not to identify direct determination of behaviour by genes. Thus, evolutionary psychology is not a form of genetic determinism. Indeed, 'Evolutionary psychologists fiercely resist the division of labor between evolutionary and cultural theory' (Sterelny and Griffiths, 1999: 325). Since the social group was a primary survival strategy for humans, so there would have been natural selection for co-operative living (Brewer and Caporael, 1990). Thus, many of the most important evolved psychological mechanisms will be social in character (Buss, 1999b). Our basic psychological mechanisms are almost certainly shared by all or most human beings (i.e. they are species-typical) though the outcomes will alter according to the environment. Thus, for evolutionary psychologists, human behaviour is shaped by two ingredients (Buss, 1999a):

1 evolved adaptations;

2 environmental input that triggers the development and activation of those adaptations.

The evolved brain

For evolutionary psychology, the human brain is conceptualized as a series of evolved information-processing mechanisms or modules that are geared to performing specific tasks. That is, our brains have developed by way of solving certain problems posed by the environments in which we evolved. When solutions were found to particular problems, they tended to be 'installed' for the foreseeable future, even though the scope of the resolution, and thus future capacities, was limited. Consequently, specific adaptations are not optimally designed for our ancestral environments let alone for contemporary conditions. Rather, adaptations survive as long as they are 'good enough' and work in the environment of their genesis.

✓ *The evolutionary time-lag means that we are operating with brain mechanisms developed within and for an environment quite different from that of contemporary culture.*

According to Buss (1999a: 47–9), an evolved psychological mechanism is a set of processes with the following properties:

- **An evolved psychological mechanism exists in the form that it does because it solved a specific problem of survival or reproduction recurrently over evolutionary history.**

- **An evolved psychological mechanism is designed to take in only a narrow slice of information.**

- **The input of an evolved psychological mechanism tells an organism the particular adaptive problem it is facing.**

- **The input of an evolved psychological mechanism is transformed through decision rules into output.**

- **The output of an evolved psychological mechanism can be physiological activity, information to other psychological mechanisms, or manifest behaviour.**

- **The output of an evolved psychological mechanism is directed toward the solution to a specific adaptive problem.**

In summary, an evolved psychological mechanism is a set of procedures within the organism that is designed to take in a particular slice of information and transform that information via decision rules into output that historically has helped with the solution to an adaptive problem. The psychological mechanism exists in current organisms because it led, on average, to the successful solution to a specific adaptive problem for that organism's ancestors. (Buss, 1999a: 49)

Domain-specific modules in the brain contribute to the shape of culture. They do this by providing the template for human thinking and the parameters of solutions to problems that we are likely to face. This includes the existence of specialized inference mechanisms. These allow for the representations that constitute culture to be transmitted from one mind to another through observation and/or interaction (Tooby and Cosmides, 1992). Of course, some aspects of culture, such as art, literature, film, music, etc., do not seem to have much to do with survival and reproduction. However, we take pleasure from shapes, colours, sounds, stories, etc., whose mechanisms evolved in relation to evolutionary tasks faced by our ancestors. These now enable us to appreciate and develop artistic endeavours (Pinker, 1997).

Some implications for cultural studies

Evolutionary psychology and neuroscience offer us useful evidence and ways of thinking about the world. For example, it is worth reflecting on the idea that we are all descended form the same ancestors and partake of the same genome (99.9 per cent shared). There may be vast tracts of cultural distance between us, but we remain members of the human species. Sometimes the cultural distance between us is apparently so vast that we see each other as different kinds of being. We appear to think in such radically divergent ways. However, the principle of shared biology may help to bridge that gap. It may underpin the desirability of cultural moves such as a declaration of human rights. Further, the roots of emotional response are biochemical. Though emotions are culturally mediated, the sharing of broad emotional reactions is one of the features that forge us together as human beings. We all feel fear and we all have the potential to love.

Evolutionary biology also suggests the likelihood that there are cultural universals. For example, all cultures use signs that have their roots in the biochemical capacities of the human brain. Subsequently, of course, we use different languages, that is, the specific forms of the universal are different. Further, all human cultures include forms of sexuality, family relations, laughter, tears, and rituals around birth, death and food. Cultural studies has been concerned with the particulars of culture and its local conjunctural character. However, there is no reason why this work cannot be set against the backdrop of cultural universals. Thus, cultural studies can explore difference and similarity.

✓ *It is the distinct and divergent ways that cultures construct meanings around sexuality, the family, death, etc., that is of interest to us even as we explore that which human beings also have in common.*

Evolutionary biology and genetic science have not received a great deal of positive attention within the humanities. This is so because they suggest that there are limits to the plasticity of human capacities and behaviours (within the time-scale of existing human history). The dilemma here is this: On the one hand, acceptance of the very real limits to human plasticity saves us from the eternal frustration of seeking after the unattainable. On the other hand, there is the danger of accepting as immutable that which is open to change.

Hence, testing the waters of cultural change is usually worthwhile. Nevertheless, we need to make judgements about when that experiment is no longer viable. Thus, feminism rightly challenged the claim that social inequality of the sexes was wholly grounded in biology and thus unalterable. However, it is now clear that there are limits set by the human body and brain to the plasticity of human gender-based behaviours (see Chapter 9). However, this is not a recipe for a return to traditional gender roles. Fifty years of cultural change in relation to sex/gender has demonstrated that some transformation is possible.

— Construct arguments suggesting that evolutionary theory must mean that there can be no human freedom of action.
— Construct an argument that evolutionary theory does not eradicate human freedom of action.
— How is it possible to hold both points of view?

BIOLOGY AND CULTURE: THE CASE OF EMOTIONS

Many of the major problems faced by western cultures involve psychological distress rather than material deprivation (which is not to say that the two do not often go hand in hand). These difficulties concern:

- **our relations with others:** *isolation, failed marriages, aggression and violence;*

- **our sense of meaninglessness:** *alienation, suicide and depression;*

- **our addictions:** *to drugs, to sex, to shopping;*

- **our mental health:** *epidemics of depression, anxiety, alcoholism.*

These problems are both biochemical and cultural. Emotional states have evolutionary roots that are triggered by cultural conditions. Further, emotional responses are socially constructed to the degree that we interpret bodily responses in cultural ways. What we require from cultural studies is an understanding of the way emotions are generated and comprehended by us.

Understanding emotion

Evolution and emotion

From an evolutionary perspective, emotions have emerged over the *longue durée* of our history and have stayed with us because they have contributed to the survival of the species (Ekman, 1980; Tooby and Cosmides, 1992). Evolution is the processes of adaptive change made by organisms in order to survive, which structure the long-term development of species. In this context, emotion is understood as a manifestation of brain biochemistry that involves a range of physiological changes. Emotions invoke circumstances that have repeatedly occurred throughout our developmental history. They deal with fundamental life tasks and help to solve problems that faced our long-gone ancestors.

On this basis, evolutionary theorists explore emotions in terms of their biological imperatives and argue that our broad orientations towards thrill-seeking, fear, anxiety, anger, addiction, sexuality etc. are genetically formed (Hamer and Copeland, 1998). Plutchik (1980), for example, argues that we have 'hard-wired' basic emotions (sadness, surprise, disgust, anger, anticipation, joy, acceptance, fear) and a number of newer emotions that are a blend of the 'basic' emotional states (friendliness, alarm, guilt, sullenness, delight, anxiety etc.). Similarly, Ekman (1980) suggests that emotions involve universal bodily responses and facial expressions that are automatic, unlearned and recognized cross-culturally.

The problem with such explanations is that emotions are reduced to physiology and genetic determination. However, evolutionary theories of emotion are not necessarily incompatible with cultural explanations. Thus, Ekman accepts that hard-wired emotions are regulated by the conventions, norms and habits that people have developed to manage emotional expression.

The emotional brain

LeDoux (1998) argues that the appropriate level of analysis of evolved psychological function is the way in which it is represented in the brain. Thus activity in the amygdala is strongly associated with anxiety and fear, the hippocampus is involved with the memory and the contextualization of events and emotion, while the frontal lobes play a significant role in the regulation of emotion. Emotions involve complex feedback mechanisms that exist between brain, the body and our conscious experience so that emotions are dynamic states.

As LeDoux acknowledges, while human consciousness and emotion are an outcome of the way the brain is organized, feelings will be different in a brain that can classify the world linguistically and a brain that cannot do so. The difference between say anxiety, fear, terror and apprehension requires cognition and language. Thus Ortony and Turner (1990) argue that we have a number of bodily responses (e.g. the heart racing) which form the components of a variety of 'emotions' that are themselves organized and named by higher cognitive functions (appraisals). In this view, there are no basic emotions, rather there is a series of primary responses that in combination, and under cognitive supervision, are held to be emotions. Thus to a set of bodily responses we add a conscious 'feeling' from our working memory and words that not only label context-specific responses as 'fear', 'anger', 'love' etc. but that can themselves set off further emotional responses.

Cognition, culture and emotion

While cognition plays a part in naming physiological response in Ortony and Turner's account, the philosopher Martha Nussbaum (2001) forwards a strong argument for placing cognitive processes at the very core of emotion. By cognition she means 'receiving and processing information', although the concept is also linked with 'mental processes' such as attention, awareness, thought and representation. Nussbaum argues that an emotion is constituted by judgements that we make in relation to objects that are of importance to our world and wellbeing. Commonly these evaluations pertain to things we cannot fully control. That is, emotions involve cognitive judgements about value, they are suffused with intelligence that appraises external objects as salient to our wellbeing as well as acknowledging our neediness and incompleteness before the world (Nussbaum, 2001).

Although cognition is not necessarily linguistic, none the less the acquisition of language gives much of our information processing, or thinking, a cultural dimension. Human emotions are culturally constructed to the degree that they are (a) formed by culturally constructed cognitions, (b) regulated through cultural interpretations and display rules and (c) named and made sense of by cultural discourses.

The cultural construction of emotion

Writers committed to social and cultural constructionism (Harré, 1986; Gergen, 1994) regard emotions as culturally formed. They cite evidence for differential emotional responses within divergent cultures and argue that discourses of emotion organize and regulate how we should understand bodily responses in given contexts. Indeed, emotions themselves are understood to be discursive constructions, i.e. emotions are brought into being by the way we talk about them. Emotions are not simply matters of individual interpretation of experience but are inevitably a part of the wider cultural repertoire of discursive explanations, resources and maps of meaning available to members of cultures.

In this vein, Potter and Wetherell (1987) have sought to demonstrate that fundamental psychological notions such as attitudes, emotions and the inner mind could be approached through the examination of a shared language. They argue that there are no 'things' that are called emotions or attitudes that lurk behind language. Rather, emotions are constituted by the rhetorical organization of linguistic and cultural repertoires by which we construct specific accounts of ourselves that invoke 'emotion'. The logic of these arguments suggests that one isn't motivated or incited to action by emotions, rather, 'one *does* emotions, or participates in them as he or she would on a stage' (Gergen, 1994: 222). Nevertheless, the languages of emotion retain value as a way of talking about the intensely meaningful as that is culturally defined, socially enacted, and personally articulated (Lutz, 1988: 5).

Emotions involve cognitive and moral judgements and the culturally approved way of acting them out. Indeed, Lutz (1988) describes emotions as 'culturally constructed judgments'. As such, emotions are subject to cultural and historical change. Thus Stearns

(1995; Stearns and Knapp, 1996) has discussed the changing character of grief in the Anglo-American world. Displays of grief were downplayed prior to the nineteenth century whereupon, during the Victorian era, it became a culturally foregrounded emotion involving public displays and rituals. However, by the early twentieth century, grieving people were once again being urged to restrain displays of grief.

Here we see that emotions are subject to rules by which people are expected to be happy at weddings and sad at funerals (feeling rules) and to enact them in culturally approved ways (display rules). Failure to do so will bring social admonishment that invokes guilt and shame, i.e. emotions implicated in social and cultural regulation. Thus Hochschild (1983) has explored the way in which flight attendants are trained to manage their feelings as an aspect of institutional emotional management in order to present a pleasant, smiling countenance to their customers.

Jeanne Tsai discusses some cultural differences between 'westerners' and 'Asians' concerning the doing of emotion (see Goleman, 2003). She argues that the greater individualism of westerners leads them to perform emotions somewhat differently than would be the case in Asian cultures. For example, in comparison to westerners, Asians tend to experience more shame and guilt when others are responsible for the events than if one had initiated them oneself. Thus an Asian cultural view of the self as grounded in social interdependence influences how emotions are constructed and experienced. Further, westerners seem to experience more 'positive' emotions than do Asians in interpersonal conflict situations, the latter are more likely to view these as a negative phenomenon.

In sum, emotion can be explored through evolutionary theory, psychological theory and cultural theory, and can be understood as being physiological, neurological and linguistic. These forms of analysis are often taken to be contradictory and mutually exclusive. However, they need not be. They might be integrated into a holistic 'circuit of emotion'.

The circuit of emotion

Cognition, physiological response and a cultural naming are all necessary components of human emotions. A sophisticated understanding of emotion grasps them as 'full system responses' (Lineham, 1993) that involve:

- **a degree of physiological hard-wiring of evolutionary/biological origin;**
- **cognitive judgements that give rise to physiological responses;**
- **appraisals that name responses as states of fear, love, etc.;**
- **the social contexts in which emotions are named, learned and displayed in culturally regulated ways;**
- **interpretations of our phenomenological experience;**
- **as motivations to act.**

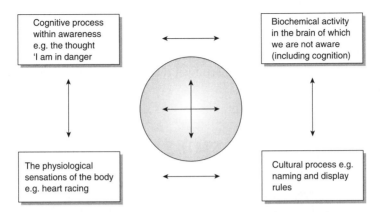

Figure 4.1   The circuit of emotion

For example, fear involves the processing of a perceived threat (cognition), an accelerated heart beat and sweaty palms (physiology) that motivates flight (action). A given social context (e.g. a boxing ring or a lecture theatre), and the cultural understandings that go with it, then shape how fear is acted out (for example, by hitting another or playing with worry beads). Giving our attention to these elements and naming them ('I know I am afraid because my legs are shaking') will shape our interpretation of the experience. Hence emotion can be understood as both cultural and biological with causal flows taking place in either direction. In other words, rather than reduce emotion to a singular necessary and sufficient component, I suggest we think about emotion in terms of a circuit of interacting elements.

The *metaphor* of the 'circuit of emotion' is an attempt to move away from determinism and reductionism along a single linear dimension (and is indebted to Du Gay et al's (1997) 'circuit of culture'). The emphasis is on the irreducible character of each moment of the circuit, which is at the same time in a relationship of mutual determination. Here, 'emotion work' is generated at each level of a circuit formed by culture (language/meaning), cognition (information processing), the brain (biochemistry and evolved psychological mechanisms), genetics (the predictability of behaviour according to DNA profiles) and the physiology of the body (heart racing, pupil dilation etc.). Each of these 'moments' is articulated to and interacts with each of the other moments. Thus, 'emotion' is not one essential entity but the outcome of interactions across a range of processes. (See Figure 4.1.)

The challenge is to grasp just how each of the processes interacts with the others. How do cultural environments shape our cognitions? For example, under what cultural conditions does one think 'I am a failure' or 'I am under threat'? What is the relationship between cognition and language? How does the cognition 'I am under threat' operate in terms of brain chemistry to generate the physiology of fear or anger? What are the display rules of anger in a given culture and how might they give rise to thoughts that change the biochemistry of the brain?

The advantage of the circuit of emotion metaphor is that it allows for analysis of the specificities of each moment of the circuit while at the same time considering the relations between them. It asserts in a holistic way that emotion is the outcome of interactions between all the moments of the circuit yet recognizes the pragmatic requirement to analyse each process in its own terms.

SMILE

© **Photographer: Chris Barker**

- *What name would you give to the emotion represented in this image?*
- *What thoughts might go with this emotion?*
- *What physical sensations might be associated with this emotion?*
- *Under what cultural circumstances is the expression of this emotion acceptable?*
- *Under what cultural circumstances would the expression of this emotion be unacceptable?*
- *Do you think the meaning of this face would alter across ethnic or national cultures?*

Draw faces that express fear, anger, disgust, sadness, joy and surprise. Ask yourself the questions above about these emotions.

Emotion as experience

The circuit of emotion is an analytic metaphor and explanatory framework. However, emotion can also be understood as an experience. The idea of experience appears somewhat paradoxically within cultural studies. On the one hand, it is crucial to understanding culture as lived and meaningful. On the other hand, one cannot understand experience without the framing work of language. That is, discourse constructs our experience as meaningful to us.

The languages of emotion 'point to' aspects of our direct embodied experience of emotion. In an existential-phenomenological sense, emotions are modes of sensuous embodied conduct made meaningful in the cultural world that may be pre-reflexive but nevertheless purposive and intentional or world directed. 'Emotion is not an accident, it is a mode of conscious existence, one of the ways in which consciousness understands (in Heidegger's sense of *verstehen*) its Being-in-the World' (Sartre, 1971: 91). Emotions constitute a point of view on the world and a mode of being that we exist in and through (Crossley, 1998).

Identity and emotion

Emotions can be understood as a form 'embodied consciousness' or 'way of being' that is lived, experienced and articulated. They involve culturally habituated practices and our interpretation of them through cultural discourses, display rules and emotion work (Denzin, 1984). These interpretations occur through culturally formed discourses related to the body via metaphors of heat and cold, pressure and release, flow and stasis etc. (Lupton, 1998). Subsequently, these narratives of emotion bring us into being as subjects and form part of our identities through, for example, learning and telling narratives of romantic love or grief. Further, identity involves emotional attachment to the narratives of our lives.

MEME THEORY

Some writers influenced by evolutionary biology have adopted the term *meme* to act as a bridge between genetic theory and culture (Blackmore, 1999; Dawkins, 1976; Dennett, 1995). A meme is understood to be the smallest cultural element that is replicated by means of the human capacity for imitation. More particularly, 'Memes are instructions for carrying out behavior, stored in the brains (or other objects) and passed on by imitation. Their competition drives the evolution of the mind' (Blackmore, 1999: 17).

A successful replicator, whether gene or meme, meets the criteria of:

- **fidelity;**
- **fecundity;**
- **longevity.**

Examples of memes would include the wheel, the alphabet, particular tunes or musical phrases, clothes fashions, books and ideas. The reproduction of a particular meme is not necessarily best for us; rather, memes are replicated simply because they can be. That is, a successful meme is one that is continuously imitated. This reproduction is advantageous to memes rather than to human beings *per se*. However, the pressures of evolutionary adaptation, and the role of our own esteem in relation to specific memes, means that the general drift of meme replication is in line with our values (themselves memes).

One of the problems associated with sociobiology (Wilson, 1975) is that it always returns to 'biological advantage'. This body of work tends to overlook the fact that culture enables the transmission from one generation to another of information and behavioural patterns in non-genetic form. Human adaptation can be cultural as well as biological. As sociobiology argues, genetic evolution has created brains that are especially concerned with sex, food and power. To a considerable extent, the memes we choose reflect those genetic concerns. However, there are many anomalies, such as celibacy, falling birth rates, adoption, contraception, serial monogamy, etc., that cannot be explained by genetic determination alone. They require a cultural – i.e. memetic – account.

> There is dispute as to whether meme replication works exactly like genetic natural selection or whether this is simply an appealing analogy.
>
> — What arguments could be put forward in support of each of these propositions?

Culture off the leash

Memes replicate independently of genes. This suggests that culture itself can be let off the leash of genetic determination. For example, the general development of language and our capacity for endless talk may be an outcome of the explosion of memes rather than of biological advantage. Blackmore suggests that the massive expansion of the human brain was the outcome of meme replication and is an example of meme–gene co-evolution. She argues that it is only when memes are transmitted horizontally (across cultures) more often than vertically (from generation to generation) that they become independent of genes.

The more ways there are to spread memes, and the faster they can go, the less constrained they will be by genes. The development of mass communications on a global scale, from the printing press through television and on to the Internet, has been a major contemporary mechanism for this process. Further, this argument suggests that memetic evolution allows human beings to be more altruistic than genes alone would have allowed.

There are more memes than there is host brain-processing power and retention capacity. Thus memetic selection must be taking place. The reason why some memes succeed and others fail is a consequence of the properties of our sensory systems and mechanisms of attention. That is, the most significant single element determining which memes proliferate lies in the parameters set by our evolved psychological mechanisms. This explains why some ideas, practices and emotional states, and not others, are passed from generation to generation and from neighbour to neighbour.

In this view, our evolved psycho-emotional processes provide the mechanism for meme selection. Biochemically driven responses, allied to discursive thought, generate emotional states that attach 'us' to particular memes (and not to others). Here the discourse of 'I' is a device for driving action and is itself a meme. This is an emotionally charged memeplex that is in a state of constant change. A memeplex is a group of memes that is reproduced together. This would include the idea of the self – a selfplex – as a set of interconnected memes. Our memes are who we *are*. Human consciousness itself is a product of memes. Each of us can be described as a massive memeplex running on the physical machinery of the human brain. Accordingly, 'The haven all memes depend on reaching is the human mind, but a human mind is itself an artifact created when memes restructure a human brain in order to make it a better habitat for memes' (Dennett, 1991: 207).

The broad implication of meme theory is that cultural change takes place as a consequence of memes doing their own thing. Note that cultural change is not to be understood as progress.

DECONSTRUCT THIS: NATURE VS. CULTURE

- *How is nature in culture?*
- *How is culture in nature?*
- *Where is the borderline between nature and culture?*

SUMMARY

In this chapter we have explored some of the arguments and debates that surround the undeniable fact that human beings are evolved animals as well as creatures who inhabit a cultural world of their own making. In carrying out this investigation, we necessarily encountered arguments about explanatory forms, in particular those of reductionism and complexity. The broad conclusions that we can draw from these discussion would include the following:

(Cont'd)

- The human brain and body are the outcome of gene – culture co-evolutionary processes.
- The human mind works according to a number of evolved psychological mechanisms that give shape to our cognitive and behavioural capacities.
- Human culture owes aspects of its parameters to these evolutionary processes.
- Human culture also has autonomous elements that develop by mechanisms of their own.
- Understanding bioculture is a matter of trying to grasp complex interrelations.
- We can fruitfully think about human beings not so much as bodies with a mind but rather as being 'thinking bodies' (Johnson, 1987).

PART TWO

THE CHANGING CONTEXT OF CULTURAL STUDIES

5 *A New World Disorder?*

KEY CONCEPTS

Cultural imperialism	*Modernity*
Disorganized capitalism	*New Social Movement*
Globalization	*Post-Fordism*
Hybridity	*Post-industrial society*
Life-politics	*Postmodernism*

There is a widespread perception that we are living through a period of radical change in our social orders. Old and trusted maps of meaning are felt to be giving way to the uncertainties of a global disorder. These multidimensional and interlinked changes concern:

- the economy;
- technology;
- politics;
- culture;
- identities.

Above all, these changes are not confined to specific nation-states. Rather, they are implicated in processes of globalization that question the very concept of bounded societies and cultures. The complexity of the changes taking place has led to a reconsideration of questions of social determination. In particular, there has been a recognition of the complex overlapping and overdetermined causes of change. These causal forces, in which culture plays a decisive role, are multidirectional and chaotic rather than singular and linear.

Many of the explanations for these changes, especially at the level of the technological and economic, have been generated from outside of the domain of cultural studies. This is reflected in the choice of writers deployed in the chapter. However, these changes form the context in which cultural studies has developed during the 1990s and beyond into the twenty-first century.

Much of the vocabulary of social and cultural change – post-Fordism, post-industrial society, postmodernization, etc. – has been absorbed into cultural studies. Further, cultural studies has tried to grasp these changes at the level of culture through exploration of consumer culture, global culture, cultural imperialism, postcoloniality, etc.

ECONOMY, TECHNOLOGY AND SOCIAL CLASS

Fordism

✓ *The post-1945 economies of the western world, and especially of Britain and America, have been dominated by 'Fordism' as an economic practice and Keynesianism as the economic policy of nation-states.*

Together, these practices add up to more than just an economic strategy. They constitute the organizing principles and cultural relations of an entire social formation. There were variations between economies and nation-states. However, the broad parameters of Fordism–Keynesianism were marked by large-scale production of standardized goods in the context of mass consumption. This required a system of relatively high wages, at the least for core workers, in order to sustain the purchasing of high-volume production. Of course, this was not the land of milk and honey. Allied to a relatively well-paid core labour force was a low-wage sector in which women and people of colour were over-represented.

Central to the mass production and mass consumption of consumer goods was a developing culture of promotion and advertising that supported the selling process. Further, full employment strategies were pursued not just as a social 'good' but as a means of keeping spending power at levels that met the capacity for production. Efficiency was sought through the techniques of 'scientific management' (Taylor, 1911), which stressed:

- **the organization of the division of labour to allow for the separation of tasks;**
- **the use of time and motion studies to measure and describe work tasks;**
- **the use of financial incentives as the prime form of worker motivation.**

As a mode of economic regulation, a degree of planning and management was required to maintain the stability of Fordism. This came about through:

- **the domination of world currencies by the USA;**
- **a degree of inter-state co-operation;**
- **the role of the state as a corporate policy maker and economic manager.**

This was a period in which the state played a significant interventionist role as creator of social welfare provisions, as corporate conflict resolver and as a significant direct employer.

Strategies took different forms in various countries. However, Britain of the 1960s was not atypical in experiencing an economic boom, especially in the South East and Midlands, with particularly heavy investment in cars and engineering. In this context, the labour movement was able to take successful industrial action to push up wages in a process dubbed 'wage drift'. Politically, the 1950s and early 1960s were marked by successive Conservative election victories. This required large sections of the working class to vote for right-of-centre parties. Some critics hailed this as the marker of a process of 'embourgeoisement' (see Goldthorpe and Lockwood, 1968), that is, the acquisition of incomes comparable to the middle class by manual workers and the adoption by them of middle-class lifestyles and values. So solid did this picture of industrial prosperity appear, that it was argued by some commentators to represent the very logic of industrialization for all societies world-wide (Kerr et al., 1973).

DRINK PRODUCTION

© Photographer: Guy Shapra | Agency: Dreamstime.com

(Cont'd)

- *What are the elements in this picture that make this a Fordist production process?*
- *Read the section on post-Fordism below, then suggest how the process in the photograph could become post-Fordist.*

Many of the elements of the economic and social configuration described as Fordism are now thought to have changed irrevocably. These changes have been given a variety of names. The three most influential (and overlapping) characterizations are known as:

1 post-Fordism;

2 the post-industrial society;

3 disorganized capitalism.

To characterize change with these concepts is to refer to shifts at the leading edges of the economy and culture. It does not imply that all production or cultural forms follow this model; rather, it represents the direction of change.

Post-Fordism

As described by Harvey (1989), the Fordist regime began to experience problems that came to a head during the early 1970s (he gives the 1972 oil crisis as the key moment). In particular, a system geared towards mass production and consumption faced the difficulties of saturated western markets. This led to a crisis of overproduction. This did not mean that everybody could have all the consumer goods that they wished for. Rather, the spending power of consumers had reached a point where they could not afford to purchase any more goods.

In addition, western economies were facing increased price competition from Japan and the Newly Industrialized Countries (NICs), including Taiwan, Korea and Singapore. This, combined with the success of the Oil Producing and Exporting Countries (OPEC) in pushing up world oil prices and the failure to stabilize the world financial markets as US hegemony weakened, led to economies blighted by stagflation (economies with nil growth but high inflation levels).

The more or less global recession that followed proved difficult to escape because of the rigidity of Fordism in relation to:

- **long-term and large-scale fixed capital investments which were built on the assumption of stable mass markets;**

- **the organization of labour markets in terms of job specialization and demarcation;**
- **state commitments to welfare spending involving large budget deficits.**

There was a perceived need by corporations to reintroduce growth and increase the rate of profit. This was to be achieved through more flexible production techniques involving new technology, the reorganization of labour and a speed-up of production/consumption turnover times.

On the level of production, the move from Fordism to post-Fordism involves a shift from mass production of homogeneous goods to small batch customization, that is, from uniformity and standardization to flexible, variable production for niche markets. Further, the costs involved in holding large buffer stocks within Fordist production processes was reduced through the system of Just-in-Time (JIT) stock management. This aimed to ensure that supplies are delivered only when required. JIT and economically viable small batch production rely on the use of new technology, for example the use of computers to order stock or to amend the machinery of production to change the 'run' capacity and/or colour, shape, style and size of the product. Further, since post-Fordism is based on the sub-contracting out of whole areas of the production process to horizontally related 'independent' companies, information technology is used to co-ordinate operations.

Reorganizing labour

Post-Fordism involves a restructuring of the labour process. It aims at multi-skilling workers and eliminating rigid job demarcation lines. The purpose is to create a more horizontal labour organization with an emphasis on worker co-responsibility. Quality control shifts from post-production testing into the very process of manufacturing. This requires the labour force to take responsibility for quality and 'continuous improvement' as a central part of their role. In some cases this involves 'quality circles' of workers who share ideas for the improvement of product calibre. All this was undertaken in the light of Japanese economic success.

The labour training required for multi-skilling is expensive. This leads companies to offer the core workforce higher long-term job security rather than waste their investment through high labour turnover. This development is epitomized in the classical imagery of post-Fordism/Japanization, by the Nissan or Toyota life-long 'company worker'. However, even if this is the case for the core workforce, about which there is doubt, such privileges do not extend to the large periphery workforce upon which post-Fordism depends. Thus, a good deal of the production process, particularly in the horizontally related supplier companies, is handled by part-time, short-contract, low-paid temporary workers whose hours yo-yo from week to week. Women, people of colour and young people are over-represented in the 'peripheral' labour force.

Outside of Japan, critics' attention has focused upon a range of 'silicon valleys' and on a region of Northern Italy known as Emilia Romagna or Third Italy. In the case of the latter, the global fashion producer Benetton was held to be the 'ideal-type' post-Fordist company (Murray, 1989a, 1989b). Here was an organization that had established a world-wide network of retail franchise operations. However, it employed only 1,500 workers in the core company, with many of these being highly skilled designers and marketing professionals. That is, Benetton did not employ a large direct workforce. Instead production and marketing depended on the use of information technology and a chain of subcontractors. The aim was to give Benetton flexibility and fast market-response times. For example, direct electronic links to their retail franchises gave the company up-to-date sales information, enabling the core operation to respond rapidly to customer demand.

KEY THINKERS

David Harvey (1935–)

British-born Harvey has worked as a Professor at Johns Hopkins University, USA and Oxford University, UK. He moved to the City University of New York in 2001, where he is Distinguished Professor in the department of Anthropology. He is one of the leading exponents of a Marxist-inspired cultural geography and the revival of interest in issues of space and place. In Harvey's account, postmodernism is not primarily an epistemological condition or an aesthetic trend but a social and spatial condition that results from crucial changes at the level of political economy. Harvey associates post-Fordism with the postmodernization of culture and, in particular, with forms of urban design and culture promoted by the 'new cultural intermediaries'.

Reading: Harvey, D. (1989) *The Condition of Postmodernity*. Oxford: Blackwell.

The Regulation School

✓ *Post-Fordism refers not just to the working practices of flexible specialization but to a new 'regime of accumulation' and an associated 'mode of social and political regulations'.*

A 'regime of accumulation' is a concept that refers to a stabilizing of the relationship between consumption and accumulation; or how much capital companies retain and how much money consumers spend. Such an analysis implies a relationship between conditions of production and social/political relations and lifestyles. This argument follows the 'regulationist' approach of Aglietta (1979). He stresses the role of social and cultural relations, and not simply the 'hidden hand' of the free market, in stabilizing the advanced capitalist economies. This includes the role the state plays in mediating production and demand.

For some writers, including Aglietta, the changes in working practices that have been described here as post-Fordism are better viewed as neo-Fordism. That is, the changes are understood to be an *extension* of Fordist practices aimed at giving it new life. Neo-Fordism involves:

- the diversification of companies into new products;

- internationalization in search of new markets;

- economies of scale;

- the intensification of labour through the intensive application of new technology and automation.

It seems likely that Fordist, neo-Fordist and post-Fordist practices are co-existing globally within and across sectors of specific economies. However, I have concentrated on post-Fordism. This is because it represents the position that has been most widely discussed and adopted within cultural studies.

Complete the grid below to compare key features of Fordism and post-Fordism.

	Fordism	Post-Fordism
Products		
Division of labour		
Marketing		
Quality control		
Stock control		
Use of technology		
Wages		
Horizontal design		
Vertical design		

'New Times'

The new configuration of production, politics, consumption, lifestyles, identities and aspects of everyday private life constitutes a condition that has been dubbed 'New Times' (Hall and Jacques, 1989). The 'New Times' approach explores a wide-ranging set of cultural, social and economic issues and the connections between them. These include:

- **flexible manufacturing systems;**
- **the customization of design and quality;**

- niche marketing;
- consumer lifestyles;
- globalization;
- new social and political movements;
- state deregulation and privatization of welfare;
- the cultural configurations of postmodernism;
- the reconfiguration of class structures.

In this context, the old certainties that linked economy, culture and politics together through the figure of class are put into doubt. It has been argued that we are witnessing a terminal decline in the manual working class, a rise in service and white-collar work, and an increase in part-time and 'flexible' labour. This is leading to new social divisions expressed as the two-thirds: one-third society. That is, two-thirds of the population are relatively well-off while one-third is either engaged in de-skilled, part-time work or forms a new 'underclass' of the unemployed and unemployable. At the same time, the cultural identities and political allegiances of class factions are increasingly unpredictable. The starkest vision of these changes has come from theorists of the post-industrial society and the more lavish thinkers of postmodernization.

Post-industrial society and the reconfiguration of class identities

For Bell (1973), a post-industrial society is characterized by the shift from industrial manu-facturing to service industries centred on information technology. This argument gives a key role to knowledge production and planning. In this view, technological change is the driving force of social change. In particular, information exchange and cultural production are seen to displace heavy industry at the heart of the economy. New production processes, and a general shift of emphasis from production to consumption, make information technology and communications *the* industries of the future. Central to these processes are the role and capabilities of computers in managing the increase in volume, speed and distance with which increasingly complex information is generated and transferred. Pivotal to conceptions of the post-industrial society are:

- the critical place of knowledge in the economy and culture;
- the shifts taking place in the kinds of work people do;
- the related changes in the occupational structure.

There has been both a sectoral redistribution of labour from the primary and secondary sectors to the service sector and a shift in the style or organization of labour towards white-collar work. That is, manual jobs are giving way to white-collar, professional and service work (Allen, 1992; Burnham, 1941), which is increasingly organized along craft rather than industrial lines. For Bell, the new class structure is centrally connected to the growing importance of knowledge and technical skills in post-industrial society. That is, 'the major class of the emerging new society is primarily a professional class, based on knowledge rather than property' (Bell, 1973: 374).

The rise of the service class

There is little doubt that the western world has seen a decline in the industrial manufacturing sectors of its economies and a rise in the service sectors, with a comparable alteration in employment patterns. Thus, the proportion of administrative, professional and technical workers in America and the UK steadily rose until it formed nearly one-third of the total workforce (Bell, 1973; Goldthorpe, 1982). This service class is not primarily involved in the direct production of commodities. Rather, they sell their skills and depend on their market power. They usually have a high degree of autonomy, working either as professional 'experts' or in directing the labour of others. Though they do not own the means of production, they may be shareholders and/or possess the ability, at least at the top of the spectrum, to manage the strategic direction of powerful companies.

Bell describes a class structure constituted by;

- **a professional class;**
- **a technician and semi-professional class;**
- **a clerical and sales class;**
- **a class of semi-skilled and craft workers.**

Noticeably absent from this list is the manual working class. This is a class to whom critics such as Gorz (1982) have said 'farewell'. Gorz's central argument is that, in the context of automation and post-industrial economies, new technologies have changed the employment patterns of societies. In particular, the majority of the population have been removed from working-class manual jobs and its associated class identity. Instead of *a* working class, we now have:

1 **a secure and privileged labour 'aristocracy';**

2 **a new cash-oriented, post-industrial 'working' class;**

3 **an unemployed underclass.**

In a similar move, Touraine (1971) places the control of information and knowledge at the heart of new social conflicts. Consequently, the dominant class is the group that is able to access and control information. It is no longer a case of 'The Ruling Class' vs. 'The Working Class'. Rather, what we have are technocrats and bureaucrats counterpoised to workers, students and consumers.

Disorganized capitalism

Theories of the post-industrial or information society have proved to be useful in pointing to key changes in western economies and societies. However, they are also problematic in a number of respects:

First, for many commentators, the scale, scope and range of the changes described are overstated geographically (different regions and countries experience change differently) and in absolute terms. Critics suggest that the changes described are confined to specific sectors of the economy and are not as widespread as they have been purported to be. For example, while there has been a shift towards information and service work, the standard capitalist patterns of labour organization still hold sway.

Second, while there has indeed been a growth in a service class, this category homogenizes a very diverse set of workers from office clerks and shop workers through to lawyers and the chief executive officers of major multinational corporations. This seems too heterogeneous a set of occupational and cultural modes to be regarded as one class. Indeed, increased fragmentation and stratification are markers of the new class formations.

Third, post-industrial society theorists rely on forms of technological determinism. That is, changes are explained by prioritizing technology as the motor of change without considering that the development and deployment of technology must be understood within a cultural, social and economic context. Not only is the very desire to develop technology cultural, but its deployment is dictated as much by questions of profit and loss as by the technology *per se.*

In contrast to post-industrial society theorists, Lash and Urry (1987) have linked economic, organizational and technological change to the restructuring and regeneration of global capitalism. Given its legacy of Marxism, and thus the significance of capitalism as a category, Lash and Urry's vision of 'disorganized capitalism' has been more readily absorbed into cultural studies than post-industrial society theory. As they argue:

> what is meant here by 'disorganized capitalism' is radically different from what other writers have spoken of in terms of 'post-industrial' or 'information' society. Unlike the postindustrial commentators we think that capitalist social relations continue to exist. For us a certain level of capital accumulation is a necessary condition of capitalism's disorganized era in which the capitalist class continues to be dominant. (Lash and Urry, 1987: 5)

Organized capitalism

Lash and Urry's work centres on a discussion of worldwide capitalism. In particular, none of the changes in economy, technology and class composition are confined to any single nation-state. Rather, they are understood to be a part of the processes of globalization. According to Lash and Urry (1987), from the mid-1870s onwards, the western world developed a series of industrial economies as part of what they call 'organized capitalism'. This was marked by:

- the concentration and centralization of industrial, banking and commercial capital in the context of increasingly regulated markets;

- the separation of ownership from control in business. This includes the development of complex bureaucratic managerial hierarchies involving new sectors of managerial, scientific and technological intelligentsia. This is held to be part of the greater ideological significance given to technical rationality and the glorification of science;

- the growth of employment in large plants and of the collective power of labour;

- the increased size and role of the state in economic management and conflict resolution;

- the concentration of industrial capitalism within relatively few nation-states, who in turn sought overseas expansion and the control of world markets;

- the development of extractive/manufacturing industry as the dominant sector, together with the growth of very large industrial cities.

Deconcentration and deindustrialization

✓ *'Disorganized capitalism' involves a world-wide deconcentration of capital through globalized production, financing and distribution.*

The growth of capitalism in the 'developing world' has led to increasing competition for the west in the extractive and manufacturing industries. This has shifted the occupational structure of First World economies towards the 'service' sector. Thus, western economies have experienced a decline in the extractive/manufacturing sectors as economies are deindustrialized. This has led directly to the decrease in the absolute and relative size of the core working class along with the emergence of a service class. This sectoral reorganization leads to a reduction in regional and urban concentration together with a rise in flexible forms of work organization and a decline in national bargaining procedures.

These changes in economic practices and class composition have an affinity with alterations in political thinking. This is manifested in the increased independence of large corporations from state regulation, the breakdown of state corporatist authority, and challenges to the centralized welfare provision. The change in the role of the state is an aspect of the general decline in the salience and class character of politics and political parties. This arises from an educationally based stratification system that disorganizes the links between occupation and class politics.

Patterns of consumption

Thus far, analysis has focused on changes centred on the structure and character of work. However, we also need to consider the linkage between changing class identities and patterns of consumption. This is a theme that has been absorbed into cultural studies via theorists of postmodern culture (see Chapter 6). Here we are concerned with two crucial dimensions:

1 **the rising absolute consumption levels available to labour;**

2 **class fragmentation and the consumer orientation of the working class.**

Thus, the majority of the population of western societies has sufficient housing, transportation and income to be in a post-scarcity situation. Consequently, it is argued, workers' identifications and identities shift from location in the sphere of production to that of consumption. While the service class continues to enjoy more consumer items and services than the working class, their experiences are of a shared *qualitative* character. This consumption-centredness of the working class becomes the medium and instrument of their fragmentation as they are internally stratified through 'taste' preferences (Crook et al., 1992). Further, they become detached, through their incomes and consumption capabilities, from the underclass.

Postmodernization

One of the more influential, if extravagant, postmodern positions is that of Baudrillard (1983a, 1983b, 1988). He argues that objects in consumer societies are no longer purchased for their use value. Rather, what is sought after are commodity-signs in the context of a society marked by increased commodification. For Baudrillard, no objects have an essential value; rather, use value itself is determined through exchange. This makes the cultural meaning of goods more significant than labour value or object utilization. Commodities confer prestige and signify social value, status and power in the context of cultural meanings that derive from the wider 'social order'. Thus, codes of similarity and difference in consumer goods are used to signify social affiliation. Objects 'speak of a stratified society'. Further, culture takes over, that is, absorbs and abolishes, the 'social' as a separate sphere of interaction.

In this view, the greater part of consumption is the consumption of signs. These signs are embedded in the growth of commodity culture, niche marketing and the creation of 'lifestyles'. In a process that Crook et al. (1992) call postmodernization (hypercommodification and hyperdifferentiation), all spheres of life are penetrated by commodification. The consequence is that external validation collapses. The choice between values and lifestyles then becomes a matter of taste and style rather than of 'authentic', socially formed cultural authority. Style is not constrained by formal canons or the mores of social strata but operates within a self-referential world of commodities.

For Featherstone (1991), this represents a consumer culture in which the creation of lifestyles is centred on the consumption of aesthetic signs. This process marks a relative shift in significance from production to consumption. Indeed, 'it is important to focus on the growing prominence of the *culture* of consumption and not merely regard consumption as derived from production' (ibid.: 13). That is, the culture of consumption has its own way of working that is not reducible to production. This logic loosens the connections between social class groups and lifestyles/identities.

Featherstone suggests that we are moving towards a society without fixed status groups. The adoption of styles of life fixed to specific social groups and divisions is becoming irrelevant. Instead, lifestyles are emerging in which 'the new heroes of consumer culture make a lifestyle a life project and display their individuality and sense of style in the particularity of the assemblage of goods, clothes, practices, experiences, appearance and bodily dispositions they design together into a lifestyle' (ibid.: 1991: 86).

The question of determination

The arguments presented as post-Fordism, post-industrial society, disorganized capitalism and postmodernization are not simply descriptions of changes in our contemporary world. They are also explanations that impute causes and determinations to sequences of events. Given its tendency to explain changes in culture in terms of changes in the economy, the power of the post-Fordist argument is jeopardized by an implicit economic reductionism. However, Hall rejects the idea that the post-Fordist paradigm involves economic reductionism. Instead, he argues, it is 'as much a description of cultural as of economic change' (Hall, 1989).

Modern culture is, he suggests, 'relentlessly material in its practices'. Nevertheless the material world of commodities 'is profoundly cultural', not least in the penetration of production processes by design, style and aesthetics. Indeed,

✓ 'rather than being seen as merely reflective of other processes – economic or political – culture is now regarded as being as constitutive of the social world as economic or political processes' (Du Gay et al., 1997: 4).

Hall argues for the articulation of a 'circuit of culture', where each moment is necessary for the next but does not determine its form. However, the Baudrillard–Crook–Featherstone formulation tends towards the 'end of the social' where 'culture takes over'. That is, they posit the decline of independently formed social relations of co-presence in the face of mediated cultural meanings and relationships of identification. For Crook et al., the relationship between economic, social, political and cultural practices should be seen as one of interpenetration and indeed the transgression by *cultural* meaning of the boundaries between them. Thus:

- **Models in which cultural processes appear as functions of 'deeper' economic or social dynamics cease to apply.**

- **Freed from their subordination, cultural components proliferate, split off and recombine.**

- **'Cultural dynamics not only reverse conventional hierarchies of material and ideal determination but play a crucial role in disrupting the autonomous developmental logics of economy, polity and society' (Crook et al., 1992: 229).**

For Hall (1988, 1989, 1997b), it is not the collapse of the social that is at stake. Rather, it is the re-articulation of the social and cultural whereby material goods double up as social signs. Here, an increasingly differentiated socially organized market yields a 'pluralization of social life [which] expands the positionalities and identities available to ordinary people' (Hall, 1988: 129). For example, Mort (1989) explores the way in which advertising and consumer culture endorse and constitute new identities such as 'career women', 'new man', Yuppies and a whole range of youth-oriented identities.

An alternative way to conceive of the determinations within social formations is to see their operation as 'rhizomorphic'. This forms a contrast to the 'root and branch' approach, in which the metaphor of the tree predominates, with causality running in straight lines. Instead, 'To be rhizomorphous is to produce stems and filaments that seem to be roots, or better yet connect with them by penetrating the trunk, but put them to new uses' (Deleuze and Guattari, 1988: 15).

Burrows, 'in all their functions of shelter, supply, movement, evasion, and breakout' (ibid.: 7), not to mention their interconnected layout, are rhizomorphic in character. This is also the case for the bulbs and tumours of potatoes. In any case, the contemporary, chaotic, rhizomorphic cultural arrangement that we are witnessing cannot be confined to the boundaries of nation-states; they are part of the new world disorder of globalization.

Draw two diagrams that illustrate the causal links in the production process of an advertisement for a car.

- The first diagram should be linear. That is, a straight line of links in a chain.
- The second diagram should be a circle that illustrates the variety of connections between each item that you put in the original causal chain.

Try this activity again but this time the causal links should be examining the production of your identity.

GLOBALIZATION

According to Robertson (1992), the concept of globalization refers us to:

- **an intensified compression of the world;**
- **our increasing consciousness of the world.**

That is, globalization is constituted by the ever-increasing abundance of global connections and our understanding of them. This 'compression of the world' can be understood in terms of the institutions of modernity. The reflexive 'intensification of consciousness of the world' can be perceived beneficially in cultural terms.

The dynamism of modernity

Modernity is a post-Middle Ages, post-traditional order marked by change, innovation and dynamism. For Giddens (1990, 1991), the institutions of modernity (Chapter 6) consist of capitalism, industrialism, surveillance, the nation-state and military power. Thus, the modern world is marked by a complex of armed industrial capitalist nation-states involved in systematic monitoring of their populations. Globalization is grasped in terms of:

- **the world capitalist economy;**
- **the global information system;**
- **the nation-state system;**
- **the world military order.**

The institutions of modernity are said to be inherently globalizing. This is because they allow for the separation of time-space and the 'disembedding', or lifting out, of social relations developed in one locale and their re-embedding in another.

A number of factors structure the patterns of time-space distanciation, that is, the processes by which societies are 'stretched' over shorter or longer spans of time and space. Of particular significance is the development of abstract clock time. This allows time, space and place (locales) to be separated from each other, enabling social relations to develop between people who are not co-present. At the same time, the development of new forms of communication and information control allow transactions to be conducted across time and space. Consequently, any given place is penetrated and shaped by social influences quite distant from it. For example, the development of money and electronic communications allows social relations to be stretched across time and space in the form of financial transactions conducted 24 hours a day throughout the globe.

Giddens likens the institutions of modernity to an uncontrollable juggernaut of enormous power that sweeps away all that stands before it. In this view, modernity originates in Western Europe and rolls out across the globe. This characterization of the relationship between modernity and globalization has been subject to the criticism that it is Eurocentric. That is, it envisages only one kind of modernity, that of the west. Featherstone (1995) argues that modernity should be seen not only in temporal terms (i.e. as an epochal social transformation) but also in spatial and relational terms. Different spatial zones of the globe have, he argues, become modern in a variety of ways. This requires us to speak of global modernit*ies* in the plural.

Featherstone suggests that Japan does not fit neatly into a tradition–modernity–postmodernity linear development. Likewise, Morley and Robins argue that 'What Japan has done is to call into question the supposed centrality of the West as a cultural and geographical locus for the project of modernity' (Morley and Robins, 1995: 160). At the height of its power, Japan had a lead in new technologies, owned significant parts of the Hollywood culture industries, pioneered post-Fordist production techniques, and was the largest creditor and net investor in the world. That is, Japan developed its own specific version of the modern (and postmodern).

Global economic flows

Many of the processes of globalization are economic in character. Thus, one half of the world's largest economic units are constituted by 200 transnational corporations. They produce between a third and a half of world output (Giddens, 1989). Automobile parts, chemicals, construction and semiconductors are amongst the most globalized industries (Waters, 1995). For example, 90 per cent of semi-conductor production is carried out by ten transnational corporations. The geopolitical centre of these companies has increasingly shifted from the USA to Japan.

World-wide financial transactions are conducted 24 hours a day enabled by the capabilities of new technologies in information transfer. Indeed, the financial sector is the most globalized of all economic practices. As the collapse of the European Exchange Rate Mechanism, Black Monday on the stock exchange and the so-called 'Asian economic meltdown' have demonstrated, states are at the mercy of the global financial markets. Globalization is, in part, constituted by planetary-scale economic activity that is creating an interconnected, if uneven, world economy.

The emergence and growth of global economic activity is not entirely new. Since at least the sixteenth century there has been an expansion of European mercantile trade into Asia, South America and Africa. However, what makes the contemporary manifestation of globalization notable is its scope and pace. It is widely held that since the early 1970s we have witnessed a phase of *accelerated* globalization marked by a new dimension of time-space compression. This was propelled by transnational companies' search for new sources of profit in the face of the crisis of Fordism.

Global recession hastened a renewed globalization of world economic activity involving the speed-up of production and consumption turnover. This was assisted by the use of information and communications technology (Harvey, 1989). Thus, accelerated globalization refers to a set of related economic activities understood as the practices of capitalism in its 'disorganized' era.

For today, consider the make-up of

- your breakfast;
- your clothes;
- any form of transport that you have used;
- any electronic items you have used.

— Where do the raw materials come from? Who made them?

Global cultural flows

✓ *Globalization is not just an economic matter but is concerned with issues of cultural meaning. While the values and meanings attached to place remain significant, we are increasingly involved in networks that extend far beyond our immediate physical locations.*

We are not of course part of a world state or unitary world culture. However, we can identify global cultural processes, of integration and disintegration, that are independent of inter-state relations. According to Pieterse, one can differentiate between a view of culture as bounded, tied to place and inward-looking, and one in which culture is seen as an outward-looking, 'translocal learning process'. He suggests that 'Introverted cultures, which have been prominent over a long stretch of history and which overshadowed translocal culture, are gradually receding into the background, while translocal culture made up of diverse elements is coming to the foreground' (Pieterse, 1995: 62).

Cosmopolitanism, argues Hebdige (1990), is an aspect of day-to-day western life. Diverse and remote cultures have become accessible, as signs and commodities, via our televisions, radios, supermarkets and shopping centres. A feature of contemporary culture is an increased level of cultural juxtapostioning, meeting and mixing. This has been enabled by:

- **patterns of population movement and settlement established during colonialism and its aftermath;**
- **the recent generalized acceleration of globalization;**
- **the globalization of electronic communications.**

Clifford (1992) has argued that we should 're-place' culture by deploying metaphors of travel rather than those of location. He includes peoples and cultures that travel and places/cultures as sites of criss-crossing travellers. There is a sense in which this has always been the case. Britain has a population drawn from Celts, Saxons, Vikings, Normans, Romans, Afro-Caribbeans, Asians, etc. Likewise the USA, whose diverse peoples have a heritage derived from native American Indians, the English, French, Spanish, Africans, Mexicans, Irish, Poles and many more. However, the accelerated globalization of late modernity has increased the relevance of the metaphor of travel because *all* locales are now subject to the influences of distant places.

Disjunctive flows

A counterpoint to the stress on travel and movement is a certain re-emergence of the politics of place. Attachment to place can be seen in the renewal of forms of Eastern European nationalism, neo-fascist politics and to some degree Islamic fundamentalism. Consequently, globalization is far from an even process of western expansion driven by economic imperatives.

Appadurai (1993) has argued that contemporary global conditions are best character-ized in term of the *disjunctive* flows of:

- **ethnoscapes;**
- **technoscapes;**
- **finanscapes;**

- **mediascapes;**

- **ideoscapes.**

That is, globalization involves the dynamic movements of ethnic groups, technology, financial transactions, media images and ideological conflicts. These flows are not neatly determined by one harmonious 'master plan'. For example, the state of the finanscape does not neatly determine the shape of the technoscape. This in turn does not decide the character of the mediascape or the ideoscape. In part this is because of the influence of a variety of ethnoscapes. That is, we have moved away from an economically determinist linear model. We have moved towards one in which the speed, scope and impact of economic and cultural flows are fractured and disconnected.

Metaphors of uncertainty, contingency and chaos are replacing those of order, stability and systematicity. Globalization and global cultural flows cannot be understood through neat sets of linear determinations. Rather, they are better comprehended as a series of overlapping, overdetermined, complex and chaotic conditions which, at best, cluster around key 'nodal points'. Unpredictable and elaborate overdeterminations have led 'not to the creation of an ordered global village, but to the multiplication of points of conflict, antagonism and contradiction' (Ang, 1996: 165). This argument, in emphasizing cultural diversity and fragmentation, runs counter to the common idea that globalization is a uniform process of cultural homogenization.

In groups, discuss the global distribution of ethnic populations (ethnoscape), computer use (technoscape), stock exchanges (finanscape), television production (mediascape) and support for consumer culture (ideoscape).

— What connections between the 'scapes' can you identify?
— What does Appadurai mean when he says that the relationships between 'scapes' are disjunctive?

Homogenization and fragmentation

Cultural imperialism and its critics

The cultural homogenization thesis proposes that the globalization of consumer capitalism involves a loss of cultural diversity. It stresses the growth of 'sameness' and a presumed loss of cultural autonomy. This is cast as a form of cultural imperialism. The argument revolves around the alleged domination of one culture by another. This is usually conceived of in *national* terms. The principal agents of cultural synchronization are said to be transnational corporations (Hamelink, 1983). Consequently, cultural imperialism is the outcome of a set of economic and cultural processes implicated in the reproduction of global *capitalism*. In this context, Robins argues:

> For all that it has projected itself as transhistorical and transnational, as the transcendent and universalizing force of modernization and modernity, global capitalism has in reality been about westernization – the export of western commodities, values, priorities, ways of life. (Robins, 1991: 25)

Herbert Schiller (1969, 1985), a leading proponent of the cultural imperialism thesis, argues that the global communications industries are dominated by US-controlled corporations. He points to the interlocking network that connects US television, defence sub-contractors and the Federal government. Schiller's case is that the mass media fit into the world capitalist system by providing ideological support for capitalism and transnational corporations in particular. They act as vehicles for corporate marketing along with a general 'ideological effect' which purportedly produces and reinforces locals' attachment to US capitalism.

No doubt the first waves of economic, military and cultural globalization were part of the dynamic spread of western modernity. Given that these institutions originated in Europe, we would have to say that modernity is a western project. The early phases of globalization certainly involved western interrogation of the non-western 'other' (Giddens, 1990). Further, as the phase of mercantile expansion gave way to more direct colonial control, European powers sought to impose their cultural forms in tandem with military and economic power. Colonial control manifested itself as

- **military dominance;**
- **cultural ascendancy;**
- **the origins of economic dependency.**

Occupied lands were converted into protected markets for imperial powers as well as sources of raw materials. Though the early twentieth century saw a series of successful anti-colonial struggles and independence movements, the economies of these countries were already integrated into the world economic order as subordinate players (Frank, 1967; Wallerstein, 1974), albeit in an uneven fashion (Worsley, 1990).

However, there are three central difficulties with the 'globalization as cultural imperialism' argument:

1 **It is no longer the case, if it ever was, that the global flows of cultural discourses are constituted as one-way traffic.**

2 **In so far as the predominant flow of cultural discourse remains from West to East and North to South, this is not necessarily a form of domination.**

3 **It is unclear that globalization is a simple process of homogenization since the forces of fragmentation and hybridity are equally as strong.**

Hybridity and complex cultural flows

European colonialism has left its cultural mark across the globe. Nowhere was this more compelling than in South African apartheid. Here a white God and the European sword combined to enforce and justify domination. European culture is evident in South Africa through language, sport, architecture, music, food, painting, film, television and the general sense amongst whites that European culture represents high culture. It is not coincidental that in a country with a wide variety of languages, English provides the most common shared point of translation.

Nevertheless, the impact of 'external' cultural influences on South Africa is more complex than the idea of a simple cultural imperialism. Consider the prevalence and popularity of American-inspired Hip-Hop and Rap music amongst black South Africans. South African rappers take an apparently non-African musical form and give it an African twist to create a form of hybridization which is now being exported back to the West. Rap, which was described here as American, can be said to have travelled to the US from the Caribbean and can trace its roots/routes back to the influence of West African music and the impact of slavery. Any idea of clear-cut lines of demarcation between the 'internal' and 'external' are swept away. Rap has no obvious 'origin' and its American form is indebted to Africa. In what sense, then, can its popularity in Soweto be called cultural imperialism?

The concept of cultural imperialism depends at heart on a notion of imposition and coercion. However, if Africans listen to some forms of western music, watch some forms of western television and buy western-produced consumer goods, which they enjoy, how can this be maintained as domination without resort to arguments that rely on 'false' consciousness (Tomlinson, 1991)? Rhizomorphic and disjunctive global cultural flows are characterizable less in terms of domination and more as forms of cultural hybridity.

✓ *Globalization is not constituted by a monolithic one-way flow from the west-to-the-rest.*

This can be seen in the impact of non-western ideas and practices on the west. For example:

- **the global impact of 'World Music';**

- **the export of telenovelas from Latin American to the USA and Europe;**

- **the creation of ethnic diasporas through population movement from South to North;**

- the influence of Islam, Hinduism, Buddhism and other world religions within the west;

- the commodification and sale of 'ethnic' food and clothing.

This adds up not only to a general decentring of western perspectives about 'progress' but also to the deconstruction of the very idea of homogeneous national cultures (Chapter 8).

The current phase of accelerated globalization is not one-directional. Rather, it is 'a process of uneven development that fragments as it coordinates – introduces new forms of world interdependence, in which, once again there are no "others"'. This involves 'emergent forms of world interdependence and planetary consciousness' (Giddens, 1990: 175). For Giddens, not only can the other 'answer back', but mutual interrogation is now possible (Giddens, 1994). Indeed, for Appadurai, existing centre–periphery models are inadequate in the face of a new 'complex, overlapping, disjunctive order' in which, 'for people of Irian Jaya, Indonesianisation may be more worrisome than Americanisation, as Japanisation may be for Koreans, Indianisation for Sri Lankans, Vietnamisation for Cambodians, Russianisation for the people of Soviet Armenia and the Baltic Republics' (Appadurai, 1993: 328).

Glocalization

Capitalist modernity does involve an element of cultural homogenization for it increases the levels and amount of global co-ordination. However, mechanisms of fragmentation, heterogenization and hybridity are also at work. 'It is not a question of *either* homogenization or heterogenization, but rather of the ways in which both of these two tendencies have become features of life across much of the late-twentieth-century world' (Robertson, 1995: 27).

Bounded cultures, ethnic resilience and the re-emergence of powerful nationalistic sentiments co-exist with cultures as 'translocal learning processes' (Pieterse, 1995). The global and the local are mutually constituting. As Robertson (1992) argues, much that is considered to be local, and counterpoised to the global, is the outcome of translocal processes. Nation-states were forged within a global system and the contemporary rise in nationalist sentiment can be regarded as an aspect of globalization.

Further, the current direction of global consumer capitalism is such that it encourages limitless needs/wants. That is, niche markets, customization and the pleasures of constant identity transformation give rise to diversity (Ang, 1996). Thus, the global and the local are relative terms. The idea of the local, specifically what is considered to be local, is produced within and by globalizing discourses. This includes capitalist marketing strategies that orientate themselves to differentiated 'local' markets. An emphasis on particularity and diversity can be regarded as an increasingly global discourse. Thus, 'the expectation of identity declaration is built into the general process of globalization' (Robertson, 1992: 175). Robertson adopts the concept of glocalization, in origin a marketing term, to express the global production of the local and the localization of the global.

Creolization

In this spirit, Ashcroft et al. (1989) argue that the hybridization and creolization of language, literature and cultural identities becomes a common theme in postcolonial literature. This marks a certain meeting of minds with postmodernism. Neither the colonial nor colonized cultures and languages can be presented in 'pure' form. They cannot be separated from each other, thereby giving rise to hybridity. This challenges not only the centrality of colonial culture and the marginalization of the colonized but the very idea of 'centre' and 'margin'.

In a Caribbean linguistic context, increasing significance has been attributed to the idea of the 'Creole continuum'; that is, a series of overlapping language usages and code switching. This process deploys the specific modes of other languages, say English and French, while inventing forms particular to itself. Creolization stresses language as a cultural practice over the abstractions of grammar or any idea of 'correct' usage.

Creolization suggests that claims of cultural homogenization do not provide a strong grounding for the arguments of cultural imperialism. Much of what is cast as cultural imperialism may be understood instead as the creation of a layer of western capitalist modernity which overlays, but does not necessarily obliterate, pre-existing cultural forms. Modern and postmodern ideas about time, space, rationality, capitalism, consumerism, sexuality, family, gender, etc. are placed alongside older discourses, setting up ideological competition between them. The outcome may be both a range of hybrid forms of identity *and* the production of traditional, 'fundamentalist' and nationalist identities. Nationalism and the nation-state continue to co-exist with cosmopolitanism and the weakening of national identities. The processes of reverse flow, fragmentation and hybridization are quite as strong as the push towards homogenization.

Globalization and power

The concepts of globalization and hybridity are more adequate than that of cultural imperialism, because they suggest a less coherent, unified and directed process. However, this should not lead us to abandon the exploration of power and inequality. The fact that power is diffused, or that commodities are subversively used to produce new hybrid identities, does not displace our need to examine it. As Pieterse argues:

> Relations of power and hegemony are inscribed and reproduced within hybridity for wherever we look closely enough we find the traces of asymmetry in culture, place, descent. Hence hybridity raises the question of the terms of the mixture, the conditions of mixing and mélange. At the same time it's important to note the ways in which hegemony is not merely reproduced but refigured in the process of hybridization. (Pieterse, 1995: 57)

For example, the cultural hybridity produced by the black diaspora does not obscure the power that was embedded in the moment of slavery or the economic push–pull of migration. As Hall (1992b) argues, diaspora identities are constructed within and by cultural power. 'This power', he suggests, 'has become a constitutive element in our own identities' (Hall, 1992b: 233). Thus, the cultural identities of rich white men in New York are of a very different order to those of poor Asian women in rural India. While we are all part of a global society whose consequences no one can escape, we remain unequal participants and globalization remains an uneven process.

— Which of the following items represent global homogenization and which stand for the maintenance of diversity? Can they do both?

- Coca-Cola;
- the Olympic Games;
- Hollywood movies;
- world music;
- Hip-Hop music
- Bollywood movies (Indian film);
- Buddhism (the fastest-growing 'religion' in the west);
- the advertising industry;
- motor car sales;
- tourism.

Modernity as loss

Tomlinson (1991) makes the case for seeing the spread of western modernity as cultural *loss*. That is, modernity does not provide adequate qualitative, meaningful and moral points of reference and experience. Tomlinson follows Castoriadis in suggesting that the western concept of development stresses 'more of everything'. In particular, the modern world provides more material goods to us, without offering us significant cultural values. There is little sense of when more is undesirable or where 'growth' might mean personal and meaningful experience rather than material gain. The people of most pre-modern societies had living traditions of family, community, morality and Gods into which they were embedded. Today, modern western-style societies have few meaningful collective traditions or communities. The conventional family is in disarray and our God(s) has been declared well and truly dead (and with no sign of imminent resurrection). In this sense, ours is a spiritually poor culture. We seem to value quantity over quality. Further, western culture is witnessing an alarming rise in addictions, mania, depression, low self-esteem and self-indulgent, self-centred behaviour. These phenomena are described by Jobst et al. (1999) as 'diseases of meaning'.

Lasch (1980, 1985) characterized the western world as a 'culture of narcissism' and later as a 'culture of survivalism'. Here self-centred individuals become increasingly apathetic as a consequence of:

- **being enmeshed in a consumer culture that offers the good life but delivers only a hollow echo of meaningfulness;**

- the rise of bureaucratic organizations that wield apparently arbitrary powers over us;

- the decline of the traditional family and its underpinning of meaningful human relations.

According to Giddens, 'Personal meaninglessness – the feeling that life has nothing worthwhile to offer – becomes a fundamental psychic problem in circumstances of late modernity' (Giddens, 1991: 9). He argues that we should understand this phenomenon in terms of a repression of the moral questions that day-to-day life poses, but which are denied answers. That is, we are separated from the moral resources necessary to live a full and satisfying existence.

Giddens explores the generation of meaninglessness as an aspect of what he calls 'the sequestration of experience'. This process involves the separation of day-to-day life from contact with experiences of sickness, madness, criminality, sexuality and death that raise potentially disturbing existential questions. That is, the development of hospitals, asylums, the 'privatization of passion' and an apparent disconnection from nature rob most people of direct contact with events and situations that link the individual life-span to broad issues of morality and death. The establishment of relative security in key domains of human life through the acceptance of routines lacks moral meaning and can be experienced as 'empty' practices.

KEY THINKERS

Anthony Giddens (1938–)

Anthony Giddens is a British-born thinker who was formerly Professor of Sociology at the University of Cambridge and Director of the London School of Economics. Giddens has sought to legitimate the project of sociology and has sometimes been critical of the impulses of cultural studies; nevertheless, his work has exerted considerable influence amongst writers in the field. Giddens's expertise in classical sociology informed his endeavours to overcome the dualism of agency and structure. His recent work argues that globalization is a consequence of the dynamism of modernity. In this context the self is a reflexive project freed from traditional constraints and in a state of continual re-invention.

Reading: Giddens, A. (1991) *Modernity and Self-Identity.* Cambridge: Polity Press.

One could then argue that it is this loss of meaningfulness that is the most potent danger posed by modernity to non-western societies. The idea of cultural imperialism also has strength where people are denied a cultural experience; that is, where particular social groups or local concerns *fail to be represented* in the media as a result of multinational control of the economics of production.

However, recognition of imbalance or loss is not the same as viewing the process of globalization as a one-way process of imperialism. As Tomlinson argues:

> Globalization may be distinguished from imperialism in that it is a far less coherent or culturally directed process. For all that it is ambiguous between economic and political senses, the idea of imperialism contains, at least, the notion of a purposeful project; the intended spread of a social system from one centre of power across the globe. The idea of globalization suggests interconnection and interdependency of all global areas which happen in a far less purposeful way. It happens as the result of economic and cultural practices which do not, of themselves, aim at global integration, but which nonetheless produce it. More importantly, the effects of globalization are to weaken cultural coherence in all individual nation-states, including the economically powerful ones – the imperialist powers of a previous era. (Tomlinson, 1991: 175)

ANTI-GLOBALIZATION PROTEST

© Photographer: Pictura | Agency: Dreamstime.com

This picture is of an anti-globalization protest in which the demonstrators have targeted capitalism.

- *What features of capitalism do you think they are objecting to? Do you agree?*
- *Read the next section on New Social Movements. Does the anti-globalization movement qualify as an NSM?*

Globalization is in part a set of supra-national processes. That is, the procedures of globalization operate at a level 'above' the nation-state. As such, it has consequences for the nation-state and its political forms. Thus, it is argued, we are witnessing decisive political changes that include alterations in the role of the state, shifts in political ideologies and the emergence of New Social Movements (NSMs)

THE STATE, POLITICS AND NEW SOCIAL MOVEMENTS

According to Giddens (1985), the modern nation-state is a container of power. It is constituted by a political apparatus recognized to have sovereign rights within the borders of a demarcated territorial area and possessing the ability to back these claims with military power. The state specializes in the maintenance of order through the rule of law and the monopoly of legitimate violence. Many citizens of nation-states have positive feelings of commitment to their national identity. The political processes of states have varied across time and space. However, some form of representative democracy is a marker of liberal democracies. In addition, a significant number of post-war states built up an edifice of welfare provision. They have also played an important role in corporate economic management. In short, the modern state can be seen to have three critical functions:

1 external defence;

2 internal surveillance;

3 the maintenance of citizenship rights.

The decline of the nation-state and the end of history?

According to a number of commentators (Crook et al., 1992; Held, 1991; Hertz, 1957), aspects of the state's functions are in decline. For example, it is argued to be increasingly difficult to legitimize the deployment of vast resources for military purposes when nuclear warfare makes military strategies a high-risk option. The state is, in this respect, unable to fully defend its citizens. Military force is increasingly irrelevant, other than as a last resort, to the solving of key economic, political and diplomatic problems. This is particularly so in the context of a post-Cold War demilitarization in which states, especially those of the former Soviet bloc, are unable to bear the costs of maintaining massive military capabilities (Shaw, 1991). In terms of its more obviously political functions,

There are four significant elements in this unravelling of the state: a horizontal redistribution of power and responsibility to autonomous corporate bodies; a vertical redistribution of power and responsibility to local councils, civic initiatives, and extra-state run enterprises; and an externalization of responsibility by shifting to supra-state bodies. (Crook et al., 1992: 38)

In Britain, decentralizing tendencies have been manifested through government privatization of major public utilities – gas, water, electricity and telecommunications – along with significant sections of the civil service. Though there are differences in the scale and scope of privatization/deregulation in different countries, the general principles have 'been followed in over 100 countries' (ibid.: 99). This includes the USA, Australia, Germany, Sweden and Poland, amongst others. In addition, decentralization has included giving schools more local autonomy and radically reducing the state's commitments to health and social security. Indeed, a growth in private health insurance and personal pension schemes marks the arrival of a 'postwelfare paradigm' (Bennett, 1990: 12).

Above all, the nation-state is embroiled in the multi-faceted processes of globalization. This can be argued to 'be corroding important functions of the modern nation-state: namely, its competence; its form; its autonomy; and its authority or legitimacy' (McGrew, 1992).

Form and competence

States are increasingly unable to manage and control their own economic policy. Nor can they protect citizens from global events such as environmental disasters. That is, the state's competence is being undermined. This leads to the development of intergovernmental or supra-governmental agencies that alter the form and scope of the state. International organizations engaged in economic and political practices that reduce the state's competence and adjust its form include, amongst others:

- the International Monetary Fund;
- the G8 summits of major economic powers;
- the European Union;
- the European Court of Human Rights;
- the United Nations;
- the International Energy Agency;
- the World Health Organization.

Autonomy

The globalization of economic and political processes means that the state is increasingly unable to maintain direct control of policy formation. Consequently, it must become an actor on the international stage of compromise and capitulation. That is, the *autonomy* of the state is increasingly restricted. Held argues that globalization exhibits a set of forces which combine to restrict the freedom of action of governments and states by blurring the boundaries of domestic politics, transforming the conditions of political decision making, changing the institutional and organizational context of national polities, altering the legal framework and administrative practices of governments and obscuring the lines of responsibility and accountability of national states themselves. These processes alone warrant the statement that the operation of states in an ever more complex international system both limits their autonomy and impinges increasingly upon their sovereignty. Any conception of sovereignty which interprets it as an illimitable and indivisible form of public power is undermined. Sovereignty itself has to be conceived today as already divided among a number of agencies, national, regional and international, and limited by the very nature of this plurality. (Held, 1991: 222)

Legitimation

The competence and autonomy of the state are being slowly undermined and at least some of its powers are being transferred to supra-state bodies. As such, the state cannot fully carry out its modern functions. It may then suffer a crisis of legitimation. Since the state cannot do what it is expected to do, people may lose faith in it.

Some critics (Gilpin, 1987) do not accept that the nation-state is being eroded. They argue that international co-operation between states and trans-state agencies increase the state's ability to direct its own fate. Further, nationalism and state military power play significant roles in international relations and show little sign of withering away. International diplomacy still operates through states rather than by-passing them. The position regarding the internal powers of the state is also ambiguous. On the one hand, states like Britain have privatized and deregulated in a process of decentralization. On the other hand, such states have taken increased authoritarian powers over questions of 'law and order', morality and internal surveillance (Gorden, 1988; Hall, 1988).

✓ *The state is changing its form, transferring some of its powers to supra-state bodies and undergoing a degree of 'legitimation crisis'. However, this is far from total and there seems to be little prospect of the state disappearing in the immediate future.*

The fall of communism

Thus far, discussion has centred on the liberal democratic states of Europe, Australia and North America. However, sweeping political and economic changes also took place in Eastern Europe in the 1980s and 1990s. During the 1970s and 1980s all the communist states experienced economic and social crises. This included:

- **falling industrial production;**
- **food and consumer goods shortages;**

- declining welfare services;

- rising crime and alcoholism;

- political dissent and mass dissatisfaction.

Subsequently, the anti-totalitarian social and political movements of Eastern Europe, spearheaded by Poland's *Solidarity* movement, took advantage of the space opened up by Soviet liberalization under Gorbachev to oust the communist establishments.

Most of the regimes of Eastern Europe have moved with varying degrees of speed towards forms of representative democracy. Further, they have espoused consumer capitalism and sought to join NATO and the European Union. Russia has embraced the west less enthusiastically than has Poland or the Czech Republic. Nevertheless, Coca-Cola and McDonald's are symbolically established in the heart of Moscow. Does this represent the final global triumph of liberal democracy and consumer capitalism?

The end of history?

The idea that the triumph of liberal democracy and capitalism is a permanent state of affairs was forwarded and popularized by Fukuyama. He argued that we faced 'the end of history as such; that is, the end point of mankind's ideological evolution and the universalization of western liberal democracy as the final form of human government' (Fukuyama, 1989: 3).

What he means by the 'end of history' is not the end to the occurrence of events. Rather, he is referring to the universal triumph of the *idea* of liberal democracy as the only viable political system (Fukuyama, 1992). The end of history is the end of ideological competition. This presumes that 'a remarkable consensus has developed in the world concerning the legitimacy and viability of liberal democracy' (Fukuyama, 1989: 22). Though Fukuyama does not expect social conflict to disappear, he argues that grand political ideologies will give way to economic management and technical problem solving. This occurs in the context of liberal-democratic states and capitalist economic and social relations.

Held (1992) raises questions about the core of Fukuyama's thesis. He argues that liberalism should not be treated as the 'unity' that characterizes Fukuyama's argument. Fukuyama neither differentiates nor decides between different versions of liberalism. He ignores ideological contestation within it. Further, argues Held, Fukuyama does not explore potential tensions between the 'liberal' and 'democratic' components of liberal democracy. For example, he does not consider the tensions between individual rights and public accountability.

In addition, Fukuyama fails to investigate the degree to which market relations, and the inequities of power and wealth to which they give rise, inhibit liberty and democracy. That is, social inequality can itself be regarded as an outcome of market power that is to the detriment of equal citizenship. Thus, 'it is far from self-evident that the existing economic system is compatible with the central liberal concern to treat all persons as "free and equal"' (Held, 1992: 24).

Held suggests that global economic inequalities, along with national, ethnic, religious and political ideologies, will continue to generate conflict. Further, these could give rise to new mass-mobilizing forces capable of legitimating new kinds of regime. However, it is difficult at present to see where, within liberal democracies, alternative economic and political *systems* are going to be generated from, either ideologically or in terms of social actors capable of system change. Held's criticisms of Fukuyama do not disrupt the claim that liberal democracy has triumphed as an idea. The demise of a 'revolutionary politics' which would realize an alternative system seems to be marked by:

- **the decline of socialism as an alternative systemic ideology;**
- **the collapse of communism;**
- **the decline of the working class as a numerical and political force;**
- **the increasing disconnection between class and politics;**
- **the rise of social and cultural movements, including ecology politics and feminism, whose political claims are reformist (in the best sense).**

On a global scale, capitalism has triumphed. As such, it is hard to see what an alternative system could or will be. Liberal and social-democratic regulatory tinkering seems to be the best that is on offer in the current climate. This is not to suggest (as would classical modernization theory) that all societies will follow the western path. There will no doubt be regional variations and the character of capitalism and political forces will take on different configurations in different parts of the world. However, it does suggest that capitalism has achieved global hegemony and that liberal democracy has triumphed in the west. This directs political activity to reformist changes within the system (see Chapter 14) and/or to New Social Movements as pressure groups.

New Social Movements

New Social Movements (NSMs) appeared in modern western societies during the 1960s. They were associated with the student movement, anti-Vietnam War protests, civil rights struggles and the women's movement. NSMs are commonly seen as encompassing feminism, ecology politics, peace movements, youth movements and the politics of cultural identity (Chapters 7–9). They are separated from the traditional class politics of labour movements.

Displacing class?

According to Touraine (1981) and Melucci (1980, 1981, 1989), contemporary radical politics is becoming detached from class determinations. Instead it is becoming organized through New Social Movements. NSMs are increasingly strident social and political collectivities based outside of the workplace. The collective identity formation of NSMs involves the accomplishment of perceived commonalty, cohesion and continuity. This is achieved through the marking of social boundaries as an aspect of collective action. As a provisional and ongoing form of identification, this has to be continually produced and reproduced over time and across space. As Melucci argues, 'Collective identity formation is a delicate process and requires continual investments' (Melucci, 1989: 34).

The forms of collective identity at the heart of New Social Movements are not those of orthodox class identification. Indeed, the rise of NSMs appears to correlate with a decline in the predictability of the relationship between class and political allegiance. Thus,

> studies of voting behaviour and political activism showed a steady decline in allegiance between the major classes or occupational categories on the one hand and the major political parties on the other. … Since the late 1960s … the class voting index has been in steady decline. (Crook et al., 1992: 139)

It is also argued that there is a reduction in trust for the major political parties. This has led to a growing interest in more direct forms of political action. Such activity involves a wider repertoire of strategy and tactics than the corporatist politics of compromise and negotiation had allowed for.

It would be a mistake to see New Social Movements as entirely replacing class politics or as an outcome of the disappearance of class. Nevertheless, it is possible to see them as a partial response to changes in the social formation. Touraine identifies a general disintegration–decomposition of industrial society, along with a decline in the workers' movement and the primacy of class politics, as contributing to New Social Movements. Though characterized by Touraine as a part of the class struggle, NSMs are distanced in language, style and class composition from the traditions of the industrial era.

> … in a society where the largest investments no longer serve to transform the organization of labour, as in industrial society, but to create new products, and beyond that, new sources of economic power through the control of complex systems of communication, then the central conflict has shifted. (Touraine, 1985: 4)

For Touraine, conflict has been displaced from the opposition of manager and worker to a wider struggle for control over the direction of social, economic and cultural development.

In particular, the axis of conflict has shifted to questions of identity, self-actualization and 'post-materialist' values.

Life-politics

According to Giddens (1992), the 'emancipatory politics' of modernity is concerned with liberation from the constraints that limit life chances. That is, 'emancipatory politics' directs its attention to the exploitative relations of class and the freeing of social life from the fixities of tradition. This includes an ethics of justice, equality and participation. In contrast, given a degree of release from material deprivation, 'life-politics' is more concerned with self-actualization, choice and lifestyle. Life-politics revolves around the creation of justifiable forms of life that will promote self-actualization in a global context. They are centred on the ethics of 'How shall we live?'

> Life-politics concerns political issues which flow from processes of self-actualization in post-traditional contexts, where globalizing influences intrude deeply into the reflexive project of the self and conversely where processes of self-realization influence global strategies. (Giddens, 1992: 214)

For Giddens, the more we 'make ourselves', the more the questions of 'what a person is' and 'who I want to be' are raised. This takes place in the context of global circumstances that no one can escape. For example, the recognition of the finite character of global resources and the limits of science and technology may lead to a de-emphasis on economic accumulation and the need to adopt new lifestyles. Likewise, developments in biological science lead us to ask questions about how to understand the nature of life, the rights of the unborn, and the ethics of genetic research. This reflexivity, involving the re-moralizing of social life, lies behind many contemporary New Social Movements.

Complete the table below.

New Social Movement	Central beliefs and aims	Forms of activity	Main symbols
1.			
2.			
3.			
4.			
5.			

Symbolic communities

According to Melucci, the organizational characteristics of New Social Movements are distinct from those that marked class politics. In particular, they are less committed to working within the established political system. Further, though the achievement of specific instrumental goals do form a part of their agenda, NSMs are more concerned with their own autonomy and the value orientation of wider social developments. Melucci casts them as having a 'spiritual' component centred on the body and the 'natural' world. This acts as a source of moral authority for the movements.

New Social Movements are more preoccupied with direct democracy and member participation than with representative democracy. They are commonly marked out by:

- **an anti-authoritarian, anti-bureaucratic and even anti-industrial stance;**
- **loose, democratic and activist-oriented organizational modes;**
- **the blurring of the boundaries between movements;**
- **overlapping flexible and shifting 'membership';**
- **'membership' that is bestowed through participation.**

New Social Movements frequently engage in 'direct action'. However, it is often not aimed at the authority and personnel of orthodox representative politics (e.g. Members of Parliament or Congress). Rather, action is directed at other actors or institutions in civil society. This includes companies, research establishments, military bases, oil-rigs, road-building projects, and so forth. New Social Movements challenge the cultural codes of institutionalized power relations. This is achieved through symbolic events and evocative language which lend themselves coherent form as an 'imagined community'.

NSMs' symbolic politics are readily disseminated by the mass media. The activities and emblems of NSMs are commonly good dramatic news events. The images generated by New Social Movements are core to their activities and blur the boundaries between their form and content. That is, many of the activities of New Social Movements are media events designed to give them popular appeal. The symbolic languages of these movements are polysemic. This gives them a broad enough message to suit the imprecision of their aims. At the same time it forms the basis of an alliance or imagined community constituted by a range of otherwise disparate people.

✓ *More than traditional modern party politics, New Social Movements are expressly a form of cultural politics (Chapter 14).*

DECONSTRUCT THIS: THE GLOBAL VS. THE LOCAL

- *What makes something global?*
- *What makes something local?*
- *Can you draw a line between the global and the local?*

SUMMARY

This chapter has described aspects of the changing world in which contemporary cultural studies operates and in which it seeks to intervene. This is an uncertain world in which metaphors of ordered and determinate relations between the economic, social, political and cultural have given way to more chaotic, rhizomorphic and disjunctive relations.

Culture, it is said, has come to play an increasingly significant role in a new globalized disorder. Indeed, Waters argues that globalization is most advanced in the sphere of culture. Signs can more easily span time and space than material goods and services. Consequently, 'we can expect the economy and the polity to be globalized to the extent that they are culturalized, that is, to the extent that the exchanges that take place within them are accomplished symbolically' (Waters, 1995: 9)

It was argued that while forces of cultural homogenization are certainly in evidence, of equal significance is the place of heterogenization and localization. Consequently, globalization and hybridity are preferred concepts to imperialism and homogeneity at the dawn of the twenty-first century. The themes of hybridity and creolization have been explored within cultural studies in relation to identities, music, youth culture, dance, fashion, ethnicity, nationality, language and the very concept of culture (all are said to be hybridized). Hybridity is one of the repeated motifs of contemporary cultural studies from Derridean deconsturction (the end of binaries where each is within the other) through postmodernism to explorations of ethnicity and postcoloniality.

We explored changes in the basis of the major world economies from Fordism to post-Fordism and the emergence of post-Industrial societies. This included:

- a degree of class decomposition;
- the rise of consumer culture;
- the emergence of new forms of lifestyle and identities.

It was argued that there has been a decline in the predictability of the relationship between class and political allegiance. There has also been a rise in New Social Movements. We

(Cont'd)

reviewed arguments that pointed to a decline in the role and competence of the nation-state. It was suggested that these developments could be understood in the context of disorganized capitalism.

Many commentators agree on the broad components of the social and cultural changes that have been described here. However, there is disagreement about their scope and significance. In particular, there has been considerable debate about whether we are experiencing an epochal shift from modernity to postmodernity, or, at the very least, the rise of a cultural and epistemological 'structure of feeling' that we can call postmodern. These themes form the basis of Chapter 6.

6   *Enter Postmodernism*

KEY CONCEPTS

Culture jamming	*Modernism*
Enlightenment	*Modernity*
Grand narrative	*Postmodernism*
Hyperreality	*Postmodernity*
Irony	*Reflexivity*

The proliferation of books on the subject of postmodernism is not simply an academic fashion. It is also a significant response to substantive changes in the organization and enactment of our social worlds. In other words, there are material grounds for taking these debates seriously. Much of the primary theoretical work on postmodernism has been produced by writers with no direct affiliation to cultural studies as a 'discipline'. Nevertheless, the debates and conceptual maps that developed as postmodernism emerged have been filtered into cultural studies. They form the context in which contemporary cultural studies has been developing and permeate the 'sites' of cultural studies investigations (Chapters 7–14). The postmodern influence in cultural studies underscores a certain break with its Marxist legacy.

DEFINING THE TERMS

Postmodern theory makes little sense outside of the associated concepts of modernity and modernism. Unfortunately, there is no consensus about what the pertinent concepts mean. For our purposes here:

✓ *Modernity and postmodernity are terms that refer to historical and sociological configurations. Modernism and postmodernism are cultural and epistemological concepts.*

In particular, the concepts of modernism and postmodernism concern:

- cultural formations and cultural experience, for example, modernism as the cultural experience of modernity and postmodernism as a cultural sensibility associated with high or post-modernity.

- artistic and architectural styles and movements, that is, modernism as a style of architecture (Le Corbusier) or writing (Joyce, Kafka, Brecht) and postmodernism in film (*Blue Velvet, Blade Runner*), photography (Cindy Sherman) or the novel (E.L. Doctorow, Salman Rushdie).

- a set of philosophical and epistemological concerns and positions, that is, thinking about the character of knowledge and truth. Modernism is associated with the enlightenment philosophy of Rousseau and Bacon along with the socio-economic theory of Marx, Weber, Habermas and others. Postmodernism in philosophy has been associated with thinkers as diverse as Lyotard, Baudrillard, Foucault, Rorty and Bauman, not all of whom would welcome that characterization. In broad terms, enlightenment thought seeks after universal truths while postmodernism points to the socio-historical and linguistic specificity of 'truth'.

THE INSTITUTIONS OF MODERNITY

Modernity is a historical period following the Middle Ages. It is a post-traditional order marked by change, innovation and dynamism. The institutions of modernity can be seen, at least in the account of Giddens (1990), to consist of;

- *industrialism* (the transformation of nature: development of the created environment);

- *surveillance* (control of information and social supervision);

- *capitalism* (capital accumulation within competitive labour and product markets);

- *military power* (control of the means of violence through the industrialization of war).

— Consider the institutions of modernity named above.
— Describe contemporary examples of each of them.

The industrial revolution

The industrial revolution in Britain transformed a pre-industrial society with low productivity and zero growth rates into a society with high productivity and increased growth. Between 1780 and 1840 the British economy changed significantly. There was a shift from domestic production for immediate use to mass consumer goods production for exchange, and from simple, family-centred production to a strict impersonal division of labour deploying capital equipment. The population trebled and the value of economic activity quadrupled (Hobsbawm, 1969). Changes also occurred in personal, social and political life: for example, alterations in working habits, time organization, family life, leisure activity, housing and the shift from rural to urban living.

Surveillance

The emergence of an industrial labour process included an increase in the size and division of labour, mechanization and the intensification of work. The workshop and factory were utilized as a means of exerting discipline and the creation of new work habits (Thompson and McHugh, 1990). That is, they marked new forms of surveillance. As Giddens puts it, 'who says modernity says not just organizations, but organization – the regularized control of social relations across indefinite time-space distances' (Giddens, 1990: 91).

Surveillance refers to the collection, storage and retrieval of information. The concept also covers direct supervision of activities and the use of information to monitor subject populations. Modernity did not invent surveillance *per se*. However, it introduced new and more complex and extensive forms of surveillance. These included shifts from personal to impersonal control. Thus, bureaucratization, rationalization and professionalization form the core institutional configurations of modernity (Dandeker, 1990).

The dynamism of capitalist modernity

The industrial organizations of modernity have been organized along capitalist lines. In the *Communist Manifesto*, first published in 1848, Marx characterized the processes of enquiry and innovation which marked capitalist modernity as the

> Subjection of nature's forces to man, machinery, application of chemistry to industry and agriculture, steam navigation, railways, electric telegraphs, clearing of whole continents for cultivation, canalisation of rivers, whole populations conjured out of the ground – what earlier century had even a presentiment that such productive powers slumbered in the womb of social labour? (Marx and Engels, 1967: 12)

The productive dynamism of capitalism spawned not just coal but nuclear power, not just trains but rockets, not just filing cabinets but computers and e-mail. Capitalism is restless in its search for new markets, new raw materials, new sources of profit and capital accumulation. It is inherently globalizing. Today the economies of all countries are integrated into the world capitalist economic order (Wallerstein, 1974).

The dynamism of modernity is such that it spreads out from its European base to encompass the globe. The western originating institutions of modernity are dynamic and globalizing because, as Giddens writes,

> The dynamism of modernity derives from the separation of time and space and their recombination in forms which permit the precise time-space 'zoning' of social life; the disembedding of social systems (a phenomena which connects closely with the factors involved in time-space separation); and the reflexive ordering and reordering of social relations in the light of continual inputs of knowledge affecting the actions of individuals and groups. (Giddens, 1990: 16–17)

Modernity fosters relations between 'absent' others. Transactions are conducted across time and space. Consequently, any given place is penetrated and shaped by social influences quite distant from it; that is, the disembedding or 'lifting out' of social relations from a local context and their restructuring across time and space. Giddens cites in particular symbolic tokens (e.g. money) and expert systems. Thus the development of money and professional knowledge allows social relations to be stretched (or distanciated) across time and space.

Modern life involves the constant examination and alteration of social practices in the light of incoming information about those practices. This reflexivity involves the use of knowledge about social life as a constitutive element of it. That is, reflexivity refers to the constant revision of social activity in the light of new knowledge; for example, the collection of statistical information about populations by governments and commerce in order to facilitate planning and marketing.

The nation-state and military power

Today we understand the world as divided into discrete nation-states. However, the nation-state is a relatively recent modern contrivance. Most of the human beings who have walked the earth did not participate in or identify with state machinery. The modern nation-state is a container of power constituted by a political apparatus recognized to have sovereign rights within the borders of a demarcated territorial area. It possesses the ability to back these claims with military power. The discourse of nationalism is a global one and nation-states emerged in relation to each other. Thus we may speak of a worldwide nation-state system (Giddens, 1985).

Nations are not just political formations. Thay are also systems of cultural representation by which national identity is continually reproduced through discursive action. National identity is a form of imaginative identification with the nation-state. This is expressed through symbols and discourses that narrate and create the idea of origins, continuity and tradition (Bhabha, 1990; Hall, 1992b).

The state specializes in the maintenance of order through the rule of law. To a considerable degree this is achieved through a monopoly of legitimate violence. Modern warfare has been underpinned by:

- **state military power;**

- **political ambition;**

- **emotional investments in national identity.**

As Giddens (1985) argues, wars are now fought with industrialized, i.e. modern, armies whose soldiers are trained, disciplined and bureaucratized. Arms supplies are produced in factories owned by capitalist corporations who engage in international arms trading.

MODERNISM AND CULTURE

The processes by which industrialism, capitalism, surveillance and the nation-state emerged we may call 'modernization'. 'Modernism' refers to the human cultural forms bound up with this modernization (Berman, 1982). Here we are concerned with modernism as a cultural experience or 'structure of feeling' (Williams, 1981).

Modernism as a cultural experience

✓ *Cultural modernism is an experience in which 'All that is solid melts into air'. This phrase, coined by Marx, suggests change, uncertainty and risk.*

Thus, industry, technology and communications systems transformed the human world and continue to do so at a breathless pace. Such transformations hold out the promise of an end to material scarcity. However, they also carry a 'darker side'. For example, electronics are the basis of modern information technologies. They are at the heart of global wealth production, communications networks and personalized information and entertainment systems. However, they are also the foundations of modern weapons systems and surveillance techniques from ICBMs to high-street CCTV.

To be modern is to find ourselves in an environment that promises us adventure, power, joy, growth, transformation of ourselves and our world – and at the same time, that threatens to destroy everything we have, everything we know, everything we are. (Berman, 1982: 15)

Risk, doubt and reflexivity

Modernists have typically displayed an optimistic faith in the power of science, rationality and industry to transform our world for the better. Not that modernism is a culture of certainty. On the contrary, the very dynamism of modernity is premised on the perpetual revision of knowledge. Modern institutions are based on the principle of doubt. All knowledge is formed as a hypothesis open to revision (Giddens, 1990, 1991). Indeed, Giddens (1994) sees modernism as a 'risk culture'. This does not, he argues, mean that modern life is inherently more risky as such. Rather, it is a reference to the way in which risk calculations play a central part in the strategic thinking of both institutions and the lives of ordinary people.

The markers of cultural modernism are:

- **ambiguity;**
- **doubt;**
- **risk;**
- **continual change.**

Indeed, these qualities are manifested in the very constitution of the modern self. 'Tradition' values stability and the place of persons in a normatively ordered and immutable cosmos. Here there is a firmness of parameters in which things are as they are because that is how they should be. By contrast, modernism values change, life planning and reflexivity. In the context of tradition, self-identity is primarily a question of social position. For the modern person, it is a 'reflexive project', that is, 'the process whereby self-identity is constituted by the reflexive ordering of self-narratives' (Giddens, 1991: 244).

By 'identity project' is meant the idea that identity is not fixed but created and built on. It is always in process, a moving towards rather than an arrival. For modernism, the self is a question not of surface appearance but of the workings of deeper structures. Consequently, metaphors of *depth* predominate. This is manifested by the ideas and concepts of psychoanalysis (including, of course, the unconscious).

Faust is one of the emblematic modern figures. This is because he was determined to *make himself* and his world even at the cost of a deal with the Devil. According to Harvey, Faust can be regarded as the literary archetype of the dilemma of modern development, that is, the interplay of creation and destruction. Faust is:

An epic hero prepared to destroy religious myths, traditional values and customary ways of life in order to build a brave new world out of the ashes of the old, Faust is, in the end, a tragic figure. Synthesizing thought and action, Faust forces himself and everyone else (even Mephistopheles) to extremes of organization, pain, and exhaustion in order to master nature and create a new landscape, a sublime spiritual achievement that contains the potentiality for human liberation from want and need. (Harvey, 1989: 16)

The *flâneur*

Another crucial figure of modernism is Baudelaire's *flâneur*. A *flâneur*, or stroller, walks the anonymous spaces of the modern city experiencing the complexity, disturbances and confusions of the streets with their shops, displays, images and variety of persons. This perspective emphasizes the *urban* character of modernism. For Baudelaire, writing of the alienated artist in 1863, the *flâneur* was one of the heroes of modern life (Baudelaire, 1964). He took in the fleeting beauty and vivid, if transitory, impressions of the crowds, seeing everything anew in its immediacy. Yet this was achieved with a certain detachment.

The *flâneur* was urban, contemporary and stylish. These are themes that are pursued by Simmel (1978) in relation to the modern concern with fashion. For Simmel, fashion represents a balancing act between individuation and absorption into the collective. It is marked as peculiarly modern by its rapid change and plurality of styles. These form a blueprint for the stylization of the self as a project. As Featherstone comments, this

directs us towards the way in which the urban landscape has become aestheticized and enchanted through architecture, billboards, shop displays, advertisements, packages, street signs, etc., and through the embodied persons who move through these spaces: the individuals who wear, to varying degrees, fashionable clothing, hair styles, make-up, or who move, or hold their bodies, in particular stylized ways. (Featherstone, 1991: 76)

The dark side of modernity

The self-image of modernism is one of:

- **continual excitement;**
- **the promise of technological and social progress;**
- **the etching away of tradition in favour of the new;**
- **urban development;**
- **the unfolding of the self.**

However, just as Faust was a troubled, destructive and tragic figure, so modernity is marked by:

- the poverty and squalor of industrial cities;

- two destructive world wars;

- death camps;

- the threat of global annihilation.

Simmel (1978) argued that, while, on the one hand, individual liberty increased, people have also been obliged to submit to a rigorous discipline and urban anonymity. This was a theme pursued by Weber (1948, 1978), whose views on the development of modern bureaucracy summed up his deep ambivalence towards the modern world.

For Weber, the march of bureaucracy was an aspect of the spread of secular rationality and rational decision-making procedures. These were based on calculability, rules and expert knowledge. These developments were bound up with the 'disenchantment' of the world in favour of economic and technical progress. The Weberian version of bureaucracy stresses impersonality, the allocation of functions, rule systems and the processes of documentation. A bureaucracy is constituted by a framework of rule-governed and ordered activities that continue irrespective of individuals and independently of their personal characteristics. The system relies on fixed and official jurisdictional areas supervised by a stable authority. Weber was convinced of the inexorable advance of bureaucracy; its rationality and efficiency as well as its encroachments on individual self-expression. Bureaucracy was the 'iron cage' of material 'progress'.

In sum, modernism as a 'structure of feeling' involves pace, change, ambiguity, risk, doubt and the chronic revision of knowledge. These are underpinned by the social and cultural processes of:

- individualization;

- differentiation;

- commodification;

- urbanization;

- rationalization;

- bureaucratization.

— Define each of the terms above.
— Give specific examples of the way in which they are associated with the rise of modern culture.

Modernism as aesthetic style

The concept of modernism also carries a narrower focus on the aesthetic forms associ-ated with artistic movements dating from the nineteenth century. Key modernist figures include Joyce, Woolf, Kafka and Eliot in literature, along with Picasso, Kandinsky and Miró in painting. It would be better to talk of modernism*s* rather than modernism. However, the general themes of artistic modernism include:

- aesthetic self-consciousness;

- an interest in language and questions of representation;

- a rejection of realism in favour of an exploration of the uncertain character of the 'real';

- a jettisoning of linear narrative structures in favour of montage and simultaneity;

- an emphasis on the value of aesthetic experience drawn from romanticism;

- an acceptance of the idea of depth and universal mythic-poetic meaning;

- the exploration and exploitation of fragmentation;

- the value and role of avant-garde high culture.

Modernism rejects the idea that it is possible to represent the 'real' in any straightforward manner. Representation is not an act of mimesis or copying of the real. Rather, it is to be understood as an aesthetic expression or conventionalized construction of the 'real'. In the context of an uncertain and changing world, modernist literature saw its task as finding the means of expression with which to capture the 'deep reality' of the world. Hence the concern with aesthetic self-consciousness, that is, an awareness of the place of form, and particularly language, in the construction of meaning. This is manifested in the experi-mental approach to aesthetic style characteristic of modernist work that seeks to express depth through fragmentation.

The problems of realism

Modernism accepts the meaningfulness of a reality that lies beneath or beyond appear-ance. Consequently, it dispenses with the idea of naturalism/realism as a form that unproblematically represents the real. For modernists, the problem with realism is that it purports to 'show things as they really are' rather than acknowledging its own status as an artifice. Further, the narrative structures of realism are organized by a 'metalanguage' of truth that privileges and disguises the editorial position rather than letting different dis-courses 'speak for themselves' and compete for allegiance (MacCabe, 1981).

Modernists require practices that reveal their own techniques and allow for reflection upon the very processes of signification. Thus, modernism's stories do not follow the established conventions of linear causality or the 'ordinary' flow of everyday time. If any one style can be said to encapsulate modernism, it is the use of *montage*; that is, the selection and assemblage of shots or representations to form a composite of jutaxposed ideas and images. This montage is not 'held together' by realist notions of time and motivation.

According to the pioneering filmmaker Eisenstein, 'while the conventional film directs emotion, intellectual montage suggest an opportunity to direct whole thought processes as well' (Eisenstein, 1951: 62). Eisenstein's techniques do not aim to conceal cinema's methods. Instead he uses the moment of the edit to create an intellectual collision between juxtaposed ideas and images that are symbolic in character. For Jean-Luc Godard, montage is used to explore the fragmented multiple discourses of the real. He encourages audiences to examine the very process by which meaning is constructed.

CASA BATILO

© Photographer: Freya Hadley

This is a picture of Casa Batilo in Barcelona, Spain, which was designed by Antonio Gaudí (1852–1926). It is in the style of Catalan Modernisme or Art Nouveau.

- *Although not strictly part of the modernist movement, the design shares features with modernism. What are they?*

- *The design also seems to prefigure features of postmodernism. Can you suggest what they might be?*

Fragmentation and the universal

Modernism incorporates the tensions between on the one hand, fragmentation, instability and the ephemeral and, on the other hand, a concern for depth, meaning and universalism. Modernist writers have commonly rejected universalism founded on God. Nevertheless, they have propounded the universals of a humanism grounded in mythic-poetic narratives (which Art has the function of uncovering and constructing). Art replaces God as the foundational narrative of human existence. For example, Joyce's *Ulysses* is regarded as the archetype of high modernist novels because of its stream of consciousness, non-realist, narrative style. Through this style, Joyce attempts to represent the real in new ways, using language to capture the fragmented character of the self. Joyce would have agreed with Nietzsche that 'God is dead', and that there can be no cosmic universals. However, he does offer us a sense that Art can draw on, and reconfigure, universal mythic-poetic meanings. Thus, a day in the life of one Dubliner is framed in terms of the universalist Ulysses of Greek myth.

The cultural politics of modernism

One route to understanding modernism as a form of cultural politics is to explore the debates about form in the work of Lukács (1972, 1977), Adorno (1977; Adorno and Horkheimer, 1979) and Brecht (1964, 1977). Lukács opposes modernism on the grounds that its concern with fragmentation, alienation and angst merely reflects the surface appearance of the world. Modernism represents for Lukács a retreat into the subjective world of angst in which the exterior world is an unchangeable horror (e.g. Kafka). Lukács charges modernism with formalism, that is, an obsession with form lacking significant content. Instead, he champions a realism which, he argues, goes beyond the world of appearance to express the true nature of reality, its underlying trends, characteristics and structures.

Adorno (1977) was influenced by the work of Lukács. However, he takes up a position diametrically opposed to him. For Adorno, the modernist works of Kafka, Beckett and Schoenberg are amongst the most radical of art forms. They 'arouse the fear that existentialism merely talks about'. Modernism is said to highlight the alienating features of capitalism. Further, it engenders a critical activity on the part of audiences. In particular, it is the form taken by modernist art that allows it to stand as a beacon of hope and a symbol of non-accommodation. This 'negativity' lies in its refusal to be incorporated by the dominant language of contemporary culture.

Brecht complicates the distinction between modernism and realism. He takes up the 'demystifying' purposes Lukács attributes to realism ('discovering the causal complexes of society'), while allying them to modernist techniques. Brecht argues that, since reality changes, so the political purposes of realism have to be expressed through new, modern forms. Brecht is laying claim to be the new, true and popular realist by using modernist forms. He is associated with the 'alienation device', for example:

- addressing the audience directly;
- staging singing spectacles;
- alluding to the constructed characteristics of plays.

These techniques aim to change the relationship between the stage and the audience so that the latter are led to reflect on meaning and the processes of signification.

Modernisms

The Lukács–Adorno–Brecht debates highlight the need to talk about modernism*s* rather than modernism. Any concept that can put Joyce, Kafka, Picasso and Brecht all in the same basket is operating at a high level of generality. However, we may say that modernism makes the whole idea of representation problematic. It deploys non-linear, non-realist modes while retaining the idea of the real. Modernism rejects metaphysical foundations. Nevertheless, it replaces them with narratives of progress and enlightenment which Art functions to illuminate. By Art is meant the work of a high culture demanding reflection and engagement from its audience. Thus, modernism retains the distinction between good and bad art, between popular culture and high culture. Whatever the differences between Lukács, Adorno, Brecht, Godard, Joyce and Eisentein, they do share the modern conception that the world is knowable and that true knowledge of it is possible. Indeed, the single biggest divide between modernism and postmodernism is their respective conceptualizations of truth and knowledge, that is, questions of epistemology.

MODERN AND POSTMODERN KNOWLEDGE

Modernity has been associated with an emancipatory project through which enlightenment reason would lead to certain and universal truths. This would lay the foundations for humanity's forward path of progress. That is, enlightenment philosophy and the theoretical discourses of modernity have championed 'Reason' as the source of progress in knowledge and society.

The enlightenment project

Enlightenment thought is marked by its belief that Reason can demystify and illuminate the world over and against religion, myth and superstition. For enlightenment thinkers, human creativity, rationality and scientific exploration mark the break with tradition that modernity heralds. The moral-political agenda of the 'project of modernity' is best encapsulated in the French Revolutionary slogan 'Equality, Liberty, Fraternity'.

✓ *In both its scientific project and its moral-political project, enlightenment philosophy sought universal truths. That is, knowledge and moral principles that applied across time, space and cultural difference.*

Enlightenment philosophy can be explored through the writings of key eighteenth-century philosophers like Voltaire, Rousseau and Hume. However, two much later and apparently contradictory streams of thought are explored here to illustrate the practical implications of enlightenment epistemology, that is, *Taylorism* and *Marxism*.

Scientific management

F.W. Taylor developed his ideas during the late 1880s and published his *Principles of Scientific Management* in 1911. He claims, on the basis of scientific knowledge, to provide the *one* best way of organizing production processes to achieve efficiency. We may summarize Taylor's main arguments thus:

- **the organization of the division of labour to allow for separation of tasks and functions;**
- **the use of time and motion studies to measure and describe work tasks;**
- **the prescription of tasks to workers in minute degrees;**
- **the use of incentive schemes and money as motivation;**
- **the importance of management in planning and control.**

The organization of production along Taylorist lines was manifested in the standardization and mechanization of factory assembly lines, for example those associated with the early days of the Ford motor company. However, the influence of Taylorism has spread much further afield than the factory. It can be seen in managerial control strategies of service industries, education systems, state administration and even mass party politics. For Braverman (1974), Taylorism is best explored as an ideology of management and control. In modified forms, it became the orthodox doctrine of technical control in both western capitalism and Soviet communism.

In short, Taylorism encapsluates that which Habermas (1972) calls the 'instrumental rationality' underpinning domination. That is, Taylorism puts the logic of rationality and science to work in the service of the regulation, control and domination of human beings. While promising material benefits, Taylorism expresses a 'dark side' of enlightenment thought.

Marxism as enlightenment philosophy

Braverman and Habermas draw considerable intellectual resources from Marxism, which can also be regarded as a child of enlightenment thought. For Marx (Chapter 1), in producing the means of subsistence through labour, 'man [*sic*] opposes himself to nature', and by 'acting on the external world and changing it, he at the same time changes his own nature' (Marx, 1961: 102). Labour is socially organized into a *mode of production* understood in terms of:

- **the organization of the means of production (factories, machinery, etc.);**
- **the specific social relations of reproduction that arise from it.**

Capitalism is a system of production premised upon the private ownership and control of the means of production. It is because of their ownership of the means of production that the bourgeoisie are able to extract from the proletariat a quantity of 'surplus value' which they appropriate. The proletariat are separated from the means of production and from the products of their own labour. Though labour epitomizes the human potential to be creative, it has become 'alien' through its subordination to capital accumulation. Thus capitalism engenders class conflict and sows the seeds of its own destruction. It is the proletariat's historical role to overthrow capitalism and in doing so liberate all people. It does this by bringing into being a new society based on need rather than exploitation. That is, capitalism is supplanted by socialist and communist modes of production.

The stress on scientific thought, historical progress, human creativity and the emancipatory role of the proletariat makes Marxism a form of enlightenment thought. However, for Habermas (1972, 1987), it differs from Taylorism in being not so much instrumental rationality as *critical* rationality. That is, Marxism deploys the logic of rationality in the service of critiquing capitalism and liberating human beings from exploitation and oppression. Nevertheless, it can be argued that Marxism also contains the 'dark side' of enlightenment thinking. Marxism continues the form of rationality by which humans seek to conquer and control nature. Thus, Adorno accused Marx of wanting to turn the whole world into a factory through the continual expansion of our productive capacities.

Scientific laws and the principle of doubt

One reading of Marx posits human history as the unfolding of an inevitable developmental logic leading from feudalism to communism. History in this sense has its own *telos*, or inevitable point to which it is moving. History is governed by the *laws* of human evolution and progress. This mechanical reading of Marxism underpins the idea of a vanguard party (the Leninist communist party) that has true knowledge of history. Consequently, the Party 'knows best' how to guide us. In other words, the seeds of Soviet totalitarianism are inherent in the epistemological base of Marxism as a philosophy of history.

In this sense, Taylorism and Marxism share a common epistemology based on the enlightenment principles of science and true knowledge. The idea that there could be 'laws of history' is a manifestation of the scientism of Marxism, that is, its wish to emulate the (alleged) scientific certainty of physics and chemistry. The confidence of modern science allows it to hail itself as 'progress', symbolized by medicine, despite the now constant threat of nuclear annihilation.

Yet modernism is ambiguous for it is far from clear that science does proceed through laws of certainty. For example:

- **Science proceeds through experimentation and the principle of falsification (Popper, 1959).**

- **Science periodically overthrows its own paradigms (Kuhn, 1962).**

- **The Einsteinian paradigm that currently predominates is one of relativity.**

Hence, Giddens (1991) regards modern science as premised on the methodological principle of doubt and the chronic revision of knowledge. Enlightenment science may have begun with the search for certain laws but is now beset with doubt and chaos.

Enlightenment thought in its many manifestations promises increased levels of material production and the abolition of want and suffering. It promotes the development of medicine, universal education, political freedom and social equality. However, the dark side of modernity is regarded by some thinkers as not merely an aberration or side-effect of enlightenment thinking but as inherent in it. Thinkers as diverse as Adorno, Nietzsche, Foucault, Lyotard and Baudrillard have criticized the impulses of modernity for heralding not progress but domination and oppression. The modern world is seen as having to give a rational account of everything – 'interrogating everything', as Foucault describes it. In this characterization, Reason leads not to alleviation of material needs or philosophical enlightenment but to control and destruction. Reason can, at the very least, be argued to have turned out to be selective and unbalanced.

The critique of the enlightenment

In their *Dialectic of Enlightenment*, Adorno and Horkheimer (1979) argue that enlightenment rationality is a logic of domination and oppression. The very impulse to control nature through science and rationality is, they argue, an impulse to control and dominate human beings. In this view, enlightenment thinking is inherently an instrumental rationality. Its logic leads not only to industrialization but also to the concentration camps of Auschwitz and Belsen. Adorno and Horkheimer characterize enlightenment thinking as positing an 'identity' between thought and its objects that seeks to capture and subsume all that is different from itself. They regard enlightenment reason as turning rationality into irrationality and deception as it eliminates competing ways of thinking and claims itself as the sole basis for truth.

> In their [Adorno and Horkheimer's] interpretation, a synthesis of instrumental rationality and capitalism employed sophisticated modes of mass communication and culture, a bureaucratized and rationalized state apparatus, and science and technology to administer consciousness and needs to ensure social integration so that the individual would act in conformity with the system's dictates. (Best and Kellner, 1991: 218)

Foucault

Adorno and Horkheimer's critique of enlightenment thought remains pertinent. However, the work of Foucault has been more influential within cultural studies.

Nietszche: truth as a mobile army of metaphors   Foucault is indebted to the philosopher Nietzsche, for whom knowledge is a form of the 'will to power'. The idea of a pure knowledge is impermissible because reason and truth are 'nothing more than the expediency of a certain race and species – their utility alone is their truth' (Nietzsche, 1967: §515). Nietzsche characterizes truth as a 'mobile army of metaphors and metonyms'. That is, sentences are the only things that can be true or false. Knowledge is not a question of true discovery but of the construction of interpretations about the world that are taken to be true.

For Nietzsche, the truth is not a collection of facts. There can be only interpretations and there is 'no limit to the ways in which the world can be interpreted'. In so far as the idea of truth has a historical purchase, it is the consequence of power, that is, of whose interpretations count as truth. Consequently, Nietzsche rejects the enlightenment philosophy of universal reason and progress.

Foucault's archaeology   Foucault's early work deploys a methodological approach described as archaeology. By this he means the exploration of the specific and determinate historical conditions under which statements are combined and regulated to form and define a distinct field of knowledge/objects. This domain of knowledge requires a particular set of concepts that delimit a specific 'regime of truth' (i.e. what counts as truth). Foucault attempts to identify the historical conditions and determing rules of formation of regulated ways of speaking about objects, that is, discursive practices and discursive formations.

Foucault (1972, 1973) argues that in the transition from one historical era to another, the social world is no longer perceived, described, classified and known in the same way. That is, discourse is *discontinuous*. It is marked by historical breaks in understanding, changes in the way objects are conceptualized and understood. Different historical eras are marked by different *epistemes*, or configurations of knowledge, that shape the social practices and social order of particular historical periods. For example, Foucault points to a rupture in the historical understanding of madness. Thus, modern reason breaks off any dialogue with madness and seeks to set up oppositions between madness and reason, the sane and the insane. In this view, history is not to be explained in terms of connections across historical periods (though breaks are never complete and are to be understood on the basis of that which already exists). Nor should it be understood in terms of the inevitable movement of history from locatable origins towards a predetermined destiny. Foucault's stress on discontinuity is an aspect of his questioning of the modern themes of genesis, teleology, continuity, totality and unified subjects.

Foucault's genealogy   Archaeology suggests excavation of the past in one specific site. Genealogy (Foucault's name for his later approach) takes the form of tracing the historical continuities and discontinuities of discourse. Here Foucault emphasizes the material and institutional conditions of discourse and the operations of power. Archaeology digs up the local sites of discursive practice. Genealogy examines the way in which discourse develops and is brought into play under specific and irreducible historical conditions through the operations of power.

> '[A]rchaeology' would be the appropriate method of the analysis of local discursivities, and 'genealogy' would be the tactics whereby on the basis of the descriptions of these local discursivities, the subjected knowledges which were released would be brought into play. (Foucault, 1980: 85)

> [Genealogy] must record the singularity of events outside of any monotonous finality ... it must be sensitive to their recurrence, not in order to trace the gradual curve of their evolution, but to isolate the different scenes where they engage in different roles ... it depends on a vast accumulation of source material. (Foucault, 1984a: 76)

Foucault's genealogical studies examine prisons, schools and hospitals in order to show the operations of power and discipline. They concentrate on the formation and use of knowledge, including the construction of the subject as an 'effect' of discourse (Chapter 7). Foucault argued that discourse regulates not only what can be said under determinate social and cultural conditions but also who can speak, when and where. Specifically, the 'regimes of truth' of modernity involve relations of power/knowledge whereby knowledge is a form of power implicated in the production of subjectivity. Crucially, Foucault argues that:

> criticism is no longer going to be practised in the search for formal structures with universal value, but rather as a historical investigation into the events that have led us to constitute ourselves and to recognize ourselves as subjects of what we are doing, thinking, saying. In that sense, this criticism is not transcendental, and its goal is not that of making a metaphysics possible: it is genealogical in its design and archaeological in its method. Archaeological – and not transcendental – in the sense that it will not seek to identify the universal structures of all knowledge or all possible moral action, but will seek to treat the instances of discourse that articulate what we think, say, and do as so

many historical events. And this critique will be genealogical in the sense that it will not deduce from the form of what we are what is impossible for us to do and know; but it will separate out, from the contingency that has made us what we are, the possibility of no longer being, doing, or thinking what we are, do, or think. (Foucault, 1984b: 45–6)

KEY THINKERS

Michel Foucault (1926–84)

Foucault is a major figure in French philosophy whose work has been influential in cultural studies. He is associated with the ideas of poststructuralism. Foucault explored the discursive practices that exert power over human bodies but without any commitment to an underlying structural order or finally determinate power. Foucault attempts to identify the historical conditions and determining rules of the formation of discourses and their operation in social practice. Much of Foucault's work is concerned with the historical investigation of power as a dispersed capillary woven into the fabric of the social order that is not simply repressive but also productive.

Reading: Foucault, M. (1979) *The History of Sexuality Vol. 1: The Will to Truth*. London: Allen Lane.

Breaking with the enlightenment   Foucault's thinking breaks with the premises of 'classical' enlightenment thought in five key ways:

1   Knowledge is not metaphysical, transcendental or universal. Rather, it is specific to particular times and spaces. Foucault talks not of truth *per se*, but of 'regimes of truth', that is, the configurations of knowledge that 'count as truth' under determinate historical conditions.

2   Knowledge is perspectival in character. There can be no one totalizing knowledge that is able to grasp the 'objective' character of the world. Rather, we both have and require multiple viewpoints or truths by which to interpret a complex, heterogeneous human existence.

3   Knowledge is not regarded as a pure or neutral way of understanding. It is implicated in regimes of power.

4   Foucault breaks with the central enlightenment metaphor of 'depth'. He argues against interpretative or hermeneutic methods that seek to disclose the hidden meanings of language. Foucault is concerned with the description and analysis

of the surfaces of discourse and their effects under determinate material and historical conditions.

5 Foucault casts doubt on the enlightenment understanding of progress. Knowledge as discourse does not unfold as an even historical evolution but is discontinuous. That is, Foucault identifies significant epistemological breaks in knowledge across time. He rejects any notion of *telos* or the inevitable direction of human history.

However, the idea that there is a clear, distinctive and final break between enlightenment and post-enlightenment thought, or between the modern and postmodern, is challenged by Foucault. He suggests that we do not have to be 'for' or 'against' the enlightenment. It is a question not of accepting or rejecting enlightenment rationality but of asking:

> What is this reason that we use? What are its historical effects? What are its limits, and what are its dangers? [If] philosophy has a function within critical thought, it is precisely to accept this sort of spiral, this sort of revolving door of rationality that refers us to its necessity, to its indispensability, and at the same time to its intrinsic dangers. (Foucault, 1984c: 249)

Postmodernism as the end of grand narratives

Foucault did not designate himself a postmodern thinker. However, other writers, most notably Lyotard, have embraced the perspectival conception of knowledge and the term 'postmodern' with greater alacrity. Lyotard argues that 'there is no unity of language, but rather islets of language, each governed by a system of rules untranslatable into those of others' (Lyotard, 1984: 61). Truth and meaning are constituted by their place in specific local language-games and cannot be universal in character. For Lyotard, the postmodern condition is not a periodizing concept, that is, the postmodern is not a historical epoch. Nor does the concept refer to the institutional parameters of modernity and postmodernity. Rather, it is

> the condition of knowledge in the most highly developed societies. I have decided to use the word postmodern to describe that condition. … it designates the state of our culture following the transformations which, since the end of the nineteenth century, have altered the rules for science, literature, and the arts. (Lyotard, 1984: xxiii)

For Lyotard, modern knowledge rests on its appeal to metanarratives, that is, grand historical stories which claim universal validity. By contrast, the postmodern, in arguing that knowledge is specific to language-games, embraces local, plural and heterogeneous knowledge*s*. The postmodern condition involves a loss of faith in the foundational schemes that have justified the rational, scientific, technological and political projects of the modern world. This is what Lyotard describes as 'incredulity toward metanarratives'.

By this he means that there remain no viable metanarratives (or elevated standpoints) from which to judge the universal truth of anything. For Lyotard, we should resist the totalizing terror of such dogmas in favour of the celebration of difference and understandings located within particular knowledge regimes.

Explain in your own words what is meant by the phrase 'incredulity toward metanarratives'.

Examples of grand narrative might be:

* Marxism;
* Science;
* Christianity.

— What features do they have in common that make them 'metanarratives'?

The end of epistemology

✓ *For postmodernism, no universalizing epistemology is possible because all truth claims are formed within discourse. There are no universal philosophical foundations for human thought or action. All truth is culture-bound.*

This is so because there can be no access to an independent object world free from language. There is no Archimedean vantage point from which to evaluate claims neutrally. Indeed, Rorty suggests that the concept of truth has no explanatory power. The notion of truth refers at best to a degree of social agreement within a particular tradition. Rorty recommends that we abandon epistemology, recognizing 'truth' as a form of social commendation (Rorty, 1989, 1991a) – a condition that Foucault described as 'being-in-the-true'.

Gergen (1994) agrees that no epistemological position is able to give universal grounding for its own truth claims. This includes modern science and postmodernism. However, he argues that the consequences of adopting a modern or postmodern epistemology are different. According to Gergen, modern truth claims are universalizing: they assert their truths for all people in all places. This has potentially disastrous disciplining consequences in which the bearers of 'truth' know best. In contrast, Gergen suggests that the consequence of saying that truths are only truths within specific language-games is to accept the legitimacy of a range of truth claims, discourses and representations of 'reality'.

Relativism or positionality?

For some commentators, postmodernism is held to be a form of relativism. That is, truth claims are said to be of equal epistemological status. Consequently, we are unable to make judgements between forms of knowledge. Gergen embraces the term 'relativism', arguing that truth is/should be an outcome of debates between competing claims. Rorty rejects relativism as self-contradictory in favour of the culturally specific character of truth, that which cultural studies would call *positionality*. He argues that there is no standpoint from which one can see across different forms of knowledge and regard them of equal value. Rather, we are always positioned within acculturalized knowledge, so that the true and the good are what we believe. For Rorty, the true and the good are judged in terms of pragmatism, that is, the consequences of adopting certain kinds of understanding. Such judgements can only be made by reference to our *values* and not to a transcendental truth. For example, science does not generate universal truths about the world. Rather, through a set of pragmatic procedures, it produces forms of knowledge that allow us to predict and control our environments to a greater degree with more or less desirable consequences.

—   How does a modern project like the physical sciences describe truth?
—   What does it mean to describe truth as a mobile army of metaphors?
—   What are the implications of a postmodern understanding of truth for science?

THE PROMISE OF POSTMODERNISM (OR MODERNITY AS AN UNFINISHED PROJECT?)

For Bauman (1991), postmodernism has the potential to give voice to a liberatory politics of difference, diversity and solidarity. He argues that the condition of postmodernity is the modern mind reflecting upon itself from a distance and sensing the urge to change. The uncertainty, ambivalence and ambiguity of the postmodern condition, argues Bauman, open up the possibility of grasping contingency as destiny. In this way we may create our own futures. To do so we must transform tolerance into solidarity,

> not just as a matter of moral perfection, but a condition of survival. ... Survival in the world of contingency and diversity is possible only if each difference recognizes another difference as the necessary condition of the preservation of its own. Solidarity, unlike tolerance, its weaker version, means a readiness to fight; and joining the battle for the sake of the other's difference, not one's own. Tolerance is ego-centred and contemplative; solidarity is socially oriented and militant. (Bauman, 1991: 256)

Politics without foundations

There are no guarantees or universal foundations for such a project. It remains only a possibility inherent in postmodern culture. As Bauman argues, liberty remains truncated, diversity thrives only in so far as the market drives it, tolerance slips into indifference and consumers replace citizens. Yet, he suggests, postmodern culture implies the need for politics, democracy, full-blown citizenship and the potential withdrawal of consent from the political edifice of the state. The postmodern mentality demands that modernity fulfil the promises of its, albeit distorted, reason.

Critics of postmodernism fear that the abandonment of foundationalism leads to irrationalism and the inability to ground any radical politics. Yet the legitimacy of a range of truth claims is in itself a political position for it signals support for pragmatic postmodern cultural pluralism. Thus, we do not require universal validations and foundations to pursue a pragmatic improvement of the human condition. We can do this on the basis of the values of our own tradition (Laclau and Mouffe, 1985; Rorty, 1991a).

These are themes of the politics of difference (Chapter 14). This is a long-term coalition cultural politics conducted in civil society, that is, clubs, pubs, schools, factories and of course the media, aimed at winning minds and changing legislation. It can be seen in terms of the politics of race, of feminism, and of queer politics, amongst others.

Modernity as an unfinished project

Postmodern 'epistemology' has not gone unchallenged. The doubt and uncertainty that characterize contemporary knowledge are seen by Giddens (1990, 1991) as the condition not of postmodernity but of a 'radicalized modernity'. In his view, relativity, uncertainty, doubt and risk are core characteristics of late or high modernity. Similarly, Habermas (1987, 1989) sees the political project of modernity as ongoing. The basis of his argument is the distinction he makes between 'instrumental reason' and 'critical reason'. He is censorious of enlightenment reason for the instrumentality by which the 'lifeworld' is colonized by 'system imperatives'; that is, the subordination of social-existential questions to money and administrative power. In this sense, Habermas views Reason as unbalanced and selective. However, the enlightenment also has a critical side, which for him is the basis of an emancipatory project which remains unfinished.

Habermas works within the tradition of critical theory. He has sought universal grounds for the validation of evaluative judgement and claims to human emancipation. He does so by arguing that all human interaction presupposes language. In the structure of speech we may find the essential grounding conditions for all forms of social organization. When we speak, suggests Habermas, we are making four validity claims:

1 **to comprehensibility;**

2 **to truth;**

3 **to appropriateness;**

4 **to sincerity.**

These claims, he argues, imply both the logical justification of truth and the social context for their rational debate. The conditions for this Habermas labels as an 'ideal speech situation'. Here competing truth claims are subject to rational debate and argument. In an 'ideal speech situation', truth is not subject to the vested interests and power plays of truth-seekers. Rather, it emerges through the process of argumentation.

The public sphere

For Habermas, our very ability to make truth claims is dependent on a democratically organized public sphere which approximates an 'ideal speech situation'. The notion of a public sphere is traced historically by Habermas as a realm that emerged in a specific phase of 'bourgeois society'. It is a space that mediates between society and the state where the public organizes itself and where 'public opinion' is formed. Habermas describes the rise of literary clubs and salons, newspapers, political journals and institutions of political debate and participation in the eighteenth century. This public sphere was partially protected from both the church and the state by the resources of private individuals. It was in principle, though not in practice, open to all. Within this sphere individuals were able to develop themselves and engage in rational debate about the direction of society.

Habermas goes on to document the decline of the public sphere. This has happened as a consequence of the development of capitalism towards monopoly and the strengthening of the state. For example, the increased commodification of everyday life by giant corporations transforms people from rational citizens to consumers. Of particular concern are the non-rational products of the advertising and public relations industries. In a parallel erosion of the public sphere, the state has taken increased power over our lives. In the economic realm it has acted as a corporate manager, and in the private realm as the manager of welfare provision and education.

The concept of the public sphere in the work of Habermas is a philosophical, historical and normative one. On the historical level there has been considerable criticism of the historical accuracy of the concept (Curran, 1991) and of the male gender bias of the bourgeois public sphere (Fraser, 1995b). Others (Thompson, 1995) have suggested that the modern media have actually expanded the public sphere. More philosophically, some postmodern critics, particularly Lyotard, argue that Habermas reproduces the totalizing discourse of 'Enlightenment Reason', ignoring its repressive character. Honneth (1985) has countered that Lyotard has a mistaken interpretation of Habermas's discursive ethics. Their purpose, he argues, lies not in the final determination of common needs, but in intersubjective agreement about the very social norms that allow different needs to be articulated and realized. By this he means that Habermas is stressing the importance of the democratic process rather than the outcome of that process.

A normative project

Whatever the historical problems with Habermas's work, as a *normative* position the idea of a public sphere retains an appeal. Postmodernists, poststructuralists and neo-pragmatists would all think Habermas mistaken in his attempt to construct a universal and transcendental rational justification for the public sphere. However, the concept retains normative political leverage. It can be justified on the pragmatic grounds of cultural pluralism rather than epistemological grounds. That is, the public sphere (or spheres) should be able to accommodate difference as a vital principle.

✓ *The emancipatory project of modernity is best served by a commitment to 'postmodern' public spheres based on difference, diversity and solidarity.*

POSTMODERN CULTURE

One may agree with Habermas that modernity has not yet passed or with Giddens (1990) that most of the elements described as postmodern were already existent in the modern. Nevertheless, there have been significant *cultural* changes in contemporary life that have been described in the language of the 'postmodern'. These social and cultural changes are at the leading edge of the society and are pointing to its future (or are already the dominant configuration). Consequently, we may refer to living in a 'postmodern era'. This does not necessarily represent a sharp break with the modern. Rather, it is a transitional period of changing economic, social and cultural patterns which are shaping the contours of the future.

The postmodern does not have to mean postmodernity (as a historical period) but rather indicates a 'structure of feeling' (Williams, 1979, 1981) and a set of *cultural* practices. Core to the postmodern 'structure of feeling' is:

- **a sense of the fragmentary, ambiguous and uncertain nature of living;**
- **an awareness of the centrality of contingency;**
- **a recognition of cultural difference;**
- **an acceleration in the pace of living.**

The reflexive postmodern

Without the certainties of traditional religious and cultural beliefs, modern life may appear as a series of proliferating choices to be made without foundations. This encourages us to be more reflexive about ourselves, since we have no certainties to fall back on. Reflexivity can be understood as 'discourse about experience' (Gergen, 1994: 71). To engage in reflexivity is to partake in a range of discourses and relationships while constructing further discourses about them. Reflexivity enables increased possibilities for the playful self-construction of multiple identities. It also requires that we compare our traditions with those of others. Consequently, postmodern culture invites the 'other' of modernity, those voices that had been suppressed by the modern drive to extinguish difference, to find ways to speak. Such voices include those of feminism, ethnic diasporas, ecologists, ravers and travellers.

Reflexivity encourages an ironic sense of the 'said before': the feeling that one cannot invent anything new but merely play with the already existent. Eco (1986) gives a good example of this with the person who cannot, without irony, say 'I love you' but prefaces it with the words 'As Barbara Cartland would say'. The thing is said, but the unoriginality acknowledged. Indeed, irony, understood as a reflexive understanding of the contingency of one's own values and culture, is the key sensibility of postmodernism. A widespread awareness of the history of film, television, music and literature promotes this feeling. For example, television has a history and repeats that history within and across channels. Thus 'television produces the conditions of an ironic knowingness' (Caughie, 1990).

Two riders need to be attached to the notion of reflexive postmodern culture as a liberatory one:

1 **Increased social and institutional reflexivity is manifested in the desire of institutions to know more about their workforce, customers and clients. This involves increased forms of surveillance, from cameras in shopping centres and 'quality management' at work, to the increased significance of marketing.**

2 **The experience of postmodern culture cannot be assumed to be the same for all people regardless of class, ethnicity, gender, nationality, etc. A more finely grained sociological analysis would need to take account of the variable experiences of postmodern culture.**

Postmodernism and the collapse of cultural boundaries

Lash (1990) identifies the shift from the 'discursive' to the 'figural' as core to the postmodern turn. By this he means that the signifying logics of the modern and postmodern work in different ways. The increasing prominence of the postmodern 'figural' is integral to the 'aestheticization of everyday life' and to the erosion of the cultural boundaries of modernity.

The modernist 'regime of signification'

- **prioritizes words over images;**
- **promulgates a rationalist world view;**
- **explores the meanings of cultural texts and distances the spectator from the cultural object.**

By contrast, the postmodern 'figural'

- **is more visual;**
- **draws from everyday life;**
- **contests rationalist views of culture;**
- **immerses the spectator in his/her desire in the cultural object.**

✓ *Postmodern culture is marked by the blurring and collapse of the traditional boundaries between culture and art, high and low culture, commerce and art, culture and commerce.*

For example, the rise in visibility and status of popular culture, hastened by the electronic media, has meant that the distinction between high and low culture is no longer viable. 'High culture becomes just one more sub-culture, one more opinion, in our midst' (Chambers, 1986: 194). Further, the collapse of attempts to sustain art/high culture: commercial/low culture distinctions, combined with the recognition of the interpretative work of active audiences, has undone the obviousness of the critique of commodity culture by both the political 'right' and 'left'.

— What is meant by (a) high culture, (b) low culture, (c) popular culture?
— What is meant by the phrase 'the distinction between high and low culture is no longer viable?

Discuss your work with other people.

Bricolage and intertextuality

Postmodern culture is marked by a historical blurring. That is, representations of the past and present are displayed together in a bricolage. Bricolage involves the rearrangement and juxtaposition of previously unconnected signs to produce new codes of meaning. Bricolage as a cultural style is a core element of postmodern culture. It is observable in architecture, film and popular music video. Shopping centres have made the mixing of styles from different times and places a particular 'trademark'. Likewise, MTV is noted for the blending of pop music from a variety of periods and locations. There has also been a notable collapse or blurring of genre boundaries within cultural products. The film *Blade Runner* is frequently cited as a movie that mixes the genres of noir, horror, sci-fi, etc. In a more contemporary vein, the films *Shrek* and the TV series *The Sopranos* and *Da Ali G Show* illustrate aspects of genre deconstruction. Further, they are double-coded (Jencks, 1986), allowing them to be understood both by the literati and by a popular audience.

Postmodern culture is marked by a self-conscious intertextuality, that is, the citation of one text within another. This involves explicit allusion to particular programmes and oblique references to other genre conventions and styles; for example, references to the film *Thelma and Louise* and the reworking of noir conventions or those of the 'road movie' in *Pulp Fiction* and *True Romance*. This intertextuality is an aspect of enlarged cultural self-consciousness about the history and functions of cultural products.

The aestheticization of everyday life

The blurring of cultural boundaries, allied to the prominence of the image, have arguably resulted in an aestheticization of urban life. Featherstone (1991) argues that this takes three critical forms:

1 **artistic subcultures which seek to efface the boundaries between art and everyday life;**

2 **the project of turning life into a work of art;**

3 **the flow of signs and images that saturate the fabric of everyday life.**

Identity projects and the aestheticization of daily life are linked together within consumer culture through the creation of lifestyles centred on the consumption of aesthetic objects and signs. This is linked to a relative shift in importance in society from production to consumption. A significant part has been played in this process by flexible (post-Fordist) forms of production that centre on small batch production, customization and niche marketing.

Postmodern aesthetics in television

✓ *Television is at the heart of image production, and the circulation of a collage of stitched-together images that is core to postmodern cultural style.*

The juxtaposition of images and meanings in television creates an electronic bricolage in which unexpected associations can occur. This is an outcome of the flow of a given channel and a reflection of multi-channel diversity. The ability of viewers to zip and zap, channel-change and fast-forward constitutes a bricolage or 'strip text' (Newcombe, 1988). Here, adopting the 'appropriate' reading attitudes and competencies is itself an aspect of postmodern culture.

Stylistically, the markers of the postmodern have been seen as:

- **aesthetic self-consciousness;**

- **self-reflexiveness;**

- **juxtaposition/montage;**

- **paradox;**

- **ambiguity;**

- **the blurring of the boundaries of genre, style and history.**

Postmodernism in the arts is seen as a reaction against modernism. However, postmodern television takes on and makes popular modernist techniques, including montage, rapid cutting, non-linear narrative techniques and the decontextualization of images.

Postmodern detectives and gangsters

The American TV 'detective' series *Twin Peaks* and *Miami Vice* are widely regarded as indicative of postmodern style. *Twin Peaks* was 'double-coded' in the commonly understood manner of postmodern texts. It involved a combination of codes which enabled it to engage with a 'concerned minority' familiar with an 'expert' language and a wider popular audience. *Twin Peaks* was postmodern in its multigeneric form, whereby the conventions of the police series, science fiction and soap opera were blended together in a way that was sometimes to be taken seriously and at other times regarded as humorous ambivalent parody (Collins, 1992). For Kellner (1992), *Miami Vice* was postmodern in two fundamental ways:

1 **its aesthetic style, by which the lighting, camera work, rock music, bright colours and exotic terrain led to intense aesthetic spectacles;**

2 **its polysemic nature, involving shifting and conflicting identities, meanings and ideologies.**

More recently, the TV series *The Sopranos* has played with the conventions of the gangster genre. In particular, it has 'cited' movies about the Mafia, including *Goodfellas* and *The Godfather*. Further, the whole drama is shot through with irony, a postmodern marker *par excellence*. This is achieved most obviously by having the central 'Godfather' figure visit a psychiatrist (a critical figure in the postmodern landscape).

The cartoon postmodern

The Simpsons has made a 'dysfunctional' American family the ironic heroes of a series that is double-coded in its appeal to children and adults. It is entertainment and a subtle reflection on American cultural life. In accordance with contemporary postmodern culture, the television set is at the heart of the Simpsons' life and its audience. The programme requires us to have a self-conscious awareness of other television and film genres as it makes a range of intertextual references. For example, *Itchy and Scratchy*, the Simpson children's favourite cartoon, parodies *Tom and Jerry*. It mocks the double standard by which television violence is simultaneously condemned and enjoyed.

The postmodern markers of ambivalence, irony and intertextuality are equally evident in the popular show *South Park*, which parodies a series of cultural stereotypes. We are presented with a range of small-minded racist and sexist characters in conjunction with a series of stereotypes of race, gender, age, body size, etc. Yet the show manages to undermine the stereotypes by making us laugh at them. The representation of the African-American chef as the sexy black soul singer, the Barry White of *South Park*, parodies the 'original' image as itself a stereotype. This is given an added intertextual dimension and ironic twist by the voice of Isaac Hayes, known for the theme song to the blaxploitation movie *Shaft*. The show walks the line between offending everyone and undermining the offence. It takes nothing seriously while making serious statements about, for example, the use of television as a child-minder.

Watch an episode of The Simpsons or South Park.

— In what ways do they illustrate multi-genre form and intertextuality?
— What genres are involved?
— How are they juxtaposed to each other?
— How do they employ irony and parody?

In a group of three or four, prepare a written and oral presentation for a new multi-genre film or TV series that you are going to 'pitch' to a film or TV company.

Culture jamming

In recent times a new form of postmodern 'politics of representation' has emerged called 'culture jamming' (or guerrilla semiotics). The strategy has roots in the 'situationist' movement of the 1960s, but came to prominence with Dery's (1993) widely circulated book *Culture Jamming* and Klein's (2001) *No Logo*. Culture jamming is the practice of subverting mass media messages, especially advertising, through artistic satire. Culture jams seek to resist consumerism by refiguring logos, fashion statements and product images in order to raise concerns about consumption, environmental damage and inequitable social practices.

Culture jamming aims to disrupt an instrumental 'technoculture' that generates consent through the use of symbols (Rheingold, 1994). It draws upon semiotic and postmodern theory to work within the systems it intends to subvert. Culture jamming does this by employing bricolage strategies of 'taking pre-existing textual fragments and modifying them so that they convey a meaning quite different than their originally intended one' (Tietchen, 2001: 114–15). 'Jammers' attempt to subvert the semiotics of the media by transforming 'the message' into its own 'anti-message'. Its supporters suggest that successful contemporary media activism resists less through simple opposition and more by using commercial rhetoric against itself, often through exaggeration (Harold, 2004).

In 1989, a group playfully called the Barbie Liberation Organization (BLO) purchased hundreds of Barbie and G. I. Joe dolls just before Christmas. They then swapped the dolls' computer chip voice boxes and returned the dolls to toy stores to be resold. When children opened their toys on Christmas morning, 'instead of Barbie chirping cheerful affirmations of American girlishness she growled, in the butch voice of G. I. Joe: "Eat lead, Cobra!" "Dead men tell no lies!" and "Vengeance is mine!" Meanwhile, Joe exclaimed: "let's plan our dream wedding"' (Harold, 2004: 198). The aim was to bring attention to the gender-based stereotyping in children's toys by reversing cultural norms.

Subverting adverts

Another example of culture jamming concerned the defacement of an advertising billboard for Berlei underwear in Sydney, Australia. The advert contained an image of a woman wearing only underwear preparing to be cut in half by a magician. Five women were charged with property damage after they added the words; 'Even if you're mutilated you'll always feel good in Berlei', to the advertising caption. The charges against the women were upheld in court but the magistrate dismissed the case without sentence or damages. Indeed, she supported the women's case that the advertisement was offensive. The public debate that followed the case raised issues about the representation of women and the level of cultural tolerance of male violence against women.

Culture jamming raises again the question of whether it is possible to subvert the ideologies and aesthetics of consumer culture from within. Certainly 'jamming' runs counter to the Frankfurt School argument that any mass-produced aesthetic is complicit in reproducing the system even when it attempts to deploy alternative discourses (Adorno and Horkheimer, 1979). Today some critics suggest that culture jammers have themselves become just another product. *Adbusters* for example, the Canadian organization devoted to ad parodies and anti-corporate analysis, now markets a line of anti-consumer products including posters, videos, postcards and T-shirts. It also has advertising slots on the television programmes *USA Today* and *MTV*. It has also launched an ambitious anti-branding campaign with an advert offering its 'blackspot' sneaker, an ethically produced alternative to the Nike swoosh (Harold, 2004).

Campaigns such as these have drawn criticism that organizations such as *Adbusters* have become merely another part of the commercial machine. 'It's become an advertisement for anti-advertising' (Klein, 1997: 42). Indeed, Klein (2001) points out that advertisers themselves have used progressive political themes as a way of promoting their products. For example, calls to celebrate diversity and more fully represent women and ethnic minorities have been accommodated by corporations such as Benetton who use it for 'hip' niche marketing. It is a moot point then whether consumers distinguish between advertisements and transgressive attempts to subvert them, or whether they simply experience one depthless culture.

Evaluating postmodern culture

The significance or insignificance of postmodern culture has been hotly debated. For some critics, contemporary culture is depthless and meaningless. However, for other writers, present-day culture is to be welcomed as popular and transgressive.

Depthless culture

For Baudrillard, postmodern culture is constituted through a continual flow of images that establishes no connotational hierarchy. Postmodern culture is argued to be flat and one-dimensional; it is literally and metaphorically 'superficial'. In this vein, Grossberg describes *Miami Vice* as 'all on the surface. And that surface is nothing but a collection of quotations from our own collective historical debris, a mobile game of trivia' (Grossberg, 1987: 29). Here is a culture in which no objects have an 'essential' or 'deep' value. Rather, value is determined through the exchange of symbolic meanings. That is, commodities have sign values that confer prestige and signify social value, status and power. A commodity is not simply an object with use value but a commodity-sign. Signs are said to be able to 'float free' from objects. Consequently, signs are able to be used in a variety of associations (as illustrated every day in television advertising). As Featherstone suggests, 'consumption … must not be understood as the consumption of use-values, a material utility, but primarily as the consumption of signs' (Featherstone, 1991: 85).

Implosions and simulations

Baudrillard's world is one in which a series of modern distinctions have broken down (sucked into a 'black hole', as he calls it). This process collapses the real and the unreal, the public and the private, art and reality. For Baudrillard, postmodern culture is marked by an all-encompassing flow of fascinating simulations and images. He calls this a hyperreality, in which we are overloaded with images and information:

> It is reality itself today that is hyperrealist. … it is quotidian reality in its entirety – political, social, historical and economic – that from now on incorporates the simulating dimension of hyperrealism. We live everywhere in an 'aesthetic' hallucination of reality. (Baudrillard, 1983a: 148)

The prefix 'hyper' signifies 'more real than real'. The real is produced according to a model that is not a given but artificially reproduced as real, a real retouched in a 'hallucinatory resemblance' with itself. The real implodes on itself. Implosion in Baudrillard's work describes a process leading to the collapse of boundaries between the real and simulations. This includes the frontier between the media and the social, so that 'TV is the world'. Television simulates real-life situations, not so much to represent the world, but to execute its own. News re-enactments of 'real-life' events blur the boundaries between the 'real' and the simulation, 'entertainment' and 'current affairs'.

According to Baudrillard, the postmodern world of communication saturation represents an over-intense advance of the world upon consciousness. The subjects of this process he describes as 'schizophrenic'. There is an over-exposure or explosion of visibility by which all becomes transparency and immediate visibility, which Baudrillard calls 'obscenity'. The television screen is the central metaphor. Here the schizoid subject of 'obscenity' becomes 'a pure screen, a switching centre for all the networks of influence' (Baudrillard, 1983b: 148).

KEY THINKERS

Jean Baudrillard (1929–2007)

French theorist Jean Baudrillard critiques structuralism and Marxism to develop his own theories of postmodernism. His key idea is that a commodity is not simply an object with use-value for exchange but a commodity-sign. For Baudrillard, postmodern culture is constituted through a continual flow of images that is one-dimensional and 'superficial'. He argues that a series of modern distinctions including the real and the unreal, the public and the private, art and reality have broken down, leading to a culture of simulacrum and hyperreality.

Reading: Baudrillard, J. (1983) *Simulations*. New York: Semiotext(e).

The cultural style of late capitalism

For Fredric Jameson (1984), who draws on the work of Baudrillard, postmodernism is implicated in a depthless sense of the present and a loss of historical understanding. We live in a postmodern hyperspace in which we are unable to place ourselves. The specific manifestations of which include:

- the cannibalization of styles from past and present;
- the loss of authentic artistic style in favour of pastiche;
- the breakdown of a firm distinction between high and low culture;
- the culture of the simulacrum or copy (for which no original existed);

- the fashion for nostalgia in which history is the object not of representation but of stylistic connotation;

- the transcending of the capacities of the individual to locate him- or herself perceptually or cognitively in postmodern hyperspace.

Jameson describes the postmodern world as marked by fragmentation, instability and disorientation. This is a view that has much in common with that of Baudrillard. However, he parts company on the level of explanation. Jameson is at pains to point out that postmodernism has genuine historical reality. He argues that postmodern cultural practices are not superficial but expressive of developments and experiences in a deep 'reality'. For Jameson, postmodernism is expressive of a world system of multinational or late capitalism. It represents the cultural style of late capitalism operating in a new global space. Late capitalism extends commodification to all realms of personal and social life, transforming the real into the image and simulacrum.

SHOPPING MALL

© Photographer: Pryzmat | Agency: Dreamstime.com

- *To what extent does the shopping mall now represent the public space of postmodern culture?*

- *What are the features of shopping malls that Jameson would describe as 'postmodern hyperspace'?*

Transgressive postmodernism

In contrast to the negative evaluations of Baudrillard and Jameson, Kaplan (1987) claims a transgressive and progressive role for postmodern culture and its collapsing of boundaries. She argues that the postmodern music video offers, in deconstructionist mode, no assured narrative position for the viewer, undermining the status of representation as real or true. This parallels Hutcheon's (1989) argument that postmodernism makes the whole idea of representation problematic even as it is complicit with it. She suggests that postmodernism 'takes the form of self-conscious, self-contradictory, self-undermining statement. It is rather like saying something with inverted commas around what is being said' (Hutcheon, 1989: 1).

✓ *Postmodernism is marked by an ironic knowingness because it explores the limitations and conditions of its own knowing.*

Collins (1992) argues that postmodernism acknowledges multiple subject positions and identities. Further, it actively encourages a conscious moving in and out of readership positions which includes playing with meaning and form. For Collins, Jameson's characterization of postmodernism as 'camp' recycling, pastiche and a loss of historical depth 'fails to account for the diversity of possible strategies of re-articulation'. These range from simple revivalism and nostalgia to 'the radicalized cover versions of pop standards by the Sex Pistols or The Clash, in which the past is not just accessed but "hijacked", given an entirely different cultural significance' (Collins, 1992: 333).

Chambers (1987, 1990) argues that rather than being the core of a 'depthless culture', commodity-signs are the raw material by which active and meaning-oriented consumers construct multiple identities. Here, consumers are self-conscious bricoleurs selecting elements of material commodities and meaningful signs and arranging them into a personal style. Thus, the postmodern can be read as the democratization of culture and of new individual and political possibilities. Other writers point to the potential of subverting the meaning of signs in consumer culture to enact a form of cultural resistance, for example, through the strategy of culture jamming (above).

DECONSTRUCT THIS: MODERNISM VS. POSTMODERNISM

- *What is modernism? What is postmodernism?*
- *What features of the modern are in the postmodern?*
- *What features of the postmodern are in the modern?*

SUMMARY

Modernity and postmodernity are periodizing concepts that refer to historical epochs. They are abstractions which broadly define the institutional parameters of social formations. In this sense, modernity is marked by the post-medieval rise of industrial capitalism and the nation-state system. These institutions of modernity are associated with the social and cultural processes of individualization, differentiation, commodification, urbanization, rationalization, bureaucratization and surveillance.

Modernism and postmodernism are cultural and epistemological concepts. As cultural concepts, they concern the experience of day-to-day living and artistic styles/movements. However, the distinction between modernism and postmodernism is less than clear. For example, it was argued that the experience of living within modernity involves pace, change, ambiguity, risk, doubt and the chronic revision of knowledge. Yet a sense of a fragmentary, ambiguous and uncertain world involving high levels of reflexivity is also a marker of postmodern culture. The stress on contingency, irony and the blurring of cultural boundaries is more obviously a marker of the postmodern. Modernism as an artistic movement and philosophy upholds the high–popular distinction in a way that postmodernism does not. At its outer edge, postmodern theorists point to the collapse of the modern distinction between the real and simulations.

As a set of philosophical and epistemological concerns, modernism is associated with the enlightenment philosophy of rationality, science, universal truth and progress. In contrast, postmodern philosophy has been associated with a questioning of these categories. For example:

- not depth but surface;
- not truth but truths;
- not objectivity but solidarity or social commendation (Rorty);
- not foundationalism but historically specific 'regimes of truth' (Foucault).

However, while Lyotard calls these philosophical positions postmodern, Foucault questioned the need to be either for or against the enlightenment. Rorty has regretted using the term 'postmodern' (since the post-enlightenment philosophy he espouses can be traced back at least as for as Nietzsche), while Giddens argues that postmodern culture is an expression of 'radicalized modernity'.

Disagreements and debates centre on whether we should describe the features of contemporary life as modernity or postmodernity. Are the artistic projects of modernism and postmodernism worlds apart, or do they share features? Is it valuable to describe the prevailing culture as postmodern? Many writers regard the questioning of philosophical

(Cont'd)

foundations of modernity as pointing to the democratic acceptance of difference and the reflexive ability to create ourselves. However, others have viewed it with trepidation. They have feared the inability to ground cultural politics, seeing postmodernism as a form of irrationalism that opens the door to the unfettered imposition of power. Likewise, some writers see consumer capitalism as releasing the possibility for creative play and identity construction. Other critics regard it as furthering the domination of global corporate power.

PART THREE

SITES OF CULTURAL STUDIES

7   *Issues of Subjectivity and Identity*

KEY CONCEPTS

Agency	*Identification*
Anti-essentialism	*Identity*
Constructionism	*Identity project*
Discourse	*Subject position*
Essentialism	*Subjectivity*

This chapter examines debates in cultural studies about subjectivity and cultural identity. In doing so, it explores the assumptions of the western 'regime of the self'. Fuelled by political struggles as well by philosophical and linguistic concerns, 'identity' emerged as the central theme of cultural studies during the 1990s. The politics of feminism, of ethnicity and of sexual orientation, amongst others, have been high-profile concerns intimately connected to the politics of identity. In turn, these struggles for and around identity necessarily raised the question: what is identity?

SUBJECTIVITY AND IDENTITY

The concepts of subjectivity and identity are closely connected and, in everyday language, virtually inseparable. However, we may make the following distinctions:

- *subjectivity*: the condition of being a person and the processes by which we become a person; that is, how we are constituted as subjects (biologically and culturally) and how we experience ourselves (including that which is indescribable);
- *self-identity*: the verbal conceptions we hold about ourselves and our emotional identification with those self-descriptions;
- *social identity*: the expectations and opinions that others have of us.

Both subjectivity and identity take narrative or story-like form when we talk about them. To ask about subjectivity is to pose the question: what is a person? To explore identity is to enquire: how do we see ourselves and how do others see us?

Personhood as a cultural production

Subjectivity and identity are contingent, culturally specific productions. For cultural studies what it means to be a person is social and cultural 'all the way down'. That is, identities are wholly social constructions and cannot 'exist' outside of cultural representations. They are the consequence of acculturation. There is no known culture that does not use the pronoun 'I' and which does not therefore have a conception of self and personhood. However, the manner in which 'I' is used, what it means, does vary from culture to culture. For Elias (1978, 1982), the very concept of 'I' as a self-aware object is a modern western conception that emerged out of science and the 'Age of Reason'. People in other cultures do not always share the individualistic sense of uniqueness and self-consciousness that is widespread in western societies. Instead personhood is inseparable from a network of kinship relations and social obligations.

The cultural repertoire of the self in the western world assumes that:

- **we have a true self;**
- **we possess an identity that can become known to us;**
- **identity is *expressed* through forms of representation;**
- **identity is recognizable by ourselves and by others.**

That is, identity is an essence that can be signified through signs of taste, beliefs, attitudes and lifestyles. Identity is deemed to be both personal and social. It marks us out as the same and different from other kinds of people. We may agree that identity is concerned with sameness and difference, with the personal and the social as understood through forms of representation. However, we will question the assumption that identity is either something we possess or a fixed thing to be found.

✓ *Identity is best understood not as a fixed entity but as an emotionally charged discursive description of ourselves that is subject to change.*

Fill in the boxes with descriptions of the different aspects of your self.

Think of many different descriptions of your (1) cultural attributes, (2) physical characteristics, (3) social relationships and (4) the spaces that you move through.

I AM ....

| 1 | 2 | 3 | 4 |

Essentialism and anti-essentialism

The western search for identity is premised on the idea that there is such a 'thing' to be found. Here identity exists as a universal and timeless core of the self that we all possess. We might say that persons have an 'essence' of the self that we call identity. Such essentialism assumes that descriptions of ourselves reflect an essential underlying identity. By this token there would be a fixed essence of femininity, masculinity, Asians, teenagers and all other social categories.

In contrast, it has been argued here that identity is cultural 'all the way down', being specific to particular times and places. This suggests that forms of identity are changeable and related to definite social and cultural conjunctures. The idea that identity is plastic is underpinned by arguments referred to as anti-essentialism. Here words are not taken as having referents with essential or universal qualities. That is, language 'makes' rather than 'finds' (Chapter 3). Identity is not a thing but a description in language. Identities are discursive constructions that change their meanings according to time, place and usage.

Self-identity as a project

For Giddens (1991), self-identity is constituted by the ability to sustain a narrative about the self. This includes the capacity to build up a consistent feeling of biographical continuity. Identity stories attempt to answer the critical questions:

- **What to do?**
- **How to act?**
- **Who to be?**

The individual attempts to construct a coherent identity narrative by which 'the self forms a trajectory of development from the past to an anticipated future' (Giddens, 1991: 75). Thus, 'Self-identity is not a distinctive trait, or even a collection of, traits, possessed by the individual. It is *the self as reflexively understood by the person in terms of her or his biography*' (Giddens, 1991: 53).

Giddens's argument conforms to our common-sense notion of identity, for he is saying that self-identity is what we as persons think it is. However, he is also arguing that identity is not a collection of traits that we possess. Identity is not something we have, nor an entity or a thing to which we can point. Rather, identity is a mode of thinking about ourselves. Of course, what we think we are changes from circumstance to circumstance in time and space. This is why Giddens describes identity as a *project*. By this he means that identity is our creation. It is something always in process, a moving towards rather than an arrival. An identity project builds on:

- **what we think we are now in the light of our past and present circumstances;**
- **what we think we would like to be, the trajectory of our hoped-for future.**

Social identities

Self-identity may be conceived of as *our* project. Nevertheless it is a sociological truism that we are born into a world that pre-exists us. We learn to use a language that was in use before we arrived. We live our lives in the context of social relationships with others. In short, we are constituted as individuals in a social process using socially shared materials. This is commonly understood as socialization or acculturation. Without acculturation we would not be persons as we understand that notion in our everyday lives. Without language the very concept of personhood and identity would be unintelligible to us.

There are no transcendental or ahistorical elements to what it means to be a person. For cultural studies identity is wholly social and cultural, for the following reasons. First, the very notion of what it is to be a person is a cultural question. For example, individualism is a marker of specifically modern societies. Second, the resources that form the material for an identity project, namely language and cultural practices, are social in character. Consequently, what it means to be a woman, a child, Asian or elderly is formed differently in different cultural contexts.

The resources we are able to bring to an identity project are historically and culturally distinct. They depend on the situational power from which we derive our cultural competencies within specific cultural contexts. It matters whether we are black or white, male or female, African or American, rich or poor, because of the differential cultural resources to which we will have had access. Here identity is a matter not only of self-description but also of social ascription.

> *Social identities* … are associated with normative rights, obligations and sanctions which, within specific collectivities, form roles. The use of standardized markers, especially to do with the bodily attributes of age and gender, is fundamental in all societies, notwithstanding large cross-cultural variations which can be noted. (Giddens, 1984: 282–3)

✓ *In sum, identity is about sameness and difference, about the personal and the social, 'about what you have in common with some people and what differentiates you from others' (Weeks, 1990: 89).*

THE FRACTURING OF IDENTITY

In a seminal article on 'the question of cultural identity', Stuart Hall (1992b) identified three different ways of conceptualizing identity, namely:

1 the enlightenment subject;

2 the sociological subject;

3 the postmodern subject.

The purpose of this section is to expand upon those conceptualizations of identity. In particular, we are concerned with tracing the development of the fractured, decentred or postmodern subject.

The enlightenment subject

The notion of persons as unique unified agents has been allied to the enlightenment, a philosophical movement associated with the idea that reason and rationality form the basis for human progress. The enlightenment subject

> was based on a conception of the human person as a fully centred, unified individual, endowed with the capacities of reason, consciousness and action, whose 'centre' consisted of an inner core. … The essential centre of the self was a person's identity. (Hall, 1992b: 275)

This view is known as the Cartesian subject and conjoined with Descartes' famous declaration 'I think, therefore I am'. It places the rational, conscious *individual* subject at the heart of western philosophy. Here the mind is regarded as having inherently *rational* capacities. This endowment allows us to experience the world and make sense of it according to the actual properties of that world.

Conceiving of the subject in this way is a matter not simply of philosophy but also of the wider cultural processes of subject and identity formation. Thus it is central to the current western account of the self to see persons as unified and capable of organizing themselves. For example, morality talk, which in western culture seeks to make intelligible and manageable the moral and ethical dilemmas that face us, is centrally concerned with questions of individual responsibility for actions. Indeed, individual responsibility is embodied in laws that hold persons accountable for their actions. It is also manifested in the organization of academic knowledge into discrete subjects. In this way the domain of psychology is held to be the workings of the individual mind and western medicine treats individual ailments. Economic theory, though concerned with social processes, has the rational, self-interested, choice-making individual at its centre.

The sociological subject

We have noted that identities are not self-generating or internal to the self but are cultural 'all the way down' because constituted through the processes of acculturation. This socialized self Hall calls the sociological subject, where the inner core of the subject was not autonomous and self-sufficient, but was formed in relation to 'significant' others, who mediated to the subject the values, meanings and symbols – the culture – of the worlds he/she inhabited. (Hall, 1992b: 275)

Our first 'significant others' are likely to be family members. From them we learn, through praise, punishment, imitation and language, 'how to go on' in social life. Thus a key assumption of the sociological view of the subject is that people are social creatures. That is, the social and the individual constitute each other. Though the self is conceived as possessing an inner unified core, this is formed *interactively* between the inner world and the outside social world. Indeed, the internalization of social values and roles stabilizes the individual and ensures that individual persons 'fit' the social structure by being stitched or 'sutured' into it.

The postmodern subject

The intellectual movement from the 'enlightenment' subject to the 'sociological' subject represents a shift from describing persons as unified wholes who ground themselves, to regarding the subject as socially formed. The social subject is not the source of itself. Nor is it a 'whole' by virtue of the truism that people take up a variety of social positions. Nevertheless, the subject is seen as having a 'core self' able to reflexively co-ordinate itself into a unity.

✓ *The decentred or postmodern self involves the subject in shifting, fragmented and multiple identities. Persons are composed not of one but of several, sometimes contradictory, identities.*

The subject assumes different identities at different times, identities which are not unified around a coherent 'self'. Within us are contradictory identities, pulling in different directions, so that our identifications are continually being shifted about. If we feel that we have a unified identity from birth to death, it is only because we construct a comforting story or 'narrative of the self' about ourselves. (Hall, 1992b: 277)

Social theory and the fractured subject

Hall argues that five major 'ruptures in the discourses of modern knowledge' have contributed to our understanding of the subject as decentred. These are:

1 Marxism;

2 psychoanalysis;

3 feminism;

4 the centrality of language;

5 the work of Foucault.

The historical subject of Marxism

Marxism, it is argued, displaces any notion of a universal essence of personhood that is the possession of each individual. This is so because 'men [*sic*] make history, but only on the basis of conditions not of their own making'. In other words, a historically specific mode of production and social relations constitutes subjects in particular ways. Hence, what it is to be a person cannot be universal. Rather, the production of subjectivity is located in a social formation of a definite time and place with specific characteristics.

Thus a feudal mode of production is based on the power of barons who own land and serfs (or lease it to peasants). Consequently the identities of barons and serfs are quite different, not only from each other, but also from the social relations and identities formed within a capitalist mode of production. Thus, capitalists (and shareholders) employ the 'free' labour of the working class rather than own slaves. What it means to be a baron, a serf, a capitalist and a worker are quite different because of the specific form of social organization of which they are a part.

Hall's interpretation of the Marxist subject could be held to be a simple sociological one were it not for the significance he attributes to the Althusserian reading of Marx, in which the place of ideology in the constitution of subjects is central. By the concept 'ideology' is meant structures of signification or 'world views' that constitute social relations and legitimate the interests of the powerful. Crucially, for Althusser, the subject formed in ideology is not a unified Cartesian subject but a shattered and fragmented one.

For Althusser, classes, while sharing certain common conditions of existence, do not automatically form a core, unified class consciousness. Instead they are cross-cut by conflicting interests and are formed and unformed in the course of actual historical development. Though I share similar working conditions with my neighbour, we do not share a homogeneous working-class identity. I am male and she is female; I am black and she is white; I am a liberal and she is a nationalist. The general point here is that subjects are formed through difference as constituted by the play of signifiers. Thus, what we are is in part constituted by what we are not. In this context, Hall's Marxism points to the historically specific character of identity and to a fractured subject formed in ideology.

Psychoanalysis and subjectivity

Hall attributes the next of his 'decentrings' to Freud and the 'discovery' of the unconscious through psychoanalysis. For Hall (1996a), psychoanalysis has particular significance in shedding light on how identifications of the 'inside' link to the regulatory power of the discursive 'outside'. Hall, along with many feminists, deploys psychoanalysis to link the 'inside' with the 'outside'. He stresses the processes by which discursively constructed subject positions are taken up (or otherwise) by concrete persons. This procedure is achieved through fantasy identifications and emotional 'investments' (Henriques et al., 1984). Indeed, this contention is central to Hall's whole conceptualization of 'identity' as

> the point of suture, between on the one hand the discourses and practices which attempt to 'interpellate', speak to us or hail us into place as the social subjects of particular discourses, and on the other hand, the processes which produce subjectivities, which construct us as subjects which can be 'spoken'. Identities are thus the points of temporary attachment to the subject positions which discursive practices construct for us. (Hall, 1996a: 5–6)

According to Freud, the self is constituted in terms of an *egos*, or conscious rational mind, a *superego*, or social conscience, and the *unconscious*, the source and repository of the symbolic workings of the mind which functions with a different logic from reason (see Chapter 1). This view of personhood immediately fractures the unified Cartesian subject. It suggests that what we do and what we think are the outcome not of a rational integrated self but of the workings of the unconscious. The unconscious is normally unavailable to the conscious mind in any straightforward fashion.

The self is by definition fractured into the ego, superego and unconscious. Thus the unified narrative of the self is something we acquire over time through entry into the symbolic order of language and culture. That is, through processes of identification with others and with social discourses we create an identity that embodies an illusion of wholeness.

For its supporters (Chodorow, 1978, 1989; Mitchell, 1974; Rose, 1997), the great strength of psychoanalysis lies in its rejection of the fixed nature of subjects and sexuality. Instead it concentrates on the construction and formation of subjectivity. Psychoanalysis also points us to the psychic and emotional aspects of identity through the concept of identification. By contrast, Nikolas Rose (1996) argues that psychoanalysis is a historically specific way of understanding persons that cannot be used to investigate the historicity of being human. He argues that 'the "interiority" which so many feel compelled to diagnose is not that of a psychological system. Rather, it is best understood as "a discontinuous surface, a kind of infolding of exteriority"' (Rose, 1996: 142). That is, the 'inside' is formed by the discourses that circulate on the 'outside'.

There is little doubt about the significance of emotion in the constitution of subjectivity and identity (see Chapter 4). However, there remains an important question mark over psychoanalysis itself. It is unclear that it is necessarily the best tool with which to explore issues of emotional identification. The scientific procedures of psychoanalysis are neither agreed nor for the most part empirically testable and repeatable. Consequently, psychoanalysis should be treated as a set of poetic, metaphorical and mythological stories with consequences. Its truths lie in its practice and its outcomes. On that front, it is fair to say that the consensus amongst the psychological profession is that other forms of analysis and treatment (e.g. cognitive behavioural therapy and construct theory) are more effective.

Further, psychoanalysis is a historically specific way of understanding persons that cannot be the basis for a universal theory. In particular, its evidential basis is drawn from a small group of nineteenth-century, middle-class Viennese women. Indeed, in so far as psychoanalysis relies on linguistic and cultural processes that are deemed to be ahistorical and universal, since they mark the psychic processes of humankind across history, then at the very least it sits uncomfortably within a cultural studies that emphasizes the cultural construction of subjectivity. Indeed, the obscurity of its language, its dubious science and its phallocentrism are real problems for psychoanalysis, particularly when other forms of psychotherapy can do its job more effectively.

Constructionism as an alternative to psychoanalysis   It is somewhat surprising that cultural studies writers have not made more of that strand of psychology that is embedded in social constructionism (e.g. Gergen and Shotter) and/or the discursive psychology that emphasizes language in the constitution of persons (e.g. Billig, Potter, Edwards, etc.). In this vein, Potter and Wetherell (1987) have sought to demonstrate that fundamental psychological notions such as attitudes, emotions and the inner mind could be approached through the examination of a shared language. In particular, they argue that there are no 'things' that are called emotions or attitudes that lurk behind language.

Here we have resources for an emergent 'cultural psychology' (Shweder, 1995) that collapses binaries like subject/object, form/content, person/environment, psyche/culture, etc. In trying to find ways to talk about the psyche and culture so that neither is by nature intrinsic or extrinsic to each other, cultural psychology conceives of the world in terms of non-linear dynamic processes with circular or dialectical feedback loops between subject/object, person/environment, psyche/culture, etc.

Feminism and difference

Feminism is a plural field of theory and politics that is constituted by competing perspectives and prescriptions for action. In general terms, feminism asserts that sexual difference is a fundamental and irreducible axis of social organization. Feminism is centrally concerned with sex as an organizing principle of social life that is thoroughly saturated with power relations subordinating women to men.

For Hall, feminism constitutes a further decentring influence on conceptions of the subject. This is so because of its challenge, through the slogan and practice of the 'personal is political', to the distinction between the 'inside' and 'outside'; the public and the private. For example, domestic violence may occur in the private domain, but is of public concern and social causality.

Feminism has interrogated the question of how we are formed as sexed subjects in the context of gendered families. It has explored how the 'inside' of gender is formed by the 'outside' of the family. Thus, what it is to be a person cannot be universal or unified since, at the very least, identity is marked by sexual difference.

In particular, poststructuralist and postmodern feminism (Nicholson, 1990; Weedon, 1997) argues that sex and gender are social and cultural constructions that are not reducible to biology. This is an anti-essentialist stance where femininity and masculinity are not essential universal and eternal categories; rather, they are understood to be discursive constructions. As such, poststructuralist feminism is concerned with the cultural construction of subjectivity *per se* and with a range of possible masculinities and femininities. What distinguishes poststructuralism is the emphasis on language, which is also central to Hall's account of fractured identity.

Language and identity

As argued in Chapter 3, language is not a mirror that reflects an independent object world ('reality'). Rather, it is a resource that 'lends form' to ourselves and our world. Here, identity is to be understood not as a fixed, eternal thing, nor as an inner essence of a person to which words refer. Instead the concept of identity refers to a regulated way of 'speaking' about persons. The idea that identities are discursive constructions is underpinned by a view of language in which there are no essences to which language refers and therefore no essential identities. That is, representation does not 'picture' the world but constitutes it for us. This is because of the following:

- **Signifiers generate meaning not in relation to fixed objects but in relation to other signifiers. According to semiotic theory, meaning is generated through relations of difference. Thus, 'good' is meaningful in relation to 'bad'.**

- **The relationship between the sounds and marks of language, the signifiers, and what they are taken to mean, the signifieds, is not held in any fixed, eternal relationship.**

- **To think about an independent object world is to do so in language. It is not possible to escape language in order to be able to view an independent object world directly. Nor can we attain a God-like vantage point from which to view the relationship between language and the world.**

- Language is relational in character. Words generate meaning not by reference to some special or essential characteristic of an object or quality. Rather, meaning is produced through the network of relationships of a language-game in use.

- Any given word includes the echoes or traces of other meanings from other related words in a variety of contexts. Meaning is inherently unstable and constantly slides away. Hence, *différance*, 'difference and deferral', by which the production of meaning is continually deferred and added *to* (or supplemented) by the meanings of other words.

This view of language has important consequences for understanding the self and identity. It cannot now be said that language directly *represents* a pre-existent 'I'. Rather, language and thinking *constitute* the 'I', they bring it into being through the processes of signification. Just as one cannot have an 'I', so one cannot 'have' an identity. Rather, one is constituted through language as a series of discourses. Language does not express an already existent 'true self' but brings the self into being.

Descartes' famous phrase 'I think, therefore I am' now becomes deeply problematic. 'I think, therefore I am' suggests that thinking is separate from and represents the pre-existent 'I'. However, since there is no 'I' outside of language, then thinking *is* being; 'I' is a position in language.

Language generates meanings through a series of unstable and relational differences. However, it is also regulated within discourses that define, construct and produce their objects of knowledge. Consequently, what we can say about the identity characteristics of, for example, a man is socially circumscribed. Identities are discursive constructions that do not refer to an already existent 'thing'. Identities are both unstable *and* temporarily stabilized by social practice and regular, predictable behaviour. This is a view influenced, as Hall argued, by the work of Foucault.

The Foucauldian subject

Foucault is said to have produced a 'genealogy of the modern subject'. That is, he has traced the derivation and lineage of subjects in and through history. Here, the subject is radically historicized; that is, the subject is held to be wholly and only the product of history. For Foucault, subjectivity is a discursive production. That is, discourse (as regulated ways of speaking/practice) enables speaking persons to come into existence. It does this by offering us subject positions from which to make sense of the world while 'subjecting' speakers to discourse. A subject position is that perspective or set of regulated discursive meanings from which discourse makes sense. To speak is to take up a pre-existent subject position and to be subjected to the regulatory power of that discourse.

Foucault describes a subject that is the product of power which individualizes those subject to it. For Foucault, power is not simply a negative mechanism of control but is *productive* of the self. The disciplinary power of schools, work organizations, prisons, hospitals, asylums and the proliferating discourses of sexuality produce subjectivity by bringing individuals into view. They achieve this by naming and fixing subjects in writing via the discourses of, for example, medicine.

For Foucault, genealogy's task 'is to expose the body totally imprinted by history and the processes of history's destruction of the body' (Foucault, 1984a: 63). The body is the site of disciplinary practices which bring subjects into being, these practices being the consequences of specific historical discourses of crime, punishment, medicine, science, sexuality, and so forth. Hence, power is generative; it is productive of subjectivity.

Foucault concentrates on three disciplinary discourses:

1 *the 'sciences'*, which constitute the subject as an object of enquiry;

2 *technologies of the self*, whereby individuals turn themselves into subjects;

3 *'dividing practices'*, which separate the mad from the insane, the criminal from the law-abiding citizen, and friends from enemies.

Disciplinary technologies arose in a variety of sites, including schools, prisons, hospitals and asylums. They produced what Foucault called 'docile bodies' that could be 'subjected, used, transformed and improved' (Foucault, 1977: 198).

Discipline involves the organization of the subject in space through dividing practices, training and standardization. It brings together knowledge, power and control. Discipline produces subjects by categorizing and naming them in a hierarchical order. It does this through a rationality of efficiency, productivity and 'normalization' (Chapter 3). In this way, we are produced and classified as particular kinds of people. Classificatory systems are essential to the process of normalization and thus to the production of a range of subjects. For example, schools demand that we be in certain places at specific times (classrooms and timetables); they supervise our activities and grade us in relation to others by judging our (alleged) abilities (e.g. examinations).

Discourses of disciplinary and bio-power can be traced historically. Consequently, we can locate particular kinds of 'regimes of the self' in specific historical and cultural conjunctures. That is, different types of subject are the outcome of particular historical and social formations. Foucault attacks the 'great myth of the interior'. He sees the subject as a historically specific production of discourse with no transcendental continuity from one subject position to another. This is an anti-essentialist position in which the subject is not unified but fractured into many 'identities'.

— Look through any 'women's magazine'. What subject positions are constructed for women?
— Look through a magazine that you judge to be aimed at men. What subject positions are constructed for men?
— Describe how such subject positions are achieved.

The articulated self

For Stuart Hall, the cumulative effect of Marxism, psychoanalysis, feminism, contemporary theories of language and the work of Foucault is to deconstruct the essentialist notion of the unified agent, that is, a subject who possesses a fixed identity as a referent for the pronoun 'I'. Instead, anti-essentialist conceptions of identity within cultural studies stress the decentred subject: the self as made up of multiple and changeable identities.

Anti-essentialism and cultural identity

Hall (1990) has usefully summarized the essentialist and anti-essentialist positions from which cultural identity can be understood. In the essentialist version, identity is regarded as the name for a collective 'one true self'. It is thought to be formed out of a common history, ancestry and set of symbolic resources. Through such optics it is possible to speak of a 'British identity' that is expressed through:

- **the symbol of the 'Union Jack';**

- **memories of the Second World War;**

- **collective rituals such as the FA Cup Final, the opening of Parliament and the nightly news.**

The underlying assumptions of this view are that collective identity exists, that it is 'a whole' expressed through symbolic representation. By this token there would be an essence of, for example, black identity based on similarity of experience.

By juxtaposing 'British' and 'black', the assumptions of an essentialist argument are immediately made problematic, for it might have been assumed that a British identity was a white Anglo-Saxon one. The presence of a substantial black (and Asian, Jewish, Chinese, Polish, etc.) population in Britain makes such an assumption impossible to sustain. Indeed, it redefines what it means to be British. Being British can involve being black with the capability to trace one's ancestry back to Africa. However, just as the concept of British identity is problematic, so too is that of black identity. It is possible to argue for cultural identifications that *connect* black populations in Africa, America, the Caribbean and Britain. However, it is also viable to trace the lines of *difference*. That is, to be black British is not the same as being black African or black American.

YOUNG BLACK MAN 1

© Photographer: Ted Denson | Agency: Dreamstime.com

- *This picture of a young black man constructs a particular type of identity. How would you describe it?*

- *In what contexts could this picture be used? Write 3–4 different captions that give it different meanings.*

- *To what extent is this image a 'stereotype'? Can you give it captions that suggest a more unconventional meaning?*

- *Compare this image to the one of the young black man in Chapter 8 (p. 273). How are they the same and different?*

Hall's anti-essentialist position regarding cultural identity stresses that as well as points of similarity, cultural identity is organized around points of difference. Cultural identity is seen not as a reflection of a fixed, natural, state of being but as a process of *becoming*.

✓ *There is no essence of identity to be discovered; rather, cultural identity is continually being produced within the vectors of similarity and difference.*

Cultural identity is not an essence but a continually shifting set of subject positions. Further, the points of difference around which cultural identities could form are multiple and proliferating. They include, to name but a few, identifications of class, gender, sexuality, age, ethnicity, nationality, political position (on numerous issues), morality, religion, etc., and each of these discursive positions is itself unstable. The meaning of Americanness, Britishness, blackness, masculinity and so forth, are subject to continual change. Their meaning is never finished or completed. Identity then becomes a 'cut' or a snapshot of unfolding meanings; it is a strategic positioning which makes meaning possible. This anti-essentialist position does not mean that we cannot speak of identity. Rather, it points us to the political nature of identity as a 'production'. It also directs us to the possibility of multiple, shifting and fragmented identities that can be articulated together in a variety of ways.

The articulation of identities

Laclau (1977) has argued that there are no *necessary* links between discursive concepts. Those connections that are forged are temporary. They are articulated and bound together by connotative or evocative links that have been established by power and tradition. The concept of articulation suggests that those aspects of social life, for example identities, that we think of as unified and eternal can instead be thought of as the unique, historically specific, temporary stabilization or arbitrary closure of meaning.

Hall (1996b) suggests that an articulation is a connection that *can* make a unity of two different elements under certain conditions. The apparent 'unity' of identity is really the articulation of different and distinct elements that under other historical and cultural circumstances, could be re-articulated in different ways. Thus, individuals are the unique, historically specific, articulation of discursive elements that are contingent but also socially determined or regulated. Since there is no *automatic* connection between the various discourses of identity, class, gender, race, age, etc., they can be articulated together in different ways. Thus, all middle-class white men do not necessarily share the same identity and identifications any more than do all working-class black women.

KEY THINKERS

Ernesto Laclau (1935–)

Laclau was born in Argentina and educated at the University of Buenos Aires and the University of Essex (UK) where he holds a chair in Political Theory. His anti-foundationalist philosophy of radical contingency is aimed at the dissolution of concepts and the weakening of the project of modernity. In particular he argues that there are no necessary links between discursive concepts and that those links that are forged are temporary articulations bound together by hegemonic practice. With Chantal Mouffe, he has developed a form of post-Marxism that has been very influential within cultural studies.

Reading: Laclau, E. and Mouffe, C. (1985) *Hegemony and Socialist Strategy: Toward a Radical Democratic Politics*. London: Verso.

Hall illustrates his argument with the case of Clarence Thomas, an African-American US Supreme Court judge with conservative political views. Anita Hill, a black woman and former colleague of Judge Thomas, accused him of sexual harassment. As Hall puts it:

> Some blacks supported Thomas on racial grounds; others opposed him on sexual grounds. Black women were divided, depending on whether their 'identities' as blacks or women prevailed. Black men were also divided, depending on whether their sexism overrode their liberalism. White men were divided, depending, not only on their politics, but on how they identified themselves with respect to racism and sexism. White conservative women supported Thomas, not only on political grounds, but because of their opposition to feminism. White feminists, often liberal on race, opposed Thomas on sexual grounds. And because Judge Thomas is a member of the judicial elite and Anita Hall,

at the time of the alleged incident, a junior employee, there were issues of social class position at work in these arguments too. (Hall, 1992b: 279–80)

Hall is making the point that identities are contradictory and cross-cut or dislocate each other. No single identity can, he argues, act as an overarching organizing identity. Rather, identities shift according to how subjects are addressed or represented. We are constituted by fractured multiple identities. This signals to Hall (1996a) the 'impossibility' of identity as well as its 'political significance'. Indeed, in the plasticity of identity lies its political significance, for the shifting and changing character of identities marks the way that we think about ourselves and others. Contestation over identity and subjectivity concerns the very way that we are formed as human subjects, that is, the kinds of people we are becoming.

Sites of interaction

Giddens (1991) argues that the multiple narratives of the self are not the outcome of the shifting meanings of language *alone*. They are also the consequence of the proliferation and diversification of social relationships, contexts and sites of interaction (albeit constituted in and through discourse – see Chapter 12).

For example, compared to the eighteenth-century peasant, modern persons have a much wider scope of relationships, spaces and places in which to interact. These include spaces and relationships of work, family and friends, but also the global resources of television, e-mail and travel. The proliferation and diversification of contexts and sites of interaction prevent easy identification of particular subjects with a given, fixed identity. Thus, the same person is able to shift across subject positions according to circumstances.

✓ *Discourses, identities and social practice in time-space form a mutually constituting set implicated in the cultural politics of identity and the constitution of humanity as a form of life.*

— List all the binary pairs used to describe people, for example, black and white.
— Is one side of the binary culturally privileged?

AGENCY AND THE POLITICS OF IDENTITY

The question of agency

The argument that identities are fractured discursive constructions is widely held within cultural studies. However, it is not without its problems. In particular, if subjects and identities are the product of discursive and disciplinary practices, if they are social and cultural 'all the way down', how can we conceive of persons as able to act and engender change in the social order? Since subjects appear within these arguments to be 'products' rather than 'producers', how shall we account for the human agency required for a cultural politics of change?

Foucault and the problem of agency

Foucault concentrates the mind on issues of discourse, discipline and power. For him, subjects are understood as discursive constructions and the products of power. Discourse regulates what can be said about persons under determinate social and cultural conditions. Specifically, the 'regimes of truth' (what counts as truth) of a disciplinary modernity involve relations of power/knowledge. That is, knowledge is a form of power implicated in the production of subjectivity. As such, Foucault provides us with useful tools for understanding the connections between subjectivity/ identity and the social order.

However, he does not develop an understanding of how and why particular discourses are 'taken up' by some subjects and not by others. Nor does he explain how a subject produced through disciplinary discursive practices can resist power (Hall, 1996a). That is, he does not supply us with an understanding of the emotional investments by which subjects are attached to discourse. As such, he does not provide us with a theory of agency. In this context, Foucault's description of subjects as 'docile bodies' whereby subjects are the 'effect' of discourse has been of concern to feminists and others involved in identity politics. This is because he appears to rob subjects of the agency required for political action.

It is arguable that Foucault's later work, which centred on 'techniques of the self', does reintroduce agency. In doing so he reintroduces the possibility of resistance and change. Here, Foucault explores how subjects are 'led to focus attention on themselves, to decipher, recognize and acknowledge themselves as subjects of desire' (Foucault, 1987: 5); that is, how the self recognizes itself as a subject involved in practices of self-constitution, recognition and reflection. This concern with self-production as a discursive practice is centred on the question of ethics as a mode of 'care of the self'.

According to Foucault, ethics are concerned with practical advice as to how one should concern oneself with oneself in everyday life: for example, what it means to be a 'good' person, a self-disciplined person, a creative person, and so forth. Ethics centre on the 'government of others and the government of oneself'. Thus, ethical discourses, which circulate independently of any given particular individual, are ways by which we constitute ourselves, bring ourselves into being (Foucault, 1979, 1984b, 1986). Ethical discourses construct subject positions which enable agency to occur. More broadly, one can argue that regulatory discourses construct subject positions of agency. That is, agency is a discursive construction exemplifying the productive character of power.

Giddens and structuration theory

The case for conceiving of subjects as active and knowledgeable agents has consistently been put by Giddens. He has been a steadfast critic of Foucault for effacing agents from the narratives of history. Giddens, drawing from Garfinkel (1967), argues that social order is constructed in and through the everyday activities and accounts (in language) of skilful and knowledgeable actors (or members).

The resources that actors draw on, and are constituted by, are social in character. Indeed, social structure (or regular patterns of activity) distributes resources and competencies unevenly between actors. That is, regularities or structural properties of social systems, which are distinct from any given individual, operate to structure what an actor is. For example, patterns of expectations about what it means to be a man or a woman, and the practices associated with gender, construct men and women differently as subjects. Gendered subjectivity then enables us to act in specifically gendered ways, for example as a mother or father.

Structuration theory (Giddens, 1984) centres on the way agents produce and reproduce social structure through their own actions. Regularized human activity is not brought into being by individual actors as such, but is continually re-created by them via the very means whereby they express themselves as actors. That is, in and through their activities, agents reproduce the conditions that make those activities possible. Having been constituted as a man or a woman by gendered expectations and practices, having learned to be a father or mother, we then act in accordance with those rules, reproducing them again.

In this context, Giddens (1984) discusses Willis's (1977) *Learning to Labour*, wherein 'the lads' are active, knowledgeable agents who resist forms of school-based power on the basis of their class affiliations and expectations. However, through the very activity of resistance, they unintentionally produce and reproduce their subordinate class position in the labour process. The lads resist school because they do not see schooling as relevant to their future lives since they expect to do working-class jobs (which they value); this leads to 'failure' at school, so that working-class jobs are precisely what they are then restricted to doing. In this way, Giddens seeks to demonstrate how persons can both be active, knowledgeable agents *and* be constituted by and reproduce social structures of, for example, class, gender and ethnicity.

The duality of structure

Central to Giddens's theory of structuration is the concept of the 'duality of structure', by which structures are not only constraining but enabling. Here, individual actors are determined by social forces that lie beyond them as individual subjects. However, those social structures enable subjects to act.

✓ *Identities are understood to be a question both of agency (the individual constructs a project) and of social determination (our projects are socially constructed and social identities ascribed to us).*

For example, what it means to be a mother in a given society may mean that we cannot undertake paid employment. In that sense we are constrained. However, the structures of motherhood also allow us to act as a 'mother', to be close to our children, to form networks with other mothers, and so forth. Likewise with language: we are all constructed and constrained by language, which pre-exists us. Yet language is also the means and medium of self-awareness and creativity. That is, we can only say what is sayable in language, yet language is the medium by which we can say anything at all.

We noted that for Foucault the subject is the 'effect' of historically specific discourses and disciplinary practices. We also observed that Foucault's work has difficulties explaining the mechanisms by which particular subjects 'take up' certain discourses and how agency could be possible. Yet, Foucault also proposed a form of agency through a discursively constructed ethics centred on the care of the self. Indeed, agency can be said to be a subject position within discourse. Giddens tends to stress agency and Foucault discipline and determination. Nevertheless, both suggest that it might be possible to think of subjects as having agency as a consequence of determination. To grasp this possibility, we need to be clearer about the concept of agency.

The concept of agency

The concept of agency has commonly been associated with notions of:

- **freedom;**
- **free will;**
- **action;**
- **creativity;**
- **originality;**
- **the very possibility of change through the actions of free agents.**

However, we need to differentiate between a metaphysical or 'mystical' notion of free agency in which agents are self-constituting (i.e. bring themselves into being out of nothingness) and a concept of agency as *socially produced*. Here, culturally generated agency is enabled by differentially distributed social resources. This gives rise to various degrees of the ability to act in specific spaces. For example, that an aspect of my identity is tied up with teaching and writing is not something that a pre-linguistic 'I' simply chose. Rather, it is the outcome of the values and discourses of my family and educational experiences which, in turn, enable me to carry out those activities as an agent. There is, then, a difference between conceptions in which acts are made by agents who are free in the sense of 'not determined' and agency as the socially constituted capacity to act.

The notion that agents are free in the sense of undetermined is untenable for two reasons:

1 **In what could an undetermined or uncaused human act consist? It would have to be something created spontaneously from nothing – a metaphysical and mystical form of original creation.**

2 There is enough historical and sociological work available, not least from Foucault and Giddens, to show that subjects are determined, caused and produced by social forces that lie outside of themselves as individuals. We are all subject to the 'impress of history' (Rorty, 1989).

Agency as making a difference

It is possible to argue that agency consists of acts that make a pragmatic difference. Here, agency is demonstrated by the enactment of X rather than Y as a course of action. Of course, precisely because agency is socially and differentially produced, some actors have more domains of action than others. Those persons whose acculturation has led them to be highly educated in a formal sense, or who have accrued wealth, may have more options for action than others. The idea of agency as 'could have acted differently' avoids some of the problems of 'free as undetermined' because the pathways of action are themselves socially constituted.

Choice and determination

To enact X rather than Y as a course of action does not mean that we have chosen it *per se*. We have simply acted. Nevertheless, questions of choice and determination remain at the heart of the debates about agency. There are a number of points to be considered here:

- As novelist Milan Kundera comments, 'We can never know what to want, because, living only one life, we can neither compare it with our previous lives nor perfect it in our lives to come' (Kundera, 1984: 8). We face a series of contingent choices and can have no certain foundations on which to base those choices.

- When we compare the outcomes of past actions, we are making *value judgements* about what is the best course of action. These values have themselves been previously socially constituted in us. The basis for our choice does not spring out of thin air but has been determined or caused by the very way we are constituted as subjects, that is, by where, when and how we came to be who we are.

- An implication of both Freud's work and contemporary neuroscience is the idea that we act and choose in ways that are determined by psychic and emotional narratives which we cannot bring wholly to consciousness. Acts are determined to some degree from outside of the consciousness of the agent.

- A good deal of the actions of modern life are routine in character. They are not thought about in a conscious discursive way but are part of taken-for-granted acts of 'going on'. Often, we do not make self-conscious choices at all but follow a socially determined, routinized path.

- There is a sense in which we can never have 'objective' knowledge of the conditions of our own actions. This is because we cannot step outside of those circumstances in order to compare our pristine selves with those conditions. Whatever we have to say about ourselves and the conditions of our existence is always already from within our socially constituted selves. The best we can do is to produce another story about our selves.

✓ *In sum, agency is determined. It is the socially constructed capacity to act and nobody is free in the sense of undetermined (in which event, one could not 'be' at all).*

Nevertheless, agency is a culturally intelligible way of understanding ourselves. We clearly have the existential experience of facing and making choices. We do act, even though those choices and acts are determined by social forces, particularly language, which lie beyond us as individual subjects. The existence of social structures (and of language in particular) is arguably an enabling condition of action. Thus, neither human freedom nor human action can consist of an escape from social determinants.

Modes of discourse

It is felicitous to consider freedom and determination as different *modes of discourse* and discursively constructed experience for the following reasons:

- We cannot escape language to achieve a God-like vantage point on an independent reality. Thus, it is pointless to ask whether people are 'really' free or 'really' determined in any absolute metaphysical sense. Rather, discourses of freedom and discourses of determination are different, socially produced narratives about human beings that have different purposes and are applicable in different ways.

- We act with the idea of freedom, and the notion of determination 'all the way down' has no bearing on this existential experience. In other words, it plays no part in our everyday practices.

- Discourses of freedom and discourses of determination are socially produced for different purposes in different realms. Thus, it makes sense to talk about freedom from political persecution or economic scarcity without the need to say that agents are free in some undetermined way. Rather, such discourses are comparing different social formations and determinations and judging one to be better than another on the basis of our socially determined values.

Originality

To hold subjectivity and identity to be contingent and determined does not mean that we are not original. While identity is a social and cultural accomplishment, our individuality can be understood in terms of the specific ways in which the social resources of the self are arranged. That is, while we are all subject to the 'impress of history', the particular form that we take, the specific arrangements of discursive elements, is unique to each individual. We have all had unique patterns of family relations, of friends, of work and of access to discursive resources. Further, it is possible to see the processes of the unconscious workings of the mind as a unique source of creativity where each human being is a 'tissue of contingencies' (Rorty, 1991b). For example, dreams can be seen as unique creative associations produced by specific individuals. Thus, no two people dream the same dream in its exactness. The self is original like the moving elements of a kaleidoscope or like a snowflake constructed from the common ingredients that make up snow.

Innovation and change

The determined or caused contingency of the self does not make the question of *innovative acts* especially problematic, for they can be understood as the practical outcomes of unique combinations of social structures, discourses and psychic arrangements. Innovation is not a quality of the act but a retrospective judgement by us on the form and outcomes of that act. This judgement is made in relation to other acts in specific historical and cultural conjunctures. Innovation is also a question of performance-in-context. That is, innovative acts are the consequence of discourses formed in one sphere of cultural life transported into another. For example, discourses of individuality and creativity formed in and through artistic practices, or in the domain of leisure activities, may have innovative and disturbing consequences in other contexts, that is, within discipline-oriented work organizations and schools or in families structured around an ideology of parental authority and control.

Innovation and change are possible because we are unique, interdiscursive individuals and because the discourses that constitute society are themselves contradictory. In the context of contemporary western societies, it is intelligible to say that we can 're-articulate' ourselves, re-create ourselves and form ourselves anew in unique ways. This does not mean that we are not caused or determined. Rather, we make ourselves singular by making new languages. We produce new metaphors to describe ourselves with and expand our repertoire of alternative descriptions (Rorty, 1991a). In so far as this applies to individuals, so it applies also to social formations. Social change becomes possible through rethinking the articulation of the elements of 'societies', redescribing the social order and the possibilities for the future.

Since, as Wittgenstein (1953) argued, there is no such thing as a private language, rethinking ourselves is a social and political activity. Change occurs through the process of rethinking and redescribing, along with the material practices that are implicated in them. Rethinking ourselves, which emerges through social practice and social contradiction, brings new political subjects and practices into being. For example, speaking of Rastafarians in Jamaica, Hall (1996b) argued that they became political subjects by learning to speak a new language. This was a language that had been adapted from the Bible and was shaped to serve their own purposes.

The concepts of agency, originality and innovation are important because they underpin the possibility of a politics of identity and social change. That is, identity politics rests on the notion that human beings can act purposefully and creatively. However, we must ask what the politics of identity can mean in the light of anti-essentialist arguments. That is, what can the politics of identity be about if there is no such thing as identity?

Anti-essentialism, feminism and the politics of identity

The politics of feminism (see Chapters 9 and 14) provides a good example of identity politics for it is based on the category of 'woman', which is said to give rise to shared interests. Some feminist writing has assumed a commonality of interests founded on a shared biology. However, such biological essentialism is bedevilled by problems.

Biology as discourse

It is difficult to see how, on the basis of biology alone, women could form a politics of common interest. It does not follow that because women have similar bodies that they share cultural or political interests. This is because biological women are divided by the social and cultural constructs of class, ethnicity, age and nationality.

For example, one of the criticisms of western feminism is that, as a broadly middle-class western movement, it does not articulate the interests of black women or women in the developing world. Further, there is in principle no access to biological truths that lie outside of cultural discourses. All knowledge, which includes understandings of biology and shared interests, must, by necessity, be formed in language and subject to discursive resources. There is no biology that is not itself a social and cultural classificatory construction. Since there is no biology outside of discourse, it is difficult to see how women's politics can be based on shared essential or 'real' biology.

This does not mean that 'everything is discourse' and that there are no bodies as such. The materiality of bodies is one of those things that is, in the Wittgensteinian sense, beyond doubt. That is, we cannot function without that assumption. As Wittgenstein argues, we may in principle imagine that every time we open a door there will be a bottomless chasm beneath us, but it makes no sense to do so; it is unintelligible to us.

As Butler (1993) argues, discourse and the materiality of bodies are indissoluble. Not only is discourse the means by which we understand what bodies are, but discourse brings bodies into view in particular ways:

> In other words, 'sex' is an ideal construct which is forcibly materialized through time. It is not a simple fact or static condition of a body, but a process whereby regulatory norms materialize 'sex' and achieve this materialization through a forcible reiteration of those norms. (Butler, 1993: 1–2)

The discourse of sex is one that through repetition of the acts it guides, brings sex into view as a necessary norm. Sex is a construction, but an indispensable one that forms us as subjects and governs the materialization of bodies.

KEY THINKERS

Judith Butler (1960–)

A US born philosopher and feminist thinker, Butler has established herself as one of the foremost writers about sex/gender, subjectivity and identity. Butler argues that 'sex' is a normative 'regulatory ideal' that produces the bodies it governs through citation and reiteration of hegemonic discourses (the heterosexual imperative) to generate a performativity that is always derivative. Butler's project involves the deconstruction of the compulsory gender matrix and she has cited drag as a parodic form that can destabilize gender norms. Nevertheless, for Butler, *all* identity categories are necessary fictions that must be interrogated.

Reading: Butler, J. (1993) *Bodies That Matter*. London and New York: Routledge.

Sex and gender

Most feminist writing has tried to evade biological determinism by relying on a conceptual division between sex and gender. Here the former concept refers to the biology of the body and the latter notion to the cultural assumptions and practices that govern the social construction of men, women and their social relations. Subsequently it is argued that it is the social, cultural and political discourses and practices of gender that lie at the root of women's inequality.

This is what Nicholson has called the 'coat-rack' view of self-identity. That is, the body is held to be a rack upon which cultural meanings are thrown. As she argues, 'one crucial advantage of such a position for feminists was that it enabled them to postulate both commonalities and differences among women' (Nicholson, 1995: 41). Further, since gender is a cultural construct, it is open to change.

However, Butler's argument that sex and the body are discursive constructs breaks down the sex–gender difference since both are socially constructed.

> In this alternative view the body does not disappear from feminist theory. Rather, it becomes a variable rather than a constant, no longer able to ground claims about the male/female distinction across large sweeps of history but still there as always a potentially important element in how the male/female distinction *gets played out in any specific society*. (Nicholson, 1995: 43–4, my emphasis)

Of course, most societies continue to operate with a binary male–female distinction. Further they often attach to this distinction cultural expectations that are detrimental to women. However, the cultural variations that exist between women, based not only on differences of class, ethnicity, age, etc., but also on differences about what it means to be a woman, suggest that there is no universal cross-cultural category of 'woman' that is shared by all women. Acceptance of the idea that sex is a cultural construct leads to the blurring of the male–female distinction. It allows for ambiguous and dual sexualites. In short, neither biological nor cultural essentialism can found a feminist politics based on a universal identity of woman.

Is a universal feminism possible?

These issues are raised by Kaplan (1997) in her discussion of the film *Warrior Marks* directed by the African-American Alice Walker and the Kenyan-born British Asian Pratibha Parmar. The film was a graphic critique of clitoridectomies in Africa that aimed to dramatize the terror and pain involved while educating women about its dangers. In doing so, the film claims that clitoridectomies are a form of torture and child abuse in violation of universal women's rights (as affirmed by the 1995 Beijing Women's Conference).

However, the adult African women in the film confidently defend clitoridectomies as a necessary part of their traditions and sacred practices. While sympathetic to the anti-clitoridectomy theme, Kaplan raises a number of potential criticisms of the film, including the arguments that it:

- **makes its points at the expense of the African women;**
- **reproduces the imperialist tradition of teaching Africans a 'better' way of living;**
- **relies on established stereotypes of Africans as exotic and savage;**
- **assumes a global women's rights and is thus essentialist.**

How can there be a universal or global feminism when there is an unbridgeable difference between these western feminists and the African women in the film? There would appear to be no shared rules or point of potential arbitration for coming to agreement as to what would constitute justice or women's rights and interests. By implication, universal women's rights are either impossible or, if declared, another version of the imperialist representation of western categories as applicable at all times and in all places.

Since all knowledge is positional or culture-bound, cultural and political discourses can in the abstract be said to be incommensurable. This is because there can be no metalanguage of translation. Feminism cannot bridge cultures but must be satisfied with being specific to times and places. However, we can recognize others as language users. If we consider languages (as culture and knowledge) as not constituted by untranslatable and incompatible rules but as learnable skills, then incommensurable languages could only be unlearnable languages. As Davidson (1984) argues, it makes no sense to say that another's language is unlearnable (and therefore untranslatable) for we would in the first place have had to have learned enough of the others' language to recognize them as language users at all.

Hence we need to encourage *dialogue* and the attempt to reach pragmatic agreements. There is no *a priori* reason why this should succeed – agreement may never be reached – but there is no *a priori* reason why it should fail either (Rorty, 1991a). Given the poverty, inequality and violence that women across the globe endure, it is difficult to believe that agreement could not reached on a range of practical issues.

DEMONSTRATION FOR WOMEN'S RIGHTS IN IRAN

© Photographer: Ariadna De Raadt | Agency: Dreamstime.com

- *This picture is of a demonstration for women's rights in Iran. What does the symbolism of the image try to convey?*

- *Many feminists see the wearing of the veil and the Burka as a sign of oppression, but some Islamic women suggest that it protects women. What arguments can you construct that support both sides of the debate?*

- *The language on the banners is in English. Why might this be so? And what implications does this have for the meaning of the picture?*

— Make a list of all the characteristics that you think:

- women have in common;
- make women different from each other.

Compare your list with other people's. Do you agree?

— What practical political issues do you think could be agreed on by:

- western women;
- western women and African women.

Compare your list with other people's. Do you agree?

The project of feminism

None of these arguments means that the project of feminism is no longer valid. Nor is it being suggested that patterns of gender inequality are not in evidence – they are (Chapter 9). Rather, it is to argue for the 'replacement of claims about women as such or even women in patriarchal societies with claims about women in particular contexts' (Nicholson, 1995: 59).

Nicholson argues that we should not regard the meaning of the word 'woman' as singular. Rather, it is best understood as part of a language-game of different and overlapping meanings. Consequently, feminism is conceived of as a coalition politics. That is, alliances are formed amongst women who come to believe that they share particular interests in specific contexts. The meaning of 'woman' in feminist politics has to be forged rather than taken as a given. The politics of identity has to be *made* rather than found.

In a not dissimilar vein, Rorty argues that feminism represents the redescription of women as subjects. The critical point of Rorty's argument is that

> injustices may not be perceived as injustices, even by those who suffer them, until somebody invents a previously unplayed role. Only if somebody has a dream, a voice, and a voice to describe the dream, does what looked like nature begin to look like culture, what looked like fate begin to look like a moral abomination. For until then only the language of the oppressor is available, and most oppressors have had the wit to teach the oppressed a language in which the oppressed will sound crazy – *even to themselves* – if they describe themselves as oppressed. (Rorty, 1995: 126)

The contention here is that the language of feminism brings oppression into view. In doing so, it expands the logical space for moral and political deliberation. Feminism does not need essentialism at all. What is required is a 'new language' in which the claims of women do not sound crazy but come to be accepted as 'true' (in the sense of a social commendation). Feminism does not involve less distorted perception. Instead it involves the generation of a new language with consequences that serve particular purposes and values. The emergence of such a language is not the discovery of universal truth. Rather, it is part of an evolutionary struggle that has no immanent teleology (i.e. no future predetermined destiny to which it must evolve).

Creating 'new languages'

Like Nicholson, Rorty regards feminism as creating 'women's experience' by creating a language rather than by finding what it is to be a woman or unmasking truth and injustice. As such, feminism is seen as a form of 'prophetic pragmatism' that imagines, and seeks to bring into being, an alternative form of community.

✓ *Feminism forges a moral identity for women as women by gaining linguistic authority over descriptions of the feminine. It does not (or should not) therefore assume that there is an essential identity for women to be found.*

In her discussion of Rorty's arguments, Fraser (1995a) suggests that he locates redescriptions exclusively in individual women. In contrast, she suggests that such redescriptions form part of a *collective* feminist politics. This must involve argument and contestation about which new descriptions will count and which women will be empowered. Thus, Fraser links feminism to the best of the democratic tradition and to the creation of a 'feminist countersphere' of collective debate and practice. In doing so, she begins to address the question of *how* a politics of identity can bring about change. This is an element of identity politics that is underplayed in Rorty's argument. These themes are taken up and elaborated in Chapter 14.

Challenging the critique of identity

The anti-essentialist conception of identities that understands them in terms of discursive constructs is the dominant strain of thinking in contemporary cultural studies. It is such an anti-essentialism that leads Hall (1990, 1996a) to describe identity as a 'cut' in language. Identity, it is argued, is best understood not as an entity but as an emotionally charged description of ourselves.

This is a view of identity and language that has much to commend it. It is an understanding based on the assumption that our maps of meaning, our culture, are learned by acquiring propositions in language. However, we also acquire a whole series of propositions in the form of practices. Further, as was noted in Chapter 3, while the meanings of language do derive from relations of difference, they are given a degree of stability by social practice. The endless play of signification is partially stabilized through the location of signs within pragmatic narratives. A meaningful expression is one that can be given a use by living human beings.

Thus, much of our bedrock of convictions is part of what Giddens (1984, 1991) calls our 'practical consciousness', that is, a condition of being that is rarely made discursively explicit but which is embedded in the practical conduct of social life. This argument can render the distinction between essentialism and anti-essentialism somewhat redundant. That is to say, it is agreed that there are in principle no essential identities. Nevertheless, in practice people act, and need to act, as if there were.

There is, then, a stream of thought within cultural studies that seeks to modify anti-essentialist conceptions of identity.

- It is argued by some writers that a discursive conception of society and identities collapses the social into language. Critics argue that everything becomes discourse and there is no material reality. However, to say that we can only have knowledge of the material world through discourse is not to say that such a material world is not present. There are indeed aspects of the world which 'are the effects of causes which do not include human mental states' (Rorty, 1989). However, we can only know them through language. Discourse and materiality are, *pace* Butler, indissociable.

- It is argued that discourse-based theories efface human agency. That is, human beings are reduced to the 'effects' of discourse. However, we tackled this question earlier in the chapter by arguing that agency is the socially constructed capacity to act. Discourse enables action by providing subject positions of agency.

- It is suggested that anti-essentialist arguments about identity are of no *practical* value. We require, it is said, a more constructive and positive account of the politics of identity based on a strategic essentialism. That is, the recognition that we act *as if* identities were stable entities for specific political and practical purposes. This point requires further elaboration.

Strategic essentialism

Appiah (1995) has suggested that we can make the argument for 'African identity' being a discursive device which can be 'deconstructed'. However, this does not mean that people do not mobilize around the idea of African identity or pan-Africanism as the means for political change and improvement. Nor does it mean that pan-Africanism may not provide a valuable device for the improvement of the human condition. Indeed, Appiah suggests that deconstructing identities from within the academy can be of little relevance to most people's lives or to the practices of political action.

That argument has some merit for practical purposes. Indeed, strategic essentialism may be what in practice happens. As Hall (1993) has argued, any sense of self, of identity, of communities of identification (nations, ethnicities, sexualities, classes, etc.) is a fiction marking a temporary, partial and arbitrary closure of meaning. Some kind of strategic cut or temporary stabilization of meaning is necessary in order to say or do anything. As Hall remarks, 'politics, without the arbitrary interposition of power in language, the cut of ideology, the positioning, the crossing of lines, the rupture, is impossible' (Hall, 1993: 136).

Nevertheless, strategic essentialism is open to the criticism that at some point certain voices have been excluded. Thus, the strategic essentialism of feminism, that it takes women to be an essential category for tactical reasons, may lead to some women, for example black or Hispanic women, saying to white women, 'you have not taken account of our differences as well as our similarities with you'. Likewise, pan-Africanism may lead to the obscuring of difference and the exclusion of certain voices. There always remains the question of where to draw the tactical line. Who, for example, is African or a woman? Strategic essentialism can lend itself towards ethnic or gender 'absolutism'. It may bypass the hybrid and syncretic character of contemporary culture and identities (Chapter 8).

✓ *The trick is to try to hold both the plasticity and the practical fixity of identity in mind at the same time, enabling one to oscillate between them.*

DECONSTRUCT THIS: AGENCY VS. DETERMINATION

- *How do people display agency?*
- *What is meant by 'determination'?*
- *How can agency be itself determined?*

SUMMARY

Identity concerns both self-identity and social identity. It is about the personal and the social. It is about ourselves and our relations with others. It has been argued that identity is wholly cultural in character and does not exist outside of its representation in cultural discourses. Identity is not a fixed thing that we possess but a becoming. It is a strategic cut or temporary stabilization in language and practice. We may understand identity as regulatory discourses to which we are attached through processes of identification or emotional investment.

The self has been understood as multiple, fragmented and decentred. This is an outcome of:

- the instability of language;
- our constitution of multiple discourses;
- the proliferation of social relationships and sites of activity.

None of these arguements needs efface human agency, provided that one understands agency as itself a socially constructed and differentially distributed set of capabilities to act. Nor do anti-essentialist arguements preclude identity politics. Such a politics is constituted through redescriptions in language and temporary strategic coalitions of people who share at least some values.

8 Ethnicity, Race and Nation

KEY CONCEPTS

Cultural identity	*Orientalism*
Diaspora	*Postcolonialism*
Ethnicity	*Race*
Hybridity	*Representation*
National identity	*Stereotype*

In this chapter we will be concerned with ethnicity, race and nationality as forms of cultural identity. Indeed, it is the exploration of the categories of race, ethnicity and nation in terms of identity that gives the cultural studies approach its distinctive edge (see Black and Solomos, 2000). For example, sociological explorations of race have concentrated on resource distribution within the context of class and political relations. Here the language has been that of 'racial and ethnic minorities' as an 'underclass' (Rex, 1970). In neo-Marxist approaches (e.g. Miles, 1982, 1989) the category of race is an ideological construct in service of world capitalism. In this context, the issue to be explored is racism rather than race *per se*. Identity politics are often seen in Marxist understandings as a diversion from the central problem of capitalism.

The cultural studies' perspective on race and ethnicity certainly acknowledges the importance of the intersections of race, ethnicity and class. However, it has sought to avoid the reduction of these categories to class and the functions of capitalism. Instead cultural studies has tended to explore:

- **the shifting character of cultural understandings of race and ethnicity in terms of representation;**

- **the cultural politics of race as a 'politics of representation';**

- the changing forms of cultural identity associated with ethnicity;
- the intersections between class, race and gender;
- the cultural legacy of colonialism.

In this context, identities are regarded as discursive–performative constructions (Chapter 7). That is, ethnic, racial and national identities are contingent and unstable cultural creations with which we identify. They are not universal or absolute existent 'things'. However, as regulated ways of speaking about ourselves, identities are not arbitrary either; rather, they are temporarily stabilized by social practice. Indeed, race, ethnicity and nationality are amongst the more enduring 'nodal points' of identity in modern western societies.

RACE AND ETHNICITY

The concept of race bears the traces of its origins in the biological discourses of social Darwinism that stress 'lines of descent' and 'types of people'. Here the concept of race refers to alleged biological and physical characteristics, the most obvious of which is skin pigmentation. These attributes, frequently linked to 'intelligence' and 'capabilities', are used to rank 'racialized' groups in a hierarchy of social and material superiority and subordination. These racial classifications, constituted by and constitutive of power, are at the root of racism.

Racialization

✓ *The idea of 'racialization' or 'race formation' is founded on the argument that race is a social construction and not a universal or essential category of biology.*

Races, it is argued (Hall, 1990, 1996d, 1997c), do not exist outside of representation. Rather, they are formed in and by symbolization in a process of social and political power struggle. Thus, observable characteristics are transformed into signifiers of race. This includes the spurious appeal to essential biological and cultural difference. As Gilroy argues:

Accepting that skin 'colour', however meaningless we know it to be, has a strictly limited material basis in biology, opens up the possibility of engaging with theories of signification which can highlight the elasticity and emptiness of 'racial' signifiers as well as the ideological work which has to be done in order to turn them into signifiers of 'race' as an open political category, for it is struggle that determines which definitions of 'race' will prevail and the conditions under which they will endure or wither away. (Gilroy, 1987: 38–9)

In Britain, America and Australia the historical formation of 'race' is one of power and subordination. That is, people of colour have occupied structurally subordinate positions in relation to every dimension of 'life-chances'. British Afro-Caribbeans, African-Americans and Australian Aboriginal peoples have been disadvantaged in:

- the labour market;

- the housing market;

- the education system;

- the media and other forms of cultural representation.

In this context, race formation (or racialization) has been inherently racist for it involves forms of social, economic and political subordination that are lived through the categories and discourses of race. The concept of racialization refers to 'those instances where social relations between people have been structured by the signification of human biological characteristics in such a way as to define and construct differentiated social collectivities' (Miles, 1989: 75).

Different racisms

As a discursive construct, the meanings of 'race' change and are struggled over. Thus, different groups are differentially racialized and subject to different forms of racism. As Goldberg argues, 'the presumption of a single monolithic racism is being displaced by a mapping of the multifarious historical formulations of *racisms*' (Goldberg in Black and Solomos, 2000: 20). For example, British Asians have historically been subject to different forms of stereotyping and have occupied a different place in the social and racial hierarchy from British Afro-Caribbeans. While British Asians may be second-class citizens, black Britons are on the third rung of the ladder. British Asians are stereotyped as doctors and shopkeepers while young Afro-Caribbean men in Britain are cast in the role of criminals.

The meanings of race differ over time and across space. For example, it has been argued (Barker, 1982) that the 'new racism' in Britain relies not on biological discourses of superiority, as in South African apartheid, but on cultural differences that exclude black people from being fully a part of the *nation*. In addition, the meanings of race differ between, say, America and Britain. In Britain, the relatively homogeneous white character of the *in situ* population was disturbed in the 1950s by the arrival of migrants from the Caribbean and Indian subcontinent. This made questions of national identity a crucial category through which racialization operated. However, West (1992) has argued that the history of the modern United States begins with the dispossession and genocide of native American peoples and continues through the long history of slavery. Thus, questions of race are posed at the very inception of the US in ways that are more longstanding, but less concerned with nationality, than in Britain.

— Consider the country that you live in. What different racial groups are there? Is there a hierarchy of power and status?
— What evidence is there of racial inequality in:

* the economy;
* the legal system;
* media representations;
* the housing market;
* immigration policy?

If you do not know, find out …

The concept of ethnicity

Ethnicity is a cultural concept centred on the sharing of norms, values, beliefs, cultural symbols and practices. The formation of 'ethnic groups' relies on shared cultural signifiers that have developed under specific historical, social and political contexts. They encourage a sense of belonging based, at least in part, on a common mythological ancestry. However, anti-essentialist arguments (Chapter 7) suggest that ethnic groups are not based on primordial ties or universal cultural characteristics possessed by a specific group. Rather, they are formed through discursive practices.

✓ *Ethnicity is formed by the way we speak about group identities and identify with the signs and symbols that constitute ethnicity.*

Ethnicity is a *relational* concept that is concerned with categories of self-identification and social ascription. Thus, what we think of as our identity is dependent on what we think we are *not*. Serbians are not Croatians, Bosnians or Albanians. Consequently, ethnicity is best understood as a process of boundary formation that has been constructed and maintained under specific socio-historical conditions (Barth, 1969). To suggest that ethnicity is not about pre-given cultural difference does not mean that such distinctiveness cannot be socially constructed around signifiers that do connote universality, territory and purity. Thus, metaphors of blood, kinship and homeland are frequently implicated in the formation and maintenance of ethnic boundaries.

A culturalist conception of ethnicity is a valiant attempt to escape the racist implications that are inherent in the historically forged concept of race. As Hall writes,

If the black subject and black experience are not stabilized by Nature or by some other essential guarantee, then it must be the case that they are constructed historically, culturally and politically – the concept which refers to this is 'ethnicity'. The term ethnicity acknowledges the place of history, language and culture in the construction of subjectivity and identity, as well as the fact that all discourse is placed, positioned, situated, and all knowledge is contextual. (Hall, 1996c: 446)

However, the concept of ethnicity does have some problems of usage and it remains a contested term. For instance, white Anglo-Saxons frequently use the concept of ethnicity to refer to other people, usually with different skin pigmentation. Consequently, Asians, Africans, Hispanics and African-Americans are held to be ethnic groups but the English or white Anglo-Saxon Americans and Australians are not. Here whiteness is seen as a taken-for-granted universal. By contrast, everyone else is understood to have been constituted by their ethnicity. However, it is important to maintain that white English, American or Australian people *do* constitute ethnic groups. As Dyer (1997) has argued, studying whiteness 'is about making whiteness strange rather than treating it as a taken for granted touchstone of human ordinariness'. Commonly, whiteness is equated with normality and thus becomes invisible so that we do not think it requires attention. Nevertheless, as Dyer notes, the recognition that whiteness is a historical invention does not mean that it can simply be wished away.

— Take 5 minutes to write down what the sign 'white' means to you.
— Form a group with others and compare the meanings that have emerged. Discuss the meaning of 'whiteness' within the whole class.
— Does the ethnicity of a person play a part in how the idea of 'white' is understood by them?

Ethnicity and power

One problem with the cultural concept of ethnicity is that some questions of power and racism may be sidelined. Ethnicity can be deployed to suggest that a social formation operates with plural and equal groups rather than hierarchical racialized groups. It has also been suggested that it diverts attention away from racism and towards the cultural characteristics of racialized minorities. Consequently, hooks (1990) and Gilroy (1987) prefer the concept of 'race' to that of ethnicity. This is not because the notion of race corresponds to any biological or cultural absolutes, but because it connotes, and refers investigation to, issues of power. In contrast, Hall (1996c) looks to a reworking of the concept of ethnicity so that we are all held to be ethnically located.

Ethnicity is constituted through power relations between groups. It signals relations of marginality, of the centre and the periphery. This occurs in the context of changing historical forms and circumstances. Here, the centre and the margin are to be grasped through the politics of representation. As Brah argues: 'It is necessary for it to become axiomatic that what is *represented* as the "margin" is not marginal at all but is a *constitutive effect of the representation itself.* The "centre" is no more a centre than is the "margin"' (Brah, 1996: 226).

Discourses of ethnic centrality and marginality are commonly articulated with those of nationality. For example, the nations of the industrialized west are often regarded as 'the centre' in relation to a 'periphery' of 'developing' nations. Further, history is littered with examples of how one ethnic group has been defined as central and superior to a marginal 'other'. While Nazi Germany, apartheid South Africa and 'ethnic cleansing' in Bosnia are clear-cut examples, the metaphor of superiority and subordination is no less applicable to contemporary Britain, America and Australia. Thus, race and ethnicity have been closely allied to forms of nationalism that conceive of the 'nation' as a shared culture requiring that ethnic boundaries should not cut across political ones (though of course they do).

AMERICAN INDIAN FLAG

© Photographer: Jim Parkin | Agency: Dreamstime.com

- *What do you think this image is saying about the relationship between the US state and the Native American people?*

- *Is there a more general message about the relationship between the nation-state and ethnic groups?*

NATIONAL IDENTITIES

The nation-state

The modern nation-state is a relatively recent invention. Indeed, most of the human species have never participated in any kind of state or identified with one. The nation-state, nationalism and national identity are not 'naturally' occurring phenomena but contingent historical-cultural formations. In particular, they are socially and culturally constructed as collective forms of organization and identification.

- The *nation-state* is a political concept that refers to an administrative apparatus deemed to have sovereignty over a specific space or territory within the nation-state system.

- *National identity* is a form of imaginative identification with the symbols and discourses of the nation-state.

Nations are not simply political formations but systems of cultural representation by which national identity is continually reproduced through discursive action. The nation-state as a political apparatus and a symbolic form also has a temporal dimension since political structures endure and change. The symbolic and discursive dimensions of national identity narrate and create the idea of origins, continuity and tradition.

Though we speak of the nation-state, it is necessary to disentangle the couplet since national cultural identities are not coterminous with state borders. Various global diasporas – African, Jewish, Indian, Chinese, Polish, English, Irish, etc. – attest to national and ethnic cultural identities that span the borders of nation-states. Further, few states have ethnically homogeneous populations. Smith (1990) not only distinguishes between *civic*/political conceptions of nations and *ethnic* ones, but is also able to list over 60 states that are constituted by more than one national or ethnic culture.

Narratives of unity

Cultures are not static entities but are constituted by changing practices and meanings that operate at different social levels. Thus, any given national culture is understood and acted upon differently by diverse social groups. For example, governments, ethnic groups and classes may perceive their own national culture in divergent ways. Further, any ethnic or class group will be divided along the lines of age and gender (Tomlinson, 1991). Thus we can ask:

- At which level should a national culture be identified?

- Which set of values within those groups are the authentic ones?

Representations of national culture are snapshots of the symbols and practices that have been foregrounded at specific historical conjunctures. This has invariably been done for particular purposes by distinctive groups of people. National identity is a way of unifying cultural diversity so that, as Hall argues,

> Instead of thinking of national cultures as unified, we should think of them as a discursive device which represents difference as unity or identity. They are cross-cut by deep internal divisions and differences, and 'unified' only through the exercise of different forms of cultural power. (Hall, 1992b: 297)

National unity is constructed through the narrative of the nation by which stories, images, symbols and rituals represent 'shared' meanings of nationhood (Bhabha, 1990).

✓ *National identity is a form of identification with representations of shared experiences and history. These are told through stories, literature, popular culture and the media.*

Narratives of nationhood emphasize the traditions and continuity of the nation as being 'in the nature of things'. They commonly stress a foundational myth of collective origin. This in turn both assumes and produces the linkage between national identity and a pure, original people or 'folk' tradition.

Compile a list of the stories, symbols and icons that construct the national identity of the country that you live in.

— How are these signs and discourses manifested in the contemporary media?

Consider a major sporting event such as the Olympics or the World Cup.

— How is national identity constructed at these events?

The imagined community

National identities are intrinsically connected to, and constituted by, forms of communication. For Anderson (1983), the 'nation' is an 'imagined community' and national identity a construction assembled through symbols and rituals in relation to territorial and administrative categories.

> It is *imagined* because the members of even the smallest nation will never know most of their fellow members, meet them, or even hear of them, yet in the minds of each lives the images of their communion. … The nation is imagined as *limited* because even the largest

of them encompassing perhaps a billion living beings, has finite, if elastic boundaries, beyond which lie other nations. … It is imagined as *sovereign* because the concept was born in an age in which Enlightenment and Revolution were destroying the legitimacy of the divinely ordered, hierarchical dynastic realm. … Finally, it is imagined as a *community* because, regardless of the actual inequality and exploitation that may prevail in each, the nation is always conceived as a deep, horizontal comradeship. Ultimately, it is this fraternity that makes it possible, over the past two centuries, for so many millions of people, not so much to kill, as willingly to die for such limited imaginings. (Anderson, 1983: 15–16)

According to Anderson, the mechanized production and commodification of books and newspapers, the rise of 'print capitalism', allowed vernacular languages to be standardized and disseminated. This provided the conditions for the creation of a national consciousness. Thus, 'Print language is what invents nationalism, not a particular language *per se*' (ibid.: 122). For the first time it was possible for the mass of people within a particular state to understand each other through a common print language. The processes of print capitalism thus 'fixed' a vernacular language as *the* 'national' language. In doing so a new imagined national community was made possible.

Communication facilitates not just the construction of a common language but also a common recognition of time, which, within the context of modernity, is an empty universal concept measurable by calendar and clock. For example, the media encourage us to imagine the simultaneous occurrence of events across wide tracts of time and space. This contributes to the concept of nation and to the place of states within a spatially distributed global system.

Criticisms of Anderson

Anderson's account is useful in linking forms of national identity with modes of communication. Nevertheless, his work falls short of specifying exactly how new print forms give rise to national sentiments (Thompson, 1995). Nor does he deal adequately with the various ways in which divergent social groups use media products and decode them in different ways. At best, Anderson shows how print media established the necessary conditions for national identity and the nation-state.

Anderson tends to overstate the unity of the nation and the strength of nationalist feeling. In doing so, he covers over differences of class, gender, ethnicity and so forth. Indeed, the proliferation and diversification of contexts and sites of interaction, constituted in and through discourse, prevent easy identification of particular subjects with a given, fixed identity. Consequently, in the context of the accelerated globalization of late modernity (Chapter 5), we have begun to talk about hybrid cultural identities rather than a homogeneous national or ethnic cultural identity. Further, the instability of meaning in language, *différance*, leads us to think of culture, identities and identifications as always a place of borders and hybridity rather than of fixed stable entities (Bhabha, 1994).

DIASPORA AND HYBRID IDENTITIES

Stable identities are rarely questioned; they appear as 'natural' and taken for granted. However, when 'naturalness' is seen to dissolve, we are inclined to examine these identities anew. As Mercer (1992) has argued, identity is hotly debated when it is in crisis. Globalization provides the context for just such a crisis since it has increased the range of sources and resources available for identity construction. Patterns of population movement and settlement established during colonialism and its aftermath, combined with the more recent acceleration of globalization, particularly of electronic communications, have enabled increased cultural juxtaposing, meeting and mixing.

According to Pieterse (1995), it is necessary to differentiate between 'culture' as bounded, that is, tied to place and inward-looking, from 'culture' as an outward-looking, 'translocal learning process'. He argues that introverted cultures are receding into the background as diverse translocal cultures come to the fore. Bounded societies and states, though very much still with us, are cut across by the circulation of global cultural discourses. Thus, Clifford (1992), amongst others, has argued that culture and cultural identities can no longer be adequately understood in terms of place. Rather, they are better conceptualized in terms of travel. This includes:

- **peoples and cultures that travel;**
- **places/cultures as sites of criss-crossing travellers.**

The idea of diaspora

In this context, new prominence is being given to the old concept of diaspora.

✓ *A diaspora can be understood as a dispersed network of ethnically and culturally related peoples.*

This notion focuses our attention on travel, journeys, dispersion, homes and borders in the context of questions about who travels, 'where, when, how and under what circumstances' (Brah, 1996: 182). Thus, 'diasporic identities are at once local and global. They are networks of transnational identifications encompassing "imagined" and "encountered" communities' (ibid.: 196). Diaspora is a *relational* concept referring to 'configurations of power that differentiate diasporas internally as well as situate them in relation to one another' (ibid.: 183).

Diaspora space as a conceptual category is 'inhabited' not only by those who have migrated and their descendants, but also by those who are constructed and represented as indigenous. In other words, the concept of *diaspora space* … includes the entanglement, the intertwining of the genealogies of dispersion with those 'staying put'. The diaspora space is the site where *the native is as much a diasporian as the diasporian is a native.* (Ibid.: 209)

According to Gilroy, the divided network of related peoples that form the diaspora is one 'characteristically produced by forced dispersal and reluctant scattering'. The idea of a diaspora

connotes flight following the threat of violence … [so that] diaspora identity is focused less on the equalizing, proto-democratic force of common territory and more on the social dynamics of remembrance and commemoration defined by a strong sense of the dangers involved in forgetting the location of origin and the process of dispersal. (Gilroy, 1997: 318)

The Black Atlantic

The concept of diaspora helps us to think about identities in terms of contingency, inde-terminacy and conflict. That is, we think of identities as being in motion rather than existing as absolutes of nature or culture. Identities are concerned with routes rather more than with roots. This is the 'changing same' of the diaspora that involves 'creolized, syncretized, hybridized and chronically impure cultural forms' (ibid.: 335).

As an example of an enacted diaspora, Gilroy (1993) introduces the concept of the Black Atlantic. Black identities cannot be understood, he argues, in terms of being American or British or West Indian. Nor can they be grasped in terms of ethnic abso-lutism (that there is a global essential black identity); rather, they should be understood in terms of the black diaspora of the Atlantic. Here, cultural exchange within the black diaspora produces hybrid identities. This involves cultural forms of similarity and differ-ence within and between the various locales of the diaspora. As Gilroy argues, black self-identities and cultural expressions utilize a plurality of histories.

Blackness is not a pan-global absolute identity, since the cultural identities of black Britons, black Americans and black Africans are different. Nevertheless, Gilroy points to *historically* shared cultural forms within the Black Atlantic. Despite the different meanings and history of 'race' that have operated in Britain, America, Africa and the Caribbean,

It may be that a common experience of powerlessness somehow transcending history and experienced in *racial* categories; in the antagonism between white and black rather than European and African, is enough to secure affinity between these divergent patterns of subordination. (Gilroy, 1987: 158–9)

For example, Rap and Hip-Hop, American-Caribbean hybrids, have become the prominent musical forms of the black diaspora and a point of identification within the Black Atlantic.

KEY THINKERS

Paul Gilroy (1956–)

Paul Gilroy was born in Bethnal Green, London, and studied at the Birmingham Centre for Contemporary Cultural Studies (CCCS). He is currently the first holder of the Anthony Giddens Professorship in Social Theory at the London School of Economics. He assumed this post in 2005, having previously been chair of the Department of African-American Studies at Yale University. Gilroy was a significant figure in bringing the study of race and racialization to the fore in cultural studies, though he was also against the very idea of classifying people into 'races'. Gilroy has written extensively about what he calls the 'changing same' of cultural identity within diaspora. He argues that black self-identities and cultural expressions utilize a plurality of histories and that we should think of identities as being in motion rather than existing as absolutes of nature or culture.

Reading: Gilroy, P. (1993) *The Black Atlantic*. London: Verso.

Types of hybridity

The concept of hybridity has proved useful in highlighting cultural mixing and the emergence of new forms of identity. However, we need to differentiate between types of hybridity. This needs to be done with reference to the specific circumstances of particular social groups. Thus, Pieterse (1995) has suggested a distinction between structural and cultural hybridization:

- *Structural hybridization* refers to a variety of social and institutional *sites* of hybridity, for example border zones or cities like Miami or Singapore. It increases the range of organizational options open to people.

- *Cultural hybridization* distinguishes cultural *responses*, which range from assimilation, through forms of separation, to hybrids that destabilize and blur cultural boundaries. This involves the opening up of 'imagined communities'.

Pieterse argues that both structural hybridization and cultural hybridization are signs of increased boundary crossing. However, they do not represent the erasure of boundaries. Thus, we need to be sensitive both to cultural difference and to forms of identification that involve recognition of similarity.

The hybridity of all culture

The concept of hybridity remains problematic in so far as it assumes or implies the meeting or mixing of completely separate and homogeneous cultural spheres. To think of British Asian or Mexican American hybrid forms as the mixing of two separate traditions is problematic because neither British, Asian, Mexican nor American culture is bounded and homogeneous. Each category is always already a hybrid form that is also divided along the lines of religion, class, gender, age, nationality and so forth.

Thus, hybridization is the mixing of that which is already a hybrid. All cultures are zones of shifting boundaries and hybridization (Bhabha, 1994). Nevertheless, the concept of hybridity has enabled us to recognize the production of new identities and cultural forms. This would include, for example, 'British Asians' and British Bhangra. Thus, the concept of hybridity is acceptable as a device to capture cultural change by way of a strategic cut or temporary stabilization of cultural categories.

Hybridity and British Asians

It is a sign of our times that forms of hybrid cultural identity are appearing all across the world, from the USA to Australia and from Europe to South Africa. In Britain, the 'place' and cultures of Asians in relation to Anglo-Saxon and Afro-Caribbean Britons have raised similar issues of purity and hybridity. Ballard (1994) documents the emergence, since the early 1950s, of Desh Pardesh, a phrase with the double meaning of 'home from home' and 'at home abroad'. He emphasizes:

- **the determination of arrivals from South Asia to pursue their own self-determined goals;**
- **the diverse and heterogeneous character of South Asian ethnicities in Britain;**
- **the changing dispositions involved in the settlers' adaptive strategies.**

The complex nature of South Asian settler cultural identities is indicated by the diverse 'origins' of these direct migrants. They came from the distinct geographical areas of the Punjab, Gujarat and Sylhet, each of which is cross-cut by differences of religion, caste, class, age and gender, as well as by an urban–rural distinction. To this we may add the presence of 'twice migrants' who arrived in Britain by way of East Africa.

From 'sojourners to settlers'

According to Ballard, migrants from South Asia to Britain transformed themselves from 'sojourners to settlers', that is, from a temporary entrepreneurial disposition involving the primacy of earning and saving money, to become permanent settlers constructing families, houses, businesses and cultural institutions. However, even when settler status was taken on board, clear boundaries were drawn between themselves and their white neighbours. In particular, the maintenance of *izzat*, or personal honour, required them to keep their distance from a culture that seemed to have little sense of family, of sexual morality, of respect for elders or personal hygiene. Indeed, 'those who mimicked English ways too closely began to be accused of being *beizzat* – without honour' (Ballard, 1994: 15).

Switching cultural codes

The emergence of British-born young 'Asians' gave rise to a generation that was much more deeply involved in transactions across ethnic boundaries than were the original migrants. Young British Asians went to school with white and Afro-Caribbean Britons, shared leisure sites, watched television and were frequently bilingual. British Asians have often been characterized as being 'between two cultures' (Watson, 1977) or caught up in a process of 'cultural conflict'. However, it is more valid to see these young people as skilled operators of cultural code switching. This is so, Brah (1996) argues, for a number of reasons:

- **The notion of 'two cultures' is incorrect because both 'British' and 'Asian' cultures are heterogeneous and stratified.**

- **There is no reason to see cultural encounters as necessarily involving clashes or conflicts.**

- **The relationship between 'British' and 'Asian' cultures is not a one-way process but multi-directional.**

- **While some Asians may experience dissonance, there is no evidence to suggest that this is widespread.**

- **Inter-generational difference should not be conflated with conflict.**

British Asian young people have developed their own home-grown syncretic or hybrid cultural forms along with political and cultural discourses of 'British Asianness'. Many of the cultural issues involved in this process have been aired in contemporary films such as *East Is East* (1999), *Bhaji on the Beach* (1993) and *Bend It Like Beckham* (2002).

In her study of Asian youth in Southall (London), Gillespie (1995) shows how young people constituted themselves, to varying degrees, as British Asian. Under some circumstances this involved identification with Britishness, at other times with aspects of Asian culture (neither being homogeneous). The circumstances of the 1990–1 Gulf War opened up ambiguities and insecurities around those points of identification. On the one hand, some young Asians identified with an Islamic 'developing nation' in conflict with the west. On the other hand, they wanted to remain within the boundaries of Britishness, the place of their birth and upbringing. The young people shifted from one subject position to another as they determined it to be situationally appropriate. This shifting within and between the discourses of Britishness and Asianness was further complicated by religious and geographical differences within Asian culture and by age, gender and class.

Multiple identities

The differences within the community studied by Gillespie prevent easy identification of particular subjects with a given, fixed identity. Thus, under certain conditions, a British Asian girl might identify herself with Asianness and argue that traditional clothes should be respected or that Asians are misrepresented on television. Yet, in the context of a discussion about relationships, she might speak from a position of western feminism to argue against the traditional patriarchal practices of some Asian men. On another occasion she may position herself as a young person, irrespective of ethnicity or gender, as she adopts the fashion and music of a specific youth subculture. A young singer puts one such range of shifting identity positions:

> 'I rap in Bengali and English. I rap on everything from love to politics. I've always been into rapping … it was rebellious, the lyrics were sensational. I could relate to that, I could identify with it. Like living in the ghetto and that. … It's from the heart. It's: "I'm Bengali, I'm Asian, I'm a woman, and I'm living here."' (Cited in Gardner and Shukur, 1994: 161)

The subject positions of this young woman involve the articulation of positions drawn from a variety of discourses and sites. At the very least she has identifications with being:

- **Bengali;**
- **English;**
- **a woman;**
- **a participant in youth culture;**
- **a devotee of Rap (an American–Caribbean hybrid, now appropriated as Anglo-Bengali).**

Thus, she is involved not only in shifting identifications but also in enacting a hybrid identity that draws on multiplying global resources.

✓ *Identities are neither pure nor fixed but formed at the intersections of age, class, gender, race and nation.*

Intersections and boundary crossings

According to Hall, the end of essentialism 'entails a recognition that the central issues of race always appear historically in articulation, in a formation, with other categories and divisions and are constantly crossed and recrossed by the categories of class, of gender and ethnicity' (Hall, 1996d: 444). We may consider this process in three fundamental ways:

1 **the multiple identities of the postmodern subject, that is, the weaving of the patterns of identity from discourses of class, race, gender, etc.;**

2 **the construction of one discourse in terms of metaphors drawn from another, that is, the construction of nation through gendered metaphors or of race in terms of class – for example, the idea of 'race' being connected to the idea of the ascent of 'Man'; further, ethnic groups may be derided as effeminate, nations be gendered as female, and absolute ethnic differences premised on the idea of blood lines and thus women's bodies;**

3 **the capability of persons to move across discursive and spatial sites of activity which address them in different ways.**

In this context, the social position of British Asian girls has particular significance. They are arguably 'special' by virtue of living across cultural boundaries and, as girls, being somewhat marginalized within male-dominated cultures. In a study of the moral discourses produced by British Asian girls watching television soap opera (Barker, 1998), it was argued that the contradictory subject positions they took up, while an aspect of logical tensions in moral discourses themselves, were also the outcome of the proliferation of discursive resources stemming from different conventions, sites and practices that were in contradiction with one another.

Gillespie (1995) discusses the way that young Asian girls use the soap opera *Neighbours* to explore the rules surrounding male–female relationships and teenage romance. This is especially significant for girls since *Neighbours* portrays young women with a greater degree of freedom than many British Asian girls can themselves expect. *Neighbours* offers the girls the pleasure of seeing more assertive women and provokes discussion about gender roles.

Read the following extract. It is taken from a research interview in which a group of British Asian girls are talking about soap opera (Barker, 1999).

—   What does the conversation tell us about:

• the place of Asian girls in British culture;
• the idea of 'hybridity'?

(Cont'd)

B: What about that thingy in *Neighbours*, Lahta?

D: That is not a typical Asian girl, did you see her with a sari on?

A: That is a joke

B: And going out with

C: That Brett

A: I know, that was taking the er [pause] mickey then, a typical Asian, they're always taking the piss of Asian or Black people, or Chinese

B: Or when they had lots of Chinese people in

C: That one had spots all over his face

B: And how long do they stay in the programme?

A: None of the other races stay in for long

D: None of the Black people stay in for long

B: In *Neighbours* is there one Black?

B: And the way her [Lahta's] brother was over-controlling her life it's not on, it's not like that in our life

A: That does not happen

B: People aren't that strict

C: And I don't think that brothers act towards their sister like that

B: I think, you know, that bit's really exaggerated. I mean you know, what's his name again, Lahta's brother?

C: Vikram

D: I mean you wouldn't see an Asian girl going to an English boy – oh I want to have it off with you

C&D: Yes, exactly

B: Well it does happen, but listen

A: The girl came from India you know

B: You know Vikram, he's a hypocrite cos do you remember when it was that party, I can't remember when, and he was dancing with Philip's wife Julie and he can't talk that his daughter, I mean sister

A: No but he didn't fancy her

C: He didn't fancy her, that was just a normal dance

A: He doesn't mind her having friends like, normal friends, but not like you know, boyfriends and trying to have it off with them

B: Yes I think that's wrong, it's the influence of everybody around her, you know Lahta she doesn't want to feel, you know, left out

A: Yes that's why Asians do this stuff sometimes

B: Yeah, sometimes, yeah

C: Why not Asians, most girls

D: Get a bad reputation and that stuff

B: I mean most girls do it at our time.

Weaving the patterns of identity

We can thus conceive of persons as operating across and within multiple subject positions. Nevertheless, some critics have worried that the critique of essentialism robs us of the tools to combat racism. This is said to be so because the very category of race seems to disappear. However, to abandon an essentialist universal condition called 'race' does not mean that the social and historical construction of race, the racialization of specific groups of human beings, need also be lost. On the contrary, the critique of essentialist arguments exposes the radical contingency of identity categories. This helps to combat the reduction of people to race by encouraging us to see all people as multifaceted. Thus:

> Employing a critique of essentialism allows African-Americans to acknowledge the way in which class mobility has altered collective black experience so that racism does not necessarily have the same impact on our lives. Such a critique allows us to affirm multiple black identities, varied black experience. It also challenges colonial imperialist paradigms of black identity which represent blackness one-dimensionally in ways that reinforce and sustain white supremacy. … When black folks critique essentialism, we are empowered to recognize multiple experiences of black identity that are the lived conditions which make diverse cultural productions possible. When this diversity is ignored, it is easy to see black folks as falling into two categories: nationalist or assimilationist, black-identifiers or white-identified. (hooks, 1990: 28–9)

As hooks submits, one of the benefits of casting off essentialism, and thus black absolutism or nationalism, is that black women do not have to subsume their critique of black masculinity. It is not a betrayal of black people to put forward a black feminist critique of black male macho (Wallace, 1979), nor is it a betrayal of women to critique white feminism from the perspective of black women (Carby, 1984; hooks, 1990). Rather, these are the processes of articulation and coalition building that are core to cultural politics (Chapter 14).

KEY THINKERS

bell hooks – aka Gloria Watkins (1952–)

hooks is an African-American feminist writer whose thinking is centrally concerned with the intersections of class, gender and race in culture and politics. Political engagement and a certain polemically oriented popular style of writing that has pedagogic and interventionist objectives mark her work. She is critical of 'white supremacist capitalist patriarchy', a phrase that echoes a concern with the abuses of male power in the context of both race and class in the contemporary USA. She is a prolific and eclectic writer whose recent work has explored rap music, film, black 'folk' culture, African-American politics, love and pedagogy.

Reading: hooks, b. (1990) *Yearning: Race, Gender and Cultural Politics*. Boston, MA: South End Press.

Anti-essentialist arguments suggest that social categories do not reflect an essential underlying identity but are constituted in and through forms of representation. Thus, a consideration of ethnicity and race directs us to issues of identity, representation, power and politics. For example, what kinds of representations are constructed of whom, by whom and for what purposes?

RACE, ETHNICITY, REPRESENTATION

Representation raises questions of inclusion and exclusion. As such, it is always implicated in questions of power. Nevertheless, Dyer (1977) points us to a useful distinction between types and stereotypes:

- *Types* **act as general and necessary classifications of persons and roles according to local cultural categories.**
- *Stereotypes* **can be understood as vivid but simple representations that reduce persons to a set of exaggerated, usually negative, characteristics.**

Stereotyping commonly involves the attribution of negative traits to persons who are different from us. This points to the operation of *power* in the process of stereotyping and to its role in the exclusion of others from the social, symbolic and moral order. Dyer suggests that 'types are instances which indicate those who live by the rules of society (social types) and those whom the rules are designed to exclude (stereotypes)' (Dyer, 1977: 29). Stereotypes concern those excluded from the 'normal' order of things and simultaneously establish who is 'us' and who is 'them'. Thus, 'stereotyping reduces, essentializes, naturalizes and fixes "difference"' (Hall, 1997c: 258).

Within the west, people of colour have often been represented as a series of *problems*, objects and victims (Gilroy, 1987). Black people are constructed as the object rather than subject of history. Unable to think or act for themselves, people of colour are not held to be capable of initiating activity or of controlling their own destiny. Subsequently, as objects and aliens from another place, black people pose a series of problems for white people, for example as a foreign contaminating cultural presence or as the perpetrators of crime.

Savages and slaves

In Britain and America the more obvious racist stereotypes echo colonial and slave history, respectively. Hall (1997c) argues that a central component of British imperial representations of black people was the theme of non-Christian savages who required civilizing by British missionaries and adventurers. These images were subsequently transformed into what he calls 'commodity racism', whereby 'images of colonial conquest were stamped on soap boxes … biscuit tins, whisky bottles, tea tins and chocolate bars' (Anne McClintock, cited in Hall, 1997c: 240). Representations of white colonial power and black 'savagery' were gendered in that the heroes of imperial Britain were male while the commodities on which such images appeared were frequently domestic and targeted at women.

> Soap symbolized this 'racializing' of the domestic world and the 'domestication' of the colonial world. In its capacity to cleanse and purify, soap acquired, in the fantasy world of imperial advertising, the quality of a fetish object. It apparently had the power to wash black skin white as well as being capable of washing off the soot, grime and dirt of the industrial slums and their inhabitants – the unwashed poor – at home, while at the same time keeping the imperial body clean and pure in the racially polluted contact zones 'out there' in the Empire. In the process, however, the domestic labour of women was often silently erased. (Hall, 1997c: 241)

Plantation images

American plantation images share the British concern with the binary of white civilization and black 'naturalness' or 'primitivism'. African-Americans have been traditionally represented as naturally incapable of the refinements of white civilization. They were by nature lazy and best fitted for subordination to whites. The social and political subordination of black people was represented as part of the inescapable, God-given order of the universe. Not that American racial stereotypes were the same as those in Britain. On the contrary, we need to recognize the existence and emergence of different, historically specific forms of racism and of the subtle typologies within given cultural contexts. In America, Donald Bogle (1973) argues that five distinct stereotypes which derive from plantation and slave images are to be found in film:

1 Toms (good blacks, submissive, stoic);
2 *Coons* (slapstick entertainers, gamblers, 'no-account' 'niggers');
3 *Mulattoes* (beautiful, sexy, exotic mixed-race women 'stained' with black blood);
4 *Mammies* (the big, strong, bossy house servant devoted and subservient to the white family);
5 *Bucks* (big, strong, violent, oversexed male renegades).

The criminalization of black Britons

In Britain, Gilroy (1987) has charted the transformations of racism in relation to the law. He argues that in the 1950s, anxiety about black criminality within the police, judiciary and press was relatively low. It concerned only the alleged association of black people with prostitution and gambling. This imagery of sexual squalor was combined throughout the late 1950s and early 1960s with the theme of housing shortages and overcrowding. During the late 1960s and the 1970s racial discourse centred on immigration. This took the form of the 'alien presence' in Britain and the 'threat' to the national culture and law that this was claimed to pose. By this time, the idea that there was something intrinsically criminal about black culture had begun to take hold. Subsequently, the imagery of black youth as dope-smoking muggers and/or urban rioters came to the fore. Hedonism, evasion of work and the criminality of black culture became the closely entwined motifs of British media racism.

In covering stories about 'mugging', journalists reproduced the assumption that street crime is solely the work of young black men (Hall et al., 1978). Journalists seek the views of the police, politicians and judges, who declare that not only is street crime on the increase, but that something must be done about it in the form of heavier policing and harsher sentences. The news media report these comments as a common-sense concern about rising crime and its association with black youth. Subsequently, the circle becomes complete when judges cite news coverage of crime as the expression of public concern. This reporting is then used to justify the harsher sentences and increased police activity that politicians and the judicial system had called for. Given that increased police activity is directed to those urban areas in which young black men live, because they are seen as the perpetrators of crime, confrontation between the police and black youth increases.

Orientalism

✓ *Racism is a matter not simply of individual psychology or pathology, but of patterns of cultural representation deeply ingrained within the practices, discourses and subjectivities of western societies.*

Edward Said (1978) illuminates the 'structural' and societal character of racism in his discussion of Orientalism. He argues that cultural–geographical entities such as the 'Orient' are not inert facts of nature. Rather, they are historically specific, discursive constructions that have a particular history and tradition. Thus 'The Orient' has been constituted by an imagery and vocabulary that have given it a particular kind of reality and presence in the west.

Orientalism is a set of western discourses of power that have constructed an Orient – have orientalized the Orient – in ways that depend on and reproduce the positional superiority and hegemony of the west. For Said, Orientalism is a general group of ideas impregnated with European superiority, racism and imperialism that are elaborated and distributed through a variety of texts and practices. Orientalism is argued to be a system of representations that brought the Orient into western learning (Said, 1978). These include Flaubert's encounter with an Egyptian courtesan. This produced an influential image of the Oriental woman who never spoke for herself, never showed her emotions and lacked agency or history, that is, the sexually beguiling dark maiden of male power-fantasy. In contrast, the Oriental male is seen as wily, fanatical, cruel and despotic.

In this respect, the contemporary elevation of 'Islam' to the role of chief bogeyman in western news follows a well-worn path. Long before the current crisis of relations between the west and Islam, Said (1981) argued that the western media represented Islamic peoples as irrational fanatics led by messianic and authoritarian leaders.

In recent years, a great deal of news coverage in the west has been devoted to:

- **the states of Afghanistan, Iran, Iraq and Libya (with a special emphasis on their alleged sponsoring of terrorism);**
- **the *fatwa* declared by Ayatollah Khomeini against Salman Rushdie;**
- **the 1990–1 Gulf War and its aftermath;**
- **the conflicts between the regime of Saddam Hussein in Iraq and the USA culminating in the war of 2003;**
- **Osama bin Laden and the tragedy of 11 September 2001;**
- **the insurgency in Iraq against the US-led coalition.**

This is not the place to debate the political origins of Islamic fundamentalism or the morality of 'terrorism'. Nor is anyone in cultural studies trying to defend the atrocities performed by some persons in the name of Islam. However, in terms of an analysis of the cultural representation of Islam within the west, we can note a certain imbalance. Thus:

- **Responsibility for the conflict between the USA and Iraq was placed firmly on the shoulders of Saddam Hussein, who was cast in the role of 'evil emperor'. There has been little exploration of the reasons Hussein may have had for his hostility towards the west and only occasional mention of the fact that this was a *secular* regime.**
- **The Taliban, Al-Qaeda and bin Laden are all portrayed as evil madmen. We are rarely told why these people think as they do, for example that bin Laden understood the presence of US troops in Saudi Arabia to be a violation of sacred Islamic ground.**
- **It is rarely reported that Islam is seen by many of its adherents as a philosophy and religion of love and peaceful co-operation.**
- **We do not seem to recognize that conflict is a two-way street and western cultural and political actions have played their part in the generation of the current crisis.**

In other words, most western politicians and media have adopted the somewhat implausible view that we in the west are angelic and that Islam is the Devil incarnate.

Television and the representation of race and ethnicity

Whites only

On one level, people of colour have simply been ignored by television. In America, it was not until the late 1960s and early 1970s that we find any black families in television drama

(Cantor and Cantor, 1992). The Kerner Commission was set up to examine the unrest that spread across urban America in the 1960s. It argued that the US news media had 'too long basked in a white world, looking out of it, if at all, with white men's eyes and a white perspective' (Kerner Commission, 1968: 389). This reflected what the Commission called 'the indifference of white America'.

In the context of 1980s Britain, the Commission for Racial Equality (1984) noted that in the USA black people were being seen more frequently on television. However, in the UK only 5 per cent of characters in TV dramas were black and only three of 62 non-white appearances constituted leading roles. For example, one criticism of British soap operas has been the representation of community as, on the whole, exclusively white, heterosexual and working class. The high-rating soap opera *Coronation Street* has had few black characters, somewhat odd for a programme with realist pretensions located in multicultural Manchester. Nor have the US soaps *Dallas, Dynasty, Days of Our Lives, The Bold and the Beautiful, Melrose Place*, etc., a good record of representing the multi-ethnic population of America. The invisibility of black people within the media is not only incompatible with the democratic role of the media, but arguably promotes white ignorance about black people and black cultures. By ignoring black people, media coverage places them outside of mainstream society, signalling them as peripheral and irrelevant.

Stereotyped representations

As media representations of people of colour increased during the 1980s and 1990s, so attention focused on the *kinds of representations* that are constitutive of ethnicity and race. For example, black people in Britain have frequently been represented by news media as a 'problem'. In particular, young black men have been associated with crime and civil disorder. In many 'comedy' programmes, images drawn from a colonial past have been deployed to suggest stupidity and ignorance. *Mind Your Language*, set in an English language class, reduced every single non-white community to a stereotype through the 'joke' that all-foreigners-are-hilarious-because-they-talk-funny (Medhurst, 1989).

In America, the first television programme to feature African-Americans was *Amos 'n' Andy*. This programme was a 'comedy' that became a symbol for the degradation of black people through the use of 'humour' based on stereotypes. Indeed, the American film and television industry has a long history of presenting stereotypical images of black people. These have been drawn from the plantation tradition of the 'Sambo' and 'Brute' slave through the smooth liberals of the 1960s to the 'Superspade' detectives of the mid-1970s.

Yet whether Sambo or Superspade, the black image on screen has always lacked the dimension of humanity. With all too few exceptions this human dimension has been lacking in the movie treatment of the black ever since the 1890s, when the first motion picture was produced. (Leab, 1976: 5)

Signs of change

These racist representations of people of colour are not to be lightly dismissed. However, an understanding of the contemporary representation of race requires recognition that change has occurred. Campbell (1995) reports that in 40 hours of American local news, 'there was no evidence of intentional, blatant bigotry' and few examples of what he calls 'old-fashioned racism' (but a good deal of more subtle modern racism). More generally, there have been attempts to construct representations of Britain, America and Australia as multicultural societies. Here a more pluralistic society is depicted in which the cultures and customs of different ethnic groups add to the richness and variety of society.

In Britain, *Empire Road* and *Desmond's*, both comedies, centred on black family life and tried to be funny without the use of racist humour. More recently *Goodness Gracious Me* and *The Kumars at No. 42* showcase British Asian humour. The soap opera *EastEnders* has portrayed a wider cross-section of ethnic communities and characters than had previously been the case. In the USA, the black Huxtable family (*The Cosby Show*) was the focal point of what was at one time the most popular prime-time comedy on television. At the same time, *EastEnders* and *The Cosby Show* have also had their critics in terms of the representation of race.

Menace to society

The problem generally remains that racism continues to be treated as an issue of personal illiberality rather than of structured inequality. Further, insufficient attention is given to the specificity of black culture within present-day representations. Contemporary representations of race in television continue to associate people of colour, specifically young men, with crime and social problems. According to Martindale (1986) and Campbell (1995), the most common portrayal of African-Americans in newscasts is as criminals connected to guns and violence. Poor blacks in particular are constructed as a 'menace to society'. They are seen as having moved beyond the limits of acceptable behaviour through their association with crime, violence, drugs, gangs and teenage pregnancy.

For Gray (1996), this process was typified by the CBS documentary *Vanishing Family: Crisis in Black America*. He argues that this programme associated normalcy with the (white) nuclear family and turned African-American families into problems. The documentary depicted a number of caring and conscientious young African-American women struggling to raise young children while a breed of feckless men hung around on street corners.

Gray makes the significant point that what might be regarded as 'positive' representations of African-Americans do not always function positively. This is particularly so when they are juxtaposed to other images of black people in the context of a wider set of representations of race. For example, the programme contained reference to what the television presenter called 'successful strong black families in America'. However, these images functioned to shift blame away from the structural and systematic character of racial inequality in America. That is, 'blame' was directed onto alleged individual weakness and moral deficiencies of poor black people rather than being located in social and cultural processes.

Thus, the meanings of 'blackness' are cumulative and intertextual. The association of black people with crime and their depiction as a constant social problem is in contrast with, and arguably reinforced by, the more positive *assimilationist* imagery of contemporary sitcoms.

Assimilationist strategies

The Cosby Show's Huxtable family and the talk show host Oprah Winfrey represent middle-class achievement and social mobility. In line with the American Dream, they suggest that success is open to all those who are talented and work for it. Consequently, African-American poverty must be at best an outcome of individual weakness and at worst a collective aspect of African-American culture. What other explanation could there be for the 'fact' that black people are overrepresented in all the statistics of poverty and urban deprivation?

As Jhally and Lewis argue, 'The Huxtables' success implies the failure of a majority of black people ... who have not achieved similar professional or material success' (Jhally and Lewis, 1992: 137). Middle-class black American sitcoms stress material success and the values of hard work, education, honesty and responsibility. However, as Gray argues, 'many individuals trapped in the underclass have the very same qualities but lack the options and opportunities to realize them' (Gray, 1996: 142).

Entman (1990) suggests that similar assimilationist strategies operate strongly within local news. For example, the use of black anchors contributes to the idea that racism no longer exists in America. The presence of black authority figures on the screen suggests that racism has been relegated to the dustbin of history. Further, their adoption of majority cultural views lends credence to the assimilationist vision. Campbell (1995) lends this argument support in the form of his qualitative analysis of local American news coverage of the Martin Luther King holiday celebrations. With one notable exception, news coverage depicted racism as a thing of the past and the holiday as a celebration of King's success rather than as a reminder to us of the failure of his historic vision to be materialized in the day-to-day reality of American life.

The ambiguities of representation

The representation of people of colour in America and Britain is riven with contradictions. Black people are, at one and the same time, characterized as at the poles of criminality and middle-class success. Race is held to be a current 'problem' and yet racism is held to be a thing of the past. As Hall remarks:

> people who are in any way significantly different from the majority – 'them' rather than 'us' – are frequently exposed to this *binary* form of representation. They seem to be represented through sharply opposed, polarized, binary extremes – good/bad, civilized/primitive, ugly/excessively attractive, repelling-because-different/compelling-because-strange-and-exotic. And they are often required to be *both things at the same time*! (Hall, 1997c: 229)

Ambiguity and ambivalence are foregrounded when the attempt is made to represent black people 'positively'. For example, the prominence given to African-American and black British sportsmen and women in the Olympics or in basketball and football is double-edged. On the one hand, this is a celebration and acceptance of black success. On the other hand, it is part of a process by which black success is *confined* to sport. Thus, black people are depicted in stereotypical fashion as primarily physical rather than mental beings.

In the world of entertainment and music, Hip-Hop, Rap and their associated videos have become one of television's most prominent genres. Rap can be said to depict the 'cultural reality' of black people's (but especially men's) experience in relation to the police, challenging what are seen as unjust authoritarian practices. Indeed, hooks suggests that:

> It is no accident that 'rap' has usurped the primary position of rhythm and blues music among young black folks as the most desired sound or that it began as a form of 'testimony' for the underclass. It has enabled underclass youth to develop a critical voice, as a group of young black men told me, a common literacy. Rap projects a critical voice, explaining, demanding, urging. (hooks, 1990: 75)

Yet Rap has also been criticized as insular, sexist, misogynist and violent even as it reformulates and extends popular music. Rap is critical and reactionary at the same time.

> As a cultural forum, rap itself is a contested terrain between different types of rap with competing voices, politics and styles ... some rap glorifies a gangster lifestyle, drugs, and misogynistic attitudes, other rap artists contest these problematic interventions, using rap to articulate quite different values and politics. (Kellner, 1995: 176)

The new ghetto aesthetic

Ambiguities are evident in a series of black-made films closely associated with Rap music, including the work of Marion Van Peebles (*New Jack City*) and John Singleton (*Boyz N the Hood*). Jacquie Jones (1996) describes them as 'The New Ghetto Aesthetic'. On the one hand, these films are significant for being Hollywood films made by African-Americans. They have also been praised for their representation of the shocking life circumstances of some African-Americans. On the other hand, they arguably 'codify a range of behaviours as uncharacteristic of the black experience as those represented in films made by whites' (Jones, 1996: 41).

Two facets of these films might be regarded as particularly problematic:

1 **the depiction of black communities as being racked by crime and violence, whose causes lie with individual pathologies and whose solution is either more police or strong father figures;**

2 **the portrayal of women in the standard bitch/ho mode, so that few are defined apart from their relationships with men.**

We get to know male characters in terms of their personal histories and emotional torments. However, women are frequently reduced to being only tough and/or sexy.

Significantly, the representation of race is frequently gendered. Thus, an exaggerated male macho style is held to be symbolic of black resistance to white power (hooks, 1992). For some black men, the adoption of a hard and excessive form of masculinity has been a response to white power. It offers a sense of self-worth and strength in the face of social disempowerment. This does not negate the undesirability of the bitch/ho binary or of 'Black Macho' (Wallace, 1979).

It is important to consider the ambiguities of representations of race so that debates are not reduced to a simple good/bad binary which elicits knee-jerk accusations of racism or demands for only positive images. After all, positive images, useful and desirable though they are in the context of stereotypes, do not necessarily undermine or displace the negative. Indeed, it is common to find that what is considered to be a 'positive' image by some people is attacked by others. For example, the British soap opera *EastEnders* and the American series *I'll Fly Away* consciously attempted to engage with realistic and positive representations of black people. They have nevertheless been seen by some commentators as problematic.

EastEnders

As a consequence of deliberate policy, *EastEnders* deploys an array of black and Asian characters rarely before seen on British television. Rather than represent people of colour as 'a problem', black characters have been enabled to take up active and significant dramatic roles. *EastEnders* represents a multi-ethnic community in ways that do not reduce black and Asian characters to one-dimensional representatives of 'the black experience'. Further, the series contained the sympathetic representation of a mixed-race relationship/marriage which, according to Bramlett-Solomon and Farwell (1996), is virtually absent from US soaps. On the other hand, the serial has been attacked for stereotyping, for example representing Asians as doctors and shopkeepers, and for ignoring the wider structural questions of racism by reducing it to individual character traits. It is also argued that the centrality of traditional white East End families and characters displaces black and Asian characters to the margins. As a consequence they can never be a part of the core of the drama (see Daniels and Gerson, 1989).

I'll Fly Away

The debate about *I'll Fly Away* centred on the representation of the central character Lily Harper. In particular, discussion surrounded her relationship to other characters and to the politics of the civil rights movement. For Karen Smith (1996), the series offered a character who, though a maid, was most definitely not a 'mammy'. Rather, Lily Harper was portrayed as an independent-minded and wise woman active in the civil rights movement. She was not subordinated to the white family for whom she worked. Smith points out that other writers have indeed seen Lily Harper as a mammy. However, for her the problem was that the network promoted the series with 'out-of-context' images that did indeed suggest that Lily was a stereotyped black maid. In other words, the Lily Harper character became, through the intertextual array of representations for different purposes, a site of contradictory and ambiguous meaning construction.

YOUNG BLACK MAN 2

© Photographer: Ted Denson | Agency: Dreamstime.com

- *This picture of a young black man constructs a particular type of identity. How would you describe it?*

- *In what contexts could this picture be used? To what extent is this a positive image? Write 3–4 different captions that give it different meanings.*

- *Compare this image to the one of the young black man in Chapter 7, page 229. How are they the same and different?*

The question of positive images

The incontestable abundance of cultural stereotypes has led many of those who suffer at their hands to seek more positive representations of people of colour and a range of other 'abjected' groups. The demand for positive images of people of colour is at heart a desire to show that black people are as 'good' or as 'human' as white people (West, 1993). However, while positive images have much to commend them in terms of the development of self-esteem, the strategy is beset by problems, namely the following:

- **It rests on an essentialist and homogenizing understanding of ethnic identity. As such, it obliterates differences of class, gender, sexuality, etc. That is, positive images of black people assume that all black people have essential qualities in common. They may not.**

- **It is impossible to know what an unambiguously positive image would consist of. We are unlikely ever to be able to agree on this. One person's commendable image is another's stereotype.**

- **The strategy rests on an epistemology of realism by which it is thought possible to bring representations of black people in line with 'real' black people. This is not viable, for the real is always already a representation. There is no access to 'real' black people.**

These arguments form part of the wider debate about what representation 'does' (Chapter 3). The demand for positive images, when manifested as a call for *accuracy* in the representation of race, stumbles over the problem of knowing what the real or accurate is. Not only is race a cultural construction, but we cannot compare the real with representations.

✓ *Representation is constitutive of race as a form of cultural identity and not a mirror or a distortion of it. Consequently, no criteria can assess the accuracy of the representation of race.*

More sustainable are arguments that revolve around the pragmatic social and political consequences of constructing and disseminating specific discursive constructions of the world. The role of criticism becomes the development of a more profound understanding of our cultural and symbolic processes and the way in which they are connected to social, political and economic *power*. The questions to be asked concern *consequences* rather than truth. Instead of seeking only positive images, we require, argues Hall (1996d), a politics of representation that:

- **registers the arbitrariness of signification;**

- **promotes representations that explore power relations;**

- deconstructs black–white binaries;

- advances the willingness to live with difference.

This process does not require universal epistemological justification for it is founded not on transcendental reason or representations of the 'real'. Rather, it is grounded in a tradition of cultural values that judges difference, diversity, solidarity, equality and democracy to be desirable ends. It is based on pragmatic comparison with other forms of social organization and not on notions of accuracy. Consequently, while continuing to critique stereotyped representations of people of colour, the issue may be one not of positive images but of the representation of *difference* and *diversity*.

Analyse the representation of race in (i) a newspaper image, (ii) a TV programme. Ask yourself the following questions:

— Who or what is the subject of the representation?
— What are the key signifiers?
— What meanings do they generate at the level of denotation and connotation?
— What is the relationship of the 'reader' to the representation?
— What relations of power are represented?
— How are representations of masculinity and femininity implicated in the construction of 'race'?
— Are there any links between race and class constructed by the representations?

Postcolonial literature

Television remains the central representational form of popular western culture and is therefore a core concern of cultural studies. However, there is also a significant strand of work that explores issues of race, ethnicity and nation within literature. This includes the current interest in postcolonial literature as exemplified by Ashcroft et al. (1989) in *The Empire Writes Back*. More than three-quarters of the people living in the world today, the authors claim, have had their lives shaped by the experience of colonialism. For Ashcroft et al., postcolonial literature is that work produced by the peoples of former European colonies.

The term 'postcolonial' might be understood to refer only to literature produced after colonization. However, it is taken here to include the colonial discourse itself. That is, the concept 'postcolonial' alludes to the world both during and after European colonization. As such, postcolonial theory explores the discursive condition of postcoloniality, that is, the way colonial relations and their aftermath have been constituted through being spoken about. Postcolonial theory explores postcolonial discourses and their subject positions in relation to the themes of race, nation, subjectivity, power, subalterns, hybridity and creolization.

While this definition is useful in defining a broad area of study, it also opens up questions for exploration. For example, the degree that a range of former colonies can now be considered postcolonial is varied and arguable (Williams and Chrisman, 1993). Thus, the literature of the USA might be seen as postcolonial in relation to Europe. However, American neo-colonial power with respect to Latin America makes the generalization that all American literature is necessarily postcolonial somewhat problematic. Further, many writers see black literature in the US as an aspect of internal colonialism/postcolonialism. Any study of postcolonial literature also needs to distinguish the work produced in former white settler colonies – Australia, Canada and New Zealand – from the literature of black Africa or the Indian subcontinent.

Models of postcolonial literature

Ashcroft et al. (1989) highlight two important models of postcolonial literature:

1 the 'national' model;

2 the 'black writing' model.

The national model centres on the relationship between a nation and its former colonizers. The paradigmatic case is the USA, where literature was part of 'an optimistic progression to nationhood' based on difference from Britain. This process involved a breaking away from metaphors of parent–child or stream–tributary that had placed American literature in a subordinate position.

However, debate rages about whether national culture is a legitimate conceptual tool or an essentialist device that unifies through the suppression of difference (e.g. of gender, class and ethnicity). Consequently, the other major exemplar cited by Ashcroft et al. is the 'black writing' model. This 'ideal type' centres on the work of the African Diaspora of the Black Atlantic, although it can be extended to include other forms of ethnic-based writing. For example, it might include Australian Aboriginal writing or that of India, since it is based on cultural criteria rather than those of nationality. It does not follow, of course, that this model escapes the problem of essentialism either.

Though it does a disservice to the complexity of the issues, we may for the current purposes reduce the themes of postcolonial literature and postcolonial theory to the two key concerns:

- domination–subordination;

- hybridization–creolization.

Domination and subordination

Issues of domination and subordination surface most directly in terms of colonial military control, genocide and economic 'under-development'. In more cultural terms, questions arise about the denigration and subordination of 'native' culture by colonial power. This includes the very language of English literature. Is English, the language of a major colonial power, a suitable tool for postcolonial writers? On the one hand, the English language can be said to carry within itself the very assumptions and concepts of colonial power. On the other hand, English has a variety of global forms leading postcolonial literature to be concerned with a range of Englishes.

Depending on which side of the above equation is stressed, a postcolonial writer might choose to either abrogate or appropriate English.

> The abrogation or denial of the privilege of 'English' involves a rejection of the metropolitan power over the means of communication. The appropriation and reconstitution of the language to new usages marks a separation from the site of colonial privilege. Abrogation is a refusal of the categories of the imperial culture. That is, a refusal of its aesthetic, its illusory standard of normative or 'correct' usage and its assumption of a traditional and fixed meaning 'inscribed' in words. … Appropriation is the process by which the language is taken and made to 'bear the burden' of one's own cultural experience, or, as Rja Rao puts it, to 'convey in a language that is not one's own the spirit that is one's own'. (Ashcroft et al., 1989: 38–9)

Domination and subordination represent a relationship that occurs not only between nations or ethnic groups but also within them. The emphasis on ethnicity in postcolonial theory literature can mask the power relations of gender. For example, images of women are significant bearers of the purity and reproduction of the nation. Further, women carry a double burden of being colonized by imperial powers and subordinated by colonial and native men. Indeed, Gayatri Spivak (1993) has argued that the 'subaltern cannot speak'. By this she means that poor women in colonial contexts have neither the conceptual language to speak nor the ear of colonial and indigenous men to listen. It is not that women cannot literally communicate, but that there are no subject positions within the discourse of colonialism which allow them to articulate themselves as persons. They are thus condemned to silence.

Hybridization and creolization

The theoretical critique of essentialism combined with the physical meeting and mixing of peoples throws the whole notion of a national or ethnic literature into doubt. That is, it is no longer clear that 'national' or 'ethnic' concepts like Indian or English have any kind of clear or stable meanings. Consequently, the hybridization and creolization of language, literature and cultural identities is a common theme of postcolonial literature and theory. For example, the concept of the 'Creole continuum' highlights the overlapping language usages and code switching common to the Caribbean. Creolization stresses language as a cultural practice and the inventions of new modes of expression particular to itself. This marks a certain meeting of minds between postcolonial theory and postmodernism.

Dialogue with the values and customs of the past allows traditions to be transformed and bring forth the new. The meaning of old words is changed and new words brought into being. Neither the colonial nor the colonized cultures and languages can be presented in 'pure' form, nor can they be separated from each other (Bhabha, 1994). This process gives rise to various forms of cultural hybridity.

✓ *Cultural hybridity challenges not only the centrality of colonial culture and the marginalization of the colonized, but also the very idea of centre and margin as being anything other than 'representational effects'.*

Postmodern Rushdie   The work of Salman Rushdie (e.g. *Midnight's Children, The Satanic Verses* and *The Moor's Last Sigh*) raises questions of hybridity and cultural representation through characters who cross or blur cultural boundaries. The non-linear narrative style of Rushdie's work derives from the oral storytelling traditions of India, yet these very same techniques are part of Rushdie's challenge to the certainties of facts and historical narrative. That is, they are histories, not *a* history, which are written or told by specific people from particular perspectives. Such a challenge has often been taken as a mark of postmodernism and Hutcheon (1989) hails Rushdie's postmodern parody. On the other hand, Berman claims Rushdie for modernism, and in particular the struggle for 'visions of truth and freedom that all modern men and women can embrace … an inner dynamism and a principle of hope' (Berman, 1982: 54). It would seem that in exploring the boundaries of cultures, their mixing and meeting, Rushdie is at one and the same time traditional, modern and postmodern.

DECONSTRUCT THIS: BLACK VS. WHITE

- *What does 'black' signify?*
- *What does 'white' signify?*
- *How do the meanings of black and white depend on each other?*

SUMMARY

It has been argued that ethnicity, race and nationality are discursive–performative constructions that do not refer to already existent 'things'. That is, ethnicity, race and nationality are contingent cultural categories rather than universal biological 'facts'.

- *Ethnicity* as a concept refers to the formation and maintenance of cultural boundaries and has the advantage of stressing history, culture and language.

- *Race* is a problematic idea because of its association with biological discourses of intrinsic and inevitable superiority and subordination. However, the idea of racialization or race formation has the advantages of stressing power, control and domination.

We noted the importance that should be given to the intersections between race, ethnicity, nation, class, age and gender. Thus, cultural identities need to be understood in terms of the articulation of these criss-crossing discourses. The ideas of race, ethnicity and nation must be explored in terms of their reliance on, and relationship to, each other, for example the manner in which the ethnic purity of nations is constituted in nationalist discourses and the role that gendered metaphors play in the construction of the nation, e.g. the fatherland, mother of the nation, etc.

The anti-essentialist argument by which identities are said to be formed within and through discourse makes the question of representation central to race, ethnicity and nation. We noted the systematic construction of black people as objects, victims, and problems. In particular, we explored a range of discourses of race and ethnicity on television, highlighting not only blatant forms of racism but also the inherent ambiguity and ambivalence of representations. Considerable stress was placed on the idea of hybridity. Cultures and identities are increasingly hybridized as specific places which are subject to distant influences and cultural mixing. For example, the African Diaspora of the Black Atlantic and the literature of the postcolonial world were used as illustrations of this process.

Above all:

If you go to analyse racism today in its complex structures and dynamics, one question, one principle above all, emerges as a lesson for us. It is the fear - the terrifying, internal fear – of living with *difference*. This fear arises as the consequence of the fatal coupling of difference and power. And, in that sense, the work that cultural studies has to do is mobilize everything that it can in terms of intellectual resources in order to understand what keeps making the lives we live, and the societies we live in, profoundly and deeply antihuman in their capacity to live with difference. (Hall, 1997d: 343)

9 Sex, Subjectivity and Representation

KEY CONCEPTS

Discourse	*Masculinity*
Femininity	*Patriarchy*
Feminism	*Performativity*
Gender	*Representation*
Identification	*Subject position*

This chapter is concerned with sex and gender, that is, with the character of men and women in contemporary societies. We shall explore the social construction of sexed subjects with particular reference to questions of cultural representation. The focus is on work influenced by feminism, poststructuralism and psychoanalysis since these are the prevailing streams of thought within cultural studies on these questions. We shall also explore the tensions between these constructionist paradigms and the findings of biochemistry.

FEMINISM AND CULTURAL STUDIES

To discuss questions of sex and gender, it is necessary to engage with a large body of feminist theory. It would be impossible to conceive of a cultural studies that did not do so. However, while feminist thinking permeates cultural studies, not all forms of feminism are to be thought of as cultural studies. Nor are all zones of cultural studies concerned with questions of gender (though many feminists might argue that they should be). Consequently, this chapter does not purport to be a history, classification or analysis of the women's movement *per se*. Rather, it is an exploration of those streams of thought within cultural studies that are concerned with sex, gender and feminism.

Franklin et al. (1991) have pointed to a number of similarities of concern between cultural studies and feminism. They draw attention to:

- **the aspirations of feminism and cultural studies to connect with social and political movements outside of the academy;**

- **a critical stance *vis-à-vis* more established disciplines such as sociology and English literature;**

- **a mutual suspicion of and challenge to established ideas of 'certain knowledge';**

- **a wish to produce 'knowledges' of and by 'marginalized' and oppressed groups, with the avowed intention of making a political intervention.**

✓ *Cultural studies and feminism have shared a substantive interest in issues of power, representation, popular culture, subjectivity, identities and consumption.*

Although the relationship between feminism and cultural studies has not always been comfortable, feminism certainly put questions of sexuality, gender, subjectivity and power at the heart of cultural studies.

Patriarchy, equality and difference

Feminism is a plural field of theory and politics that has competing perspectives and prescriptions for action. In general, feminism asserts that sex is a fundamental and irreducible axis of social organization which, to date, has subordinated women to men. Thus, feminism is centrally concerned with sex as an organizing principle of social life and one that is thoroughly saturated with power relations. Feminists have argued that the subordination of women occurs across a whole range of social institutions and practices. That is, the subjection of women is understood to be a structural condition. This structural subordination of women has been described by feminists as patriarchy, a concept that has connotations of male-headed family, mastery and superiority.

As a movement, feminism has been concerned with two key issues. First, to win citizen rights such as voting and equality before the law. Second, to influence cultural representations and norms in ways that are beneficial to women. Feminists have constructed a range of analysis and political strategies by which to intervene in social life in pursuit of the interests of women. They have been broadly categorized as:

- **liberal feminism;**

- **difference feminism;**

- **socialist feminism;**

- poststructuralist feminism;
- black feminism;
- postcolonial feminism;
- postfeminism.

These categories are not set in stone and indeed do a disservice to feminism in so far as they erect unhelpful and inflexible divisions. However, as explanatory devices, they do point to variations in base assumptions and emphasis about what constitutes the interests of women.

Liberal and socialist feminism

Liberal feminists regard differences between men and women as socio-economic and cultural constructs rather than the outcome of an eternal biology. They stress the need for equality of opportunity for women in all spheres. This is a goal that, within the liberal democracies of the west, is held to be achievable inside the broad structures of existing legal and economic frameworks (e.g. Mackinnon, 1987, 1991). In contrast, socialist feminists point to the interconnections between class and gender, including the fundamental place of gender inequalities in the reproduction of capitalism. The subordination of women to men is seen as intrinsic to capitalism, so that the full 'liberation' of women would require the overthrow of capitalist organization and social relations. It is argued that women's domestic labour is core to the reproduction of the workforce both physically (feeding, clothing, care, etc.) and culturally (learning appropriate behaviour such as time-keeping, discipline, respect for authority, etc.). Further, women are said to form a supply of cheap and flexible labour for capitalism that is more easily 'returned to the home' when required. Thus, core to socialist feminism is a stress on the 'dual role' (domestic labour and paid labour) of women in the reproduction of capitalism (Oakley, 1974).

Difference feminism

Liberal and socialist feminists stress equality and sameness. However, difference feminism asserts that there are essential distinctions between men and women. These fundamental and intractable differences are variously interpreted as cultural, psychic and/or biological. In any case, difference is celebrated as representing the creative power of women and the superiority of their values over those of men (Daly, 1987; Rich, 1986). As such, difference feminism has developed a tendency towards separatism.

One criticism of difference feminism, and indeed of the concept of patriarchy, is that the category of woman is treated in an undifferentiated way. 'The trouble with patriarchy', as Rowbotham (1981) argued, is that it obscures the differences between individual women and their particularities in favour of an all-embracing universal form of oppression. Not only do all women appear to be oppressed in the same way, but also there is a tendency to represent them as helpless and powerless. These are assumptions challenged by black feminists, who have argued that a white middle-class movement has overlooked the centrality of race and colonialism.

Black and postcolonial feminism

Black feminists have pointed to the differences between black and white women's experiences, cultural representations and interests (Carby, 1984; hooks, 1992). They have argued that colonialism and racism have structured power relationships between black and white women, defining women as white. Gender intersects with race, ethnicity and nationality to produce different experiences of what it is to be a woman. In a postcolonial context, women carry the double burden of being colonized by imperial powers and subordinated by colonial and native men. Thus, Spivak (1993) holds that the 'subaltern cannot speak'. She is suggesting that for poor women there are no subject positions within the discourse of colonialism which allow them to speak.

Poststructuralist feminism

Feminists influenced by poststructuralist and postmodern thought (Nicholson, 1990; Weedon, 1997) have argued that sex and gender are social and cultural constructions that are not to be explained in terms of biology or to be reduced to functions of capitalism. This anti-essentialist stance suggests that femininity and masculinity are not universal and eternal categories but discursive constructions. That is, femininity and masculinity are ways of describing and disciplining human subjects. As such, poststructuralist feminism is concerned with the cultural construction of subjectivity *per se*, including a range of possible masculinities and femininities. Femininity and masculinity, which are a matter of how men and women are represented, are held to be sites of continual political struggle over meaning.

✓ *Given its stress on culture, representation, language, power and conflict, poststructuralist feminism has become a major influence within cultural studies.*

Postfeminism

The fundamental argument of feminism is that women are oppressed and subjugated by men as a consequence of being women. That is, all women are oppressed by all men. Thus, feminism pointed to structural inequalities in the economy and in the institutions of social and cultural power. Further, it suggested that certain forms of male attitudes and behaviour (contempt, violence, sexual harassment) could oppress women. Despite decades of feminist action, many continue to argue that little or nothing has changed for women even within western culture.

However, Rosalind Coward (1999) has described feminism as 'a movement blind to its own effectiveness'. She lists the following achievements:

- **significant gains for women in the economy;**
- **an increased visibility for women in the cultural sphere;**
- **a transformation of knowledge in academia;**
- **changes in sexual attitudes and behaviour;**
- **the reform of pay and divorce laws;**
- **the recognition of male loss and vulnerability;**
- **the understanding that women can wield sexual power.**

It is not being suggested that spheres of gender inequality and injustice are not still in evidence – they are. Rather, what is being argued is that the central tenets of feminism have been absorbed into the culture and surpassed. Women are not *necessarily* oppressed by dint of being women. Not all men are oppressors and it is unhelpful to understand gender relations in terms of 'women vs. men'. What is required is constructive dialogue and structural change where required.

The idea of postfeminism suggests that the most significant and systematic institutional barriers to women's participation in politics and culture have been removed in the west. Women are citizens and have equal legal rights with men. Postfeminist women are now entitled to enjoy cultural life as they choose. Postfeminists want to escape the sense that women are passive victims of patriarchy, which they suggest was the inference inherent in previous feminist campaigning. The performance of victim identity reinforces the myth that women are the 'weaker sex', they say, and risks perpetuating the power dynamic inherent between victim and perpetrator (or victim and voyeur). Orr (1997) suggests that postfeminism stresses the ability of women to make personal choices. As such, postfeminism advocates a libertarian form of feminism founded on women's autonomy. Influential postfeminist writing includes Naomi Wolf's *Fire with Fire* (1994), Rene Denfield's *The New Victorians* (1995) and Catharine Lumby's *Bad Girls* (1997).

There are, of course, other feminist writers who would disagree with this argument. They would point to continued inequality for women in the workplace and the reproduction of cultural representations and practices that exclude or demean women.

— Make a list of the social and cultural gains that women have made over the last 40 years.
— Make a list of the areas in which women are still disadvantaged in our culture.
— Compare your lists and discuss the degree to which feminism has been successful in promoting the interests of women.

SEX, GENDER AND IDENTITY

Identification of oneself as male or female is a foundation stone of a self-identity that is widely held to be the outcome of particular bodies and their attributes. Common sense encompasses a form of biological reductionism suggesting that the biochemical and genetic structures of human beings determine the behaviour of men and women in quite definite and specific ways. Men are commonly held to be more 'naturally' domineering, hierarchically oriented and power-hungry, while women are seen as nurturing, child rearing and domestically inclined. By contrast, many writers in cultural studies and other humanities have argued for the complete plasticity of sex and gender. That is, the influence of biology has been rejected in favour of understanding masculinity and femininity as cultural constructions.

These apparently opposite ways of understanding are commonly grasped as a question of nature vs. nurture. However, to set up the issues relating to nature and culture as opposed binaries is not a useful way to approach the subject.

✓ *Arguments for the cultural construction of gendered identity and the evidence for a genetic core to sexual difference are not necessarily contradictory stances.*

Biochemical similarity amongst women (and difference from men) is able to co-exist with cross-cultural divergence for the following reasons:

- **Cultural difference operates 'on top of' genetic similarity.**

- **Biological predispositions have different outcomes in divergent contexts.**

- **Human culture and human biology have co-evolved and are indivisible (see Chapter 4).**

- **The language of biology and the language of culture have different purposes and achieve different outcomes.**

The language of biology enables us to make behavioural and bodily predictions. At the same time, what it means to be gendered remains a cultural question. On the one hand, there is evidence that points to the *predictability* of a range of male and female capabilities and behaviour that derives from genetics. On the other hand, there are also clear indications that masculinity and femininity are changeable. We can make a distinction between identity as a social construction, a representation with which we emotionally identify, and those human capacities and behaviours that correlate highly with certain biochemical structures of the brain. The language of culture helps to re-cast the way we talk about and perform 'sex' and 'gender'.

The science of sex

There is a considerable body of evidence to suggest genetic and biochemical difference between men and women in relation to language ability, spatial judgement, aggression, sex drive, ability to focus on tasks or to make connections across the hemispheres of the brain (Hoyenga and Hoyenga, 1993; Moir and Moir, 1998). 'Feminist' psychologist Diane Halpern begin her review of the literature holding the opinion that socialization practices were solely responsible for apparent sex differences in thinking patterns. However,

> After reviewing a pile of journal articles that stood several feet high and numerous books and book chapters that dwarfed the stack of journal articles, I changed my mind … there are real, and in some cases sizeable, sex differences with respect to some cognitive abilities. Socialization practices are undoubtedly important, there is also good evidence that biological sex differences play a role in establishing and maintaining cognitive sex differences, a conclusion I wasn't prepared to make when I began reviewing the relevant literature. (Halpern, 1992: xi)

Genetic science and biochemistry suggest that there are material, i.e. chemical, limits to behavioural possibilities. It is thought that hormones shape our brain structure so that men and women have different patterns of brain activity. Indeed, the core of the argument that biochemistry determines male and female behaviour lies in the evidence for differential male and female brain structures and capabilities (Christen, 1991; Moir and Jessel, 1991; Moir and Moir, 1998). There is also considerable evidence that:

- **women are more verbal, co-operative and organized then men;**
- **men show greater spatial, mathematical and motor skills than women.**

It is argued that the brains of the two sexes are organized in distinct ways that give rise to differences in a range of abilities. Thus, women have more of their brain dedicated to verbal matters and item memory. Men are said to possess greater spatial and mathematical abilities (Kimura, 1996). Men and women also use their brains in different ways. Men specialize their key brain functions on one side of their cerebral matter (e.g. verbal performance on the left and spatial skills on the right). Women are more able to communicate across the two hemispheres of the brain. For men, this has the advantage of concentrated focus on specific tasks but the disadvantage of lower levels of integration and cross-referencing. By contrast, women excel in connecting the emotional and reasoning aspect of the mind. Much of this argument is confirmed by Functional MRI scans that locate the active parts of the brain while subjects carry out specific tasks. Evidence also suggests that men have lower 'arousal thresholds' than women, who are able to pay greater focused attention to events and more swiftly than are men.

The predominance of evidence suggests that different kinds of brain organization are the result of hormone exposure in the womb rather than of cultural training. Over 30 world-wide studies show that girls who are born with congenital adrenal hyperplasia (CAH) as a consequence of exposure to high levels of 'male hormones' in the womb exhibit styles of play more commonly seen amongst boys. Thus, CAH girls have better spatial and mathematical skills than the average girl does. Greater levels of testosterone and lower levels of serotonin in men appear to unpin the evidence that:

- **Men are greater risk-takers.**
- **Men have a higher propensity to find multiple partners.**
- **Men are more disposed to anger and less to empathy.**
- **Men are less inclined to verbalize emotions.**

Biochemical evidence suggests that we are not blank sheets at birth. Consequently, we cannot remake ourselves into anything we want to. Some aspects of being can be changed and some cannot. As the old saying goes: wisdom lies in knowing the difference. Nevertheless, biochemical arguments should not be used as an excuse not to test the limits of the culturally possible.

✓ *Questions of culture and language remain of central significance in understanding sex and gender.*

At stake are the cultural questions 'What is a woman?' and 'What is a man?'

— Make two lists under the following headings:

1 How to identify a man
2 How to identify a woman

— 'Score' each item 1–10 for the degree to which the characteristic is changeable where 1 equals the most plastic and 10 the least.
— Discuss your work with others in a group.

Women's difference

An essentialist answer to the question 'What is a woman?' takes the category 'woman' to be a reflection of an underlying identity based on either biology or culture. Thus, Collard and Contrucci's (1988) ecofeminist *Rape of the Wild* relies on biological essentialism. They argue that all women are linked by childbearing bodies and innate ties to the natural earth that support egalitarian, nurturance-based values. Likewise Rich (1986), who celebrates women's difference from men, locating its source in motherhood. This is condemned in its historical modes of oppression but celebrated for its female power and potentialities.

Most of the arguments that celebrate women-cultures are linguistic and cultural rather than biological. Grosz (1995), for example, argues that 'difference feminism' has been misunderstood as essentialist and that difference from a pre-given norm is not a kind of metaphysical 'pure difference'. Difference feminism in this instant is based on signifiers of the female body. For example, Daly's (1987) *Gyn/Ecology* links women to nature, stresses the material and psychological oppression of women, and celebrates a separate woman-culture. Much of her argument revolves around the language used to describe women and its power over them.

A clearly culturally founded argument for women's difference comes from Gilligan (1982). In her study of moral reasoning she argues that while men are concerned with an 'ethic of justice', women are more centred on an 'ethics of care'. Women, it is argued, develop for cultural reasons 'a different voice' from men, a voice that stresses context-specific forms of argument in contrast to the more abstract thinking of men. Gilligan argues that western cultural norms have validated men's understanding of morality and ethics at the expense of women's, which has been cast as deficient. Gilligan's critics see in her work essentialist claims about universal patterns of moral development.

Irigaray and womanspeak

A psychoanalytically inspired philosophical route to understanding difference comes from Luce Irigaray, who theorizes a presymbolic 'space' or 'experience' for women that is unavailable to men. This domain is constituted by a feminine *jouissance* or sexual pleasure, play and joy, which is outside of intelligibility. Irigaray (1985a, 1985b) has been at the forefront of attempts to write the unwritable, to inscribe the feminine through *écriture féminine* (woman's writing) and *le parler femme* (womanspeak).

Irigaray speculates on what she understands to be the 'Otherness' of the feminine. This she seeks to ground in the female body. In particular, she turns to the mother–daughter relationship of the pre-Oedipal imaginary as the source of a feminine that cannot be symbolized (because it precedes entry into the symbolic order and the Law of the Father – see

Chapters 1 and 7). For Irigaray, woman is outside the specular (visual) economy of the Oedipal moment and thus outside of representation (i.e. of the symbolic order). Given that the symbolic lacks a grammar that could articulate the mother–daughter relationship, the feminine, according to Irigaray, can return only in its regulated form as man's 'Other'.

Irigaray proceeds by way of deconstructing western philosophy. This is a philosophy that she reads as guaranteeing the masculine order and its claims to self-origination and unified agency. That is, western philosophy is said to be phallocentric. Irigaray explores the feminine as the constitutive exclusion of philosophy. That is, 'woman' is not an essence *per se* but rather that which is excluded. Here the feminine is understood to be the unthinkable and the unrepresentable (other than as a negative of phallocentric discourse).

In trying to read philosophical texts for their absences, Irigaray is faced with the problem of trying to critique philosophy for its exclusions while using the very language of that philosophy. Her strategy is to 'mime' the discourse of philosophy, that is, to cite it and talk its language but in ways that question the capacity of philosophy to ground its own claims. Womanspeak mimes phallocentrism only to expose what is covered over (Irigaray, 1985b).

KEY THINKERS

Luce Irigaray (1932–)

Irigaray was born and educated in Belgium, though she has spent a considerable period of her working life in France. She is currently Director of Research in Philosophy at the Centre National de la Recherche Scientifique in Paris. She engages in philosophy, linguistics, and psychoanalysis to explore the operations of patriarchy and the exclusions of women. Irigaray proceeds by way of deconstructing western philosophy which she critiques for its exclusions while 'miming' the discourse of philosophy; that is, she talks its language but in ways that question the capacity of philosophy to ground its own claims. Her style varies from the lyrical and poetic to the political and didactic.

Reading: Irigaray, L. (1985) *This Sex Which Is Not One*. Trans. C. Porter and C. Burke. Ithaca, NY: Cornell University Press. (1st published in French in 1977.)

For Irigaray's supporters, she represents a bold attempt to assert the specificity of the feminine but for her detractors she posits an essentialism that mirrors patriarchal discourse itself.

The social construction of sex and gender

Unlike Irigaray, Linda Alcoff regards any emphasis on a special and benign female character as mistaken. She argues that such essentialism 'is in danger of solidifying an important bulwark for sexist oppression: the belief in innate "womanhood" to which we must all adhere lest we be deemed either inferior or not "true" women' (Alcoff, 1989: 104).

Equality, rather than difference, is also stressed in the work of Catherine Mackinnon (1987, 1991), who castigates the idea of a woman-culture as 'making quilts'. She argues that women's subordination is a matter of social power founded on men's dominance of institutionalized heterosexuality. Though not all men have equal power and not all women are subject to the same forms of oppression, her summation of feminist arguments stresses equality: 'We're as good as you. Anything you can do, we can do. Just get out of the way' (Mackinnon, 1987: 32).

Joan Scott has argued that the equality–difference debate relies on a false binary since it is possible for equality and difference to co-exist. 'Equality is not the elimination of difference, and difference does not preclude equality' (Scott, 1990: 137–8). That is, sameness is not the only ground for claims to equality and difference is the condition for all identities.

A good deal of sociological, cultural and feminist writing, including Mackinnon's, has sought to challenge biological determinism through the conceptual division between sex and gender. Sex is taken to be the biology of the body while gender refers to the cultural assumptions and practices that govern the social construction of men and women. Subsequently, it is the social, cultural and political discourses and practices of gender that are said to lie at the root of women's subordination. However, the sex–gender distinction is now itself the subject of criticism.

✓ *Since gender is a cultural construct, it is said to be malleable in a way that biology may not be.*

Sex as a discursive construct

The distinction between sex as biology and gender as a cultural construction is broken down on the grounds that there is in principle no access to biological 'truths' that lie outside of cultural discourses. Thus, there can be no biological 'sex' that is not also cultural. Sexed bodies are always already represented as the production of regulatory discourses (see Butler's arguments later in the chapter). In this view, the body does not disappear,

> Rather, it becomes a variable rather than a constant, no longer able to ground claims about the male/female distinction across large sweeps of history but still there as always a potentially important element in how the male/female distinction gets played out in any specific society. (Nicholson, 1995: 43–4)

For poststructuralists, the cultural variations that exist between women (and between men) suggest that there is no universal cross-cultural category of 'woman' (or 'man') that is shared by all. Rather, there are multiple modes of femininity (and masculinity) which are enacted not only by different women, but, potentially, by the same woman under different circumstances. The claim is that sex and gender are infinitely malleable in principle, even though in practice they are moulded and regulated into specific forms under particular historical and cultural conditions.

SEXED SUBJECTS

Within cultural studies the argument that femininity and masculinity are malleable social constructions has taken its inspiration either from the work of Foucault (Weedon, 1997) or from psychoanalysis. We shall trace these apparently contradictory arguments (Foucault was opposed to psychoanalysis), culminating in Judith Butler's attempt to unite them.

Foucault: subjectivity and sexuality

For Foucault, subjectivity is a discursive production. That is, discourse (as regulated ways of speaking/practice) offers speaking persons subject positions from which to make sense of the world. In doing so, discourse also 'subjects' speakers to the rules and discipline of those discourses. A subject position is that perspective or set of regulated discursive meanings from which discourse makes sense. To speak is to take up a subject position and to be subjected to the regulatory power of that discourse.

Foucault propounds an anti-essentialist argument in which there are no universal ahistorical subjectivities. To be a man or a woman is not the outcome of biological determinism or universal cognitive structures and cultural patterns. Gender is historically and culturally specific, subject to radical discontinuities over time and across space. This does not mean that one can simply pick and choose genders or that gender is a matter of random chance. Rather, we are gendered through the power of regulated and regulatory discourses.

Sex and the discursive construction of the body

The body and sexuality are major themes in Foucault's work. He argued that sexuality was a focal point for the exercise of power and the production of subjectivity in western societies. Subjectivity is coterminous with sexuality since subjects are constituted through the production of sex and the control of the body. Foucault is concerned with 'the overall "discursive fact", the way in which sex is "put into discourse"' (Foucault, 1979: 11). He suggests that discourses of polymorphous sexualities have proliferated and been disseminated through:

- medicine;
- the church;
- psychoanalysis;
- education programmes;
- demography.

The proliferating discourses of sexuality *produce* particular subjectivities by bringing them into view via the discourses of, for example, medicine. These discourses analyse, classify and regulate sexuality in ways that produce sexed subjects and construct sexuality as the cornerstone of subjectivity. For example, he argues that from the early eighteenth century onwards, women's bodies were subject to the discourses of modern science. These discourses produced women as hysterical and nervous subjects while reducing them to their reproductive system.

Foucault maintains that the confessional, developed by Catholicism, has been adapted and taken over by other institutions to become the basis of discursive 'subjection'. Therapy would be one example, as would TV talk shows such as *The Jerry Springer Show* and *The Oprah Winfrey Show*. Nevertheless, according to Foucault, wherever discursive power operates, so also does resistance become possible, not least through the production of 'reverse discourses'. For example, medics and clerics put the idea of homosexuality into discourse in order to condemn it. However, the very discursive production of a homosexual subject position allowed homosexuals to be heard and to claim rights.

Select a contemporary toy for discussion.

— In what ways does the toy embody discourses of gender for its consumer:

(a) as a visual object;
(b) as an object used to generate play activities for children?

The feminist critique of Foucault

Foucault has been subject to feminist criticism for neglecting 'to examine the gendered character of many disciplinary techniques' (McNay, 1992: 11). It is argued (Bartky cited in McNay, 1992) that Foucault treats bodies as gender-neutral with little specificity beyond a male norm. He does not, for example, explore how men and women are related differently to the disciplinary institutions he describes.

While these criticisms have force, McNay tempers them by pointing out the dangers of positing a completely different history and experience of repression for women. Male and female bodies have been worked on in historically specific ways, However, this should not lead us, she argues, to propose an eternal and essential opposition between the sexes.

Foucault's description of subjects as 'docile bodies', whereby subjects are the 'effect' of discourse, has been of concern to feminists because it appears to rob subjects of the agency required for an emancipatory project. However, it is arguable that Foucault's later work centred on 'techniques of the self' does reintroduce agency and the possibility of resistance and change. Foucault is led to consider how 'man [*sic*] proposes to think his own nature when he perceives himself to be mad; when he considers himself to be ill; when he conceives of himself as a living, speaking, labouring being' (Foucault, 1987: 6–7). This concern with self-production as a discursive practice is centred on the question of ethics as a mode of 'care of the self'.

Ethics and agency

According to Foucault, morality is concerned with systems of injunction and interdiction constructed in relation to formalized codes. Ethics are concerned with practical advice as to how one should concern oneself with oneself in everyday life (Foucault, 1979, 1984b, 1986). While morality operates through a set of imposed rules and prohibitions, ethics is concerned with the actual practices of subjects in relation to the rules that are recommended to them. These rules are enacted with varying degrees of compliance and creativity.

Foucault explores the space between a system of laws and an individual's ethical practices that permits a degree of freedom to subjects in forming their individual behaviour. In particular, he points to an ethics of self-mastery and 'stylization' that is drawn from the character of relationships themselves rather than from external rules of prohibition. Thus does Foucault attribute a degree of individual autonomy and independence to subjects, even while pointing to the indissociability of subjectivity from social and cultural constraints. McNay argues that this more dynamic conception of the self enables the exploration of a variety of sexualities and suggests a route for feminist political activity: 'Foucault's idea of practices of the self parallels developments in feminist analysis of women's oppression that seek to avoid positing women as powerless victims of patriarchal structures of domination' (McNay, 1992: 66).

Foucault's work has been criticized for its inability to explain why some discourses are 'taken up' by subjects and others are not. Consequently, some critics have looked for ways to connect the discursive 'outside' with the psychic 'inside'. For Stuart Hall (1995, 1996a), identity is the point of 'suture' between a domain of discursive operations and the realm of the imaginary or unconscious. To explain this process, he and others have turned to psychoanalysis.

Psychoanalysis, feminism and sexed subjectivity

Regulating sexuality

Amongst Freud's oft-quoted sayings are two apparently contradictory phrases whose interrogation may help us to grasp the implications of psychoanalysis for questions of sexual identity. On the one hand, Freud suggests that 'anatomy is destiny'. However, on the other hand, he describes human sexuality as involving 'polymorphous perversity', that is, the capability of taking on any number of forms.

According to Freud, the libido or sexual drive does not have any pre-given fixed aim or object. Rather, through fantasy, any object, which includes persons or parts of bodies, can be the target of desire. An almost infinite number of sexual objects and practices are within the domain of human sexuality. Subsequently, Freud's work is concerned to document and explain the *regulation* and repression of this 'polymorphous perversity'. This ordering is achieved through the resolution (or not) of the Oedipus complex, so that heterosexual gendered relationships become the norm.

Anatomy is argued to be destiny not because of genetic determination but because bodily differences are signifiers of sexual and social differentiation.

✓ *Anatomy is destiny because it is hard to escape the regulatory scripts that surround the signifiers of bodily difference.*

It is quite clear that, as years of feminist writing have argued, bodies *do* matter.

Chodorow: masculinity and femininity

According to Nancy Chodorow (1978, 1989), Freud demonstrates that:

- **There is nothing inevitable about our sexual object choices and identifications.**
- **Sexual identity is formed through a developmental process in the context of our first relationships.**
- **Our sexualities are regulated in ways that are particularly costly for women.**

For Chodorow, the theory of the Oedipus complex is a demonstration of the reproduction of male dominance and male contempt for women. She argues that, in the context of patriarchy, mothers treat boys as independent and outgoing persons. Conversely, girls are loved more narcissistically as being like the mother. Boys' separation involves identification with the father and the symbolic Phallus as the domain of social status, power and independence. A form of masculinity is produced that stresses externally oriented activity. This comes at the price of covering over an emotional dependence on women and weaker skills of emotional communication. In contrast, girls have acquired a greater surety with the communicative skills of intimacy through introjection of, and identification with, aspects of their mothers' own narratives. The traditional cost is a greater difficulty with externally oriented autonomy.

Chodorow argues that these sexed subjectivities are not universals of the human condition. Indeed, psychoanalysis shows us that the formation of sexual love objects and of the relations between men and women is formed in the context of historically specific family configurations. Over time, new forms of subject and new forms of masculinity and femininity could be forged.

Phallocentric psychoanalysis

For cultural studies there remains the vexed question of the phallocentric (i.e. male-centred) character of psychoanalysis. Freud's assertion that women would 'naturally' see their genitals as inferior is highly problematic. This is also the case for the claim that genital heterosexual activity that stresses masculine power and feminine passivity is the normal form of sexuality. Further, in Lacan's reworking of Freud, the Oedipal moment marks the formation of the subject in the symbolic order and into the Law of the Father.

That is, the power of the Phallus is understood to be necessary to the very existence of subjects. Here the symbolic Phallus:

- **acts as the 'transcendental signifier' of the power of the symbolic order;**

- **serves to split the subject from desire for the mother, thus enabling subject formation;**

- **marks the necessary interruption of the mother–child dyad and the subject's entry into the symbolic (without which there is only psychosis);**

- **allows the subject to experience itself as a unity by covering over a sense of lack.**

For some critics (Irigaray, 1985a, 1985b), the centrality of the Phallus to Lacan's argument renders 'woman' an adjunct term. By contrast, for Mitchell (1974) and Chodorow (1978, 1989), Freud's patriarchal assumptions are an expression of his value system and not inherent to psychoanalysis *per se*. Psychoanalysis could be cleansed of these assumptions and the historical specificity of its categories recognized and reworked. For them, psychoanalysis offers a deconstruction of the very formation of gendered identity in the psychic and symbolic domains of patriarchal societies.

Indeed, Rose (1997) argues for the fundamentally symbolic character of the Phallus in Lacan's work. That is, the function adopted by the Phallus as a 'transcendental signifier' could be taken up by other objects in alternative socio-cultural circumstances. It is, she says, the place of the Phallus in language and culture which counts, not any specific Phallus/penis or parent–child relationship. Thus, the particular kinds of psychic resolutions that psychoanalysis describes are not universals of the human condition but historically and culturally specific.

Julia Kristeva: the semiotic and the symbolic

The Lacanian-influenced psychoanalyst who has perhaps attracted the most attention within feminist cultural studies is Julia Kristeva (see Kristeva, 1986c). This is for a number of reasons:

- Kristeva's work is centrally concerned with signs/semiotics, that is, with the symbolic order of culture.

- Her work is organized around questions of subjectivity and identity, which are critical issues for cultural studies.

- She is a practising psychoanalyst and is of interest as psychoanalysis undergoes a revival within cultural studies.

- Her work explores the way that psychic forces are intertwined with cultural texts through (a) the identifications or investments that subjects make in texts and (b) the place they have in the production of texts.

KEY THINKERS

Julia Kristeva (1941–)

Kristeva was born in Bulgaria and schooled in Marxism and Russian formalism. She emigrated to France where she initially studied with Roland Barthes and wrote for the avant-garde journal *Tel Quel*. Working as a professor at both the universities of Paris and Columbia (New York), she developed a critique of structuralism and a methodology she calls 'semanalysis'. Through this she seeks to explore signification and 'set categories and concepts ablaze' as part of transgressing the dominant symbolic order. A practising psychoanalyst, her work is particularly concerned with gender and subjectivity.

Reading: Kristeva, J. (1986) 'Revolution in Poetic Language', *The Kristeva Reader*, ed. T. Moi. Oxford: Blackwell.

Kristeva distinguishes between the 'semiotic chora', which is presymbolic, and the 'thetic' or symbolic sphere. For Kristeva, subjects are 'always *both* semiotic *and* symbolic' (Kristeva, 1986a: 93). What she calls the 'subject-in-process' is an interplay between the 'semiotic' and the symbolic. Language is the symbolic (thetic) mechanism by which the body can signify itself (as a signified ego). This involves the regulation of the (presymbolic) semiotic by the symbolic. Nevertheless, the semiotic returns in the symbolic order as a transgression of it and appears, for example, in certain kinds of (modernist) literary and artistic practice through the rhythms, breaks and absences in texts. This presymbolic 'feminine' is not the preserve of women *per se,* for Kristeva holds a firmly anti-essentialist view of sexual identity.

Deconstructing sexual identity   Kristeva has argued that 'To believe that one "is a woman" is almost as absurd and obscurantist as to believe that one "is a man"' (cited in Moi, 1985: 163). We may identify with gendered identities but one cannot *be* a woman in an essentialist ontological sense. Sexual identities as opposites can only come into being after entry into the symbolic order. That is, sexual identity is not an essence but a matter of representation.

According to Kristeva, a small child faces the choice of mother-identification, and subsequent marginality within the symbolic order, or father-identification, giving access to symbolic dominance but wiping out the plenitude of pre-Oedipal mother-identification. These choices face both male and female infants. Consequently, degrees of masculinity and femininity are said to exist in biological men and women. Femininity is a condition or subject position of marginality that some men, for example avante-garde artists, can also occupy. Indeed, it is the patriarchal symbolic order that tries to fix all women as feminine and all men as masculine, rendering women as the 'second sex'. Kristeva advocates a position in which the dichotomy man/woman belongs to metaphysics.

Kristeva is suggesting that the struggle over sexual identities takes place within each individual. Rather than a conflict between two opposing male–female masses, sexual identity concerns the balance of masculinity and femininity within specific men and women. This struggle, she suggests, could result in the deconstruction of sexual and gendered identities understood in terms of marginality within the symbolic order. This argument stresses the singularity and multiplicity of persons as well as the relativity of symbolic and biological existence.

✓   *'The time has perhaps come to emphasize the multiplicity of female expressions and preoccupations' (Kristeva, 1986b: 193).*

Kristeva maintains not only that women occupy a range of subject positions but also that a new symbolic space and subject position are opening up for them. In particular, she suggests that a new space is now available for women to intermingle motherhood (and difference) with the politics of equality and the symbolic order.

Judith Butler: between Foucault and psychoanalysis

Kristeva's attempt to deconstruct sexual identity is one shared by Judith Butler. Foucault rejected psychoanalysis as yet another network of disciplinary power. However, Butler has attempted to work with and between the work of Foucault and psychoanalysis. She accepts the Foucauldian argument that discourse operates as a normative regulatory power that produces the subjects it controls. However, she also suggests a return to psychoanalysis in order to pursue 'the question of how certain regulatory norms form a "sexed" subject in terms that establish the indistinguishability of psychic and bodily formation' (Butler, 1993: 22). Butler deploys psychoanalysis to discuss how regulatory norms are invested with psychic power through processes of identification.

In Foucauldian fashion, Butler argues that discourse defines, constructs and produces bodies as objects of knowledge. Discourse is the means by which we understand what bodies are.

> The category of 'sex' is, from the start, normative; it is what Foucault has called a 'regulatory ideal'. In this sense, then, 'sex' not only functions as a norm, but is part of a regulatory practice that produces the bodies it governs, that is, whose regulatory force is made clear as a kind of productive power, the power to produce – demarcate, circulate, differentiate – the bodies it controls. Thus, 'sex' is a regulatory ideal whose materialization is compelled, and this materialization takes place (or fails to take place) through certain highly regulated practices. In other words, 'sex' is an ideal construct which is forcibly materialized through time. It is not a simple fact or static condition of a body, but a process whereby regulatory norms materialize 'sex' and achieve this materialization through a forcible reiteration of those norms. (Ibid.: 1–2)

The discourses of sex are ones that, through repetition of the acts they guide, bring sex into view as a necessary norm. Sex is a construction, but an indispensable one that forms subjects and governs the materialization of bodies.

The performativity of sex

Butler conceives of sex and gender in terms of citational performativity, with the performative being 'that discursive practice which enacts or produces that which it names' (Butler, 1993: 13). This is achieved through citation and reiteration of the norms or conventions of the 'law' (in its symbolic, Lacanian sense). A performative is a statement that puts into effect the relation that it names, for example, within a marriage ceremony 'I pronounce you …'

For Butler, 'sex' is produced as a reiteration of hegemonic norms understood as a performativity that is always derivative. The 'assumption' of sex, which is not a singular act or event but an iterable practice, is secured through being repeatedly performed. Thus, the statement 'It's a girl' initiates a process by which 'girling' is compelled.

This is a 'girl', however, who is compelled to 'cite' the norm in order to qualify and remain a viable subject. Femininity is thus not the product of choice, but the forcible citation of a norm, one whose complex historicity is indissociable from relations of discipline, regulation, punishment. (Ibid.: 232)

Performativity is not a singular act for it is constituted by a reiteration of a set of norms. Nor should it be understood as a performance given by a self-conscious, intentional actor. Rather, the performance of sex is compelled by a regulatory apparatus of heterosexuality that reiterates itself through the forcible production of 'sex'. Indeed, the very idea of an intentional sexed actor is a discursive production of performativity itself. 'Gender is *performative* in the sense that it constitutes as an effect that very subject it appears to express' (Butler, 1991: 24).

Identification and abjection

Butler combines this reworking of discourse and speech act theory with psychoanalysis. This leads her to argue that the 'assumption' (taking on) of sex involves identification with the normative phantasm (idealization) of 'sex'. Sex is a symbolic subject position assumed under threat of punishment (e.g. of symbolic castration or abjection).

The symbolic is a series of normative injunctions that secure the borders of sex (what shall constitute a sex) through the threat of psychosis and abjection (an exclusion, a throwing out, a rejection). For Butler, identification is understood as a kind of affiliation and expression of an emotional tie with an idealized fantasized object (person, body part) or normative ideal. It is grounded in fantasy, projection and idealization.

Identification constitutes an exclusionary matrix by which the processes of subject formation simultaneously produce a constitutive outside. That is, identification with one set of norms, say heterosexuality, repudiates another, say homosexuality. Indeed, Butler's work is particularly concerned with the abjection of gay and lesbian sexuality by the heterosexual 'imperative'. She is also at pains to argue that identifications are never complete or whole. Identification is with a fantasy or idealization. Consequently, it can never be coterminous with 'real' bodies or gendered practices; there is always a gap or slipping away of identification. Like Rose (1997), psychoanalysis highlights for Butler the very *instability* of identity.

Drag: recasting the symbolic

Some feminists, for example Irigaray and to some extent Kristeva, regard resistance to heterosexual masculine hegemony as rooted in the presymbolic 'imaginary'. This is understood to be a zone that exists before the acquisition of language. By contrast, Butler argues for the necessity of recasting the symbolic itself as that set of regulatory norms that govern sex. Though the symbolic regulates identificatory practices, this process is never complete. It involves only *partial* identifications. Consequently, Butler is able to theorize a space for change in which the very notions of 'masculinity' and 'femininity' can be rethought.

Butler argues that drag can destabilize and recast gender norms through a re-signification of the ideals of gender (Butler, 1990). Through a miming of gender norms, drag can be subversive to the extent that it reflects on the performative character of gender. Drag suggests that all gender is performativity and as such destabilizes the claims of hegemonic heterosexual masculinity as the origin that is imitated. That is, hegemonic heterosexuality is itself an imitative performance which is forced to repeat its own idealizations. That it must reiterate itself suggests that heterosexuality is beset by anxieties that it can never fully overcome. The need for reiteration underlines the very insecurity of heterosexual identifications and gender positions. However, Butler's arguments are indicative of only one possible subversive activity for, as she points out, drag is at best always ambivalent and can be itself a reiteration and affirmation of the Law of the Father and heterosexuality.

DRAG QUEEN

© Photographer: Karen Struthers | Agency: Dreamstime.com

- *What are the features of this image that suggest that we are looking at (a) a man and (b) a woman?*

- *Do you agree with Judith Butler that Drag illustrates the performativity of sex?*

The discipline and the fiction of identity

Ambivalence pervades Butler's discussion of identity categories *per se* and the notion of 'queer' in particular. The word 'queer' has been rearticulated and resignified by ACT-UP, Queer Nation and other communities of queer politics to deflect its injurious effects and turn it into an expression of resistance. However, Butler argues that identity categories of this type cannot be rearticulated (redefined) in any way. Nor can the effects of rearticulation be controlled, since they are always open to further resignifications.

Thus, the use of the term 'queer' as an affirmative has proved politically useful. However, it continues to echo its past pejorative usage. Further, Butler argues that we need to be attentive to the exclusions and abjections that *any* identity category enacts. This includes the notion of 'queer', which arguably establishes a false unity between gay men and gay women that may not resonate within all communities.

✓ *For Butler, all identity categories are necessary fictions which, though we continue to use them, should simultaneously be interrogated.*

MEN AND MASCULINITY

Most of this chapter is centred on women and the pertinent debates within feminism and cultural studies. However, reflection upon the social construction of gender must apply to men as well as women. As Giddens writes:

> In Western culture at least, today is the first period in which men are finding themselves to be men, that is, as possessing a problematic 'masculinity'. In previous times, men have assumed that their activities constituted 'history', whereas women existed almost out of time, doing the same as they always had done. (Giddens, 1992: 59)

What it is to be male varies across time and space so that masculinity can be understood as a cultural construct.

✓ *In particular, we must speak of masculinities rather than a masculinity since not all men are the same (Connell, 1995). Masculinity is also marked by difference.*

The sense that masculinity is not an unchanging given of nature has sparked a growing research interest into men and masculinity (e.g. Biddulph, 1994; Connell, 1995;

Connell et al., 1982; Farrell, 1993; Johnson and Meinhof, 1997; Nixon, 1997; Pfeil, 1995; Seidler, 1989). The central areas of interest have been:

- **cultural representations of men and masculinity;**
- **the character of men's lives as they experience them;**
- **the problems that men face in contemporary culture.**

In general terms, traditional masculinity has encompassed the values of strength, power, stoicism, action, control, independence, self-sufficiency, male camaraderie/mateship and work, amongst others. Devalued were relationships, verbal ability, domestic life, tenderness, communication, women and children.

— Describe and discuss examples of the kinds of men who embody the traditional values of masculinity as named above.
— What kinds of masculinities are represented in contemporary culture that are at odds with these traditional forms?

Since the enlightenment, men have traditionally associated masculinity with metaphors of reason (Seidler, 1989). Factories that were run by clock time rather than on the basis of seasonal rhythms demanded discipline and control. Managers and bureaucrats, mainly men, were to operate with impersonal, task-oriented hierarchical rules. Modernity is an epoch not just of external domination but also of self-control. 'As men it is difficult not to be "control freaks"'. This is the history we inherit' (ibid.: 63).

Reason, control and distance are central metaphors of contemporary masculinity. Control over other people and control over themselves. Distance from other people and distance from themselves. In particular, the association of rationality with masculinity involves the self-discipline of, and distance from, the feminized language of emotions.

The modernist division of labour gave men the role of providing the wages of survival and women the domestic duties of child-rearing and housekeeping. Consequently, the language of modernity stresses the gulf between the feminine-coded private world and the masculine-coded public. In the latter, men have been acculturated to seek esteem through public performance and the recognition of achievement. This can take many forms, from violence through sport to educational qualifications and occupational status. It also lends itself to hyper-individualism, competitiveness and separation from the relational, for it is 'I' who must perform and 'I' who will take the glittering prize. Performance orientation of this kind – from work to sexuality – is manifested in grandiosity, on the one hand, and deep feelings of inadequacy and depression, on the other (for the performances are never outstanding enough to satisfy the internal parents).

These traditional values of masculinity may no longer be serving men well. Some of the problems men face can be understood as an outcome of the incompatibility between ascendant notions of masculinity and that which is required to live contentedly in the contemporary social world. Indeed, it is significant that Giddens (above) talks about the discovery of a 'problematic masculinity', since it is on the linked notions of 'men's problems' and 'men as a problem' that attention has focused.

MODERN YOUNG MAN

© **Photographer: Dreamstime Agency | Agency: Dreamstime.com**

- *What do you think this image is trying to say about modern young men?*
- *To what extent is this a representation of unconventional masculinity?*
- *To what extent does it also reproduce conventional masculinity?*

Problematic masculinity

The view that men are problems is a result of the apparent destructiveness of contemporary men – the move from being naughty boys to being bad men. However, bad men often turn out to be better described as 'sad men', the damaged goods of industrial society.

For Warren Farrell (1993), men are the 'disposable gender'; they die in war and from suicide more often than women and are also the most common victims of violence, overwork and mental illness. Of course, men also commit over 90 per cent of convicted acts of violence and comprise over 90 per cent of the inmates of jails (Biddulph, 1994). Men are also more likely to be obese; to be diagnosed with mental disorders as a child; to be HIV positive; to have an accident; and to be the victim of suicide. Either way, according to Steve Biddulph, there are very few happy men.

Biddulph argues that the central problems of men's lives, as he sees it – loneliness, compulsive competition and lifelong emotional timidity – are rooted in the adoption of impossible images of masculinity that men try, but fail, to live up to. These idealized images are formed in the absence of a loving father to act as a living male role model.

These arguments are echoed by John Lee, whose central claim is that 'our fathers were not there for us emotionally, physically, or spiritually – or at all' (Lee, 1991: xv). Without the guidance and training that a loving father can give, men don't learn enough of the skills required for living, including the ability to give and receive.

The roots of male addiction

Terrence Real (1998) argues that 48 per cent of men in the USA are at some point in their lives implicated in depression, suicide, alcoholism, drug abuse, violence and crime. In Australia, a survey suggested that:

- **Over 35 per cent of boys in school year 10 had been 'binge drinking' in the previous two weeks.**

- **At least 45 per cent of the male population under 24 drink to a degree hazardous or harmful to them (National Drug Strategy, 1995).**

Psycho-therapeutic work (e.g. McLean et al., 1996: Rowe, 1997) suggests that low self-esteem (itself an outcome of family life), along with the self-perceived failure to meet cultural expectations of achievement, lies at the root of depression and drug abuse amongst men. For Real (1998), men's violence, sex addiction, gambling, alcohol and drug abuse is a form of self-medication; that is, an attempted defence (achieved through 'merging' or self-elevation) against covert depression stemming from shame and 'toxic' family relationships. Addiction and other forms of compulsive behaviour, including the 'workaholism' of high achievers, offer a source of comfort and a defence against anxiety. Thus, Giddens argues that addictions – as compulsive behaviour – are narcotic-like 'time-outs' that blunt the pain and anxiety of other needs or longings that cannot be directly controlled. Addiction is the 'other side' of the choice and responsibility that go with the autonomous development of a self-narrative (or identity). In circumstances in which traditional guidance (for example, about what it is to be a man) has collapsed, these lifestyle decisions become a potentially 'dread-full' process of 'making oneself'.

Men's apparent predilection for addiction and self-destruction at the dawn of the twenty-first century needs to be understood within the context of modern life and its increasing stress on the self-regulation of emotions. According to Giddens (1992), men's predominance in the public domain and their association with 'reason' has been accomplished at the cost of their exclusion from the 'transformation of intimacy'. Intimacy is largely a matter of emotional communication. The evident difficulties men have talking about relationships, which requires emotional security and language skills, are rooted in a culturally constructed and historically specific form of masculinity.

✓ *Boys are treated by parents as independent, so that a framework of masculinity emerges that stresses externally oriented activity (e.g. work and sport). This comes at the price of a masked emotional dependence on women and weak skills of emotional communication.*

The betrayal of the modern man

Even Susan Faludi, author of a radical critique of masculinity as a 'bedrock of misogyny' (Faludi, 1991), is now giving more sympathetic observance to men's lives (Faludi, 1999). Her story centres on the 'promise of postwar manhood' and its subsequent 'betrayal'; that is, the loss of the unstated covenant that men had presumed gave them a valued place in the social order. Forged through war and work, the modern man, argues Faludi, was acculturated to value being *useful* at work, to his family and to the community at large. A man was expected to be in control, the master of his destiny, a person who makes things happen. Further, as a man, he was able to develop and rely on solidarity with other men.

The Second World War proved to be the 'last gasp' of the useful and dutiful male as the ideal of manhood. The post-war American baby-boomer generation was offered a 'mission to manhood' that revolved around the conquest of space, the defeat of communism, a brotherhood of organizational men and a family to provide for and protect. However, 'the boy who had been told he was going to be the master of the universe and all that was in it found himself master of nothing' (Faludi, 1999: 30).

Downsizing, unemployment, the Vietnam and Korean Wars, feminism and a decline in public concern with space travel all undermined the confidence and security of post-war American men. In particular, what Faludi calls 'ornamental culture' signalled the end of a utilitarian role for men. Ornamental culture is a culture of celebrity, image, entertainment and marketing, all underpinned by consumerism. In this context, masculinity becomes a matter of personal display rather than the demonstration of the internal qualities of inner strength, confidence and purpose. Manhood has become a performance game to be won in the marketplace.

In the absence of an alternative vision of manhood that could provide a new sense of meaning and purpose in the world, Faludi documents a series of 'men in trouble':

- shipyard workers who have lost not only their source of income but also their craftsmanship, pride and solidarity;

- corporate executives and middle managers who watch their consumer dream of the house, the pool, the car and the cosy family threatened by the onset of recession;

- young men – both black and white – who seek purpose in celebrity and, failing to find either, turn instead to crime;

- Christian men who look to reassert their symbolic status as head of the family even as their wives pack up and leave;

- disillusioned casualties of the Vietnam War who, expecting to return as heroes, find themselves to be social pariahs, leaving them wounded once more even after the bullets have ceased flying.

All these and more appear as the distressed and confused men who inhabit the ghostly landscape of the contemporary USA. In that context, the countercultural model of confrontation that revolved around an enemy that could be 'identified, contested, and defeated' may not be the best way forward for men or women, argues Faludi. Instead men need to find new ways of being men or, rather, new ways to be human that bestow masculinity as a side-effect of doing and living in a manner that brings respect, esteem and self-worth.

GENDER, REPRESENTATION AND MEDIA CULTURE

For most writers within cultural studies, masculinity and femininity are not essential qualities of embodied subjects. Rather, they are understood to be matters of representation. Sexual identity is constituted by ways of speaking about and disciplining bodies. This theme of representation is a trope of cultural studies that is also manifested in the study of gender within popular culture.

A good deal of feminist writing in the field of culture has been concerned with the representation of gender and of women in particular. As Evans (1997) comments, in the first place there was a concern to demonstrate that women had played a part in culture, and in literature in particular, in the face of their omission from the canon of good works.

This was coterminous with a concern for the kinds of representations of women which had been constructed; that is, 'the thesis that gender politics were absolutely central to the very project of representation' (ibid.: 72).

Early feminist studies made the realist epistemological assumption that representation was a direct expression of social reality and/or a potential and actual distortion of that reality. That is, representations of women reflected male attitudes and constituted mis-representations of 'real' women (see Tuchman et al., 1978). This is known as the 'images of women perspective'. However, later studies informed by poststructuralism regard all representations as cultural constructions and not as reflections of a real world. Consequently, concern centres on how representations signify in the context of social power with what consequences for gender relations. This exploration of 'women as a sign' (Cowie, 1978) we may call the 'politics of representation'.

Images of women

The concept of the stereotype occupies a prominent place within the 'images of women' perspective. A stereotype involves the reduction of persons to a set of exaggerated, usually negative, character traits. 'Stereotyping reduces, essentializes, naturalizes and fixes "difference"' (Hall, 1997c: 258). Through the operation of power, a stereotype marks the boundaries between the 'normal' and the 'abjected', 'us' and 'them'. Given the large body of work within the 'images' approach, the examples offered here should be regarded only as indicative of the kind of studies accomplished.

The bitch, the witch and the matriarch

An early example of the 'images of women' approach is Diana Meehan's (1983) analysis of women on US television. Her study combined a quantitative analysis, which counted the number and kind of representations of women, with a qualitative interpretation of women's roles and power(lessness) within those representations. She suggested that representations on television cast 'good' women as submissive, sensitive and domesticated while 'bad' women are rebellious, independent and selfish. Meehan identifies the following as common stereotypes:

- *the imp*: rebellious, asexual, tomboy;
- *the good wife*: domestic, attractive, home-centred;
- *the harpy*: aggressive, single;
- *the bitch*: sneak, cheat, manipulative;
- *the victim*: passive, suffers violence or accidents;
- *the decoy*: apparently helpless, actually strong;

- *the siren*: sexually lures men to a bad end;
- *the courtesan*: inhabits saloons, cabarets, prostitution;
- *the witch*: extra power, but subordinated to men;
- *the matriarch*: authority of family role, older, desexed.

She concludes that 'American viewers have spent more than three decades watching male heroes and their adventures, muddied visions of boyhood adolescence replete with illusions of women as witches, bitches, mothers and imps' (ibid.: 131).

Affirmation and denial

US television is not the only villain in the story: Gallagher's (1983) survey of women in the media suggests a consistent *global* depiction of women as commodified and stereotyped into the binary images of 'good' and 'bad'. For example, Krishnan and Dighe (1990) argue that affirmation and denial were the two main themes evident in their study of the representation of women on Indian television. The affirmation they describe is of a limited definition of womanhood as passive and subordinate, that is, being tied to housework, husbands and children. The denial is of the creativity, activity and individuality of women, particularly in relation to work and the public sphere.

Krishnan and Dighe report that men in television fiction were the principal characters in much larger numbers than women (105 men to 55 women). Further, while men were represented in a range of occupations, most women (34) were depicted as housewives. Each of the principal characters was described on the basis of 88 polar opposite personality attributes and analysis revealed that the most common characteristics ascribed to men and women were as in Table 9.1.

Table 9.1   Attributes of masculinity and femininity on Indian television

Male characters	Female characters
self-centred	sacrificing
decisive	dependent
self-confident	anxious to please
seeing a place in the larger world	defining the world through family relations
rational and conniving	emotional and sentimental
dominant	subordinate
paternal	maternal

Source: Krishnan and Dighe, 1990

Women of Bollywood

According to Krishnan and Dighe (1990), the representation of the idealized woman on Indian television is drawn from traditional Hindu sources which also provide the ideal moral universe for popular Hindi films (Mishra, 1985).

The title of the Hindi film *Suhaag* connotes a symbol of marriage, which is the leit motif of a movie which acts as a guide as to what constitutes a virtuous woman (Bahia, 1997; see also Dasgupta and Hedge, 1988, and Rajan, 1991, as sources of the following discussion). This includes the characteristics of chastity, patience and selflessness, which are exemplified by the central character. Thus, 'Maa', abandoned by her villainous husband, nevertheless brings up her sons without straying from traditional boundaries. Throughout the film it is Maa's role to bring up her sons in the correct and respectable way at whatever cost to herself. Despite her husband's lack of acknowledgement of her existence, when he later reappears, Maa subordinates herself to him despite his continual betrayal of her trust. Above all things, she must seek to save her marriage, without which she has no identity.

The Taming of the Shrew

The critique of the cultural representation of women is not confined to popular culture but also includes the 'Arts'. For example, McLuskie (1982) discusses how Shakespeare's *Taming of the Shrew* involves the treatment of women as commodities within a pattern of luxury consumption and aristocratic lifestyle. Shakespeare's work is culturally significant for its place in 'high' culture, which is assured through the education system. McLuskie argues that the whole notion of 'taming' is ideological, as Petruchio tames Kate as he would an animal. All the 'jokes' are at Kate's expense and the play requires Petruchio's systematic destruction of her will through his puns. That he has the right to 'tame' Kate and that she is his property is made clear in the following extract from Petruchio:

> I will be master of what is mine own.
> She is my goods, my chattels; she is my house,
> My household stuff, my field, my barn,
> My horse, my ox, my ass, my any thing,
> And here she stands. Touch her whoever dare,
> I'll bring my action on the proudest he
> that stops my way in Padua. (III, ii, 229–35)

Analyse a set of adverts or a television drama that constructs femininity and masculinity.

— How are gendered identities achieved?
— What techniques are used?
— What roles are assigned to men and women?

The problem of accuracy

Illuminating though such studies are, the 'images of women' approach presents us with an epistemological problem. Namely, it asserts the truth and falsity of representations. For example, Gallagher (1983) describes the world-wide representation of women as demeaning, damaging and *unrealistic*. As Moi comments, an 'images of women' approach 'is equivalent to studying *false* images of women constructed by both sexes because the "image" of women in literature is invariably defined in opposition to the "real person" whom literature somehow never quite manages to convey to the reader' (Moi, 1985: 44–5). The central problem is that the 'real' is always already a representation (Chapter 3).

Consequently, later studies become concerned less with representational adequacy and more with a 'politics of representation'. This approach explores the subject positions constructed by representations.

✓ *Here the marginality or subordination of women is understood as a constitutive effect of representation realized or resisted by living persons.*

Subject positions and the politics of representation

A subject position is that perspective or set of regulated and regulatory discursive meanings from which the text or discourse makes sense. It is that subject with which we must identify in order for the discourse to be meaningful. In identifying with this subject position, the text subjects us to its rules; it seeks to construct us as a certain kind of subject or person. For example, in the context of advertising:

> Addressing us in our private personae, ads sell us, as women, not just commodities but also our personal relationships in which we are feminine: how we are/should be/can be a certain feminine woman, whose attributes in relation to men and the family derive from the use of these commodities. … A woman is nothing more than the commodities she wears: the lipstick, the tights, the clothes and so on are 'woman'. (Winship, 1981: 218).

The slender body

Among the more powerful and influential representations of women within western culture is that of the 'slender body'. This discourse has become a disciplinary cultural norm (Bordo, 1993). Slenderness and a concern with diet and self-monitoring are preoccupations of western media culture with its interest in a 'tighter, smoother, more constrained body profile'. Consequently, adverts target bulge, fat or flab and the desirability of flat stomachs and cellulite management. As Susan Bordo argues, the slender body is a gendered body for the subject position of the slender body is female. Slenderness is a contemporary ideal for female attractiveness so that girls and women are culturally more prone to eating disorders than are men.

Paradoxically, advertising culture offers us images of desirable foods while proposing that we eat low-calorie items and buy exercise equipment. In the face of this contradiction, the capacity for self-control and the containment of fat is posed in moral as well as physical terms. The choice to diet and exercise leading to the production of a firm body is a symbol not only of gendered identity but also of the 'correct' attitude. The failure to exert such control, symbolically manifested in obesity and anorexia, is disciplined through, among other things, television talk shows that feature portrayals of 'eating disorders' or the struggles of the obese to lose weight. *The Oprah Winfrey Show*, for example, has placed the presenter's struggle with weight gain at the centre of its strategy to humanize her.

The independent mother

Texts construct subject positions about and for women. However, we should not imagine that these representations remain static. Thus Katherine Woodward (1997) discusses the changing representation of motherhood in contemporary culture. She notes the emergence of a new representation of the 'independent mother' that is not an idealized domesticated figure concerned only with child care. Rather, this contemporary representation of motherhood is also supportive of autonomy and work for women/mothers. Woodward argues that the pleasures of this subject position lie in the fantasy of being a mother *and* having a career *and* being able to explore one's individuality *and* looking attractive.

Representing persons with AIDS

The politics of representation and sexuality have also been explored in the context of AIDS. Douglas Crimp (1992) argues that the typical portraits of PWAs (people with AIDS), particularly as it relates to so-called 'risk' groups, are of gay men in tight 501s, prostitutes on the streets, Afro-Caribbeans and drug addicts who are depicted as an 'arm-with-a-needle-in-it'. These persons are contrasted to 'ordinary' heterosexuals – ordinary in that they are white, heterosexual and do not shoot drugs. In trying to convince the white heterosexual population that AIDS is a danger, health promotion imagery stereotypes gays and other so-called 'risk' groups.

Even attempts to humanize PWAs and to help us understand suffering are riddled with problems. Crimp (1992) suggests that:

- **Images of PWAs tend to reinforce a sense of hopelessness. Whatever we learn about PWAs always includes the fact of their death and the ravages of the disease on their bodies.**

- **PWAs are presented as *passive victims*, whereas current treatment regimes are increasingly enabling PWAs to live longer, more productive lives.**

- **There is a lack of representations of people *living* with AIDS.**

- **Images of PWAs nearly always involve a brutal invasion of privacy as they are exploited for a public spectacle and morality play.**

- **PWAs are portrayed in terms of a narrative of their private tragedies and kept firmly within those bounds.**

As Benson (1997) suggests, there are serious issues of representation at stake here. How to address the fact that gay communities have borne the brunt of AIDS without depicting a 'gay plague'? How to acknowledge suffering without demonizing PWAs? How to talk about 'living with AIDS' when there is dying?

Madonna's performance

Cultural theorists have been interested not only in subject positions that seek to fix the character of sexuality but also in those that destabilize them. Kaplan (1992) explores the ambiguity of Madonna as a text that deconstructs gender norms. Her concern is with a politics of the signifier. That is, with the exploration of sex as an unstable but regulated performance.

For Kaplan, Madonna is able to 'alter gender relations and to destabilize gender altogether' (ibid.: 273). Thus Madonna's videos:

- **seek to empower women by exhorting them to take control of their lives;**

- **play with the codes of sex and gender to blur the boundaries of masculinity and femininity.**

Kaplan argues that Madonna's videos are implicated in the continual shifting of subject positions. This involves the production of stylized and mixed gender signs that question the boundaries of gender constructs. This, she argues, is a politics of representation that centres on sex and gender as unstable 'floating' signifiers.

Kaplan argues that Madonna's video 'Express Yourself' continually shifts the focus of the camera, to adopt a variety of subject–viewer positions. Consequently, identification is dispersed and becomes multiple. Body boundaries are violated and gender norms crossed. For example, Madonna mimes the male filmmaker Fritz Lang, only to open her jacket to reveal a bra.

Raunch culture

Madonna is also a significant point of reference for the postfeminist interest in so-called 'raunch' culture. The porn star Jenna Jamison (whose book *How to Make Love Like a Porn Star* became a bestseller), pop singer Christina Aguilera and 'celebrity' Paris Hilton have also been mentioned as influential figures in the profile of raunch culture. Raunch advocates sexual provocativeness and promiscuousness by women as women. It liberally employs references to pornography and celebrates sexual objectification and physicality. Levy (2005) observes that women identifying within this 'culture' speak of their rights to objectify sexuality like a man, including looking at and enacting pornography. They reject the idea that women should behave as victims and claim the right to do whatever they want to their bodies and to look how they wish to look. This includes the use of plastic surgery should they so wish. Levy describes how such women employ discourses of empowerment and it is in this sense that raunch culture has been celebrated as postfeminist. The argument is that, as women, they no longer have to be concerned about objectification by men *per se*. Rather, they are entitled to rejoice in their own sexuality and to act on it in just as assertive, and even predatory, a way as men. One might describe raunch culture as postfeminist party-time.

This argument stands diametrically opposed to the more traditional feminist case against sexually explicit material such as pornography. Dworkin (1993) and MacKinnon (1995), for example, campaigned against pornography as a form of female oppression. Dworkin describes pornography as: 'a process of dehumanization, a concrete means of changing someone into something' (Dworkin, 1993: 2). MacKinnon (1995) suggests that pornography acts in objectifying women twice, first when it is made and, second, when it is viewed.

— Organize a class debate about either pornography or 'Raunch culture'. Do they empower women or demean them?
— Design an advertising campaign that undermines classical gender roles.

The question of audiences

The discussion above has concentrated on forms of textual analysis focusing on the subject positions offered to readers. However, a new range of reception studies has stressed the active audience, that is, the way viewers construct, negotiate and perform a multiplicity of meanings and gendered identities. Rather than regard audiences as reproducing textual subject positions and meanings, we need to consider what concrete people in specific locations actually do with texts. We must be concerned, then, not simply with textual devices that produce a variety of modes of femininity and masculinity but also with the extent to which textual subject positions are 'taken up' by concrete women and men (see Chapter 10).

DECONSTRUCT THIS: MASCULINITY VS. FEMININITY

- *What are the characteristics of masculinity?*
- *What are the characteristics of femininity?*
- *How do the characteristics of the one depend on the other?*

SUMMARY

Within cultural studies, sex and gender are held to be social constructions intrinsically implicated in matters of representation. They are matters of culture rather than of nature. There is a strand of feminist thinking that stresses the essential differences between men and women. However, most cultural studies writers have chosen to explore the idea of the historically specific, unstable, plastic and malleable character of sexual identity. This does not mean that one can simply throw off sexual identities with ease and take on others. Sex can be understood as a social construction. However, it is one that constitutes us through the impositions of power and the identifications of the psyche. That is, social constructions are regulated and have consequences. Further, we noted that there is a considerable body of evidence that points to a place for biochemical explanations of human behaviour.

Sexual *identity* is held to be not a universal biological essence but a matter of how femininity and masculinity are spoken about. Thus, both feminism and cultural studies must be concerned with matters of sex and representation. For example, cultural studies has explored the representation of women in popular culture and within literature. It has argued that women across the globe are constituted as the second sex, subordinated to men. That is, women have subject positions constructed for them that place them in the patriarchical work of domesticity and beautification or, increasingly (within the west), of being a mother and having a career and being able to explore one's individuality and looking attractive. Women in postcolonial societies carry the double burden of having been subordinated by colonialism and native men. Nevertheless, we also noted the possibility of destabilizing representations of sexed bodies (drag and Madonna).

While texts construct subject positions, it does not follow that all women or men take up that which is offered. Rather, reception studies have stressed the negotiations between subject and text, including the possibility of resistance to textual meanings. Indeed, such studies have often celebrated the values and viewing culture of women. This shift from text to audience, from image to talk, is discussed in Chapter 10. Where we explore the place of television as a textual resource available to concrete persons who identify or otherwise with the subject positions texts offer.

10   Television, Texts and Audiences

KEY CONCEPTS

Active audience	*Glocalization*
Commodification	*Ideology*
Convergence	*Popular culture*
Deregulation	*Synergy*
Genre	*Text*

The development and institutionalization of cultural studies has long been intertwined with that of media studies. In particular, television, the major form of communication in most western societies, is one of cultural studies' prolonged concerns. No other medium can match television for the volume of popular cultural texts it produces and the sheer size of its audiences.

Television is a resource open to virtually everybody in modern industrialized societies and an increasing one in the 'developing' world. It is a source of popular knowledge about the world and increasingly brings us into contact, albeit in a mediated way, with ways of life other than our own. Television is implicated in 'the provision and the selective construction of social knowledge, of social imagery, through which we perceive the "worlds", the "lived realities" of others, and imaginarily reconstruct their lives and ours into some intelligible "world-of-the-whole" ' (Hall, 1977: 140). Though we are currently witnessing the rise of new digital media (see Chapter 11), television remains the most widely accessible mass media. As Thompson has argued:

> We must not lose sight of the fact that, in a world increasingly permeated by the products of the media industries, a major new arena has been created for the process of self-fashioning. It is an arena which is severed from the spatial and temporal constraints of face-to-face interaction and, given the accessibility of television and its global expansion, is increasingly available to individuals world-wide. (Thompson, 1995: 43)

Television needs to be understood in terms of:

- **texts (programmes);**
- **the relationship between texts and audiences (audience research);**
- **political economy (organizations/industry);**
- **patterns of cultural meaning.**

This argument points to the desirability of a multidimensional and multiperspectival approach to the understanding of television. This is one that would seek to avoid reductionism by grasping the connections between the economic, political, social and cultural dimensions of the medium.

TELEVISION AS TEXT: NEWS AND IDEOLOGY

News is one of the principal texts of television. It appears on just about every television network across the globe. Indeed, it is the subject of entire globally distributed channels, including Cable News Network (CNN). The production of news holds a strategic position in debates about television for its presumed, and often feared, influence on public life. This concern has been heightened by the emergence of global cross-border television.

Putting reality together

Television news is not a reflection of reality so much as 'the putting together of reality' (Schlesinger, 1978).

✓ *News is not an unmediated 'window-on-the-world' but a selected and constructed representation constitutive of 'reality'.*

The selection of items for inclusion as news and the specific ways in which a story is constructed are never neutral or objective. They are always a particular version of events. News narratives concern explanations for the way things are. They offer us frameworks of understanding and rules of reference about the way the world is constructed. It follows that news selection criteria tell us about the binding and justifying 'world view' that is being assembled and disseminated.

The first selection concerns the topics that news covers. For Anglo-American news, Hartley (1982) identifies these as:

- **politics;**
- **the economy;**
- **foreign affairs;**
- **domestic affairs;**
- **sport;**
- **'occasional' stories.**

These topics define the news paradigm. We may note a significant omission; namely the domain of the personal/sexual. In other words, news defines itself as concerned with public events.

A second moment of selection concerns the constitution of the topic. Thus, politics is defined as being about government and mainstream political parties with a stress on personalities. The economy is circumscribed as being about the stock exchange, trade figures, government policy, inflation, money supply and so forth. Foreign affairs means intergovernmental relations. Domestic news is subdivided into 'hard' stories – conflict, violence, industrial disputes – and 'soft' human interest stories. The category of 'sport' has traditionally been constituted by male professional sport.

For the manufacture of a story within a topic, we can turn to Galtung and Ruge's (1973) pioneering work on news values, that is, the values that guide the selection processes. Galtung and Ruge identify four prime news values of the *western* world:

1 **reference to elite nations;**
2 **reference to elite persons;**
3 **personalization;**
4 **negativity.**

The unexpected is a significant news value. However, it is even more so if it has negative consequences involving elite persons of an elite nation. A scandal about the private life of the President of the USA is more 'newsworthy' than successful crop figures in Malawi.

— Rank the items listed below 1–10 as you think they would be selected for a TV news programme in (a) London, (b) Sydney, (c) New Delhi. In each case make one list for a commercial station and another for a public broadcast station.

- US President visits London for security talks with the British Prime Minister.
- Flood waters sweep across South India killing 25,000 people.

(Cont'd)

- Sydney Roosters win the Australian Rugby League Grand Final.
- Lassie the dog gets drunk every night with his owner at the local pub.
- Little-known Indian actress wins a part in the next Star Wars movie.
- Genetically modified seeds can produce a ten-fold increase in crop yields, says Australian scientist.
- Eighty-year-old man knocked down and killed by a passing car on the streets of Bombay.
- US government announces interest rate rises of 1 per cent.
- Pakistan conducts a nuclear test explosion.
- England loses World Cup semi-final.

— Discuss with others your reasons for the order you have arrived at.
— What conclusion do you draw about the character of news values and the 'realism' of the news?

The manipulative model

Explanations for how and why the news promotes some world views and not others come in a variety of forms. In the manipulative model, the media are seen as a reflection of a class-dominated society. Here ideology is said to be consciously introduced by media controllers. This happens as a direct result of the concentration of ownership in the hands of people who are part of the 'establishment' or through direct government manipulation and/or informal pressure. There have been examples of direct manipulation of the news. However, this is too crude a model of the media in the context of western plural democracies because of:

- **the quasi-independence granted to operational controllers and journalists;**

- **legal constraints placed on news organizations;**

- **the sophistication of audiences.**

The pluralist model

Western journalists and news organizations themselves often stress a pluralist model. This argument suggests that market forces lead to a plurality of outlets and to a multiplicity of voices addressing different audiences. Concentration of media ownership does not lead to direct proprietorial control because of the independence of professional staff. What the media pay attention to is determined by audience choice through the mechanisms of the market. Audiences, aware of a range of political views and presentational styles within the media, choose to buy or watch that which they already agree with.

A pluralist model recognizes that the media are not simply manipulated by their owners. However, this paradigm arguably bends the stick too far. Increasing media concentration belies arguments about pluralism. Further, there is considerable evidence of the systematic exclusion of some world views in favour of others (see 'Gulf War news' below). Indeed, the increasing reliance on advertising in television systems may lead to a stress on immediacy, entertainment and the omission of certain types of news programmes such as documentaries (Blumler, 1986; Dahlgren, 1995).

The hegemonic model

Within cultural studies the hegemonic model has been popular. Any given culture is constructed in terms of a multiplicity of streams of meaning. However, it is argued that there is a strand of meanings that can reasonably be called ascendant or dominant (Hall, 1977, 1981; Williams, 1973). The process of making, maintaining and reproducing these authoritative sets of meanings and practices has, after Gramsci (1968), been dubbed cultural hegemony (see Chapter 2).

Within a hegemonic model, ideological processes in news production are not the result of direct intervention by owners or even a conscious attempt at manipulation by journalists. Rather, they are an outcome of the routine attitudes and working practices of staff. News journalists learn the conventions and codes of 'how things should be done'. This involves the reproduction of ideology (or 'justifying world views') as common sense. For example, Hall et al. (1978) argue that reliance on 'authoritative sources' leads to the media reproducing primary definers' accounts as news. Primary definers are taken to be politicians, judges, industrialists, the police, and so forth, that is, official agencies involved in the making of news events. In translating the primary definitions of news, the media, as secondary definers, reproduce the hegemonic ideologies associated with the powerful. They also translate them into popular idioms.

Hall et al. (1978) argue that in constructing stories about 'mugging', journalists reproduce the racist assumption that street crime is the work of young black men. Journalists seek the views of police, politicians and judges who declare that not only is street crime on the increase, but that something must be done about it. The solution is posed in the form of heavier policing and harsher sentences. The news media report such comments as common-sense concern about rising crime and its association with black youth. The circle becomes complete when judges cite news coverage of crime as the expression of public concern. They use media coverage to justify the harsher sentences and increased police activity that they and politicians had called for.

Subsequently, police activity is directed into areas in which young black men live. This is because they have been seen as the perpetrators of crime. One consequence of this process is the fuelling of confrontation between the police and black youth.

Agenda setting

The media draw off and constitute consensual assumptions about the world in a process of agenda setting. They define what constitutes news by delineating between that which is important and that which is outside of the news paradigm. Hall et al. (1981) argue that many current affairs programmes do offer balance in terms of the time given to different political views. However, the very field of 'politics' has already been set up as concerning established political procedures, that is, Parliament or Congress. Green politics, revolutionary politics and feminist concerns with domestic life usually fall outside of the established view of what politics and balance are about.

Gulf War news

The 1990–1 Gulf conflict was seen on television screens all over the world and marked the arrival of Cable News Network (CNN) as a world-wide news service. The news coverage of the war was a highly managed and selective affair as journalists were not able to move and report freely. Their numbers were limited and those that were present were carefully shepherded by the military.

The most enduring motif on television of the 1990–1 Gulf War was that of technologically 'smart' weapons able to hit targets with pinpoint accuracy. However, Mowlana et al. (1992) suggest that Iraq was subjected to carpet bombing of a greater tonnage than that which was dropped in the entire Second World War. They also suggest that only 7 per cent of the tonnage dropped was 'smart', and of these 10 per cent missed their targets. Further, Morrison's (1992) content analysis of CNN, Sky News and UK terrestrial television documents the evidence that only 3 per cent of the news coverage was of 'the results of military action in terms of human casualties' and only 1 per cent of the visual images of television were of 'death and injury'.

Television was deficient in providing an adequate explanation for the war. Rather 'the event itself – war – appears to swamp the news and did so at the expense of discussion about either the initial invasion of Kuwait in August 1990, or the presentation of a historical perspective on the war' (Morrison, 1992: 68). By concentrating on the 'glamour' of high tech weaponry and the immediate military objectives of the war, television often obscured the reason that lay behind the conflict. Over a decade later the news management of the US-led coalition invasion of Iraq in 2003 was more sophisticated still. The so-called 'embedding' of journalists with combat forces was designed not only to encourage journalists to develop empathy with soldiers but also to allow for an even greater control of news output.

Yet, the role of television in both wars has not been wholly supportive of US policy. President George Bush Sr's decision to stop the 1990–1 Gulf War short of a full-scale invasion of Iraq was arguably a consequence of his fear that images of slaughter and fleeing Iraqi forces would turn public opinion against him. In 1990–1 there was little alternative to CNN news coverage of the war. Today, CNN coverage is rivalled not only by BBC 24 news but more importantly still by the Arabic station Al-Jazeera. Significantly, Al-Jazeera can claim 35 million viewers and up to an 80 per cent audience share in the Middle East (*The Sydney Morning Herald Magazine*, 29 March 2003). The resources that Al-Jazeera has at its disposal are paltry in comparison to those of CNN. Nevertheless, it is offering an alternative coverage of the war to that of the major western channels and demonstrates that the globalization of television, though unbalanced in favour of the west, does involve countervailing forces. Further, as television reports daily on the carnage in Iraq, so public support for the US-led occupation is declining, even in America.

The Gulf Wars of 1990–1 and 2003 illustrate the way that news stories commonly build upon themselves. That is, a contemporary news narrative will usually be related to a similar one from the past in order to make it more comprehensible. Thus, the attacks on the World Trade Center on September 11, 2001 spawned US president George Bush's 'War Against Terrorism'. Subsequently, coverage of tensions with Iraq during 2002–3 were placed in the context of both the 'War on Terrorism' and the 1991 Gulf War. In this way Saddam Hussein and the Iraqi regime were understood to be terrorists akin to Al-Qaeda and the conflict of 2002 was cast as 'unfinished business' from 1991.

Presentational styles

Television news is constituted not only by its choice of topics and stories but also by its verbal and visual idioms or modes of address. Presentational styles have been subject to a tension between an informational-educational purpose and the need to entertain us. Current affairs programmes are often 'serious' in tone, with adherence to the 'rules' of balance. However, more popular programmes adopt a friendly, lighter idiom. Here we are invited to consider the impact of particular news items from the perspective of the 'average person in the street'. Contemporary political coverage has come to rely on the staged sound-bite, resonant phrase or telling image.

Dahlgren (1995) argues that growing commercial competition has tilted television towards popular formats. He cites increased use of faster editing tempos and 'flashier' presentational styles. These include the use of logos, sound-bites, rapid visual cuts and the 'star quality' of news readers. A stress on immediacy in the presentation of news is a specific and recent development in global news. Electronic news gathering (ENG) technology allows television to bring accounts of global events to the screen as they happen. Lightweight cameras, digital video editing and the multiskilling of television personnel allow for speed and flexibility. Now we even get news footage from mobile phones, shortening the 'threshold' time of what constitutes news.

Within the traditional news programme, there has been a proliferation of new popular formats. These would include the tabloid-style news broadcast, the political talk show, the vox-pop audience participation format and the 'infotainment' magazine shows of breakfast and daytime television (Dahlgren, 1995). These programmes rely on a rapid turnover of items, emblematic visuals and a sense of proximity through the location of news in everyday experience (the human interest story).

Popular formats can be said to enhance understanding by engaging an audience unwilling to endure the longer verbal orientation of older news formats. However, they arguably work to reduce understanding by failing to provide the structural contexts for news events. We quickly learn *what* has happened (or at least a version of it) but not *why* it has happened.

TELEVISION AS TEXT: SOAP OPERA AS POPULAR TELEVISION

Television news is an obvious arena of political and ideological interest. However, cultural studies has also been concerned with popular television, that is, game shows, police and hospital dramas, sport, reality TV, music and soap opera. I take the latter as my example of a popular television form much explored within cultural studies.

Soap opera as a genre

The general features of soap opera as a genre can be summarized (see Allen, 1985, 1995; Ang, 1985; Buckingham, 1987; Dyer et al., 1981; Geraghty, 1991) thus:

- *Open-ended narrative forms*: Soap opera, as a long-running serial, has a potentially unlimited time period in which to tell its stories. There is not the sense of closure to be found in the feature film or the 13-episode series.

- *Core locations*: Most soaps establish a sense of geographical space that the audience can identify with and to which the characters return again and again. Thus *Neighbours* utilizes the Melbourne suburbs while *Coronation Street* and *EastEnders* are set in fictionalized working-class areas of major British cities.

- *The tension between the conventions of realism and melodrama*: Soap opera utilizes the conventions of both realism and melodrama. Indeed, they can be differentiated from each other in terms of the balance struck between these conventions. Realism refers to a set of conventions by which drama appears to be a representation of the 'real world' with motivated characters, recognizable locations and believable social problems. The narrative techniques deliberately hide and obscure their own status as constructs, denying their artificiality in order to present themselves as 'real'. In contrast, melodrama is constituted through a heightened sense of the dramatic, with a focus on emotions and 'life's torments'. Here characters have insufficient motivation from a 'realist' point of view. Reinforced by the use of a certain elevated acting style, dramatic music and lingering close-up shots, the story-lines contain a variety of twists and turns that would stretch the credibility of a realist narrative. In the context of melodrama, viewers are propelled along a roller-coaster ride of emotional ups and downs.

- *The pivotal themes of interpersonal relationships*: Marriages, divorces, break-ups, new alliances, arguments, acts of revenge and acts of caring lie at the core of the soap opera. They provide the narrative dynamic and emotional interest. Given the stress in soaps on the personal sphere, it is understandable that the family forms the mythic centre of the soap opera. It is mythic because though 'family' is a major theme and most of the characters take up family roles (available in plot terms for a marriage, divorce, relationships), only a limited number of characters actually live in a conventional nuclear family. The imaginary ideal of the family is constantly shattered by the arguments, affairs and divorces that are so necessary a part of the soap opera. These features named above are markers of soap opera in general. However, it is important to recognize that the genre works in different ways under different national circumstances. For example, Geraghty (1991) draws attention to the different treatment of 'the family' in US and British soaps. The former, she argues, adopt a patriarchal model of the family that centres on men's efforts to hold the family together in the face of crisis. Here the family is intimately connected to questions of property, power and money. In British soaps, there is a tradition of strong women characters who offer selfless support to others, most notably a breed of feckless men. Thus, the moral and practical task of family survival falls on female shoulders.

SOAP

© Photographer: Andrea Hall | Agency: Dreamstime.com

- *This image is entitled 'Soap'. What assumptions does it make about:*

— *the audience for soap opera*
— *the purpose of watching soap opera and*
— *the value of soap opera?*

- *Do you agree with those assumptions?*

KEY THINKERS

Ien Ang (1954–)

Ang's pioneering study of the way an audience reads television, *Watching Dallas*, became one of the cornerstones of the 'active audience' stream within cultural studies. Ang has continued to write widely on the themes of media, culture, migration and globalization. She has continued to maintain a substantial empirical emphasis in her work, which includes an interest in ethnicity and migrant cultures in Australia and the Asia-Pacific region. She is Professor of Cultural Studies and Director of the Centre for Cultural Research at the University of Western Sydney, Australia.

Reading: Ang, I. (1985) *Watching Dallas: Soap Opera and the Melodramatic Imagination*. London: Methuen.

Women and soap opera

Feminist writers have often suggested that soap opera is a women's space in which women's motivations are validated and celebrated. It has been argued (Ang, 1985; Geraghty, 1991; Hobson, 1982) that the central themes of soap opera – interpersonal relationships, marriages, divorces, children, and so forth – chime with the traditionally domestic concerns of women. Thus, soap opera is held to be a space in which women's concerns and points of view are validated and from which women take pleasure.

Soap operas deploy a variety of strong and independent-minded women characters. However, while the private sphere may be celebrated, women are frequently confined to it. The financially independent woman in the soap is a relatively recent and limited phenomenon. Additionally, the use of glamour and the physical appearance of women to enhance soaps is subject to the criticism that the representation of women is for the male gaze. Women may be strong in soaps, but that strength is frequently put at the service of the family and the men within it.

As commentators have argued, there is both protest and acceptance by women in soap opera (Geraghty, 1991). Indeed, television frequently involves *contradictory ideologies* that compete with each other. For example, in telenovelas (Latin American soaps) women are often presented as adjuncts of men. That is, they are economically and socially dependent on men so that daughters are directed to marry according to the father's wishes. On the other hand, telenovelas often depict women denouncing and resisting domination in a variety of ways (Vink, 1988). The family in soap opera is also handled in a contradictory way. It is idealized yet also shown to be tearing itself apart. Women are the victims of the claustrophobia of family life and, in a sense, the saviours of that which is valuable about it, that is, the care and concern.

Soap opera and the public sphere

The emphasis on the family in soap opera may lead to the general exclusion of issues located in the public sphere, a potential implication of which is that personal and family relations are deemed more important than wider social and structural issues. If we are happy in the family, nothing else matters, or it matters only in terms of its private implications for individuals. Whether it be in response to such criticism or not, soaps have begun to engage with public issues like racism, AIDS, crime and unemployment. This would seem to be a welcome development, though Geraghty (1991) expresses concern that the increasing role of male characters and the entrance of the teenager as a key soap concern may be upsetting the orientation of soaps to women viewers.

— Outline the key elements of a new soap opera designed for the international television market.

You should name (a) four locations, (b) six characters, (c) three story-lines.

Do this activity in a group if possible.

THE ACTIVE AUDIENCE

No consideration of television would be complete without exploring the evidence provided by audience research. However, empirical evidence never simply 'speaks for itself' in an unambiguous way but is framed within particular theoretical perspectives. The framework that has dominated audience research within the cultural studies tradition has been the 'active audience' paradigm.

✓ *The active audience 'tradition' suggests that audiences are not cultural dopes but are active producers of meaning from within their own cultural context.*

The active audience paradigm developed in reaction to the numerous ways in which audiences had been studied with the built-in assumption that watching television was passive in character and that the meanings of television were unproblematically taken up by viewers. This would include the considerable volume of research which argued that audiences imitated violence on television, or which used statistical correlations to 'prove' that watching television had certain 'effects' on audiences. The stress on the audience's active engagement with television was also a reaction to a textual strand in cultural studies which implied that one could 'read off' audience understandings from a close examination of the meanings embodied in television texts.

The proponents of the active audience approach argued that statistical and behavioural approaches were mistaken modes by which to study television audiences. It was suggested instead that watching television is a socially and culturally informed activity that is centrally concerned with *meaning*. Audiences are active creators of meaning in relation to television (they do not simply uncritically accept textual meanings). They do this on the basis of previously acquired cultural competencies forged in the context of language and social relationships. Further, it was argued that texts do not embody one set of unambiguous meanings but are themselves polysemic, that is, they are carriers of multiple meanings. Only some of these meanings are taken up by audiences. Indeed, differently constituted audiences will work with different textual meanings. Thus the active audience paradigm represented a shift of interest:

- **from numbers to meanings;**
- **from textual meaning to textual meanings;**
- **from the general audience to particular audiences.**

There is now a good deal of mutually supporting work on television audiences within the cultural studies tradition from which the following conclusions can be drawn:

- **The audience is conceived of as active and knowledgeable producers of meaning not products of a structured text.**

But …

- **Meanings are bounded by the way the text is structured and by the domestic and cultural context of the viewing.**
- **Audiences need to be understood in the contexts in which they watch television in terms of both meaning construction and the routines of daily life.**
- **Audiences are easily able to distinguish between fiction and reality; indeed they actively play with the boundaries.**
- **The processes of meaning construction and the place of television in the routines of daily life alter from culture to culture and in terms of gender and class within the same cultural community.**

These conclusions about the character of audiences have been reached by way of two mutually supporting routes: theoretical work and empirical research. On the theoretical front, the encoding–decoding model proved to be of major significance.

Encoding–decoding

Hall (1981) conceives of the process of television encoding as an articulation of the linked but distinct moments in a circuit of meaning. Each of the moments in this circuit has its specific practices which are necessary to the circuit but which do not guarantee the next moment (Figure 10.1).

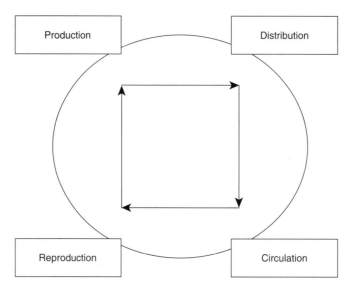

Figure 10.1   Hall's (1981) 'Circuit of Television'

Though meaning is embedded at each level, it is not necessarily taken up at the next moment in the circuit. In particular, the production of meaning does not ensure consumption of that meaning as the encoders might have intended. This is because television messages, constructed as a sign system with multi-accentuated components, are polysemic. In short, television messages carry multiple meanings and can be interpreted in different ways. That is not to say that all the meanings are equal among themselves. Rather, the text will be 'structured in dominance' leading to a 'preferred meaning', that is, the one to which the text guides us.

The audience is conceived of as socially situated individuals whose readings will be framed by shared cultural meanings and practices. To the degree that audiences share cultural codes with producers/encoders, they will decode messages within the same framework. However, where the audience is situated in different social positions (e.g. of class and gender) with different cultural resources, it is able to decode programmes in alternative ways. Hall (1981) proposed, after Parkin, a model of three hypothetical decoding positions:

1   *the dominant–hegemonic encoding/decoding* which accepts the 'preferred meanings';

2   *a negotiated code* which acknowledges the legitimacy of the hegemonic in the abstract but makes its own rules and adaptations under particular circumstances;

3   *an oppositional code* where people understand the preferred encoding but reject it and decode in contrary ways.

Audiences do not merely reproduce textual meaning but *produce new meaning*. The text may structure aspects of meaning by guiding the reader, but it cannot fix meanings, which are the outcome of the oscillations between the text and the imagination of the reader. This argument was popularized within cultural studies by the early work of Morley and Ang.

The *Nationwide* audience

Morley's (1980) research into the audience for the British news 'magazine' programme *Nationwide* was based on Hall's encoding–decoding model. It aimed to explore the hypothesis that decodings varied by socio-demographic factors (class, age, sex, race) and by their associated cultural competencies and frameworks. This investigation has its methodological problems, which Morley (1992) acknowledges. Nevertheless, the study suggests a multitude of audience readings that cluster around key decoding positions as constituted by class. For example, dominant decodings were made by a group of conservative print managers and bank managers. Negotiated readings were made by a group of trades union officials. The latter's readings remained negotiated rather than oppositional because they were specific to a particular industrial dispute while remaining within the general discourse that strikes were a 'bad thing for Britain'. According to Morley, oppositional decodings were made by a group of shop stewards, whose political perspectives led them to reject wholesale the discourses of *Nationwide*. Opposition was also expressed by a group of black further education students, who felt alienated from the programme by virtue of its perceived irrelevance to their lives.

KEY THINKERS

David Morley (1949–)

Morley, a professor at Goldsmith College, University of London, and a former member of the Birmingham Centre of Contemporary Cultural Studies was a key figure in the development of the 'active audience' paradigm within cultural studies. His early work on television audiences during the 1980s combined a theoretical justification of ethnographic methods with empirical studies of audience readings. Morley has also written on the gendered character of television viewing, the absorption of technology into everyday cultural life, and globalization and cultural identity.

Reading: Morley, D. (1992) *Television, Audiences and Cultural Studies.* London and New York: Routledge.

Watching Dallas

Ang's (1985) study of *Dallas* and its audience was carried out amongst women viewers in the Netherlands. It involved a 'symptomatic' analysis (i.e. searching for the attitudes which lie behind texts) of letters written to her about watching the soap. Ang begins by exploring the tension between the ideas of an active audience and the potential structuring of meaning by the text. Her central argument is that *Dallas* viewers are actively involved in the production of meaning and pleasure. In doing so, they generate a range of responses that are not reducible to either the structure of the text, an 'ideological effect' or a political project.

Fiction, says Ang, is a way of enjoying the here and now. It involves playing with one's feelings in a movement between involvement and distance, acceptance and protest. It is also an experience mediated by the 'ideology of mass culture', which places *Dallas* in an inferior relationship to other cultural activities. This led viewers to adopt a range of viewing positions:

- **feeling guilty about watching *Dallas*;**

- **an ironic stance to stave off the contradiction of liking *Dallas* and seeing it as 'trash';**

- **arguing that it was acceptable to watch the programme if you were 'aware of the dangers';**

- **defending themselves on the grounds that they had the right to hold whatever cultural tastes they so wished.**

Ideology and resistance

It has often been assumed that the active nature of the audience undercuts the role of ideology in television. That is, audience activity makes reception and the generation of meaning less problematically tied to textual construction and issues of power. Thus, there has been a tendency to see the reproduction of ideology as associated with passive audiences and to link the active audience with resistance to ideology. However, while evidence suggests that television viewers understand a good deal about the grammar and production processes of television, and that on the level of television *form* they are extremely sophisticated and literate, this does not necessarily prevent them from producing and reproducing forms of ideology.

Research carried out amongst British Asian teenage viewers of soap opera in the UK (Barker, 1998, 1999; Barker and André, 1996) suggested that they are both active *and* implicated in the reproduction of ideology about the family, relationships and gender.

Indeed, audience activity is a *requirement* for the engagement with and reproduction of ideology. As Silverstone (1994) suggests, audiences are *always* active but whether this results in a challenge to ideologies has to be empirically determined case by case and not to be taken for granted.

✓ *Audience activity can deconstruct 'preferred' meaning only when alternative discourses are available. Thus, the self becomes a site of struggle over meaning and significance.*

TELEVISION AUDIENCES AND CULTURAL IDENTITY

Watching television is constitutive of and constituted by forms of cultural identity (Chapter 7). Television is a resource for the construction of cultural identity just as audiences deploy their cultural identities and cultural competencies to decode programmes in their own specific ways. As television has become globalized, so the place of television in the constitution of ethnic and national identities has taken on a particular significance (Barker, 1999).

The export of meaning

Liebes and Katz (1991) conducted a large-scale study of how viewers from a range of cultural and ethnic backgrounds generate meaning as they watch television fiction. The study involved 65 focus discussion groups from various ethnic communities and sought to explore the cross-cultural dimensions of viewing of the US soap opera *Dallas*. The groups were constituted by Arabs, Russian Jews, Moroccan Jews and Israeli kibbutz members in Israel, plus a group of Americans and Japanese situated in their country of origin.

Liebes and Katz argue that their study provides evidence of divergent readings of television narratives founded in different cultural backgrounds. In particular, they explore the differences between 'referential' and 'critical' approaches to the programme across different groups. Overall, referential statements outweighed critical statements three to one.

- *By 'referential' they mean an understanding that reads the programme as if it were referring to 'reality'.*
- *By 'critical' they mean an awareness of the constructed nature of the programme.*

Liebes and Katz argue there were distinct differences between ethnic groups in the levels of each type of statement. They concluded that Americans and Russians were particularly critical. However, the critical awareness displayed by Americans was largely centred on questions of form and production context, based on their greater understanding of the business of television. Americans were less critical in terms of themes/content. Arab groups were said to have a high sensitivity to the 'dangers' of western culture and of western 'moral degeneracy'.

The Liebes/Katz research suggests that audiences draw on their own sense of national and ethnic identity when decoding programmes. American television is not uncritically consumed by audiences with the destruction of 'indigenous' cultural identities as the inevitable outcome.

Localizing the global

In a similar vein, Miller (1995) argues that it would be a mistake to think that a Trinidadian audience's engagement with the US soap opera *The Young and the Restless* is simply the consumption of American consumer culture. He recounts the ways in which the soap opera is 'localized'; that is, made sense of and absorbed into local practices and meanings. In particular, the gossip and scandal (specifically that of a sexual nature) which are core concerns of the soap opera's narrative resonate with the Trinidadian concept of 'bacchanal'. According to Miller, 'bacchanal' is a deeply rooted folk concept fusing ideas of confusion, gossip, scandal and truth. The concerns of the soap thus 'collude with the local sense of truth as exposure and scandal' (ibid.: 223).

That television is uneven and contradictory in its impact is illustrated by Lull's research in China. According to Lull (1991, 1997), television was introduced into China by a government hoping to deploy it as a form of social control and cultural homogenization. However, it has turned out to play quite the opposite role. Although the Chinese government has attempted to use television to re-establish social stability after the Tiananmen Square protests of 1989, it has instead become a central agent of popular resistance.

Television has amplified and intensified the diversity of cultural and political sentiments in China by presenting alternative views of life. Driven by the need to attract larger audiences, television has become a cultural forum of competing ideas. This has developed as commercial and imported dramas have been juxtaposed with China's own economic difficulties. Further, not only are programmes themselves polysemic, but audiences have become adept at reading between the lines of official pronouncements. For Lull, the challenge to autocratic rule raised by the Chinese resistance movement, with its stress on freedom and democracy, could not have happened without television.

✓ *Television circulates texts and discourses on a global scale. However, its consumption and use as a resource for the construction of cultural identities always take place in a local context.*

GOAL!

© Photographer: Ran Rosman | Agency: Dreamstime.com

Italian fans celebrate at the football world cup.

- *How does television make the world cup both a global event and a moment of local national identification?*

- *Why do television companies want to screen the world cup?*

- *What role has sports TV played in the development of cable and satellite television?*

Audiences, space and identity

The cultural significance of television lies not only in textual meanings and interpretations, but also in its place within the rhythms and routines of everyday domestic life. In particular, watching television is something we commonly do in specific domestic spaces, for example the 'living room'. Of particular interest is:

- the manner in which broadcasting provides ritual social events wherein families or groups of friends watch together and talk before, during and after programmes;

- the connection between such rituals, the spaces in which they are watched and the production of cultural identities.

Space, as Massey (1994) argues, is not 'empty' but is produced culturally by social relations (Chapter 12). For example, Scannell (1988) has argued that television plays a role in the construction of national space by bringing major public events into the private world of viewers. In doing so, it constructs a national calendar that organizes, co-ordinates and renews a national public social world. Such events might include the FA Cup Final, Wimbledon, the opening of Parliament and the last night of the Proms in Britain; and Congressional elections, the Superbowl and 4th July celebrations in America. Of course, the forces of globalization are now setting such national events within an international context.

Family space and global space

Morley's (1986) study *Family Television* pointed to the gendered nature of watching television in the home. He suggested that power and control over programme choice lies mostly with men. He argues that men and women have different viewing patterns and preferences. For example, men have more attentive viewing styles than women, who are engaged in other domestic activities. Drama and fiction feature more in the preferences of women than men, for whom sport and news are more central.

More recently, the connections between television, space and daily routines have been explored by Lull (1991, 1997) in a Chinese context. Here limited domestic space means that the introduction of a television set into a household has considerable impact. When the television is on, it cannot be escaped from, so that watching television has to be a collective family experience. Consequently, family routines now include a specific time to watch TV. Thus, the arrival of television has altered family relationships, introducing potential conflict over what is watched, when and by whom. The regulation of children's viewing was a particular issue.

In contrast to Lull's stress on the home as a place, Meyrowitz (1986) is concerned with global space. He suggests that electronic media alter our sense of the 'situational geography' of social life. This means that we inhabit a virtual world-wide space in which new forms of identification are forged. The core of his argument is that electronic media break the traditional bonds between geographic place and social identity. This is a consequence of the way the mass media provide us with increasing sources of identification that are situated beyond the immediacy of specific places. Meyrowitz's arguments raise questions about television, culture and identity in the context of accelerated globalization.

THE GLOBALIZATION OF TELEVISION

By globalization (see Chapter 5) is meant a set of processes that are leading to the compression or shrinking of the world, that is, to an ever-increasing abundance of global connections and our understanding of them. The globalization of television involves technology, economics, institutions and culture. Television may be considered global in respect of:

- **the various configurations of public and commercial television, which are regulated, funded and viewed within the boundaries of nation-states and/or language communities;**

- **the technology, ownership, programme distribution and audiences of television, which operate across the boundaries of nation-states and language communities;**

- **the circulation by television of similar narrative forms and discourses around the world.**

The globalization of television is an aspect of the dynamic expansionist logic of capitalism in its quest for new commodities and new markets. Television stands at the centre of wider commercial activities, being core to the expansion of consumer capitalism. There are at least one billion television sets world-wide, watched by more than 2.5 billion people per day in over 160 countries. The USA has the highest density of televisions per head of the population, with 99 per cent of American households owning at least one television set. Seventy-four per cent of these homes have two or more sets (Nielson Media Research, 1999, www.nelsonmedia.com/reports_available/reports.html). However, since the mid-1980s the fastest growth area for television set ownership has been the 'developing world' and it is now China that claims the highest number of television households (*Screen Digest*, May 1998).

✓ *There is little doubt that television is a global phenomenon in its production, dissemination and viewing patterns – and one that grows daily.*

The political economy of global television

Political economy is concerned with the power and the distribution of economic and social resources. For current purposes this translates into:

- **a concern with who owns and controls the production and distribution mechanisms of television;**

- **the consequences of patterns of ownership and control for the cultural landscape.**

Murdock and Golding (1977) have argued that the ownership of communications by private capital is subject to a general process of concentration via conglomeration. This produces multimedia corporations that are part of a wider process of capital conglomeration. Murdock (1990) distinguishes three basic kinds of conglomerates operating in the communications field:

1 industrial conglomerates;

2 service conglomerates;

3 communications conglomerates.

These operate in the context of changes in the communications industries centred on the processes of synergy, convergence and deregulation (Dyson and Humphreys, 1990; Thussu, 2000).

Synergy and television ownership

During the 1990s there was a good deal of diversification by financial, computer and data processing companies into telecommunications. This process created multimedia giants who dominated key sectors of the market. Companies needed the financial power that can come from mergers to undertake the massive investment required in order to be players in the global market. The 1989 merger of Time and Warner created the largest media group in the world. Time Warner then grew further still in 1995 through the acquisition of Turner Broadcasting (CNN) and the subsequent merger with America Online.

The prime reason for these developments is the search for synergy. This involves the convergence or bringing together of various elements of television and other media at the levels of production and distribution so that they complement each other to produce lower costs and higher profits. The preoccupation with combining software and hardware can be seen when films are marketed simultaneously with pop music soundtracks and virtual reality video games all owned by the same company. This is now not so much the exception as the rule. No communications organization represents that synergy better than Rupert Murdoch's News Corporation.

The acquisition by News Corporation of the Hong Kong-based Star TV for $525 million gave Murdoch a satellite television footprint over Asia and the Middle East. Allied to other television holdings, notably BSkyB (UK) and Fox TV (USA and Australia), News Corp's television interests have a global reach of some two-thirds of the planet. It is not just the spatial breadth of the corporation's ownership that is significant, it is also the potential link-ups between its various elements. In Twentieth Century Fox and Star TV, Murdoch acquired a huge library of film and television product that he can channel through his network of distribution outlets. He hopes to create a lucrative global advertising market. At the same time, Murdoch is able to take advantage of cross-promotion. That is, he can use his newspapers to promote his television interests by giving space in his press holdings to the sporting activities covered by his television channels.

— Design an 'ideal-type' global communications corporation that maximizes the possibilities for synergy.
— Draw the organization in the form of a map and illustrate the cross-links with arrows.

Deregulation and reregulation

Synergy and convergence have been made to happen by the captains of industry and enabled by politicians. Multimedia conglomerates have existed for many years. However, the scope of their activities has been allowed to widen by governmental relaxation of the regulations restricting cross-media ownership and the entry of new players. This does not mean that all regulations have been abolished; rather, the television and telecommunications industries have been reregulated. Significantly, the new regulations are considerably less stringent than their predecessors. This has been occasioned by a number of factors:

- the growth of 'new' communication technologies has invalidated the natural monopoly argument since digital technology allows frequencies to be split and alternative delivery systems employed;

- the upholding by court rulings in various countries of the legal rights to communicate and the adoption of diversity as a key public principle;

- a new governmental enthusiasm for the market, including a preference for the funding of television by commercial means rather than through taxation.

Thus it was the relaxation of television and newspaper ownership rules that allowed Murdoch to launch Fox Cable TV in America. It also enabled him to own both newspapers and television companies in the UK. Similarly, deregulation has allowed AT&T, the biggest telephone operator in America, to participate in the television market. This was a domain from which it had previously been excluded by law.

Outside of America, public service broadcasting and political regulation in a national context marked the 'old order' of television. Today the 'new order' in television involves:

- the co-existence of public and commercial broadcasting;

- the deregulation of commercial television;

- the increasing emergence of multimedia transnational companies;

- pressure on public service television to operate with a commercial logic.

These are the world-wide trends that underpinned the emergence of a global electronic culture.

> — What are the arguments for and against the deregulation of the television market?
> — What are the arguments in favour of retaining a public service television broad-caster?
>
> Assess the arguments.

GLOBAL ELECTRONIC CULTURE

✓ *In the age of electronic reproduction, culture is able to come to us via the screen, video, radio, etc. We are no longer required to explore it in the context of ritualized spaces.*

In the context of globalization, culture can be seen to span time and place. Thus, cultural artefacts and meanings from different historical periods and geographical places can mix together and be juxtaposed. The values and meanings attached to place remain significant. However, the networks in which people are involved extend far beyond their physical locations. For some critics this involves mixing, matching and cultural exchange; for others it is a form of cultural domination.

Media imperialism

Schiller (1969, 1985) makes the case that the media fit into the world capitalist system by providing ideological support for capitalism, and for transnational corporations in particular. The media are seen as vehicles for corporate marketing, manipulating audiences to deliver them to advertisers. This is allied to the assertion of a general ideological effect by which media messages create and reinforce audience attachment to the status quo.

Concerns about media and cultural imperialism have been fuelled by a limited number of dated studies of the global television trade which have concluded that programming flows are dominated by the USA (Varis, 1974, 1984). Certainly America is the major exporter of television programmes, a position enabled by the economics of the industry. This allows US producers to cover much of their costs in the domestic market, leaving exports as profit. However, 'more and more nations are producing an increasing proportion of their own programming', a significant number of which are 'doing over half of their own programming, both in the total broadcast day and during primetime' (Straubhaar, 1996: 293).

Regionalization

The US can claim 'at least 75 per cent of the world-wide television programme exports' (Hoskins et al., 1995). However, there has been a distinct move towards *regionalization* of markets on the basis of shared language, culture and historical trade links. Thus the majority of US media product goes to seven countries: Australia, Canada, France, Germany, Italy, Japan and the UK (Waterman, 1988). Straubhaar (1996) argues that there are a number of 'geo-cultural' markets emerging. These include those based in Western Europe, Latin America, the Francophone world of France and its former colonies, an Arabic world market, a Chinese market and a South Asian market. Further, these markets are not necessarily bounded by geographical space but involve diaspora populations distributed across the world. For example, the Indian film industry serves not only the Indian subcontinent but also areas of Africa, Malaysia, Indonesia and Europe.

The US-media imperialism argument does not take on board the contradictory, unpredictable and heterogeneous meanings that active audiences are able to take from television. Television does play a direct role in the penetration of cultures by meaning systems from elsewhere. However, rather than involving the obliteration of local conceptions, the process is better understood as one in which local meanings are overlaid by alternative definitions. This relativizes both and creates new senses of ambiguity and uncertainty (Ferguson, 1990). We are seeing a set of economic and cultural processes dating from different historical periods, with different developmental rhythms, being overlaid upon each other. This process creates global disjunctures as well as new global connections and similarities (Appadurai, 1993; Smith, 1990).

— Write down your top ten favourite television programmes.
— Ask three other people (friends and relatives with different tastes would help) to do the same.
— Go through the TV guide and identify the country of origin for each programme. What conclusions might you draw?

The global and the local

Television can be said to be global in its circulation of similar narrative forms around the world: soap opera, news, sport, quiz shows and music videos can be found in most countries. Soap opera, for example, is a global form in two senses:

1 It is a narrative mode *produced* in a variety of countries across the globe.

2 It is one of the most exported forms of television *viewed* in a range of cultural contexts.

The global attraction of soap opera can be attributed to:

- the apparently universal appeal of open-ended narrative forms;
- the centrality of personal and kinship relations;
- the emergence of an international style embedded in the traditions of Hollywood.

However, the success of soap opera also reflects the possibilities offered to audiences of engaging in local or regional issues located in recognizable, 'real' places. For example, South African television screens a good deal of American and Australian soap opera. However, it is also possible to watch the locally produced *Generations.*

The tensions between the poles of the global and the local are highlighted by, on the one hand, the enormous global popularity of soaps like *Neighbours* and *The Bold and the Beautiful* and, on the other hand, the failure of these very same soaps in particular countries (e.g. *Neighbours* in America). As Crofts (1995) has pointed out, the global success, and failures, of soap opera depends on the specificities of soap opera as a televisual form and the particularities of the conditions of reception. We have certainly witnessed the emergence of an international primetime soap opera style, including high production values, pleasing visual appearances and fast-paced, action-oriented narrative modes. Nevertheless, many soaps retain local settings, regional language audiences and slow-paced, melodramatic story-telling.

Likewise, news exhibits global similarities as well as local differences. Straubhaar's (1992) cross-cultural study concluded that 'what is news' is 'fairly consistent' from country to country. Data collected by Gurevitch et al. (1991) about the Eurovision News Exchange and the 36 countries which regularly use it suggest that the availability of common news footage and a shared professional culture has led to 'substantial, but not complete' convergence of news stories. This may reflect 'the drift towards an international standardization of basic journalistic discourses' (Dahlgren, 1995: 49), together with the domination of global news agendas by western news agencies.

However, the fact that western news agencies tend to supply 'spot news' and visual reports without commentary allows different interpretations of events to be dubbed over the pictures. This leads to what Gurevitch et al. (1991) call the 'domestication' of global news. This is regarded as a 'countervailing force to the pull of globalization'.

Beyond specific genres like soap opera and news, the global multiplication of communications technologies has created an increasingly complex semiotic environment. This is one in which television produces and circulates an explosive display of competing signs and meanings. This process creates a flow of images and juxtapositions that fuse news, views, drama and reportage into an electronic bricolage (Williams, 1974).

✓ *The globalization of television has contributed to the construction of a collage of images from different times and places which has been dubbed postmodern.*

Global postmodern culture

Lash (1990) identifies the shift from the 'discursive' to the 'figural' as core to the postmodern turn. By this he means that the signifying logics of the modern and postmodern work in different ways. For Lash, the modernist 'regime of signification':

- prioritizes words over images;
- promulgates a rationalist world view;
- explores the meanings of cultural texts;
- distances the spectator from the cultural object.

In contrast, the postmodern 'figural':

- puts stress on the visual;
- draws from everyday life;
- contests rationalist views of culture;
- immerses the spectator in his/her desire for the cultural object.

We may conclude that the globalization of the essentially *visual* medium of television forms a central part of the postmodern cultural turn.

Hutcheon argues that postmodernism 'takes the form of self-conscious, self-contradictory, self-undermining statement. It is rather like saying something with inverted commas around what is being said' (Hutcheon, 1989: 1). In other words, postmodernism is a form of ironic knowingness. It is ironic because it explores the limitations and conditions of its own knowing. The stylistic markers of the postmodern in television have been seen as:

- aesthetic self-consciousness/self-reflexiveness;
- juxtaposition/montage/bricolage;
- paradox/ambiguity/uncertainty;
- intertextuality and the blurring of genre boundaries;
- irony, parody and pastiche.

The techniques of postmodern television include montage, rapid cutting, non-linear narrative techniques and the de-contextualization of images. Programmes that have commonly been identified with the postmodern decentre the importance of linear narrative in favour of a new look and feel in which image takes preference over story-telling (Kellner, 1992). Self-conscious intertextuality involves explicit allusion to particular programmes and oblique references to other genre conventions and styles. An example would be the explicit reference to the films *Thelma and Louise* and *Halloween* in the TV cartoon *The Simpsons*. This intertextuality is an aspect of enlarged, cultural self-consciousness about the history and functions of cultural products.

The Simpsons has been widely acclaimed as an example of the postmodern in television. Here a 'dysfunctional' American family are the ironic heroes of a series which is, on the one hand, simply a cartoon and, on the other hand, a set of subtle reflections on American life and culture. It is not coincidental that the centre of the Simpsons' life is the television set, nor that the programme makes a series of intertextual references to other television programmes and genres. Indeed, *The Simpsons* requires us to be aware of a range of other television and film genres. Thus, the ending of one episode is entirely an ironic reworking of the final sequence of *The Graduate*. Further, *Itchy and Scratchy,* a cartoon watched by the Simpson children, parodies *Tom and Jerry*. It mocks the double standard by which we seem to condemn television violence even as we lap it up.

> — Watch a TV programme or film that you think is known for its use of intertextuality (e.g. Blade Runner, Pulp Fiction, The Sopranos).
>
> — Identify the following:
>
> • genres that are referred to or imitated;
> • characters from other books, plays, films, etc.;
> • lighting, camera work and styles taken from other films and programmes;
> • homage to or reference to other books or films.

Hyperreality and TV simulations

A more apocalyptic view of postmodern culture is taken by Baudrillard (1983a, 1983b). For him, television is the heart of a culture marked by an all-encompassing flow of fascinating simulations and facsimiles, that is, a hyperreality in which we are overloaded with images and information. This is a world where a series of modern distinctions – the real and the unreal, the public and the private, art and reality – have broken down, or been sucked into a 'black hole'.

For Baudrillard, 'hyperreality' is produced according to a model. It is not a given but is artificially reproduced as real. Thus, the prefix 'hyper' signifies 'more real than real': a real retouched in a 'hallucinatory resemblance' with itself. Baudrillard describes a process leading to the collapse of boundaries, which he calls 'implosion', between the media and the social. Here the news and entertainment blur into each other and 'TV is the world'. Thus, television simulates real-life situations, not so much to represent the world as to execute its own. For Baudrillard, postmodern television is flat and one-dimensional, its continual flow of images and simulacra having no connotational hierarchy. It is both literally and metaphorically 'superficial'.

In contrast, for Kellner television is meaningful and does not represent 'a black hole where all meaning and messages are absorbed in the whirlpool' (Kellner, 1992: 156). Rather, he argues for the integrating central role of television as myth and ritual celebrating dominant values and modes of thought and behaviour. As such, he suggests that television provides models by which people construct their attitudes, values and consequent actions.

Consumer culture

Globalization, consumer culture and postmodernism are closely allied phenomena for the following reasons:

- **Globalization has involved the 'displacement' of the west and its philosophical categories from the centre of the universe; indeed, some have seen the collapse of western classifications as *the* marker of postmodernism.**

- **The rise in visibility and status of popular culture, hastened by electronic media, has meant that the distinction between high and low culture is no longer viable.**

- **The blurring of the boundaries between art, culture and commerce, allied to the rising prominence of the postmodern 'figural', has resulted in a general aestheticization of everyday life (Featherstone, 1991, 1995).**

The development of global television as a fundamentally commercial form has placed that core activity of consumer culture, visual-based advertising, at the forefront of its activities (Mattelart and Mattelart, 1992). Television is pivotal to the production and reproduction of a *promotional culture* focused on the use of visual imagery to create value-added brands or commodity-signs. Indeed, Wernick argues that cultural phenomena which serve to communicate a promotional message of some type or other have become 'virtually co-extensive with our produced symbolic world' (Wernick, 1991: 184). The phrase 'Coca-Cola culture' encapsulates the global reach of this promotional culture and highlights the alleged link between global capitalism, advertising and cultural homogenization. That is, for some critics, global processes represent a form of cultural homogenization. This is particularly so in the field of consumer culture, where Coca-Cola, McDonald's, Nike and Microsoft Windows circulate world-wide.

However, the global circulation of consumer goods should not lead us to assume that their impact is the same the world over. Consumer goods are subject through the processes of glocalization to a variety of meanings on the level of local consumption. This should prevent us from equating Coca-Cola culture with homogeneous cultural identities. Indeed, it is the juxtaposition of Windows and ox-drawn carts, *The Simpsons* and *Hum Log* (an Indian soap opera), Hollywood and Bollywood, *Faithless* and traditional dance music that suggests the idea of a global postmodern.

Creative consumption

The majority of cultural studies writers have taken a more positive view of cultural consumption than does Baudrillard. They have stressed the creative potential inherent in contemporary television and consumer culture. For example, Chambers (1987) and Hebdidge (1988) have discussed the ways in which commodities, including television, form the basis of multiple identity construction. They have emphasized the active and meaning-oriented activity of consumers, who act as bricoleurs selecting and arranging elements of material commodities and meaningful signs. Likewise, Fiske (1987) argues that popular culture is constituted by the meanings that people make with it rather than those identifiable within the texts. Indeed, he sees popular culture as a site of semiotic warfare and of popular tactics deployed to evade or resist the meanings produced and inscribed in commodities by producers.

Paul Willis (1990) argues that the processes of commodification underpin a 'common culture' in the consuming practices of young people. Rather than meaning being inherent in the commodity, he points to the construction of meaning and value in actual usage. This he calls 'grounded aesthetics'. For Willis, contemporary culture is not meaningless or superficial surface but involves the active creation of meaning by all people as cultural producers. Willis takes the familiar line that audiences (he is talking about young people in particular) are sophisticated readers of images, having learned to play with interpreting television codes.

In this way, the contemporary television world can be read not as a one-dimensional hyperreality but as a democratic and creative culture. The creative play through which such cultural forms are produced and consumed offers democratizing possibilities. The production of popular music, film, television and fashion may be in the hands of transnational capitalist multimedia corporations. However, texts are altered and managed at the level of consumption by people who are active producers of meaning.

DECONSTRUCT THIS: TEXT VS. AUDIENCE

- How do texts construct an audience?
- How does an audience construct a text?
- How is it possible to distinguish between textual meanings and those generated by an audience?

SUMMARY

Television has been a long-standing concern of cultural studies. This is because of its central place in the communicative practices of western societies and its proliferation across the globe. These concerns have become increasingly acute as global television turns away from public service broadcasting towards a commercial television that is dominated by multimedia corporations in search of synergy and convergence.

The globalization of the institutions of television is paralleled by the world-wide circulation of key television narratives and genres. These include news, soap opera, music television, sport and game shows. These texts are set within an advancing 'Promotional' and postmodern culture marked by bricolage, intertextuality and genre blurring.

Attention was paid to the values constructed by television programmes, including hegemonic versions of world news that exclude alternative perspectives. However, it was also argued that television programmes are polysemic; they contain many meanings that are commonly contradictory. Thus, audiences can explore a range of potential meanings. Further, evidence was given to suggest that audiences are active producers of meaning and do not simply take on board those textual meanings identified by critics. Hence, global television is better understood as the promotion of bricolage and hybridity rather than as cultural imperialism.

The significance of television is not confined to textual meanings for it is situated and sustained within the activities of everyday life. The political economy and programme flows of television may be global. However, watching television is situated within the domestic practices of the day to day. In particular, it was argued that the domestic space of the home is a site for the construction and contestation of wider cultural identities, including those of gender.

Digital Media Culture

KEY CONCEPTS

Convergence	*Identity*
Cyberspace	*Information economy*
Cyborgs	*Intertextuality*
Digital divide	*Public sphere*
Hypertext	*Virtual reality*

Since its inception, cultural studies has been concerned with the mass media and the place they occupy at the centre of public life and culture. Indeed, contemporary western cultures are now media saturated. Today the media continue to be implicated in the selective provision of social knowledge and imagery through which we grasp our world. Yet alongside the conventional mass media a new digital universe is emerging, some of which is miniaturized and niche marketed. The significance of this is not confined to textual meanings, for it is situated and sustained within the routine activities of everyday life.

Jane is a newly enrolled university student. She conducts research on the Internet, submits word-processed assignments that she has completed on her laptop, and has her marks stored in a central digital database. To fund her studies, she works part-time in a call-centre. Her social life is organized through her mobile phone or via MSN, and the personalized sound-track to her life is downloaded on to an mp3 player. When she can grab a spare moment she likes to play computer games, watch videos on YouTube, and update her My Space site. Thirty years ago students at that same university did none of these things. Yet today, like Jane, almost every reader of this book will encounter computers and other electronic media on a daily basis. We are in the midst of a digital revolution that is transforming our world.

DIGITAL MEDIA

Digital technology organizes information electronically into bytes, or discrete bundles of information. This enables more information to be stored and processed at greater speed than by any other other medium in human history. This information can be compressed during transmission and decompressed on arrival, allowing data to travel at greater speed over larger distances. Digital media also enable cultural representations to be endlessly and cheaply reproduced without loss of quality. The impact of new technologies in general, and digital processes in particular, can be summed up in terms of speed, volume and distance, that is, more information handled at greater speed and distributed over larger distances. The term 'digital technology' encompasses computers and all its functions, including information storage in databases, information processing and the Internet. It also covers digital equipment such as USB data storage devices, cameras, mp3 players and some types of cinema and television.

Digital divides

Although digital media are ubiquitous in western culture, we do need to qualify our sense of living in a computerized world. First, while the capacity to download film and video from the Internet exists, broadcast television (whether analogue or digital) remains at the core of our leisure time, even in advanced industrial countries. The 'end of television' predicted by some prophets of the new digital age is nowhere in sight. It may happen in the future but not any time soon. Second, the use of digital media is unevenly distributed in western culture. More young people than adults aged over 40 play computer games and own mp3 players; more men than women access the Internet, and wealth inevitably marks a break between the digital 'haves' and 'have nots'. Third, the 'digital divide' created by the distribution of wealth is magnified on a global scale. When we talk about a digital world, it is worth remembering that:

✓ *'the majority of non-Western nations and nearly 97 percent of the world's population remain unconnected to the net for lack of money, access, or knowledge.' (Trend, 2005: 2)*

Nonetheless the impact of digital media within the post-industrial societies of the world has been substantial. With it a large and growing literature has emerged which examines its significance. Since it is not possible to explore here all the concerns writers have raised about digital culture, we will investigate only a few emblematic issues. First, we will investigate the question of democracy and cyberspace; second we will examine the issue of identity with particular reference to both gaming and cyberfeminism; and third we will explore issues related to the political economy of cyberspace, including the significance of the mobile phone in the era of digital convergence. Each of these issues is marked by another digital divide, this time between utopia and dystopia. When it comes to digital culture, writers seem to love it or hate it.

Cyberutopia

Cyberspace is a spatial metaphor for the 'nowhere' place in which the electronic activities of computers, cable systems and other digital communications technologies occur. The concept, which is said to have been coined by William Gibson (1984), can be understood as referring to a computer-generated, collective hallucination which constructs the virtual space of electronic culture. Wertheim (1999) notes that enthusiasts of cyberspace often imagine it as utopian space 'above and beyond' the culture, history and problems of our times.

Utopian voices often envisage cyberspace as a disembodied heavenly place, suggests Wertheim. This image is enabled by the fact that cyberspace is not clearly located in the physical world, yet it remains a very real, day-to-day social space for large numbers of people. In particular, a key utopian proposition about the Internet is that it is open to all people regardless of sex, gender, age, class or nationality because within it we are free from body scrutiny. Poster (1997), for example, hails the Internet as a space of democratization because acts of discourse are multidirectional and not constrained by the marks of gender and ethnicity that are visible in face-to-face communication.

Some critics have gone further and imagined the Internet as a transcendent democratic medium with a universal language. That is, the Internet is imagined as a space in which we are able to communicate freely with one another across the divisions of class, race, nationality, gender, language and geography. Heaven indeed. Yet any genuine cultural studies' analysis of cyberspace must grasp it as a product of its historical time and place. Of course, this may involve new modes of communication, interaction and identity construction in a novel form of social space. However, questions of gender or race in cyberspace must be explored as simultaneously drawing on and articulating with identity formation in the discourses and interactions of the wider cultural sphere. Digital culture is not separate from 'ordinary' culture.

While some writers imagine cyberspace as a free utopia, others envision it to be an Orwellian nightmare of *1984* proportions. In this view, the potential of digital technology to be a tool for Big Brother style centralized surveillance and control becomes the basis for anxiety. This is because electronic cameras and audio devices can track populations and digital databases can store immense amounts of information about them. Already state tax, social security and crime agencies use sophisticated software to cross-reference information about us from amongst the various government databases. This is done in the name of preventing fraud and apprehending criminals. But how long will it be before the same methods are deployed as a standard tool for identifying and 'managing' political dissidents, critics ask.

Information bomb

The digital universe is overflowing with information. Optimists hail this as a wondrous expansion of human knowledge. This underpins a utopian vision of the Internet as a space where we can educate ourselves and pursue our own interests and pastimes. In this view, cyberspace is a dominion of playful identity construction where anything is possible. On the more pessimistic side of the debate are sceptics who envisage us as lost souls in an unnavigable sea of information. As we become overloaded and disorientated by this ocean of data, we come to rely on others to 'select' and manage it for us.

And with information comes disinformation: perhaps deployed by governments or, more likely still, by big multinational companies who use it to further their interests in a global marketplace of their own creation. Indeed, Virilio warns of an 'information bomb' in which the sheer volume and velocity of electronic data will inevitably give rise to 'a generalized kind of accident, a never-seen-before accident' (Virilio, 2005: 25). Previous shifts in technology gave rise to automobile collisions, plane crashes and nuclear power station meltdowns. So, argues Virilio, the absolute velocity, complexity and interactivity of electronic data will spawn a new kind of accident of which stock market collapse is merely a slight prefiguration.

— What kind of information accident might Virilio be thinking of?
— Write a one-page short story or newspaper report entitled 'Digital Disaster'.

CYBERSPACE AND DEMOCRACY

There is a widespread perception that the Internet is an inherently democratic technology. Two central arguments are put forward in support of the view that the Internet is a vehicle for extending democracy in social and cultural life. The first is that cyberspace will enhance existing conceptions and practices of democracy. According to this vision, the core principles and practices of the public sphere remain unchanged but wider dissemination of information and interactive discussion will lead to a better educated and more active electorate. It is also suggested that electronic voting and Internet plebiscites will enable liberal democracy to work better.

The second contention is that the Internet will transform and enlarge our very notion of what democracy is, as it generates novel spaces in which fresh voices can be heard. In this view the public sphere is expanded and takes on multiple forms that open up new places from which to speak. This enables previously excluded groups to participate in democratic processes and draws new aspects of social life into the political process. Indeed, the possibility is held out that some as yet unimagined form of radical democracy might emerge in cyberspace. Our discussion here revolves around the arguments that the Internet will enable this more radical scenario to emerge.

Although theorists disagree over the form the public sphere takes, it continues to be understood as a space for the democratic exchange of ideas (see Chapter 14). Many critics fear that contemporary culture no longer contains the interactive spaces for democratic dialogue once enabled by cafés, town halls, public squares and universities. At best the popular media, especially television, constitute the public sphere through the dissemination of information and the formation of public opinion (Hartley, 1992; Thompson, 1995). However, the conventional mass media remain fundamentally centralized one-way communication systems; for example, audience dialogue with television is minimal. By contrast, its adherents argue that the Internet will enable radically decentralized and interactive forms of communication that will expand public democracy.

The democratic vision

The first argument in support of the Internet as a vehicle for radical democracy lies in the character of the technology. The Internet is a decentralized network of networks, through which, so it is said, anyone can make a phone call, write a message and /or set up a web page.

✓ *As such the Internet is hailed as a new social space that is not subject to control by any one centre of power, rather the Net is held to be intrinsically open and democratic.*

This, it is argued, will support wider democratic processes because it enables the circulation of information and encourages dialogue. Further, the process of Internet democracy will infiltrate into the wider society because as Net users experience democratic discussion, so they will demand it in other spheres of their life.

A second argument supporting the Internet's capacity to enhance democracy concerns the character of hypertext, which is the common mode of organizing and presenting signs. Hypertext is constituted by a series of textual blocs made up of writing, pictures, diagrams and sound that are connected together by electronic links. Here one text refers you to another, which elaborates or comments on the initial text. Thus on entering a web site we are offered multiple menu options and inter-site links.

When we read a book or watch a television programme, the text inevitably imposes a hierarchical sequence of meanings upon us because we must progress from start to finish. However, hypertext allows us to construct multiple pathways through a series of information nodes and networks. Anyone who uses hypertext puts their interests at the centre of the investigation rather than following someone else's preordained agenda. In this way intertextuality is built into the architecture of hypertext.

Intertextual hypertext

The concept of intertextuality refers to the accumulation and generation of meaning across texts, where all meanings depend on other meanings that have been generated in alternative contexts. A text has no single meaning or original source but is made up of a set of already existing cultural quotations. In other words, textual meaning is unstable and cannot be confined to single words, sentences or particular texts. All meaning is open to negotiation rather than being the consequence of natural forces or authoritative pronouncement (Barthes, 1967). As such, Landow (2005) argues that hypertext does not permit one tyrannical voice to dominate but is intrinsically multivocal, both assuming and requiring an active reader.

Charles Ess (1994) argues that hypertext may lead to a democratization of society. He suggests that Hypertext enables the open, non-hierarchical communication necessary for the 'ideal speech situation'. As described by Habermas (1989), an 'ideal speech situation' is a domain of democratic debate where truth claims are subject to rational arbitration rather than determination by the power of vested interests (see Chapter 14).

KEY THINKERS

Jürgen Habermas (1929–)

Habermas is a Professor of Philosophy at the University of Frankfurt, Germany. He stands in the tradition of the Frankfurt School. However, he does not dismiss enlightenment reason *per se*, but distinguishes between instrumental reason and critical reason. The former subordinates social-existential questions of the 'lifeworld' to the 'system imperatives' of money and administrative power. The latter provides the basis of the unfinished emancipatory project of modernity. A critic of postmodernism, Habermas has sought universal grounds for human emancipation through communicative processes including the 'ideal speech situation' and the 'public sphere'.

Reading: Habermas, J. (1989) *The Structural Transformation of the Public Sphere*. Cambridge, MA: MIT Press.

For Ess, hypertext will enable the development of a public sphere approximating an ideal speech situation because it cannot impose one textual meaning on a reader but invites them into an open, multi-voiced conversation. As such, Ess regards hypertext as an intrinsically democratic mode of communication that will penetrate everyday discourse. In doing so it will set up the conditions for democratic communication within communities.

Web 2:0 participation

There is currently talk amongst Internet users about what is being called web 2:0. It is argued that new developments on the Net are being built around user participation in building up large, shared databases through platforms rather more than the centralized publisher control of applications like Netscape. Often cited examples of this are Bit torrent, eBay and Wikipedia. Bit torrent enables peer-to-peer sharing of files, notably music, which all users can download and listen to, while eBay facilitates buying and selling between individuals. Wikipedia involves the continual creation of encyclopaedic data that is provided by its users and relies on trust.

As new users add content to sites like Wikipedia or the now defunked Napster music-sharing site, so the network resources are strengthened. In most cases this is based not so much on a principle of democratic participation, but on the business model that allows users to build value. Nonetheless, adherents welcome it as a form of cultural participation from 'below' which harnesses collective intelligence. The other participatory development of web 2:0 is the rise of blogging. What makes blogs more significant than simple personal web sites is that new technology called RSS means that blogs are easily networked together and users are notified when other blogs are updated. Thus blogs moved from being just easy places to self-publish to an emerging community of discussion. Because the 'blogosphere' is linked together and self-referential, their collective attention is highly influential on search engines.

'We can be heroes'

It is not just the Internet that is promising a new era of democratic cultural participation but so too are many other kinds of digital technology. For example, miniaturization is making hand-held movie cameras, sound recording devices and mixing equipment cheaper, more readily available and relatively easy to use. Enthusiasts suggest that this will make us all cultural producers or at the very least we will not have to rely on giant multi-national corporations. For example, You Tube enables all of us to make a video and put it up on the Internet if we so wish. The band Arctic Monkeys and the film *Kenny* exemplify even more lasting success with do-it-yourself cultural production.

The Arctic Monkeys are a Sheffield (UK) based band that did not have a record company. Instead they placed mp3 files of their music on the Internet. Fans began to download the files and pass the word around about the band's music. The process began to snowball until the band had generated a sizable worldwide fan base, and a record company. As another example, *Kenny* is a comedic Australian film about portable toilets and family relationships. First-time filmmakers made it using digital equipment with a largely non-professional cast. The movie became a huge hit in Australia and overseas, scooping numerous awards. Of course, these stories of cultural success are heart-warming, but they do not necessarily mean that we can all be in bands or make films. We may not have the necessary skills, talent or resources to do so.

Cyberactivism

A number of writers have hailed the Internet as enabling new forms of political activism that draw in previously marginalized communities, thereby enhancing and extending democracy. Evans (2005), for example, points out that e-mail and list servers have become the everyday tools of feminist activist organizations. This argument also applies to peace activists, ecologists, human rights organizations and web sites that mobilize populations for political action (e.g. moveOn.org and Getup.org). The new phenomenon of personal web sites dedicated to writing known as 'blogging' is also seen as a support for democratic activism. Blogs allow anyone to put their point of view and through them we may learn about events from an angle previously denied us. For example, the world has heard Iraqi versions of the war in their country through blogs. Blogging also helps activists to find each other and link up on a global scale.

While the embrace and use of technologies is important, Evans (2005) argues that the most interesting developments are those that challenge the foundations of virtual spaces. For example, access to information is a significant issue, particularly as more and more web sites demand payment for data. Evans notes that 'free and open software' (FOSS) and the 'Creative Commons' are two ways that have sought to close the digital divide. They have done this by making access and the exchange of ideas easier through reducing costs and resisting regulation. The Creative Commons group, for example, has developed a new range of licences that were launched on the Internet in 2001. They are designed to protect the interests of individual cultural producers while promoting a creative community and furthering public culture. Commons licences are less restrictive than copyright legislation but do depend on voluntary adoption.

Sassen (2002) suggests that the Internet is a powerful medium for 'non-elites' to contribute to a more democratic civil society and globalized cross-border activism. Through the Internet, local issues can become part of a network of global connections while still remaining specific to local concerns. She notes that cyberspace is often a more concrete space for the articulation of social struggles than many orthodox national political systems. This is because it accommodates a broader range of issues and persons than more traditional discourses and institutions.

For example, domestic and family-related institutions such as clinics and schools have traditionally isolated women from the public domain. But now women can be situated in local spaces such as the household, the school or neighbourhood centre and still engage in global political conversations. Further, the globalization of communications technologies like the Internet have opened up the public sphere not only to women but also to non-government organizations such as charities, lobby groups and others in pursuit of social justice. The ecology and peace movements, for example, make extensive use of the Internet as a vehicle both for disseminating information and organizing activists.

Meme wars

One of the purposes of cyberactivism is to persuade other people of the merits of their arguments. It is part of what Marxist cultural studies has called 'ideological conflict' or counter-hegemonic struggle. However, some writers concerned with digital media have understood the process using different concepts. With the explosion of information that is taking place in cyberspace has come the idea that we are in the midst of an 'information war'. One radical activist 'zine' described the notion in this way:

> Traditionally, war has been fought for the territory/economic gain. Information Wars are fought for the acquisition of territory indigenous to the Information Age, i.e. the human mind itself. …. In particular it is the faculty of the imagination that is under the direct threat of extinction from the onslaughts of the multimedia overload……WHOEVER CONTROLS THE METAPHOR GOVERNS THE MIND. ('No' cited in Bey, 2005: 119)

A distinguishing feature of the thinking about an information war is that it does not simply concern the need to get access to information or to make information available. Rather it is about the ability to make one's own message highly memorable amidst the ocean of available data. The concept of the meme (Chapter 4) has been appropriated to grasp this process and thus the struggle for hearts and minds in cyberspace has been dubbed 'meme wars'.

The idea of a meme grew from evolutionary theory and is understood to be the cultural equivalent of a gene (Blackmore, 1999; Dawkins, 1976). However, meme replication occurs independently from genes. A meme is the smallest cultural item that is replicated through the human capacity for imitation. A successful meme is one that is constantly and faithfully replicated because it best 'fits' the evolved capacities of our brains. Think for example of that song which just won't get out of your head. Memes include the alphabet, tunes or musical phrases, fashions, books and ideas (like 'the meme').

It is argued that the development of digital communications on a global scale has enlarged the number of memes available and their capacity for reproduction (Blackmore, 1999). However, there are more memes around than the human brain is able to process and retain, so selection must take place. The degree of match between the properties of a meme and our brains explains why some memes survive and others do not. The evolved psychological mechanisms of our brains, particularly mechanisms of attention and memory, enable some ideas and practices to continue while leaving others to wither.

One implication of meme theory is that cultural change takes place without our conscious choice. Another is that if you want people to pay attention to your message, it is necessary to make it memorable. This after all is what advertising seeks to do. Memes then can be seen as part of the wider promotional culture.

✓ *The lesson for cyberactivists is the need to generate distinctive and unforgettable messages or lose the meme wars to consumer culture and government agencies.*

Indeed, while some writers envisage a new age of political and cultural democracy, others are less optimistic about the possibilities offered by digital media.

The limitations to cyber democracy

Papacharissi (2002) notes that increased access to information and the rise of online political groups and activist web sites appear to support claims that the Internet advances democracy. However, she also suggests that unequal access (the digital divide) and 'flaming' online (enraged, abusive and nonsensical exchanges) provide evidence for the limitations of the Internet as a political space. Papacharissi highlights three particular areas of concern:

1 the ability of democratic forces to distribute information on the Internet;

2 the ability of the Internet to bring people of diverse backgrounds together;

3 the Internet's future in a capitalist era.

While the Internet has provided a new political space for debate, Papacharissi suggests that it is still plagued by the inadequacies of the broader political system. In particular, a few key voices representing the usual political persuasions use their power and resources to dominate discussions. The Internet does provide fast, cheap and easy connectivity between government and civilians, which facilitates instant polling and citizen feedback to politicians. However, this does not necessarily promote open debate or ease political inequalities. A majority of Internet users are not conservatives, yet she cites evidence to suggest that conservatives dominate political discourse in cyberspace. Anti-democratic white supremacists, for example, have appropriated some of the most effective uses of online space to promote their views. Liberal or progressive forces seem to be less effective in disseminating information.

The Internet does appear to offer a space in which people from diverse backgrounds can connect with each other. But a space for interaction does not necessarily lead to more diverse political discussion. It can lead instead to fragmentation and the emergence of parallel, disconnected voices as each interest or identity group talks amongst itself and fails to communicate beyond its borders. Do Palestinians and Israelis, Gay men and evangelical Christians, the peace movement and the military ever talk to each other online? Further, even where online political discussion does occur, this may fuel a feeling that political processes are occurring but deliver few tangible achievements. The Internet can then give rise to the *illusion* of dissent in the face of actual powerlessness. There are many web sites warning about global warming and explaining what governments and individuals can do about it, but it is unclear that major progress has been made by politicians and the captains of industry.

There is a great deal of talk on the Internet but does it always further political debate? It is unclear, for example, whether personal blogs, My Space and web sites about movies necessarily contribute to democracy. Freedom of information is certainly a cornerstone of democracy, but much user-generated material is of dubious cultural or political value, argues Papacharissi. Users can just as easily be characterized as passive, disinterested bystanders turning away from democracy as the engaged citizens of a new digital democracy. Further, the sheer volume of material on the Internet can obscure that which is of worth. It can be hard to see the wood for the trees.

Cyber capitalism

The Internet exists within a capitalist world driven by profit seeking and dominated by a powerful consumer culture. The concern regarding democracy is that the World Wide Web will become a commodified sphere of entertainment and selling rather than of political discussion. In particular, advertising is invading the Internet not only as a source of revenue, but also as a culture. Indeed, the whole digital world is fast becoming the cutting edge of capitalist consumer culture. The digital surface of western culture is now constituted by visual-based consumer images and meanings; a promotional culture plastered with the signs of Coca-Cola, Nike, Google and Microsoft.

The suggestion is that the Internet will further the development of a visual promotional culture that relies on emotive forms of persuasion and not on well-formed argument. The Internet may become yet another domain of the depthless commodity-sign, promoting only itself (see Chapters 6 and 10). This would be to the detriment of a democratic public sphere based on rational debate. Further, the Arts, identity-based groups and more marginalized political forces are unlikely to be supported by advertising.

These concerns grew in 2006 with the willingness of the online search engine Google to put its business interests before freedom of information. Google apparently agreed to limit the data and sites available to users in China in order to appease an anti-democratic government, which held the key to its entry into the market. In addition, Google has bought You Tube and is suggesting that advertising will be a prominent part of its revenue stream. It is hard to believe Time Warner or News Corporation when they say that we are in control of the web. That Google, Microsoft and Yahoo are the most accessed web sites does not suggest a citizen-controlled Internet. By building huge information portals and having an interest in a range of online activities including news, e-mail, chat rooms and video streams, the big players can direct traffic through the web. We might think we are surfing freely through the web but actually we are being channelled into the limited options chosen by powerful commercial interests.

INFORMATION GRAVEYARD

© Photographer: Brian Mcentire | Agency: Dreamstime.com

This image is entitled 'Information Graveyard'.

- *What is it asking us to consider about the disadvantages of the digital revolution?*
- *What does it tell us about the culture that we live in?*

Intellectual property

The concern that the commercialization of the Internet and digital media in general will diminish the public sphere is reinforced by the extension and utilization of copyright laws. Copyright gives cultural producers control over the use and revenue stream of published material. This prevents others from profiting from work they have not contributed to and gives producers an incentive to create new work. This is of particular significance in the digital age where electronic culture can be reproduced with little or no added cost. However, the protection granted to producers must be balanced against the needs of public culture and future creative endeavours. Copyright has traditionally been of limited duration so that after a specified period the material becomes freely available to all. This enables new producers to use it creatively and enriches public culture through libraries, educational institutions and art galleries.

The first eighteenth-century US copyright laws were limited to 14 years but were subsequently increased incrementally until, in 1962, Congress increased them to 70 years. In 1975 they were raised again to the life (of the author) plus 50 years and in 1998 the bar was raised to life plus 70 years. US copyright law is of global significance for two reasons: first because US producers are the major player in the digital media age and second because the US has sought to impose its laws through free trade agreements with other nations (e.g. Australia which has adopted the life plus 70 rule). It is significant that the life plus 70 law came into being just as the Disney Micky Mouse character was about to be freed of copyright restrictions. In other words, critics argue that copyright laws are being used to further the commercial interests of multinational media corporations and reduce the raw material for future cultural production (Moore, 2005).

The extension of copyright law in the digital age helps major commercial cultural producers but it harms small-scale creative talent and public culture. The extra incentive for the individual creator is trivial, argues Richardson (2004), but it limits the pool of resources that new creators draw on and furthers the interests of monopoly profit. In addition, there is a net cost to public culture because libraries and educational institutions end up paying more in copyright fees, or they and we go without significant cultural resources.

Alongside the extension of copyright law, there has been a criminalization of intellectual property infringement and anti-circumvention provisions to regulate, compute, code and protect digital copyright material (Moore, 2005). Much of this is designed to restrict the use of commercial material by peer-to-peer software like Bit torrent and Internet sites like You Tube. That is, copyright law is being used to limit the participatory cultural democracy hailed as web 2:0 in order to protect the commercial interests of corporate power. In particular, copyright ownership is at the core of a globalized trade in cultural commodities and the development of pay-per-use culture.

Democracy in the balance

Overall, we can characterize 'democracy' in cyberspace as a 'see-saw struggle' between citizens and the interests of economic and political elites (Moore, 1999). The possibilities for democracy in cyberspace are enormous but the contemporary hegemony of global capitalism casts a huge shadow of doubt over these hopes. If commercial interests with deep pockets get their way, then the Internet will not become a utopia of democratic Net users. Politically, the Internet could enhance 'the use of electronic networking to bring about a more direct form of democracy … to look for more net supported plebiscites and "official" online debates in deciding issues of government policy' (Moore, 1999: 55). But equally, cyberspace could turn out to be the ideal instrument for power and control by consumer capitalism and entrenched political forces.

— Write down 3 arguments that support a utopian vision of the Internet and other digital technology.
— Write down 3 arguments that support a dystopian or nightmare vision of the new digital world.
— Join with 3 other people to discuss and compare your lists. Which vision is supported by the strongest arguments – utopia or dystopia?

COMPUTER GAMING

Research paths

Computer gaming is a widespread leisure activity these days, and a multi-million dollar business. By contrast, research into electronic game playing is a very recent and relatively modest enterprise. Early work was quantitative in character and dominated by the 'effects' paradigm, which understands audiences as passive receivers of unambiguous messages (see Chapter 10). Like its forerunner television audience research, investigations into computer games were obsessed with violence and whether or not 'real world' aggression had its origins in the virtual universe. According to Smith (2002), there was insufficient evidence to support a direct causal link between violence and gaming playing, though this remains a matter of debate.

In recent times writers have brought a more cultural, meaning-oriented approach to understanding gaming derived from hermeneutic philosophy and literary theory (Aarseth, 1997). In particular, the interactive character of computer games makes them a valuable site to explore the active relationship between author, text and reader. However, even this will be limited, argues Aarseth, if the application of a pre-existing set of literary concepts to games doesn't grasp their game-specific dynamics. Aarseth (2002) argues that an investigation of the hermeneutic circle of 'games in virtual environments' would need to explore:

- *Game-play*: psycho-social explorations of players' motives and actions;

- *Game-structure*: investigations into the design and the rules of the game; and

- *Game-world*: literary/cultural examination of characters and narratives.

In particular, he advocates the need to expand investigation beyond text analysis of games into an exploration of game players and the performative skills required. Text analysis isolated from an understanding of active meaning-producing players and the specifics of game performances can lead to mistaken conclusions about the cultural impact of games. For example, the unsubstantiated idea that the actions of the young men responsible for the Columbine High School massacre in the USA could in some way be attributed to playing violent video games (Finn, 2000).

Addicted to games

The cultural theorist Asa Berger (2002) explores video games as a popular cultural phenomenon through a combination of textual and 'bio-psychosocial' analysis. He draws the conclusion that electronic gaming is associated with social isolation, violence and addiction.

> If video games are becoming interactive movies, it means that people who play them, the gamers, will become the heroes or heroines, or villains and villainesses of the new game/movies. We may find this playing so intriguing and addictive that we neglect other aspects of our lives, including loved ones. (ibid.: 109)

Berger acknowledges that gamers are part of a larger gaming community but he envisions it only as a virtual network lacking the authenticity of a 'real community'. This connection between gaming and lonely, anti-social men (for the most part) chimes with a popular media view. However, this claim is not substantiated with empirical research into game players and relies on theoretical argument and text analysis. It echoes the limitations of textual analysis in television studies that did not undertake active audience research and, as such, warrants caution regarding its conclusions.

Gaming and identity

In contrast to Berger's pessimism lie the utopian dreams of writers who see cyberspace as a dominion in which to play with identity free of social constraints.

✓ *It is argued that by enabling players to mask their worldly identities, virtual space allows a range of identity performances that are not tied to material bodies.*

In this way we can transcend our class, gender or race. Since no one can see you in cyberspace, no one can judge you based on your cultural characteristics.

The problem, of course, is that actors in cyberspace remain tied to the everyday material world whose impact on the virtual universe persists. Balsamo (2000), for example, suggests that far from being a free counter-cultural space, virtual reality is reproducing the power relations of broader cultural forces. The idea of the 'body' in cyberculture is still marked by gender and race, she argues, because of the tendency to reproduce familiar and comfortable ideas. Innovative technologies are not necessarily used to forge new ideas but are more likely to reinforce the traditional hegemonic narratives about the gendered, race-marked body.

Between the idea of freedom from the material world and simple reproduction of it lies the most interesting cultural writing on electronic identity. This explores the manner in which social forces of class, gender and race continue to be inscribed in cyberspace generally, and gaming in particular, but in transformed ways.

Cyberspace race

Nakamura (2000) explores the way race is 'written' and 'read' by players within LambdaMOO, an online textual, character-driven community. She does this through a form of ethnographic study. Nakamura is particularly concerned with whether cultural rules about race have been transformed in this new social space. While players are utopian about the absence of race within the game, Nakamura sees not a lack of racism but new shifting forms of online stereotyping.

The first act in any gaming community of this type is to create a character through textual description. In the LambdaMOO gender is required (although it comes with three options: male, female and indeterminable) but race is not even an optional descriptor. This might suggest that race has been dispensed with in the community. However, Nakamura argues that race becomes implied in two ways; first, as hair and eye colour which usually indicate race; second, because when racial signifiers are not given, the character is usually seen as white. Nakamura suggests that gaming involves an illusion of freedom and choice, but that assumptions drawn from 'real life' (RL) about race continue.

Where game players do denote the race of their character, it is often an occasion for stereotyping. For example, when 'Asian' is used in combination with 'male', Nakamura finds what she describes as character 'tourism', in which white people 'pass' online as Manga-style violent masculine characters. This then becomes the virtual face of 'Asianness' and the 'real life' complexities of race are absent and suppressed. For Nakamura, gender-cross dressing and race tourism are doubly repressive for Asian female characters who become sexualized and submissive playthings. The complex actualities of gender and race in Asian women are absent, she argues.

Playing multiple identities

Turkle (1995) discusses the ways in which the conditions of postmodern multiple identities are enabled and enacted in Multi User Dimensions (MUDs). The idea of multiple identities refers to the way people take on different and potentially contradictory identifications at varied times and places. Since all of us have multiple identifications of class, gender, sexuality, age, ethnicity and nationality, we are best understood as being composed not of one but of several identities that are not unified around a coherent 'self' (see Chapter 7).

Turkle argues that MUDs give people the opportunity to play with identities and to try out new ones; in MUDs she suggests, one can be many. This displaces the notion of an authentic identity and decentres the self without limit. For Turkle, the multiplicity and heterogeneity of online identities are rooted in the new social experiences of postmodern culture. She points out that play has always been an important way of discovering who one is and wishes to be. As such, a MUD can be a laboratory for the construction of identities. Of course, experiments do not always have welcome outcomes and while Turkle describes players who have delighted in invention, she points to others whose game-life has merely highlighted the limitations and inadequacies of their 'real life'.

One of the more discussed aspects of playing with identity through games is the evidence that significant numbers of RL males pose as women in virtual environments. Some players say that this is not particularly significant and is simply done for fun. However, Turkle suggests that virtual 'cross-dressing' is often a more psychologically complex phenomena. For example, she discusses an RL man whose female game character allows him to experiment with an assertiveness he feels unable to enact in daily life. The man told Turkle that in his everyday world the assumptions surrounding masculinity make standing up for himself an act of aggression and 'being a bastard', whereas as a virtual female, assertiveness is read as appropriately modern. Turkle also draws attention to an RL woman whose virtual male character allows her to take on a self-confident voice that is denied her elsewhere.

In *My Tiny Life*, Julian Dibbell (1998) discussed his first experience of cyber cross-dressing when he entered the LambdaMOO as Samantha, the central female character from the 1960s TV show *Bewitched*. Dibbell's online and offline friend Sebastiano takes 'Samantha' on a tour of the woodlands community (which is within one of the wall hangings of the mansion which is the main space for LambdaMOO). The woodlands have become the site for a 'sort of subcommunity for Lambda's queer contingent'. It would seem that in a reproduction of 'real life', non-hegemonic groups retreat to specific 'suburbs' within Lambda's many rooms and spaces.

Dibbell then discusses the feelings and sensations he feels in Samantha's skin. He notes that he often feels excited with new morphs of character in virtual space, but with the Samantha character Dibbell felt the transformation had greater depth. It was as if their bodies melded, he says. He felt poised, charming and feminine and the gender identification felt very tangible. We might ask then how such feelings are possible when Dibbell was simply typing and reading at his computer? Where do all of these emotions of 'Samantha-ness' and femininity come from when all that has occurred is a shift in the character in a textual online virtual space?

Turkle argues that boundary crossing between the real and the virtual, including the playing-out of multiple identities, calls forth a moral discourse. For example, does cyber sex with a character who is not one's 'real life' partner constitute infidelity? She suggests that a culture of simulation may help us to achieve a vision of multiple but integrated identity that provides us with the joy of accessing our many selves. On the other hand, she warns of the danger of being lost in cyberspace and mistaking the dream for the real world.

—   Is it possible to write a character that is without gender or race?
—   Try writing a short story or a description of a virtual game that has characters without such characteristics. Then consider whether you have been successful.
—   Try asking another person to read your story to see if they make any assumptions about gender and race.

Cyberfeminism

The ambiguity of gender identity in virtual reality has led some thinkers to wonder if cyberspace offers new opportunities for feminism. Plant (2000), for example, suggests that cyberspace offers the possibility of ending the world view that has supported two thousand years of patriarchy. Patriarchy refers to a social order in which there is recurrent and systematic domination by men over subordinated women across a wide range of social institutions and practices.

Plant points to the fluidity of interlinked networks that evade centralized structures, and to online identities that are shiftable and blurred as aiding a new feminist cyber-awareness. The invisibility of the body that cyberspace allows enables a fluidity of identity which is useful, she argues, when identity – as a woman – is a liability. Further, she suggests that the network thinking style of cyberspace has made the masculine single-mindedness of patriarchy obsolete. Instead, she suggests that a shifting contextual existence, which has always been necessary for women, becomes the norm in cyberculture. Plant is aware that Net culture is dominated by men but believes that it still offers possibilities for feminists.

Cyborg manifesto

Plant's case represents a continuation of the hopeful line of argument pioneered by Donna Haraway (1985) in her famous essay 'A Manifesto for Cyborgs'. A cyborg is a hybrid composed of machine and organism and is a feature of both fiction (for example 'The Borg' in *Star Trek*) and social reality (humans who use heart pacemakers). There is also a sense in which by entering into a virtual world generated by a machine, one becomes a cyborg. Haraway describes her essay as an ironic political myth that is faithful to feminism and socialism. The essay celebrates the confusion of boundaries that cyborgs represent and, in particular, the partiality, irony and oppositional perversity she sees in them.

KEY THINKERS

Donna Haraway (1944–)

American feminist Donna Haraway trained as a scientist and her cultural writings reflect her continued concern with the epistemological and social issues raised by science. She rejects the claims of science, and some branches of feminism, to hold the God-like neutral knowledge of a disembodied gaze. She advocates 'partial perspectives' that recognize their inherent limitations and remind us that no single perspective is complete. She rejects the distinction between sex and gender on the grounds that biology is a partial perspective that privileges sexuality. She describes herself in terms of multiple identities that include the cyborg; a position that, she argues, has advantages for women.

Reading: Haraway, D. (1991) *Simians, Cyborgs, and Women: the Reinvention of Nature.* Cambridge: Polity Press.

Cyborgs blur the boundaries between organisms and machines, as well as between humans and other animals, to the extent that the division between culture and nature collapses. When all is artifice, argues Haraway, the position of universal transcendent knowledge claimed by 'man' can no longer be sustained. The category 'nature' does not refer to an independent object world but rather is a strategy for maintaining political boundaries. As such, the very concepts of man, woman, black and white are shown to be constructions. There is nothing natural that binds the cultural qualities of 'female' to women or holds women together as a homogeneous group.

Haraway's argument is in accord with the anti-essentialist, poststructuralist feminist theory discussed in Chapter 9. That is, no essential womanhood exists and the politics of feminism must rely on self-conscious coalitions and not on natural identification. Cyborg feminist writing then celebrates the hybrid, the marginalized and the partial in ways that undermine the central dogma of phallocentrism (or privileged male knowledge that reduces and dominates all others as different and inferior).

CYBORG BEAUTY

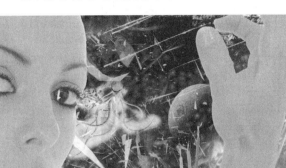

© **Photographer: Jaimie Duplass| Agency: Dreamstime.com**

- *Describe the key elements of this image. What kind of genre style does it construct?*

- *Analyse the image as a representation of women.*

- *Do you think this is what Haraway had in mind?*

Representation and regulation

It is often argued that the majority of Internet users are men and, as Stone (1991) points out, there is a politics of representation in the cyberspace that is largely in the hands of young male computer engineers and programmers. She argues that men are constructing a Cartesian world view in cyberspace: that is, one in which they hold a privileged position of God-like knowledge and where conventional hierarchical binaries of gender and race are reproduced once more. After all, stereotypes of large-breasted, sexy young women do abound in cyberspace games, and the Internet is awash with pornography. This raises the question of whether the Internet should be subject to greater public regulation.

An infamous case of 'rape' within LambdaMOO raises issues about gender and regulation. According to Dibbell (1998), the incident centred on a character called Mr Bungle who resided in the MOO as a weird, grubby clown living in the dungeons of the mansion. The original creators of the character were a group of male university students. A series of violent and forced rapes occurred online that were attributed to Mr Bungle hacking into other characters and making them carry out sexual acts without their knowledge or consent.

Dibbell describes the way that some players wanted real-life consequences to flow from these virtual acts. This poses interesting questions about reality and cyberculture. This was a textual environment and yet the outrage felt by those affected was real. The lack of immediate physicality in one social space does not necessarily negate ideas, feelings and the power relationship that exist between people. There is a form of power structure within LambdaMOO in that the 'wizards' have an overseer role. When the rape was committed, they were called upon to pass judgement. A form of regulation took place through the enactment of new 'laws' and indeed a system of organized politics emerged within the game community.

Laura Miller (1995), who says that she was not upset by the Mr Bungle incident, suggests that complaints about the treatment of women on the Internet fall into three types:

1 that women are subject to unwanted sexual attention;

2 that an abrasive style of online discussion repels women; and

3 that women are singled out for hostile treatment.

She argues that the case for regulating the Internet takes place in a context where cyberspace is described as a frontier realm of limitless possibilities and few social controls. This spatial metaphor resonates with the American Western narrative, suggesting a world of freedom from the demands of society. However, the Western myth also calls for the 'civilization' of the lawless society of men to protect women and children.

Miller argues that women have the right to be protected against crime but should be wary of suggestions that they require 'special protections'. She argues that such a claim is based on the idea that women are naturally weak and unable to participate in public discourse. Instead, like Plant and Haraway, she hails cyberspace as a realm that demonstrates the culturally constructed character of gender. She adds that if and when the virtual world portrays women in unacceptable ways or treats them dismissively, then they should be met with the protests of robust women.

— Is there a case for government regulation of the Internet? Or should the Internet be free of legal controls?
— If you think it should be regulated, what in particular would you want to regulate and how could this be achieved?

THE GLOBAL ECONOMY OF CYBERSPACE

Governments are not the only social force that seeks to shape cyberspace. Indeed, they are perhaps less significant than the global capitalist corporations who are forging the new global information economy.

✓ *Growth in the world economy now depends on digital technology and fuels its expansion.*

Manuel Castells (1993) has been one of the foremost theorists of 'the information economy'. He describes five interrelated features that characterize the new global economy, as detailed below.

The information economy

Castells first points to the increasingly important role of *information and applied knowledge* in the modern economy. The greater the complexity and productivity of an economy, the more significant is its informational component and the value of new knowledge. This includes science and managerial know-how. For example, the high salaries of chief executive officers and the emphasis placed on managerial education reflect the fact that economic growth is increasingly understood to be the outcome of more efficient combination of the factors of production.

The second shift in the economies of advanced capitalist societies has been *the move from material production to information-processing activities* both as a proportion of Gross National Product and as a percentage of the working population engaged in it. The digital manipulation of symbols plays an increasing part in economic activity and the quality of information is a major strategic factor in productivity.

A third feature of the new information economy is a profound change in the organization of production. This is *the move from standardized mass production to flexible customized production* (see Chapter 5). Here information technology is the foundation for flexibility and adaptability in response to changing and diversified markets.

The fourth dynamic of the new economy is the fact that it is *global in scale*. Although nation-states are still important realities, economic thinking and practices are played out globally. That is, we are witnessing the interpenetration of national economies and economic activities so that national characteristics become features of a global system.

Finally, it is vital to note that the transformation of the world economy is taking place through *a technological revolution*. The core of this transformation is in information technology constituted by microelectronics, informatics and telecommunications. The microchip revolution has been stimulated by economic change and has simultaneously formed its material base. It is digital technology in particular that enables economies to process the vast amount of information they require and to create flexible production processes.

Private space

We talk about cyberspace and the global economy as if they were naturally given phenomenon. But our understanding of space has always been tied to our cultural assumptions. In particular, ideas about property and the state have been founded on the ownership of space to the degree that they actually define what space is. For example, the eighteenth- and nineteenth-century enclosure movement in England turned common land into private property, paving the way for capitalist agriculture. And the formation of nation-states depended on their sovereign control of territory. Today legal and technical definitions of space are reinforcing the private capitalist control of cyberspace as a dimension of the global information economy (Graham, 2002).

First, the ownership and exclusive occupation of 'geotechnical spaces' such as radio spectrums and telecommunications infrastructure are enabling the private control of social spaces. It is global capitalist corporations who own and manage much of the vital technology of cyberspace, both hard and software. Think of IBM, General Electric, Microsoft and Apple, for example.

Second, far-reaching legal rulings are enabling the private ownership of 'intellectual property' so that information has become the raw material of cyber economies. This includes web sites where we pay for data from academic papers to mp3 music files, but also includes fundamental dimensions of human life such as language and DNA. Some biotech companies actually claim ownership rights over the human genome.

Third, the commodification of cyberspace as the leading edge of the global information economy reinforces the reduction of human values to matters of price. There is very little that is not bought and sold on the Internet, including human life. As cyberspace becomes a marketplace, so it is simultaneously flooded with advertising material in its many guises. The convergence of technology, information, entertainment and consumer culture is epitomized by the new generation of mobile phones.

Convergence and the mobile phone

One of the contemporary buzzwords around digital media is convergence. This refers to the breakdown of boundaries between both technologies and corporations. With the latter, synergy is sought through mergers and takeovers, giving rise to multimedia corporations. Technological convergence refers to the way that former functions that had previously been produced and used separately merge into one. It is largely digital technology that enables this to occur. The long-term vision is of an 'information super-highway', that is, screens that bring together television with computers linked to cable or wireless systems that will enable us to:

- **watch television;**

- **order and pay for shopping;**

- **transfer e-money;**

- **keep an eye on our bank accounts;**

- **call up a selection of films;**

- **search the World-Wide Web for information.**

Much of this is already available to those who know how to do it and can pay for it, or more commonly, can access the files illegally. However, these functions are not yet integrated into an easy-to-use commercial desktop system. The more immediate prospect is for convergence of functions in and around the mobile phone.

The mobile phone

The digital cellphone is ubiquitous in contemporary culture and is fast becoming the communications focal point of our lives. The new generation of mobile phones are being transformed into multimedia platforms. They are becoming data casters at the centre of consumer entertainment industries. Phone calls, video download, photography, gaming, music and Internet connection are all being built into mobiles.

Phones with 5 gigabytes of memory mean that you can store phenomenal amounts of information. Faster networks will allow us to communicate this data more freely. Handheld digital devices like music players, digital cameras, or PSP Nintendo devices are now moving into the mobile phone, as it becomes a converged device. Indeed, it has been suggested that the new mobile will spell the death of the iPod. During June 2006 more music capable phones were sold than iPods. That mp3 players are themselves relatively new devices that most people have not yet acquired only goes to illustrate the speed of commercial and technological change.

Marketing executives are targeting the 13–27 age group, the so-called Generation C, for whom the mobile phone is the primary device for connecting with friends and continuing their social networks. Pundits suggest that the mobile phone will become the fulcrum around which 'digital public spaces' revolve. A digital public space is a domain where you allow information about yourself to be made publicly available. This might include Internet sites such as My Space or simply a digital photograph of ourselves that we circulate to others.

The power of the phone will not only enable simply downloading video or music but will also offer an interactive experience. For example, GPS location devices in mobile phones will allow people to know where they are and give information about that place. This is heralding the development of location-based games using mobile phones as both a navigation and story-telling device. The phone would pinpoint a location and receive gaming instructions related to this environment. A game story would be told that might, for example, place aliens at the railway station. This style of gaming would blur the boundaries between 'reality' and the 'game'.

Location devices are not just about games, however. They can be used to pinpoint users for the purposes of surveillance and/or marketing. This raises the fear that mobile phones could be used for the purposes of political surveillance. More likely still, they will be used to track mobile users, leisure habits and spending patterns as a precursor to targeted advertising. After all, the mobile phone is big consumer business. At present advertising via mobile phones is limited, not least because users don't want to pay for receiving them. But in due course it is likely that we will see advertising on mobile phones in the context of subscription services or simply appearing as a text message. There is already a UK service in which users receive free phones in return for agreeing to accept advertising.

The world's quickest growing mobile phone market is in India, which has been adding some 5 million new subscribers per month. There are already over 100 million mobile users, and this number is expected to grow to 300 million by 2010. Mobile entertainment in 2005 was about a $16 billion business, of which half was accounted for by music. Over the next four years that figure will rise to at least $45 billion and then upwards towards $124 billion (www.abc.net.au/rn/mediareport). Given the control of mobile technology and entertainment content by giant US-based corporations, the explosion of the Indian digital market raises again the question of cultural imperialism.

Digital imperialism

Cultural imperialism involves the domination of one culture by another and is widely associated with the leading role played in the global economy by multinational corporations of American origin. In Chapter 10 we saw that Schiller (1985) and other critics regard the globalization of television as a form of western cultural imperialism. He makes a similar argument in relationship to the global information highway. He points out that the US is taking control of the digital communications sector through the formation of multimedia integrated global corporations. These companies stand to run both technological and content sides of new media.

Time Warner, AT&T, Microsoft and their competitors are not concerned about social inequality but rather focus on revenue, argues Schiller. However, profits come from those with the income to purchase the services they sell. The globalized information economy and the digital media that accompany it are widening the gap between the rich and poor as US corporate control of information gives them a preeminent place in a global economy that eludes national control. The increasingly large and visible economic gap between the rich and poor both between nations and within the borders of states will fuel discontent, argues Schiller. This has the potential to destabilize governments and generate waves of refugees at the borders of the advanced industrial nations.

Culturally, Schiller points out that English has become the world's second most spoken language and more significantly still the language of the Internet. With the spread of English comes the ready adoption of Anglo-American ideas, he argues, and so the free flow of ideas in practice means the ascendance of US cultural products. This process weakens local cultures and furthers western economic interests. It also makes the economically developed countries even more attractive destinations for economic and political migrants.

The broad thrust of Schiller's case clearly has some validity. It is hard to deny the place of English on the Internet or the preeminent place of global capitalism. Nonetheless, it is subject to the same kinds of criticisms made of his media imperialism thesis in Chapter 10 and requires greater complexity of cultural argument. Schiller tends to ignore the unevenness of western influence and too easily reads-off cultural implications from economic trends. For example, the worldwide spread of English is as likely to give rise to hybrid cultures as to straightforward cultural imperialism. Evidence about call-centre operators in India working with western clients suggests that they remain keen to maintain and strengthen their more traditional cultural practices as well as to learn English.

DECONSTRUCT THIS: REAL LIFE VS. VIRTUAL REALITY

- *What is our definition of the real?*
- *What is our understanding of the virtual?*
- *Can we easily locate the borders between them?*

SUMMARY

In this chapter we have explored aspects of the newly emerging universe of digital media. We began by noting that despite a widespread perception that we live in an electronic world, the vast majority of the human species do not have access to the appropriate technology. Even within the advanced industrial countries, there is a digital divide between men and women, rich and poor.

Many fans of the Internet hope that it will herald a new era of democracy. This is because Internet technology and hypertext are both fundamentally non-hierarchical in character. It is

(Cont'd)

also argued that the Net will enable new cultural voices to be heard and advance the case of progressive political action. Less optimistic critics fear that cyber politics merely reproduces the hegemonic power of the 'real world' and gives the illusion of change where none is really happening.

Virtual gaming is one of the newly emerging sites for academic research, though it is not yet clear what research methods and language will yield the best results. To date the questions of representation and identity have concerned many writers, especially feminists. Unsurprisingly, no clear consensus has emerged about whether digital media are places to play and experiment with multiple identities or whether they again reproduce conventional cultural identities and their attendant power plays. On the whole, feminists seem to welcome cyberspace as a place where gender can be redefined, but there remain dissenters from this view.

Cyberspace has its material foundations in computer technology, which is central to the global information economy. Both digital hardware and the software that is deployed within it are produced and sold by multinational corporations whose concerns are not democracy, multiple identities or feminism but profit. Many writers fear that the democratic political and cultural potential of digital media, which might allow us all to be cultural producers, will be lost to an entertainment-driven consumer culture in the context of global capitalism.

12 Cultural Space and Urban Place

KEY CONCEPTS

Cyberspace	*Post-industrial society*
Global city	*Postmodernism*
Information society	*Space*
Place	*Symbolic economy*
Political economy	*Urbanization*

Since the 1970s there has been a growing interest within social and cultural theory in questions of space and place. Previously, modern theory was more interested in time, seeing this as the dynamic field of social change. By contrast space was regarded as dead, fixed and immobile, traversed by the movement of history. As Foucault remarked, 'a whole history remains to be written of spaces – which would at the same time be the history of powers – both these terms in the plural – from the great strategies of geopolitics to the little tactics of the habitat' (Foucault, cited in Soja, 1995b: 14).

In this chapter we will consider the meanings of space and place, including the manner in which they are constituted by social relations of power. Subsequently we will explore some of the cultural questions related to cities as a specific formation of sociocultural places. Attention will be paid to:

- the political economy of global cities;

- the symbolic or cultural economies of urban regeneration;

- the emergence of postmodern cities as contested spaces;

- the idea that cities can be read as texts;

- the virtual world of cybercities.

SPACE AND PLACE IN CONTEMPORARY THEORY

As Giddens (1984) argues, understanding the manner in which human activity is distributed in space is fundamental to analysis of social and cultural life. Human interaction is situated in particular spaces that have a variety of social meanings. For example, a 'home' is divided into different living spaces – front rooms, kitchens, dining rooms, bedrooms, etc. These spaces are used in diverse ways and within them are carried out a range of activities with different social meanings. Accordingly, bedrooms are intimate spaces into which we would rarely invite strangers, whereas a sitting room or lounge is deemed the appropriate space for such an encounter.

Giddens (1984) deploys Goffman's (1969) concepts of 'front' and 'back' regions to illustrate a fundamental divergence in social-spatial activity. Front space is constituted by those places in which we put on a public 'on-stage' performance. Here we act out stylized, formal and socially acceptable activities. Back regions are those spaces where we are 'behind the scenes'. In this context we prepare for public performance or relax into less formal modes of behaviour and speech. The social division of space into front and back regions or into the appropriate uses of kitchens, bedrooms and lounges is of course *cultural*. Distinct cultures design homes in different ways, allocating contrasting meanings or modes of appropriate behaviour.

— Draw an outline map of (1) a house and (2) a place of work.
— Name each room and write in:

  • the activities that commonly occur in that room,
  • the connotations of the room,
  • the back space–front space usages of the room,
  • the gendered character of the room.

Time-geography

The socio-cultural world is spatially organized into a range of places in which different kinds of social activity occur:

• places of work;

• places of leisure;

• places of sleep;

- places to eat;

- places to shop, and so forth.

Given the complexity of contemporary life, it is a requirement on us all to move across and through these spaces and places. Time-geography (Hagerstrand, 1973) has been concerned to map the movements and pathways of persons through physical environments. It traces the variety of social activities that occur and the constraints which material and social factors place on the patterns of our movement.

A simple time-geography might include my catching a train from one town to another. This might be followed by a short walk to my place of work, where I enter through the front doors and move along a corridor to my office. Here I stay for an hour working behind my desk. Later I move to a lecture hall, and from there to the canteen and subsequently the library. On my return home I call in at the supermarket to do some shopping before going to the cinema. During the course of these movements I encounter a series of physical limitations – distance, walls, traffic jams – and social expectations – those surrounding the performance of a lecture, for example. As I do so, I cross paths with a variety of other people – students, librarians, checkout operatives, etc. – each of whom has his or her own daily time-space paths. As Gillian Rose puts it:

> Time-geography traces the routinized paths of individuals in timespace, and is especially interested in the physical, technological, economic and social constraints on such movement. It claims to demonstrate how society as a whole is constituted by the unintended consequences of the repetitive acts of individuals. (Rose, 1993: 75)

The account of space and social relations presented thus far has a good deal to recommend it. In particular, it points to the spatial distribution of social activities and to the situated character of all social action. However, there is a telling grammar in play that situates the social *in* space or *across* space at given moments of time. This implies that space is a flat surface across which history moves. That is, time and space are held to be radically opposed to each other. Physics and social theory have both questioned this assumption.

— Write a time–space geography of your life yesterday.

Time-space

✓ *Following Einstein's theory of relativity, space and time are not to be thought of as separate entities but as inextricably interwoven.*

Space is not an absolute but is relationally defined. Thus, at least two particles are required for space to occur. Further, time is constituted by the movement of these particles, which simultaneously establishes both time and space. It is not that time moves across a static space, but that space and time constitute each other, requiring us to speak of time-space. In principle, then, time-space is relationally formed through the interrelations of objects. It follows that social space is also relationally constituted out of the simultaneous co-existence of social relations and interactions. From this point, Massey (1994) proposes five arguments about space:

1   **Space is a social construct.**

2   **The social is spatially constructed.**

3   **Social space is not static but dynamic. It is constituted by changing social relations.**

4   **Space is implicated in questions of power and symbolism, that is, the 'power-geometry' of space.**

5   **Social space implies 'a simultaneous multiplicity of spaces: cross-cutting, intersecting, aligning with one another, or existing in relations of paradox or antagonism' (Massey, 1994: 3).**

Space and place

Thus far, I have used the language of space and place as if they were interchangeable terms, whereas it is usually thought necessary to distinguish between them. Giddens (1990) characterizes space and place in terms of absence–presence, where place is marked by face-to-face encounters and space by the relations between absent others. Space refers to an abstract idea, an empty or dead space that is filled with various concrete, specific and human places. Thus, home is a place where I meet my family with regularity, whereas e-mail or letters establish contact between absent persons across space. In a not dissimilar move, Seamon (1979) regards the place called home as the product of physical presence and social rituals. However, the absence–presence distinction, while suggestive, seems a bit stark. As Harvey (1993) remarks, place has a rather richer range of metaphorical meanings than are encompassed by presence.

We may distinguish between space and place on the grounds that the latter are the focus of human experience, memory, desire and identity. That is, places are discursive constructions which are the target of emotional identification or investment (Relph, 1976).

> Home … is a manifestation of an investment of meaning in space. It is a claim we make about a place. It is constructed through social relations which are both internal and external and constantly shifting in their power relations. (Silverstone, 1994: 28)

The social construction of place

Whatever conceptual distinction between space and place we may settle for, the most significant question to ask (Harvey, 1993) is: by what social processes is place constructed? Two examples will suffice: Massey's (1994) arguments about gendered space, and Nzegwu's (1996) discussion of the city of Lagos.

Gendered space

Gender is an organizing principle of social life thoroughly saturated with power relations. Thus, it follows that the social construction of space will be gendered. As Massey (1994) suggests, gender relations vary over space: spaces are symbolically gendered and some spaces are marked by the physical exclusion of particular sexes.

The classical western gendering of space is manifested in the division between 'home' and 'workplace'. This distinction is articulated with the 'private' and the 'public'. Thus, the home is regarded as the domain of the 'private' and the feminine. Sites of paid work have been coded masculine within the public sphere. Homes have been cast as the unpaid domain of mothers and children, connoting the secondary values of caring, love, tenderness and domesticity. In contrast, places of paid work have been regarded as the domain of men, connoting the primary values of toughness (either physically or mentally), hardness, comradeship and reality. While this crude spatial map has been changing as gender relations are being transformed, much of this cultural coding remains.

Massey argues that: 'The limitation of women's mobility, in terms of both space and identity, has been in some cultural contexts a crucial means of subordination' (Massey, 1994: 179). She notes that as a child she was struck by the way large tracts of the Mersey flood plain had been given over to playing fields for boys. This was a place to which she did not go. Further, within the art gallery, to which she did go, her place was quite different from that of men. For them, Massey argues, this place of high culture was a domain in which to gaze at pictures of naked women. Today, cricket, rugby and football remain as primarily (though not solely) male practices in male spaces. More threateningly, certain streets, parks and pubs are not safe for women to enter alone, especially at night. Thus, attempts by some women to 'reclaim the night' are essentially spatial practices.

Masculine modernism   The rise of modernism in aesthetic form is deeply associated with the spatial and social organization of the city. For example, modernism's figure of the *flâneur* or stroller is one who walks the anonymous spaces of the modern city (see also Chapter 6). Here he experiences the complexity, disturbances and confusions of the streets with their shops, displays, images and variety of persons. Massey argues that these city spaces and the modernist experience were deeply gendered. The experience of the *flâneur* and of modernism was one of male-coded public spaces from which women were excluded (e.g. the boulevards and cafés) or entered only as objects for male consumption. Thus:

- The *flâneur* was a male figure who walked spaces from which women were largely excluded.

- The *flâneur's* gaze was frequently erotic, and women were the object of that gaze.

- The paintings of modernism are often of women and spatially organized in such a way as to privilege a male-coded sense of a 'detached' (but not disinterested) view.

The multiple spaces of Lagos

Nzegwu's (1996) study of Lagos, Nigeria, is a multi-levelled analysis which directs our attention to the way that spaces and places, cities and homes, are constructed. Here class, gender, race, ethnicity, colonialism, modernization, multinational capitalism, urban planning, military power and government intervention have all played their part. Nzegwu sets out to show that cultural desires and symbolic representations are central to the evolution of urban space as sites of contestation and interaction. Thus, an analysis of space reveals the presence of value systems and their transformatory impact.

According to Nzegwu, Lagos is more than a place of residence or domicile; it is *ile* (home). Thus, a recovery of Yoruba ideas of land and *ile* is key to understanding the character of the contemporary city. Central to the notion of *ile* as homespace is the family. Yoruba architectural style spatially organizes families into interlocking, horizontally organized households and compounds which stress an expansive conception of kinship. Land, which is regarded as sacred, is viewed as belonging to an entire lineage and not as a commodity for sale to the highest bidder. Nzegwu argues that the cultural beliefs underpinning Yoruba conceptions of land encouraged a 'freestyle' approach to urban space. This approach, enacted as a warren of interconnected subhouses, courtyards and decorated walls, is different from the regimented gridiron order of western urban space. Further, given the emphasis on lineage within Yoruba spatial organization, the typical modernist zonal distribution of city spaces into distinct parts for the rich and poor was largely absent from their communities.

Postcolonial city   The annexation of Lagos as a British colony led to the introduction of a land-law system underpinned by a commodity logic. 'Modern' western restructuring guided colonial and post-colonial responses to the influx of diverse ethnic groups and the subsequent demand for new housing. The colonial solution to housing needs was revealing of endemic racism in that it:

- **kept European dwellings apart from Africans;**

- **built houses which in design and location disrupted Yoruba family organization.**

The small size of the houses built for 'natives' and the high densities of these homes restricted the extended family, preventing the traditional expansion of courtyards and buildings. Yoruba organization of space involved multiple, horizontally distributed sites of power for both men and women. By contrast, western vertical buildings coded an order of power and gender relations which hierarchically formalized domestic space. This privileged men, as reflected, in for example, the master bedroom and the drawing room, with the kitchen, in which women's domestic work took place, hidden from view. This was most unlike Yoruba life.

By 1960, when independence was established for Nigeria, Lagos had been reorganized along modern grid-lines. This divided the city into racially segmented areas including low-density European zones, high-density poor-quality African sectors, a Brazilian quarter and a commercial district. Later, as colonial influence declined, the European sectors were taken over by upper-class Nigerian families who maintained the trappings of colonial power.

Also figurative of class ascendancy was the arrival of towering skyscrapers of modernist design in the central and commercial districts. These buildings symbolically and materially epitomized the presence of powerful multinational capitalist corporations and their ethos of investment, trade and commerce. This process had been encouraged by the military government as a sign of 'development'. Of course, such development has its losers as well as its winners. Thus, the significant spaces between the high-rise buildings were contested and taken over by the poor, market traders and financial hustlers. Indeed, with the economic downturn in the 1980s and 1990s, class polarization widened, crime increased and walls grew up around the premises of the wealthy.

CITIES AS PLACES

✓ *Space is a construction and material manifestation of social relations which reveals cultural assumptions and practices.*

Our continuing example will be that of cities as places. Western academic explorations of urban life are virtually coterminous with the emergence of modern social science, especially the discipline of sociology. All three of the so-called 'founders' of sociology – Durkheim, Marx and Weber – regarded urbanization as one of the key features of capitalist industrialization, viewing it with a certain ambivalence.

Durkheim hoped that urban life would be a space for creativity, progress and a new moral order. However, he feared that it was to be the site of moral decay and anomie. For Weber, urban life was the cradle of modern industrial democracy whilst also engendering instrumental reason and the 'iron cage' of bureaucratic organization. Marx viewed the city as a sign of progress and the great leap of productivity which capitalism brought about. Nevertheless, he also observed that urban life was a site of poverty, indifference and squalor. A more positive modernist view of urban life was held by Simmel. For him the city was the birthplace of the aesthetic of modernism and the escape from the controls of tradition. In short, the city can be regarded as both product and symbol of modernity. The ambivalence of Durkheim, Weber and Marx is indicative of the Janus-face of modernity itself (Chapter 6).

The Chicago School

The breakthrough in establishing urban studies as a specific field of enquiry came with Robert E. Park and fellow members of the 'Chicago School', Ernest Burgess and Louis Wirth. Although differing in a number of respects, these writers, Burgess in particular, cast their work in the language of 'science' and sought after the 'underlying laws' of urban life. Burgess's prime metaphor for the city was that of the organism struggling for survival and undergoing evolutionary change in the context of a specific environment. This is a functionalist, 'urban ecology' approach to cities in which concentric urban zones were territories to be fought over, invaded and altered before the establishment of a new equilibrium. According to Burgess:

> The typical processes of expansion of the city can best be illustrated, perhaps, by a series of concentric circles, which may be numbered to designate both the successive zones of urban extension and the types of areas differentiated in the process of expansion. (Burgess, 1967: 50)

Burgess's 'ideal-type' construction of the city expands radially from the Central Business District (CBD). Each subsequent zone is inhabited by a particular type or class of people and activities. As we move outward from the CBD, we pass through:

- **a zone of transition;**
- **a belt of working-class housing;**
- **a zone of high-class dwellings;**
- **a commuter belt of satellite towns.**

In effect, various social class groups are allocated specific residential zones by income selection. Although originally constructed from fieldwork in Chicago, Burgess's urban map was taken to be a general model of city growth. In particular, it was said to demonstrate the 'tendency of each inner zone to extend its area by invasion of the next outer zone' (ibid.: 50). Although using the language of invasion and succession, Burgess took an essentially optimistic view of urban life, seeing it as inevitably progressive.

Wirth displays a more cultural than ecological approach to urban life. He was primarily concerned with urbanism as a way of life and a form of social existence. In particular, he was interested in the cultural and lifestyle diversity of urban living. This he saw as promoting impersonality and mobility (social and spatial) as people lost a sense of 'place' and stable social relationships.

According to Wirth, urban living was based on having large numbers of people living in close proximity without really knowing one another. This required them to conduct instrumental transactions and passing encounters leading to superficial, transitory, competitive relationships. From this grows a sense of alienation and powerlessness. However, Wirth also points to the way city dwellers form associations with each other based on lifestyle, culture and ethnicity. Indeed, so-called 'community studies' was to argue that cities developed a range of communities or urban villages of tight-knit social relations. These would include Italian-Americans in Boston (Gans, 1962) and working-class neighbourhoods in London (Young and Willmott, 1962).

Photocopy a map of the city that you live in.

Using the signs on the plan and your own cultural knowledge, mark out the following:

- the socio-economic categories of the residential zones;

- the main shopping areas;

- the main industrial areas;

- the main business zone;

- the main zones of leisure activity.

— Does your city conform to the patterns of the Chicago School? If not, in what ways does it differ?

Criticisms of urban studies

There are a number of problems with these early versions of urban studies, namely:

- **the functionalism and spurious science;**

- **the overgeneralization from American cities, and particularly Chicago, to elsewhere;**

- **the greater variety of urban life than the ecology model acknowledged;**

- **a stress on the idea that *where* you live is the central factor in determining *how* you live, so that space is determinate of culture and economy.**

Thus, Gans (1968) argued that the crucial factor shaping lifestyle was not so much the locality where people live but their social class and place in the 'family life cycle'. This argument is closer to the views of those for whom the structures and transformations of capitalism are the prime forces that shape city life, that is, the contemporary emphasis on political economy in the emergence of the global city.

POLITICAL ECONOMY AND THE GLOBAL CITY

The work of Harvey (1973, 1985) and Castells (1977, 1983) stresses the structuring and restructuring of space as a created environment through the spread of industrial capitalism. They argue that the geography of cities is the result not of 'natural forces' but of the power of capitalism in creating markets and controlling the workforce.

Capitalism and the urban environment

Capitalist corporations continually promote commodification and the search for new markets. This makes them sensitive to questions of location and their relative advantages. Lower labour costs, weaker unionization and tax concessions lead firms to favour some places over others as locations for plants, markets and development. Similarly, the need to find alternative forms of investment, and the particular conditions of markets and state intervention, assist some sectors of the economy (and thus some places) in gaining the upper hand.

For Harvey, the state has played a major role in the reproduction of capitalism and its shaping of the urban environment. For example, the post-war expansion of suburbia was an outcome, at least in part, of:

- tax relief given to home-owners and construction firms;
- the setting up of lending arrangements by banks/building societies;
- the laying down of the transport, telecommunications and welfare infrastructure.

For Castells, these homes, schools, transport services, leisure facilities and welfare provisions are an aspect of the 'collective consumption' inherent to capitalism and the creation of an urban environment conducive to business.

The city is said to be the site of a class struggle engendered by capitalism. This is marked by contestation over the control of space and the distribution of resources, for example the conflicts over the cutting of welfare spending during the restructuring of capitalism in the 1980s and 1990s. Indeed, for Harvey and Castells, the reorganizing of the city is an aspect of the restructuring of capitalism on a global scale. This illustrates the place of urban life in the long line of dependency and exploitation constitutive of world-wide capitalism. As King argued:

> All cities today are 'world cities', yet they have not just assumed that role overnight. The agenda for urban history which perceives them in this way is clearly vast. Yet such a perspective would enable urban problems, economic, social and physical, to be seen in a much more realistic light. ... The cosy viewpoint of looking at our cities from within must be replaced by the more uncomfortable view of seeing them from outside. (King, 1983: 15)

According to Harvey (1989), the global recession of the 1970s hastened a renewed globalization of world economic activity. This involved a significant speed-up of production and consumption turnover times. Assisted by the use of information and communication technology, a new post-Fordist 'regime of accumulation' was established (Chapter 5). Lash and Urry (1987) describe this restructuring of capitalism on a global scale as a 'disorganized' set of global flows of capital, resources and people. They point to the deconcentration of capital through globalized production, financing and distribution. At the same time, western economies have experienced a decline in the extractive/manufacturing sectors as economies are deindustrialized. This has led to a decrease in the absolute and relative size of the core working class in tandem with the emergence of a service class. Like Harvey, Lash and Urry stress the rise in flexible forms of work organization and a decline in national bargaining procedures.

Global cities

In this context, the restructuring of urban space can be explored in terms of the emergence of global cities and the place of 'culture' in urban regeneration. Underpinning the concept of the global city is the sense that the urban world and global economy are dominated by a small number of important centres. These act as command and control points for an increasingly dispersed set of economic activities. These centres – London, New York, Tokyo, Seoul, Los Angeles, Frankfurt, Paris, Singapore – have significance not because of population size or volume of business but because key personnel and activities are located within them. That is, they are sites for the accumulation, distribution and circulation of capital. Thus, information and decision-making functions are more telling than mere size.

According to Clarke (1996), ten cities host the headquarters of nearly half of the world's largest 500 transnational manufacturing corporations. The top four cities, London, New York, Tokyo and Seoul, account for 156 of these. He suggests three reasons behind the emergence and patterning of global cities:

1 growth in the number and range of the institutions of global capital;

2 geographical concentration of capital;

3 the extension of global reach via telecommunications and transport.

Finance and banking have become the crucial facets of a city's claim to global significance. For example, the manufacturing sector of the UK is relatively small (in planetary terms). Nevertheless, London is a world city because it is the prime centre for and supplier of financial services to global markets. After New York, perhaps the major financial centre, London has the largest stock exchange in the world. All the world's top 100 banks are represented there.

Tokyo's global status was originally based on the research-led, government-protected microelectronics industry and the flexible production methods it pioneered. On the back of this success, Tokyo developed as a commercial centre through the transnationalization of the capital it had accumulated and subsequently exported to nearby Asian economies (Korea, Taiwan, etc.) and to Europe and the USA.

The post-industrial global city

Sassen (1991, 1996) explores the variety of spaces that make up the urban forms of the contemporary post-industrial global city as symbolized by New York, London and Tokyo. These include the high-rise CBD, the declining post-industrial zones, and the spaces of ethnicity. The contrast between the homogeneity of the high-rise offices of the CBD and the diversity of the urban forms which mark immigrant communities reveals how power inscribes itself in the urban landscape. 'One represents technological advance and cosmopolitan culture, the other economic and cultural backwaters' (Sassen, 1996: 24). Of course, 'advanced' and 'backward' are relational concepts and representational effects. As Sassen argues, the so-called 'backwaters' are a vital part of the economic and cultural life of cities and deeply intertwined with the self-nominated 'advanced' sectors.

The increasing globalization of capitalism gives rise to the need for command, control and co-ordination nodal centres that constitute the core of 'global cities'. This is manifested spatially and architecturally in the high-rise, high-density office developments of the downtown districts of New York, London and Tokyo. These centres, constituted by the offices of large multinational corporations, require servicing by suppliers, sub-contractors and consultancy firms, etc. Thus, around the command posts grow other layers of economic activity. These include the small firms and labour force of separate ethnic communities whose physical and cultural presence represents another aspect of globalization. Consequently, the expansion of global economic activity is premised, in part, on local informal (i.e. unregulated) economic activity (Sassen, 1991, 1996).

THE SYMBOLIC ECONOMY OF CITIES

While Harvey and Sassen focus on political economy, Zukin explores the symbolic and representational aspects of cites.

> To ask 'whose city?' suggests more than a politics of occupation; it also asks who has the right to inhabit the dominant image of the city. This often relates to real geographical strategies as different social groups battle over access to the center of the city and over symbolic representations in the center. (Zukin, 1996b: 43)

Questions concerning the symbolic economy of cities focus on three fundamental issues:

1 The relationship between representations and 'readings' of social groups that mark inclusion and exclusion. For example, particular districts, streets, parks or buildings whose symbolism marks zoning and the materialization of social rules. Thus, the unwritten 'keep out' which the high-rise corporate buildings of the CBD signs to the poor, blacks and Latinos in North American cities.

2 Economic redevelopment, including the transformation of wharfs and canals into shopping centres or areas of leisure activity. This process signifies the role of the symbolic economy in material economic power.

3 The role played by representations in the constitution of place whereby a vibrant symbolic economy attracts investment, giving particular cities comparative advantages over rivals.

✓ *Urban spaces and places are formed by the synergy of capital investment and cultural meanings.*

Zukin (1991) argues that the increasing significance of the symbolic economies of cities is rooted in the long-term relative decline of urban areas in comparison with suburbs, the expansion of financial speculation, the growth of cultural consumption, the arrival and visibility of 'ethnic immigration', and the marketing of identity politics. This leads her to suggest that we cannot understand cities without considering:

- how cities use culture as an economic base;

- how capitalizing on culture spills over into the privatization and militarization of public space;

- how the power of culture is related to the aesthetics of fear. (Zukin, 1996a)

Cultural economics

Culture plays an economic role in a number of ways:

- It acts as a *branding* for a city, associating it with desirable 'goods': for example, movie representations of the New York skyline; the meeting houses of the American Revolution hosted by Boston; the Bridge, Opera House and harbour of Sydney; the art culture of Florence; the 'mother of parliaments' in London; and the high-tech neon of Tokyo.

- The *culture industries*, including film, television, advertising agencies and the music business lend glamour to cities, bringing direct employment and other economic benefits.

- The museums, restaurants, shops, theatres, clubs and bars of cities provide convivial *consumption spaces* for business meetings and tourism. For example, Paris is a 'world city' not for its manufacturing or financial clout but because its architectural history and gastronomic reputation attract international conventions and organizational headquarters.

The discussion about urban regeneration and the symbolic economies of cities has centred on North American cities. However, the place of culture in urban restructuring is also prominent in a European context. For example, the British city of Birmingham has attempted to shift its internal centre of power and public space so as to reposition itself in the symbolic culture and economic order of Europe and the world. The city's hosting of the G8 summit and Eurovision Song Contest in 1998 within its International Convention Centre (ICC) and canal development area was a sign of its success. It was also a part of its strategy as the city plastered itself with the slogan 'Birmingham Welcomes the World'. As Tim Hall (1997) argues, the redevelopment of Birmingham exemplifies the tactics by which 'peripheral' places use cultural strategies to win investment.

For Birmingham, this strategy involved the opening up of a series of spectacular 'flagship' spaces based on technical excellence, prestige, modern design and professionalism. There was a stress on display. This included the ICC, the shops, restaurants and waterside walkways surrounding the canal basin. An important cultural symbol was the Symphony Hall, associated as it is with the high cultural world of classical music and the spectacle of performance. Thus, 'the city imagined itself within certain cultural spaces, those of high culture, international culture and spectacle' (Hall, 1997). Subsequently, Birmingham attempted to circulate these discourses through the media, linking civic identity to the processes of transformation and the colonization of the future.

BIRMINGHAM CANAL BASIN

© **Photographer: Freya Hadley**

- *This is a picture of the regeneration of the Birmingham (UK) canal basin. What have the urban planners tried to achieve, and for what purpose?*

- *Find out about the role of Birmingham and canals in the industrial revolution. Why would tourists want to visit the area?*

Look up the following cities in tourist brochures or on the Internet:

- Beijing;
- Berlin;
- Cape Town;
- London;
- New York;
- Paris;
- San Francisco;
- São Paulo;
- Sydney;
- Tokyo.

— What cultural icons are associated with each of them?
— What are the connotations of each icon? That is, what do they sign about the kind of city we are meant to understand it to be?

The creative industries

Since the late 1990s, the notion of the 'creative industries' has emerged to promote the strategy of using culture to generate urban economic growth. The central idea is to group cultural, commercial and industrial activities together in order to better develop their creative potential. The term 'creative industries' was first coined in 1997 in the UK by the incoming Labour Government. It has since been widely adopted throughout Europe, North America, Australia, New Zealand and in Eastern Asia (Jones et al., 2004).

The UK Government's 'Creative Industries Task Force' defined the creative industries as 'those industries which have their origins in individual creativity, skill and talent and which have a potential for wealth and job creation through the generation and exploitation of intellectual property' (Department of Culture, Media and Sport, 1998). The Task Force also identified 13 categories to be included under the collective creative umbrella: advertising, architecture, the art and antiques market, crafts, design, designer fashion, film and video, interactive leisure software, music, the performing arts, software and computer services, and television and radio. Offshoot terms include 'cultural industries', which includes cultural tourism, heritage, museums, libraries, sports and hobbies; and 'creative clusters', which describes geographic concentrations of interconnected firms and institutions in a particular industry or sector.

The creative industries are seen by their supporters to be powerful forces in the movement of advanced industrial economies away from the production of goods and services to the creation of ideas and knowledge. It is also argued that they simultaneously further social and cultural development and even rejuvenate hitherto marginalized types of cultural production (Cunningham, 2004; Matheson, 2006).

The rise of the creative class

Two publications have emerged as the manifesto of the creative industries: *The Rise of the Creative Class* (2002) by Richard Florida, an academic, and *The Creative City* (2000; first published 1994) by policymakers Landry and Bianchini. Florida and Landry have become successful as urban economic development consultants. Florida (2002) argues that contemporary cities must attract the new 'creative class' whom he identifies as the prime movers of economic development. According to Florida, the successful cities and regions of the future will be the ones most endowed with the 3T's: technology, talent and tolerance. Pools of creative talent are said to be at least as important as stocks of technology in driving urban and regional development. According to Florida, the cultural atmosphere of a city is equally as significant as its technological labour markets in drawing creative talent to it. He argues that cultural tolerance attracts creative talent, which in turn stimulates technological innovation and generates growth.

However, critics think the idea of the creative industries have been overinflated and they are sceptical about how successful they will be in stimulating economic growth. It has also been suggested that Florida's celebrity status and the globalization of the idea of the creative industries privileges Anglo-American narratives over local circumstances (Gibson and Klocker, 2004). Some writers have argued that the creative drive is hostile to traditional suburban family lifestyles as it links economic growth to alternative lifestyles (Kotkin and Siegal, 2004). Critics have also suggested that the creative industries do little to disrupt the conservative economic orthodoxies that create and widen the socio-ecnomic inequalities of class, race and gender. Peck (2005) is particularly scathing about Florida, arguing that his programme actually fortifies the inequities of neo-liberalism by giving it a soft, cultural, tolerant veneer. For example, the creative industries are part of the private sector and doing little to restore declining public cultural space.

Privatizing public space

Zukin's (1996a) prime example of the privatization of public space is the evolution and transformation of the public park. The major cities of the western world all have parks and squares. These were built, usually during the nineteenth century, as places of public access where people could meet, walk, talk and participate in a common culture. Often these collective spaces were created in celebration of civic achievements and as monuments to public figures. Today, it is argued, these spaces are on the decline. The new arenas of public meeting, public culture and the public sphere are situated in private commercial spaces – the private park, the shopping mall and the simulated theme world. This is the product of a combination of factors, including:

- the inability or unwillingness of city government to fund and maintain public spaces;

- increased levels of everyday fear surrounding perceptions of rising crime in general and public assault and robbery in particular (often linked to ethnic and racial tensions);

- the rise of the leisure industries and an increased involvement of private security and leisure companies in the management of 'public' space.

Zukin (1996a) gives a number of examples, including Bryant Park, New York, where a once flourishing public space had become a litter-filled danger zone inhabited by drug users, homeless people and other victims of urban poverty. Under the auspices of a privately funded restoration company, the park was 'cleaned up' and redesigned. Entertainment was introduced, opening hours restricted, and security guard patrols were established to oversee the park. This scheme and others like it have been successful in creating 'safe' public space that is popular and busy during key times of the day. Equally, the consequence has been to turn the park into a visual and spatial representation of middle-class public culture inhabited by mainly white office workers.

The public culture of private elites

Zukin's concern is that public culture – if such can be said to exist – is shaped by private sector elites. This poses three problems:

1 Only certain profitable sites will be developed, that is, those with the potential to enhance property prices or retail business.

2 Control of access to these 'public' spaces is in the hands of security regimes. These organizations explicitly exclude 'undesirable' social groups, that is, the urban poor, in which people of colour are overrepresented.

3 There is an attempt to control the total environment through population flow and control of a symbolic culture conducive to commerce. This is exemplified by shopping malls and theme parks. Accordingly,

> Disneyland and Disney World are two of the most significant public spaces of the late 20th century. They transcend ethnic, class, and regional identities to offer a national public culture based on aestheticizing differences and controlling fear. (Zukin, 1996a: 49)

Disney: fantasy and surveillance

The Disney landscape provides a multimedia experience representing a tourist attraction and a symbolically desirable lifestyle. This is a 'public' culture where civility and social interaction occur in the context of a security regime in which there are no guns, no homeless people and no drugs. Disney's idealized and fantasized 'Main Street USA' presents to us in symbolic and imaginary form the pleasurable aspects of urban life while removing the fear. It is a far cry from the 'real' streets of New York. Disney World, through its private management, spatial control and stimulating/simulated visual culture, is the new model for public space. These principles are echoed in numerous shopping malls. For Zukin, Disney World is important because it confirms and consolidates the significance and power of culture as a form of commerce and social control. It imposes a form of meaning and manages social diversity through a combination of visual imagery and physical spatial control.

Disney World has been defended on the grounds that it is a safe, defensible public space. However, critics influenced by Baudrillard have attacked it for its hyperreality, its collapsing of the real and the fake (and indeed its celebration of the fake). Others have reviled Disney World for being all too real in its total control of space through the use of its own rules, vocabulary, norms, security force and even sanitation workers – most of whom are the relatively low-paid workforce of an ever-increasing service sector (Zukin, 1996a). This arguably marks the postmodernization of contemporary life (Chapter 6).

THE POSTMODERN CITY

✓ *'A postmodern urbanization process can be defined as a summative depiction of the major changes that have been taking place in cities during the last quarter of the twentieth century.' (Soja, 1995a: 60)*

As Watson and Gibson (1995) remark, every city in the world is to some degree postmodern. However, for Soja (1989, 1995a), the 'quintessential' case of postmodern urbanization is Los Angeles. This city represents for him an 'extraordinary intensity' of urban restructuring and a 'comprehensive vividness' of change. Although too much has been made of LA as 'the future', it stands in the literature as the city that 'must be discussed'.

Postmodern urbanization

For Soja, postmodern urbanization does not imply total transformation of the urban landscape into something wholly new. Rather, the postmodern city has continuities with its past. On the other hand, the concept of the postmodern does suggest 'something more than piecemeal reform'. Soja argues that we can see in Los Angeles six intertwined processes and relationships that together produce a composite postmodern urban geography. These are as follows:

1 *Fordist to post-Fordist urbanization*: The move from Fordism to post-Fordism (Chapter 5) involves a move from mass production and consumption of standardized goods to small batch production. This is achieved through flexible specialization geared towards niche markets. For Soja, the key processes are ones of deindustrialization and reindustrialization, which forge dramatic changes in the foundations of the urban economy. The reindustrialization of Los Angeles is constituted by the development of high-technology industries, including aerospace and electronics (situated outside of the old industrial zones), and by the growth of low-skill, labour-intensive, design-sensitive industries. Though once clustered in Downtown, these businesses are increasingly dispersed across the urban landscape. In addition, the growth of the finance, insurance and real-estate business is a marker of LA's postmodern restructuring. Together, these developments have reorganized not only the economic base of LA but also the residential areas. This has included the emptying out of the centre and the urbanization of suburbia.

2 *Globalization and the formation of world cities*: Los Angeles is an especially vivid example of the world city as a finance/trade centre. It is marked by global, but particularly Japanese, inward investment. It is also the location of 'the most

culturally heterogeneous population ever agglomerated in any city in the world' (Soja, 1995a: 130). A city which was once 80 per cent Anglo is now at least one-third foreign-born, many of whom are the backbone of a cheap and weakly organized labour force essential to the growth of the LA economy.

3   *A combination of decentralization and recentralization*: The urban form of the post-modern city is said by Soja to be significantly different from its predecessors. He argues that it no longer conforms to the concentric rings of the Chicago School. Nor does it resemble the late modern 'disjointed metropolis' constituted by a central business district, an inner city poor zone and a series of sprawling suburbs. Rather, while these areas continue to exist, the postmodern city has juggled them around. The 'inner city' poor zone is not necessarily located within the physical inner city. The residential suburbs are increasingly the site of new forms of industrial development. This is the outcome of a restructuring and redistribution of jobs, affordable housing, transport systems and lines of racial/ethnic divide.

4   *New patterns of social fragmentation, segregation and polarization*: Post-Fordism, deindustrialization, globalization and the reconfiguration of the spatial geography of the city are bound up with the changing social structure of urban life. This includes new patterns of fragmentation, segregation and polarization. For Soja this involves increasing social, economic and cultural inequality. A complex new social kaleidoscope leads to creative cross-cultural mixing in the arts, business and politics. However, it also generates even greater depths of despair, impoverishment, crime and violence. In particular, an enlarging managerial technocracy, a shrinking middle class and a growing base of the homeless, welfare dependants and cheap labour now mark the social landscape.

5   *The increasingly 'carceral' city*: The postmodern kaleidoscopic city has become increasingly ungovernable. This has led to walled-in estates, armed guards, patrolled shopping centres, surveillance cameras and wire fences, all aimed at keeping the threatening spectre of crime, violence and ethnic difference at bay. LA is marked by turf wars of gangs and police, the latter armed with the latest technology of control. However, Soja also points to an increasing politics of place, including greater neighbourhood participation in local municipal issues.

6   *A new mode or regulation involving the rise of hyperreality and simulacra*: The most obviously postmodern aspect of Soja's argument refers to the emergence of a new form of social control, or mode of regulation, constituted by a transformed 'urban imaginary'. This is a new epistemology in which the relationship between image and reality is blurred or even deconstructed. The most visible example is the growing significance of the hyperreal or simulacrum. According to Soja, it is not the production of hyperreal Hollywood or Disneyland that is significantly new, but rather the proliferation and dissemination of the hyperreal into

ordinary everyday life. This is evidenced by the vocabulary of spin doctors, virtual reality, cyberspace, sound-bites and pop culture.

Urban change: suburbs and edge cities

Soja attempts to map the postmodern city from the elevated heights of the metaphorical mountain-top. He works with the language of globalization and macro-economic restructuring. However, patterns of change can also be understood through the more localized language of urban studies with its vocabulary of the inner city, suburbs, gentrification and edge cities.

The 'modern' Anglo-American city has commonly been discussed in terms of a poor, non-white, inner-city zone of decay paralleled by the growth of suburbs populated by a predominantly middle class. Typically, this involved a degree of 'white flight' from the city to the suburbs and the emptying out of the inner city. At its most extreme, a city like Detroit (USA) has a poor black inner zone with whole sections not supplied with basic services like electricity and water. In the popular imagination these are dangerous places of gang wars, drug abuse and crime.

KEY THINKERS

Edward Soja (1935–)

Soja is a Professor of Urban Planning at the University of California Los Angeles. His work has focused on urban restructuring in Los Angeles and more broadly on the critical study of cities and regions. His work brings together political economy and critical cultural studies and is often designated as postmodern. He is particularly interested in the way issues of class, race, gender, and sexuality intersect the spatiality of social life to create a cultural politics of difference and identity. His writing focuses on the way social scientists and philosophers think about space, time and geography.

Reading: Soja, E. (1989) *Postmodern Geographies: The Reassertion of Space in Critical Social Theory*. London: Verso Press.

Soja's argument is that residential suburbs have become the site of industrial activity while so-called 'inner-city' poverty is increasingly located across the urban landscape. Further, some parts of the inner city, especially those areas that have suffered most from deindustrialization, have been taken over by middle-class groups who have benefited from the regeneration of dockland areas or taken to 'loft living' (Zukin, 1988), that is, *gentrification*. This has involved an increase in house prices and the generation of cultural activities based on the lifestyles of a 'college-educated generation'. The displacement of lower income groups has inevitably followed.

Edge cities are urban places of residence and work that have grown up on the outer rims of established cities. Usually of middle-class suburban character, edge cities have emerged in spaces that often have no designated name or immediate local government structures. These urban areas have resisted being incorporated into established places. This has allowed the American middle classes to achieve, or at least lobby for, lower tax rates and reduced public administration. This includes the privatization of local government. Edge cities are not just suburbs but places of work and economic activity. This is significant for, according to Zukin, edge city development in America indicates

> a major reversal of meaning between the city and its suburbs. Until quite recently, we thought of cities as the economic heartland whose vast wealth nourished a surrounding, and clearly subordinate, regional culture. The city had sleek office towers; the suburbs had poky commuter trains. The city had theaters and concert halls for original performances; the suburbs had mass culture's derivative shopping centers and drive-in movies. This socio-spatial differentiation repeated the pattern of form following function, with 'suburbanization' considered a form of consumption derived from the city's productive functions. More critical, however, is the fact that the city has always financed the suburbs. Investment by the city's banks builds highways and shopping centers. Employment in the city's offices pays mortgages on the suburban homes. And the concentration of 'social problems' in the city fuels the exodus outward into the suburbs of all those people who can afford to move away. Even in the glossiest cultural representations, it was never imagined that the suburbs would compete with the city as a source of productive wealth, a landscape of economic power. (Zukin, 1991: 135–6)

Urban unrest

The kind of urban change typically seen in the USA, and to some extent in the UK and Australia, is argued by its critics to be driven by the agenda of the professional and managerial middle class and large corporate business. This has increased and intensified social polarization, as manifested by the abandonment of an 'underclass' to mass unemployment, drug trafficking, poverty and homelessness. Here are the conditions for the urban rioting witnessed in the UK during the 1980s (Toxteth, Handsworth, Brixton, Tottenham) and of course in LA in 1992.

The popular image is of black or Latino urban rioters located in the inner city. However, McGuigan (1996a) notes that significant numbers of the people involved are white and from working-class estates on the edges of urban areas. In either case, cities must be considered as contested areas. Consequently, in parallel to urban unrest, there has been an increase in techniques of surveillance and control. Again, the paradigm case is Los Angeles, described vividly by Mike Davis (1990) in his book *City of Quartz*. Here he offers an apocalyptic vision of Los Angeles marked by the following features:

- a city built on the myth of sunshine and the good life;

- property and land prices as the central dynamic and social value;

- rapid population increase and surburbanization;

- the decay of infrastructure and the development of pollution and other environmental problems;

- an indifferent, selfish middle class bent on tax reductions and reduced public expenditure;

- a corrupt political establishment which, though divided along ethnic lines and increasingly fragmented, still holds enormous power;

- the growing influence of LA as a global city in the sway of Japanese capital;

- growing social and economic polarization, poverty, low pay and urban unrest;

- gangland crime and high-tech policing;

- commuter belts and urban wastelands;

- severe racial divisions and discriminatory practices;

- a racist police force committed to an ongoing, because inherently flawed, 'war on drugs' which has virtually curfewed non-Anglo youth.

Fortress LA

These factors represent the conditions for riots and underpin the construction of the city as Fortress LA. Davis argues that, in post-liberal Los Angeles,

> the defense of luxury lifestyles is translated into a proliferation of new repressions in space and movement, undergirded by the ubiquitous 'armed response'. This obsession with physical security systems, and, collaterally, with the architectural policing of social boundaries, has become a zeitgeist of urban restructuring, a master narrative in the emerging built environment of the 1990s. (Davis, 1990: 223)

For Davis, LA merges urban design, architecture and police apparatus into a comprehensive security endeavour. Here fear becomes a function of the security mobilization itself.

He cites the redesign and rebuilding of the Downtown area in which street frontage is denuded, pedestrians carefully channelled, 'undesirable' sectors cut off from access, and certain 'types of people' (notably people of colour and the poor) 'discouraged' and excluded. Parallel with this 'cleansing' of Downtown there has, he argues, been a deliberate strategy of 'containment' of the poor into designated spaces where they can be policed and harassed. This has included banning cardboard shelters and even avoiding the erection of public toilets in designated areas.

The concern for security has been elevated to the point where it structures the design of buildings. This is exemplified by the 'fortified' public library and the ever-increasing number of gated and guarded residential facilities. Increasingly, contemporary residential security in Los Angeles depends on private security services and an implicit division of labour between private police and the public LAPD. The latter concentrates on high-tech surveillance and information gathering, leaving much of the 'leg work' to commercial organizations.

DOWNTOWN LOS ANGELES

© Photographer: Byron Moore | Agency: Dreamstime.com

- *What are the features that make LA a contemporary postmodern city?*
- *What does the image tell us about the place and source of power in the city?*

The excitement of the city

Davis's account is a useful, informative and frightening antidote to unreflective celebrations of cities as places of unrestricted cultural mixing and merging. At the same time, a pessimistic stance oriented by political economy pointing only to the problems of urban life misses the specifically cultural aspects of cities and the pleasures they offer. For those in a position to enjoy them, cities offer:

- **unrivalled opportunities for work and leisure;**
- **the context for mixing and meeting with a range of different kinds of people;**
- **cultural excitement, uncertainty and the possibility of the surprise encounter.**

In big cities, as nowhere else, one can eat, listen to music, go to the movies, dress up, set off on travels and play with identities.

— What are the things about cities that:
- bring people together;
- keep people apart;
- support people;
- cause people to suffer?

— How might these factors be different according to age, gender, class and race?

CYBERSPACE AND THE CITY

✓ *The heterogeneous pleasures and representations of contemporary urban life are increasingly derived from a growing electronic culture.*

The culture of the western world is increasingly constituted through an electronic medium of film, television, virtual reality games, electronic arcades, PCs and the Internet. This is a heavily 'mediatized' (Thompson, 1995) culture in which the spaces of social and cultural interaction are separated from specific social and geographical places. The potential exists for electronic culture to offer more flexibility and scope in the construction of identity projects. However, electronic technologies are also the means for increased surveillance and control.

The concept of cyberspace, commonly attributed to novelist William Gibson (1984), suggests the 'nowhere' space where e-mails pass, electronic money transfer takes place, digital messages move and web sites are accessed (Chapter 11). 'A conceptual "spaceless place" where words, human relationships, data, wealth status and power are made manifest by people using computer-mediated communications technology' (Ogden, 1994: 715).

The main technologies of electronic culture are computers, cable systems, satellites, television, video and virtual reality technology. These technologies form the domain of 'telematics', that is, services and infrastructures that link computers and digital technologies over telecommunication links. The central features of these technologies are:

- electronics;

- abundance;

- speed;

- convergence;

- plurality;

- interactivity.

Electronic technology provides more information and services at increased speed across greater distances to more people. Some services are interactive, though at present this is at a relatively low level. The idea of PC-TV or the 'information superhighway', highlights the issue of technological convergence, that is, technologies which had been produced and used separately start to merge into one. Technological convergence is enabled by digital technology. This allows information to be electronically organized into bytes, or discrete bundles of information, which can be compressed during transmission and decompressed on arrival. Thus, a good deal more information can travel at greater speed over larger distances.

The information superhighway

The current model of electronic development is the Internet. Originally set up by the US military, the Internet is a communications infrastructure of linked but decentred computer terminals with no central regulatory authority. The Internet has a number of different levels of use: e-mail, newsgroups, web sites and online services with the last two being the most rapidly expanding areas. It has been estimated that there are around 5 million Internet host computers with probably 25–30 million users.

To date, the Internet has largely involved free access. However, this is changing as multinational corporations develop subscription services and web sites or explore the possibilities of setting up their own 'information superhighways'. Here one would be able to order and pay for shopping, transfer e-money, keep an eye on one's bank account, call up a selection of films, videos and programmes and search the web for information. Both

Microsoft and News Corporation have ambitions to develop their own information superhighway in which the television would be the visual terminal for a whole range of services and activities (Figure 12.1). Indeed, the component parts of this picture are already being put in place in the USA, where 34 per cent of the population have PCs and 40 per cent of these have modems (required to access the Internet).

Electronic urban networks

According to Graham and Marvin, there are three key areas of analysis for exploring the relationship between telecommunications and cities, namely:

1 the functional and material tensions between the fixity of urban places and the mobility supported by telecommunications and electronic spaces;

2 the social struggles which develop over the shaping of urban places and electronic spaces;

3 the issues surrounding social representation, identity and perception in cites and telecommunications. (Graham and Marvin, 1996)

Traditionally, cities have been regarded as relatively fixed places whose great strength lay in their overcoming of the 'frictional distance of space'. That is, cities brought together the elements of industrialization, work and leisure. Cities reduced the need to transport people and goods over long distances. However, since electronic technology is able to overcome distance in an instant, it creates new networks and new senses of time and space.

> The idea of telecommunications as 'distance-shrinking' makes it analogous to other transport and communication improvements. However, in doing so the idea fails to capture the essential essence of advanced communications, which is not to reduce the 'friction of distance' but to render it entirely meaningless. When the time taken to communicate over 10,000 miles is indistinguishable from the time taken to communicate over 1 mile, then 'time-space' convergence has taken place at a fairly profound scale.
> (Gillespie and Williams, 1988: 1317)

As Castells (1989) argues, the new geometry of production, consumption and information flows denies the meaning of place outside of its position in a network. Specifically, cities are the electronic hubs of a new global information economy. Urban areas are the nodal points of social, technological, cultural and economic networks. Further, the growth of telematics as integral to cities is an aspect of the deindustrialization and restructuring of global economies in which information is the key commodity of post-industrial 'information cities' (Chapters 5 and 11). Telematics supports the dispersal of economic activity across the 'megalopolis' and indeed the planet.

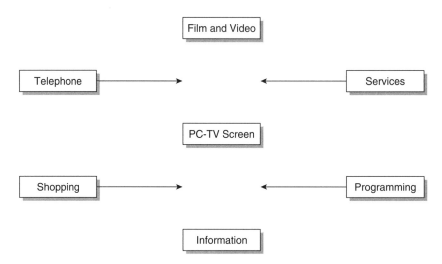

Figure 12.1 Television as the visual terminal of the information superhighway

KEY THINKERS

Manuel Castells (1942–)

Spanish-born Manuel Castells is Professor of Sociology and Professor of City and Regional Planning at the University of California, Berkeley. He has published over 20 books and was one of the founders of the New Urban Sociology. His publications include studies of urban social movements, and of urban and regional changes brought about by information technology and economic restructuring. He is considered a world expert on the information age and addressed the United Nations' Economic and Social Council on information technology and global development.

Reading: Castells, M. (1989) *The Informational City: Information Technology, Economic Restructuring and the Urban–Regional Process*. Oxford: Blackwell.

The informational city

For Castells (1989, 1994), we are witnessing epochal changes driven by the agenda of a professional and managerial class. This is constituted by:

- the technological revolution of computers and information transfer;

- the emergence of an 'information society' with economic, social, military and cultural capabilities being information-based;

- the emergence of a global economy operating in real time on a planetary scale;

- the significance of cities as command centres of the global economy, including competition for relative advantage;

- increased social polarization between regions of the world (North–South) and within cities divided by race and class (the dual city).

Telematics challenges the fixity of cities while increasing social polarization and conflictual struggles over the meaning of technologies and city spaces. On the horizon lies an increasing distance between the information-rich and the information-poor. Electronic technology is also at the heart of social control and surveillance as manifested by:

- the increased use of CCTV cameras in urban centres;

- security systems surrounding houses;

- police helicopters using infra-red cameras;

- the use of electronic shopping cards that record information for store management regarding consumer spending patterns.

The computerized credit card, the home computer, and the sophisticated television system that permits home banking, shopping, opinion polls, and so on also allow corporations to collect massive amounts of information on users. … How much money you have, what you like to buy, your views on capital punishment, your preference for president or laundry detergent – the new technology is used to draw detailed marketing profiles of individual households for what is called … precise targeting of potential buyers. (Mosca, 1988: 6)

In short, the development of electronic technologies that are intrinsic to contemporary cities is bound up with issues of social power and conflict. Cities are terrains of contestation in which various ethnic, class, gender and organizational agents struggle to shape the social and built environment. This is manifested in disputes over the redevelopment of inner cities, docklands or downtown areas. It is also evident in the debates about whether the Internet will remain a free dispersed network of computers accessible in principle by all or a commercially dominated, pay-per-view complex.

Electronic homes in global space

One of the urban places that electronic technologies threaten to change is the home. As Castells suggests:

> homes … are becoming equipped with a self-sufficient world of images, sounds, news, and information exchanges. … Homes could become disassociated from neighbour-hoods and cities and still not be lonely, isolated places. They would be populated by voices, by images, by sounds, by ideas, by games, by colors, by news. (Castells, 1985: 34)

For some writers, we are heading towards a new domestic-centred society based on home-working, interactive teleservices and the 'smart' home. That is, the family residence becomes a terminal in a range of electronic flows emanating from, for the most part, transnational corporations.

The home is one of the major locations of electronic culture by which we can become armchair travellers. Electronic culture spans time and place, coming to us via the screen, video, radio, etc. Cultural artefacts and meanings from different historical periods and geographical places can mix together and be juxtaposed. Thus, while the values and meanings attached to place remain significant, the networks in which people are involved extend far beyond their physical locations (Chapters 5 and 10).

This is the postmodern culture of visual bricolage, intertextuality, aesthetic self-consciousness, paradox, ambiguity, irony, parody, pastiche, montage, rapid cutting, non-linear narrative techniques and the decontextualization of images (Chapter 10). It includes the blurring of the boundaries between art, culture and commerce. This is allied to the rising prominence of the postmodern 'figural', resulting in a general aestheticiza-tion of everyday life (Featherstone, 1991, 1995).

THE CITY AS TEXT

Most of the approaches to the city that we have explored thus far fail to register the prob-lematic notion of representation that underpins them. They tend to assume that they are offering us an accurate picture of the city over and against ideological distortions. However,

✓ *Representing the city involves the techniques of writing – metaphor, metonym and other rhetorical devices – rather than a simple transparency from the 'real' city to the 'repre-sented' city.*

For example, we have seen the city described in the languages of:

- plant life and ecology (the Chicago School);
- economic development, restructuring and investment (Harvey);
- power and surveillance (Davis);
- symbolic culture, suburbanization and gentrification (Zukin);
- postmodernism (Soja);
- information technology (Castells).

In the context of the 'crisis of representation' (Chapter 3), accounts of the city have increasingly been recast in the language of poststructuralism. This approach makes issues of representation more problematic and reads 'the city' as text. According to Rob Shields,

> while we may happily speak of the 'reality' of the city as a thing or form, they are the result of a cultural act of classification. We classify an environment as a city, and then 'reify' that city as a thing. The notion of 'the city', *the city itself is a representation*. It is a gloss on an environment which designates by fiat, resting only on the assertion of the self-evidence that a given environment is 'a city'. (Shields, 1996: 227)

There is no unmediated access to 'the real'. What counts as true and as real is the outcome of discursive constructions that bring the objects of knowledge into view through the processes of classification. Representations of cities – maps, statistics, photographs, films, documents, etc. – make the city available to us. However, we then discuss these representations as if the city were a thing, a clear-cut object external to human cultural representation. Shields argues that representations summarize the complexity of the city and displace the physical level of the city onto signs – simulacra which present themselves as 'reality'. These representations, which give meaning to places, are political because they are linked to normative notions, that is, to what is appropriate social behaviour.

Classified spaces

Representations of the spatial divisions of cities are symbolic fault-lines of social relations by which people come to think about the world through the built environment. That is, the cultural representation and classification of city zones as, say, black or white, working class or middle class, safe or dangerous, business or residential, glamorous or squalid are concrete cultural abstractions through which the world is lived. These are *poetic* representations with definite consequences that raise questions about what is hidden and what is shown. A politics of representation needs to ask about the operations of power that are brought to bear to classify environments. By revealing only some aspects of the city, representations have the power to limit courses of action or frame 'problems' in certain ways.

There is a tendency to represent the city in terms of public spaces rather than domestic ones. Thus, much of the world of women and children is rendered invisible, for the easily discernible city is the old male public sphere. Likewise, representations of 'dangerous places' which play on fear (commonly associated with people of colour) fail to acknowledge that so-called 'dangerous places' are so only to certain people or at certain times. This poststructuralist-informed account of representation and the city tends to analysis in which:

- the social and the spatial are indivisible;

- the city is constituted and lived through representation;

- a decentred account of the social is offered – that is, there are a series of available sites in which the urban is produced. Thus, 'the city is *many* cities' (Westwood and Williams, 1997: 6).

The city which is not one

Shields (1996) argues that we should view the city as a complex surface of activities and interactions. These can be explored through a multidimensional analysis and dialogic representation that does not seek to synthesize or overcome contradictions but instead juxtaposes and celebrates a diversity of opposing voices. The languages used to describe the city are, it is argued (Tagg, 1996), also languages of the city, that is, the languages of social science which emerged from the modern city. These function as discursive formations that, in a cultural sense, produce the city since they have no common prior object. The discursivity of the city is multiple and heterogeneous. This is the city which, in Tagg's (1996) phrase, with its echoes of Irigaray, 'is not one'.

Choose a film in which a city features prominently (some examples might be: Blade Runner, Nashville, Manhattan, Beijing Bicycle).

— How is the city represented? That is, what do we learn about the city and how is that achieved?
— From whose point of view are we seeing the city? Might other people see it differently?

DECONSTRUCT THIS: PLACE VS. SIGN

- *How do places shape the use of signs?*
- *How do signs construct places?*
- *How can you distinguish between meaning (sign) and object (place)?*

SUMMARY

This chapter has explored the growing concern in cultural studies with questions of space and with cities in particular. It was argued that space and place are social and cultural constructions, with the latter marked by human emotional investment and identification. Space and place are always matters of the social relations of class, gender, ethnicity, etc., that is, places of power marked by contestation over their meanings. The city is never one thing but rather is manifested and read as a series of contested spaces and representations – cities rather than the city.

From the perspective of political economy, we noted the emergence of global cities as command points of the world economy. It was argued that the restructuring of cities is an aspect of the reorganization of the global economy. We also explored the symbolic economies of cities as playing a role in their restructuring and regeneration. Thus, urban places sought comparative advantage through the acquisition of symbolic capital.

We discussed the trends of postmodern urbanization towards fragmentation, polarization, surveillance, control, conflict and simulacra. These, together with the development of suburban edge cities, the privatization of public space in the context of reduced public spending and growing urban unrest, mark the direction and growth of cities in the twenty-first century. However, we also noted that the city is a place of excitement, fun, strange encounters and the mixing and matching of playful identities.

13 Youth, Style and Resistance

KEY CONCEPTS

Authenticity	*Homology*
Bricolage	*Moral panic*
Bricoleur	*Resistance*
Commodification	*Style*
Distinctions	*Subculture*

The post-war western world has been marked by the emergence and proliferation of distinct musical forms, fashion styles, leisure activities, dances and languages associated with young people. The question of youth cultures has a significant place in cultural studies. The first wave of postgraduates at the Centre for Contemporary Cultural Studies (CCCS) Birmingham, UK – Hebdige, Clarke, Cohen, McRobbie, Willis, Grossberg, etc. – were themselves part of the 'babyboomer' rock generation. Youth culture was 'their' culture, and taking it seriously formed part of the validation of popular culture in the face of high cultural disdain (Chapter 2).

The Birmingham group's analysis of youth subcultures, *Resistance through Rituals* (Hall and Jefferson, 1976), was a landmark publication in cultural studies. Further, the cultural studies network remains one populated by students and lecturers who have personal and professional engagements with popular music, style and fashion.

The study of youth cultures raises a number of significant concerns and themes which echo down and across the pathways of cultural studies, namely:

- the cultural classification of persons into social categories (youth);

- the demarcations of class, race and gender;

- the questions of space, style, taste, media and meaning (i.e. issues of culture);

- **the place of consumption within capitalist consumer societies;**
- **the vexed question of 'resistance'.**

These themes will structure our exploration of youth cultures. However, we should note that cultural studies has tended to explore the more spectacular youth cultures, that is, the visible, loud, different, avant-garde youth styles that have stood out and demanded attention. This has been to the detriment of sociological explorations of what the majority of young people do with their time. This chapter is no exception to that general rule.

THE EMERGENCE OF YOUTH

Common sense tells us that youth is a natural and inevitable marker of a biologically determined age, that is, an organically founded classification of persons who as a consequence of their age hold specific social positions. However, sociologists such as Talcott Parsons have challenged this view.

✓ *Youth is not a universal category of biology. Rather, it is a changing social and cultural construct that appeared at a particular moment of time under definitive conditions.*

Youth as moratorium

For Parsons (1942, 1963), youth or adolescence is a social category which emerged with the changing family roles generated by the development of capitalism. In pre-capitalist societies, he argues, the family fulfilled all the major biological, economic and cultural functions of social reproduction. The transition from childhood to adulthood was marked by rites of passage and there was not an extended period of youth or adolescence. With the emergence of specialized, universalized and rationalized occupational and adult roles in capitalist society, there was a discontinuity between the family and the wider society. Such a rupture needed a cultural space of transition, training and socializing for young people. This marked not only the category of youth but also a moratorium of 'structured irresponsibility' between childhood and adulthood. Here youth culture was able to emerge.

The specificity of youth as a social position between childhood dependence and adult responsibility can be seen in the institutions of the family, education and work. For example, youth is regarded as undergoing preparation for the inevitability of leaving home and joining the adult world. Young people are granted some greater responsibilities than children but are still subject to adult control. This view leads to a set of significant assumptions and classifications of youth by agencies of social control – politicians, policymakers and youth professionals. These include the following:

- Youth is a unitary category, with certain psychological characteristics and social needs common to an age group.

- Youth is an especially formative stage of development, where attitudes and values become anchored to ideologies and remain fixed in this mould for life.

- The transition from childhood dependence to adult autonomy normally involves a rebellious phase. This is understood to be part of a cultural tradition transmitted from one generation to the next.

- Young people in modern societies experience difficulty in making successful transitions and require professional help, advice and support to do so. (Cohen, 1997: 182)

Youth as cultural classification

Cultural studies writers would agree that the concept of youth has no universal meaning to it. However, the 'biological age' deployed by Parsons is itself part of a cultural classificatory system. It is not simply a naturally fixed point upon which social expectations are hung. Youth as an age has no unified characteristics, nor is it a secure transitional stage. This much is apparent if we ask the following questions:

- When does youth start and end biologically?

- Are all 16-year-olds biologically and culturally the same?

- What do all 25-year-olds have in common?

- Why is it that young people seem to be different in New York, New Delhi and Rio de Janeiro?

- How can it be that a section of the adult population over 40 strives to be youthful?

- How is it possible that the period of 'youth' seems to be getting longer in western societies?

> Discuss the above questions in a group.
>
> — What conclusions can you draw about the unified nature of the category of youth?

Youth is not so much a biological category overlaid with social consequences as a complex set of shifting cultural classifications marked by difference and diversity. As a cultural construct, the meaning of youth alters across time and space according to who is being addressed by whom. Youth is a discursive construct. It is formed by the organized and structured way we talk about and bring into being youth as category of persons. Of particular significance are discourses of style, image, difference and identity.

The ambiguity of youth

However we seek to define it, youth remains an ambiguous concept. Even legal definitions are uneven. Across the globe the ages at which a person can buy alcohol, consent to sexual intercourse, engage in homosexual practices and vote for governments differ. Physical age is thus being deployed imprecisely and differentially as a marker to define, control and order social activity (James, 1986). As Sibley argues, youth remains a contested ambivalent classification wedged between the boundaries of childhood and adulthood:

> The limits of the category child vary between cultures and have changed considerably through history within western, capitalist societies. The boundary separating child and adult is a decidedly fuzzy one. Adolescence is an ambiguous zone within which the child/adult boundary can be variously located according to who is doing the categorizing. Thus, adolescents are denied access to the adult world, but they attempt to distance themselves from the world of the child. At the same time they retain some links with childhood. Adolescents may appear threatening to adults because they transgress the adult/child boundary and appear discrepant in 'adult' spaces. … [T]he act of drawing the line in the construction of discrete categories interrupts what is naturally continuous. It is by definition an arbitrary act. (Sibley, 1995: 34–5)

For Grossberg, what matters is the way that the ambiguous category of youth is articulated with other discourses. These would include, for example, music, style, power, responsibility, hope, the future, Americanness, etc. As he argues, 'The issue is not whether the various discourses about youth are referentially accurate, but that they are themselves part of the context in which youth is organized' (Grossberg, 1992: 199).

Trouble and fun

Many adults view youth as merely a state of transition. However, young people have invested in it as a privileged site in which to foreground their own sense of difference. This includes a refusal to identify with the perceived boredom of routinized everyday life. Youth has became an ideological signifier charged with utopian images of the future. On the other hand, it is also commonly feared as a potential threat to existing norms and regulations. Thus is youth 'ambivalently valued' (Grossberg, 1992).

Dick Hebdige (1988) remarks that youth has been constructed within and across the discourses of 'trouble' (youth-as-trouble: youth-in-trouble) and/or 'fun'. For example, through the figures of football hooligans, motorbike boys and street corner gangs, youth has been associated with crime, violence and delinquency. Alternatively, youths have been represented as playful consumers of fashion, style and a range of leisure activities. This is figured by the partygoer, the fashion stylist and, above all, by the consuming 'teenager'. According to Hebdige, the teenager drives a wedge between childhood and adulthood. It represents the commodification of youth, that is, the creation of the youth consumer market forged on the back of the surplus cash that working-class youth has at its disposal.

YOUTH SUBCULTURES

The concept of the 'teenager' has framed much popular discourse on youth. However, cultural studies was drawn instead to the analytic concept of subculture.

✓ *The concept of subculture is a mobile one constitutive of its object of study. It is a classificatory term that attempts to map the social world in an act of representation.*

Thus, subcultures do not exist as authentic objects but have been brought into being by subculture theorists (Redhead, 1990; Thornton, 1995). Consequently, we might ask not so much what a subculture is, but rather how the term has been used. For cultural studies, the culture in subculture has referred to a 'whole way of life' or 'maps of meaning' which make the world intelligible to its members. The 'sub' has connoted notions of distinctiveness and difference from the dominant or mainstream society. Hence, the notion of an authentic subculture depends on its binary opposite, that is, the idea of an inauthentic, mass-produced mainstream or dominant culture.

> The defining attribute of 'subcultures', then, lies with the way the accent is put on the distinction between a particular cultural/social group and the larger culture/society. The emphasis is on variance from a larger collectivity who are invariably, but not unproblematically, positioned as normal, average and dominant. Subcultures, in other words, are condemned to and/or enjoy a consciousness of 'otherness' or difference. (Thornton, 1995: 5)

Subterranean values

As Thornton argues, another significant resonance of the prefix 'sub' is that of subaltern or subterranean. Subcultures have been seen as spaces for deviant cultures to renegotiate their position or to win space for themselves. Hence, in much subcultural theory the question of 'resistance' to the dominant culture comes to the fore. This was initially conceived of within cultural studies through the category of class. However, it was later expanded to include questions of gender, race, sexuality, etc.

The resonances of subterranean values, of deviance and of class, were absorbed into cultural studies through an engagement with the American sociology of 'delinquency'. In particular, the Chicago School explored 'juvenile delinquency' as a collective set of behaviours organized in and through subcultural class values. Young people's publicly troublesome behaviour was understood not as individual pathology, nor as the outcome of an undifferentiated 'youth'. Instead it was conceived of as a collective practical solution to the structurally imposed problems of class. In this context, various scenarios were advanced regarding the character of 'delinquency'; namely that it was:

- a rejection and inversion of the middle-class values of work, success and money that was enacted by working-class young people in order to cope with their perceived deficiencies in those terms (Cohen, 1955);

- the enactment and emphasis on subterranean working-class values, especially those of leisure, which were deviant only from the perspective of middle-class social controllers (Matza and Sykes, 1961; Miller, 1958);

- the attempt by working-class young people to enact the values of success, wealth and power (Merton, 1938) and/or of leisure and hedonism (Cloward and Olin, 1960) via alternative routes. This was required, given that the socially approved paths were blocked off by the structures of class.

Magical solutions

Cultural studies theorists agreed that conceptualizing 'youth' as a homogeneous group was to be rejected in favour of analysing class differences and their articulation with the values of the dominant or mainstream culture. Subcultures were seen as magical or symbolic solutions to the structural problems of class. Or, as Brake was later to express it, 'subcultures arise as attempts to resolve collectively experienced problems resulting from contradictions in the social structure … they generate a form of collective identity from which an individual identity can be achieved outside that ascribed by class, education and occupation' (Brake, 1985: ix).

Brake goes on to consider five functions that subcultures may play for their participants:

1 providing magical solutions to socio-economic structural problems;

2 offering a form of collective identity different from that of school and work;

3 winning space for alternative experiences and scripts of social reality;

4 supplying sets of meaningful leisure activities in contrast to school and work;

5 furnishing solutions to the existential dilemmas of identity.

Consider two contemporary youth cultures.

— Describe the specific activities that meet each of the five functions named above.

Homologies

In this context, the concept of homology was applied by Paul Willis (1978) to describe the 'fit' between:

- **a structural position in the social order;**
- **the social values of subcultural participants;**
- **the cultural symbols and styles by which they expressed themselves.**

The concept of homology connects a located lived culture as a set of 'constitutive relationships' to 'the objects, artefacts, institutions and systematic practices of others which surround it' (Willis, 1978: 189). Homological analysis, which is synchronic, records snapshots of social structures and cultural symbols. It involves two levels of related analysis: the examination of the social group and the examination of their preferred cultural item.

> Essentially it is concerned with how far, in their structure and content, particular items parallel and reflect the structure, style, typical concerns, attitudes and feelings of the social group. Where homologies are found they are actually best understood in terms of structure. It is the continuous play between the group and a particular item which produces specific styles, meanings, contents and forms of consciousness. (Willis, 1978: 191)

Subcultural participants are not held to understand homologies in the way the cultural theorist does. Nevertheless, the creativity and cultural responses of groups are not random but expressive of social contradictions. 'They "understand" in the logic of cultural action something of their own conditions of existence' (ibid.: 170). Sacred objects that lie at the heart of a profane culture provide the coded value-systems of a coherent subculture.

Motorbike boys

Willis holds that 'the ensemble of the bike, noise, rider *on the move*' expressed the motorbike boys' culture, values and identities. 'The solidity, responsiveness, inevitableness, the *strength* of the motorcycle matched the concrete, secure nature of the bikeboys' world' (ibid.: 53). The motorcycle underwrites the boys' commitment to tangible things, to roughness and power, so that 'the surprise of its fierce acceleration, the aggressive thumping of the unbaffled exhaust, matches and symbolizes the masculine assertiveness, the rough camaraderie, the muscularity of language, of their style of social interaction' (ibid.: 53).

According to Willis, subcultures live out important criticisms and insights into contemporary capitalism and its culture. For example, hippies subvert and reorganize industrial capitalism's linear, ordered and disciplinary sense of time. Motorbike boys' 'taming of a fierce technology for a symbolic human purpose' shows us the 'terror of gigantic technologies' of capitalism. It expresses alienation and a profound loss of human scale. Consequently, the creative, expressive and symbolic work of subcultures can be read as forms of resistance.

KEY THINKERS

Paul Willis (1945–)

Paul Willis was a postgraduate student at the Birmingham Centre for Contemporary Cultural Studies and has been associated with the emergence of cultural studies. In particular, he has been one of cultural studies' foremost proponents of ethnographic research into culture as sensual lived experience. On a theoretical level, Willis has been influenced by both Marxism and the ideas of 'culturalism'. His *Learning to Labour* (1977) is an ethnographic study of 'The Lads', and the way a group of working-class boys reproduce their subordinate class position. Later in *Common Culture* (1990) he examined the creative symbolic practices of young people at the moment of consumption.

Reading: Willis, P. (1977) *Learning to Labour*. Farnborough: Saxon House.

Resistance through rituals

As Hebdige (1979) argues, the concept of homology, crossed with that of bricolage, was to play a significant part in CCCS's seminal book on youth cultures, *Resistance through Rituals* (Hall and Jefferson, 1976). Bricolage describes 'the re-ordering and recontextualization of objects to communicate fresh meanings' (Clarke, 1976: 177). That is, objects that already carry sedimented symbolic meanings are resignified in relation to other artefacts in a new context. Clarke points to the construction of the Teddy Boy style through a combination of the otherwise unrelated Edwardian upper-class look, the bootlace tie and brothel-creepers. Likewise, the boots, braces, cropped hair, stayprest shirts and Ska music of Skinheads were a stylistic symbolic bricolage which communicated a 'hardness, masculinity and working classness' (Clarke et al., 1976). This theme is said to resonate with the group's situated social relations in a homological unity.

The double articulation of youth

In this analysis, youth subcultures are explored as stylized forms of resistance to hegemonic culture. Youth is constituted through a 'double articulation' to parent working-class culture and to the dominant culture. The parent working-class culture is said to develop its own distinctive ways of being and modes of meaning in relation and in opposition to hegemonic culture.

> In relation to the hegemony of a ruling class, the working class is, by definition, a subordinate social and cultural formation. ... Of course, at times, hegemony is strong and cohesive, and the subordinate class is weak, vulnerable and exposed. But it cannot, by definition, disappear. It remains as a subordinate structure, often separate and impermeable, yet still contained by the overall rule and domination of the ruling class. The subordinate class has developed its own corporate culture, its own forms of social relationships, its characteristic institutions, values, modes of life. (Clarke et al., 1976: 41)

Working-class resistance is subject to historical ebb and flow. However, it never entirely disappears for it is placed in a position of structural defence and resistance to the hegemonic culture. Youth cultures are said to 'share the same basic problematic' in relation to the dominant culture as the parent working-class culture. Nevertheless, they simultaneously seek to differentiate themselves from it. That is, subcultures involve the expression of difference from and identification with the parent culture.

Youth has a specific generational consciousness and lives the class problematic in sets of institutions and experiences that are distinct from the parent culture. Youth subcultures are marked, it is argued, by the development of particular styles, that is, the active organization of objects with activities and attitudes through the modes of dress, music, ritual and argot. This involves a process of resignification through bricolage. Here commodities, which are also cultural signs, become organized into new codes of meaning. Youth subcultures are said to 'win space' for themselves from the parent and dominant cultures through symbolic resolutions of the class contradictions they face.

Teds, Mods and Skins

It is suggested in *Resistance through Rituals* that Teddy Boy expropriation of upper-class style 'covers the gap' between manual working-class experience and the 'all-dressed-up-and-nowhere-to-go' Saturday night experience. Similarly, the fetishization of style and consumption by Mods 'covers the gap' between the never-ending weekend and the resumption of boring Monday morning, dead-end work. It was further argued that subcultures were a response to the decline of traditional British working-class values and spaces. This loss of space was coterminous with the disappearance of jobs and the redevelopment of established housing communities, marking the dawn of a post-industrial society. *Resistance through Rituals* suggests that certain youth subcultures sought to reinvent the lost community and values of the working class through stylization.

Thus, skinheads were held to be enacting an imaginary recapturing of working-class male 'hardness' through their cropped hair, boots, jeans and braces. Their style stressed the resources of working-class collectivism and territoriality through the coherence and loyalty of 'the gang' of mates. Thus, a stylistic ensemble is a form of symbolic resistance forged on the terrain of hegemonic and counter-hegemonic struggle. However, there is no subcultural solution to low pay, boring routine work and miseducation. Consequently, youth subcultural 'resolutions' remain at the level of symbolic ritual.

Signs of style

One of the problems with the concept of homology as deployed by Clarke et al. (1976) is that it threatens to become a form of reductionism. That is, the analysis appears to explain youthful style in terms of class structures. Here, style is derived from and explained through class. In contrast, Hebdige (1979) interrogates style on the level of the autonomous play of signifiers. In doing so, he asserts the specificity of the semiotic and cultural while retaining the concepts of bricolage and resistance.

For Hebdige, style is a signifying practice that, in the case of spectacular subcultures, is an obviously fabricated display of codes of meaning. This is said to act as a form of semiotic resistance to the dominant order.

✔ *Through the signification of difference, style constitutes a group identity. This is achieved through the transformation of the signs of commodities through the process of bricolage.*

> Subcultures represent 'noise' (as opposed to sound): interference in the orderly sequence which leads from real events and phenomena to their representation in the media. We should therefore not underestimate the signifying power of the spectacular subculture not only as a metaphor for potential anarchy 'out there' but as an actual mechanism for semantic disorder; a kind of temporary blockage in the system of representation. (Hebdige, 1979: 90)

British Punk was Hebdige's favoured exemplar. He argued that Punk was not simply responding to the crisis of British decline manifested in joblessness, poverty and changing moral standards; it *dramatized* it. Punk appropriated the media language of crisis and recycled it in corporeal and visual terms. Punk style was an expression of anger and frustration cast in a language generally available but now resignified as symptomatic of a cluster of contemporary problems.

It was an especially dislocated, self-aware and ironic mode of signification. It

> reproduced the entire sartorial history of post-war working class youth cultures in 'cut up' form, combining elements which had originally belonged to completely different epochs ... punk style contained distorted reflections of all the major postwar subcultures. (Hebdige, 1979: 26)

As bricolage signifying noise and chaos at every level, Punk style was, for Hebdige, ordered and meaningful. Punk was a 'revolting style' which created an ensemble of the perverse and abnormal: safety pins, bin liners, dyed hair, painted faces, graffitied shirts and the iconography of sexual fetishism (leather bondage gear, fishnet stockings, etc.). Through disordered dancing, cacophonous sound, desecrating lyrics, offensive language and anarchic graphics, Punk 'did more than upset the wardrobe. It undermined every relevant discourse' (ibid.: 108).

Consider two contemporary youth cultures.

— Do they have a unique and specific style associated with them?
— If so, describe what this style consists of in terms of (a) objects, (b) signs, (c) meanings.
— If they do not have a specific style associated with them, how are they distinguished from other youth groups?

Critiques of subcultural theory

Stanley Cohen (1980) argued that 'youth' in the hands of cultural studies theorists was always something more than itself. He comments that it is not possible to be a 'mere' delinquent any more, as a result of CCCS's overstretched concept of resistance. Style, he suggests, is overinflated as resistance while resistance is reduced to questions of style. Style is robbed of its elements of fun and flattened down to become only a political question. Similarly, Laing (1985) argued that Punk was primarily a musical genre which Hebdige reduces to a signifying practice in the name of contestable political purposes.

Cohen expresses a fundamental problem with the work of Hall and Jefferson (1976) and Hebdige (1979) (but less so Willis). He suggests that 'The nagging sense here is that these lives, selves and identities do not always coincide with what they are supposed to stand for' (Cohen, 1980: xviii). The problem is one of relating the analysts' structural interpretation to the meanings held by knowing subjects. He suggests that not only are the interpretations offered by Hebdidge and others disputable, but also that young people are made to 'carry too much'. At heart, the criticism is that CCCS failed to engage with members' accounts of subcultural involvement (Widdicombe and Wooffitt, 1995).

The substantive criticism of CCCS subcultural theory from within cultural studies concerned its framing of youth subcultures as mainly white, male and working class. It was argued that CCCS celebrated spectacular youth cultures while handily glossing over strands of racism and sexism.

This is held to be an aspect of:

- **subcultural theorists' over-commitment to the subcultures;**
- **an emphasis on the spectacular at the expense of the routine;**
- **a stress on meaning and style over pleasure and fantasy.**

In the end, whatever we take youth to be, it is certainly divided by class, race and gender as much as age, attitudes or style unites it.

YOUTHFUL DIFFERENCE: CLASS, GENDER, RACE

The self-damnation of the working class

One of the most widely read and enduring texts in cultural studies is Willis's *Learning to Labour*. Using ethnographic methods, Willis seeks to explore the question of 'how working-class kids get working-class jobs [and] why they let themselves' (Willis, 1977: 1). He follows a group of working-class boys, 'the lads', as they resist the discipline and promises of schooling through messing-up, evasion and a refusal to behave according to the expectations of the school authorities. These boys are contrasted with the 'ear'oles' (as nominated by the lads), who, with expectations of long-term gains, work co-operatively with teachers.

The lads' understandings and actions involved what Willis calls 'penetrations' and 'limitations'. In Willis's view, the lads called the bluff on the 'teaching paradigm', which promises personal growth and social advancement in return for compliance and docility. They grasped the unpleasant fact that education is a pathway to 'success' for a limited few that only rarely includes working-class boys like them. Consequently, they see no point in 'playing the game'. Rather, they 'have a laugh' at the expense of teachers and the 'ear'oles'. More effort is put into their pursuit of the pleasures of leisure and sexuality.

However, the lads' perspective is also tragically limited and constitutes a form of 'self-damnation'. In recursive fashion, the structures of class (which are implicated in the lads' consciousness) are reproduced and enacted through the boys' own actions. Their positive valuation of manual labour and the perceived uselessness of mental labour lead to a refusal to engage with school work. The result is that the lads deliver themselves to working-class jobs.

Gendered youth

The great strength of Willis's study is its articulation of 'youth' with and through class. However, this is also a limitation in so far as the working class in question is held to be exclusively white and male. McRobbie and Garber argued that:

> Very little seems to have been written about the role of girls in youth cultural groupings. They are absent from the classic subcultural ethnographic studies, the pop histories, the personal accounts and the journalistic surveys of the field. When girls do appear, it is either in ways which uncritically reinforce the stereotypical image of women … or they are fleeting and marginally presented. (McRobbie and Garber, 1991: 1)

McRobbie and Garber are not dismissing the value of subcultural studies. Indeed, they explicitly retain the stress on class, school, leisure and subculture. However, they are raising the profile of gender issues by suggesting that:

- **Girls have been ignored by male researchers.**
- **Girls have been marginalized and subordinated in male subcultures.**
- **Girls' youth cultures are structurally located in a different place from those of boys.**

McRobbie and Garber criticize Willis's (1978) exploration of motorbike culture as dismissive of girls, who, it is claimed, are evaluated only in terms of their relationships to men. Angela McRobbie also argues that the language of 'the lads' in *Learning to Labour* is 'unambiguously degrading to women' (McRobbie, 1991a: 23). She suggests that Willis fails to confront this and side-steps the way in which working-class male resistance to oppressive class structures is constructed in and through violence to women. 'A fully sexed notion of working-class culture would have to consider such features more centrally' (ibid.: 22). She further argues that Hebdige's exploration of youth culture (see above) involves a 'usage of "style" [which] structurally excludes women' (ibid.: 25).

Another space for girls

McRobbie and Garber argued that if women are marginal to spectacular subcultures, it is because they are marginal to the male world of work. Further, they are discouraged from 'loitering on street corners'. Instead, women are central to the family and to an alternative female youth culture of magazines, pop music, posters and bedrooms. In her early work, McRobbie is still suspicious of the consumer culture from which this 'girl-culture' stems.

For example, the magazine *Jackie* (McRobbie, 1991b) is held to operate through the codes of romance, domesticity, beauty and fashion. This serves to define the world of the personal sphere as the prime domain of girls. *Jackie*, argues McRobbie, presents 'romantic individualism' as the ethos *par excellence* of the teenage girl (ibid.: 131). In her account of working-class girls, McRobbie (1991c) explores the way in which this culture of femininity is used by girls to create their own space while at the same time securing them for boyfriends, marriage, the family and children.

Later, in conjunction with the general shift in cultural studies from a concern with text to a focus on consumption, McRobbie (1991d) critiques her own reliance on the analysis of documents. She suggests that girls are more active and creative in relation to girls' magazines and other forms of consumer culture than she had given them credit for. She points to the productive, validating and inventive bricolage of fashion style that women originate and to the dynamic character of shopping as an enabling activity (McRobbie, 1989).

McRobbie argues that the active and changing character of femininity is marked by the transformation of girls' magazines in response to the 'sophisticated and discerning young consumer' (McRobbie, 1991d). This involved a shift of attention from romance to pop, fashion and more a self-confident sexuality. McRobbie underscores the productive role of fantasy in marking the transition from pre-pubertal femininity to adolescent femininity. This includes its capacity to leave gaps and spaces open for individual interjection. She sees youth magazines marketed for girls as a space for the politics of feminism and exhorts students to look for jobs within them. No doubt in doing so, it would help to be white, like the assumed audience for most British girls' magazines of the time.

KEY THINKERS

Angela McRobbie (1951–)

Another former member of the Centre for Contemporary Cultural Studies (CCCS), Angela McRobbie is currently Professor of Communications at Goldsmiths College, University of London. Her research work on the relationship between teenage girls and magazines in the 1970s involved ideological textual analysis. She later produced work that put a greater stress on their active meaning making and consuming practices of girls. More recently she has explored many other areas of contemporary culture, including fashion, modern art and pop music.

Reading: McRobbie, A. (1991) *Feminism and Youth Culture*. London: Macmillan.

PUNK GIRL

© Photographer: Ralph Daniels | Agency: Dreamstime.com

- *How might we describe this 'punk girl' as enacting resistance through ritual?*
- *What place does the image give to girls in the subcultural world?*
- *Does the image conform to McRobbie's analysis of girls in subcultures?*

Racialized youth

✓ *'We can watch, played out on the loaded surfaces of British working-class youth cultures, a phantom history of race relations since the war' (Hebdige, 1979: 45).*

That is, British youth cultures can be read as 'a succession of differential responses to the black immigrant presence in Britain' (ibid.: 29).

For example:

- Teddy Boys juxtaposed black rhythm and blues with aristocratic Edwardian style while being implicated in attacks on West Indians.

- Mods sought to emulate the 'cool' style of West Indians as they adopted soul music.

- Skinheads appropriated dress items, argot and music from West Indians while gaining a reputation for racism.

- Punk found resonances in black youths' rejection of Britishness and authority. Reggae was embraced by Punk at the same time as it produced musical forms that were black music's antithesis.

Hebdige sees in Reggae, sound systems and the signs of Rastafarianism resources for resistance to white culture and racial subordination. Reggae is said to encompass the transgressive features of black speech and African rhythms. As such, it is understood as a living record of black–white relations from slavery through to the present. Rastafarianism involves a 'profound subversion of the white man's religion' through appropriation and reversal of the Bible. Together, Reggae and Rasta 'proclaimed unequivocally the alienation felt by many young black Britons' (ibid.: 36).

There are numerous aspects of black culture that have been articulated with youth culture. However, Mercer's (1994) discussion of black hair as 'style politics' is of particular interest for its resonances with Hebdige's (1979) exploration of the concept of style.

The artifice of black hair

Hair, Mercer remarks, is never a straightforward fact of nature but a symbolic artifice of culture. Hair is cut, groomed and shaped. As such it involves declarations about the self and society. In particular, hair is a key ethnic signifier second only to skin. Through hair, racist discourses have cast 'black' on the side of nature, wildness and ugliness. By contrast, 'white' has been positioned on the side of culture, civilization and beauty. Strategies for revalorizing the ethnic signifier of black hair have taken two fundamental forms, argues Mercer: one emphasizing *natural* looks and the other *artifice*.

The Afro and Dreadlock styles asserted themselves as natural against the claim that black hair can only be beautiful if cultivated through straightening and other techniques. As such, these hairstyles:

- valorized the materiality of the texture of black hair;
- reconstructed a symbolic link with Africa;
- resonated with anti-colonial, postcolonial and anti-racist struggles.

However, it is a romanticized and imaginary Africa that the Afro brings into play. Mercer argues that there was nothing particularly African about the Afro. Indeed, he suggests that the Afro was dependent on European conceptions of Africa and nature. Consequently, the tactical reversal involved in the claim that black is naturally beautiful depends on the same association of Africa with nature as do racist and imperial discourses. Further, once commodified as a style, the Afro was neutralized as a signifier of opposition.

Mercer does not condemn straightened black hairstyles as imitative of white culture. Rather, he sees them as indicative of black innovation. Diasporian black hair involves the creolizing and radical transformation of western forms. Black hairstyles within the west refract elements from white and black cultures through processes of exchange, appropriation, imitation and incorporation. Black style is a manifestation of shared experience and an encoded refusal of passivity. This is achieved by way of active inflection and recoding of hegemonic conventions.

The Conk, for example, did not copy anything. While suggesting resemblance with white people's hair, it nevertheless emphasized difference through artifice. For Mercer, black style encoded a set of subversive messages to those in the cultural know. The diversity of black hairstyles testifies to an inventive, improvisational aesthetic and to the value of cultural plurality.

> Consider Rap and Hip-Hop as forms of contemporary youth culture.
>
> — Describe the way in which gender and race are manifested in the specific activities associated with them.

SPACE: A GLOBAL YOUTH CULTURE?

Youth is a cultural category differentially articulated with (constructed in relation to) class, gender and race. In addition, youth is understood as a spatial matter, that is, youth may be produced differently in divergent spaces and places. Youth is enacted in clubs, pubs, schools and parks. This gives rise to a range of meanings and behaviours. The street and the shopping mall have become significantly charged and contested zones involving young people. Indeed, these are amongst the few quasi-autonomous spaces that young people can create for themselves.

However, they are also areas in which adults may contest a youthful presence as being a threat to order. At home, questions of privacy and personal boundaries manifested through issues of noise, door locks, tidiness and the hour of comings and goings are the stuff of generational family politics. There has also been a growing interest in globalization and the apparently transnational space of 'youth culture'.

For some critics the emergence of brands like Nike, Levi, PlayStation, Coca-Cola and MTV, alongside international pop stars, represents the commodification and subsequent homogenization of youth culture. For others, global cultural developments, including those connected to youth, are more chaotic and syncretic in character, representing creative hybrid cultures (Chapters 5 and 8).

Rapping and raving around the globe

Rap, argues Gilroy, is

> a hybrid form rooted in the syncretic social relations of the South Bronx where Jamaican sound-system culture, transplanted during the 1970s, put down new roots and, in conjunction with specific technological innovations, set in train a process that was to transform black America's sense of itself and a large portion of the popular music industry as well. (Gilroy, 1987: 144)

In addition, Rap can trace its routes along pathways that include the influence of West African music and the impact of slavery. As American, Jamaican, West African, South African, British, Indian, German and Icelandic (amongst others), Rap cannot be said to have any obvious point of origin or authenticity. Rap is always already a cultural hybridization marked by rhizomorphic cultural flows.

In Britain, Asian youths have produced their own hybrid forms of Ragga–Banghra–Reggae–Rap cross-overs. Indeed, African-American and black British fashion, music and dance styles are appropriated by Asian youths into their lifestyles (Gillespie, 1995). For Mercer, these 'emerging cultures of hybridity, forged among the overlapping African, Asian and Caribbean diaspora' (Mercer, 1994: 3), are a challenge to white western authority. They are also ways of living with and in 'conditions of crisis and transition'.

✓ *Communications technologies have constructed commodities, meanings and identifications of youth culture that cut across the boundaries of races or nation-states: global Rap, global Rave and global Salsa.*

Champion (1997) recounts the expansion of Rave culture in the unlikely setting of the conservative and rock-dominated American Midwest. Raving, which she describes as America's new outlaw culture, adapts to local environments. This form of music had travelled to Wisconsin via Chicago, Detroit, Ibiza, London, Manchester and the UK dance scene. As Champion explains 'Dance culture is a virus which mutates as it spreads, and in the Midwest they have taken rave and made it their own' (ibid.: 114). In a Wisconsin context, cars take on a prominent role (absent in the British scene) in a pastiche of *American Graffiti*. Young people dance the night away not so much in warehouses (Britain) or bunkers (Germany) but on ski slopes and in cowsheds.

Syncretic global youth

Doreen Massey highlights some of the issues raised by the emergence of a global youth culture. She recounts how she had been interviewing a group of Mayan women in the Yucatán (Mexico). She then turned away from this picture of apparently authentic and indigenous culture to be confronted by a dozen young people playing computer games and listening to western music. 'Electronic noises, American slang and bits of Western music floated off into the night-time jungle' (Massey, 1998: 121).

Massey argues that while this youth culture of Yucatán Maya is not a closed 'local' culture, it is not an undifferentiatedly global (or American) one either. It is a product of interaction in which the terms 'local' and 'global' are themselves in dispute. In each particular youth culture the mix of the global and the local will be different. Indeed, what is or is not a global status symbol for youth will vary by location.

What is at stake is not just an understanding of youth but the place of culture. Culture is less a matter of locations with roots than of hybrid and creolized cultural routes in global space. Youth cultures are not pure, authentic and locally bounded; rather, they are syncretic and hybridized products of interactions across space. They are 'constellations of temporary coherence (and amongst such constellations we can identify local cultures) set within a social space which is the product of relations and interconnections from the very local to the intercontinental' (ibid.: 125).

Global interconnections are always imbued with power and the terms of cultural mixing are uneven. It is American popular culture that is valued by Mayan youth as the symbol of international status. Equally, the cultural traffic is not all one-way. The Afro-Caribbean-originated 'Red, Green and Gold' of Rastafarianism became a diasporian sign of resistance and solidarity. Some First World young people have been politically engaged in issues of global inequity (e.g. Live Aid). International youth culture puts a particular twist on Clifford's (1992) notion of 'travelling cultures'. Here culture is conceptualized in terms of peoples and cultures that travel and places/cultures as sites of criss-crossing travellers. For example, 'checking out the planet' (Desforges, 1998) in a search for authenticity is a growing strand of youth culture. Here, travel is framed as the experience of a series of differences that form the basis of a narrative of self-development. These tales of adventure then accrue cultural capital upon the return home. However, no place is an untouched authentic site for the traveller to discover. All places are always already marked out and signed as to their significance (Culler, 1981). Travelling is a branch of tourism (not in itself an inauthentic practice) and not a different category.

Steve Redhead (1990) extends the challenge to the authenticity of youth culture. He suggests that any clear-cut distinction between the media, the culture industries and an oppositional and authentic youth subculture is problematic. This is so because the latter is 'heavily influenced and shaped by the global leisure industry, of which pop is now structurally so much an integral part' (Redhead, 1990: 54). The 'death of youth culture' is marked by the end of the relevance of the concept of an authentic subculture that played such a prominent part in cultural studies' understanding of youth.

SHINJUKU GIRLS

© Photographer: Freya Hadley

- *This is an image of subcultural style in Shinjuku, Tokyo. Can this be described as resistance through ritual?*
- *What do these girls have in common with 'Punk girl' on p. 420?*
- *How are they different?*
- *Is there a global youth culture?*

AFTER SUBCULTURES

Sarah Thornton (1995) articulates a set of criticisms of subcultural theory. She argues the following:

- **Youth cultural difference is not necessarily resistance.**
- **Differences are classifications of power and distinctions of taste.**

- Subcultural theory relies on unsustainable binaries, namely mainstream–subculture, resistance–submission, dominant–subordinate.
- Youth cultures are not formed outside and opposed to the media.
- Youth cultures are formed within and through the media.
- Youth cultures are not unified but marked by internal differences.
- Youth cultures mark not the politicization of youth but aestheticization of politics.

These criticisms are not simply indicators of the blind-spots of subcultural theory. Rather, they are also markers of the new analytic attitude towards the leisure activities of young people (with dance cultures as the most common object of enquiry). Redhead suggests that the concept of subculture is 'no longer appropriate – if, indeed, it ever was – to conceptual apparatuses' needed to explain pop music culture's developments since the publication of Hebdige's major book in 1979' (Redhead, 1997a: x). The 'end of subcultures' is announced not because distinctive cultures of youth do not occur. Instead it indicates that:

1 Youth cultures are increasingly fragmented.

2 The idea of a grass-roots, media-free authentic subculture cannot be sustained.

Media spotlights

The deviancy theory from which CCCS's subcultural work drew inspiration accords the mass media a role of considerable significance. The concepts of 'moral panics' and 'deviant amplification' (Cohen, 1972; Young, 1971) attribute to media coverage a central role in the creation and sustaining of youth subcultural deviancy. The media are said to latch on to a particular group of young people and label their behaviour as deviant, troublesome and likely to reoccur. That is, youth are labelled as contemporary 'folk devils'. The public response is a moral panic that seeks to track down and punish deviant youth culture. Young people respond with increased deviancy, so that a cycle of labelling, amplification and deviancy is set in motion.

Many of these themes are echoed in the work of CCCS subcultural theorists. Thus Mods, Punks and Skins are seen to be the media 'folk devils' of the day. In this model it is assumed that the media work on previously existing subcultural activities. These youth cultures are held to exist in authentic distinct and pristine form prior to media intervention. That is, subculture theory perceived youth culture to be 'outside' of the media and opposed to it. In contrast, contemporary theorists suggest that youth cultures are always 'inside' the media. They are dependent on the media even as they wish to deny it.

Cultural studies and sociologies of 'moral panic' tend to position youth cultures as innocent victims of negative stigmatization. But mass media 'misunderstanding' is often an objective of certain sub-cultural industries, rather than an accident of youth's cultural pursuits. 'Moral panic' can therefore be seen as a form of hype orchestrated by culture industries that target the youth market. (Thornton, 1995: 136)

Media devils and subcultural hero(in)es

Thornton argues that the idea of an authentic culture formed outside of the media is a resilient but misguided one. This is because 'the distinctions of youth subcultures are, in many cases, phenomena of the media' (ibid.: 116).

✓ *Media are integral to the formation of subcultures and to young people's formulations of their own activities.*

For example, the notion of the 'underground' is defined against the mass media and delights in 'negative' media coverage. There is nothing more likely to kill the pleasures of subculture membership than mass media approval. Indeed, radio or TV bans and/or ironic mocking performances are the highlights of subcultural lifestyles. A devil in the media will be a hero(ine) in the subculture. Indeed, Punk and House were marketed by subcultural entrepreneurs and record companies in and through moral panics or distinctions of 'hipness' that they helped to foster (Thornton, 1995).

It is not that the media, and the tabloid press in particular, do not engage in the production of moral panics. Headlines like 'Acid House Horror', 'Ban This Killer Music' and 'Drug-Crazed Acid House Fans' (Redhead, 1997b) attest that they do. Such coverage frames and disseminates subcultures as events worthy of attention. Subsequently, record companies exploit this notoriety for marketing purposes. However, subculture studies, argues Thornton, have tended to suggest that youth subcultures are subversive until the moment they are represented by the media. In contrast, she argues that in the perpetual search for significance, subcultures 'become politically relevant only when framed as such. Derogatory media coverage is not the verdict but the essence of their resistance' (Thornton, 1995: 137).

Postmodernism: the end of authenticity

Youth cultures are thoroughly embroiled in surveillance, the mass media and the cultural industries. Consequently, claims to authenticity by members and subculture theorists look dubious. This understanding presents a problem for a concept of style that relied on originality, purity and authenticity as the basis of its claim to be 'resistance'.

Previous theorists of postwar popular music, youth culture and deviance (whether Cultural Studies or Radical, or New Deviancy, or Deviancy Theory traditions) have tended to look beneath or behind the surfaces of the shimmering mediascape in order to discover the 'real', authentic subculture, apparently always distorted by the manufactured press and television image, which in turn becomes 'real' as more and more participants act out the media stereotypes. This 'depth model' is no longer appropriate – if it ever was – for analysing the surfaces of the (post)modern world, a culture characterized by shallowness, flatness and hyperreality. (Redhead, 1993: 5)

Style, it is now argued, involves bricolage without reference to the meanings of originals. Style has no underlying message or ironic transformation. It is the look and only the look. Merely another mode of fashion. Pastiche rather than parody (Muggleton, 1997). For Jameson (1984), this cannibalization of styles from the past and present represents a loss of artistic depth in favour of a superficial pastiche. This Baudrillardian version of postmodernism suggests that 'Contemporary popular culture is merely a seductive sign-play that has arrived at the final referent: the black hole of meaninglessness' (Chambers, 1987: 5). However, the birth of youth fashion and style in the media does not reduce style to meaninglessness. The end of authenticity is not the death of meaning. Postmodern bricolage involves the creative recombination of existing items to forge new meanings. Here, 'post-subculturalists' can 'revel in the availability of subcultural choice' (Muggleton, 1997: 198).

Postmodern bricoleurs

Chambers (1987, 1990) and Hebdige (1988) discuss ways in which commodities form the basis of multiple identity construction. They emphasize the meaning-oriented activity of consumers, who act as bricoleurs selecting and arranging elements of material commodities and meaningful signs.

… postmodernism, whatever form its own intellectualizing might take, has been fundamentally anticipated in the metropolitan cultures of the last twenty years: among the electronic signifiers of cinema, television and video, in recording studios and record players, in fashion and youth styles, in all those sounds, images and diverse histories that are daily mixed, recycled and 'scratched' together on that giant screen which is the contemporary city. (Chambers, 1987: 7)

This creativity takes place 'inside the whale' of postmodern consumer capitalism. Here the binary divisions of inside–outside and authentic–manufactured collapse. Consequently:

- **Style is on the surface.**
- **Culture is an industry.**
- **Subcultures are mainstream.**
- **High culture is a subculture.**
- **The avant-garde is commercial pop art.**
- **Fashion is retro.**

Discuss each of the statements on page 428 in a group.

— Do you agree that the statement has validity?
— Can you give a concrete example of each one?
— What do you understand by the concept of 'authenticity'?
— In what way does each of the statements undermine the concept of authenticity?

Thus postmodern culture is marked by:

- 'ironic knowingness' (Caughie, 1990);

- deconstruction of authenticity and fixity (Kaplan, 1987);

- the creative juxtaposing of second-hand clothes styles (McRobbie, 1989); and/or

- radicalized strategies of rearticulation (Collins, 1992).

Claims to authenticity

The deconstruction of authenticity at the level of theory does not prevent participants in youth subcultures from laying claim to it. Indeed, empirical research suggests that claims to authenticity are at the heart of contemporary youth subcultures and club cultures. In Widdicombe and Wooffitt's (1995) interviews with a range of subcultural 'members', participation is explained by reference to the emergence and maintenance of a 'true' inner self. Members' own 'deepness' and 'authenticity' is constructed in relation to the claimed inauthenticity and shallowness of others. Authenticity, then, is an accumulated social achievement.

Distinctions of taste

Rock has always made declarations of artistic authenticity on the basis of live performance. In doing so it has disparaged dance music and disco in particular. By contrast, dance music, through a long process of enculturalization, has authenticated the record and the DJ over live performance (Thornton, 1995). Subsequently, club cultures are marked by a whole series of internal authenticity claims and distinctions.

Club cultures are *taste cultures* … club cultures embrace their own hierarchies of what is authentic and legitimate popular culture … club cultures are riddled with cultural hierarchies … which can be briefly designated as: the authentic versus the phoney, the 'hip' versus the 'mainstream', and the 'underground' versus 'the media'. (Thornton, 1995: 3–4)

Thornton follows Bourdieu (1984) in claiming that distinctions are never simply statements of equal difference. Rather, they entail claims to authority, authenticity and the presumed inferiority of others. This argument is based on the concept of *cultural capital*, that is, the accumulated knowledge that confers power and status. For example, education and/or the ability to talk knowledgeably about high culture has traditionally been a form of upper-middle-class cultural capital. Cultural capital is distinguished from *economic capital* (wealth) and *social capital* (whom you know). In the context of club cultures, Thornton suggests that it makes sense to talk of *subcultural capital* to designate the way that clothes, records, haircuts, dance styles and knowledges confer status and power on young people.

Subcultural capital involves distinctions between 'us' (alternative, cool, independent, authentic, minority) and 'them' (mainstream, straight, commercial, false, majority). It also involves distinctions within club culture: knowing the latest releases and dances, wearing the most fashionable clothes, seeing the coolest DJs, attending the right clubs. So fast-moving is contemporary club culture as it undergoes metamorphosis after metamorphosis that maintaining subcultural capital is a highly skilled task.

✓ *Consumption is a creative and productive process.*

CREATIVE CONSUMPTION

Critics invariably take different views on the validity and radicalness of youth cultural activities. Thus one review of the German dance scene argues that 'In the equal, loving space of the rave, young people are creating a potential blueprint for the whole of society to follow' (Richard and Kruger, 1998: 173). These authors consider the Techno scene to be offering a utopian critique of contemporary society. However, Reynolds (1997) considers that the Rave dream of transracial, cross-class unity has fallen foul of Rave music's fixation with its own sensations.

Clearly these authors are opposed in their assessments of Rave culture. More significantly, they do not supply any empirical evidence with which to substantiate their arguments. By contrast, during the 1980s and 1990s a critical mass of consumption studies built up which argued that textual analysis (in its very broadest sense) could not tell us which meanings are brought into play by actual readers/audiences/consumers.

It was argued that audiences are active creators of meaning, bringing previously acquired cultural competencies to bear on cultural texts. Audiences are not thought to be cultural dopes but are active producers of meaning from within their own cultural contexts. Fiske (1987), in particular, argued that popular culture is constituted not by texts but by the meanings that people produce with them. Certainly, political economy and textual analysis form part of any investigation of the power of the culture industries. However, they do not determine cultural significance or invalidate the power active audiences have as producers of meaning.

Common culture

One of the more wide-ranging studies of the consuming practices of young people is Paul Willis's (1990) *Common Culture*. Willis argues that young people have an active, creative and symbolically productive relation to the commodities that are constitutive of youth culture. Meaning, he suggests, is not inherent in the commodity but is produced through actual usage. This he calls 'grounded aesthetics':

> ... the specifically creative and dynamic moments of a whole process of cultural life, of cultural birth and rebirth. ... This is a making specific of the ways in which the received natural and social world is made human to them and made, to however small a degree (even if finally symbolic), controllable by them. (Willis, 1990: 22)

For Willis, contemporary culture is not meaningless or superficial surface. Rather, it involves the active creation of meaning by all people as cultural producers. 'The symbolic creativity of the young is based in their everyday informal life and infuses with meaning the entirety of the world as they see it' (ibid.: 98). Through a series of interviews with young people it is proposed that they:

- **have an active and creative relation to television;**
- **are sophisticated and inventive viewers of advertising;**
- **assert their personal competencies through dancing and the customization of fashion;**
- **transform and recode the meanings of everyday objects.**

Ironically, it is capitalism and the expansion of consumerism that have provided the increased supply of symbolic resources for young people's creative work. Capitalism (in the world of work) may be that from which escape is sought. However, it also provides the means and medium (in the domain of consumption) by which to do so. Consumerism is an active not a passive process (Willis, 1990).

In response, McGuigan (1992) argued that Willis represents an uncritical embracing of the pleasures of consumer sovereignty in the marketplace. According to McGuigan, Willis has lost his conviction that there are grounds for criticizing the current order or for providing alternative visions. Others (Silverstone, 1994) have suggested that audiences/consumers are *always* active but that this does not guarantee a challenge to the hegemonic order.

Whether activity produces a challenge or acquiescence is ultimately a case-by-case empirical question. The evidence that young consumers are active creators of meaning is overwhelming, nevertheless, agency and activity do not have to imply resistance. They can also signify active appropriation of hegemonic values. Activity may be *required* to take up ideology. Indeed, it is unclear what 'resistance' means in a postmodern, post-authentic world.

RESISTANCE REVISITED

Stuart Hall writes that:

> [t]here are many different kinds of metaphors in which our thinking about cultural change takes place. These metaphors themselves change. Those which grip our imagination, and, for a time, govern our thinking about scenarios and possibilities of cultural transformation, give way to new metaphors, which make us think about these difficult questions in new terms. (Hall, 1996e: 287)

Metaphors of change are tools rather than analytic categories of truth and falsity. Hall (1996e) suggests that metaphors of change do two things:

1 They allow us to imagine what it would be like if the prevailing cultural hierarchies were transformed.

2 They help us to 'think' the relationship between the social and the symbolic.

✓ *The question of 'resistance' is a matter of utility and value rather than truth or falsity.*

Resistance is conjunctural

Hall (1996e) argues that the strength of *Resistance through Rituals* lay in its conception of resistance as relational and conjunctural. That is, resistance is not thought of as a singular and universal act that defines itself for all time. Rather, resistance is constituted by repertoires whose meanings are specific to particular times, places and social relationships. If we are to consider youth culture as 'resistance', we need to ask some basic questions:

- **What or who is youth culture resisting?**
- **Under what circumstances is resistance taking place?**
- **In what form is resistance manifested?**
- **Where is resistance sited?**

— Give answers to the above questions with reference to (a) Rap (b) Heavy Metal (c) dance culture (d) Hippie culture.

Resistance as defence

For Bennett, 'Resistance is an essentially defensive relationship to cultural power that is adapted by subordinate social forces in circumstances where the forms of cultural power in question arise from a source that is clearly experienced as external and other' (Bennett, 1998: 171). That is, resistance issues from relationships of power and subordination where a dominating culture is seeking to impose itself on subordinate cultures from without. Consequently, resources of resistance are to be located in some measure outside of the dominating culture. Bennett argues that the merit of *Resistance through Rituals* was that it saw spectacular youth cultures as essentially defensive reactions to a new aggressive phase of capitalist expansion. Resistance was rooted in the conditions of working-class culture, which stands as a distinct space opposed to ruling-class culture.

For Bennett, this is a productive characterization of resistance because it is clear about the who, where and when of resistance. This involves a bipolar construction of the field of power: the ruling class and the working class; hegemony and subordination. This is contrasted to those formulations of resistance which, Bennett argues, are unspecific and romantic about its character, seeing virtually any response to power as resistance (his target is de Certeau, see below).

Inside the whale

However, we might see the bipolarity of Bennett's reading of resistance as less a strength than a problem. Capitalism is the stated target for resistance yet our discussion of youth culture has suggested that none of young people's cultural texts, symbols and artefacts function outside of capitalism. As bricoleurs of commodities, young people are immersed in, not separated from, consumer capitalism and the mass media. If resistance is taking place, it is happening inside the whale. Youth cultures are not authentic alternative spaces of resistance but places of *negotiation*. Here the positions of resistance are strategic and themselves enabled by the structures of power (Best, 1997).

For Hall, the strength of *Resistance through Rituals* lay in its conception of resistance 'as challenges to and negotiations of the dominant order which could not be assimilated to the traditional categories of revolutionary class struggle' (Hall, 1996e: 294). Hall is making the case that resistance is not best understood as a simple reversal of the order of high and low, of power and its absence. Contemporary cultural theory, Hall argues, has given up on the idea of pure transcendence.

Instead, ambivalence and ambiguity occupy the space of resistance. This process is exemplified by the transgressive character of the 'carnivalesque'. The carnivalesque is a temporary reversal of the order of power enacted through rituals, games, mockeries and profanities. By these means the polite is overthrown by the vulgar and the king usurped by the fool. However, the power of the 'carnivalesque' for Hall lies not in a simple reversal of distinctions. Rather, it resides in the invasion of the high by the low that creates 'grotesque' hybrid forms. Here the challenge is not simply to the high by the low but to the very act of cultural classification by power.

This is a challenge Hall also attributes to the concept of the 'popular', which transgresses the boundaries of cultural power (for it is of value though classified as low). In doing so, it is said to expose the arbitrary character of cultural classification. In this way, aspects of youth culture could be seen as transgressive popular culture and/or carnivalesque subversions of the order of power.

Hiding in the light

Hebdige (1988) applies Foucauldian ideas regarding the micro-relations of power to the construction of youth as trouble and fun. In particular, he argues that the nineteenth-century impulse to control, penetrate and supervise has been carried over into the production of youth. Youth subcultures respond to surveillance by making a 'spectacle' of themselves for the admiring glances of strangers (and the media in particular). Hebdige goes on to offer three propositions regarding youth cultures:

1 **Youth is only present when its presence is regarded as a problem. When young people go 'out of bounds', they get noticed and become visible. This allows them to 'play with the only power at their disposal – the power to discomfort, to pose … a threat'.**

2 **New forms of power produce new forms of powerlessness and new types of resistance. Consequently, the politics of youth and the micro-politics of pleasure cannot be collapsed into old/existing organized political activity.**

3 **The politics of youth culture is a politics of gesture, symbol and metaphor that deals in the currency of signs. As such, it is ambiguous and there can be no authoritative interpretation of it for it is underneath authorized discourses. Thus,**

Subculture forms at the interface between surveillance and the evasion of surveillance. It translates the fact of being under scrutiny to the pleasure of being watched, and the elaboration of surfaces which takes place within it reveals a darker will to opacity, a drive against classification and control, a desire to exceed. (Hebdige, 1988: 54)

Hebdige argues that subculture is neither an affirmation nor a refusal. It is a declaration of independence and of alien intent. It is at one and the same time an insubordination of and conformation to powerlessness. It is a play for attention and a refusal to be read transparently.

GRAFFITI ARTIST

© Photographer: David Davis | Agency: Dreamstime.com

- *Does 'graffiti' represent 'art' or 'vandalism'?*
- *In what way is this women 'hiding in the light'?*

Tactics and strategies

An alternative account of resistance with considerable currency within cultural studies is that of Michel de Certeau (1984). This work has been popularized through the writing of Fiske (1987, 1989a, 1989b, 1989c). De Certeau's work has the merits of conceptualizing the resistive practices of everyday life as always already in the space of power. For de Certeau, as with Foucault (1980), there are no 'margins' outside of power from which to lay an assault on it or from which to claim authenticity. Rather, the poetic and illegible practices of the popular are forms of resistance that make creative and adaptive play inside power.

De Certeau makes the distinction between the strategies of power and the tactics of resistance. A *strategy* is the means by which power marks out a space for itself distinct from its environs and through which it can operate as a subject of will. Thus, the power of an enterprise involves the creation of its own space and the means by which to act separately from its competitors, adversaries, clients, etc. By contrast:

> a *tactic* is a calculated action determined by the absence of a proper locus. No delimitation of an exteriority, then, provides it with the condition necessary for autonomy. The space of a tactic is the space of the other. Thus it must play on and within a terrain imposed on it and organized by the law of a foreign power. … It does not, therefore, have the options of planning a general strategy and viewing the adversary as a whole within a distinct visible, and objectifiable, space. It operates in isolated actions, blow by blow. It takes advantages of opportunities and depends on them, being without any base where it could stockpile its winnings, build up its own position, and plan raids. (De Certeau, 1984: 36–7)

Tactics are the plays of the poacher, the ruses and deceptions of everyday life using the resources of 'the other' which seek to make space habitable. These include the devious productions of consumption, which 'insinuates itself everywhere, silently and almost invisibly, because it does not manifest itself through its own products, but rather through its ways of using the products imposed by a dominant economic order' (ibid.: xii–xiii). For example, youth cultures take the commodities of record companies, clothes manufacturers and magazines and, in the spaces of clubs, pubs and streets, make them their own. That is, young people invest these products with their own meanings, thereby negotiating their own place in the world.

Banality in cultural studies

De Certeau's conception of resistance has the merit of displacing the idea of a monolithic and impenetrable culture industry that imposes its meanings on a passive set of consumers. This is a position also advanced in the work of Chambers, Willis and Fiske.

However, for its critics, this line of argument runs the risk of turning almost every piece of pop culture and youth style into resistance. According to Morris (1996), it leads to a 'banality in cultural studies' by which an endless series of writers find resistance in popular culture at every turn. She parodies this as a formulation in which 'people in modern mediatized societies are complex and contradictory, mass cultural texts are complex and contradictory, therefore people using them produce complex and contradictory culture' (Morris, 1996: 161).

For Morris, what is missing is a balance sheet of gains and losses, of hope and despair. What is required, she suggests, is a critical edge which can articulate the notion that 'they always fuck us over' while constructing a space in which we can posit the utopian. Likewise for Bennett (1998), resistance in the work of Fiske and de Certeau does not distinguish sufficiently between types of resistance under sociologically and historically specific circumstances. It is not sufficiently conjunctural.

Resistance: the normative stance of cultural critics

At this stage we might usefully ask two questions of the concept of resistance:

1 **Is resistance constituted by any acts contrary to power, or must they be in the service of particular goals or *values?* Is it enough to make subcultural noises, or must those noises, in order to constitute resistance, be in pursuit of values (e.g. of equality or diversity)?**

2 **Must resistance be a matter of consciousness and intentionality? Can resistance be identified by critics and analysts even though actions might not be conceived of in this way by subcultural participants?**

Resistance could be understood in terms of one force meeting another where both are forces and resistances. That is, the idea of resistance could simply be descriptive of the balance of forces (a use sometimes encountered in Foucault). We may have no interest in the outcome of resistive forces. However, in the context of cultural studies, to describe an act as resistance is a matter not of truth or falsity but of utility and value. Cultural studies has a commitment to a cultural politics of insubordination and the politics of difference. Consequently, resistance is *a normative* concept with 'success' measured strategically against normative criteria. That is, resistance has to be in pursuit of named values.

For example, Skinheads were conceived as resisting middle-class power in the name of the values of working-class solidarity or masculinity. Punks were resisting the normal semantic order in the name of difference and diversity. Of course, it is another matter to claim success for resistance: what did Punks achieve against what criteria? The merit of the values that are defined as resistance is also a matter of contention. While cultural studies critics might value 'working class', they are unlikely to value the 'masculinity' of Skinheads. Thus, resistance is doubly a matter of value: the identification of the values which resistance upholds, and our identification with those values.

✓ *Resistance is not a quality of an act but a category of judgement about acts.*

Consequently, it is possible and legitimate for critics to identify resistance when participants do not understand it in this way. Resistance is a distinction of value which classifies the classifier (to paraphrase Bourdieu, 1984). It is a judgement that reveals the values of the cultural studies critic just as youth culture is an analytic category of adults.

DECONSTRUCT THIS: MAINSTREAM CULTURE VS. SUBCULTURE

- *What makes a cultural activity mainstream?*
- *What makes an activity subcultural?*
- *How do each of the key terms depend on each other?*

SUMMARY

Although less widely discussed in cultural studies than the eternal triumvirate of class, gender and race, age is a significant marker of social classification and stratification. The descriptors child, youth, adolescence, adult, elderly, pensioner, etc., are identity categories that carry connotations regarding capabilities and responsibilities. Youth is a cultural classification of an elastic age band that has been ambiguously coded by adults to indicate 'trouble' and 'fun'. Youth carries adult hopes for the future but also incites fear and concern.

The early work of British cultural studies concerned itself with the idea of spectacular youth subcultures. These were understood to be the manifestation of symbolic resistance to the class hegemonic order. Subcultures as distinct domains of subterranean values were argued to offer magical solutions to the structural problems of class. Three main analytic tools were foregrounded:

1 the concept of *homology*, by which subcultural symbolic objects were held to be expressions of the underlying concerns and structural positions of youth groups;
2 the concept of *bricolage*, by which previously unconnected symbols are juxtaposed to create new meanings;
3 the concept of *style*, a bricolage of symbols constituting a coherent and meaningful expression of subcultural values.

Contemporary commentators on the youth scene, particularly those focused on dance culture, now question the usefulness of the concept of subculture. They argue that youth culture is increasingly fragmented and 'incoherent', with the notion of an authentic subculture no longer viable. It is not that distinct clusterings of fashion, dance, music and other manifestations of youth cultural style cannot be found; rather, it is that they are 'inside' not 'outside' of mass-mediated consumer capitalism. They are best understood as marked by internal distinctions of taste (and claims to authenticity) rather than as coherent expressions of resistance or opposition.

This argument does not lead youth into the black hole of insignificance. Rather, the creative usage of commodities to achieve a postmodern 'cut 'n' mix' by active, productive consumers represents a set of meaningful activities. Indeed, the production of hybrid youth cultures is an increasingly global phenomenon that challenges any conception that culture has a secure place in the world. Whether this can be regarded as 'resistance' is a moot point. It depends on who is said to be resisting what by whom under particular circumstances. Resistance is relational, conjunctural and normative.

14 Cultural Politics and Cultural Policy

KEY CONCEPTS

Citizenship	*Hegemony*
Cultural policy	*Ideology*
Cultural politics	*Power*
Deconstruction	*Pragmatism*
Governmentality	*Public sphere*

This chapter is concerned with the related issues of cultural politics and cultural policy. We begin by exploring 'cultural politics' in the context of the cultural studies 'tradition' since its formation as an institutionalized mode of study and research. This involves consideration of the way concepts drawn from Gramsci have informed cultural studies and their modification in the light of poststructuralism. In particular, we will consider the 'politics of difference' and the 'politics of representation' in relation to ethnicity, citizenship and the public sphere.

The discussion of cultural politics will be followed by debates critical of cultural studies regarding:

- **the relationship of textual cultural studies to political economy;**
- **the need to develop cultural policy.**

We will review arguments that suggest that cultural studies has been insufficiently centred on cultural policy and has, as a consequence, become a marginalized academic concern. We will consider the relation between cultural criticism, essentially a textual practice, and the pragmatic politics of policy formation and implementation.

CULTURAL STUDIES AND CULTURAL POLITICS

Cultural studies is a multi-disciplinary or even post-disciplinary field of enquiry which blurs the boundaries between itself and other disciplines. However, since cultural studies does not wish to be thought of as 'anything' (Hall, 1992a), it has sought to differentiate itself through its politics. Cultural studies consistently claims to be centred on issues of power, politics and the need for social change. Indeed, cultural studies has aspirations to form links with political movements outside of the academy. Thus,

✓ *Cultural studies is a body of theory reflexively produced with the idea that this process is a political practice.*

For cultural studies, knowledge is never a neutral or objective phenomenon, but a matter of positionality. This is what Gray describes as 'Who can know what about whom, by what means and to what purposes' (Gray, 1997: 94).

Naming as cultural politics

In broad terms we may consider cultural politics to be about:

- **the power to name;**
- **the power to represent common sense;**
- **the power to create 'official versions';**
- **the power to represent the legitimate social world. (Jordan and Weedon, 1995: 13)**

— Give examples of each of the items above using gender, race or class as examples. That is to say, what does it mean to name 'being a man'? How is that made into common sense, and so forth?

One of the central arguments of cultural studies is that its object of study, culture, is a zone of contestation over meaning. That is, within the field of culture divergent understandings of the world have fought for ascendancy and the pragmatic claim to truth. In particular, meaning and truth in the domain of culture are constituted within patterns of power. It is in this sense that the 'power to name' and to make particular descriptions stick is a form of cultural politics.

Issues of cultural representation are 'political' because they are intrinsically bound up with questions of power. Power, as social regulation that is productive of the self, enables some kinds of knowledge and identities to exist and not others. It matters whether we are black or white, male or female, African or American, rich or poor, because of the differential cultural resources by which we will have been constituted and to which we will have access.

For example, to describe women as full human beings and citizens with equal social rights and obligations is quite a different matter from regarding them as sub-human domestic workers with bodies designed to please men. To use the language of citizenship to describe women is a different representation of common sense and official ideology from one in which they are described as whores, tarts and servants. The language of citizenship legitimates the place of women in business and politics. The language of sexual and domestic servitude denies this place, seeking to confine women to the traditional spheres of domesticity and as objects of the male gaze.

CULTURAL POLITICS: THE INFLUENCE OF GRAMSCI

Discussion about cultural politics during the 1970s and 1980s was framed within a vocabulary drawn from Antonio Gramsci (1968, 1971) (see also Chapter 2). The most significant concept within Gramscian cultural studies is hegemony. Here, a 'historical bloc' of ruling-class factions is said to exercise 'social authority' and 'leadership' over subordinate classes. This is achieved through the winning of consent. Hegemony involves those processes of meaning-making by which an ascendent or authoritative set of representations and practices is produced and maintained.

Winning hegemony

It is central to Gramscian analysis that hegemony involves education and the winning of consent rather than the use of brute force and coercion alone. The state is not conceived here as a crude arm of the ruling class. Nevertheless, it is held to be implicated in the production of class hegemony. Gramsci makes a distinction between:

- the *'night-watchman state'* as a repressive apparatus reliant on the army, the police and the judicial system;

- the *'ethical state'*, which plays an educative and formative role in the creation of citizens and the winning of consent.

Though force remains an option for social control, during times of relative stability it takes a back seat to the unifying role of ideology.

POLICE LINES

© Photographer: Freya Hadley

- *What is the role of violence in maintaining the modern state?*

- *When does the state use violence? Against whom is violence used? For what purposes is violence used?*

- *What is the relation between violence and the generation of consent in the modern state?*

After Gramsci, cultural studies adopted the view that ideology is rooted in the day-to-day conditions of popular life. Here ideology was understood to be constituted by maps of meaning that support the power of particular social groups. For Gramsci, ideologies provide people with rules of practical conduct and moral behaviour. Ideologies are both lived experience and a body of systematic ideas whose role is to organize and bind together a bloc of diverse social elements in the formation of hegemonic and counter-hegemonic blocs. Ideological hegemony is the process by which certain ways of understanding the world become so self-evident or naturalized as to render alternatives nonsensical or unthinkable.

In the Gramscian view, the common-sense and popular culture through which people organize their lives and experience becomes the crucial site of ideological contestation. This is the place where hegemony, understood as a fluid and *temporary* series of alliances, needs to be constantly rewon and renegotiated. The creation and dissolution of cultural hegemony is an ongoing process and culture a terrain of continuous struggle over meanings.

The deployment of Gramscian concepts proved to be of long-lasting significance because of the central importance given to popular culture as a site of ideological struggle. Further, while the concept of hegemony was originally utilized in relation to social class, its scope became broader as it encompassed the power relations of sex, gender, race, ethnicity, age and national identity. Notions of ideology and hegemony also became pertinent to feminism, postcolonial theory, the politics of race, queer theory, etc.

KEY THINKERS

Antonio Gramsci (1891–1937)

Gramsci was an Italian Marxist theorist and political activist whose main contribution to cultural studies has been his application of Marxism to modern western societies. In particular, he developed and deployed the concepts of ideology and hegemony in ways that gained considerable currency within cultural studies during its formative years in the 1970s. Gramsci was influential in developing a non-reductionist Marxism that explored meaning and ideas as developmental forces that were not explicable in economic terms alone, hence his significance to western Marxists who were interested in culture.

Reading: Gramsci, A. (1968) *Prison Notebooks*. London: Lawrence & Wishart.

The role of intellectuals

Gramscian thinking places cultural analysis and ideological struggle at the heart of western politics. Thus, by implication it elevates cultural studies to a place of preeminence for those who are concerned with social change. Indeed, it places a special premium on the work of intellectuals and their relations with other participants in social struggle. Here Gramsci offers a significant distinction between 'traditional' intellectuals and 'organic' intellectuals.

Traditional intellectuals are those persons who fill the scientific, literary, philosophical and religious positions in society. This would include those working in universities, schools, churches, the media, medical institutions, publishers and law firms. Though traditional intellectuals may be drawn from different class backgrounds, their status, position and functions lead them to view themselves as independent of any class allegiances or ideological role. However, for Gramsci they produce, maintain and circulate those ideologies constitutive of hegemony that become naturalized as common sense. For example, numerous analyses of contemporary media output (Chapter 10) have argued for the ideological role of journalists, television producers and other media intellectuals.

By contrast, *organic intellectuals* are said to be a constitutive part of the working-class (and later feminist, postcolonial, African-American, etc.) struggle. They are said to be the thinking and organizing elements of the counter-hegemonic class and its allies. As Gramsci puts it, as a new class develops, it creates 'organically ... one or more strata of intellectuals which give it homogeneity and an awareness of its own function, not only economic but also in the social and political fields' (Gramsci, 1971: 5). Gramsci has an expansive notion of the organic intellectual. Consequently, this role is not to be played only by those situated within the educational world, but also by trade unionists, writers, campaigners, community organizers, teachers, and so forth.

Cultural studies as a political project

As cultural studies developed, many of its adherents adopted the model of organic intellectuals. Thus, cultural studies was conceived of as an intellectual project aimed at providing wider social and political forces with intellectual resources in the 'ideological struggle'. Here cultural studies sought to play a 'de-mystifying role' by pointing to the constructed character of cultural texts. It aimed to highlight the myths and ideologies embedded in texts in the hope of producing subject positions and real subjects opposed to subordination. Indeed, as a political theory, cultural studies hoped to organize disparate oppositional groups into an alliance of cultural politics.

The emergence of cultural studies as an institutionally located enterprise did not coincide with an upsurge of class struggle. Consequently, it has been the 'new' social and political movements of identity politics that have provided cultural studies with its alleged constituency. Even then, it is debatable whether cultural studies has been connected with these movements in any 'organic' way. Rather, as Hall (1992a) has commented, cultural studies intellectuals acted 'as if' they were organic intellectuals or in the hope that one day they could be. Others, notably Bennett (1992), have been more sanguine in questioning whether cultural studies has ever been conceivable in terms of organic intellectuals.

— Which of the following would you describe as 'an intellectual':

* a professor;
* a school teacher;
* a public relations manager;
* a priest;
* a journalist;
* a police officer;
* a doctor;
* a trades union organizer;
* a human rights campaigner;
* a lawyer?

— What are the criteria for deciding whether someone is an intellectual?
— What functions do intellectuals perform within a culture?

Gramscian texts

One of the seminal texts of cultural studies, *Resistance through Rituals* (Hall and Jefferson, 1976), encapsulates the Gramscian thrust of cultural studies in its title. Here, youth subcultures are explored as stylized forms of resistance to hegemonic culture. It was argued that certain youth subcultures had developed in reaction to the decline of traditional working-class values, spaces and places. That is, youth subcultures sought to reinvent through stylization the lost community and values of the working class. Skinheads were held to be recapturing in an imaginary way the tradition of working-class male 'hardness' through their cropped hair, boots, jeans and braces. This was combined with a stress on the resources of working-class collectivism and territoriality through the coherence and loyalty of 'the gang' of mates.

Style is read as a form of symbolic resistance forged on the terrain of hegemonic and counter-hegemonic struggle. However, it is always a limited form of resistance. This is because symbolic resources cannot overcome the structural position of the working class. They cannot abolish unemployment, educational disadvantage, low pay or urban regeneration. This would require a more fully articulated and organized anti-capitalist politics of resistance and insurrection.

Gramscian themes of ideology, hegemony, resistance and containment are also apparent in *Policing the Crisis* (Hall et al., 1978). This book explores the 1970s moral panic in the British press surrounding street robbery. The authors explore the articulation of 'mugging' with race and the alleged black threat to law, order and the British way of life. Specifically, the text sets out to:

- dispute the association of mugging with an alien black presence and to offer alternative explanations;

- give an account of the political, economic, ideological and racial crisis of Britain which formed the context of the moral panic;

- demonstrate the ideological work done by the media in constructing mugging and connecting it with concerns about racial disorder;

- illustrate the popularization of hegemonic 'ideology' through the professional working practices of the media;

- explicate the argument that the moral panic around mugging facilitated the move into the 'exceptional state' of an authoritarian 'law and order' society.

Hall (1988) expands on these core arguments in his Gramscian exploration of the success of Thatcherism in Britain. Thatcherism represented the most right-wing government Britain had seen in the post-war period, yet also one of its most popular. Hall describes this as an 'authoritarian populism' whose great strength was its ability to sustain popular support for an authoritarian and moralistic state bent on rolling back the boundaries of welfare provision and trade unionism. Hall imputes this success to an ideological struggle that transformed common sense so that it embraced the virtues of 'possessive individualism'. Thatcherism (see Hall and Jacques, 1989) exploited a very real popular sense of:

- the intrusion of the state into personal life;

- the inefficiency of welfare provision;

- the increased levels of personal choice engendered by consumer capitalism;

- the changing class structure.

The Gramscian influence in cultural studies can also be seen in a series of textual analyses related to ideology in news and current affairs (Brunsdon and Morley, 1978), soap opera (Dyer et al., 1981), advertising (Williamson, 1978) and popular film (Bennett et al., 1986). It also framed the turn to audience research through Hall's (1981) essay on encoding–decoding and Morley's research (1980) into the *Nationwide* audience (Chapter 10). However, the whole terrain of cultural studies and cultural politics was to shift considerably under the influence of poststructuralism, postmodernism and the politics of difference.

THE CULTURAL POLITICS OF DIFFERENCE

The central arguments of poststructuralism and postmodernism are discussed elsewhere in the text, notably Chapters 3 (language), 6 (postmodernity) and 8 (identity). Consequently, I shall not repeat them at length here. However, I do wish to draw attention to those facets of poststructuralist and postmodern arguments that have been absorbed into cultural studies, prompting a revision of Gramscian modes of thinking. These would include:

- **the constitutive place of language and discourse within culture;**
- **the discursive construction of identity and social life;**
- **the anti-essentialist character of all social categories;**
- **the 'no-necessary' correspondence between discursive elements;**
- **the dispersed character of power that is central to all social relationships;**
- **the decline of grand narratives (notably of Marxism) and totalizing fields of enquiry;**
- **a stress on micro-fields of political power and resistance;**
- **the significance given to New Social Movements and identity politics;**
- **the instability of meaning in language** (*différance*);
- **a stress on the politics of difference.**

New languages of cultural politics

✓ *The assimilation of poststructuralist thinking has led cultural studies to an understanding of 'politics' that is centred on the power of discourse to describe and regulate cultural identities and social action.*

Cultural politics is now held to involve the struggle over 'naming' and the power to redescribe ourselves in what Rorty (1989) calls 'new languages'. These questions of cultural power translate into the practical purposes of identity politics when, for example:

- **African-Americans challenge the representation of black people as marginal and criminalized;**
- **women redescribe themselves as citizens of equal standing with men;**

- the 'Gray Panthers' voice the discontents of forgotten and excluded older people (see www.graypanthers.org);
- gays and lesbians stage 'Gay Pride' events throughout the country.

Social change becomes possible through rethinking and redescribing the social order and the possibilities for the future. Since there is no such thing as a private language, then redescription is a social and political activity. This 'rethinking' of ourselves emerges through social practice and, more often than not, through social contradiction and conflict. In doing so, it brings new political subjects and practices into being. For example, in relation to Rastafarians in Jamaica, Hall has argued that:

> Rasta was a funny language, borrowed from a text – the Bible – that did not belong to them; they had to turn the text upside-down, to get a meaning which fitted their experience. But in turning the text upside-down they remade themselves; they positioned themselves differently as new political subjects; they reconstructed themselves as blacks in the new world: they *became* what they are. And, positioning themselves in that way, they learned to speak a new language. And they spoke it with a vengeance. ... [T]hey only constitute a political force, that is, they *become* a historical force in so far as they are constituted as new political subjects. (Hall, 1996b: 143–4)

The theorization of the 'new' cultural politics of difference has come from a number of directions. However, the work of Laclau and Mouffe (1985) and Hall (1988, 1990, 1992a, 1996a) has been of particular significance. Each retains the concept of hegemony but reworks it into a form of post-Marxism that draws on poststructuralist theory. Post-Marxism is said to selectively retain that which is held to be valuable in Marxism but to have superseded it. Thus, Marxism is no longer held to be the primary grand narrative of our time as it once was for cultural studies.

The politics of articulation

Following Derrida, Laclau and Mouffe take meaning to be inherently unstable. That is, *différance* – 'difference and deferral' – whereby the production of meaning is continually deferred and added to (or supplemented) by the meanings of other words (Chapter 3). For example, if you look up a word in a dictionary, you will be referred to other words in an infinite process.

This process involves the continual supplementarity of meaning, that is, the continual substitution and adding of meanings through the play of signifiers. This understanding challenges the identity of words with fixed meanings. Thus, key cultural categories such as 'women', 'class', 'society', 'identities', 'interests', etc., are no longer conceived of as single unitary objects with fixed meanings or single underlying structures and determinations.

Consequently, for Laclau and Mouffe, the 'social' is constituted through a series of discursive differences involving multiple points of power and antagonism. These particularities of authority and conflict do not cohere (as in Marxism and Gramscian theory) around class and the mode of production. The social is not an object but a field of contestation in which multiple descriptions of self and others compete for ascendancy. It is to be thought of not as a totality but as a set of contingently related aggregates of difference articulated or sutured together.

Articulation (Chapter 3) refers to the temporary juxtaposition or unity of discursive elements which do not have to 'go together'. Articulation is the form of the connection that can make a unity of two different elements under certain conditions. For example, we commonly speak of the nation as 'a society'. However, not only can a country's people never meet, but also they are fundamentally *different* in terms of class, gender, sexuality, race, age, political persuasion, morality, etc. Here, the nation is a discursive device for unifying difference through identification with, for example, the signs 'England' or 'Australia'. For Laclau and Mouffe, it is the role of ideology and of hegemonic practices to try to fix difference, that is, to put closure around the unstable meanings of signifiers in the discursive field in order to stabilize what, for example, masculinity or American identity means.

No class-belonging

Points of closure or temporarily stabilized meaning are said to be plural. This leads Laclau and Mouffe to put aside the final determination of class and the economic. For them, economic relations do not determine cultural meanings (which can be articulated together in a variety of ways). From this it follows that Laclau and Mouffe regard the Gramscian concept of hegemony as mistakenly centred on class. Instead, they stress that history has neither a prime agent of social change nor one central point of antagonism. For Laclau and Mouffe, ideology has no 'class-belonging' (Barrett, 1991) and the social has no single originatory point or underlying principle of determination that fixes the field of differences. Instead, hegemonic and counter-hegemonic blocs are formed through temporary and strategic alliances of a range of discursively constructed subjects and groups of interest.

The prime agents of social change, it is argued, are not so much classes (though they play a part) as cultural movements that have developed from a proliferation of new social antagonisms. These movements are centred less in the workplace than class and more in the spaces of consumption, welfare and habitat. In this context, the ideology of liberal democracy is reworked to stress a broader sphere of 'social rights'. In pursuit of those rights, a new political axis is sought around the struggles of 'urban, ecological, anti-authoritarian, anti-institutional, feminist, anti-racist, ethnic, regional or ... sexual minorities' (Laclau and Mouffe, 1985: 159).

The 'cut' in language

Language involves a potentially endless and infinite proliferation of meanings. Thus, Hall (1993) has argued that any sense of self, of identity or of communities of identification (nations, ethnicities, sexualities, classes, etc.) are necessary fictions marking a temporary, partial and arbitrary closure of meaning. It is possible, given the instability of language, to go on redescribing what it means to be a 'woman' for ever in an endless process of supplementarity. However, in order to say anything (to mark significance), and in order to take action, a temporary closure of meaning is required.

Thus, feminist politics need at least momentary agreement about what constitutes a woman and what is in women's interests under particular circumstances. For Hall, there has to be a full stop, or cut in the flow of meaning, albeit a provisional one, for cultural politics to be possible.

✓ *Identities and identifications may be culturally constructed fictions. However, they are necessary to human culture and its associated politics.*

All the social movements which have tried to transform society and have required the constitution of new subjectivities, have had to accept the necessarily fictional, but also the fictional necessity, of the arbitrary closure which is not the end, but which makes both politics and identity possible. [This is] a politics of difference, the politics of self-reflexivity, a politics that is open to contingency but still able to act … [T]here has to be a politics of articulation – politics of hegemonic project. (Hall, 1993: 136–7)

According to West (1993), the 'new cultural politics of difference' proceeds by way of the following:

- *Deconstruction*: A reading of texts that challenges the tropes, metaphors and binaries of rhetorical textual operations. For example, the binaries of male/female and white/black, in which the former term is privileged as 'the good', are first overturned and subsequently put into a productive tension. In short, deconstruction (Chapter 1) helps us to see the political assumptions of texts.

- *De-mythologization*: Highlighting the social construction of metaphors that regulate descriptions of the world and their possible consequences for classifying the social. That is, mapping the metaphors by which we live and their link with politics, values, purposes, interests and prejudices. De-mythologization shows why we must speak not of History but histories, not of Reason but historically contingent forms of rationality.

- *De-mystification*: Describing and analysing the complexity of institutional and other power structures in order to disclose options for cultural politics and cultural policy. For West, such 'prophetic criticism' requires social analysis that is explicit and partisan in its moral and political aims. Further, the development of critical positions and new theory must be linked with communities, groups, organizations and networks of people who are actively involved in social and cultural change.

DIFFERENCE, ETHNICITY AND THE POLITICS OF REPRESENTATION

Emblematic of the 'politics of difference' is work on 'new ethnicities' (Chapter 8) in which ethnicity:

- **defines new spaces for identities;**
- **constitutes new hybrid identities;**
- **insists on the specificity and positionality of all knowledge and identities.**

Ethnic identity is a discursive construction, that is, a description in language, rather than a reflection of an essential, fixed, natural state of being (Hall, 1990, 1992a, 1996a). For Hall, a reworking of the concept of ethnicity helps us to explore cultural practices within specific historical and political conjunctures. This helps us to understand that we are all ethnically located (Hall, 1996d). As such, an exploration of ethnicity must concern itself with the relations between groups that define each other in the context of power. Ethnicity is concerned with relations and representations of centrality and marginality in the context of changing historical forms and circumstances.

Invisibility and namelessness

According to West (1993), the central cultural problematic for the black diaspora is one of 'invisibility and namelessness', that is, a relative lack of power to represent themselves as complex human beings and to contest the negative stereotypes that abound. Responses to this problem have involved the adoption of a number of strategies that we might call:

- **the demand for positive images;**
- **the search for multiculturalism;**
- **the adoption of anti-racism;**
- **the politics of representation.**

Positive images

The demand for positive images can be understood as the need to show that black people are 'really as good as' or 'as human as' white people. This needs to be grasped in the context of the negative stereotypes and assimilationist expectations of white society. However, this strategy entails a number of problems:

- **Assimilation requires that people of colour adopt the 'way of life' of Anglo culture. This would involve losing their own cultural and social specificity in a bid to gain white acceptance.**

- **This response promotes a homogenization of black people that tends to obliterate differences of class, gender, region, sexuality, etc.**

- **It rests on a reflectionist or realist conception of representation by which it is thought possible to bring representation closer to 'real' black people. This is an impossibility since representations of race are always already constructions (Chapters 3 and 8).**

- **Representations are always matters of contestation. Consequently, it is difficult to know what an unambiguously positive image would look like.**

Multiculturalism and anti-racism

The multiculturalist strategy also demands positive images but gives up the requirement for assimilation. Instead, ethnic groups are held to be of equal status and have the right to preserve their cultural heritage. Multiculturalism aims to celebrate difference. For example, the teaching of multi-faith religious education, the performance of rituals and the promotion of ethnic food become facets of educational policy.

This strategy has much to commend it. However, the process of relativizing cultures can, in the context of institutionally racist social orders, overlook the dimension of power. The day-to-day experiences of racism in relation to housing, employment and physical violence may slip from view. In contrast, the anti-racist argument is said to highlight the operations of power and challenge the ideological and structural practices that constituted racist societies. This includes contesting racist language in school books and the overrepresentation of black pupils in school exclusions and suspensions.

The politics of representation

The philosophy and strategies of multiculturalism and anti-racism have their merits. However, they both rest on essentialist versions of black identity and thus homogenize experience to the signifier 'black'. As Hall (1996d) has commented, black identity is not an essentialist category but one that had to be learned. Consequently, he has looked towards a 'politics of representation' which registers the arbitrariness of signification and seeks the willingness to live with difference. Rather than demand positive images alone, a politics of representation explores representations which themselves enquire into power relations and deconstruct the very terms of a black–white binary. Hall (1996d, 1997c) has seen such a politics in Hanif Kureishi's screen play *My Beautiful Laundrette*, the photography of Robert Mapplethorpe, the work of filmmaker Isaac Julien and the emergence of hybrid identities.

A politics of representation is double-coded. On the one hand, it concerns questions of discourse, images, language, reality and meaning. On the other hand, questions of representation are part of the discourse of democracy, citizenship and the public sphere. Indeed, the concept of citizenship is a mechanism for linking the micro-politics of representation/identity with the official macropolitics of institutional and cultural rights.

Thus, Mercer argues that 'The concept of citizenship is crucial because it operates in the hinge that articulates civil society and the state in an open-ended and indeterminate relationship' (Mercer, 1994: 284). From within the British Asian context, Parekh highlights what a stress on citizenship and cultural rights might mean for the politics of 'new ethnicities'.

> First, cultural diversity should be given public status and dignity. ... Second, minorities can hardly expect to be taken seriously unless they accept the full obligations of British citizenship. ... Third, the minority communities must be allowed to develop at their own pace and in a direction of their own choosing. ... Fourth, like individuals, communities can only flourish under propitious conditions. ... Fifth, the distinct character of ethnic communities needs to be recognized by our legal system. (Parekh, 1991: 194–5, cited in McGuigan, 1996a: 152)

DIFFERENCE, CITIZENSHIP AND THE PUBLIC SPHERE

According to Dahlgren (1995), citizenship is a form of identity and one aspect of our multiple selves. He argues that a civic 'identity of citizenship' holds together a diversity of values and lifeworlds within a democratic framework. The identity of citizenship may be the only thing we have in common. However, a commitment by diverse groups to the procedures of democracy and to intersubjectively recognized rights and duties of citizenship in the social, civil and political domains advances democracy and provides the conditions for particularistic identity projects. This involves the 'hegemony of democratic values' developed in the public sphere.

— Discuss and define the meanings of the following terms:

- identity of citizenship;
- procedures of democracy;
- intersubjectively recognized rights and duties.

— In conclusion: what does it mean to be a citizen?

Habermas and the public sphere

For Habermas (1989), the public sphere is a realm that emerged in a specific phase of 'bourgeois society'. It is constituted as:

- **a space that mediates between civil society and the state;**
- **a place where the public organizes itself;**
- **an arena in which 'public opinion' is formed.**

Within this sphere individuals are able to develop themselves and engage in debate about the direction of society. Habermas goes on to document what he sees as the decline of the public sphere in the face of the development of capitalism towards monopoly and the strengthening of the state. Nevertheless, he attempts to ground its renewal in the notion of an 'ideal speech situation' where competing truth claims are subject to rational debate and argument. Thus the public sphere is conceived as a space for debate based on conversational equality.

However, as Fraser (1995b) has argued, no such conditions exist in practice. Rather, social inequality means that citizens are denied equal access to the public sphere. Subordinate groups do not have participatory parity and the space to articulate their own languages, needs and demands. According to Fraser, Habermas's modern conception of the public sphere requires interlocutors to bracket status differences, to confine discussion to questions of the public good (barring private concerns), and to create only one, because common, public sphere.

However, social inequality cannot be bracketed, many private issues are public (e.g. domestic violence), and there are competing versions of the public good. Consequently, Fraser argues that a postmodern conception of the public sphere should accept the desirability of multiple publics and multiple public spheres while at the same time working to reduce social inequality. She argues that feminism represents such a 'counter-public sphere' of debate and political activity.

The democratic tradition

The concept of the public sphere does not require Habermas's attempt to construct universal and transcendental rational justification for it. The defence of the public sphere is *normative* and pragmatic rather than epistemological. That is, it can be warranted through the values associated with cultural human rights and cultural pluralism and does not require metaphysical foundations. One supports a democratic public sphere because one believes it to be good rather than true or the destiny of the species.

456 SITES OF CULTURAL STUDIES

✓ *Principles that the democratic tradition regards as good include the values of justice, diversity, liberty and solidarity.*

The concepts of *justice* and *diversity* suggest the need for cultural pluralism and the representation of the full range of public opinions, cultural practices and social and geographical conditions. *Liberty* and *solidarity* suggest forms of sharing and cooperation that are genuine and not enforced, that is, they imply supportive liberality and togetherness rather than coercive control.

Radical democracy

The values of justice, tolerance, solidarity and difference, formed on the historically contingent grounds of a western democratic political tradition, are also those which drive Laclau and Mouffe's vision of 'radical democracy', whose aim is 'A society where everyone, whatever his/her sex, race, economic position, sexual orientation, will be in an effective situation of equality and participation, where no basis of discrimination will remain and where self-management will exist in all fields' (Mouffe, 1984: 143). The achievement of this vision demands the articulation of 'chains of equivalence' under what Mouffe (1992) calls the 'hegemony of democratic values'. By this is meant that the 'democratic revolution' proposes the idea of equality and difference. Divergent manifestations of inequality and disparate forms of oppression are by a logic of comparison put on the same footing. That is, inequalities of gender, of class, of race, of nation, etc., are given equal priority and require to be linked up in the formation of counter-hegemonic practices.

Consider the following:

— Is the public sphere expanding or contracting?
— In what ways is the public sphere today different to what it was the eighteenth century?
— What forces are at work in expanding or contracting cultural democracy in the contemporary world?
— Why is the contemporary public sphere not constituted as one of equals?

QUESTIONING CULTURAL STUDIES

The cultural politics of difference as constituted by a politics of representation has been subject to the criticism that it overlooks material inequalities and relations of power. It is said to lack a political economy of housing, labour markets and educational achievement (McGuigan, 1996b). Critics claim that cultural studies fails to grasp the material circumstances and power relations that pertain between people. Consequently, it is said to lack the means to bring about change. An overly textual and populist cultural studies is argued to be unable to engage in cultural policy. The most common targets of such criticism have been:

1 textual deconstruction;
2 active audience research that celebrates the 'productive' capacities of readers.

The critique of cultural populism

Cultural studies has, of course, many critics who are 'external' to the paradigm (Ferguson and Golding, 1997). However, we shall concern ourselves only with those broadly sympathetic to the overall project, for example Jim McGuigan's (1992, 1996a, 1996b) critiques of 'cultural populism'. McGuigan's argument is that cultural studies rightly took issue with the 'mass culture' arguments of the Frankfurt School and the 'cultural elitism' of Leavisism (Chapter 2) that denigrated popular culture as unworthy of either participation or study. This critique took two fundamental forms: first, the philosophical attack on high–low cultural boundaries; second, the marking of the moment of consumption as itself a moment of meaningful production.

However, McGuigan argues that the increased 'postmodernization' of culture has itself collapsed the high–low division and that the celebration of the productive and resistive capacities of audiences has gone too far. Indeed, he argues that it has become complicit with the ideology of consumer sovereignty. Cultural studies, it is argued, is unable to critique the products of consumer culture because it has lost sight of any profound conception of cultural value from which to critique texts. Further, it over-endows audiences with the cultural competencies to deconstruct ideology. In particular, it fails to note the uneven distribution of such competencies across the divisions of class, gender, ethnicity, ages, etc. Consequently, cultural studies is unable to offer, at the level of either analysis or policy, any transformative alternative to the market as it stands.

McGuigan's central target is John Fiske (1987, 1989a, 1989b), who had argued that popular culture is constituted by the meanings that people make rather than those identifiable within texts. For Fiske, popular culture is a site of semiotic warfare and of popular tactics deployed to evade or resist the meanings produced and inscribed in commodities by producers. McGuigan accuses Fiske of a retreat from critical thinking and an abandonment of any form of political economy. This is said to have led to the acceptance of the free market and consumer capitalism. Ang has countered that recognition of the plural meanings that audiences produce is not an abandonment of the need to explore media institutions or texts. Rather, it is the sign of a new problematic; namely, the need to enquire about 'the way in which cultural contradiction, inconsistency and incoherence pervade contemporary, postmodern culture' (Ang, 1996: 11).

A multiperspectival approach

McGuigan asks cultural studies to engage more thoroughly with the political economy of culture, that is, with questions of ownership, institutions, control and power. This would enable cultural studies to explore more fully the ways in which the moment of production inscribes itself in the range and meanings of cultural products. McGuigan argues for a multiperspectival approach that interrogates the relationships between political economy, representations, texts and audiences alongside an engagement with cultural policy. Also supportive of a multiperspectival approach, Kellner (1997) recommends political economy to textual cultural studies as being able to:

- show how cultural production takes place within specific historical, political and economic relations which structure textual meanings;

- highlight the way capitalist societies are organized according to a dominant mode of production centred on commodification and the pursuit of profit;

- call attention to the fact that culture is produced within vectors of domination and subordination;

- illuminate the limits and range of political and ideological discourses and texts possible at specific historical conjunctures.

Thus, a textual analysis of Madonna (see Chapter 9) would concentrate on her sign value and audience responses in order to engage with questions of ideology and resistance. However, it would also need to take account of the fact that she has 'deployed some of the most proficient production and marketing teams in the history of popular music' (Kellner, 1997: 118). This argument does not in itself displace the analysis of Madonna as a sign. Consequently, Kellner rightly suggests that the divide between cultural studies (as textual studies) and political economy is a false one.

The circuit of culture

The call to utilize the methods of political economy may be a timely reminder of its uses (and abuses). Nevertheless, the case is overstated, for political economy has never really disappeared from cultural studies. A series of cultural studies texts produced in the 1990s and involving Stuart Hall put the notion of a multiperspectival approach based on the 'circuit of culture' at their core (see Figure 2.2). This model is a development of Hall's earlier encoding–decoding model published in 1981, and has been operative within cultural studies for a long time. Thus, much of the cultural studies versus political economy debate appears to be overstated.

The argument is that each of the moments of the circuit – representation, regulation, consumption, production and identity – is articulated together and productive of meanings that are necessary for the continuation of the circuit but insufficient to determine the form and content of other instances.

✓ *The challenge is to grasp just how the moment of production inscribes itself in representation in each case without assuming that it can be 'read-off' from economic relations.*

We would also be interested in how culture or representation is implicated in the forms and modes of organization that production takes. That is, we need to grasp the ways in which that which we call 'the economic' is formed culturally.

The debate about textual politics and political economy is a contemporary version of a relatively old debate. However, the call for a turn to cultural policy is a more radical and recent event for cultural studies. Cultural studies has not taken cultural policy or the possibility of working with state or commercial organizations very seriously. Indeed, it has often seemed contemptuous of such an idea. Cultural studies has held cultural politics to be constituted by the long-haul building of anti-hegemonic coalitions outside of mainstream institutions (which have been regarded as somewhat corrupting). However, during the 1980s and 1990s a significant discussion about cultural policy was prompted by the work of Tony Bennett (1998).

THE CULTURAL POLICY DEBATE

Bennett (1992) argues that the textual politics with which cultural studies has been engaged ignores the institutional dimensions of cultural power. He urges cultural studies to:

- **adopt a more pragmatic approach;**
- **work with cultural producers;**
- **put questions of policy creation at its heart.**

For Bennett, cultural politics centres on *policy* formulation and enactment within the institutions that produce and administer the form and content of cultural products. This would include organizations like the Arts Council in the UK, museums, government departments of education/arts/culture/media/sport, etc., schools, institutions of higher education, theatre administration, television organizations (public and commercial), record companies and advertising agencies.

Redirecting the cultural studies project

Bennett is critical of cultural studies for displacing its politics on to the level of signification and text. This, he argues, has been at the expense of a material politics of the institutions and organizations that produce and distribute cultural texts. For Bennett, cultural studies has been overly concerned with consciousness and the ideological struggle as conceived through Gramsci and not enough with the material technologies of power and of cultural policy. He argues that cultural studies needs to:

- understand itself as located in the higher education system as an arm of government;

- conceptualize culture as constituting 'a particular field of government' and social regulation;

- identify the different 'regions' of culture and their managerial operations;

- study the different technologies of power and forms of politics associated with different domains of cultural practice;

- accord cultural policy a more central place in its cosmology;

- work with other 'governmental' organizations of culture to develop policy and modes of strategic intervention, since we are not discussing the relations between two separate realms (critique and the state) but, rather, the articulations between two branches of government, each of which is deeply involved in the management of culture' (Bennett, 1998: 6).

Governmentality

Bennett's arguments depend on a specific notion of culture and governmentality drawn from an interpretation (for some, contentious) of Foucault. As Foucault stated:

By this word [governmentality] I mean three things:

1   The ensemble formed by the institutions, procedures, analyses and reflections, the calculations and tactics that allow the exercise of this very specific albeit complex form of power, which has as its target population, as its principal form of

2   The tendency which, over a long period and throughout the west, has steadily led towards the pre-eminence over all other forms (sovereignty, discipline, etc.) of this type of power which may be termed government, resulting, on the one hand, in the formation of a whole series of specific governmental apparatuses, and, on the other, in the development of a whole complex of *savoirs*.

3   The process, or rather the result of the process, through which the state of justice of the Middle Ages, transformed into the administrative state during the fifteenth and sixteenth centuries, gradually becomes 'governmentalized'. (Foucault, 1991: 102–3)

The concept of governmentality is commonly associated with the operations of the state. However, it is better understood in the broader sense of regulation throughout the social order, or, to put it in Foucault's preferred manner, the 'policing' of societies by which a population becomes subject to bureaucratic regimes and modes of discipline.

Governmentality is a growing aspect of the micro-capillary character of power, that is, the multiplicity of force relations that are not centralized but dispersed. This includes modes of regulation that operate through medicine, education, social reform, demography and criminology and by which a population can be categorized and ordered into manageable groups. The state is held to be a more or less contingent collection of sometimes conflicting institutions and apparatuses. The 'bureau' is understood to be an autonomous 'technology for living' organized around its own faculties and possessing its own modes of conduct.

Culture and power

The concept of governmentality stresses that processes of social regulation do not so much stand over and against the individual but are constitutive of self-reflective modes of conduct, ethical competencies and social movements. Culture in this reading is understandable in terms of governmentality since 'the relations of culture and power which most typically characterize modern societies are best understood in the light of the respects in which the field of culture is now increasingly governmentally organized and constructed' (Bennett, 1998: 61).

For Bennett, culture is caught up in, and functions as a part of, cultural technologies that organize and shape social life and human conduct. A cultural technology is part of the 'machinery' of institutional and organizational structures that produce particular configurations of power/knowledge.

✓   *Culture is a matter not just of representations and consciousness but of institutional practices, administrative routines and spatial arrangements.*

Here are some cultural organizations:

- a film production company;
- a book publisher;
- a museum of contemporary art;
- a school.

For each of the above write down and discuss:

— What issues of the 'politics of representation' might be involved?
— What questions of 'the politics of institutional practices' might be involved?

The domains of culture and governmentality to which Bennett most often refers are education and museums. For example, he argues that cultural studies must be understood as a part of the expansion of higher education. In particular, cultural studies is said to be a part of a university curriculum that addressed students who entered it without the traditional resources of 'high culture'. This widening of the curriculum was, argues Bennett, already well under way in schools long before cultural studies emerged. Thus, cultural studies is understood to be an arm of reforming and regulatory government.

Museums are explored for their self-conscious deployment of culture's alleged 'civilizing effects', which are utilized in order to regulate working-class subjectivities and modes of behaviour. In particular, museums have aimed to produce self-regulating persons (notably men) who were to become better citizens through the formation and policing of 'new' subjectivities. In this sense, culture is 'a reformer's science'.

KEY THINKERS

Tony Bennett (1947–)

Bennett's early work continued the Gramscian tradition within cultural studies, particularly in relation to television and popular culture. Subsequently Bennett has been critical of the Gramscian stream of cultural studies as over-emphasizing signification and consciousness at the expensive of the pragmatic considerations of cultural policy. As Director of the Australian Key Centre for Cultural and Media Policy at Griffith University, Bennett played a significant part in promoting cultural policy as a goal for cultural studies. He is currently a Professor at the Open University (UK).

Reading: Bennett, T. (1998) *Culture: A Reformer's Science*. St Leonards, NSW: Allen & Unwin.

Foucault or Gramsci?

Bennett compares his Foucauldian conceptualization of culture focused on governmentality with a Gramscian version of cultural studies centred on the concepts of ideology, consciousness and the winning of consent (i.e. a version of culture centred on meaning and representations). Revisionist Gramscian cultural studies – or 'the politics of articulation' – is, argues Bennett, overtly and overly discursive. In particular, the struggles in culture are seen as operating primarily at the level of language and ideology. In contrast, for Bennett's Foucault, the order of relations between practices (which are contingently established) must be charted through a dense materialism.

In Gramscian theory, argues Bennett, the conceptualization of descending flows of ideology (hegemony) leads to the attempt to organize generalized struggles of the subordinate against a single source of power, that is, counter-hegemonic struggles. By contrast, for Foucault, there is no single originatory source of power. Rather, power is held to be dispersed and conflict is specific to a 'region' of culture and the particular technologies pertaining to it.

For Bennett, the Gramscian tradition has accorded little attention to the specificities of cultural institutions, technologies and apparatuses. Instead it has concentrated on textual analysis and the personal rewards of a certain 'ethical style' which unduly celebrates notions of marginality. By contrast, in Bennett's reading, Foucault demands a 'politics of detail' in order to be effective in relation to governmental technologies, cultural policy and cultural technologies.

According to Bennett, Gramscian cultural studies hankers after the 'organic intellectual' with his/her pivotal role in the intellectual armoury and political co-ordination of social movements. Bennett argues that such a vision is an impossibility. This is because the primary location of cultural studies in the higher education system means that intellectuals are an arm of governmentality. Thus, they are not able to function as organic intellectuals whose knowledge is required to have grown directly out of and in conjunction with specific communities and movements. At best, cultural studies can provide 'the development of forms of work – of cultural analysis and pedagogy – that could contribute to the development of the political and policy agendas associated with the work of organic intellectuals' (Bennett, 1998: 33).

For Bennett, the concept of governmentality leads intellectuals to focus on the specifics of cultural practices and technologies. Although he concedes that such work points in many directions, the privileged route for Bennett is 'towards the bureau'. This is because it is within the machinery of government, or so he argues, that the work of organic intellectuals is carried out. Rather than bypass the existing forms of social administration, cultural studies is urged to answer the bureaucrat's question, 'What can you do for us?'

Cultural studies might usefully envisage its role as the 'training of cultural technicians' who are less committed to cultural critique and alterations in consciousness and more inclined to 'modifying the functions of culture by means of technical adjustments to its governmental deployment' (Bennett, 1992: 406).

Policy and the problem of values

Bennett's work offers a *prima facie* case for taking the pragmatic politics of cultural organizations seriously. However, even if we are convinced by the need for an engagement with cultural policy, questions remain unanswered, namely:

- **What political and social values will guide our policy work?**

- **What as a consequence are the 'targets' we are trying to achieve?**

Bennett might argue that the latter is context- and technology-specific. That is, the aims of cultural policy depend on the particular kind of cultural technology and organization under consideration. Nevertheless, when truth is a pragmatic question of what is taken to 'count as truth' (as Bennett says it is), then truths and actions are formed within and through social *values*. The problem is that Bennett does not make clear what values his cultural policy would pursue. Is he committed to the values of equality, justice, liberty, solidarity, etc.? Is he adopting a liberal democratic strategy, or is he, like Hall, Laclau and Mouffe, committed to the politics of difference and 'radical democracy'?

— What do you understand by the following concepts:

- equality;
- liberty;
- justice;
- diversity?

Discuss them with other people and try to come to agreement on definitions.

— How would these values inform a cultural policy in relation to:

- television;
- education;
- the Arts?

Shifting the command metaphors of cultural studies

Stuart Cunningham (1992a, 1992b, 1993) has been more forthright about his commitment to social democracy and the values of liberty, equality and solidarity as the motor of a new reformism. He advances a 'social democratic view of citizenship and the trainings necessary to activate and motivate it' (Cunningham, 1993: 134). This would involve a shift in the 'command metaphors' of cultural studies 'away from the rhetorics of resistance, oppositionalism and anti-commercialism on the one hand, and populism on the other, towards those of access, equity, empowerment and the divination of opportunities to exercise appropriate cultural leadership' (ibid.: 137–8).

Cunningham (1992b) argues that an increased policy sensitivity in cultural studies would lead to:

- greater attention being paid to the modes of interaction between cultural politics and *institutional* politics – an example would be feminist social reform initiated within government agencies and bureaucracies;

- a reconstructed *textual* analysis which could engage with the important policy issues of 'quality', 'excellence', 'diversity', etc., which form a significant aspect of the broadcasting debate in particular;

- *reception* work, which, rather than seeking cultural authenticity, would be committed to charting audience tastes with a view to cultural maintenance and a renewed sense of citizenship.

The horizon of the thinkable

Cunningham's work has the merits of being clear about the necessity of cultural studies being normative and in particular his commitment to social democratic citizenship. Nevertheless, one might wish to take issue with the specific values or policy proposals he advances. For example, Cunningham argues that as a matter of cultural policy, we should take seriously national content regulations in television advertising in order to boost (Australian) national identity. He speaks as if Australian national identity were a fixed phenomenon that would be boosted by Australian content. However, since there is no essential Australian national identity (Chapter 7), we need to ask about the kind of national identity (if any) we find desirable and what kind of exclusions are enacted by all forms of identity and policy regulation. While we might think it desirable to advance citizenship, this ought not to be on the exclusionary grounds of nationality and ethnicity.

The point is not to dispute Cunningham's concern for policy or the significance of television as an object of policy. Rather, it is to raise again the question of *values* in relation to policy by querying his specific analysis of television and national identity. As Morris (1992) argues in another context, Cunningham makes assumptions about what progressive ends are instead of opening them up for debate. Under changing socio-cultural contexts we need to keep reconsidering the values that make a policy orientation worthwhile. This is the continuing importance of cultural theory and criticism.

O'Regan (1992a, 1992b) makes a similar point in describing Bennett and Cunningham's work as 'a pragmatic politics as the horizon of the thinkable'. For O'Regan, their policy initiative remains bound within current ways of thinking rather than letting us challenge and expand our purposes through inventing 'new languages' (Rorty, 1989) or what he calls 'agenda setting social research'. In short, O'Regan is advocating the role of critical intellectuals in formulating the value goals of policy, so that, for example, research on social class may inform and secure policy aimed at equality and equal opportunity. As he argues:

> Cultural criticism and policy certainly are different, but they are both part of the policy process. Rather than berating cultural criticism, it is more productive to locate the particular form, direction and nature of the criticism and analyse its contribution to policy. The social power of the cultural critic may be difficult to mobilize; but such figures may shape the public agenda in ways that provide policy with valuable resources and arguments. (O'Regan, 1992b: 530–1)

Criticism and policy

Morris (1992) argues that for feminists involved in the academy, bureaucracies and policy initiatives (praised by Cunningham), there is always a 'critical outside' of feminism, that is, an unregulated site from which the actions of professional feminists can be scrutinized and criticized. This means, she argues, that feminism rarely falls for the binary logic of criticism *or* policy that marked the policy debate.

There is no necessary reason why cultural studies cannot attend to the important pragmatic calls of policy without relinquishing the role that 'critical cultural theory' has to play. Similarly, if it takes politics rather than posturing seriously, then cultural criticism does need to engage with cultural policy. To this end, I want briefly to explore a strand of thought which may have a useful part to play in the debate, that is, the American tradition of pragmatist philosophy and its current revival in the hands of Richard Rorty. Since pragmatism is a stream of thought that has not been strongly represented within cultural studies, though its influence is growing, readers may take this to be the expression of a personal predilection.

GREEN DEMONSTRATION

© **Photographer: Freya Hadley**

- *Can we describe the Green movement as a New Social Movement?*
- *To what extent does the Green movement represent a 'critical outside'?*
- *What relationship would you expect between the Green movement and policymakers in meeting the challenge of climate change?*

NEO-PRAGMATISM AND CULTURAL STUDIES

There are many versions of pragmatist philosophy that can be traced through the work of Peirce, James, Dewey and others. West regards the following as the best definition of pragmatism:

> Pragmatism could be characterized as the doctrine that all problems are at bottom problems of conduct, that all judgements are, implicitly, judgements of value, and that, as there can be ultimately no valid distinction of theoretical and practical, so there can be no final separation of questions of truth of any kind from questions of the justifiable ends of action. (C.I. Lewis, cited in West, 1993: 109)

Pragmatism and cultural studies

Pragmatism shares with the poststructuralist strand of cultural studies an anti-foundationalist, anti-representationlist, anti-realist view of truth. However, this is combined with a commitment to pragmatic social reform.

✓ *Pragmatism suggests that the struggle for social change is a question of language/text and of material practice/policy action.*

Like cultural studies, pragmatism attempts to render contingent that which appears 'natural' as a part of the process of developing a 'better' world. However, unlike the revolutionary rhetoric of the 'cultural left', pragmatism weds itself to reformism. Unlike much of the cultural left, but in common with cultural policy arguments, pragmatism regards liberal democracies as the best kind of system the world has yet come up with.

This stance requires us to work within liberal democracies even as they are urged to do better. In this sense, pragmatism has a 'tragic' view of life for it does not share the utopian push of Marxism. In contrast, it favours a trial-and-error experimentalism that seeks new ways of doing things. In particular, pragmatism pursues new ways of being that can be described as 'better', where 'better' registers a measurement of practices against our values.

As with postmodern cultural studies, pragmatism is against 'grand theory'. As such it is in agreement with Lyotard's 'incredulity towards metanarratives'. Pragmatists have a radically contingent view of the world where truth ends with social practice. However, this does not mean that all theory is to be jettisoned; rather, local theory becomes a way of redescribing the world in normative ways. In other words, it envisages possible new and better ways of doing things.

Since pragmatism sees the universe as always 'in the making', so the future has ethical significance. We can, it is argued, make a difference and create new, better futures. In this sense, pragmatism insists on the irreducibility of human agency even as it recognizes the causal stories of the past. Pragmatism shares with poststructuralist, post-Marxist cultural studies the idea that social and cultural change is a matter of 'politics without guarantees'. Here, without recourse to Marxism's 'laws of history', politics is centred on ethical commitment and practical action.

Richard Rorty: politics without foundations

Rorty (1980, 1989, 1991a, 1991b) has consistently spelled out a philosophy that combines an anti-representationalist view of language with an anti-foundational politics (see Chapter 3).

Anti-representationalism

Anti-representationalism means that we cannot understand language as representing the world in ways that correspond to the material world. For Rorty, 'no linguistic items represent any non-linguistic items' (Rorty, 1991a: 2).

Anti-foundationalism

Anti-foundationalism means that we cannot found or justify our actions or beliefs in any universal truths. Human history has no telos, or inevitable historical point to which it is unfolding. Rather, human 'development' is the outcome of numerous acts of chance and environmental adaptation that make the 'direction' of human evolution contingent. 'Progress' or 'purpose' can only be given meaning as a *retrospectively* told story.

Contingency, irony, solidarity

Rorty argues that we do not require universal foundations to pursue a pragmatic improvement of the human condition. Instead this is pursued on the basis of the values of our own tradition. Indeed, we cannot escape values any more than we can ground them in metaphysics. Consequently, a historically and culturally specific value-based politics is an inevitable and inescapable condition of human existence.

For Rorty (1989), the contingency of language underpins the stance of irony. Here irony means holding to beliefs and attitudes which one knows are contingent and could be otherwise, that is, they have no universal foundations. In turn, this irony leads us to ask about what kind of human being we want to be (for no transcendental truth and no transcendental God can answer this question for us). This includes questions about us as individuals – who we want to be – and questions about our relations to fellow human beings – how shall we treat others? For Rorty, these are pragmatic questions requiring political-value responses. They are not metaphysical or epistemological issues.

Truth as social commendation

Rorty argues that most of the beliefs that we hold to be 'true' are indeed 'true'. However, to say that something is true is not to make an epistemological statement about correspondence between language and reality. Rather, it is to deploy a consensual term that refers to degrees of agreement and co-ordination of habits of action. To say that something is not necessarily true is to suggest that someone has come up with a better way of describing things. Here the idea of 'better' refers to a value judgement about the consequences of describing the world in this way (including its predictive power).

For Rorty, knowledge is a matter not of getting a true or objective picture of reality but of learning how best to cope with the world. We produce various descriptions of the world and use those that seem best suited to our purposes. In this view, continued redescription of our world and the playing-off of discourses against each other is a pragmatically desirable thing to do because of the following:

- **It offers the possibility of an enlargement of the self and the improvement of the human condition through comparison between different actual practices.**

- **'Our minds gradually grow larger and stronger and more interesting by the addition of new options – new candidates for belief and desire, phrased in new vocabularies' (Rorty, 1991a: 14).**

- **We are encouraged to listen to the voices of others who may be suffering, where the avoidance of suffering is taken to be the paramount political virtue.**

In sum, scientific, philosophical or cultural analysis cannot offer final single resolutions of questions. Our vocabularies are only final in the sense of currently without tenable challenge. While stories are always formed within the conceptual terms of 'our' cultural tradition, we must remain open to the possibility of new vocabularies that persuade us to look at the world differently.

Forging new languages

The struggle to have 'new languages' accepted in the wider social formation is the realm of cultural politics. For example, Rorty argues that feminism represents the redescription of women as subjects. The critical point of his argument is that

> injustices may not be perceived as injustices, even by those who suffer them, until somebody invents a previously unplayed role. Only if somebody has a dream, a voice, and a voice to describe the dream, does what looked liked nature begin to look like culture, what looked liked fate begin to look like a moral abomination. For until then only the language of the oppressor is available, and most oppressors have had the wit to teach the oppressed a language in which the oppressed will sound crazy – *even to themselves* – if they describe themselves as oppressed. (Rorty, 1995: 126)

Thus, the language of feminism brings oppression 'into view' and expands the logical space for moral and political deliberation. In this sense, feminism (and all forms of identity politics) does not need essentialism or foundationalism. What is required are 'new languages' in which the claims of women do not sound crazy but come to be accepted as 'true' (in the sense of a social commendation). As such, feminism does not involve less distorted perception. Rather, it is a language with consequences that serve particular purposes and values. The emergence of such a language is not the discovery of universal truth in opposition to ideology but is part of an evolutionary struggle which has no pre-determined destiny.

Prophetic pragmatism

Rorty regards feminism as fashioning 'women's experience' by creating a language rather than by finding what it is to be a woman or 'unmasking' truth and injustice. As such, feminism is a form of *prophetic pragmatism* that imagines, and seeks to bring into being, an alternative form of community. Feminism forges a moral identity for women as women by gaining semantic authority over themselves and not by assuming that there is a universal essential identity for women waiting to be found.

Fraser (1995a) concurs with Rorty's pragmatism but argues that he locates the redescriptions involved exclusively in individual women. In contrast, she suggests that such redescriptions are best seen as a part of a *collective* feminist politics. Such a politics must involve argument and contestation about which new descriptions will count and which women will be empowered. Fraser links feminism with the best of the democratic tradition and to the creation of a 'feminist counter-sphere' of collective debate and practice.

West (1993) is, like Fraser, a cultural critic sympathetic to pragmatism. However, he worries about Rorty's failure to analyse *power* and to deploy sociological kinds of explanations. This, it is argued, prevents Rorty from being able to identify the realistic and pragmatic collective routes for social change. This is perhaps the major criticism of Rorty's pragmatism, with West locating Rorty's analysis at the level of de-mythologization rather than demystification. Foucauldians will share this concern with the place of power in social life.

Private identities and public politics

Rorty argues for the kind of society which will 'make it as easy as possible for people to achieve their wildly different private ends without hurting each other' (Rorty, 1991b: 196). He wants to forge social institutions that best allow different and diverse private identity projects to prosper. This argument suggests the need for dialogue and underpins the procedural arguments for a diverse and plural public sphere of citizens. That is, our best chance of pursuing a private identity project may be to live in a culture that prides itself on being heterogeneous.

Rorty advocates both a politics of 'new languages' and political action on the level of institutions and policy. The 'Left', Rorty argues, is, or should be, 'the party of hope' (Rorty, 1998: 14) in the struggle for social justice. However, 'In so far as the Left becomes spectorial and retrospective, it ceases to be a Left' (ibid.:). It is Rorty's contention that to a major extent the cultural left has become a spectator left. That it is more interested in theorizing than in the practical politics of material change. The cultural left, he suggests, prefers knowledge to hope. It imagines that it can somehow 'get it right' on the level of theory and has given up on the practical task of making democratic institutions once again serve social justice. This is not to discount the fact that 'The cultural Left has had extraordinary success. In addition to being centers of genuinely original scholarship, the new academic programs have done what they were, semi-consciously, designed to do: they have decreased the amount of sadism in our country' (ibid.: 80–1). Consequently, while there has been little legislative change for social justice, 'the change in the way we treat one another has been enormous' (ibid.). For example, 'It is still easy to be humiliated for being a woman in America, but such humiliation is not so frequent as it was thirty years ago' (ibid.: 81–2). However, for Rorty the contemporary left remains more interested in cultural power than in economic, social and political power. Further, it has given up on practical reform in favour of an abstract and wholly theoretical revolutionary desire to overturn the 'system'.

Rorty concurs with the anti-representationalism of Nietzsche, Foucault and Derrida, the most influential philosophers within cultural studies. However, while they adopt a revolutionary tone, Rorty talks of reformism and pragmatic social experimentalism. Overall, the Rortian thesis combines:

- a commitment to the cultural politics of difference, that is, to language-based re-descriptions of the world which expand the realm of democratic cultures;

- a commitment to the need for the public policy that supports democracy and social justice.

✓ *A cultural politics of representation and a cultural policy orientation need not, within liberal-democratic states, be opposed.*

The implications of pragmatism for cultural studies

Much that Rorty has to say about truth and knowledge is in accordance with the predominant voices within cultural studies. The main points of difference tend to be in regard to the methods by which one seeks to forward social justice. Rorty puts more stress than many cultural studies writers do on the routine politics of liberal democracies. He is committed to the development of values such as hope rather than upon the expansion of theory in relation to social objectives.

Overall, a pragmatist cultural studies would hold to the following ideas:

- There are no universal metaphysical truths that can found theory or political action.

- Truth is a social and cultural construction.

- Language is central to meaning and culture.

- Truth inheres in local stories not in grand narratives.

- Personal projects and identity politics require us to write new stories about ourselves.

- It is necessary to engage in the politics of liberal democracies at the level of the state and thus also in the formation of cultural policy.

- The development of personal self-reflection and irony is to be welcomed in liberal democracies because it furthers tolerance and solidarity.

- It is necessary to develop hope in the struggle for social justice.

DECONSTRUCT THIS: CULTURAL CRITICISM VS. CULTURAL POLICY

- *How can cultural criticism shape cultural policy?*
- *How does cultural policy impact on cultural criticism?*
- *Do we need to distinguish between the generation of criticism and the production of policy?*

SUMMARY

In this chapter we have explored a number of different ways in which cultural studies has conceived of cultural politics inside and outside of the academy. Cultural politics was defined as the power to name and represent the world, where language is constitutive of the world and a guide to action. Cultural politics can be conceived of as a series of collective social struggles organized around class, gender, race, sexuality, age, etc., that seeks to redescribe the social in terms of specific values and hoped-for-consequences.

In the course of the chapter we encountered a number of conceptualizations of cultural politics operating within the broad frame of the struggle over and within meaning. For example, we noted the influential 'Gramscian moment' in cultural studies and its revision by Laclau, Mouffe and Hall towards a politics of difference. This involved:

- a move away from class as the central axis of politics;
- an acceptance of the contingent anti-essential character of social classifications and political alliances;
- a move towards the 'politics of articulation' and 'the politics of representation'.

We noted a number of challenges to the cultural politics of difference. In particular, we concentrated on Bennett's call for cultural studies to engage more productively in cultural policy formation and implementation. This argument was based on an interpretation of Foucault's concept of 'governmentality' whereby culture is an arm of government and a 'reformer's science'. At the same time, we noted a sense in which the cultural policy call seemed to downplay the question of values and the need for critical intellectual enquiry. Finally, we briefly explored pragmatism as a philosophy that might offer a route for uniting the politics of difference and representation with cultural policy.

Glossary

The Language-Game of Cultural Studies

SIGNPOSTS TO THE COMMON USAGE OF KEY TERMS

Acculturation: A set of social processes by which we learn how to 'go on' in a culture through the acquisition of the language, values, norms and maps of meaning that constitute a way of life.

Active audience: The capability of audiences to be dynamic creators and producers of meaning rather than being passive receptors of those generated by texts.

Agency: The socially determined capability to act and make a difference. This idea is not to be confused with a self-originating transcendental subject.

Anti-essentialism: Words are not held to have referents with essential or universal qualities; rather, meaning is generated through the relationship between signs. Consequently, being discursive constructions, categories change their meanings according to time, place and usage. For example, since words do not refer to essences, identity is not a fixed universal 'thing' but a description in language.

Articulation: A temporary unity of discursive elements that do not have to 'go together'. An articulation is the form of the connection that can make a unity of two different elements under certain conditions. Articulation suggests expressing/representing and a joining together so that, for example, questions of gender may connect with race but in context-specific and contingent ways.

Authenticity (claims): A claim that a category is genuine, natural, true and pure. For example, that the culture of a place is authentic because uncontaminated by tourism or that a youth culture is pure and uncorrupted by consumer capitalism. Closely related to the notion of essentialism in that authenticity implies immaculate origins.

Body (The): The body is normally understood to be the physical flesh and bones of an organism. However, within cultural studies the body is also held to be stylized and performed, that is worked over by culture. Thus, we are constantly called upon to perform, 'body work' in the form of, for example, diets, exercise and cosmetic surgery.

Bricolage: The rearrangement and juxtaposition of previously unconnected signifying objects to produce new meanings in fresh contexts. A process of re-signification by which cultural signs with established meanings are reorganized into new codes of meaning.

Bricoleur: Someone who constructs a bricolage (above). Within cultural studies the term has most commonly been applied to those who stylize themselves using the clothing and artefacts of popular culture.

Capitalism: A dynamic and globalizing system of industrial production and exchange based on private property and the pursuit of profit. For Marxism, capitalism is an exploitative order that gives rise to the social relations of class conflict.

Citizenship: A form of identity by which individuals are granted a sense of belonging, social rights and obligations within political communities. Citizenship articulates civil society and the state.

Class: A classification of persons into groups based on shared socio-economic conditions. Class is a relational set of inequalities with economic, social, political and ideological dimensions. Marxism has defined class as a relationship to the means of production. Post-Marxists have seen class as a discursively formed collective subject position.

Codes (cultural): A system of representation by which signs and their meanings are arranged by cultural convention to temporarily stabilize significances in particular ways. Traffic light signs are coded in a sequence red (stop), amber (pause), green (go). Objects are commonly gender-coded: washing machine (female), drill (male), cooker (female), car (male).

Commodification: The process associated with capitalism by which objects, qualities and signs are turned into commodities, where a commodity is something whose prime purpose is sale in the marketplace.

Conjunctural (analysis): A form of analysis which is historically and contextually specific. An exploration of the assemblage, coming together or articulation of particular forces, determinations or logics at specific times and places.

Constructionism: A generic name given to anti-essentialist theories that stress the culturally and historically specific social creation of meaningful categories and phenomena. This is in contrast to theories that appeal to universal and biological explanations for phenomena.

Convergence: This concept refers to the breaking down of barriers between technologies and industrial sectors. The most common usage within cultural studies relates to the communications industries and thus to the information superhighway. The mobile phone is increasingly a site for the convergence of previously separate functions such as phone calls, photography, playing music and connecting to the Internet.

Cultural identity: A snapshot of unfolding meanings relating to self-nomination or ascription by others. Thus, cultural self-identity can be understood as a description of ourselves with which we identify. Social identity would refer to the descriptions others have of us. Cultural identity relates to the nodal points of cultural meaning, most notably class, gender, race, ethnicity, nation and age.

Cultural imperialism: Said to involve the domination of one culture by another, leading to the suppression and potential obliteration of the dominated culture. It is usually conceived of in terms of the ascendancy of specific nations and/or global consumer capitalism.

Cultural materialism: Concerned to explore how and why meanings are inscribed at the moment of production. It involves the exploration of signification in the context of the means and conditions of its production. Cultural materialism is concerned with the connections between cultural practices and political economy.

Cultural policy: Procedures, strategies and tactics that seek to regulate and administer the production and distribution of cultural products and practices. Practitioners of cultural policy seek an engagement with the institutions, organizations and management of cultural power.

Cultural politics: Concerned with issues of power in the acts of naming and representation that constitute our cultural maps of meaning. Cultural politics is concerned with the contestation over the meanings and resources of culture. It involves the writing of new languages by which to describe ourselves in the belief that they will have desirable social consequences.

Cultural studies: An interdisciplinary or post-disciplinary field of enquiry that explores the production and inculcation of maps of meaning. A discursive formation, or regulated way of speaking, concerned with issues of power in the signifying practices of human formations.

Culturalism: An approach to the study of culture associated with Raymond Williams that stresses an anthropological and historically informed analysis. There is a stress on the 'ordinariness' of culture and the active, creative capacity of common people to construct shared meaningful practices.

Culture: The concept of culture does not represent an entity in an independent object world. It is best thought of as a mobile signifier that enables distinct ways of talking about human activity. The concept of culture is thus political and contingent. In so far as cultural studies has a distinguishing take on the concept of culture, it is one that stresses the intersection of power and meaning. Culture can also be understood as overlapping maps of criss-crossing discursive meaning which form zones of temporary coherence and shared but always contested significance in a social space. The production and exchange of meanings, or signifying practices, leading to that which is distinctive about a way of life.

Culture jamming: The practice of subverting the semiotics of the media by turning commercial rhetoric against itself. Culture jamming is an act of cultural resistance that modifies logos and advertisements in order to convey a meaning different from the one intended. It transforms media messages into their opposite in order to raise political concerns.

Cyberactivism: The use of the Internet, and particularly e-mail, www sites and blogs, as vehicles for political agitation.

Cyberdemocracy: This concept refers both to the idea that digital media could contribute to democratic processes, through, for example, electronic voting, and to the possibilities that the Internet and other digital media could be spheres of democratic participation in their own right.

Cyberspace: A spatial metaphor for the 'nowhere' place in which the electronic activities of computers, cable systems and other digital communications technologies occur. The concept refers to the virtual space of electronic culture. A computer-generated collective hallucination.

Cyborg: An entity that is part organism and part machine and as such blurs the boundaries between them. Cyborgs appear regularly in science fiction such as *The Terminator* series of films. Human beings are cyborgs as they use technology to support them; for example, contact lenses, heart pacemakers and prosthetic limbs.

Deconstruction: To take apart, to undo, in order to seek out and display the assumptions, rhetorical strategies and blind-spots of texts. The dismantling of hierarchical binary oppositions such as reality/appearance, nature/culture, reason/madness, in order to show: (a) that one part of the binary is devalued as inferior; (b) that the binary serves to guarantee truth; and (c) that each part of the binary is implicated in the other.

Deregulation: Refers in a communications context to the relaxation of state prescriptions governing the ownership and content of the media. It involved the replacement of such regulations with others that were less stringent in their restrictions. Thus deregulation is better described as re-regulation.

Diasporas: Dispersed networks of ethnically and culturally related peoples. The concept is concerned with ideas of travel, migration, scattering, displacement, homes and borders. It commonly, but not always, connotes aliens, displaced persons, wanderers, forced and reluctant flight.

Différance: After Derrida, 'difference and deferral'. Meaning is said to be unstable and never complete since the production of meaning is continually deferred and added to by the meanings of other words. This involves the continual supplementarity of meaning, the substitution and adding of meanings through the play of signifiers.

Difference: Non-identical, dissimilar, distinction, division, otherness, variance. Difference is the mechanism for the generation of meaning. Difference is not an essence or attribute of an object but a position or perspective of signification.

Digital divide: The communications revolution is driven by digital technology such as computers, cameras, music players and mobile phones. However, class, gender, race and nationality restrict access to this technology. The gap between those who have access to digital technology and those who do not is called the digital divide.

Discourse: For Foucault, from whom cultural studies derives its usage of this term, discourse 'unites' both language and practice. The idea refers to the production of knowledge through language which gives bounded meanings to material objects and social practices. Material objects and social practices are given meaning or 'brought into view' by language and are thus discursively formed. Discourse constructs, defines and produces the objects of knowledge in a regulated and intelligible way while excluding other forms of reasoning as unintelligible.

Discursive formation: A pattern of discursive events that refer to, or bring into being, a common object across a number of sites.

Disorganized capitalism: A reorganization of capitalism on a world-wide scale involving the dispersal of capital through globalized production, financing and distribution. In the west this has been associated with deindustrialization, a sectoral shift towards the service sector and a rise in flexible forms of work organization.

Distinctions (of taste): A concept associated with Bourdieu. Here distinctions of cultural taste are understood to be classifications based on lines of power. Distinctions are never simply statements of equal difference but entail claims to authority and authenticity.

Emotions: Emotions are the consequence of interaction between brain biochemistry cognitive classificatory functions and cultural meaning. They involve physiological changes, learned responses and cognitive appraisal activities. Emotion involves both universal bodily responses and learned cultural differences in expression and display.

Encoding–decoding: Encoding refers to the organization of signs into codes, while decoding refers to the process by which readers generate meaning from them. The encoding–decoding model of communication as developed by Stuart Hall suggests that whatever analysis of textual meanings a critic may undertake, it is far from certain which of the identified meanings, if any, will be activated by actual readers/audiences/consumers.

Enlightenment (The): A stance in eighteenth-century European philosophy that sought after universal truths in search of the improvement of the human condition that it called progress. The powers of Reason – especially science – to demystify the world were at the centre of the project. The moral-political agenda of the enlightenment was one of equality, liberty and fraternity.

Epistemology: The domain of intellectual enquiry that is concerned with the source and status of knowledge. Thus, the question 'what is truth?' is an epistemological issue.

Essentialism: Essentialism assumes that words have stable referents so that social categories reflect an essential underlying identity. By this token there would be stable truths to be found and an essence of, for example, femininity. Here words refer to fixed essences and thus identities are regarded as stable entities.

Ethnicity: A cultural term for boundary formation between groups of people who have been discursively constructed as sharing values, norms, practices, symbols and artefacts and are seen as such by themselves and others. Closely connected to the concept of race.

Ethnography: An empirical and theoretical approach that seeks detailed holistic description and analysis of cultures based on intensive participative fieldwork. Qualitative small-scale and detailed exploration of the norms, values and artefacts of culture as they are connected to the wider social processes of a 'whole way of life'.

Evolution: The processes of adaptive change through natural selection made by organisms in order to survive, which structure the long-term development of the species. Natural selection is the inevitable outcome of the interaction of phenotypic variation, differential fitness and heritability.

Evolutionary psychology: Concerned with the evolution of the cognitive mechanisms that arose as fitness-enhancing effects in the context of our ancestral environments and that oversee behaviour. Here the foundations of culture are held to be the evolved psychological mechanisms that utilize and work over social and cultural inputs.

Femininity: A discursive-performative construction that describes and disciplines the cultural characteristics associated with what it means to be a woman; that is, culturally regulated behaviour regarded as socially appropriate to women.

Feminism: (a) Diverse body of theoretical work; (b) social and political movement. Feminism aims to examine the position of women in society and to further their interests.

Foundationalism: The attempt to give absolute universal grounds or justifications for the truth of knowledge and values.

Gender: The cultural assumptions and practices that govern the social construction of men, women and their social relations. Gender is a matter of how men and women are represented and performed.

Genealogy: Concerned with derivation and lineage. A Foucauldian usage in cultural studies examines power and the historical continuities and discontinuities of discourses as they are brought into play under specific and irreducible historical conditions.

Genome: A genome or genotype is the total collection of genes, or digitally encoded chemical information, that an organism carries.

Genre: A regulated narrative process producing coherence and credibility through patterns of similarity and difference.

Global city: Urban conglomerations acting as command and control points for dispersed sets of economic activities. They are sites of accumulation, distribution and circulation of capital as well as nodal points of information exchange and decision-making processes.

Globalization: Increasing multi-directional economic, social, cultural and political global connections across the world and our awareness of them. Globalization is associated with the institutions of modernity and time-space compression or the shrinking world.

Glocalization: A term used to express the global production of the local and the localization of the global; that is, the way in which the global is already in the local and the production of the local is generated by a global discourse.

Governmentality: A form of regulation throughout the social order by which a population becomes subject to bureaucratic regimes and modes of discipline. The institutions, procedures, analyses and calculations that form specific governmental apparatuses and forms of knowledge which are constitutive of self-reflective conduct and ethical competencies.

Grand narrative: An overarching story or metanarrative that claims universal validity as a foundational scheme that justifies the rational, scientific, technological and political projects of the modern world. Examples would be Marxism, Christianity and science.

Hegemony: A temporary closure of meaning supportive of the powerful. The process of making, maintaining and reproducing the governing sets of meanings of a given culture. For Gramsci, hegemony implies a situation where a 'historical bloc' of ruling-class factions exercise social authority and leadership over the subordinate classes through a combination of force and, more importantly, consent.

Holism: A methodological approach that insists on the non-separability of the parts from the whole in which the properties of the whole are not fully determined by the properties of its parts. The whole is always more than the sum of its parts and the designation of levels is a device for understanding that can only be used in the context of a well-defined analytic arrangement or metaphor designed to achieve particular purposes.

Homology: Synchronic relationship by which social structures, social values and cultural symbols are said to 'fit' together; that is, the way in which the structure and meanings of symbols and artifacts parallel and reflect the concerns of a social group.

Hybridity: The mixing together of different cultural elements to create new meanings and identities. Hybrids destabilize and blur established cultural boundaries in a process of fusion or creolization. Hybrid identities include British-Asians and Chinese-Australians.

Hyperreality: A reality effect by which the real is produced according to a model so that representations become more real than the real. The distinction between the real and a representation collapses or implodes. A simulation or artificial production of real life that executes its own world to constitute reality.

Hypertext: The organization of signs within computer software which forms a network of information pathways. It is made up of a series of interlinked textual blocs where one text refers you to another, for example multiple menu options or worldwide web links.

Identification: The process of forming contingent and temporary points of attachment or emotional investment which, through fantasy, partially suture or stitch together discourses and psychic/emotional forces.

Identity: A temporary stabilization of meaning or description of ourselves with which we emotionally identify. Identity is a becoming rather than a fixed entity involving the suturing or stitching together of the discursive 'outside' with the 'internal' processes of subjectivity. Points of temporary attachment to the subject positions which discursive practices construct for us.

Identity politics: The forging of 'new languages' of identity combined with acting to change social practices, usually through the formation of coalitions where at least some values are shared. Feminism can be understood as a form of identity politics.

Identity project: The ongoing creation of narratives of self-identity relating to our perceptions of the past, present and hoped-for future.

Ideology: The concept of ideology is best understood as the 'binding and justifying ideas' of any social group. It is commonly used to designate the attempt to fix meanings and world views in support of the powerful. Here ideology is said to be constituted by maps of meaning that, while they purport to be universal truths, are historically specific understandings which obscure and maintain the power of social groups (e.g. class, gender, race).

Information society (economy): A concept used to designate a society in which information is the key commodity of a post-industrial economy where economic, social, military and cultural capabilities are information-based. The management of information replaces the manufacturing sector as the key economic driver. This is a global economy driven by a digital technological revolution.

Intertextuality: The accumulation and generation of meaning across texts, where all meanings depend on other meanings. The self-conscious citation of one text within another as an expression of enlarged cultural self-consciousness.

Irony: A reflexive understanding of the contingency or lack of foundations of one's own values and culture that is said to be a feature of the postmodern condition. The self-knowledge that what is being said or done has been said and done before. The doubleness of a self-undermining statement by which the already known is spoken in inverted commas.

Language-game: Whereby the meaning of words is located in their usage in a complex network of relationships, rather than being derived from some essential characteristic or referent. Meaning is contextual and relational. It depends on the relationships between words that have 'family resemblances' and on specific utterances in the context of pragmatic narratives.

Life-politics: Concerned with reflexivity, self-actualization, choice and lifestyle in pursuit of qualitatively better ways to live. Life-politics revolves around the creation of justifiable forms of life involving less emphasis on economic accumulation and more on the need to re-moralize social life and adopt new lifestyles.

Marxism: A body of thought derived from the work of Karl Marx which stresses the determining role of the material conditions of existence and the historical specificity of human affairs. Marxism, which has focused on the development and dynamics of capitalism and class conflict, makes claims to be an emancipatory philosophy of equality.

Masculinity: A discursive-performative construction that describes and disciplines the cultural characteristics associated with what it means to be a man; that is, culturally regulated behaviour regarded as socially appropriate to men.

Mass culture: Pejorative term used to suggest the inferiority of commodity-based capitalist culture as inauthentic, manipulative and unsatisfying. The concept draws its power from the contrast with high culture and/or an alleged authentic people's culture.

Meme: The smallest cultural element that is replicated by means of the human capacity for imitation. Memes are cultural instructions for carrying out behaviour stored in the brains and passed on by imitation. Human consciousness is said to be a product of memes.

Modernism: (a) The cultural experience of modernity marked by change, ambiguity, doubt, risk, uncertainty and fragmentation; (b) artistic style marked by aesthetic self-consciousness, montage and the rejection of realism; (c) philosophical position by which certain knowledge is sought after, even though it is recognized as subject to continual and chronic revision.

Modernity: A post-traditional, post-medieval historical period marked by the rise of industrialism, capitalism, the nation-state and forms of surveillance.

Moral panic: A social process by which the media latch on to a culturally identified group and label their behaviour as troublesome and likely to recur. The public response is a moral panic that seeks to track down and punish the deviant culture.

Multimedia corporations: Media corporations operating across the range of media outlets.

Multiple identities: The assumption of different and potentially contradictory identities at different times and places that do not form a unified coherent self. We do not *have* multiple identities; rather, we *are* constituted as multiple. Nevertheless, we construct narratives of unity so that we appear to ourselves as being 'One'.

Myth: Story or fable that acts as a symbolic guide or map of meaning and significance in the cosmos. After Barthes, the concept implies the naturalization of the connotative level of meaning.

Narrative: A sequential account or purported record of events ordered across time into a plot. The concept of narrative refers to the form, pattern or structure by which stories are constructed and told.

National identity: A form of imaginative identification with the nation-state as expressed through symbols and discourses. Thus, nations are not only political formations but also systems of cultural representation, so that national identity is continually reproduced through discursive action.

New Social Movements: Provisional symbolic and political collectives that stress democratic participation and ethics-based action located outside of the workplace and distinct from class. Encompasses the feminist movement, ecology politics, peace movements, youth movements and the politics of cultural identities.

News values: The values that structure the selection of news items and their presentation.

Orientalism: That set of western discourses which constructed an Orient in ways that depend on and reproduce the positional superiority and hegemony of the west. A system of representations impregnated with European superiority, racism and imperialism that brought the idea of 'The Orient' into western learning.

Patriarchy: The recurrent and systematic domination of men over subordinated women across a range of social institutions and practices. The concept carries connotations of the male-headed family, mastery and superiority.

Performativity: Discursive practice that enacts or produces that which it names through citation and reiteration of the norms or conventions of the 'law'. Thus, the discursive production of identities through repetition and recitation of regulated ways of speaking about identity categories (e.g. masculinity).

Phallocentrism: Male-centred discourse, that is, from the perspective of masculinity. Here the Phallus is held to be the symbolic transcendental universal signifier of source, self-origination and unified agency.

Phenotype: A concept drawn from evolutionary biology that refers to the manifested morphology, physiology and behaviour of an organism. Phenotypic effects are the consequence of the interaction between genes and the environment.

Place: Socially constructed site or location in space marked by identification or emotional investment. Bounded manifestations of the production of meaning in space.

Political economy: A domain of knowledge concerned with power and the distribution of economic resources. Political economy explores the questions of who owns and controls the institutions of economy, society and culture.

Politics: Concerned with the numerous manifestations and relations of power at all levels of human interaction. Cultural studies has been particularly concerned with the 'politics of representation': the way that power is implicated in the construction, regulation and contestation of cultural classifications through the temporary stabilization of meaning.

Polysemic: Signs carry many potential meanings. Signs do not have transparent and authoritative meaning by dint of reference to an independent object world but depend on actual usage within a dialogic relationship between speaker and listener. The 'multi-accentuality' of signs is the site of attempts by social convention and social struggles to fix meaning.

Popular culture: Widespread and common public texts. The meanings and practices produced by popular audiences. As a political category, the popular is a site of power and the struggle over meaning. The popular transgresses the boundaries of cultural power and exposes the arbitrary character of cultural classification through challenging notions of high/low.

Positionality: Indicating that knowledge and 'voice' are always located in time, space and social power. The concept of positionality refers us to the who, where, when and why of speaking, judgement and comprehension.

Postcolonialism: Critical theory that explores the discursive condition of post-coloniality, that is, colonial relations and their aftermath. Postcolonial theory explores postcolonial discourses and their subject positions in relation to themes of race, nation, subjectivity, power, subalterns, hybridity and creolization.

Post-Feminism: The fundamental argument of Post-Feminism is that the central tenets of feminism have been absorbed into western culture and surpassed. Post-feminist writers have suggested that most of the systematic barriers to women's advancement have been removed in the west and that women are not neccessarily oppressed by dint of being women. Post-feminism opposes the idea that women are passive victims of Patriarchy.

Post-Fordism: This term marks the movement from an economy based on the mass production of standardized goods for an aggregated market (Fordism) to one in which the leading edge of the economy is marked by small-scale customized production for niche markets. Post-Fordism is founded on the flexibility of labour and the individualization of consumption patterns. From a production- to consumption-oriented society.

Post-industrial society: A concept suggesting that industrialized societies are witnessing a shift of locus from industrial manufacturing to service industries centred on information technology. Information production and exchange along with the displacement of significance from production to consumption are said to be markers of the post-industrial society.

Post-Marxism: After Marxism, by which Marxism is no longer held to be the primary explanatory narrative of our time. The superseding of Marxism in cultural studies through the selective retention of that which is held to be valuable in it. A form of anti-essentialist Marxism based on discourse theory.

Postmodernism: (a) Cultural style marked by intertextuality, irony, pastiche, genre blurring and bricolage; (b) philosophical movement which rejects 'grand narratives' (i.e. universal explanations of human history and activity) in favour of irony and local knowledges.

Postmodernity: (a) A historical period after modernity marked by the centrality of consumption in a post-industrial context; (b) a cultural sensibility which rejects 'grand narratives' in favour of local truths within specific language-games.

Poststructuralism: 'After structuralism' involving both critique and absorption. Poststructuralism absorbs structuralism's stress on the relational character of language and the production of significance through difference. Poststructuralism rejects the idea of a stable structure of binary pairs; rather, meaning is always deferred, in process and intertextual. Poststructuralism rejects the search for origins, stable meaning, universal truth and the 'direction' of history.

Power: Commonly thought of in terms of a force by which individuals or groups are able to achieve their aims or interests against the will of others. Power here is constraining (power over) and a zero-sum model (you have it or you do not) organized into binary power blocs. However, cultural studies has, after Foucault, stressed that power is also productive and enabling (power to) and that power circulates through all levels of society and all social relationships.

Power/knowledge: After Foucault, knowledge is understood to be not neutral or universal but historically specific and always implicated in questions of social power. Power and knowledge are mutually constitutive.

Pragmatism: A philosophical tradition that adopts an anti-foundationalist, anti-representationlist and anti-realist view of truth and knowledege. Here all problems are problems of conduct and all judgements are implicitly judgements of value. Pragmatism has a radically contingent view of the world where truth ends with social practice and progress is a retrospective value judgement based on trial-and-error experimentalism.

Psychoanalysis: A body of thought and therapeutic practice developed from the work of Freud that argues that the human subject is divided into the ego, superego and unconscious. Psychoanalysis within cultural studies has been deployed to explore the construction and formation of sexed subjectivity.

Public sphere: A space for democratic public debate and argument that mediates between civil society and the state, in which the public organizes itself, and in which 'public opinion' is formed.

Race: A signifier indicating categories of people based on alleged biological characteristics, including skin pigmentation. A 'racialized group' would be one identified and subordinated on the grounds of race as a discursive construct.

Rationality: Refers to the idea that the grounds on which beliefs are held are coherent, logical and compatible with experience. Rationality is not a universal metaphysical foundation but a form of social commendation founded on cultural procedures that is deployed to justify beliefs and action.

Realism: (a) An epistemological claim that the truth is identifiable as that which corresponds to or pictures the real; (b) a set of aesthetic conventions by which texts create 'reality effects' and purport to represent the real.

Reductionism: By which one category or phenomenon is likened to and explained solely in terms of another category or phenomenon. In particular, cultural studies has argued against economic reductionism, by which cultural texts are accounted for in terms of political economy.

Reflexivity: A process of continuous self-monitoring. The use of knowledge about social life as a constitutive element of it. Discourse about experience and revision of social activity in the light of new knowledge.

Representation: By which signifying practices appear to stand for or depict another object or practice in the 'real' world. Better described as a 'representational effect' since signs do not stand for or reflect objects in a direct 'mirroring' mode. Representations are constitutive of culture, meaning and knowledge.

Resistance: A category of normative judgement about acts. Resistance issues from relationships of power and subordination in the form of challenges to and negotiations of the ascendant order. Resistance is relational and conjunctural.

Self-identity: The way we think about ourselves and construct unifying narratives of the self with which we emotionally identify; that is, a reflexive discursive construction of self.

Semiotics: The study (or 'science') of signs and signification.

Sex: Sex has been taken to refer to the biological markers of male and female bodies while gender concerns the cultural assumptions and practices which govern the social construction of men and women. Butler holds that sex and gender can both be taken to be discursive-performative social constructions.

Signification: The processes of generating meaning through the organization of a system of signs (signifying system).

Signifieds: Concepts, ideas, sense, significance, meaning.

Signifiers: The form or medium of signs, for example a sound, an image, the marks that form a word on the page.

Signifying practices: Meaning-producing activities. The production and exchange of signs generating significance, that is, meaning, sense and importance.

Signs: Marks and noises that generate or carry meaning through their relationship with other signs. Signs stand in for or represent concepts.

Simulacrum: Imitation or copy without an original or referent. The simulation becomes more real than the real; the reality of simulation is the measure of the real.

Social: Of or in society, where society is held to be the organization of human association and relationships through rule-governed interactions. Here, the social is held to be an autonomous sphere of activity. However, many cultural studies theorists hold the 'social' to have no proper object of reference, being a sign constituted through a series of discursive differences. For them, the social is not an object but a field of contestation in which multiple descriptions of self and others compete for ascendancy.

Social formation: The social is conceived of as a concrete, historically produced complex assemblage composed of different practices (ideological, political, economic). A social formation is said to consist of levels of practice, each of which has its own specificity, that are articulated together in particular conjunctures where there is no necessary or automatic correspondence or relationship to each other.

Social identity: Discursively constructed social expectations, normative rights and obligations that are ascribed to individuals as constituting who they are. The notion of what it is to be an individual is social and cultural in character and identity is formed from social and cultural resources, notably language.

Space: Space is defined by the relationship between at least two particles. Social space is a dynamic, multitudinous and changing social construction constituted in and through social relations of power.

Stereotype: Vivid but simple representations which reduce persons to a set of exaggerated, usually negative, character traits. A stereotype is a form of representation that essentializes (i.e. suggests that categories have inherent and universal characteristics) others through the operation of power.

Strategic essentialism: Acting 'as if' identities were stable for specific political reasons, for example accepting the category of 'woman' to be a stable unity for the purposes of mobilizing women in feminist political action.

Structuralism: A body of thought (derived from the study of language) that is concerned with the structures of signs that allow linguistic performance to be possible. A structuralist understanding of culture is concerned with the 'systems of relations' of an underlying structure that forms the grammar which makes meaning possible (rather than actual performance in its infinite variations).

Structure: Regularities or stable patterns. The rules and conventions that organize language (*langue*). Recurrent organization and patterned arrangements of human relationships (social structure). Structures are 'virtual' in that they derive from the way we represent the social world rather than being 'things'.

Style: A signifying practice involving the organization of objects in conjunction with activities and attitudes through active bricolage to signify difference and identity. Associated with youth subcultures and the display of codes of meaning through the transformation of commodities as cultural signs.

Subculture: Groups of persons so labelled who share distinct values and norms which are held to be at variance with dominant or mainstream society. Subcultures offer maps of meaning which make the world intelligible to its members.

Subject positions: Empty spaces or functions in discourse from which the world makes sense. The speaking subject is dependent on the prior existence of discursive positions since discourse constitutes the 'I' through the processes of signification.

Subjectivity: The condition and processes of being a person or self. For cultural studies, subjectivity is often regarded, after Foucault, as an 'effect' of discourse because subjectivity is constituted by the subject positions which discourse obliges us to take up. The characteristics of agency and identity that discursive subject positions enable for a speaking subject.

Surveillance: The monitoring and collection of information about subject populations with an eye to the supervision and regulation of activities.

Symbolic: A sign whereby one item stands in for or represents another.

Symbolic economy: On the one hand, this idea refers to the organization of signs into meaningful representations. On the other hand, it suggests the way in which the symbolic practices of culture are also productive activities of a monetary economy.

Symbolic order: Regulated and patterned forms of significance or meaning constituted by the relations of difference between signs; that is, the structuring of the signs and representations that constitute culture.

Synergy: The bringing together of previously separate activities or moments in the processes of production and exchange to produce higher profits. Manifested in the formation of multinational multimedia corporations.

Text: The everyday usage of the term refers to writing in its various forms so that books and magazines are texts. However, it is an axiom of cultural studies that a text is anything that generates meaning through signifying practices. Hence, dress, television programmes, images, sporting events, pop stars, etc., can all be read as texts.

Theory: Narratives that seek to distinguish and account for the general features which describe, define and explain persistently perceived occurrences. Theory is a tool, instrument or logic for intervening in the world through the mechanisms of description, definition, prediction and control. Theory construction is a self-reflexive discursive endeavour that seeks to interpret and intervene in the world.

Truth: Common sense, and realist epistemology, understands truth to be that which corresponds to or pictures the real in an objective way. Constructionism, of which cultural studies is a manifestation, argues that truth is a social creation. Cultural studies speaks of 'regimes of truth', a Foucauldian term meaning that which comes to count as truth through the operation of power. For Rortian pragmatism, truth is a social commendation suggesting a consensual term of approval inseparable from values.

Under erasure: A Derridean term which forms part of the vocabulary of deconstructionism. To place a word under erasure is to indicate that word is inaccurate or mistaken but remains one that we cannot escape using. This suggests the undecidability of metaphysical binary oppositions.

Urbanization: The social, economic and cultural practices that generate metropolitan zones. The concept of urbanization implies the turning of the countryside into a cityscape as one of the key features of capitalist industrialization.

Virtual reality: Virtual reality is a representation of a world within digital media. The term implies that the virtual is 'near to' or an 'approximation of' reality. However, in an epistemological sense it is no different from other representations. In social practice, virtual reality refers to both a textual universe in cyberspace and computer-generated images of greater depth and complexity.

References

Aarseth, E.J. (1997) *Cybertext: Perspectives on Ergodic Literature*. London: Johns Hopkins. University Press.

Aarseth, E.J. (2002) 'Playing Research: Methodological Approaches to Game Analysis'. *The 5th International Digital Arts Conference, Melbourne DAC*. Melbourne: RMIT.

Abercrombie, N., Lash, S. and Longhurst, B. (1992) 'Popular Representation: Recasting Realism' in S. Lash and J. Friedman (eds) *Modernity and Identity*. Oxford: Blackwell.

Adorno, T.W. (1941) 'On Popular Music'. *Studies in Philosophy and Social Science*, IX (1).

Adorno, T.W. (1977) 'Commitment' in E. Bloch (ed.) *Aesthetics and Politics*. London: New Left Books.

Adorno, T.W. and Horkheimer, M. (1979) *Dialectic of Enlightenment*. London: Verso.

Aglietta, M. (1979) *A Theory of Capitalist Regulation: The US Experience*. London: Verso.

Alasuutari, P. (1995) *Researching Culture: Qualitative Method and Cultural Studies*. London: Sage.

Alcoff, L. (1989) 'Cultural Feminism versus Post-Structuralism: The Identity Crisis in Feminist Theory' in M. Malson, J. O'Barr, S. Westphal-Wihl and M. Wyer (eds) *Feminist Theory in Practice and Process*. Chicago: University of Chicago Press.

Allen, J. (1992) 'Post-Industrialism and Post-Fordism' in S. Hall, D. Held and T. McGrew (eds) *Modernity and Its Futures*. Cambridge: Polity Press.

Allen, R. (1985) *Speaking of Soap Operas*. Chapel Hill, NC: University of North Carolina Press.

Allen, R. (ed.) (1995) *To Be Continued …: Soap Opera around the World*. London and New York: Routledge.

Althusser, L. (1969) *For Marx*. London: Allen Lane.

Althusser, L. (1971) *Lenin and Philosophy and Other Essays*. London: New Left Books.

Anderson, B. (1983) *Imagined Communities: Reflections on the Origins and Spread of Nationalism*. London: Verso.

Ang, I. (1985) *Watching Dallas: Soap Opera and the Melodramatic Imagination*. London: Methuen.

Ang, I. (1996) *Living Room Wars*. London and New York: Routledge.

Ang, I. and Stratton, J. (1996) 'On the Impossibility of a Global Cultural Studies: "British" Cultural Studies in an International Frame' in D. Morley and D.-K. Chen (eds) *Stuart Hall*. London: Routledge.

Appadurai, A. (1993) 'Disjuncture and Difference in the Global Cultural Economy' in P. Williams and L. Chrisman (eds) *Colonial Discourse and Post-Colonial Theory*. Hemel Hempstead: Harvester Wheatsheaf.

Appiah, K. (1995) 'African Identity' in L. Nicholson and S. Seidman (eds) *Social Postmodernism*. Cambridge: Cambridge University Press.

Arnold, M. (1960) *Culture and Anarchy*. Cambridge: Cambridge University Press.

Ashcroft, B., Griffiths, G. and Tiffin, H. (1989) *The Empire Writes Back*. London and New York: Routledge.

Bahia, K. (1997) 'An Analysis of the Representation of Femininity in Popular Hindi Film of the 1980s and 1990s'. Unpublished dissertation, University of Wolverhampton, UK.

Bakhtin, M. (1984) *Rabelais and his World*. Bloomington, IN: University of Indiana Press.

Ballard, R. (ed.) (1994) *Desh Pardesh: The South Asian Presence in Britain*. London: Hurst & Co.

Balsamo, A. (2000) 'The Virtual Body in Cyberspace' in D. Bell, and B. Kennedy (eds) *The Cybercultures Reader*. London: Rouledge.

Barker, C. (1998) '"Cindy's a Slut": Moral Identities and Moral Responsibility in the "Soap Talk" of British Asian Girls', *Sociology*, 32 (1).

Barker, C. (1999) *Television, Globalization and Cultural Identities*. Milton Keynes: Open University Press.

Barker, C. and André, J. (1996) 'Did You See? Soaps, Teenage Talk and Gendered Identity', *Young: Nordic Journal of Youth Research*, 4 (4).

Barker, M. (1982) *The New Racism*. London: Junction Books.

Barrett, M. (1991) *The Politics of Truth: From Marx to Foucault*. Stanford, CA: Stanford University Press.

Barth, F. (1969) *Ethnic Groups and Boundaries*. London: Allen & Unwin.

Barthes, R. (1967) *The Elements of Semiology*. London: Cape.

Barthes, R. (1972) *Mythologies*. London: Cape.

Barthes, R. (1977) *Image, Music, Text*. Glasgow: Fontana.

Baudelaire, C. (1964) *The Painter of Modern Life and Other Essays*. Oxford: Phaidon Press.

Baudrillard, J. (1983a) *Simulations*. New York: Semiotext(e).

Baudrillard, J. (1983b) *In the Shadow of the Silent Majorities*. New York: Semiotext(e).

Baudrillard, J. (1988) *America*. London: Verso.

Bauman, Z. (1991) *Modernity and Ambivalence*. Cambridge: Polity Press.

Bell, D. (1973) *The Coming of the Post-Industrial Society*. New York: Basic Books.

Bennett, R. (1990) *Decentralization, Local Governments and Markets*. Oxford: Clarendon Press.

Bennett, T. (1992) 'Putting Policy into Cultural Studies' in L. Grossberg, C. Nelson and P. Treichler (eds) *Cultural Studies*. London and New York: Routledge.

Bennett, T. (1998) *Culture: A Reformer's Science*. St Leonards, NSW: Allen & Unwin.

Bennett, T., Martin, G., Mercer, C. and Woollacott, J. (eds) (1981) *Popular Television and Film*. London: British Film Institute.

Bennett, T., Mercer, C. and Woollacott, J. (eds) (1986) *Popular Culture and Social Relations*. Milton Keynes: Open University Press.

Benson, S. (1997) 'The Body, Health and Eating Disorders' in K. Woodward (ed.) *Identity and Difference*. London and Thousand Oaks, CA: Sage.

Berger, A. (2002) *Video Games: A Popular Culture Phenomenon*. New Brunswick: Transaction Publishers.

Berman, M. (1982) *All That Is Solid Melts into Air*. New York: Simon & Schuster.

Best, B. (1997) 'Over-the-Counter-Culture: Retheorizing Resistance in Popular Culture' in S. Redhead with D. Wynne and J. O'Connor (eds) *The Clubcultures Reader: Readings In Popular Cultural Studies*. Oxford: Blackwell.

Best, S. and Kellner, D. (1991) *Postmodern Theory: Critical Interrogations*. Basingstoke and London: Macmillan.

Bey, H. (2005) 'The Information War' in D. Trend (ed.) *Reading Digital Culture*. Oxford: Blackwell.

Bhabha, H. (1990) *Nation and Narration*. London and New York: Routledge.

Bhabha, H. (1994) *The Location of Culture*. London and New York: Routledge.

Biddulph, S. (1994) *Manhood*. Sydney: Finch.

Black, L. and Solomos, J. (2000) *Theories of Race and Racism: A Reader*. London and New York: Routledge.

Blackmore, S. (1999) *The Meme Machine*. Oxford: Oxford University Press.

Blumler, J. (1986) *Television in the United States: Funding Sources and Programming Consequences*. Leeds: University of Leeds.

Bogle, D. (1973) *Toms, Coons, Mulattoes, Mammies and Bucks: An Interpretative History of Blacks in American Films*. New York: Viking Press.

Bordo, S. (1993) *Unbearable Weight: Feminism, Western Culture and the Body*. Berkeley: University of California Press.

Bourdieu, P. (1984) *Distinction: A Social Critique of the Judgement of Taste*. Cambridge, MA: Harvard University Press.

Brah, A. (1996) *Cartographies of Diaspora*. London: Routledge.

Brake, M. (1985) *Comparative Youth Culture: The Sociology of Youth Culture and Youth Subcultures in America, Britain and Canada*. London: Routledge & Kegan Paul.

Bramlett-Solomon, S. and Farwell, T. (1996) 'Sex on Soaps: An Analysis of Black, White and Interracial Couple Intimacy' in V. Berry and C. Manning-Miller (eds) *Mediated Messages and African American Culture*. London and Thousand Oaks, CA: Sage.

Braverman, H. (1974) *Labor and Monopoly Capitalism*. New York: Monthly Review Press.

Brecht, B. (1964) 'A Short Organum for the Theatre' in J. Willett (ed.) *Brecht on the Theatre: The Development of an Aesthetic*. London: Eyre Methuen.

Brecht, B. (1977) 'Against George Lukács' in E. Bloch (ed.) *Aesthetics and Politics*. London: New Left Books.

Brewer, M. and Caporael, L. (1990) 'Selfish Genes Versus Selfish People: Sociobiology as Origin Myth', *Motivation and Emotion*, 14: 237–43.

Brunsdon, C. (1990) 'Problems with Quality', *Screen*, 31 (1).

Brunsdon, C. and Morley, D. (1978) *Everyday Television: 'Nationwide'*. London: British Film Institute.

Buckingham, D. (1987) *Public Secrets: EastEnders and Its Audience*. London: British Film Institute.

Burgess, E. (1967) 'The Growth of the City: An Introduction into a Research Project' in R. Park and E. Burgess (eds) *The City*. London: University of Chicago Press.

Burnham, J. (1941) *The Managerial Revolution*. New York: Doubleday.

Buss, D. (1999a) *Evolutionary Psychology: The New Science of the Mind*. Needham Heights, MA: Allyn & Bacon.

Buss, D. (1999b) 'Evolutionary Psychology: A New Paradigm for Psychological Science' in D. Rosen and M. Luebbert (eds) *Evolution of the Psyche*. Westport: Praeger.

Butler, J. (1990) *Gender Trouble*. New York and London: Routledge.

Butler, J. (1991) 'Imitation and Gender Subordination' in D. Fuss (ed.) *Inside/Out: Lesbian Theories, Gay Theories*. London: Routledge.

Butler, J. (1993) *Bodies That Matter*. London and New York: Routledge.

Campbell, C. (1995) *Race, Myth and the News*. London and Thousand Oaks, CA: Sage.

Cantor, M. (1991) 'The American Family on Television: From Molly Goldberg to Bill Cosby', *Journal of Comparative Family Studies*, 22 (2).

Cantor, M. and Cantor, J. (1992) *Prime Time Television: Content and Control*. London and Newbury Park, CA: Sage.

Carby, H. (1984) 'White Woman Listen' in Centre for Contemporary Cultural Studies (ed.) *The Empire Strikes Back*. London: Hutchinson.

Castells, M. (1977) 'The Class Struggle and Urban Contradictions: The Emergence of Urban Protest Movements in Advanced Industrial Societies' in J. Cowley, A. Kaye, M. Mayo and A. Thompson (eds) *Community or Class Struggle?* London: Stage 1.

Castells, M. (1983) *The City and the Grassroots*. London: Edward Arnold.

Castells, M. (1985) 'High Technology, Economic Restructuring and the Urban–Regional Process in the United States', in M. Castells (ed.) *High Technology, Space and Society*. London and Newbury Park, CA: Sage.

Castells, M. (1989) *The Informational City: Information Technology, Economic Restructuring and the Urban–Regional Process*. Oxford: Blackwell.

Castells, M. (1993) 'The New Informational Economy in the New International Division of Labor' in M. Carnoy (ed.) *The New Global Economy in the Information Age*. University Park, PA: Pennsylvania State University Press.

Castells, M. (1994) 'European Cities, the Informational Society, and the Global Economy', *New Left Review*, 204.

Caughie, J. (1990) 'Playing at Being American', in P. Mellencamp (ed.) *Logics of Television: Essays in Cultural Criticism*. London: British Film Institute.

Chambers, I. (1986) *Popular Culture: The Metropolitan Experience*. London: Methuen.

Chambers, I. (1987) 'Maps for the Metropolis: A Possible Guide to the Present', *Cultural Studies*, I (1).

Chambers, I. (1990) 'Popular Music and Mass Culture' in J. Downing, A. Mohammadi and A. Sreberny-Mohammadi (eds) *Questioning the Media*. London: Sage.

Champion, S. (1997) 'Fear and Loathing in Wisconsin' in S. Redhead with D. Wynne and J. O'Connor (eds) *The Clubcultures Reader: Readings in Popular Cultural Studies*. Oxford: Blackwell.

Chodorow, N. (1978) *The Reproduction of Motherhood*. Berkeley: University of California Press.

Chodorow, N. (1989) *Feminism and Psychoanalytic Theory*. Cambridge: Polity Press.

Christen, Y. (1991) *Sex Differences: Modern Biology and the Unisex Fallacy*. New Brunswick: Transaction Publishers.

Clarke, D. (1996) *Urban World/Global City*. London: Routledge.

Clarke, J. (1976) 'Style' in S. Hall and T. Jefferson (eds) *Resistance through Rituals: Youth Subcultures in Post-War Britain*. London: Hutchinson.

Clarke, J., Hall, S., Jefferson, T. and Roberts, B. (1976) 'Subcultures, Cultures and Class' in S. Hall and T. Jefferson (eds) *Resistance through Rituals: Youth Subcultures in Post-War Britain*. London: Hutchinson.

Clifford, J. (1988) *The Predicament of Culture. Twentieth-Century Ethnography, Literature, and Art*. Cambridge, MA: Harvard University Press.

Clifford, J. (1992) 'Traveling Cultures' in L. Grossberg, C. Nelson and P. Treichler (eds) *Cultural Studies*. London and New York: Routledge.

Clifford, J. and Marcus, G. (eds) (1986) *Writing Culture*. Berkeley: University of California Press.

Cloward, R. and Ohlin, L.E. (1960) *Delinquency and Opportunity*. New York: Free Press of Glencoe.

Cohen, A.K. (1955) *Delinquent Boys: The Subculture of the Gang*. London: Collier Macmillan.

Cohen, P. (1997) *Rethinking the Youth Question: Education, Labour and Cultural Studies*. London: Macmillan.

Cohen, S. (1972) *Folk Devils and Moral Panics: The Creation of the Mods and Rockers*. London: MacGibbon & Kee.

Cohen, S. (1980) 'Symbols of Trouble: An Introduction to the New Edition' in S. Cohen, *Folk Devils and Moral Panics: The Creation of the Mods and Rockers*. London: Martin Robertson.

Collard, A. with Contrucci, J. (1988) *Rape of the Wild*. London: The Women's Press.

Collins, J. (1989) *Uncommon Cultures*. London and New York: Routledge.

Collins, J. (1992) 'Postmodernism and Television' in R. Allen (ed.) *Channels of Discourse, Reassembled*. London and New York: Routledge.

Commission for Racial Equality (1984) *Report into Ethnic Minorities on Television*. London: Commission for Racial Equality.

Connell, R.W. (1995) *Masculinities*. Cambridge: Polity Press.

Connell, R.W., Ashendon, D.J., Kessler, S. and Dowsett, G.W. (1982) *Making the Difference: Schools, Families and Social Division*. Sydney: Allen & Unwin.

Coward, R. (1999) *Sacred Cows*. London: HarperCollins.

Cowie, E. (1978) 'Women as Sign', *M/F*, 1.

Crimp, D. (1992) 'Portraits of People with AIDS' in L. Grossberg, C. Nelson and P. Treichler (eds) *Cultural Studies*. London and New York: Routledge.

Crofts, S. (1995) 'Global *Neighbours*?' in R. Allen (ed.) *To Be Continued …: Soap Opera around the World*. London and New York: Routledge.

Crook, S., Pakulski, J. and Waters, M. (1992) *Postmodernization*. London and Thousand Oaks, CA: Sage.

Culler, J. (1976) *Saussure*. London: Fontana.

Crossley, N. (1998) 'Emotions and Communicative Action' in G. Bendelow and S.J. Williams (eds) *Emotions in Social Life: Critical Themes and Contemporary Issues*. London: Routledge.

Culler, J. (1981) 'Semiotics of Tourism', *American Journal of Semiotics*, 1.

Cunningham, S. (1992a) *Framing Culture*. Sydney: Allen & Unwin.

Cunningham, S. (1992b) 'The Cultural Policy Debate Revisited', *Meanjin*, 51 (3).

Cunningham, S. (1993) 'Cultural Studies from the Viewpoint of Cultural Policy' in A. Gray, A. and J. McGuigan (eds) *Studying Culture*. London: Arnold.

Cunningham, S. (2004) 'The Creative Industries after Cultural Policy: a Genealogy and Some Possible Preferred Futures', *International Journal of Cultural Studies*, 7 (1).

Curran, J. (1991) 'Rethinking the Media and the Public Sphere' in P. Dahlgren and C. Sparks (eds) *Communication and Citizenship*. London and New York: Routledge.

Dahlgren, P. (1995) *Television and the Public Sphere*. London and Newbury Park, CA: Sage.

Daly, M. (1987) *Gyn/Ecology*. London: Women's Press.

Dandeker, C. (1990) *Surveillance, Power and Modernity*. Cambridge: Polity Press.

Daniels, T. and Gerson, J. (eds) (1989) *The Colour Black*. London: British Film Institute.

Dasgupta, D. and Hedge, R. (1988) 'The Eternal Receptacle: A Study of the Mistreatment of Women in Hindi Film' in R. Ghanially (ed.) *Women in Indian Society*. London and Newbury Park, CA: Sage.

Davidson, D. (1984) *Inquiries into Truth and Interpretation*. Oxford: Clarendon Press.

Davis, M. (1990) *City of Quartz: Excavating the Future of Los Angeles*. London: Verso.

Dawkins, R. (1976) *The Selfish Gene*. Oxford: Oxford University Press.

Dawkins, R. (1995) *River Out of Eden: A Darwinian View of Life*. New York: Basic Books.

de Certeau, M. (1984) *The Practice of Everyday Life*. Berkeley: University of California Press.

Deleuze, G. and Guattari, F. (1988) *Thousand Plateaus: Capitalism and Schizophrenia*. Minneapolis: University of Minneapolis Press.

Denfield, R. (1995) *The New Victorians: a Young Woman's Challenge to the Old Feminist Order*. St Leonards, NSW: Allen & Unwin.

Dennett, D. (1991) *Consciousness Explained*. Boston: Little Brown.

Dennett, D. (1995) *Darwin's Dangerous Idea: Evolution and the Meanings of Life*. London: Penguin.

Denzin, N.K. (1984) *On Understanding Emotion*. San Francisco: Jossey Bass.

Department of Culture, Media and Sport (DCMS) (1998) *The Comprehensive Spending Review: A New Approach to Investment in Culture*, DCMS. London. www.culture.gov.uk/Reference_library/

Derrida, J. (1976) *Of Grammatology*. Baltimore: Johns Hopkins University Press.

Derrida, J. (1980) *La Carte Postale*. Chicago: University of Chicago Press.

Dery, M. (1993) *Culture Jamming: Hacking, Slashing and Sniping in the Empire of Signs*. Westfield, NJ: Open Media.

Desforges, L. (1998) '"Checking Out the Planet": Global Representations/Local Identities and Youth Travel' in T. Skelton and G. Valentine (eds) *Cool Places: Geographies of Youth Cultures*. London and New York: Routledge.

Dibbell, J. (1998) *My Tiny Life*. @.www.juliandibbell.com. Accessed 7/4/06.

Du Gay, P., Hall, S., Janes, L., Mackay, H. and Negus, K. (1997) *Doing Cultural Studies*. London and Thousand Oaks, CA: Sage.

Dworkin, A (1993) 'Pornography Happens to Women'. Transcript of a speech given at the University of Chicago, 6 March 1993. Accessed 8/4/02. htttp://www.nostatusquo.com/ACLU/dworkin/pornHappens.html

Dyer, R. (1977) *Gays and Film*. London: British Film Institute.

Dyer, R. (1997) 'Seeing White', *Times Higher Education Supplement*, 27 June.

Dyer, R., Geraghty, C., Jordan, M., Lovell, T., Paterson, R. and Stewart, J. (1981) *Coronation Street*. London: British Film Institute.

Dyson, K. and Humphreys, J. (eds) (1990) *Political Economy of Communications*. London and New York: Routledge.

Eagleton, T. (1984) *The Function of Criticism*. London: Verso.

Eco, U. (1986) *Travels in Hyperreality*. London: Picador.

Eisenstein, S. (1951) *Film Form*. London: Dobson.

Ekman, P. (1980) 'Biological and Cultural Contributions to Body and Facial Movement in the Expression of Emotions', in A.O. Rorty (ed.) *Explaining Emotions*. Berkeley: University of California Press.

Elias, N. (1978) *The History of Manners: The Civilizing Process, Vol. 1*. Oxford: Blackwell.

Elias, N. (1982) *State Formation and Civilization: The Civilizing Process, Vol. 2*. Oxford: Blackwell.

Entman, R. (1990) 'Modern Racism and the Images of Blacks in Local Television News', *Critical Studies in Mass Communication*, 7 (4).

Ess, C. (1994) 'The Political Computer: Hypertext, Democracy, and Habermas' in G. Landow (ed.) *Hypertext/theory*. Baltimore: Johns Hopkins University Press.

Evans, K. (2005) 'Cybergirls: hello…are you out there?' in S. Wilson (ed.) *Defending our Dreams: Global Feminist Voices for a New Generation*. London: Zed Books.

Faludi, S. (1991) *Backlash: The Undeclared War against American Women*. London: Vintage.

Faludi, S. (1999) *Stiffed: The Betrayal of the American Man*. London: Chatto & Windus.

Farrell, W. (1993) *The Myth of Male Power*. Sydney: Random House.

Featherstone, M. (1991) *Consumer Culture and Postmodernism*. London and Newbury Park, CA: Sage.

Featherstone, M. (1995) *Undoing Culture: Globalization, Postmodernism and Identity*. London and Newbury Park, CA: Sage.

Ferguson, M. (1990) 'Electronic Media and the Redefining of Time and Space' in M. Ferguson (ed.) *Public Communication: The New Imperatives*. London and Newbury Park, CA: Sage.

Ferguson, M. and Golding, P. (eds) (1997) *Cultural Studies in Question*. London and Newbury Park, CA: Sage.

Finn, M. (2000) 'Computer Games and Narrative Progression', *M/C: A Journal of Media and Culture*. www. media-culture.org.au/0010/narrative.txt.

Fiske, J. (1987) *Television Culture*. London: Methuen.

Fiske, J. (1989a) *Understanding Popular Culture*. London: Unwin Hyman.

Fiske, J. (1989b) *Reading the Popular*. London: Unwin Hyman.

Fiske, J. (1989c) 'Everyday Quizzes, Everyday Life' in J. Tulloch and G. Turner (eds) *Australian Television: Programs, Pleasures and Politics*. London and Sydney: Allen & Unwin.

Fiske, J. (1992) 'British Cultural Studies' in R. Allen (ed.) *Channels of Discourse, Reassembled*. London and New York: Routledge.

Florida, R. (2002) *The Rise of the Creative Class: And How It's Transforming Work, Leisure, Community and Everyday Life*. New York: Basic Books.

Foucault, M. (1972) *The Archaeology of Knowledge*. New York: Pantheon.

Foucault, M. (1973) *The Birth of the Clinic*. London: Tavistock.

Foucault, M. (1977) *Discipline and Punish*. London: Allen Lane.

Foucault, M. (1979) *The History of Sexuality, Vol. 1: The Will to Truth*. London: Allen Lane.

Foucault, M. (1980) *Power/Knowledge*. New York: Pantheon.

Foucault, M. (1984a) 'Nietzsche, Genealogy, History' in *The Foucault Reader*, ed. P. Rabinow. New York: Pantheon.

Foucault, M. (1984b) 'On the Genealogy of Ethics: An Overview of Work in Progress' in *The Foucault Reader*, ed. P. Rabinow. New York: Pantheon.

Foucault, M. (1984c) 'What Is the Enlightenment?' in *The Foucault Reader*, ed. P. Rabinow. New York: Pantheon.

Foucault, M. (1984d) *The Foucault Reader*, ed. P. Rabinow. New York: Pantheon.

Foucault, M. (1986) *The Care of the Self: The History of Sexuality, Vol. 3*. London: Penguin.

Foucault, M. (1987) *The Uses of Pleasure: The History of Sexuality, Vol. 2*. Harmondsworth: Penguin.

Foucault, M. (1991) 'Governmentality' in G. Burchill, C. Gordon and P. Miller (eds) *The Foucault Effect: Studies in Governmentality*. Hemel Hempstead: Harvester Wheatsheaf.

Frank, A. (1991) *At the Will of the Body*. New York: Houghton Mifflin.

Frank, A.-G. (1967) *Capitalism and Underdevelopment in Latin America*. London and New York: Monthly Review Press.

Franklin, S., Lury, C. and Stacey, J. (1991) *Off-Centre: Feminism and Cultural Studies*. London: HarperCollins.

Fraser, N. (1995a) 'From Irony to Prophecy to Politics: A Reply to Richard Rorty' in R.S. Goodman (ed.) *Pragmatism*. New York: Routledge.

Fraser, N. (1995b) 'Politics, Culture and the Public Sphere: Towards a Postmodern Conception' in L. Nicholson and S. Seidman (eds) *Social Postmodernism*. Cambridge: Cambridge University Press.

Freud, S. (1977) *Three Essays on Sexuality. The Pelican Freud Library, Vol. 7*. Harmondsworth: Penguin.

Fukuyama, F. (1989) 'The End of History?', *The National Interest*, 16.

Fukuyama, F. (1992) *The End of History and the Last Man*. Harmondsworth: Penguin.

Fullan, M. with S. Stiegelbauer (1991) *The New Meaning of Educational Change*. London: Cassell.

Gadamer, H.-G. (1976) *Philosophical Hermeneutics*. Berkeley: University of California Press.

Gallagher, M. (1983) *The Portrayal and Participation of Women in the Media*. Paris: UNESCO.

Galtung, J. and Ruge, M. (1973) 'Structuring and Selecting News' in S. Cohen and J. Young (eds) *The Manufacture of News*. London: Constable.

Gans, H. (1962) *The Urban Villagers*. Glencoe, IL: Free Press.

Gans, H. (1968) 'Urbanism and Suburbanism as Ways of Life' in R.E. Pahl (ed.) *Readings in Urban Sociology*. Oxford: Pergamon Press.

Gardner, K. and Shukur, A. (1994) 'I'm Bengali, I'm Asian, and I'm Living Here' in R. Ballard (ed.) *Desh Pardesh: The South Asian Presence in Britain*. London: Hurst & Company.

Garfinkel, H. (1967) *Studies in Ethnomethodology*. Englewood Cliffs, NJ: Prentice Hall.

Geertz, C. (1973) *The Interpretation of Cultures*. New York: Basic Books.

Geraghty, C. (1991) *Women in Soap*. Cambridge: Polity Press.

Gergen, K. (1994) *Realities and Relationships*. Cambridge, MA and London: Harvard University Press.

Gibson, C. and Klocker, N. (2004) 'Academic Publishing as "Creative" Industry, and Recent Discourses of "Creative Economies": Some Critical Reflections', *Area*, 36 (4).

Gibson, W. (1984) *Neuromancer*. London: HarperCollins.

Giddens, A. (1979) *Central Problems in Social Theory*. London: Macmillan.

Giddens, A. (1984) *The Constitution of Society*. Cambridge: Polity Press.

Giddens, A. (1985) *The Nation-State and Violence*. Cambridge: Polity Press.

Giddens, A. (1989) *Sociology*. Cambridge: Polity Press.

Giddens, A. (1990) *The Consequences of Modernity*. Cambridge: Polity Press.

Giddens, A. (1991) *Modernity and Self-Identity*. Cambridge: Polity Press.

Giddens, A. (1992) *The Transformation of Intimacy*. Cambridge: Polity Press.

Giddens, A. (1994) 'Living in a Post-Traditional Society' in U. Beck, A. Giddens and C. Lash (eds) *Reflexive Modernization*. Cambridge: Polity Press.

Gillespie, A. and Williams, H. (1988) 'Telecommunications and the Reconstruction of Regional Comparative Advantage', *Environment and Planning*, A20.

Gillespie, M. (1995) *Television, Ethnicity and Cultural Change*. London and New York: Routledge.

Gilligan, C. (1982) *In a Different Voice*. Cambridge, MA: Harvard University Press.

Gilpin, R. (1987) *The Political Economy of International Relations*. Princeton: Princeton University Press.

Gilroy, P. (1987) *There Ain't No Black in the Union Jack*. London: Unwin Hyman.

Gilroy, P. (1993) *The Black Atlantic*. London: Verso.

Gilroy, P. (1997) 'Diaspora and the Detours of Identity' in K. Woodward (ed.) *Identity and Difference*. London and Thousand Oaks, CA: Sage.

Goffman, E. (1969) *The Presentation of Self in Everyday Life*. Harmondsworth: Penguin.

Goffman, E. (1974) *Frame Analysis*. New York: Harper & Row.

Goffman, E. (1979) *Gender Advertisements*. London: Macmillan.

Goldthorpe, J. (1982) 'On the Service Class, its Formation and Future' in A. Giddens and G. Mackenzie (eds) *Social Class and the Division of Labour*. Cambridge: Cambridge University Press.

Goldthorpe, J. and Lockwood, D. (1968) *The Affluent Worker*. Cambridge: Cambridge University Press.

Goleman, D. (2003) *Destructive Emotions and How We Can Overcome Them: a Dialogue with the Dalai Lama*. London: Bloomsbury.

Gorden, D. (1988) 'The Global Economy: New Edifice or Crumbling Foundations?', *New Left Review*, 168.

Gorz, A. (1982) *Farewell to the Working Class*. London: Pluto Press.

Graham, P. (2002) 'Space and Cyberspace: on the Enclosures of Consciousness' in J. Armitage and J. Roberts (eds) *Living with Cyberspace: Technology and Society in the 21st Century*. London: Continuum.

Graham, S. and Marvin, S. (1996) *Telecommunications and the City: Electronic Spaces, Urban Places*. London: Routledge.

Gramsci, A. (1968) *Prison Notebooks*. London: Lawrence & Wishart.

Gramsci, A. (1971) *Selections from the Prison Notebooks*, edited by Q. Hoare and G. Nowell-Smith. London: Lawrence & Wishart.

Gray, A. (1997) 'Learning from Experience: Cultural Studies and Feminism' in J. McGuigan (ed.) *Cultural Methodologies*. London and Thousand Oaks, CA: Sage.

Gray, A. (2003) *Research Practice for Cultural Studies*. London: Sage.

Gray, H. (1996) 'Television, Black Americans, and the American Dream' in V. Berry and C. Manning-Miller (eds) *Mediated Messages and African American Culture*. London and Thousand Oaks, CA: Sage.

Gribbin, J. (1998) *Almost Everyone's Guide to Science*. London: Phoenix.

Grossberg, L. (1987) 'The In-difference of Television', *Journal of Communication Enquiry*, 10 (2).

Grossberg, L. (1992) *We Gotta Get Out of This Place: Popular Conservatism and Postmodern Culture*. London and New York: Routledge.

Grossberg, L., Nelson, C. and Treichler, P. (1992) 'Cultural Studies: An Introduction' in L. Grossberg, C. Nelson and P. Treichler (eds) *Cultural Studies*. London and New York: Routledge.

Grosz, E. (1995) *Space, Time and Perversion: Essays on the Politics of Bodies*. St Leonards: Allen & Unwin.

Gurevitch, M., Levy, M. and Roeh, I. (1991) 'The Global Newsroom: Convergence and Diversities in the Globalization of Television News' in P. Dahlgren and C. Sparks (eds) *Communication and Citizenship*. London and New York: Routledge.

Gutting, G. (1999) *Pragmatic Liberalism and the Critique of Modernity*. Cambridge: Cambridge University Press.

Habermas, J. (1972) *Knowledge and Human Interests*. London: Heinemann.

Habermas, J. (1987) *The Philosophical Discourse of Modernity*. Cambridge: Polity Press.

Habermas, J. (1989) *The Structural Transformation of the Public Sphere*. Cambridge, MA: MIT Press.

Hagerstrand, T. (1973) 'The Domain of Human Geography' in R.J. Chorley (ed.) *Directions in Geography*. London: Methuen.

Hall, S. (1972) *On Ideology: Cultural Studies 10*. Birmingham: Centre for Contemporary Cultural Studies.

Hall, S. (1977) 'Culture, the Media and the Ideological Effect' in J. Curran, M. Gurevitch and J. Woollacott (eds) *Mass Communications and Society*. London: Edward Arnold.

Hall, S. (1981) 'Encoding/Decoding' in S. Hall, D. Hobson, A. Lowe and P. Willis (eds) *Culture, Media, Language*. London: Hutchinson.

Hall, S. (1988) *The Hard Road to Renewal*. London: Verso.

Hall, S. (1989) 'The Meaning of New Times' in S. Hall and M. Jacques (eds) *New Times: The Changing Face of Politics in the 1990s*. London: Lawrence & Wishart.

Hall, S. (1990) 'Cultural Identity and Diaspora' in J. Rutherford (ed.) *Identity: Community, Culture, Difference*. London: Lawrence & Wishart.

Hall, S. (1992a) 'Cultural Studies and its Theoretical Legacies' in L. Grossberg, C. Nelson and P. Treichler (eds) *Cultural Studies*. London and New York: Routledge.

Hall, S. (1992b) 'The Question of Cultural Identity' in S. Hall, D. Held and T. McGrew (eds) *Modernity and Its Futures*. Cambridge: Polity Press.

Hall, S. (1993) 'Minimal Selves' in A. Gray and J. McGuigan (eds) *Studying Culture*. London: Edward Arnold.

Hall, S. (1995) 'Fantasy, Identity, Politics' in E. Carter, J. Donald and J. Squires (eds) *Cultural Remix: Theories of Politics and the Popular*. London: Lawrence & Wishart.

Hall, S. (1996a) 'Who Needs Identity?' in S. Hall and P. du Gay (eds) *Questions of Cultural Identity*. London: Sage.

Hall, S. (1996b) 'On Postmodernism and Articulation: An Interview with Stuart Hall' in D. Morley and D.-K. Chen. (eds) *Stuart Hall*. London: Routledge.

Hall, S. (1996c) 'Gramsci's Relevance for the Study of Race and Ethnicity' in D. Morley and D.-K. Chen (eds) *Stuart Hall*. London: Routledge.

Hall, S. (1996d) 'New Ethnicities' in D. Morley and D.-K. Chen (eds) *Stuart Hall*. London: Routledge.

Hall, S. (1996e) 'For Allon White: Metaphors of Transformation' in D. Morley and D.-K. Chen (eds) *Stuart Hall*. London: Routledge.

Hall, S. (1997a) 'The Work of Representation' in S. Hall (ed.) *Representations*. London and Thousand Oaks, CA: Sage.

Hall, S. (1997b) 'The Centrality of Culture: Notes on the Cultural Revolutions of Our Time' in K. Thompson (ed.) *Media and Cultural Regulation*. London: Sage.

Hall, S. (ed.) (1997c) 'The Spectacle of the Other' in S. Hall (ed.) *Representations*. London and Thousand Oaks, CA: Sage.

Hall, S. and Jacques, M. (eds) (1989) *New Times: The Changing Face of Politics in the 1990s*. London: Lawrence & Wishart.

Hall, S. and Jefferson, T. (eds) (1976) *Resistance through Rituals: Youth Subcultures in Post-War Britain*. London: Hutchinson.

Hall, S., Critcher, C., Jefferson, T., Clarke, J. and Roberts, B. (1978) *Policing the Crisis: Mugging, the State and Law and Order*. London: Macmillan.

Hall, S., Hobson, D., Lowe, A. and Willis, P. (eds) (1981) *Culture, Media, Language*. London: Hutchinson.

Hall, T. (1997) '(Re)placing the City: Cultural Relocation and the City as Centre' in S. Westwood and J. Williams (eds) *Imagining Cities*. London: Routledge.

Halpern, D. (1992) *Sex Differences in Cognitive Abilities*. London: Lawrence Erlbaum Associates.

Hamelink, C. (1983) *Cultural Autonomy in Global Communications*. New York: Longman.

Hamer, D. and Copeland, P. (1998) *Living with Our Genes*. New York: Doubleday.

Hammersley, M. and Atkinson, P. (1983) *Ethnography: Principles and Practice*. London: Tavistock Books.

Hancock, P., Hughes, B., Jagger, E., Paterson, K., Russel, R., Tulle-Winton, E. and Tyler, M. (2000) *The Body, Culture and Society: An Introduction*. Buckingham: Open University Press.

Haraway, D. (1985) 'A Manifesto for Cyborgs: Science, Technology, and Socialist Feminism', *Socialist Review*, 5 (2).

Haraway, D. (1991) *Simians, Cyborgs, and Women: the Reinvention of Nature*. Cambridge: Polity Press.

Harold, C. (2004) 'Pranking Rhetoric: "Culture Jamming" as Media Activism', *Critical Studies in Media Communication*, 21 (3).

Harré, R. (ed.) (1986) *The Social Construction of Emotion*. Oxford: Blackwell.

Hartley, J. (1982) *Understanding News*. London: Methuen.

Hartley, J. (1992) *The Politics of Pictures*. New York: Routledge.

Harvey, D. (1973) *Social Justice and the City*. London: Edward Arnold.

Harvey, D. (1985) *The Urbanization of Capital*. Oxford: Blackwell.

Harvey, D. (1989) *The Condition of Postmodernity*. Oxford: Blackwell.

Harvey, D. (1993) 'From Place to Space and Back Again: Reflections on the Condition of Postmodernity' in J. Bird, B. Curtis, T. Putnam, G. Roberston and L. Tickner (eds) *Mapping the Futures: Local Cultures, Global Change*. London and New York: Routledge.

Hebdige, D. (1979) *Subculture: The Meaning of Style*. London and New York: Routledge.

Hebdige, D. (1988) *Hiding in the Light*. London: Comedia.

Hebdige, D. (1990) 'Fax to the Future', *Marxism Today*, January.

Held, D. (1991) 'Democracy, the Nation-State and the Global System' in D. Held (ed.) *Politcal Theory Today*. Cambridge: Polity Press.

Held, D. (1992) 'Liberalism, Marxism and Democracy' in S. Hall, D. Held and T. McGrew (eds) *Modernity and Its Futures*. Cambridge: Polity Press.

Henriques, J., Holloway, W., Urwin, C., Venn, C. and Walkerdine, V. (1984) *Changing the Subject: Psychology, Social Regulation and Subjectivity*. London: Methuen.

Hertz, J. (1957) 'The Rise and Demise of the Territorial Nation-State', *World Politics*, ix.

Hobsbawn, E.J. (1969) *Industry and Empire*. Harmondsworth: Penguin.

Hobson, D. (1982) *Crossroads: Drama of a Soap Opera*. London: Methuen.

Hochschild, A.R. (1983) *The Managed Heart: The Commercialization of Human Feeling*. Berkeley, CA: University of California Press.

Hoggart, R. (1957) *The Uses of Literacy*. Harmondsworth: Penguin.

Honneth, A. (1985) 'An Aversion against the Universal', *Theory, Culture & Society*, 2 (3).

hooks, b. (1990) *Yearning: Race, Gender and Cultural Politics*. Boston, MA: South End Press.

hooks, b. (1992) *Black Looks: Race and Representation*. Boston, MA: South End Press.

Hoskins, C., McFadyen, S., Finn, A. and Jackel, A. (1995) 'Film and Television Co-productions: Evidence from Canadian–European Experience', *European Journal of Communication*, 10 (2).

Hoyenga, K. and Hoyenga, K.T. (1993) *Gender-Related Differences*. New York: Allyn & Bacon.

Hutcheon, L. (1989) *The Politics of Postmodernism*. London and New York: Routledge.

Irigaray, L. (1985a) *Speculum of the Other Woman*. Ithaca, NY: Cornell University Press.

Irigaray, L. (1985b) *This Sex Which Is Not One*. Ithaca, NY: Cornell University Press.

Iser, W. (1978) *The Act of Reading: A Theory of Aesthetic Responses*. London and New York: Routledge & Kegan Paul.

James, A. (1986) 'Learning to Belong: The Boundaries of Adolescence' in A.P. Cohen (ed.) *Symbolizing Boundaries: Identity and Diversity in British Cultures*. Manchester: Manchester University Press.

Jameson, F. (1984) 'Postmodernism or the Cultural Logic of Late Capitalism', *New Left Review*, 46.

Jencks, C. (1986) *What Is Post-Modernism?* New York: Academy/St Martins Press.

Jhally, S. and Lewis, J. (1992) *Enlightened Racism: The Cosby Show, Audiences, and the Myth of the American Dream*. Boulder, CO: Westview Press.

Jobst, K., Shostak, D. and Whitehouse, P.J. (1999) 'Diseases of Meaning: Manifestations of Health and Metaphor', *Journal of Alternative and Complementary Medicine*, 6 (2): 125–6.

Johnson, M. (1987) *The Body in Mind: The Bodily Basis of Meaning, Imagination and Reason*. Chicago: Chicago University Press.

Johnson, S. and Meinhof, U. (eds) (1997) *Language and Masculinity*. Oxford: Blackwell.

Jones, J. (1996) 'The New Ghetto Aesthetic' in V. Berry and C. Manning-Miller (eds) *Mediated Messages and African American Culture*. London and Thousand Oaks, CA: Sage.

Jones, P., Comfort, D., Eastwood, I. and Hillier, D. (2004) 'Creative Industries: Economic Contributions, Management Challenges and Support Initiatives', *Management Research News*, 27 (11/12): 134–45.

Jordan, G. and Weedon, C. (1995) *Cultural Politics: Class, Gender, Race and the Postmodern World*. Oxford: Blackwell.

Kaplan, E. (1987) *Rocking Around the Clock: Music Televison, Postmodernism and Consumer Culture*. Boulder, CO: Westview Press.

Kaplan, E. (1992) 'Feminist Criticism and Television' in R. Allen (ed.) *Channels of Discourse, Reassembled*. London and New York: Routledge.

Kaplan, E. (1997) *Looking for the Other: Feminism, Film and the Imperial Gaze*. London and New York: Routledge.

Kellner, D. (1992) 'Popular Culture and the Construction of Postmodern Identities' in S. Lash and J. Friedman (eds) *Modernity and Identity*. Oxford: Blackwell.

Kellner, D. (1995) *Media Culture: Cultural Studies, Identity and Politics between the Modern and the Postmodern.* London and New York: Routledge.

Kellner, D. (1997) 'Overcoming the Divide: Cultural Studies and Political Economy' in M. Ferguson and P. Golding (eds) *Cultural Studies in Question.* London and Newbury Park, CA: Sage.

Kerner Commission (1968) *Report of the National Advisory Committee on Civil Disorders.* New York: E.P. Dutton.

Kerr, C., Dunlop, K., Harbison, F. and Mayers, C. (1973) *Industrialism and Industrial Man.* Harmondsworth: Penguin.

Kimura, D. (1996) 'Sex, Sexual Orientation and Sex Hormones Influence Human Cognitive Function', *Current Opinion in Neurobiology,* 6 (2): 259.

King, A.D. (1983) 'The World Economy Is Everywhere: Urban History and the World System' in *Urban History Yearbook (1983).* Leicester: Leicester University Press.

Klein, N. (1997) 'Subvertising: Culture Jamming Re-emerges on the Media Landscape', *Village Voice,* 6 May.

Klein, N. (2001) *No Logo: No Space, No Choice, No Jobs.* London: Flamingo.

Kotkin, J. and Siegal, F. (2004) 'Too much froth', *Blueprint* 6.

Krishnan, P. and Dighe, A. (1990) *Affirmation and Denial: The Construction of Femininity on Indian Television.* London and Newbury Park, CA: Sage.

Kristeva, J. (1986a) 'Revolution in Poetic Language' in *The Kristeva Reader,* ed. T. Moi. Oxford: Blackwell.

Kristeva, J. (1986b) 'Women's Time' in *The Kristeva Reader,* ed. T. Moi. Oxford: Blackwell.

Kristeva, J. (1986c) *The Kristeva Reader,* ed. T. Moi. Oxford: Blackwell.

Kuhn, T.S. (1962) *The Structures of Scientific Revolutions.* Chicago and London: University of Chicago Press.

Kundera, M. (1984) *The Unbearable Lightness of Being.* London and Boston: Faber & Faber.

Lacan, J. (1977) *Écrits: A Selection.* London: Tavistock.

Laclau, E. (1977) *Politics and Ideology in Marxist Theory.* London: New Left Books.

Laclau, E. and Mouffe, C. (1985) *Hegemony and Socialist Strategy: Toward a Radical Democratic Politics.* London: Verso.

Laing, D. (1985) *One Chord Wonders: Power and Meaning in Punk Rock.* Milton Keynes: Open University Press.

Landow, G. (2005) 'Hypertext and Critical Theory' in D. Trend (ed.) *The Digital Culture Reader.* Oxford: Blackwell.

Landry, C. and Bianchini, F. (2000) *The Creative City.* London: Earthsian Publications.

Lasch, C. (1980) *The Culture of Narcissism.* London: Arnold.

Lasch, C. (1985) *The Minimal Self.* London: Picador.

Lash, S. (1990) *Sociology of Postmodernism.* London and New York: Routledge.

Lash, S. and Urry, J. (1987) *Disorganized Capitalism.* Cambridge: Polity Press.

Leab, D. (1976) *From Sambo to Superspade.* New York: Houghton Mifflin.

Leach, E. (1974) *Lévi-Strauss.* Glasgow: Collins.

Leavis, F.R. and Thompson, D. (1933) *Culture and the Environment.* London: Chatto & Windus.

LeDoux, J. (1998) *The Emotional Brain.* London: Phoenix.

Lee, J. (1991) *At My Father's Wedding.* New York: Bantam Books.

Levy, A. (2005) *Female Chauvinist Pigs: Women and the Rise of Raunch Culture*. Melbourne: Schwartz Publishing.

Liebes, T. and Katz, E. (1991) *The Export of Meaning*. Oxford: Oxford University Press.

Lineham, M. (1993) *Cognitive-Behavioural Treatment for Borderline Personality Disorder*. New York: The Guilford Press.

Lukács, G. (1972) 'Ideology of Modernsim' in D. Lodge (ed.) *Twentieth-Century Literary Criticism*. London: Longman.

Lukács, G. (1977) 'Realism in the Balance' in E. Bloch (ed.) *Aesthetics and Politics*. London: New Left Books.

Lull, J. (1991) *China Turned On: Television, Reform and Resistance*. London: Routledge.

Lull, J. (1997) 'China Turned On (Revisited): Television, Reform and Resistance' in A. Sreberny-Mohammadi, D. Winseck, J. McKenna and O. Boyd-Barrett (eds) *Media in a Global Context*. London: Edward Arnold.

Lumby, C. (1997) *Bad Girls: the Media, Sex and Feminism in the 90s*. St Leonards, NSW: Allen & Unwin.

Lupton, D. (1998) *The Emotional Self*. London: Sage.

Lutz, C. (1988) *Unnatural Emotions: Everyday Sentiments on a Micronesian Atoll and their Challenge to Western Theory*. Chicago: University of Chicago Press.

Lyotard, J.-F. (1984) *The Postmodern Condition*. Manchester: Manchester University Press.

MacCabe, C. (1981) 'Realism and the Cinema: Notes on Some Brechtian Themes', *Screen*, 5 (2).

McGrew, A. (1992) 'A Global Society?' in S. Hall, D. Held. and T. McGrew (eds) *Modernity and Its Futures*. Cambridge: Polity Press.

McGuigan, J. (1992) *Cultural Populism*. London: Routledge.

McGuigan, J. (1996a) *Culture and the Public Sphere*. London: Routledge.

McGuigan, J. (1996b) 'Cultural Populism Revisited' in M. Ferguson and P. Golding (eds) *Cultural Studies in Question*. London and Newbury Park, CA: Sage.

McGuigan, J. (1997a) 'Introduction' in J. McGuigan (ed.) *Cultural Methodologies*. London: Sage.

McGuigan, J. (ed.) (1997b) *Cultural Methodologies*. London: Sage.

Mackinnon, C. (1987) *Feminism Unmodified*. Cambridge, MA and London: Harvard University Press.

Mackinnon, C. (1991) 'Difference and Domination' in K. Bartlett and R. Kennedy (eds) *Feminist Legal Theory*. Boulder, CO and London: Westview Press.

Mackinnon, C. (1995) *Only Words*. London: Harper Collins.

McLean, C., Carey, M. and White, C. (eds) (1996) *Men's Ways of Being*. Boulder, CO: Westview Press.

McLuskie, K. (1982) 'Feminist Deconstruction: The Example of Shakespeare's *Taming of the Shrew*', *Red Letters*, 12.

McNay, L. (1992) *Foucault and Feminism*. Cambridge: Polity Press.

McRobbie, A. (1989) *Zoot Suits and Second-Hand Dresses*. London: Macmillan.

McRobbie, A. (1991a) 'Settling Accounts with Subcultures' in A. McRobbie, *Feminism and Youth Culture*. London: Macmillan.

McRobbie, A. (1991b) '*Jackie*: Romantic Individualism and the Teenage Girl' in A. McRobbie, *Feminism and Youth Culture*. London: Macmillan.

McRobbie, A. (1991c) 'Working-Class Girls and the Culture of Femininity' in A. McRobbie, *Feminism and Youth Culture*. London: Macmillan.

McRobbie, A. (1991d) '*Jackie* and *Just Seventeen* in the 1980s' in A. McRobbie, *Feminism and Youth Culture*. London: Macmillan.

McRobbie, A. and Garber, J. (1991) 'Girls and Subcultures' in A. McRobbie, *Feminism and Youth Culture*. London: Macmillan.

Martindale, C. (1986) *The White Press in Black America*. Westport, CT: Greenwood Press.

Marx, K. (1961) *Karl Marx: Selected Writings in Sociology and Social Philosophy*, T. Bottomore and M. Rubel (eds). London: Pelican.

Marx, K. and Engels, F. (1967) *The Communist Manifesto*. London: Penguin.

Marx, K. and Engels, F. (1970) *The German Ideology*. London: Lawrence & Wishart.

Massey, D. (1994) *Space, Place and Gender*. Cambridge: Polity Press.

Massey, D. (1998) 'The Spatial Construction of Youth Cultures' in T. Skelton and G. Valentine (eds) *Cool Places: Geographies of Youth Cultures*. London and New York: Routledge.

Matheson, B. (2006) 'A Culture of Creativity: Design Education and the Creative Industries', *Journal of Management Development*, 25 (1): 55–64.

Mattelart, M. and Mattelart, A. (1992) *The Carnival of Images*. New York: Bergin & Garvey.

Matza, D. and Sykes, G. (1961) 'Juvenile Delinquency and Subterranean Values', *American Sociological Review*, 26.

Mayr, E. (1982) *The Growth of Biological Thought: Diversity, Evolution and Inheritance*. Cambridge: Cambridge University Press.

Medhurst, A. (1989) 'Laughing Matters: Introduction' in T. Daniels and J. Gerson (eds) *The Colour Black*. London: British Film Institute.

Meehan, D. (1983) *Ladies of the Evening: Women Characters of Prime-Time Television*. Metuchen, NJ: Scarecrow Press.

Melucci, A. (1980) 'The New Social Movements: A Theoretical Approach', *Social Science Information*, 19 (2).

Melucci, A. (1981) 'Ten Hypotheses for the Analysis of New Movements' in D. Pinto (ed.) *Contemporary Italian Sociology*. Cambridge: Cambridge University Press.

Melucci, A. (1989) *Nomads of the Present*. London: Hutchinson Radius.

Mercer, K. (1992) '"1968": Periodizing Postmodern Politics and Identity', in L. Grossberg, C. Nelson and P. Treichler (eds) *Cultural Studies*. London and New York: Routledge.

Mercer, K. (1994) *Welcome to the Jungle: New Positions in Black Cultural Studies*. London and New York: Routledge.

Merton, R.K. (1938) 'Social Structure and Anomie', *American Sociological Review*, 3.

Meyrowitz, J. (1986) *No Sense of Place*. Oxford: Oxford University Press.

Miles, R. (1982) *Racism and Migrant Labour*. London: Allen & Unwin.

Miles, R. (1989) *Racism*. London: Routledge.

Miller, D. (1995) 'The Consumption of Soap Opera: *The Young and the Restless* and Mass Consumption in Trinidad' in R. Allen (ed.) *To Be Continued …: Soap Opera around the World*. London and New York: Routledge.

Miller, L. (1995) 'Women and Children First: Gender and the Setting of the Electronic Frontier' in J. Brook and I. Boa (eds) *Resisting Virtual Life*. San Francisco: City Light Books.

Miller, W.B. (1958) 'Lower Class Culture as a Generating Milieu of Gang Delinquency', *Journal of Social Issues*, 14.

Mishra, V. (1985) 'Toward a Theoretical Critique of Bombay Cinema', *Screen*, 26.

Mitchell, J. (1974) *Psychoanalysis and Feminism*. London: Allen Lane.

Moi, T. (1985) *Sexual/Textual Politics: Feminist Literary Theory*. London and New York: Routledge.

Moir, A. and Jessel, D. (1991) *BrainSex: The Real Differences between Men and Women*. London: Mandarin.

Moir, A. and Moir, B. (1998) *Why Men Don't Iron: The Real Science of Gender Studies*. London: HarperCollins Publishers.

Moore, R. (1999) 'Democracy and Cyberspace' in B. Hague and B. Loader (eds) *Digital Democracy: Discourse and Decision Making in the Information Age*. London: Routledge.

Morley, D. (1980) *The Nationwide Audience*. London: British Film Institute.

Morley, D. (1986) *Family Television: Cultural Power and Domestic Leisure*. London: Comedia.

Morley, D. (1992) *Television, Audiences and Cultural Studies*. London and New York: Routledge.

Morley, D. and Chen, D.-K. (eds) (1996) *Stuart Hall*. London: Routledge.

Morley, D. and Robins, K. (1995) *Spaces of Identity: Global Media, Electronic Landscapes and Cultural Boundaries*. London and New York: Routledge.

Morris, M. (1992) 'A Gadfly Bites Back', *Meanjin*, 51 (3).

Morris, M. (1996) 'Banality in Cultural Studies' in J. Storey (ed.) *What Is Cultural Studies? A Reader*. London and New York: Edward Arnold.

Morrison, D. (1992) *Television and the Gulf War*. London: John Libbey.

Mort, F. (1989) 'The Politics of Consumption' in S. Hall and M. Jacques (eds) *New Times: The Changing Face of Politics in the 1990s*. London: Lawrence & Wishart.

Mosca, V. (1988) 'Introduction: Information in the Pay Society' in V. Mosca and J. Wasko (eds) *The Political Economy of Information*. Madison: University of Wisconsin Press.

Mouffe, C. (1984) 'Towards a Theoretical Interpretation of "New Social Movements"' in S. Hanninen and L. Palden (eds) *Rethinking Marx*. New York and Bagnolet: International General/IMMRC.

Mouffe, C. (1992) 'Democratic Citizenship and the Political Community' in C. Mouffe (ed.) *Dimensions of Radical Democracy*. London: Verso.

Mowlana, H., Gerbner, G. and Schiller, H. (eds) (1992) *Triumph of the Image: The Media's War in the Persian Gulf*. Boulder, CO: Westview Press.

Muggleton, D. (1997) 'The Post-Subculturalist' in S. Redhead (ed.) *Subcultures to Clubcultures: An Introduction to Popular Cultural Studies*. Oxford: Blackwell.

Murdock, G. (1990) 'Redrawing the Map of the Communications Industries: Concentration and Ownership in the Era of Privatisation' in M. Ferguson (ed.) *Public Communication: The New Imperatives*. London and Newbury Park, CA: Sage.

Murdock, G. and Golding, P. (1977) 'Capitalism, Communications and Class Relations' in J. Curran, M. Gurevitch and J. Wollacott (eds) *Mass Communications and Society*. London: Edward Arnold.

Murray, R. (1989a) 'Fordism and Post-Fordism' in S. Hall and M. Jacques (eds) *New Times: The Changing Face of Politics in the 1990s*. London: Lawrence & Wishart.

Murray, R. (1989b) 'Benetton Britain' in S. Hall and M. Jacques (eds) *New Times: The Changing Face of Politics in the 1990s*. London: Lawrence & Wishart.

Nakamura, L. (2000) 'Race in/for Cyberspace: Identity Tourism and Racial Passing on the Internet' in D. Bell and B. Kennedy (eds) *The Cybercultures Reader*. London: Rouledge.

National Drug Strategy (1995) *Household Survey.* Canbera: Commonwealth Government of Australia.

Neale, S. (1980) *Genre.* London: British Film Institute.

Newcombe, H. (1988) 'One Night of Prime Time' in J. Carey (ed.) *Media, Myth, Narrative.* London and Newbury Park, CA: Sage.

Nicholson, L. (ed.) (1990) *Feminism/Postmodernism.* London and New York: Routledge.

Nicholson, L. (1995) 'Interpreting Gender' in L. Nicholson and S. Seidman (eds) *Social Postmodernism.* Cambridge: Cambridge University Press.

Nietzsche, F. (1967) *The Will to Power.* New York: Random House.

Nietzsche, F. (1968) 'On Truth and Lie in the Extra Moral' in W. Kaufman (ed.) *The Portable Nietzsche.* London: Viking Penguin. p. 46.

Nixon, S. (1997) 'Exhibiting Masculinity' in S. Hall (ed.) *Representations.* London and Thousand Oaks, CA: Sage.

Norris, C. (1987) *Derrida.* Cambridge, MA: Harvard University Press.

Nussbaum, M. (2001) *Upheavals of Thought: The Intelligence of Emotion.* Cambridge: Cambridge University Press.

Nzegwu, N. (1996) 'Bypasssing New York in Re-Presenting Eko: Production of Space in a Nigerian City' in A.D. King (ed.) *Re-presenting the City.* London: Macmillan.

Oakley, A. (1974) *Housewife.* London: Allen Lane.

Ogden, M. (1994) 'Politics in a Parallel Universe: Is There a Future for Cyberdemocracy?', *Futures,* 26 (7).

O'Regan, T. (1992a) '(Mis)taking Policy: Notes on the Cultural Policy Debate', *Cultural Studies,* 6 (3).

O'Regan, T. (1992b) 'Some Reflections on the "Policy Moment"', *Meanjin,* 51 (3).

Orr, C. (1997) 'Charting the Currents of the Third Wave', *Hypatia,* 12 (3).

Ortony, A. and Turner, T.J. (1990) 'What's Basic about Basic Emotions?' *Psychological Review,* 97: 315–31.

Papacharissi, Z. (2002) 'The Virtual Sphere, The Internet as a Public Space', *New Media and Society,* 4 (1).

Parekh, B. (1991) 'British Citizenship and Cultural Difference' in G. Andrews (ed.) *Citizenship.* London: Lawrence & Wishart.

Parsons, T. (1942) 'Age and Sex in the Social Structure of the United States', *American Sociological Review,* 7.

Parsons, T. (1963) 'Youth in the Context of American Society', *American Sociological Review,* 27.

Pears, D. (1971) *Wittgenstein.* London: Fontana.

Peck, J. (2005) 'Struggling with the Creative Class', *International Journal of Urban and Regional Research,* 29 (4).

Pfeil, F. (1995) *White Guys.* London: Verso.

Rheingold, H. (1994) 'Culture Jamming', *Whole Earth Review,* 82.

Pieterse, J. (1995) 'Globalization as Hybridization' in M. Featherstone, S. Lash and R. Robertson (eds) *Global Modernities.* London and Newbury Park, CA: Sage.

Pinker, S. (1997) *How the Mind Works.* New York: Norton.

Plant, S. (2000) 'On the Matrix: Cyberfeminist Simulations' in D. Bell and B. Kennedy (eds) *The Cybercultures Reader.* London: Routledge.

Plutchik, R. (1980) 'Emotion: A General Psychoevolutionary Theory' in R. Plutchik and H. Kellerman (eds) *Emotion: Theory, Research and Experience.* New York: Academic Press.

Popper, K. (1959) *The Logic of Scientific Discovery.* London: Hutchinson.

Poster, M. (1997) 'Cyberdemocracy: The Internet and the Public Sphere' in D. Porter (ed.) *Internet Culture.* London: Routledge.

Potter, J. and Wetherell, M. (1987) *Discourse and Social Psychology: Beyond Attitudes and Behaviour.* London and Thousand Oaks, CA: Sage.

Poulantzas, N. (1976) *Political Power and Social Classes.* London: New Left Books.

Rajan, S.R. (1991) *Ideal and Imagined Women.* London: Routledge.

Real, T. (1998) *I Don't Want to Talk About It: Men and Depression.* Dublin: Newleaf.

Redhead, S. (1990) *The End-of-the-Century Party: Youth and Pop Towards 2000.* Manchester: Manchester University Press.

Redhead, S. (1993) *Rave Off: Politics and Deviance in Contemporary Youth Culture.* Aldershot: Avebury.

Redhead, S. (1997a) 'Introduction: Reading Pop(ular) Cult(ural) Stud(ie)s' in S. Redhead with D. Wynne and J. O'Connor (eds) *The Clubcultures Reader: Readings in Popular Cultural Studies.* Oxford: Blackwell.

Redhead, S. (1997b) 'PopTime, Acid House' in S. Redhead (ed.) *Subcultures to Clubcultures: An Introduction to Popular Cultural Studies.* Oxford: Blackwell.

Relph, E. (1976) *Place and Placelessness.* London: Pion.

Reynolds, S. (1997) 'Rave Culture: Living Dream or Living Death' in S. Redhead (ed.) *Subcultures to Clubcultures: An Introduction to Popular Cultural Studies.* Oxford: Blackwell.

Rex, J. (1970) *Race Relations in Sociological Theory.* London: Routledge & Kegan Paul.

Rich, A. (1986) *Of Woman Born.* London: Virago Press.

Richard, B. and Kruger, H.H. (1998) 'Ravers Paradise? German Youth Cultures in the 1990s' in T. Skelton and G. Valentine (eds) *Cool Places: Geographies of Youth Cultures.* London and New York: Routledge.

Richardson, M. (2004) 'Downloading Music off the Internet: Copyright and Privacy Law in Conflict', *Journal of Law and Information Science,* 13 (1): 90–106.

Robertson, R. (1992) *Globalization.* London and Newbury Park, CA: Sage.

Robertson, R. (1995) 'Glocalization: Time–Space and Homogeneity–Hetrogeneity' in M. Featherstone, S. Lash and R. Robertson (eds) *Global Modernities.* London and Newbury Park, CA: Sage.

Robins, K. (1991) 'Tradition and Translation: National Culture in its Global Context' in J. Corner and S. Harvey (eds) *Enterprise and Heritage: Cross-currents of National Culture.* London: Routledge.

Rorty, R. (1980) *Philosophy and the Mirror of Nature.* Cambridge: Cambridge University Press.

Rorty, R. (1989) *Contingency, Irony and Solidarity.* Cambridge: Cambridge University Press.

Rorty, R. (1991a) *Objectivity, Relativism, and Truth: Philosophical Papers, Vol. 1.* Cambridge: Cambridge University Press.

Rorty, R. (1991b) *Essays on Heidegger and Others: Philosophical Papers, Vol. 2.* Cambridge: Cambridge University Press.

Rorty, R. (1995) 'Feminism and Pragmatism' in R.S. Goodman (ed.) *Pragmatism.* New York: Routledge.

Rorty, R. (1998) *Achieving Our Country.* Cambridge, MA: Harvard University Press.

Rose, G. (1993) *Feminism and Geography*. Cambridge: Polity Press.

Rose, J. (1997) *Sexuality in the Field of Vision*. London: Verso.

Rose, N. (1996) 'Identity, Genealogy, History' in S. Hall and P. du Gay (eds) *Questions of Cultural Identity*. London and Newbury Park, CA: Sage.

Rowbotham, S. (1981) 'The Trouble with Patriarchy' in R. Samuel (ed.) *People's History and Socialist Theory*. London: Routledge.

Rowe, D. (1997) *Depression*. London: Routledge.

Said, E. (1978) *Orientalism*. London: Routledge.

Said, E. (1981) *Covering Islam*. London and New York: Routledge.

Sartre, J.-P. (1971) [1939] *Sketch for a Theory of Emotion*. London: Methuen.

Sassen, S. (1996) 'Rebuilding the Global City: Economy, Ethnicity and Space' in A.D. King (ed.) *Re-presenting the City*. London: Macmillan.

Sassen, S. (2002) 'Mediating Practices: Women with/in Cyberspace' in J. Armitage and J. Roberts (eds) *Living with Cyberspace: Technology and Society in the 21st century*. New York: Continuum.

Saussure, F. de (1960) *Course in General Linguistics*. London: Peter Owen.

Scannell, P. (1988) 'Radio Times: The Temporal Arrangments of Broadcasting in the Modern World' in P. Drummond and R. Paterson (eds) *Television and Its Audiences*. London: British Film Institute.

Schiller, H. (1969) *Mass Communications and the American Empire*. New York: Augustus M. Kelly.

Schiller, H. (1976) *Communication and Cultural Domination*. New York: M.E. Sharpe.

Schiller, H. (1985) 'Electronic Information Flows: New Basis for Global Domination?' in P. Drummond and R. Patterson (eds) *Television in Transition*. London: British Film Institute.

Schlesinger, P. (1978) *Putting Reality Together*. London: Constable.

Scott, J. (1990) 'Deconstructing Equality vs. Difference' in M. Hirsch and E. Fox Keller (eds) *Conflicts in Feminism*. London and New York: Routledge.

Seamon, D. (1979) *A Geography of the Life World*. London: Croom Helm.

Seidler, V. (1989) *Rediscovering Masculinity: Reason, Language and Sexuality*. London: Routledge.

Shaw, M. (1991) *Post-Military Society*. Cambridge: Polity Press.

Shields, R. (1996) 'A Guide to Urban Representation and What to Do About It: Alternative Traditions in Urban Theory' in A.D. King (ed.) *Re-presenting the City*. London: Macmillan.

Shilling, C. (1993) *The Body and Social Theory*. London and Thousand Oaks, CA: Sage.

Shilling, C. (1997) *Re-forming the Body: Religion, Community and Modernity*. London and Thousand Oaks, CA: Sage.

Shweder, R. (1995) 'Cultural Psychology: What Is It?' in N. Rule Goldberger and J. Bennet Veroff (eds) *The Culture and Psychology Reader*. New York and London: New York University Press.

Sibley, D. (1995) *Geographies of Exclusion*. London: Routledge.

Silverstone, R. (1994) *Television and Everyday Life*. London and New York: Routledge.

Simmel, G. (1978) *The Philosophy of Money*. London: Routledge & Kegan Paul.

Smith, A.D. (1990) 'Towards a Global Culture?' in M. Featherstone (ed.) *Global Culture*. London and Newbury Park, CA: Sage.

Smith, J.H.(2002) 'Computer Game Research 101: a Brief Introduction to the Literature', *Game Research: the Art, Business and Science of Computer Games*. www.game-research.com/art_computer_game_research. asp

Smith, K. (1996) 'Advertising Discourse and the Marketing of *I'll Fly Away*' in V. Berry and C. Manning-Miller (eds) *Mediated Messages and African American Culture.* London and Thousand Oaks, CA: Sage.

Soja, E. (1989) *Postmodern Geographies: The Reassertion of Space in Critical Theory.* London: Verso.

Soja, E. (1995a) 'Postmodern Urbanisation: The Six Restructurings of Los Angeles' in S. Watson and K. Gibson (eds) *Postmodern Cities and Spaces.* Oxford: Blackwell.

Soja, E. (1995b) 'Heterotopologies: A Rememberance of Other Spaces in the Citadel-LA' in S. Watson and K. Gibson (eds) *Postmodern Cities and Spaces.* Oxford: Blackwell.

Spivak, G. (1976) 'Translator's Introduction' in J. Derrida, *Of Grammatology.* Baltimore: Johns Hopkins University Press.

Spivak, G. (1993) 'Can the Subaltern Speak?' in P. Williams and L. Chrisman (eds) *Colonial Discourse and Post-Colonial Theory.* Hemel Hempstead: Harvester Wheatsheaf.

Stearns, P.N. (1995) *American Cool: Constructing a Twentieth Century Emotional Style.* New York; New York University Press.

Stearns, P.N. and Knapp, M. (1996) 'Historical Perspectives on Grief' in R. Harré and W.G. Parrott (eds) *The Emotions: Social, Cultural and Biological Dimensions.* London: Sage.

Sterelny, K. and Griffiths, P. (1999) *Sex and Death: An Introduction to Philosophy of Biology.* Chicago and London: The University of Chicago Press.

Stone, A. (1991) 'Will the Real Body Please Stand Up? Boundary Stories about Virtual Cultures' in M. Benedikt (ed.) *Cyberspace: First Steps.* Cambridge, MA: MIT Press.

Storey, J. (1993) *Cultural Theory and Popular Culture.* Edinburgh: Edinburgh University Press.

Straubhaar, J. (1992) 'What Makes News? Western, Socialist, and Third World Television Newscasts Compared in Eight Countries' in F. Korzenny and S. Ting Toomey (eds) *Mass Media Effects across Cultures.* London and Newbury Park, CA: Sage.

Straubhaar, J. (1996) 'Distinguishing the Global, Regional and National Levels of World Television' in A. Sreberny-Mohammadi, D. Winseck, J. McKenna and O. Boyd-Barrett (eds) *Media in a Global Context.* London: Edward Arnold.

Tagg, J. (1996) 'The City Which is Not One' in A.D. King (ed.) *Re-presenting the City.* London: Macmillan.

Taylor, F. (1911) *Principles of Scientific Management.* New York: Harper.

Thompson, E. (1963) *The Making of the English Working Class.* New York: Vintage.

Thompson, J. (1995) *The Media and Modernity.* Cambridge: Polity Press.

Thompson, P. and McHugh, D. (1990) *Work Organization: A Critical Introduction.* London: Macmillan.

Thornton, S. (1995) *Club Cultures: Music, Media and Subcultural Capital.* Cambridge: Polity Press.

Thussu, D.K. (2000) *International Communication: Continuity and Change.* Cambridge: Polity Press.

Tietchen, T. (2001) 'Language Out of Language: Excavating the Roots of Culture Jamming and Postmodern Activism from William S. Burroughs' *Nova* Trilogy', *Discourse,* 23 (3): 107–29.

Todorov, T. (1977) *The Poetics of Prose.* Ithaca, NY: Cornell University Press.

Tomlinson, J. (1991) *Cultural Imperialism.* London: Pinter Press.

Tooby, J. and Cosmides, L. (1992) 'The Psychological Foundations of Culture' in J. Barkow, L. Cosmides and L. Tooby (eds) *The Adapted Mind.* Oxford: Oxford University Press.

Touraine, A. (1971) *The Post-Industrial Society.* New York: Random House.

Touraine, A. (1981) *The Voice and the Eye: An Analysis of Social Movements.* Cambridge: Cambridge University Press.

Touraine, A. (1985) 'An Introduction to the Study of New Social Movements', *Social Research*, 52 (4).

Trend, D. (ed.) (2005) *Reading Digital Culture.* Oxford: Blackwell.

Tuchman, G., Daniels, A.K. and Benit, J. (eds) (1978) *Hearth and Home: Images of Women in the Mass Media.* New York: Oxford University Press.

Turkle, S. (1995) *Life on the Screen.* New York: Simon & Schuster.

Turner, B. (1996) *The Body and Society: Explanations in Social Theory.* London and Thousand Oaks, CA: Sage.

Turner, G. (1990) *British Cultural Studies: An Introduction.* London: Unwin Hyman.

Turner, G. (1992) 'It Works for Me: British Cultural Studies, Australian Cultural Studies, Australian Film' in L. Grossberg, C. Nelson and P. Treichler (eds) *Cultural Studies.* London and New York: Routledge.

Varis, T. (1974) 'Global Traffic in Television', *Journal of Communication*, 24 (1).

Varis, T. (1984) 'International Flow of Television Programmes', *Journal of Communication*, 34 (1).

Vink, N. (1988) *The Telenovela and Emancipation.* Amsterdam: Royal Tropical Institute.

Virilio, P. (2005) 'Speed and Information: Cyberspace Alarm!' in D. Trend (ed.) *Reading Digital Culture.* Oxford: Blackwell.

Vološinov, V.N. (1973) *Marxism and the Philosophy of Language.* London: Seminar Press.

Wallace, M. (1979) *Black Macho.* London: Calder.

Wallerstein, I. (1974) *The Modern World System.* New York: Academic Press.

Waterman, D. (1988) 'World Television Trade: The Economic Effects of Privatization and New Technology', *Telecommunications Policy*, June.

Waters, M. (1995) *Globalization.* London: Routledge.

Watson, J. (ed.) (1977) *Between Two Cultures.* Oxford: Blackwell.

Watson, S. and Gibson, K. (1995) 'Introduction' to S. Watson and K. Gibson (eds) *Postmodern Cities and Spaces.* Oxford: Blackwell.

Weber, M. (1948) *From Max Weber.* London: Routledge & Kegan Paul.

Weber, M. (1978) *Economy and Society: An Outline of Interpretative Sociology.* Berkeley: University of California Press.

Weedon, C. (1997) *Feminist Practice and Poststructuralist Theory.* Oxford: Blackwell.

Weedon, C., Tolson, A. and Mort, F. (1980) 'Introduction to Language Studies at the Centre' in S. Hall, D. Hobson, A. Lowe and P. Willis (eds) *Culture, Media, Language.* London: Hutchinson.

Weeks, J. (1990) 'The Value of Difference' in J. Rutherford (ed.) *Identity: Community, Culture, Difference.* London: Lawrence & Wishart.

Wernick, A. (1991) *Promo Culture.* London and Newbury Park, CA: Sage.

Wertheim, M. (1999) *The Pearly Gates of Cyberspace, A History of Space from Dante to the Internet.* Sydney: Doubleday.

West, C. (1992) 'The Postmodern Crisis of the Black Intellectuals' in L. Grossberg, C. Nelson and P. Treichler (eds) *Cultural Studies.* London and New York: Routledge.

West, C. (1993) *Keeping Faith.* London and New York: Routledge.

Westwood, S. and Williams, J. (1997) 'Imagining Cities' in S. Westwood and J. Williams (eds) *Imagining Cities*. London: Routledge.

Widdicombe, S. and Wooffitt, R. (1995) *The Language of Youth Subcultures*. Hemel Hempstead: Harvester Wheatsheaf.

Williams, P. and Chrisman, L. (eds) (1993) *Colonial Discourse and Post-Colonial Theory*. Hemel Hempstead: Harvester Wheatsheaf.

Williams, R. (1965) *The Long Revolution*. London: Penguin.

Williams, R. (1973) 'Base and Superstructure in Marxist Cultural Theory', *New Left Review*, 82.

Williams, R. (1974) *Television: Technology and Cultural Form*. London: Fontana.

Williams, R. (1979) *Politics and Letters: Interviews with New Left Review*. London: New Left Books.

Williams, R. (1981) *Culture*. London: Fontana.

Williams, R. (1983) *Keywords*. London: Fontana.

Williams, R. (1989) *Resources of Hope*. London: Verso.

Williamson, J. (1978) *Decoding Advertisements*. London: Marion Boyars.

Willis, P. (1977) *Learning to Labour*. Farnborough: Saxon House.

Willis, P. (1978) *Profane Culture*. London: Routledge & Kegan Paul.

Willis, P. (1980) 'Notes on Method' in S. Hall, D. Hobson, A. Lowe and P. Willis (eds) *Culture, Media, Language*. London: Hutchinson.

Willis, P. (1990) *Common Culture*. Milton: Keynes: Open University Press.

Wilson, E.O. (1975) *Sociobiology: The New Synthesis*. Cambridge, MA: Harvard University Press.

Winship, J. (1981) 'Sexuality for Sale' in S. Hall, D. Hobson, A. Lowe and P. Willis (eds) *Culture, Media, Language*. London: Hutchinson.

Wittgenstein, L. (1953) *Philosophical Investigations*. Oxford: Blackwell.

Wittgenstein, L. (1969) *On Certainty*. New York: HarperTorch Books.

Wolf, N. (1994) *Fire with Fire*. Canada: Vintage.

Wolff, J. (1980) *The Social Production of Art*. London: Macmillan.

Woodward, K. (1997) 'Motherhood: Identities, Meanings and Myths' in K. Woodward (ed.) *Identity and Difference*. London and Thousand Oaks, CA: Sage.

Worsley, P. (1990) 'Models of the Modern World System' in M. Featherstone (ed.) *Global Culture*. London and Newbury Park, CA: Sage.

Young, J. (1971) *The Drugtakers: The Social Meaning of Drug Use*. London: Paladin.

Young, M. and Willmott, P. (1962) *Family and Kinship in East London*. Harmondsworth: Penguin.

Zukin, S (1988) *Loft Living: Culture and Capital in Urban Change*. London: Century Hutchinson.

Zukin, S. (1991) *Landscapes of Power: From Detroit to Disneyworld*. Berkeley: University of California Press.

Zukin, S. (1996a) *The Culture of Cities*. Oxford: Blackwell.

Zukin, S. (1996b) 'Space and Symbols in an Age of Decline' in A.D. King (ed.) *Re-presenting the City*. London: Macmillan.

Index

Please note that page references to non-textual information such as photographs are in *italic* print. Titles of publications beginning with 'A' or 'The' will be filed under the first significant word. Numbers (e.g. 20) are filed as if spelled out (e.g. twenty). Page numbers containing major reference to thinkers are in **bold** print.